The Book of Temples

Spiritual Places Around the World

gestalten

Contents

Building Faith

Spiritual Architecture for the World and What Lies Beyond

Since time immemorial, humanity has felt the need to give faith a home. Across all continents, it has created special places to worship its gods and communicate with them. And how wonderful, diverse, and breathtaking these places are!

The Book of Temples takes readers on a journey to holy places around the world: to shrines in Africa, sacred sites in the Middle East, and traditional temples in Asia. It explores the diversity of places of worship across the Americas and examines how Europe transformed spiritual ideas into physical reality. Through the architecture of the world's belief systems, we are brought closer to the traditions and convictions that have shaped—and continue to shape—entire epochs, cultures, and continents.

Temples are places where the soul of a community becomes visible. Here, people celebrate their shared faith, come closer to one another and to themselves. From the earliest cult sites to modern places of worship, every temple is a snapshot of architectural innovation and cultural identity at a particular moment in time. Their designs speak of ancient symbolism and legends, of transformation, power, and conquest, of new homelands and the merging of traditions. The convergence of major religions can be seen in the Hindu and Buddhist elements of the temples at Angkor Wat in Cambodia (pp. 10–15), in the symbiosis of Christian and Islamic styles in the Hagia Sophia in Turkey (pp. 130–135), or in the Hanging Temple of Hengshan in China (pp. 40–45), masterfully integrated into a cliffside and uniting elements of various faiths.

Some of the temples featured here are considered architectural and technical masterpieces of their time, such as the Temple of the Great Jaguar in Guatemala (pp. 88–91), renowned for its towering stepped design and its significance in Mayan ceremonial life. Other houses of worship, however, were built primarily through spiritual dedication, overcoming all contemporary expectations and challenges. Construction on the Sagrada Família in Spain (pp. 136–141) has been ongoing since 1882, a timeline that still pales in comparison to the 632 years it took to build Cologne Cathedral in Germany (pp. 160–163). Religious minorities worldwide often built their temples in difficult political and social circumstances. Synagogues emerged in the Jewish diaspora, persecuted Buddhist monks created remote cave monasteries, and Christians in Japan constructed hidden chapels under threat of death. These structures stand as testaments to an unwavering will to preserve both faith and culture.

The Birth of an Architectural Idea

Every architectural innovation stems from the idea of making an unseen world tangible through space and form. Neanderthals, it is believed, used natural cave structures for ritual purposes while *Homo sapiens* constructed the very first buildings, structures that not only provided shelter but also carried spiritual significance, marking the beginnings of spatial design and aesthetics. Gradually, *Homo sapiens* became *Homo faber*—the creative human being—expressing emotions through stone and art.

With the advent of settled life around 10,000 BCE, architecture changed fundamentally. Sacred sites, such as Göbekli Tepe in what is now Turkey, soon laid the proverbial foundation for a social and religious order that, for the first time, had a fixed place. Some 7,000 years later, this gave rise to the megalithic cultures of Europe, whose most famous monument is Stonehenge, where architectural knowledge was already used for astronomical alignments. The idea of reaching the divine through structures became a fundamental part of human creation, and increasingly, people sought to connect with higher powers.

Gods Taking Residence

Parallel to the development of complex societies in Europe, the first monumental structures—ziggurats in Mesopotamia, pyramids in Egypt—emerged, marking technical and aesthetic milestones. On the Indian subcontinent, early temple structures in the second millennium BCE laid the foundation for a design approach that seamlessly blended spirituality and artistry. Simple structures evolved into magnificent Hindu temples that have become the breathtaking sites we know today.

By the 8th century BCE, the Greek gods as we know them were already believed to reside on Mount Olympus, and people built temples to them with clear proportions and column orders that remain iconic examples of classical architecture. Shortly thereafter, the Romans adopted many Greek design elements and expanded them with innovative techniques like the arch and the dome, as seen in structures like the Pantheon in Rome (pp. 182 – 185). Meanwhile, in Asia, a diverse array of styles developed that made use of local materials and techniques to create spiritual spaces.

A New Worldview

The monotheistic religions—Judaism, Christianity, and Islam—introduced new architectural forms. After the destruction of the Second Temple in Jerusalem by the Romans in 70 CE, Judaism survived in the diaspora, transforming from temple-based worship to rabbinic Judaism centered on the Torah. Today, the Western Wall (pp. 250 – 253) remains a place of mourning for the loss of the temple. Synagogues, particularly in the Middle Ages, were often designed discreetly but still served vital cultural and religious functions.

Christianity spread rapidly through the Roman Empire despite early persecution, producing remarkable churches in every era—from the early basilicas of late antiquity to the massive Romanesque structures, soaring Gothic cathedrals, and ornate churches of the Renaissance and baroque periods, as well as the innovative sacred buildings of the last two centuries. Islam, too, developed its own architectural language, characterized by majestic mosques, graceful minarets, and intricate ornamentation. As Islam spread from the Arabian Peninsula to North Africa, Southern Europe, and Asia, it merged local building traditions with Islamic stylistic elements, creating a stunning diversity of sacred architecture, as exemplified by the Great Mosque of Djenné in Mali (pp. 202 – 205).

Death and Rebirth

Where new religions encountered local traditions, the protective hand of the divine must have seemed distant, especially during the colonial era, when countless sacred sites were repurposed or destroyed, and left to fade from cultural memory. At the same time, breathtaking churches and sanctuaries emerged, combining Indigenous and Christian style elements, particularly in South America.

The temples encountered by missionaries were often expressions of a harmonious understanding of humanity, nature, and the cosmos. In Chichén Itzá, Mexico, the Mayan Temple of Kukulkán (pp. 92 – 95) continues to captivate visitors with its precise construction and astronomical alignment. The Aztecs held the ancient city of Teotihuacán, built by an earlier civilization, in great reverence and wove its pyramids into their spiritual narratives. The most famous Inca site, Machu Picchu (pp. 108 – 113), survived the colonial era purely by chance—the Spanish never discovered the remote, mystical city in the Andes.

On the African continent, meanwhile, religions before the arrival of Christianity and Islam were deeply rooted in nature. In Nigeria, the still-preserved Sacred Grove of Osun-Osogbo (pp. 220 – 225) tells the story of the Yoruba people's devotion to their river goddess. On the other side of the continent, the monolithic churches of Lalibela in Ethiopia (pp. 230 – 235), carved directly into the rock, hide an ancient form of Orthodox Christianity in the mountains. In North America, on the other hand, there are few built temples. Many Indigenous peoples found the sacred in mountains, springs, and rock formations. At Mesa Verde in Colorado, the Ancestral Puebloans conducted ceremonies and engaged in spiritual practices tied to their deep connection with the land. In places like Nan Madol in Micronesia or Rapa Nui (pp. 114 – 117), distinct spiritual traditions developed, while in New Zealand, the Māori continue to honor their ancestors at traditional Marae. These sacred sites, long overlooked or deliberately ignored, are now gaining increasing international recognition. Preservation efforts, such as those spearheaded by UNESCO, help protect such sacred places and honor their invaluable significance.

The Book of Temples is an invitation to retrace humanity's spiritual journey through architecture and become immersed in its myriad stories, beliefs, and sacred spaces. The following pages visit select temples that represent the world's countless sites of lived faith, cherished and visited for centuries by believers, spiritual seekers, lovers of architecture, and history enthusiasts alike. They tell of the power of faith to move mountains, and of its temples, which bring the divine closer to us in a thousand forms. While the names of their great architects or patrons are often well known, the workers who actually put their hands to the task—digging foundations, placing stone upon stone, setting mosaics, carving reliefs, painting stained glass windows, and crafting doors—remain in the shadows. It is to them, to those whom the world owes these magnificent temples, that this book is dedicated. They have offered us a sense of belonging and given faith, in all its forms, abiding residence.

Marianne Julia Strauss combines her love for travel with places that touch and inspire. In this, her fifth collaboration with gestalten, she once again explores the meaning, beauty, and soul of the world's most fascinating cultural landmarks.

Traditions of Wisdom and Harmony

In the sacred sites of Asia, the intertwining of great religions is visible in the fantastic chronicles carved in stone.

As the cradle of several major world religions, Asia offers a fascinating insight into the spiritual history of humanity through its sacred sites. From the early temples of Hinduism to Buddhist monasteries, Taoist sanctuaries, and the ornate mosques of Central Asia, these structures vividly reflect the religious, cultural, and political developments of their time.

Before the development of Hinduism, Asia was a vast patchwork of Indigenous belief systems that regarded nature itself—mountains, springs, forests—as sacred. The present-day veneration of holy rivers like the Ganges and the divinity granted certain animals, especially cows, have their roots in these early systems of belief. After the consolidation of Hinduism around 1500 BCE, people began constructing magnificent temples for their numerous deities. Although appearing much later, Meenakshi Temple in Madurai (pp. 20 – 23) is one such site, and stands as a remarkable example of the artistry of Dravidian architecture. The development and spread of Buddhism outside of India in the 3rd century BCE also led to the construction of awe-inspiring temples and monasteries, such as the spectacular Tiger's Nest in Bhutan (pp. 56 – 61). In Japan, Buddhism evolved further into meditative schools like Zen, embodied in minimalist structures such as Kinkaku-ji (pp. 36 – 39).

While the great religions flourished in South Asia, China saw the rise of its own spiritual traditions in the 6th century BCE, with Confucianism laying the foundation for moral conduct and social order. Simultaneously, Taoism emerged, which centered on the Tao, the universal way that permeates the world. Taoist temples, like the Temple Complex on Mount Laojun (pp. 46 – 49), are breathtaking examples of the often elusive harmony between humanity and nature.

Starting in the 7th century CE, Islam spread from Arabia along trade routes to Central and Southeast Asia. Mosques, as well as necropolises like the Shah-i-Zinda in Uzbekistan (pp. 80 – 85), reflect the fusion of Islamic art with local traditions. Thousands of miles away, Southeast Asia also showcases enduring examples of Islamic architecture that blend traditional and modern stylistic elements.

Today, in the modern era, Asia remains a continent that preserves its spiritual traditions while continually reinterpreting them. From modern Bahá'í houses of worship to futuristic mosques and Buddhist temples, old teachings are skillfully translated into innovative architectural forms.

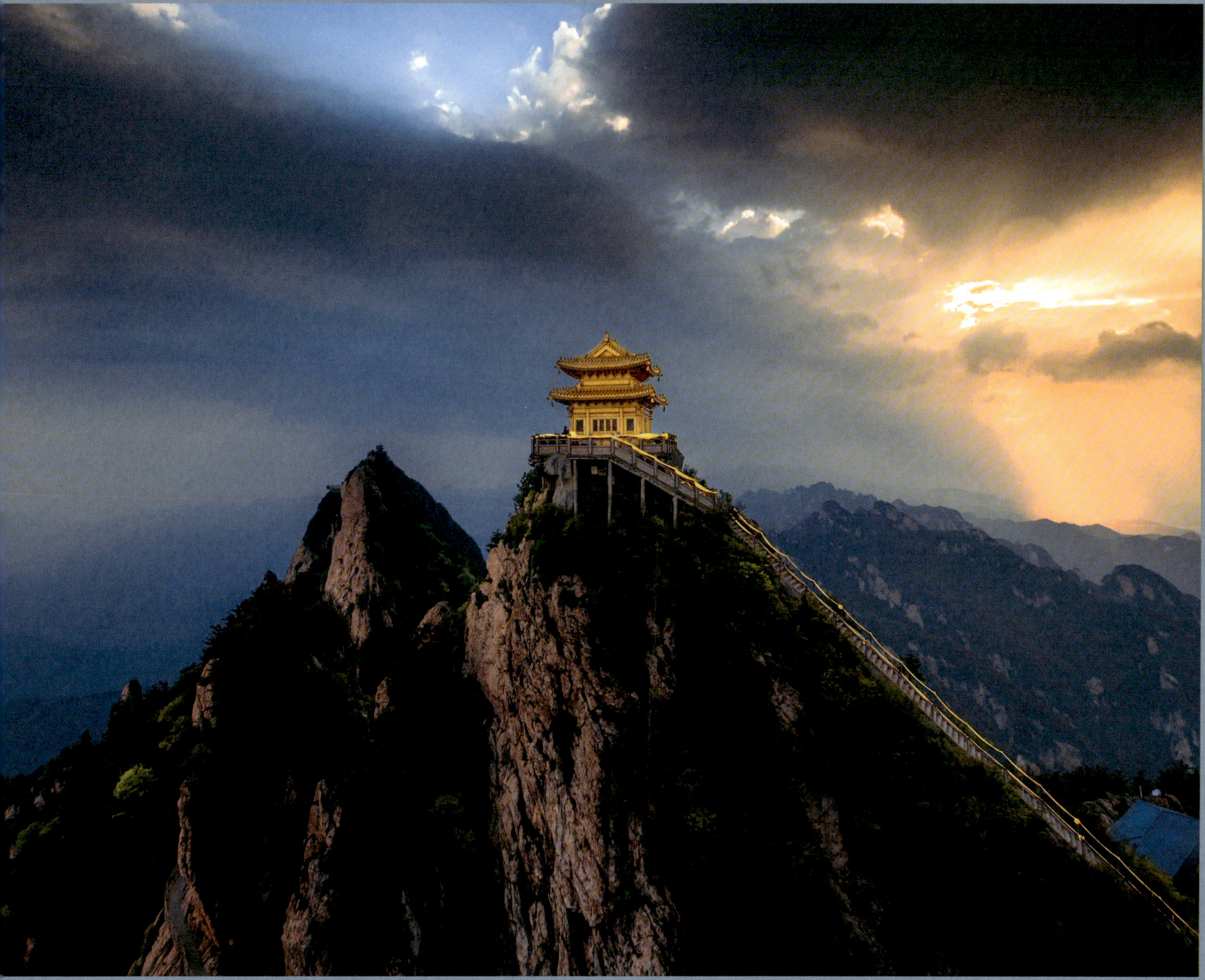

ASIA

Angkor Wat

A Divine Reflection

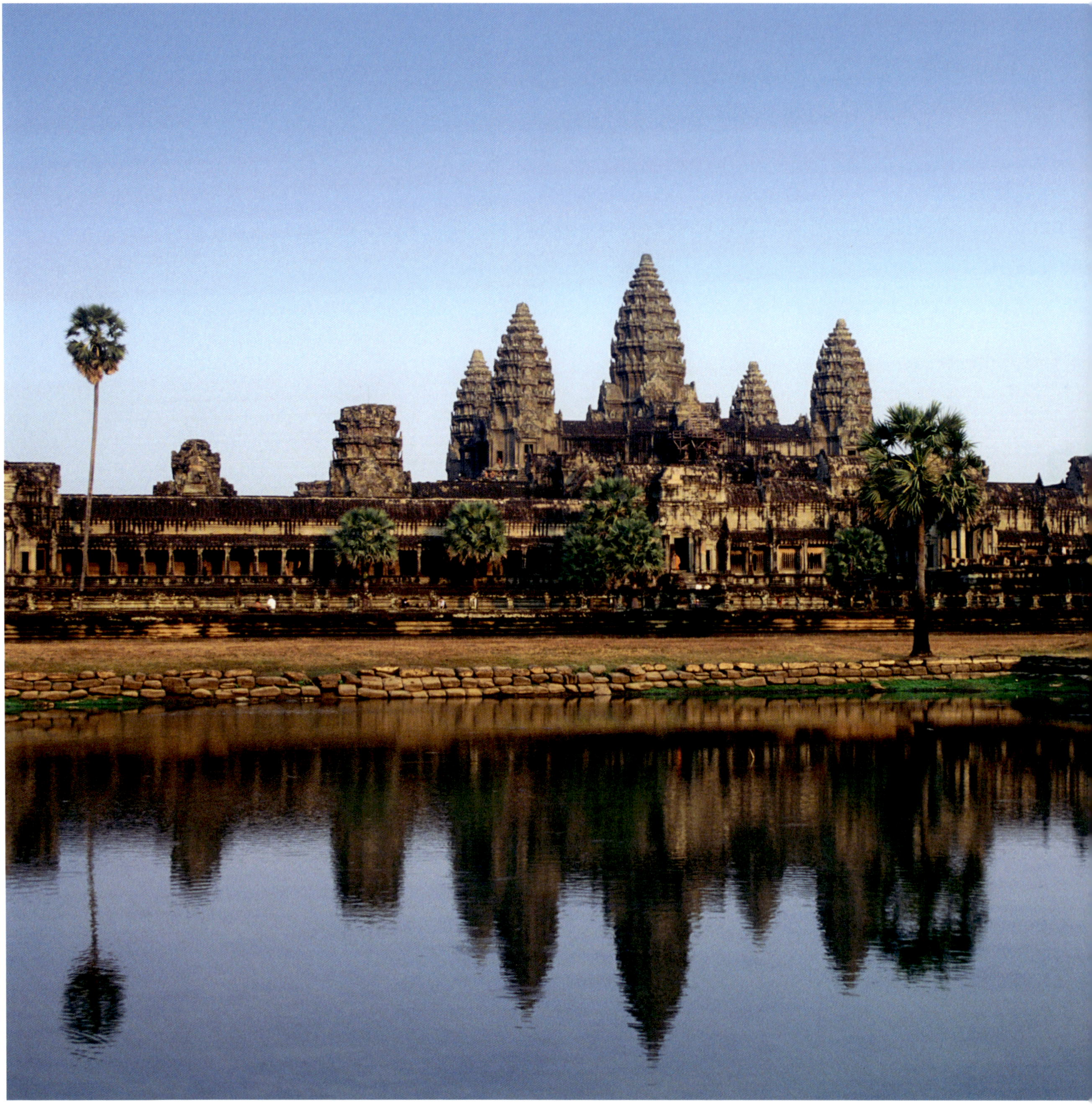

Built: 12th century CE,
Siem Reap, Cambodia

Every corner of the world's largest religious monument invokes the transcendent.

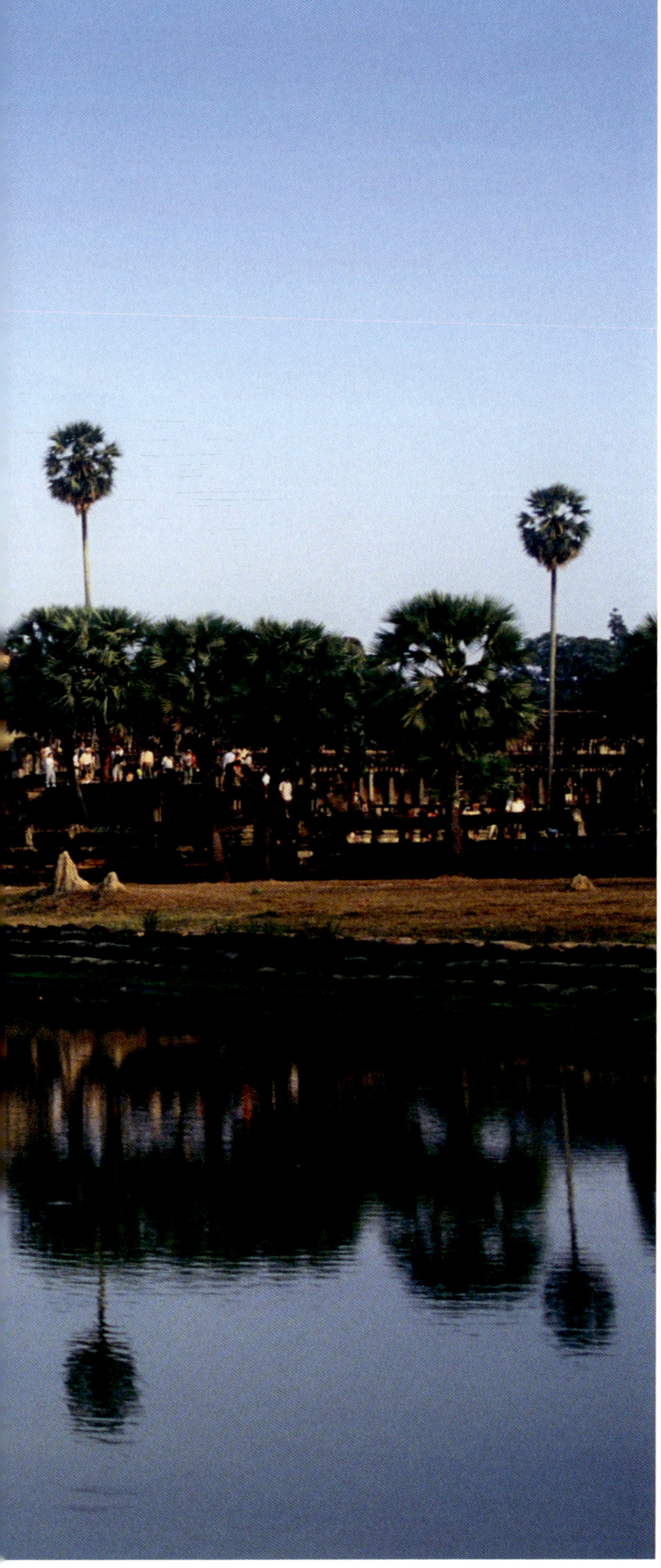

It's impossible to overstate the mystical allure of Angkor Wat: the spiritual geometry of the world's largest temple complex reveals both the vastness and intricacy of an entire cosmology. Its numberless towers, columns, canals, and reservoirs are infused with the prayers and hopes of the faithful, and glow with a rich symbolism.

The architecture of Angkor Wat reflects the Hindu concept of *Rta,* which imagines the entire universe as governed by the forces of movement and interdependence. Everything follows this cosmic order, which is maintained by the three main deities: Brahma, Vishnu, and Shiva. These gods represent the cycle of creation, preservation, and destruction that keeps the universe in perpetual balance. Angkor Wat is designed to reflect this cosmic geometry, its construction an attempt to create on earth a rendering of the divine. Its five towers symbolize Mount Meru, the sacred mountain at the center of the universe. The surrounding moat represents the cosmic sea from which existence sprung, and the walls are adorned with epic scenes from the *Mahabharata* and *Ramayana.*

The vision that guided the construction of Angkor Wat can be traced back to King Suryavarman II of the Khmer Empire. It is believed that workers carried millions of sandstone blocks from the distant Phnom Kulen, each block so precisely carved that they fit together without mortar. Astonishingly, in just 30 years the temple complex was complete.

In the 14th century, as Buddhism gained influence in Cambodia, Angkor Wat transformed into a Buddhist monastery. Alongside the depictions of Hindu deities, countless statues and reliefs of Buddha appeared. But the empire's decline had already begun, and by the 15th century, Angkor was largely abandoned. Trees began to reclaim the temple, their roots embedding themselves in the sacred walls. Although Angkor Wat was never entirely forgotten by the locals, and even saw continuous use by Buddhist monks, it remained largely unknown in the West. It wasn't until the 19th century, when the French explorer Henri Mouhot wrote about the temple, that Angkor Wat captured global attention.

Today, this sprawling, UNESCO-protected temple complex is one of the world's most famous tourist attractions, whose likeness even graces the Cambodian flag. Those who restored the temple in the 20th century consciously chose not to remove the majestically gnarled trees that had overtaken the architecture, a nod to the forces of movement and interdependence that govern the universe.

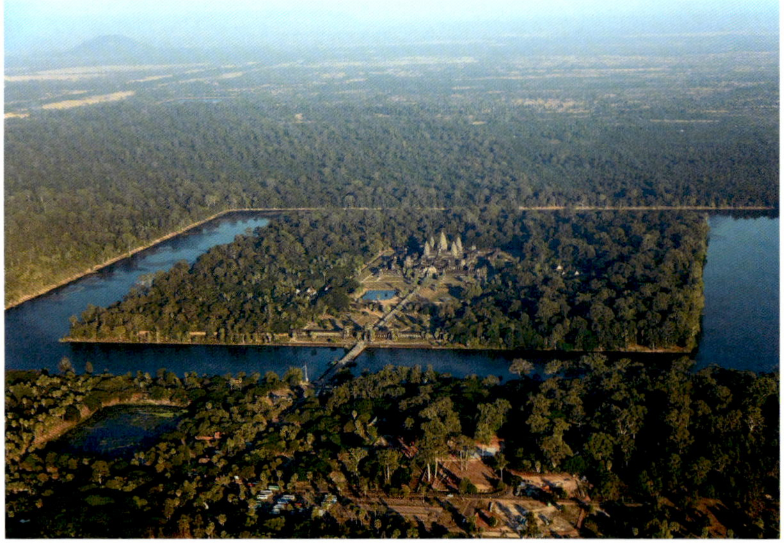

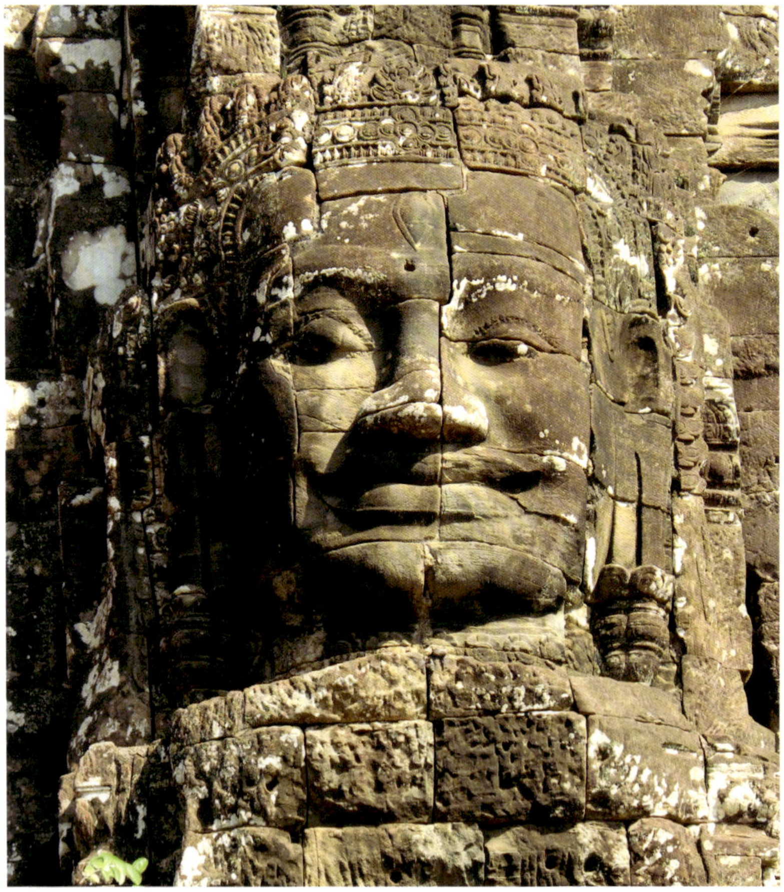

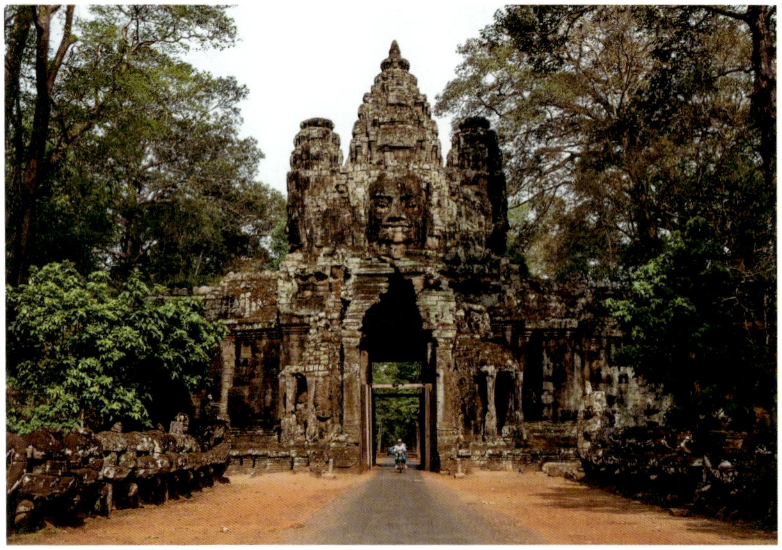

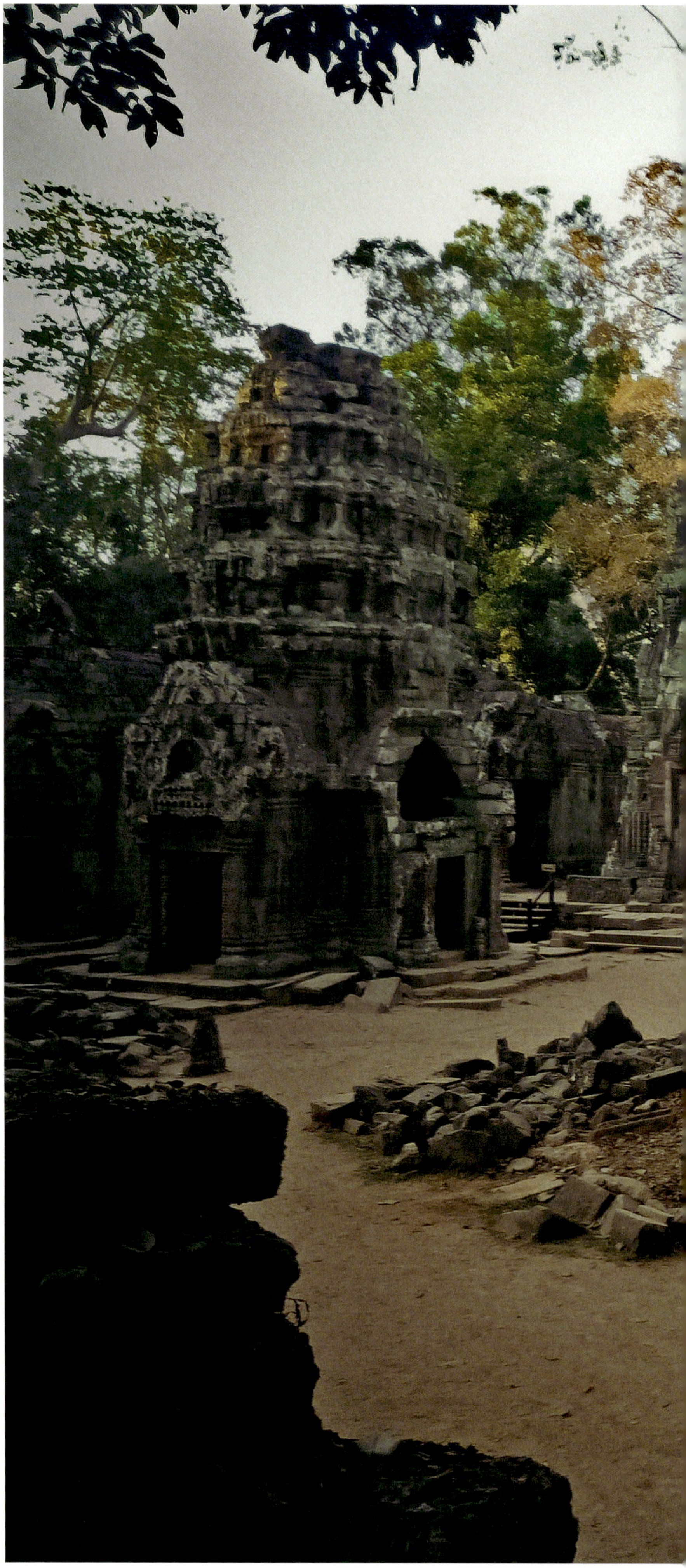

Top The temples of Angkor Wat are surrounded by a broad moat, symbolizing the cosmic oceans.
Middle Thousands of intricate reliefs tell tales of the Hindu epics.
Bottom Behind the majestic temple gates lies a sacred universe.

Siem Reap, Cambodia

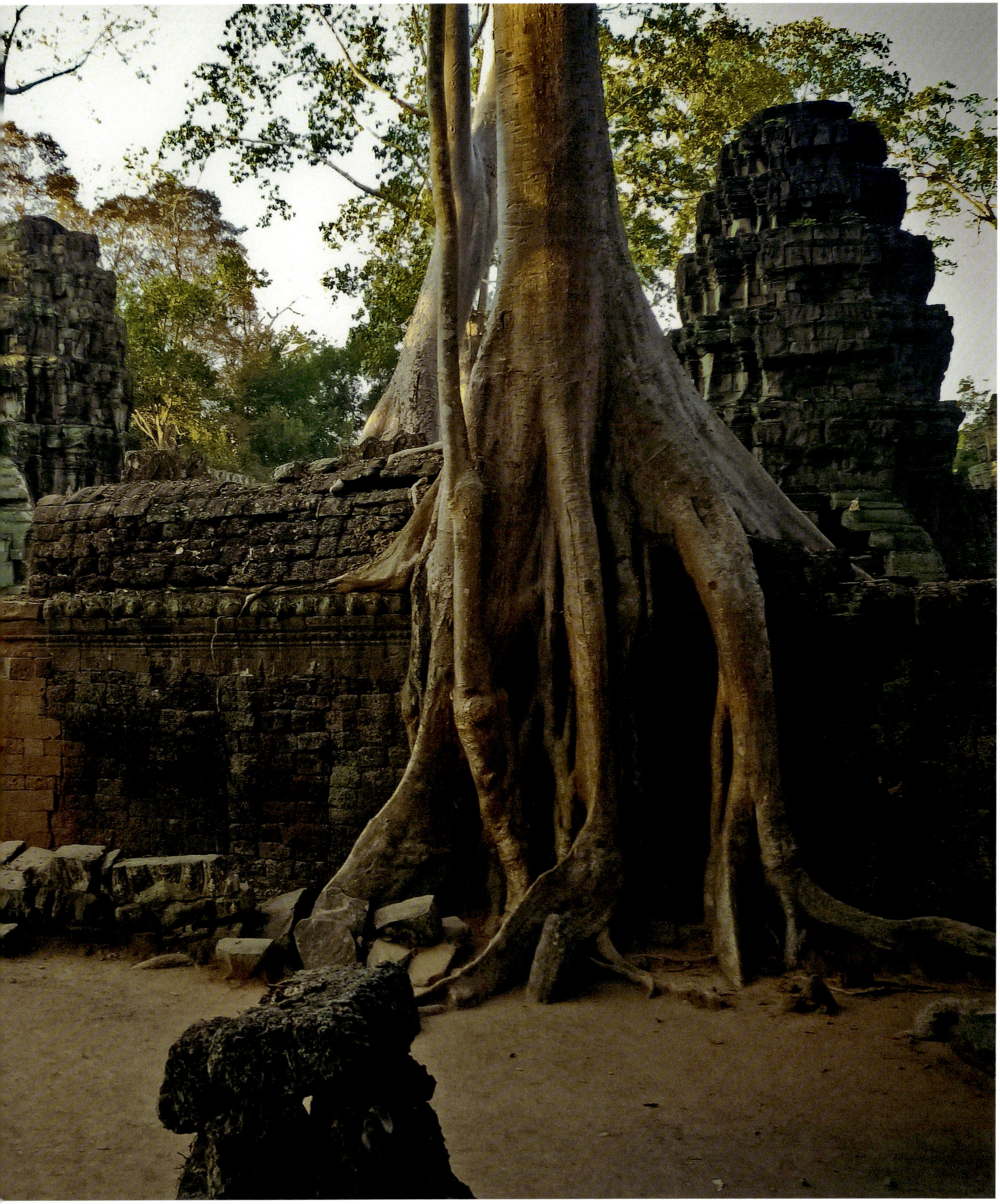

Above The roots of strangler fig trees decoratively intertwine with the stones of Angkor Wat. They stabilize some structures while eroding others.

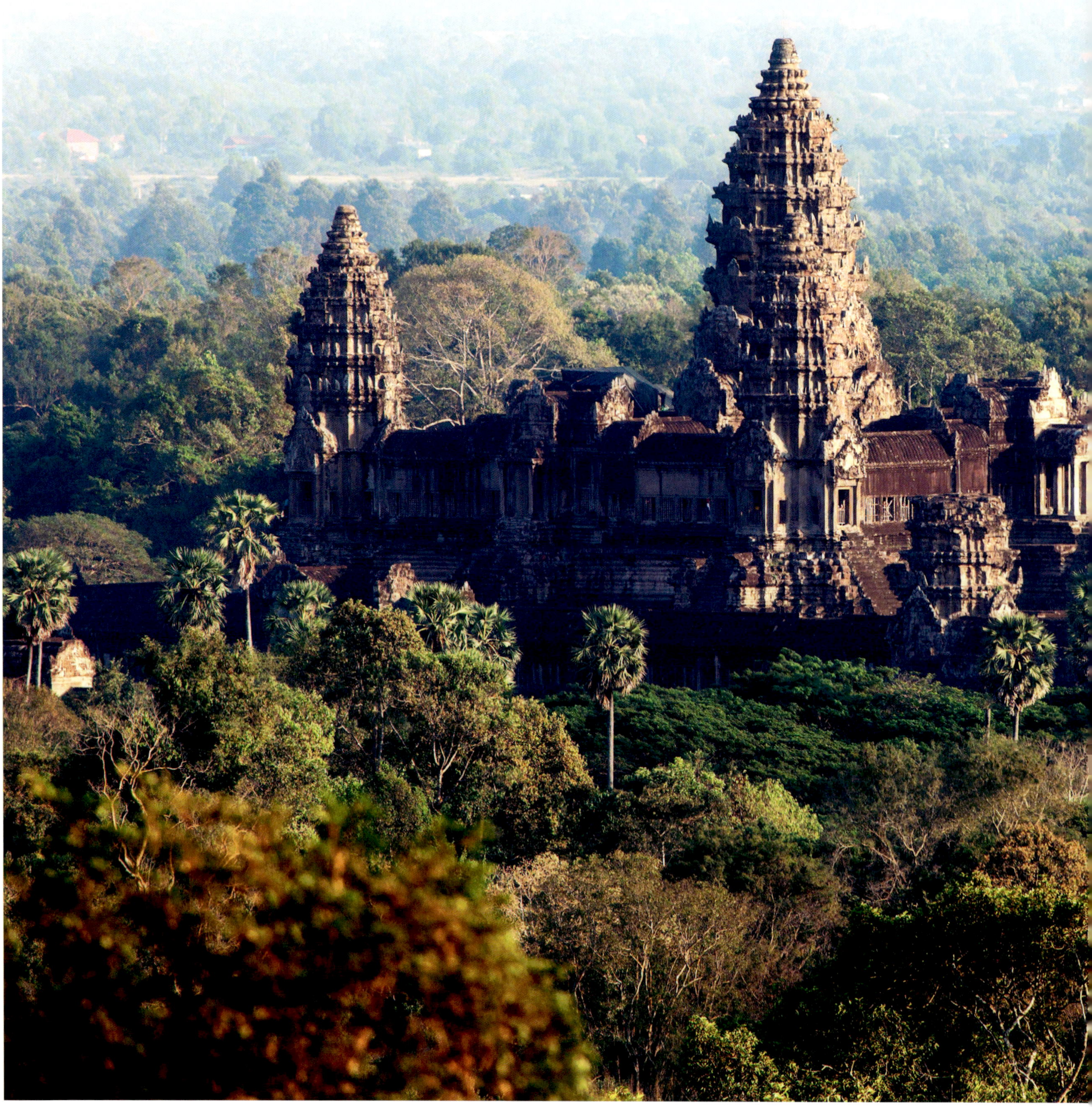

Above Unusually, Angkor Wat is aligned to the west, not the east. Could this be due to the worship of Vishnu, who is associated with the west?

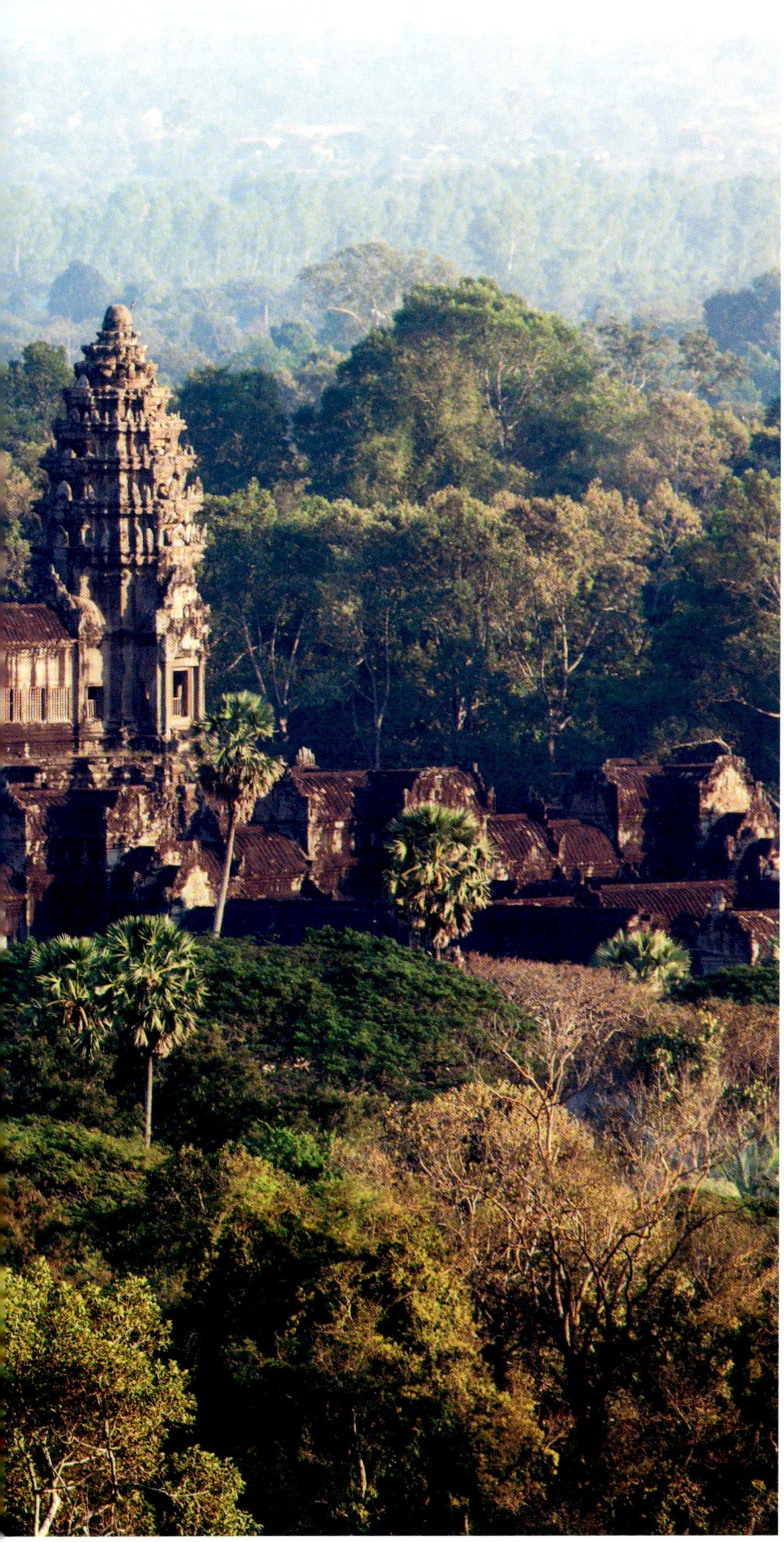

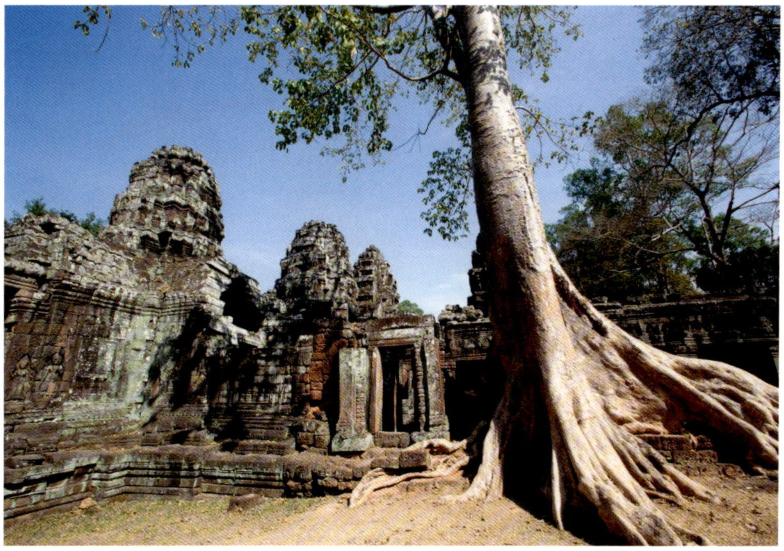

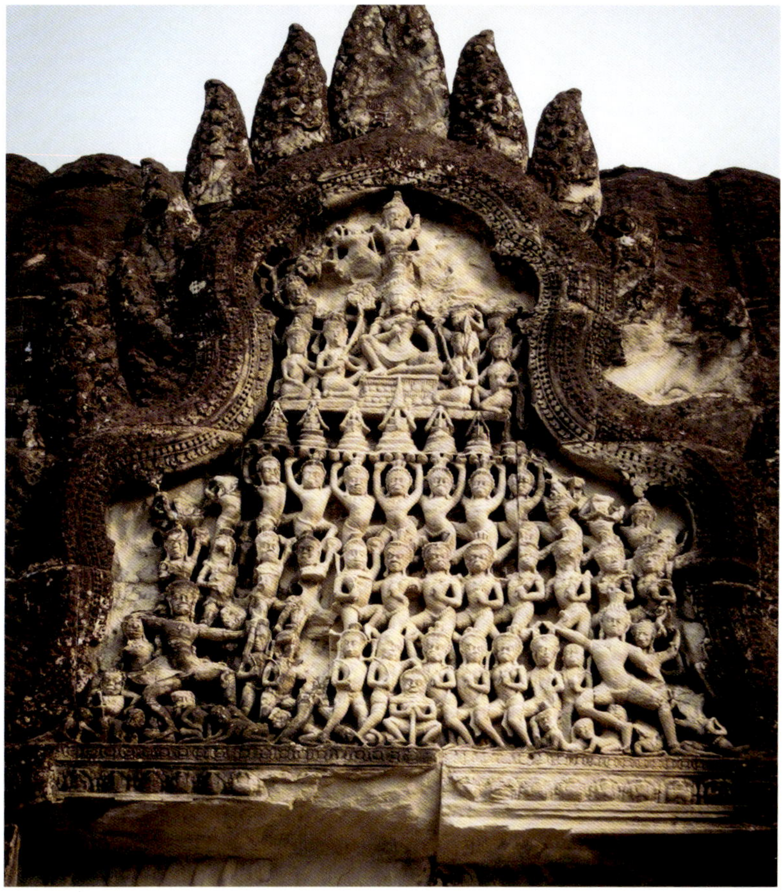

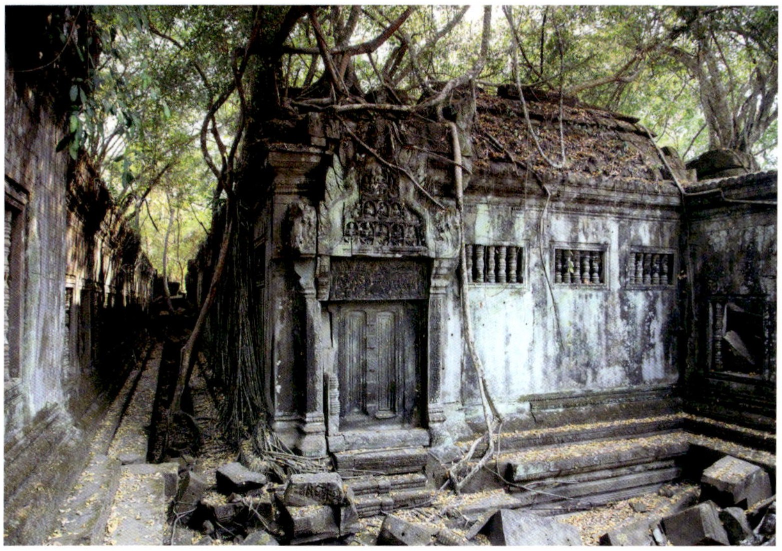

Top Especially at the temple of Ta Prohm, trees merge with the ruins, creating a unique atmosphere.
Middle Here, ancient Hindu myths have been immortalized in stone.
Bottom The temples are a prime example of Khmer architecture.

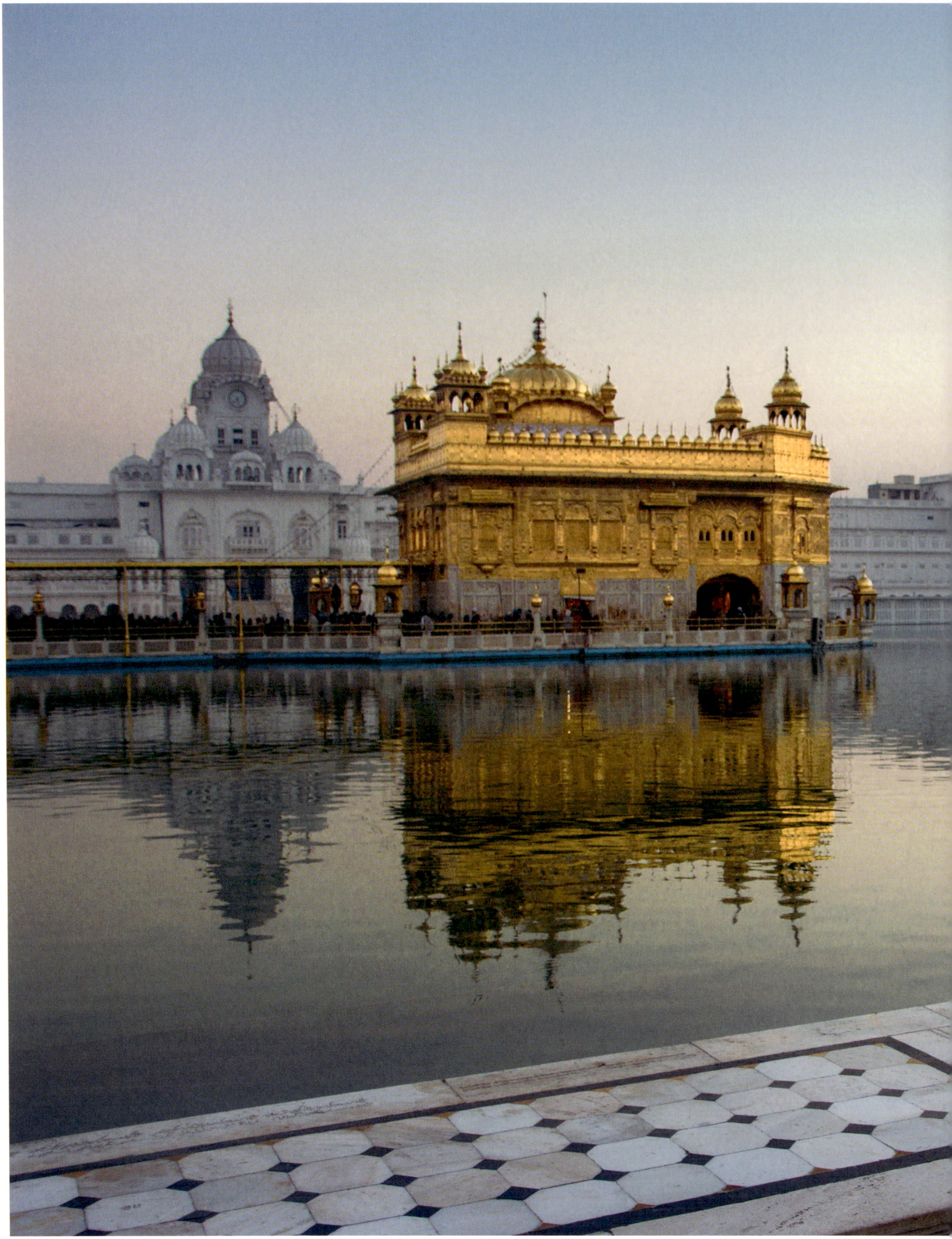

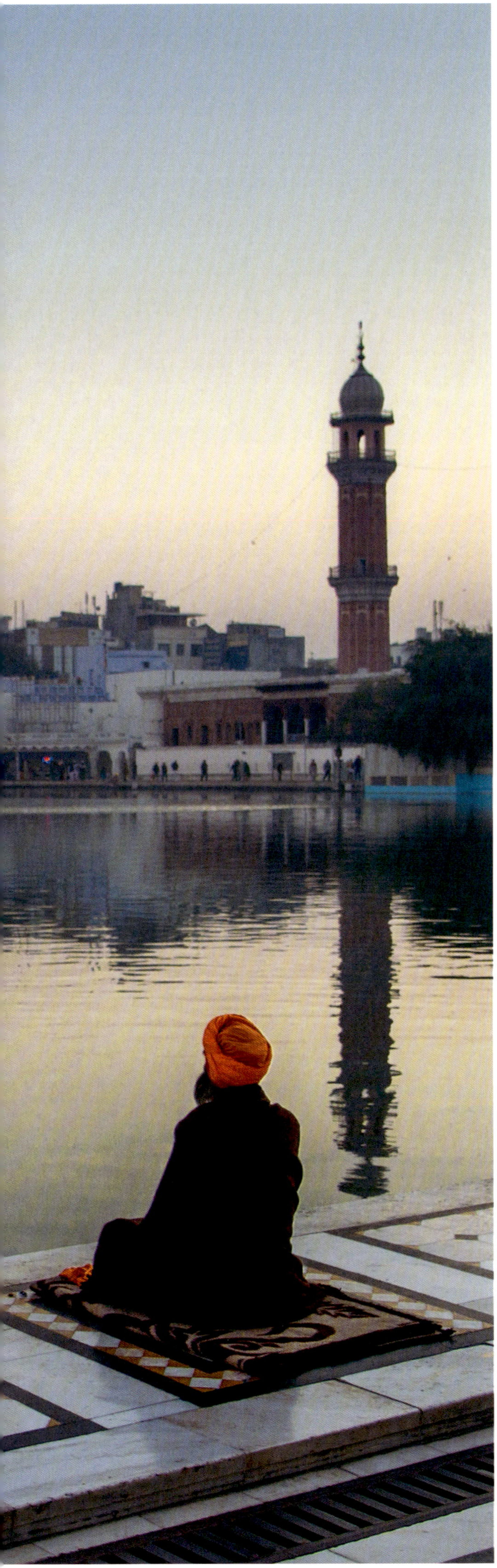

Harmandir Sahib

Gold for All the World

Built: between 1581 and 1604 CE, Amritsar, India

Under the glittering domes of Harmandir Sahib, the most sacred site in the Sikh religion, people of all origins, classes, and religions are welcome.

The air is filled with the scent of fresh chai, fried food, and incense. The hot, dusty atmosphere of Amritsar vibrates with the honking of scooters and the calls of street vendors. Amidst this vibrant hustle and bustle lies the spiritual heart of Sikhism: Harmandir Sahib, the "Golden Temple." Under its shimmering roof, no distinctions between caste, social background, or religion are made. Here, community is lived in the truest sense.

Guru Arjan, the fifth Sikh Guru, deliberately designed the temple as a sacred place of worship for all, and its architecture still reflects his vision today. Each of the four entrances of Harmandir Sahib face a cardinal direction, a gesture of openness toward pilgrims from differing lands. Unlike many religious structures, the temple is built not on an elevated platform but lower, perhaps in the spirit of humility it values in its visitors. The surrounding water basin, Amrit Sarovar ("Pool of Nectar") invites pilgrims to bathe in its waters—it is believed that the water possesses healing powers, and blesses those who enter with a pure heart.

Enshrined inside the temple is the sacred text of Sikhism, known as Guru Granth Sahib. This poetic scripture is revered as the eternal Guru of the Sikhs, and contains the wisdom of the human Gurus that preceded it. Every morning, the book is carried in a solemn ceremony from its resting place in the Akal Takht, the highest religious seat of the Sikhs, to the temple, where it is read and sung until evening. At the close of day, the book returns to the Akal Takht in a sacred procession.

Whether a spiritual sojourner or ordinary traveler, all who visit Harmandir Sahib are invited to a free meal at the *langar,* the temple's community kitchen. Up to 100,000 meals are served daily, making this particular *langar* the largest in the world. This tradition of feeding the community, also initiated by Guru Arjan, embodies the principle of *seva*—selfless service. In the 16th century, it was revolutionary for people of different castes and religions to eat together, especially in a society deeply divided by social and religious barriers. To this day, this practice is upheld as a symbol of social cohesion and inclusion.

The central values of Sikhism include equality, service to others, and humility, as well as justice, and devotion. These teachings are embodied and brought to life in the Harmandir Sahib, a temple that invites one to live in harmony with the community as well as the divine.

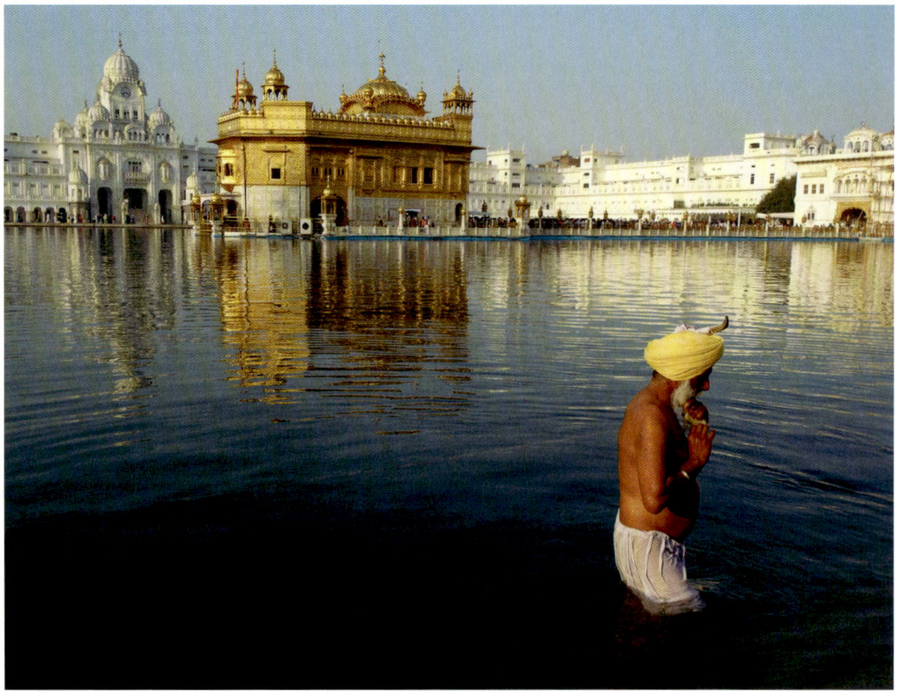

Under the golden roof of the temple, no distinctions are made based on caste, social background, or religion. Here, community is lived in the truest sense.

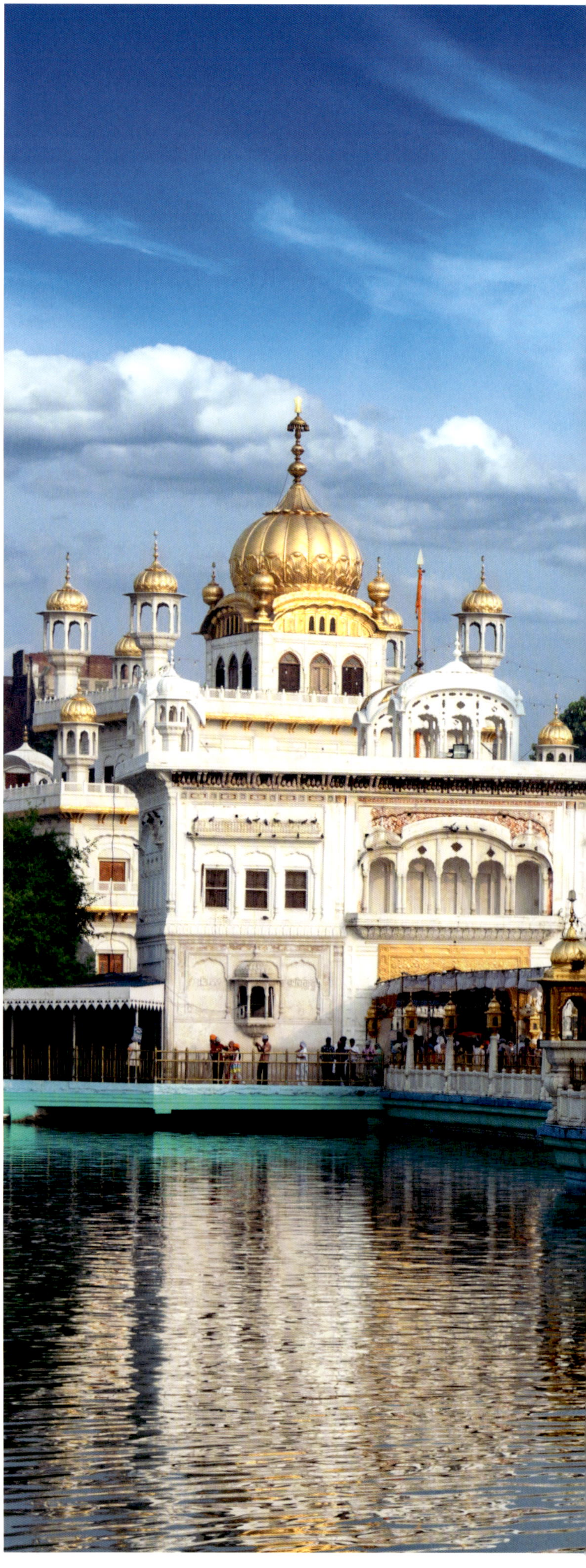

Amritsar, India

Left According to Sikh belief, the water of the Amrit Sarovar blesses those who enter with a pure heart.

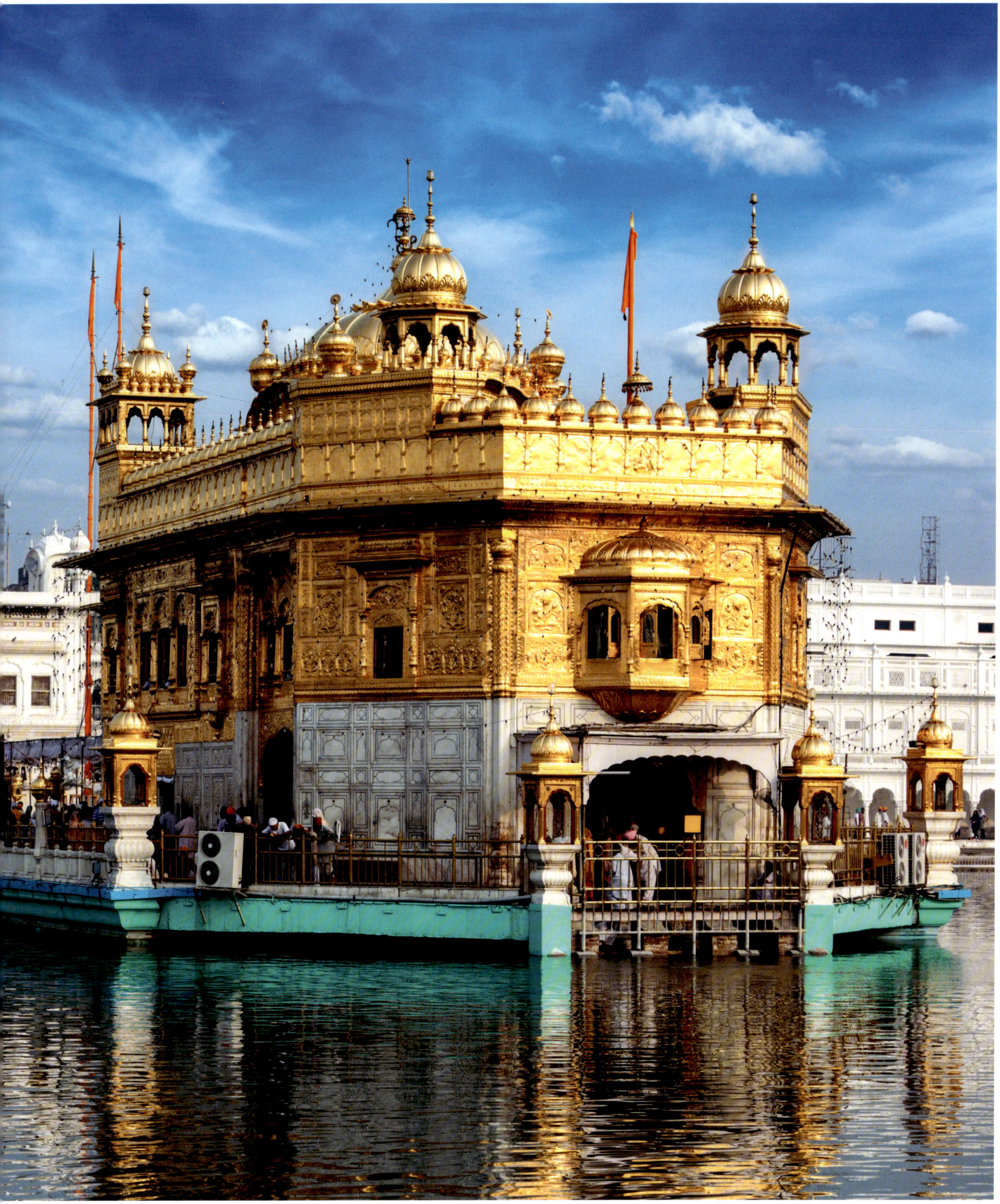

Above In the 19th century, Maharaja Ranjit Singh, the most significant ruler of the Sikh Empire, had the upper floors and domes of the Harmandir Sahib covered with gold.

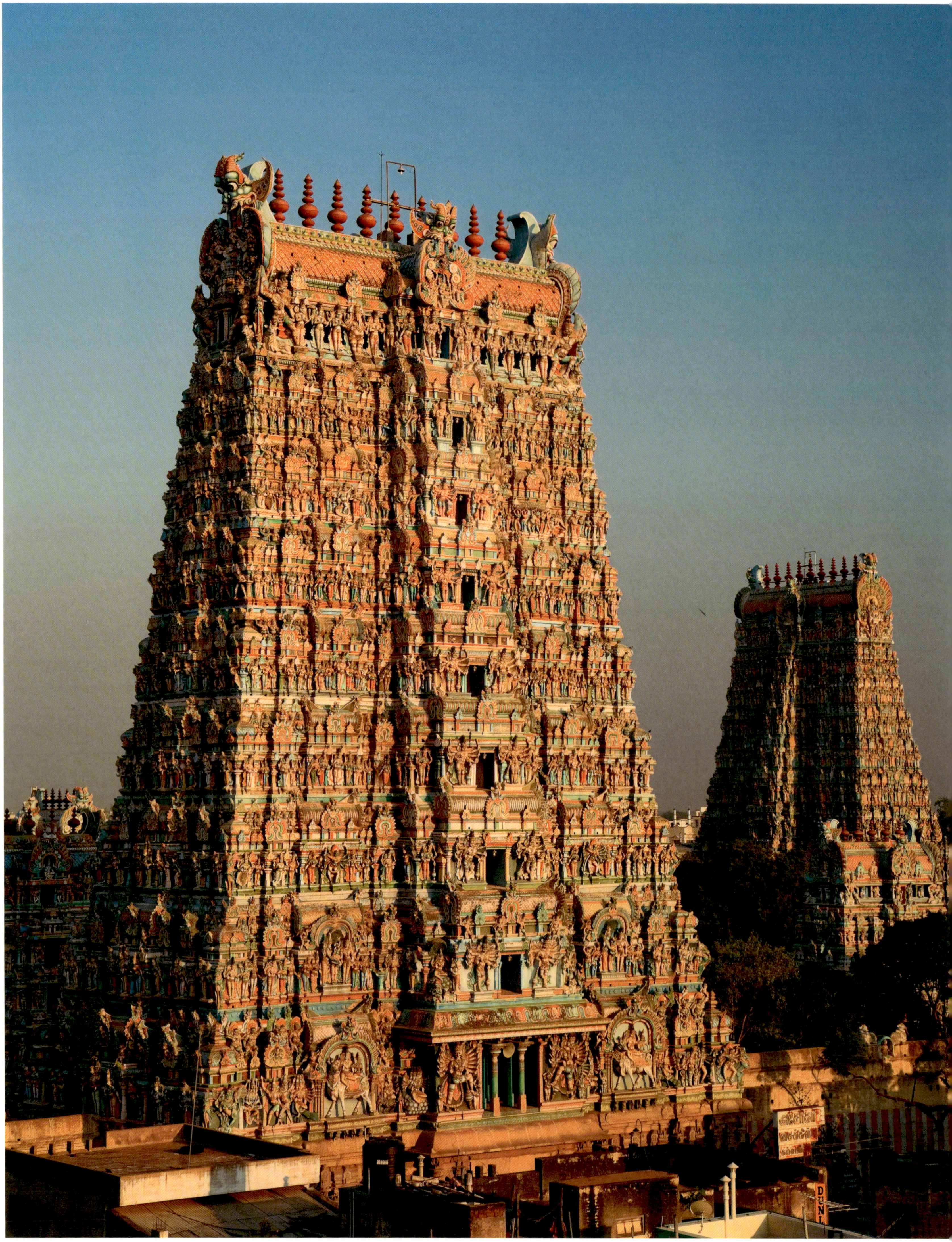

Meenakshi Temple

For a Goddess with Divine Eyes

Built: 6th century CE, rebuilt 16th and 17th centuries CE, Madurai, India

In the sacred pond of the temple, where a golden lotus blooms at its center, the heavenly Devas are said to have once bathed.

In the heart of Madurai, one of South India's most ancient cities, rises the magnificent—and staggeringly intricate—Meenakshi Temple. Dedicated to the Goddess Meenakshi, an incarnation of Parvati, and her beloved Shiva, worshipped here as Sundareshvara, this temple celebrates divine love and union. Meenakshi, a revered goddess with beautifully shaped, fish-like eyes, embodies fertility and love, and is one of the rare female deities in Hinduism to have a temple in her honor. The entire site celebrates the celestial union of Meenakshi and her lover Sundareshvara: each evening, the idol of Sundareshvara is carried in a grand procession to the silver chamber of his goddess, only to return to his own sanctum during morning prayers.

The Meenakshi Temple exemplifies Dravidian architecture. Four gorgeous, intricately carved main entrances—the largest of the temple's 14 *gopurams*—provide access to the sprawling complex. These vibrant towers are covered in thousands of colorful statues that depict gods, demons, and mythical beings. Each figure, vital to the overarching story, is painted in vivid hues that are refreshed every twelve years. In the interior, the Hall of a Thousand Pillars, a richly ornamented space with 985 exquisitely carved columns, serves as both a museum and a sanctuary for meditation. At the temple's core lies the Potramarai Kulam, a sacred pond with a golden lotus at its center. According to legend, the heavenly Devas once bathed in its waters, imbuing it with profound spiritual significance. Devotees often perform ritual ablutions here, aligning themselves with divine purity and heightening their awareness of the soul's sanctity. The golden lotus stands as a symbol of spiritual enlightenment, and entering these sacred waters is believed to bring blessings and success.

For the people of South India, the Meenakshi Temple holds as much cultural and spiritual significance as the Taj Mahal does for the North. It serves as both a sacred space for prayer and tradition and a vibrant hub of art, culture, and Hindu history. Originally built in the 6th century—according to legend, by survivors of the mythical continent Kumari Kandam—the temple was destroyed by invaders in the 14th century, and magnificently rebuilt in the 16th and 17th centuries.

Each year, millions of pilgrims journey to Madurai, drawn by the spiritual aura of this holy site. They come to marvel at its awe-inspiring architecture, towering *gopurams*, intricate sculptures, and splendid halls—but, above all, to feel the power and splendor of Meenakshi and Sundareshvara's divine love.

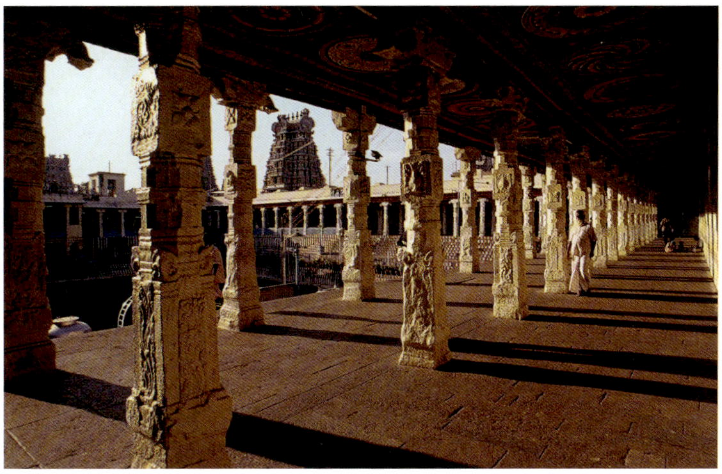

Opposite Meenakshi Temple is renowned for its 14 *gopurams*.
Above About 15,000 pilgrims visit the temple daily.

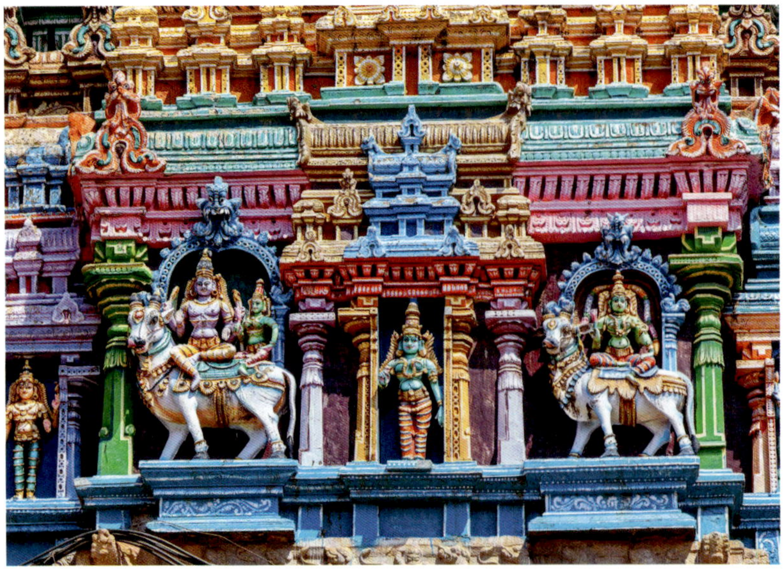

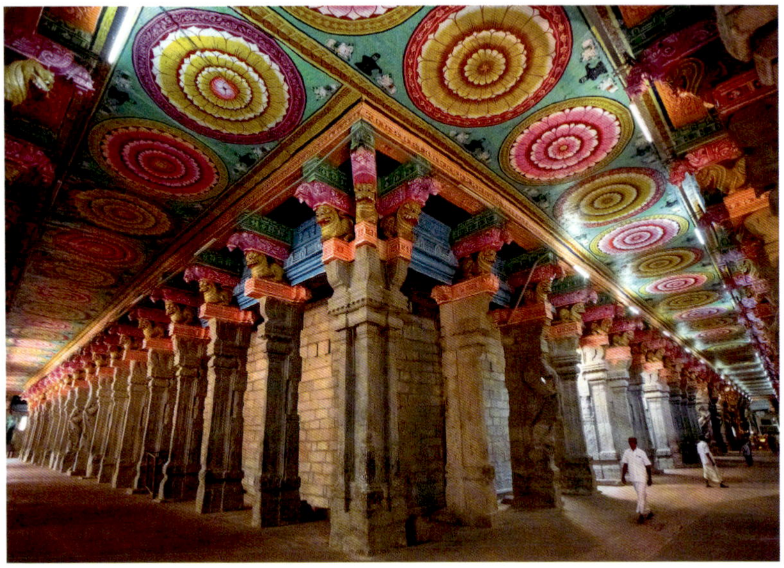

For the people of South India, Meenakshi Temple holds as much cultural and spiritual significance as the Taj Mahal does for the North.

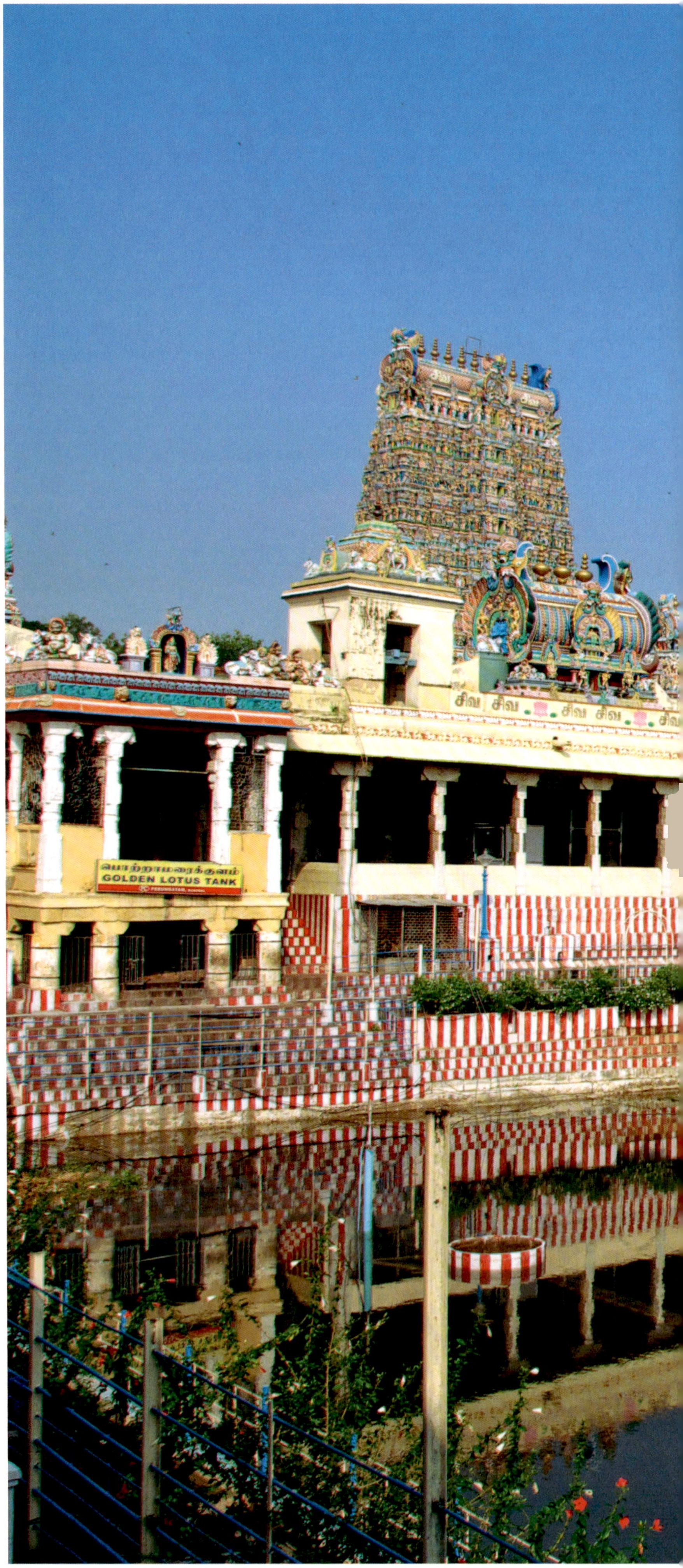

Top The myths of the Hindu pantheon shine in a thousand colors at Meenakshi Temple.
Bottom The magical "Hall of a Thousand Pillars" is a must-see.

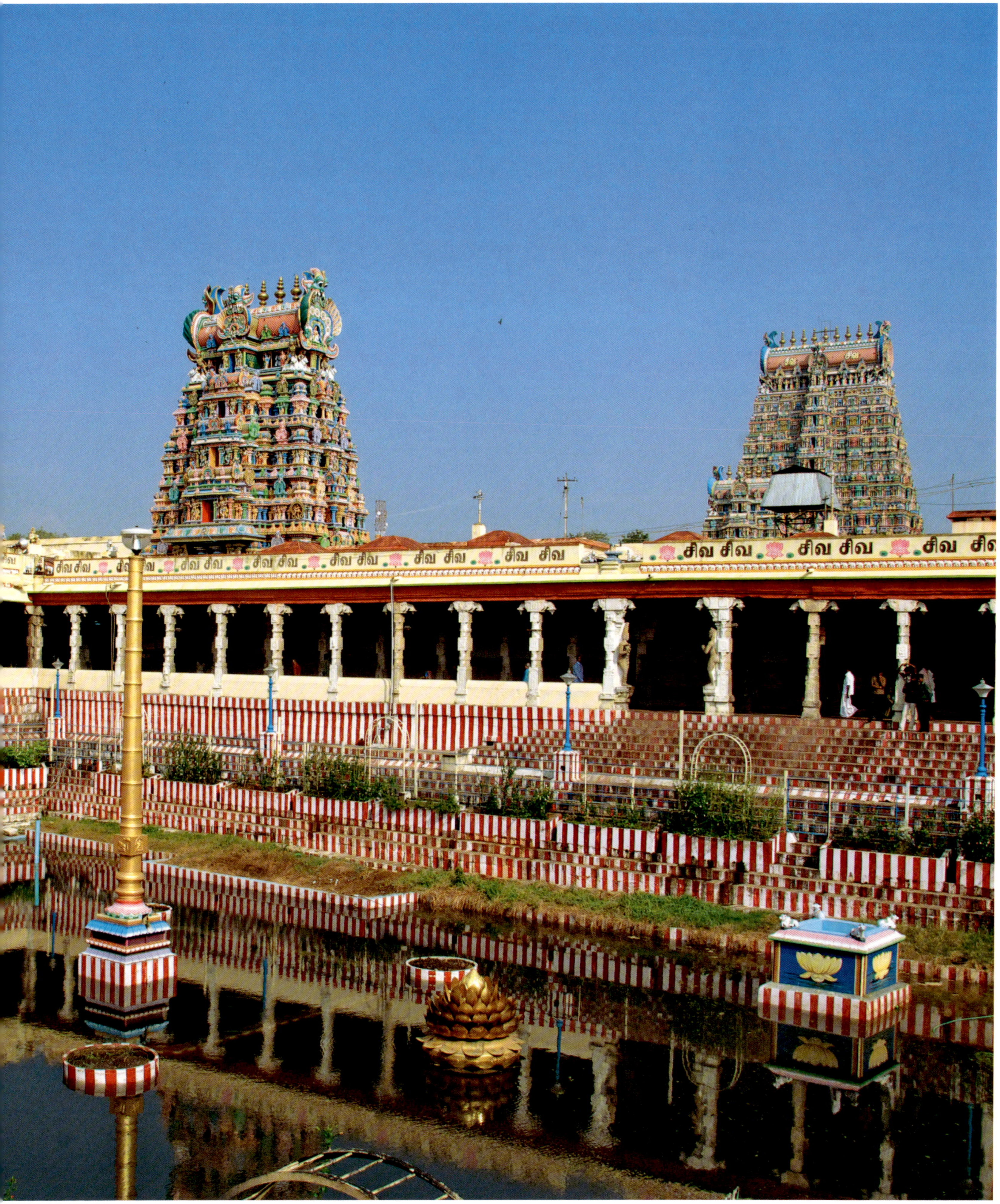

Above Within the temple, the sacred pond Potramarai Kulam is used by pilgrims for ritual cleansing and symbolizes purity, enlightenment, and the removal of worldly impurities.

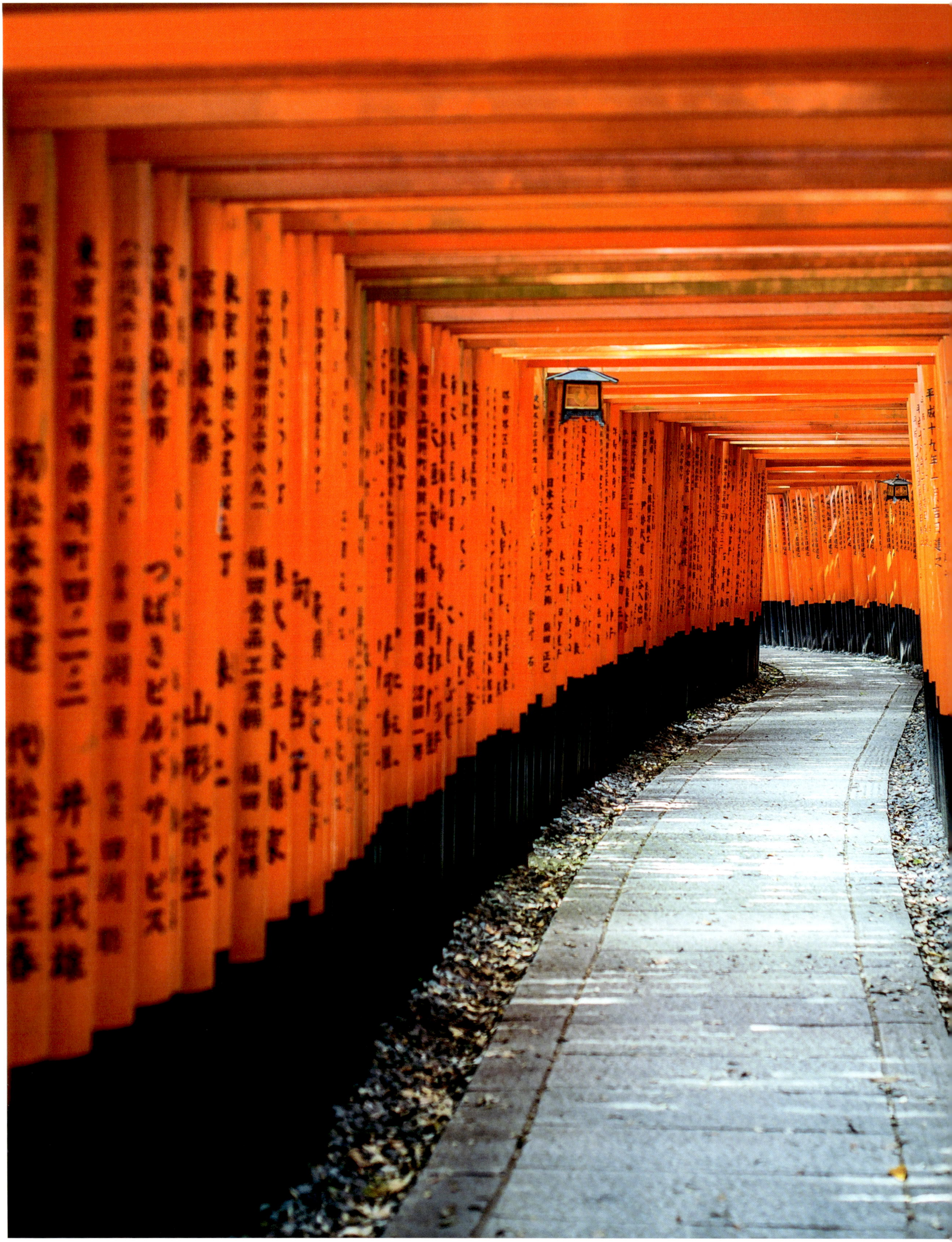
東京都立川市幸町四ノ二ノ二
つばきビルドサービス

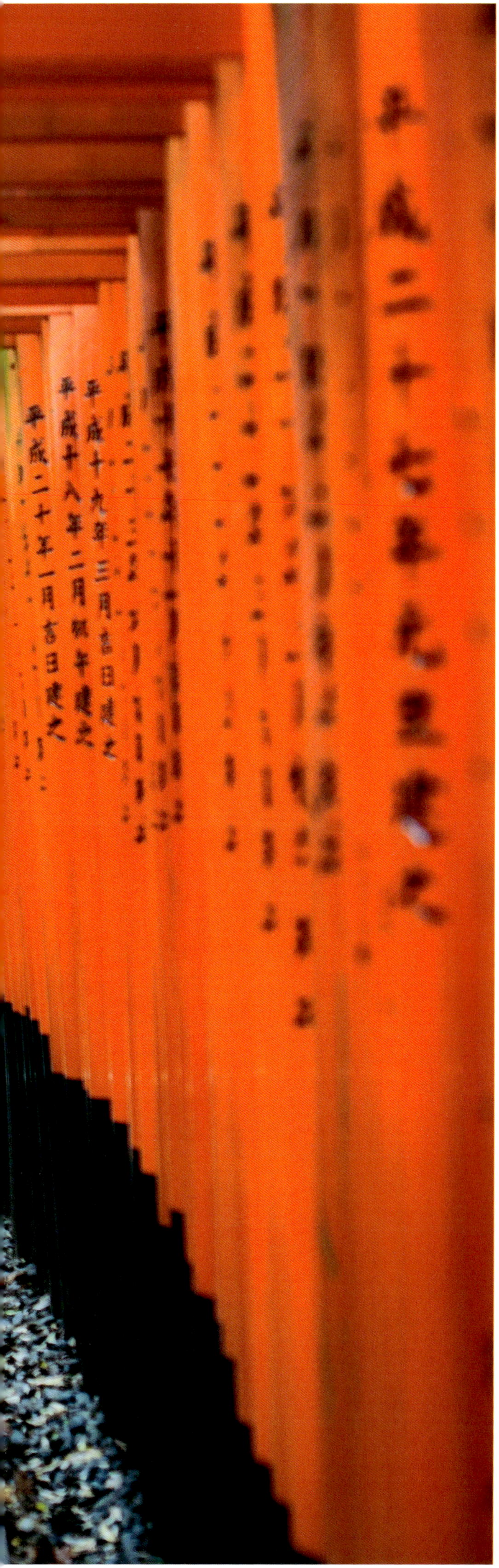

Fushimi Inari Shrine

Where the Fox Spirits Watch

Built: 8th century CE, Kyoto, Japan

For over 1,300 years, worshippers have visited the shrine to pray for sustenance and well-being.

A staggering succession of gates frame the path to the summit of *Inariyama,* or Mount Inari. Known as the "Path of a Thousand *Torii,*" it winds up the slopes, passing numerous smaller shrines along the way. At the base of the mountain lies one of Japan's most significant Shinto shrines: Fushimi Inari-taisha. Here, for centuries, the deity Inari has been invoked for bountiful harvests and prosperity.

Painted vermillion, a color traditionally used as protection against evil forces, the *torii* of Mount Inari symbolize the transition from the human world to the spiritual. They are donated to the site as a gesture of gratitude for fulfilled wishes, or as a plea for future blessings. The further one follows the *torii* up the mountain, the deeper one ventures into the spiritual dimension of the shrine. Hundreds of stone statues of *kitsune,* or fox spirits, guard the faithful as messengers of Inari. In Japanese mythology, foxes are considered wise and cunning beings capable of shape-shifting and trickery. Here, on the grounds of Fushimi Inari Shrine, many *kitsune* carry a key in their mouths, symbolizing access to the granaries where precious rice is stored. Other *kitsune* carry jewels, which represent spiritual enlightenment.

The path continues through shaded forests, passing small shrines. Along the way, one finds breathtaking views of the ancient imperial city of Kyoto. In the *Yamashirokoku Fudoki,* an ancient provincial account, it is written that the legendary Irogu no Hatanokimi practiced archery here. When he shot an arrow at a rice cake, the cake miraculously transformed into a white swan and flew to the summit of Mount Inari. At the spot where the bird landed, an auspicious event occurred: rice began to grow. In gratitude, Irogu no Hatanokimi built a shrine at that very place. Today, only a *shinseki* remains at the summit, marking where the shrine once stood. Yet, the deity's presence remains, both on the mountaintop and at the current shrine at the mountain's base.

Most visitors take a brief walk along the *torii*-adorned paths at the foot of the mountain. However, those with more time and a deeper interest in the spiritual heritage of the site embark on the roughly two-hour hike to the summit. Today, Fushimi Inari-taisha is at the heart of a network of around 30,000 Inari-dedicated shrines spread across Japan. Yet with its thousands of vermillion gates and attendant fox spirits, it remains the most mystical and iconic.

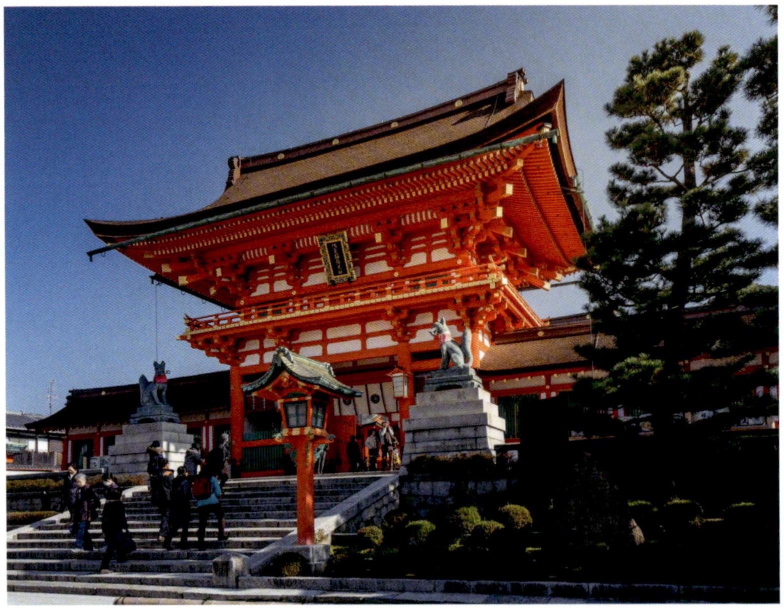

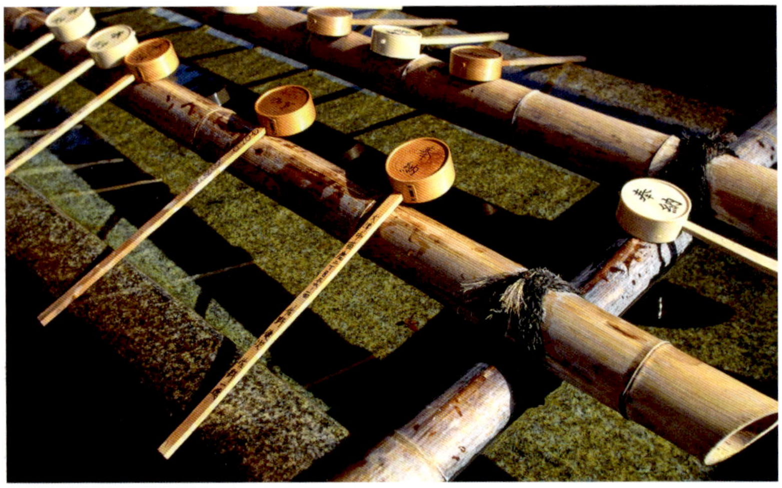

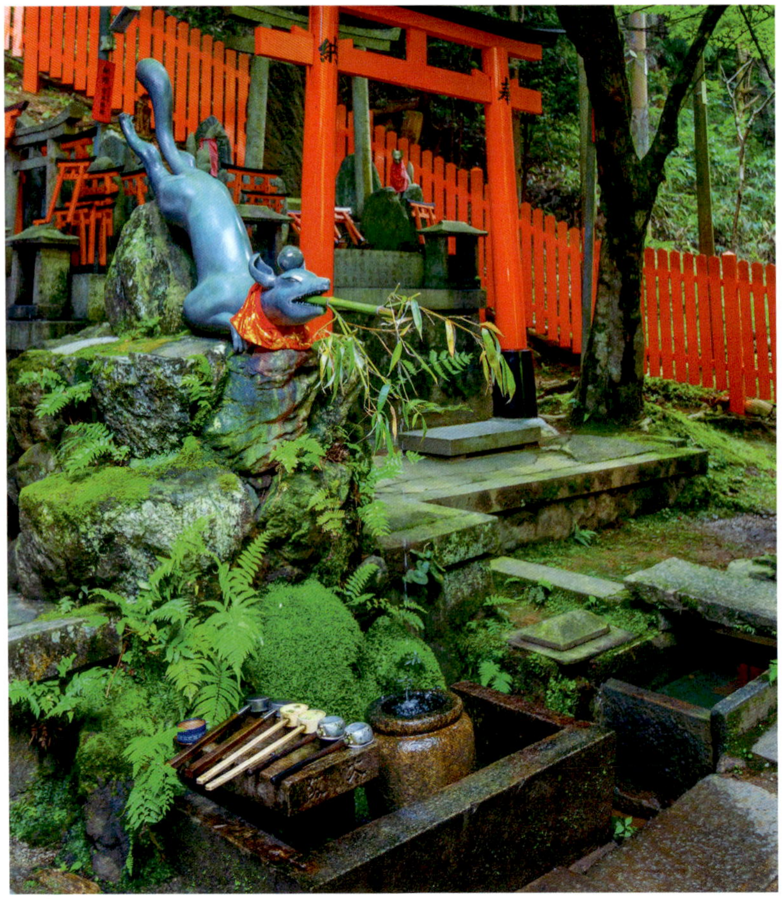

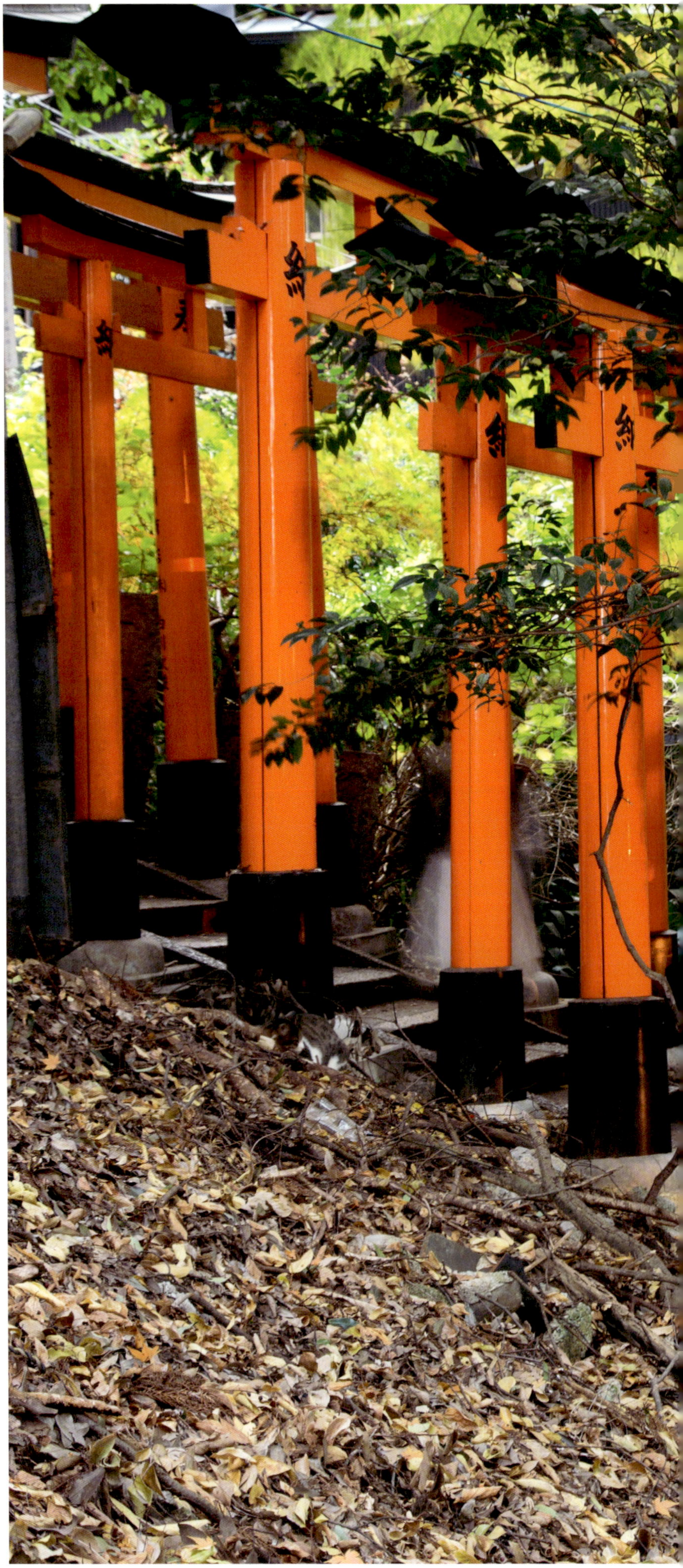

Top Stone statues of *kitsune*, or fox spirits, greet visitors from the sides of the stairs.
Middle The ladles are used for the purification ritual.
Bottom Each *torii* was donated to honor the deity Inari.

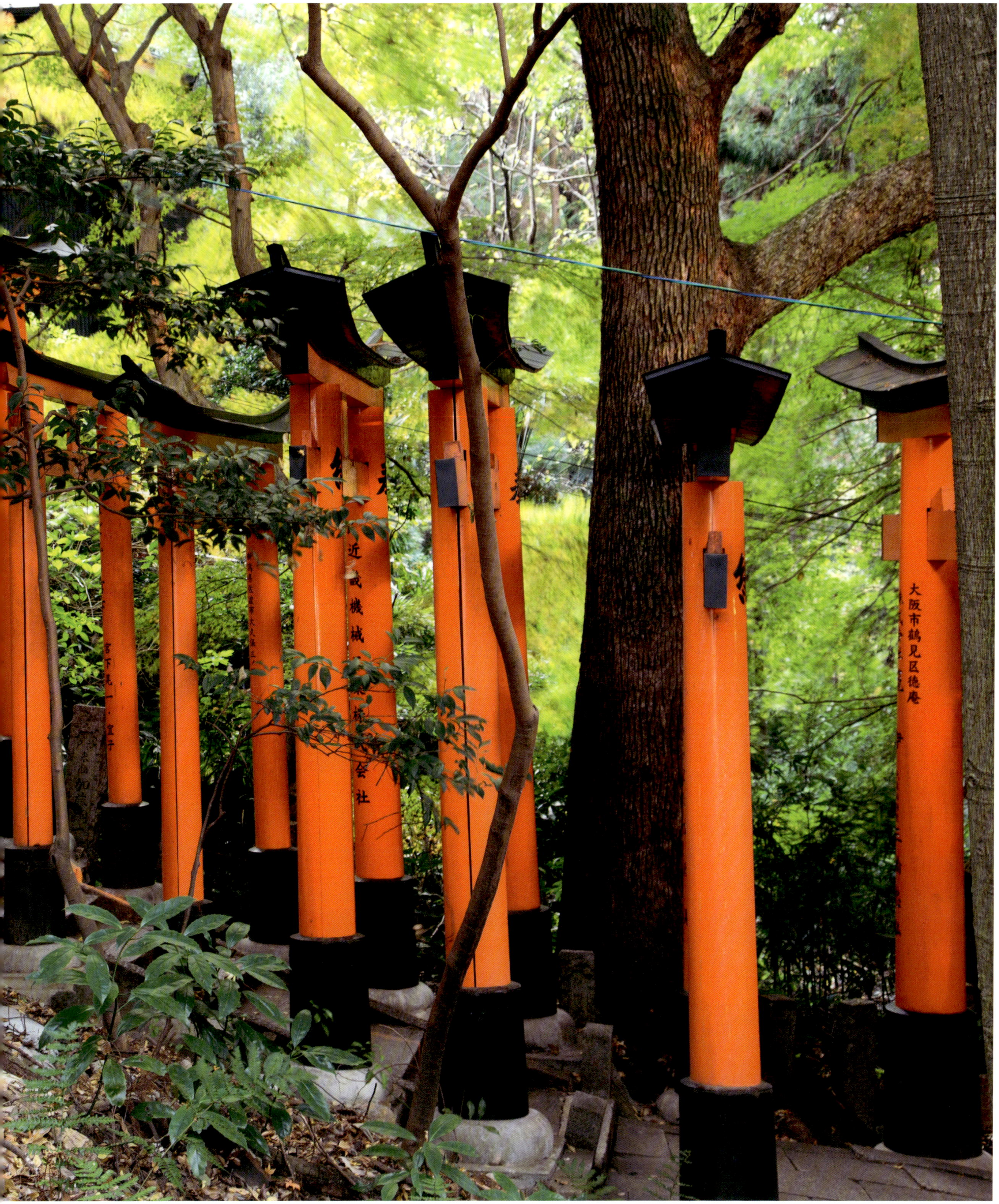

Above The famous "Path of a Thousand *Torii*" winds its way up to the summit of Mount Inari in vibrant hues, symbolizing the transition from the human world to the realm of the gods.

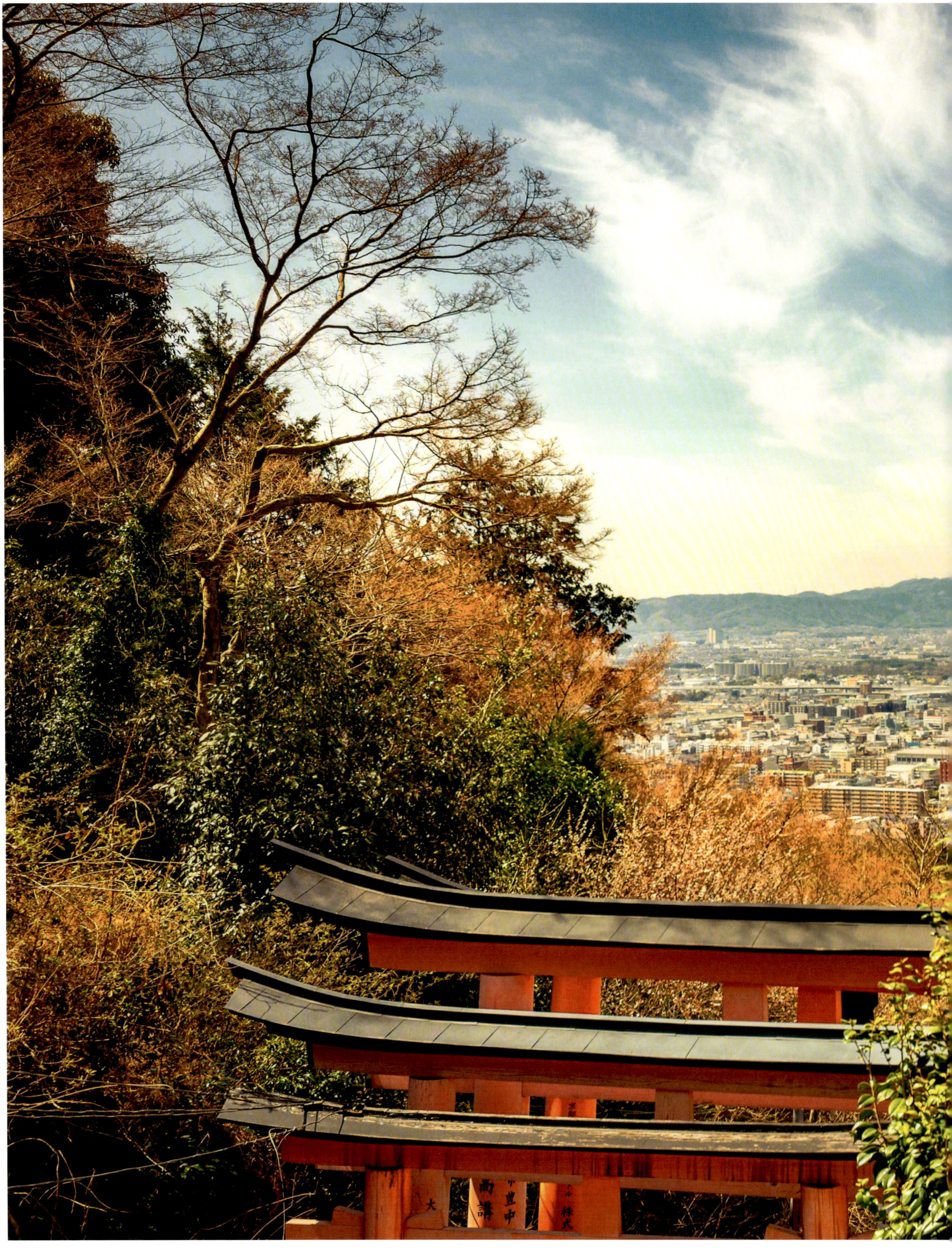

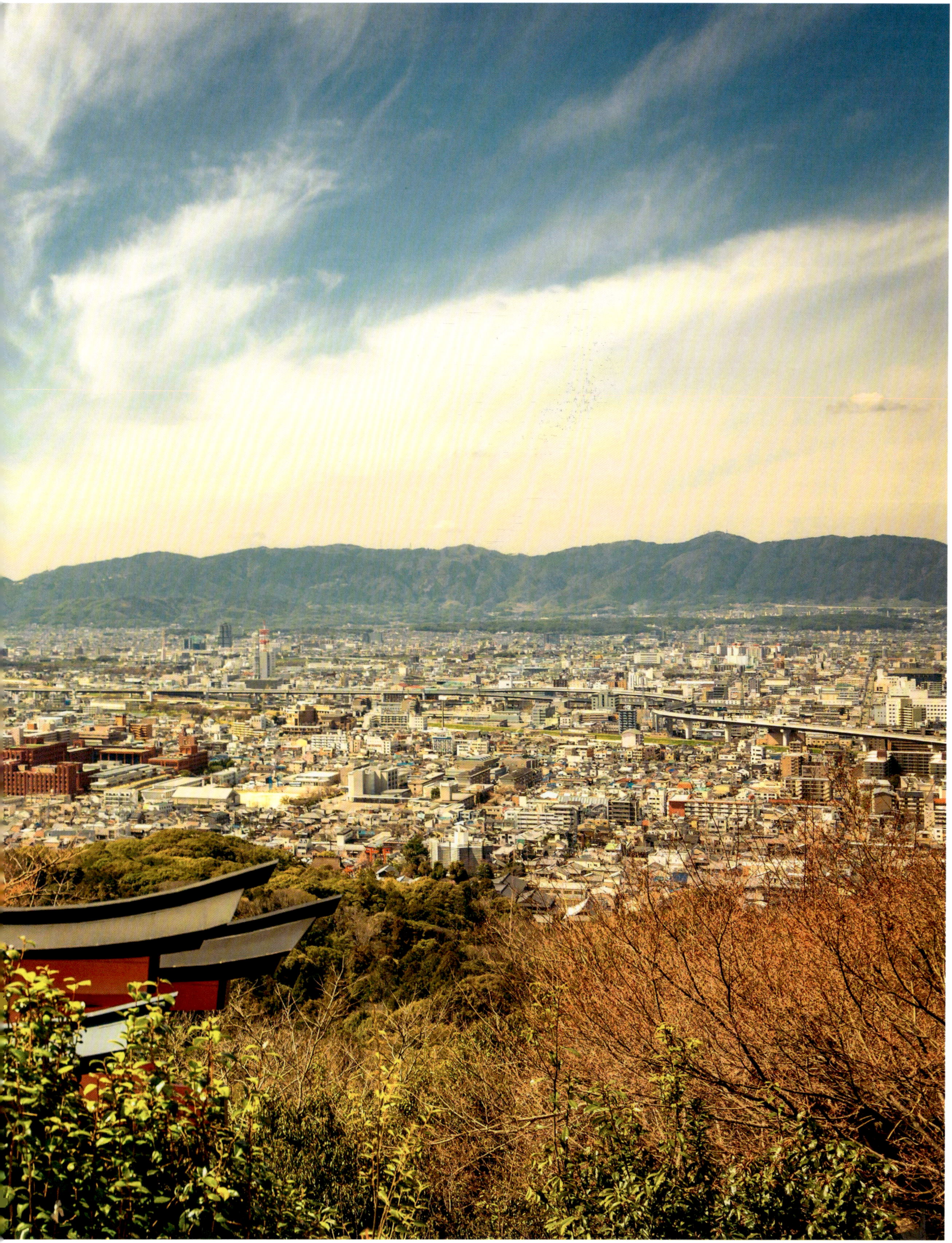

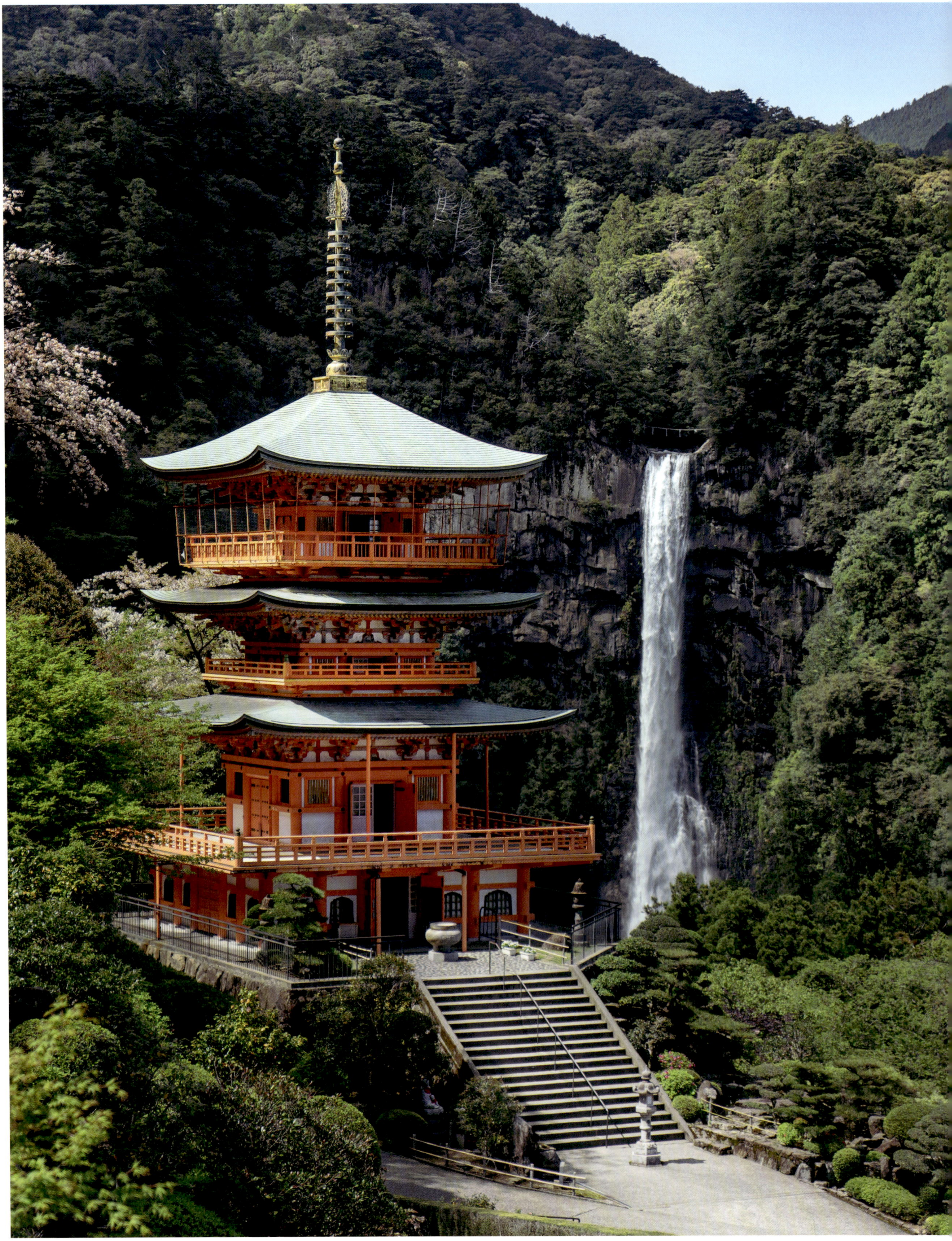

Seiganto-ji

Between Symmetry and Syncretism

Built: 4th century CE,
rebuilt in the 16th century CE,
Nachikatsuura, Japan

Buddhism and Shintoism could hardly have chosen a more picturesque setting for their convergence.

A dazzling tableau, the three tiers of the vibrant red pagoda of Seiganto-ji rise into the sky above the primeval forest of Nachi, while behind it, the sacred waters of Nachi-no-Otaki cascade 436 feet (133 meters) down the mountainside. Seiganto-ji is one of the most stunning temples along the Kumano Kodō, the ancient Japanese pilgrimage route. As an expansive complex that includes the Nyorindō (main hall), the renowned three-tiered pagoda, and the Ryuhoden (treasure hall), it carries a rich and storied history.

According to legend, Seiganto-ji, the "Temple of Crossing the Blue Shore," was founded in the 4th century by the monk Ragyō Shōnin. While meditating at the waterfalls, he was visited by Kannon, the Bodhisattva of Compassion, and decided to build a structure in her honor. Yet even before this, the waterfalls were regarded as sacred. Local lore holds that the kami spirit Hiryū Gongen, the "Flying Waterfall Avatar," resides here—a Shinto deity embodying the purity and power of the waters. Over the centuries, the Buddhist veneration of Kannon and the Shinto reverence for Hiryū Gongen blended into a unique and harmonious vision. Seiganto-ji became a place where Shinto and Buddhism were not seen as opposites but as complementary forces, united in their connection to nature and compassion.

The present Seiganto-ji was carefully rebuilt in the 16th century after the original temple was destroyed during the Sengoku period, a time of civil war and upheaval in Japan. Surrounded by lush greenery, the temple exudes understated elegance and harmonious symmetry. Its pagoda, with its simple yet striking three-tiered structure and gracefully curving roofs, appears almost painted onto the landscape. The main hall, or Nyorindō, is a quintessential example of Momoyama-era architecture. Its standout feature is the *waniguchi* drum, the largest of its kind in Japan, symbolizing the link between heaven and earth and playing a central role in the temple's rituals. Just a short distance away lies the Ryuhoden, or treasure hall, which houses intricately crafted sutra cylinders, statues, and altar fittings unearthed by archaeologists near the waterfall.

The steady sound of Nachi-no-Otaki's cascading waters provides a meditative rhythm for visitors of Seiganto-ji. Indifferent to the temple's turbulent history, the waters plunge into the depths below, embodying, as they go, both divine nature and impermanence—an extraordinary fusion of both the Buddhist and Shinto traditions.

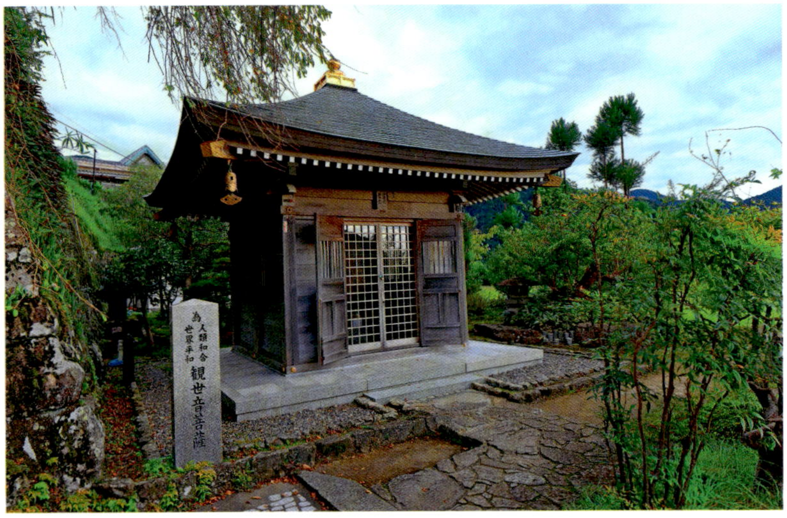

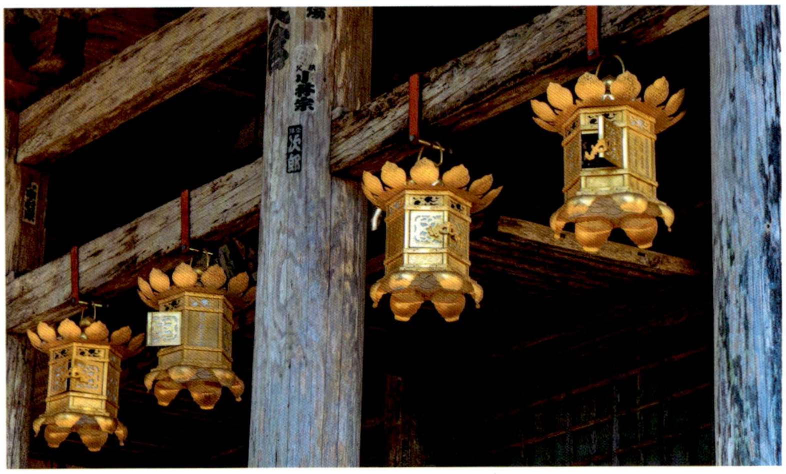

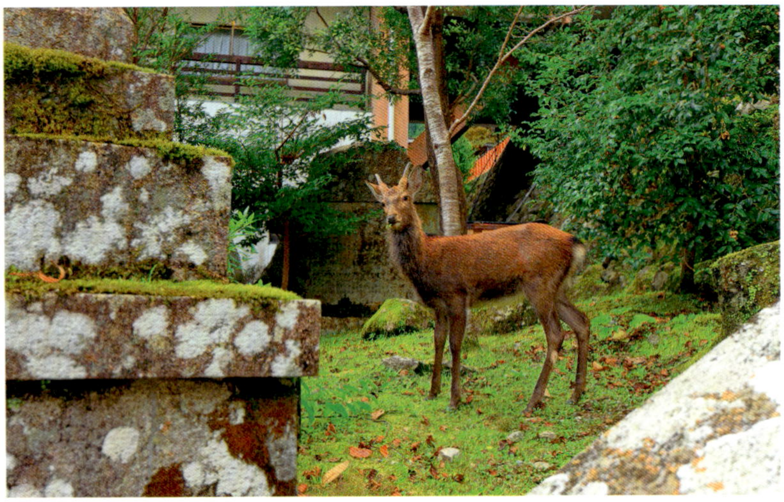

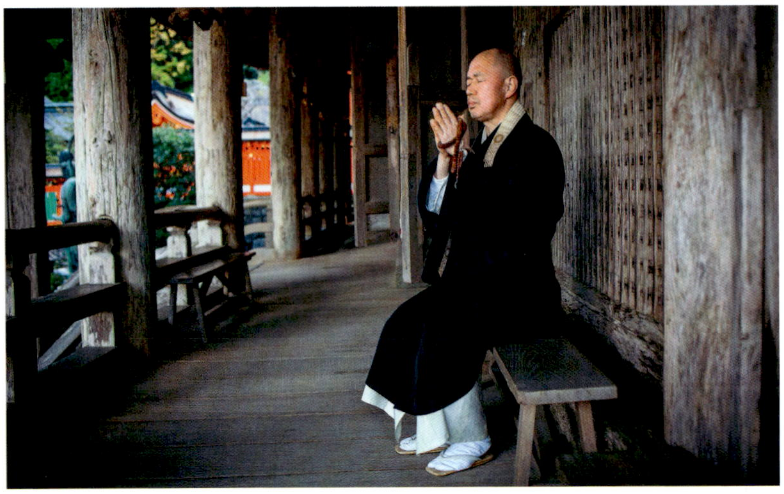

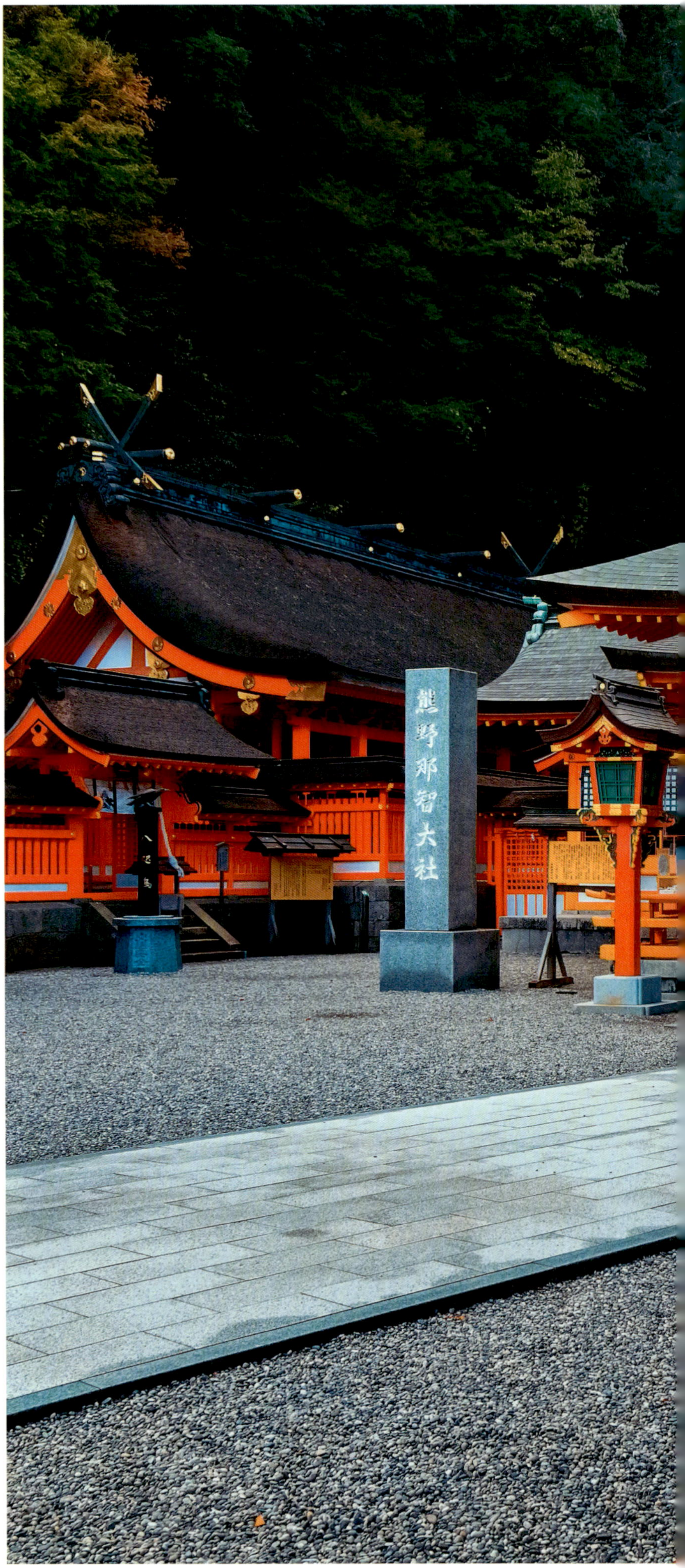

Nachikatsuura, Japan

Top Visitors will find numerous shrines on the temple grounds.
Upper middle Traditional temple lanterns adorn the wooden beams.
Lower middle The proximity to nature attracts animal visitors as well.
Bottom Seiganto-ji marks the start of the Saigoku Kannon Pilgrimage.

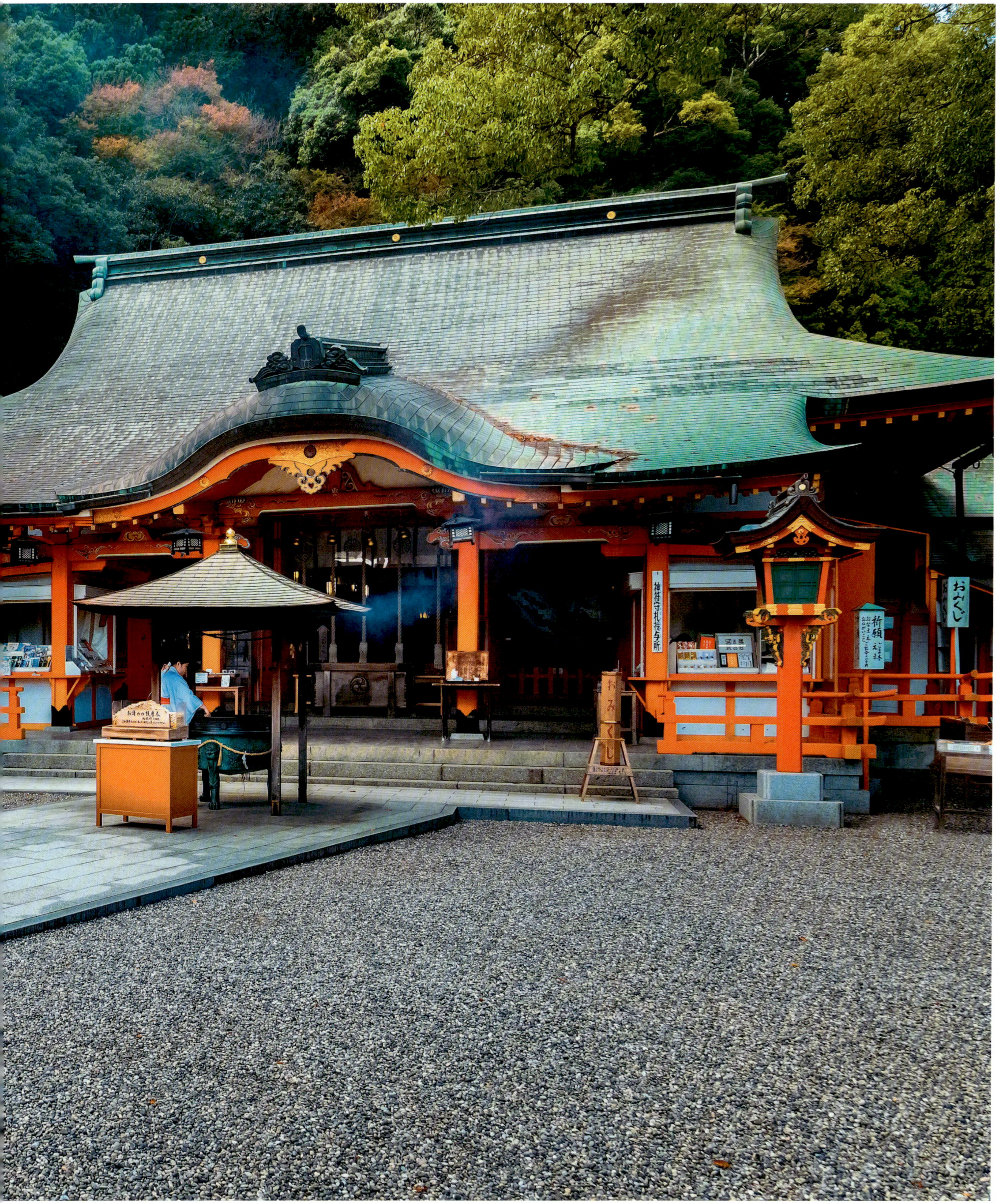

Above Since 2004, the temple complex of Seiganto-ji has been part of UNESCO's "Sacred Sites and Pilgrimage Routes in the Kii Mountain Range".

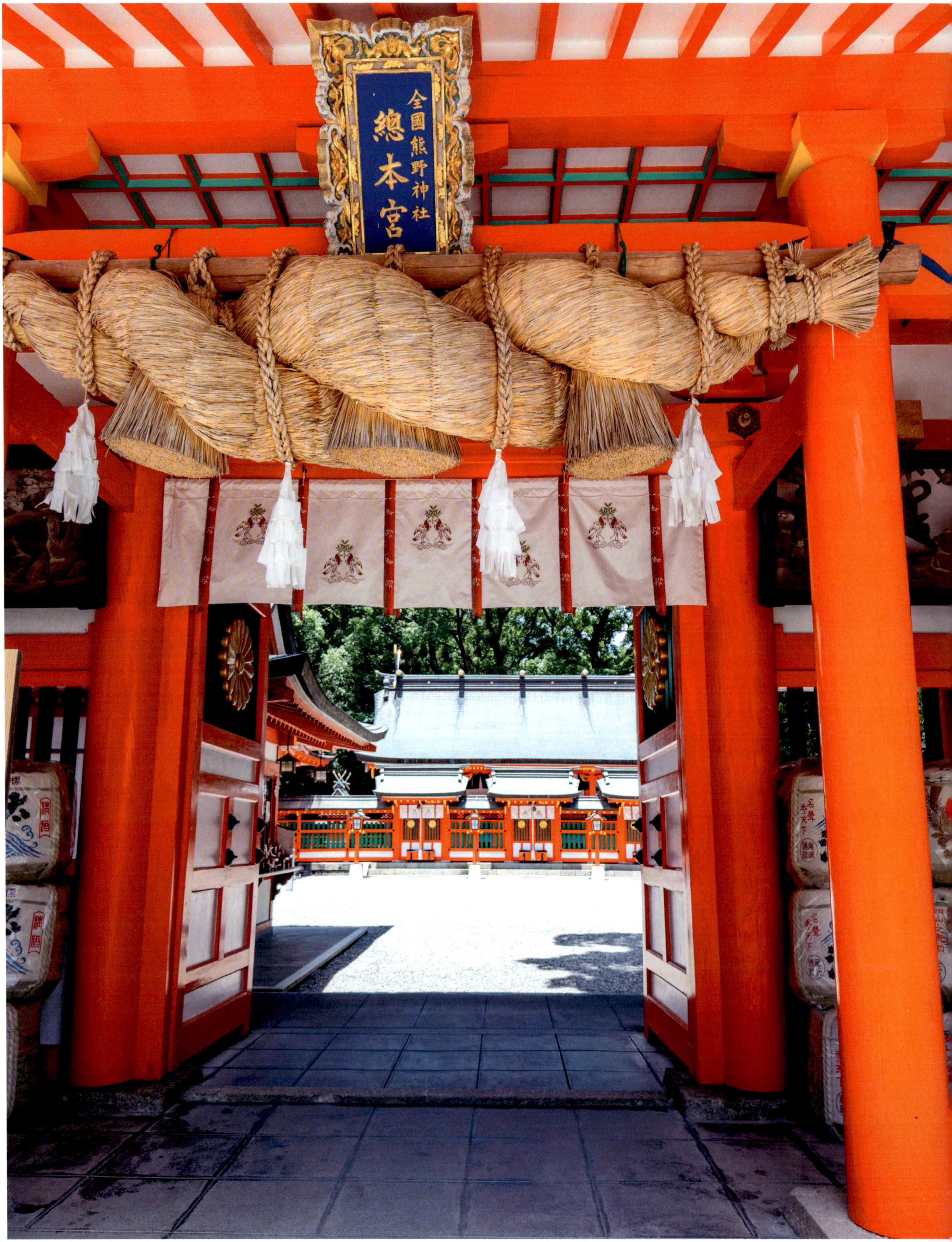
全國熊野神社
總本宮

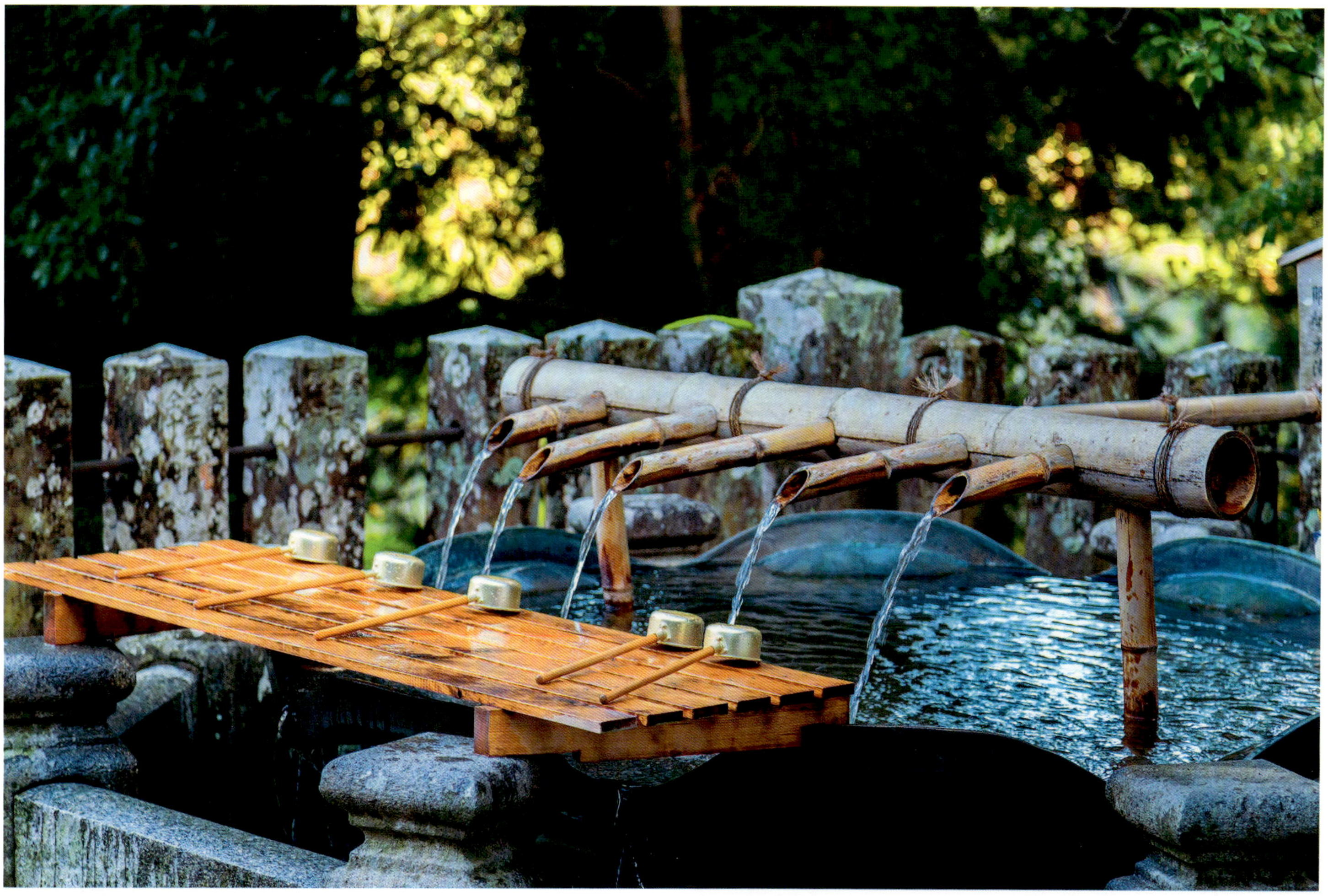

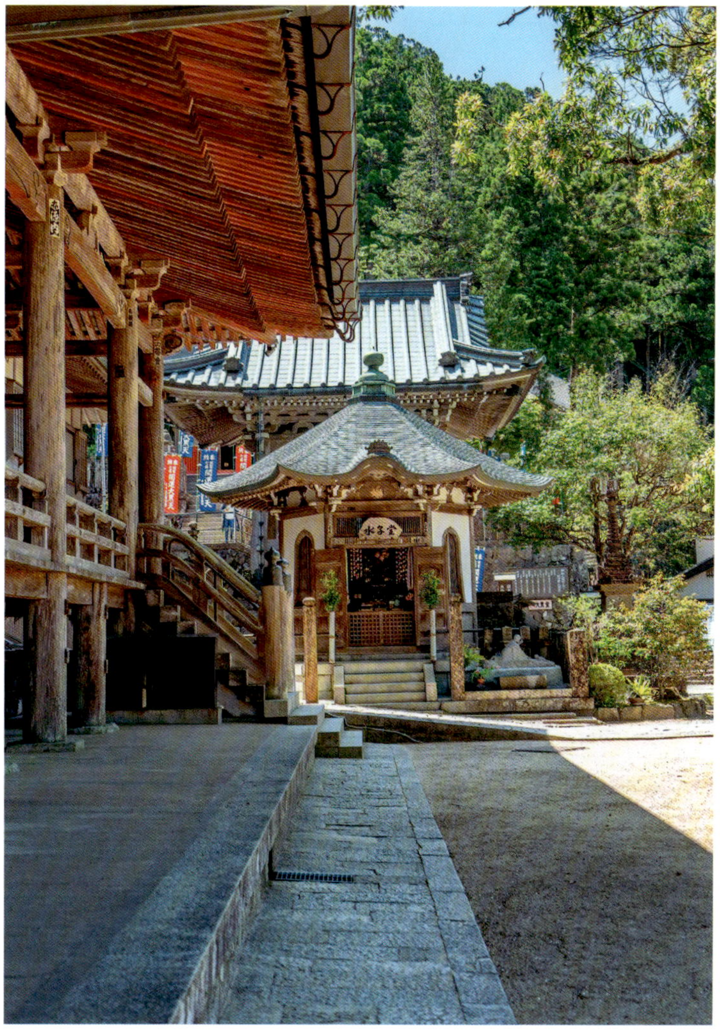

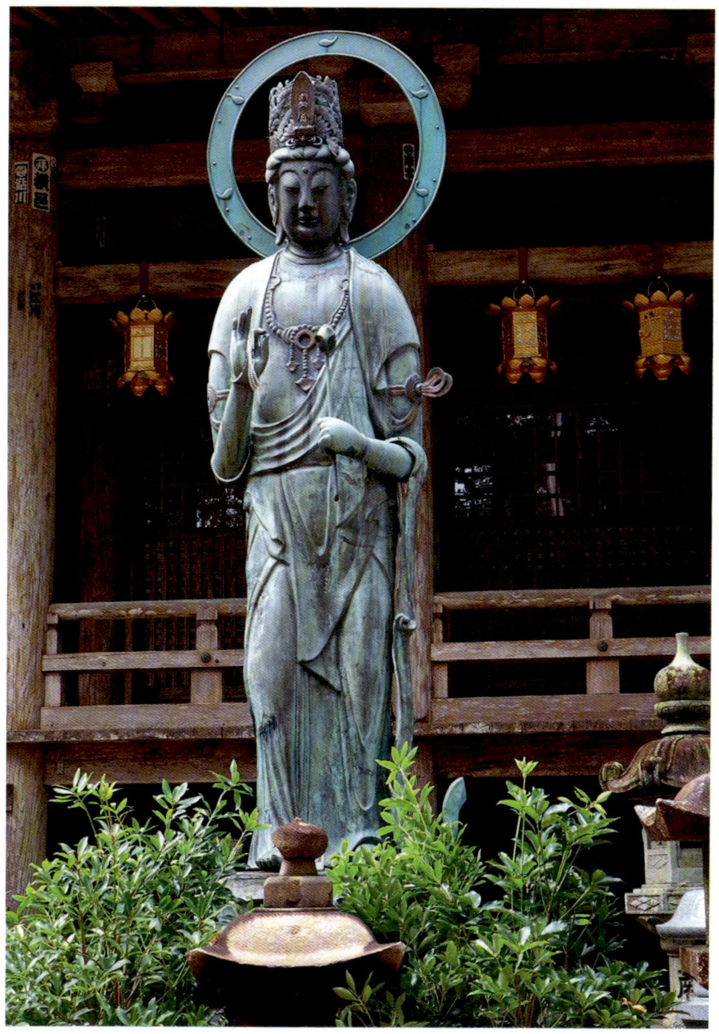

Opposite The doors of Seiganto-ji are wide open to visitors.
Top The water invites pilgrims to undertake spiritual purification.
Bottom left Buddhist and Shinto elements merge here.
Bottom right A Buddha statue watches over the temple.

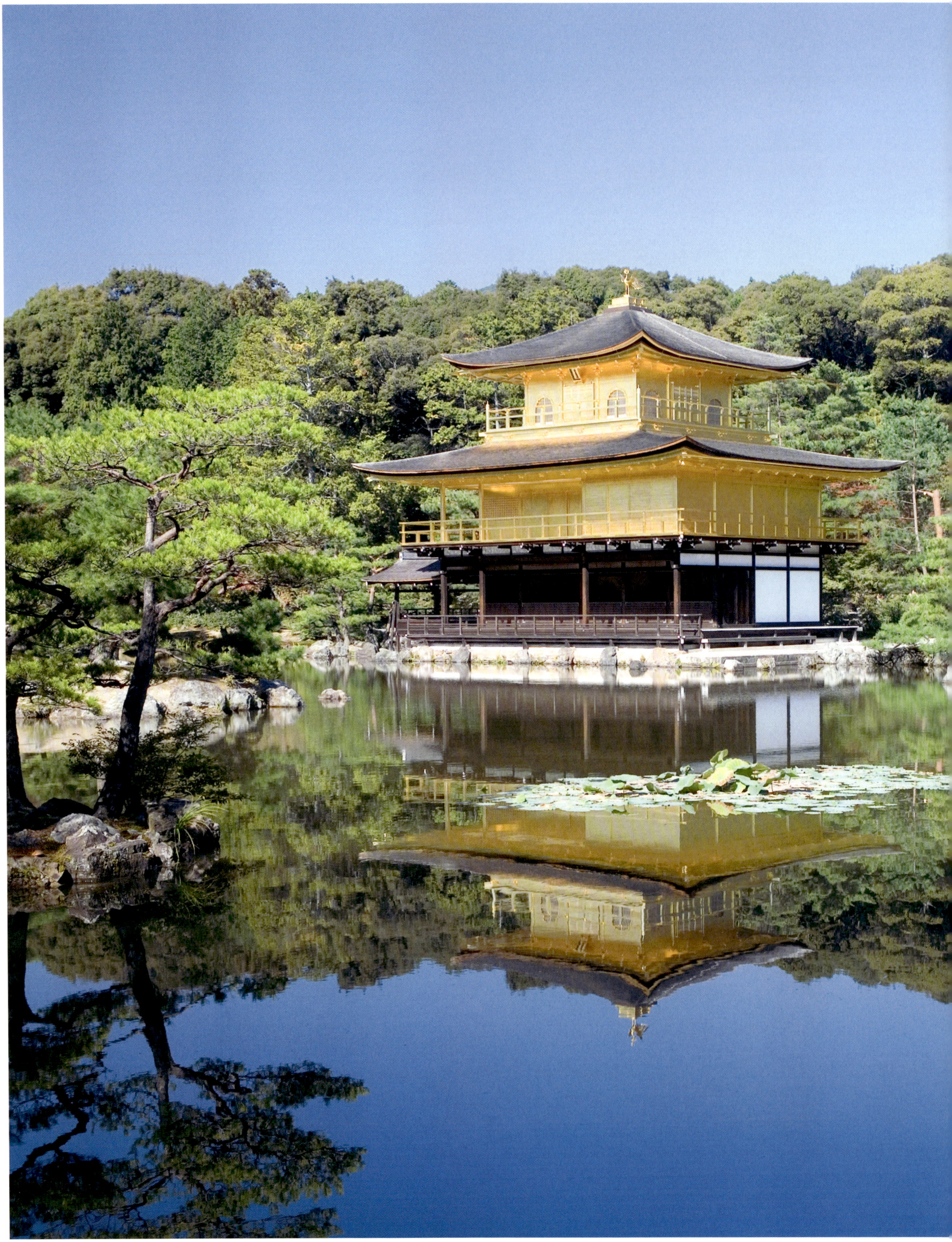

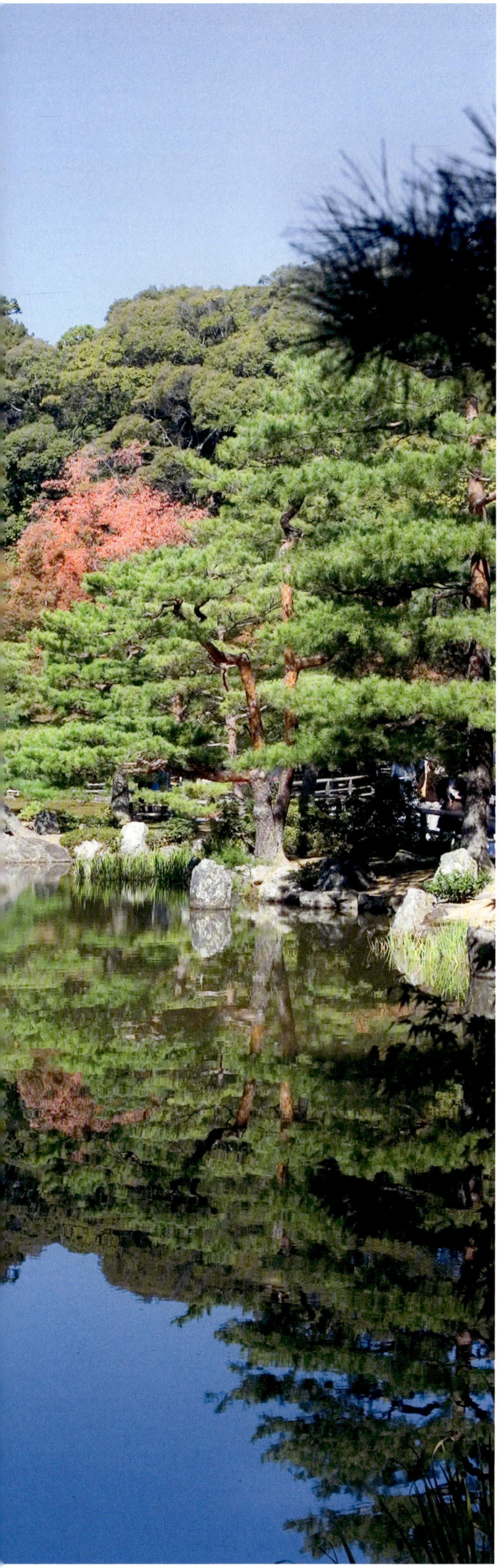

Kinkaku-ji

Mirror of the Mind

Built: 14th century CE, rebuilt in 1955 CE, Kyoto, Japan

Gazing into the still waters of this temple's pond, one might just catch a glimpse of their true self.

Kinkaku-ji's golden pavilion is reflected so perfectly in the calm waters of the Kyōko-chi pond that, from afar, the temple appears doubled. The building is a masterpiece of Japanese architecture, embodying the principles of Zen down to the smallest detail.

Each of its three stories represents a different architectural tradition and cultural influence. The sense of simplicity, openness, and naturalness that permeates the first story recalls the *shinden-zukuri* style popular during the Heian period. The second story, reflective of the *buke-zukuri* style associated with samurai residences and whose exterior is covered in gold leaf, offers a feeling of both discipline and transience. The top story, the "Cupola of the Ultimate," is modeled after a Zen meditation hall and continues with gold-leaf inside and out—a touch designed to purify the minds of those who meditate.

Surrounding the pavilion lies the garden of Kinkaku-ji, a space where Zen tradition comes to life. The design emphasizes harmony between humanity and nature and invites visitors to engage in mindful awareness. Each stone and plant has been precisely placed to create the ideal setting for practice. The garden's paths guide visitors through shifting perspectives, allowing them to experience the principle of impermanence and the ever-changing nature of the world.

The Kyōko-chi pond, encircling the pavilion, offers visitors a kind of mental mirror, and a welcome opportunity to look within. For the student of Zen, attaining a clear mind, one that reflects the true nature of things without distortion, is a primary goal. Kyōko-chi's tranquil waters, and the interplay between the temple and the pond's reflection, invite contemplation of one's inner reality and its reflections in the world.

The temple, now protected as a UNESCO World Heritage Site, has been damaged and rebuilt several times over the centuries—most recently, in 1950, after falling victim to arson. Yet even in these darker moments lies a Zen lesson: nothing is solid, all is in flux, and permanence is an illusion. Destruction and renewal are integral, unavoidable aspects of existence. What temple could embody these principles more powerfully than Kinkaku-ji?

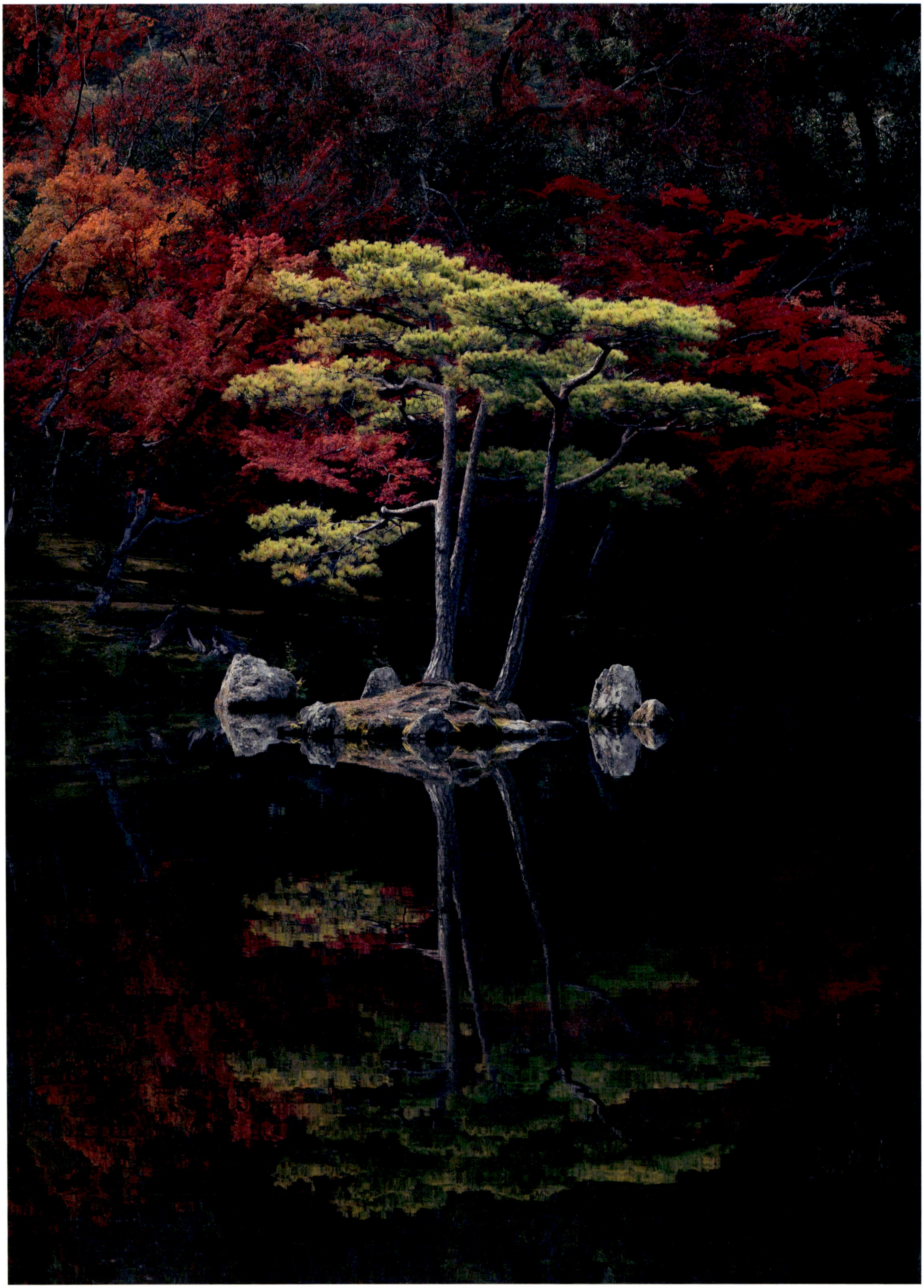

Above Encircling the pavilion, the Kyōko-chi pond embodies the profound concept of the "mirror of the mind," reflecting the true essence of things with serene and undisturbed clarity.

Kyoto, Japan

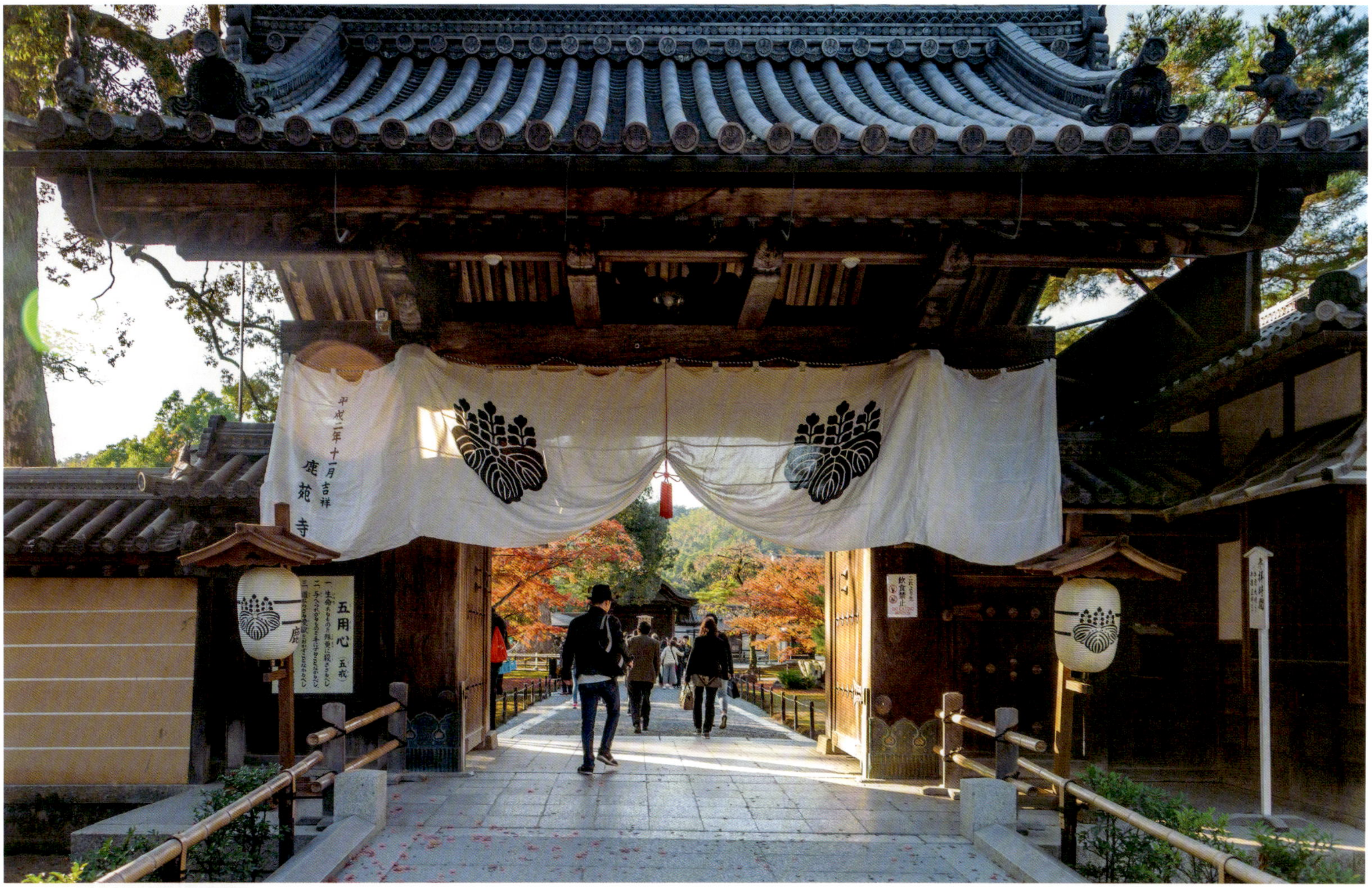

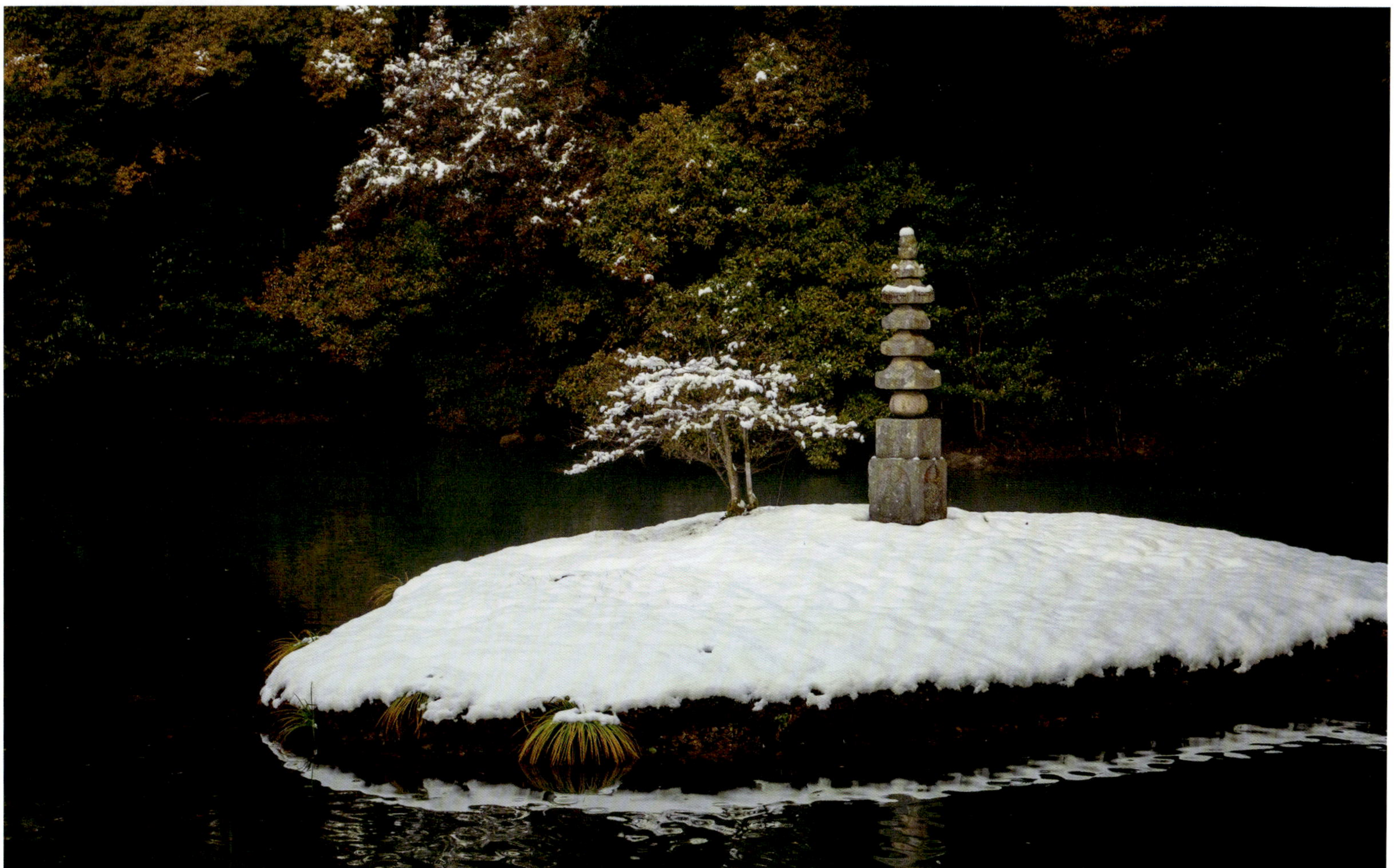

Top Originally built in 1397 as the retirement villa of the shogun Ashikaga Yoshimitsu, the temple was later converted into a Zen temple. *Bottom* Visitors to the Golden Pavilion are invited to reflect on the transience of all forms, and attune their minds to the present.

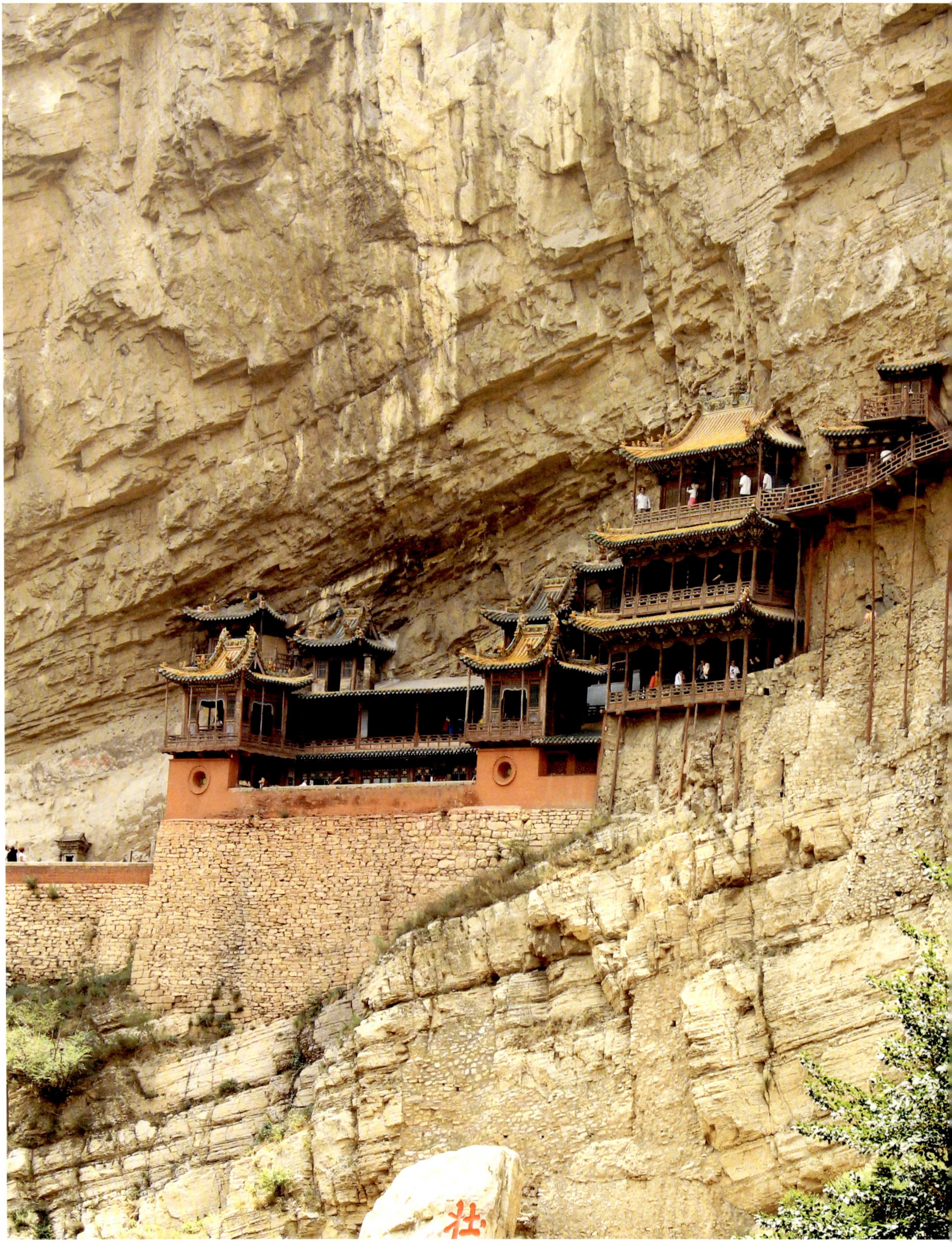

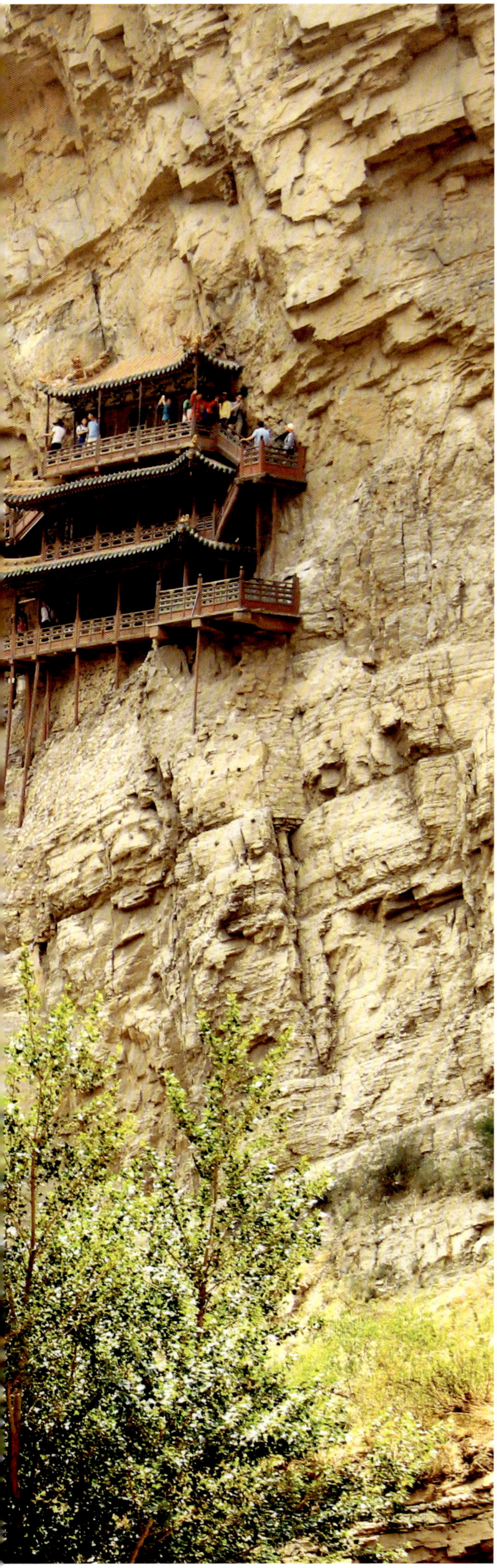

Hanging Temple of Hengshan

Between Heaven, Earth, and Three Spiritual Traditions

Built: 5th century CE, Shanxi Province, China

For this remote place of worship, the laws of gravity seem mysteriously suspended.

Temples often serve as a bridge between heaven and earth, but few structures take this as literally as the Hanging Temple of Hengshan. Perched 246 feet (75 meters) above the ground, it clings to a steep cliff near the foot of Hengshan, a mountain in the Shanxi province. Defying gravity for over 1,500 years, the Hanging Temple, also known as *Xuankong Si,* is a lofty and awe-inspiring feat of engineering. Yet the temple also stands as a symbol of openness and tolerance: under its roof, the three major philosophical and religious traditions of China—Buddhism, Taoism, and Confucianism—are equally represented and honored.

The temple's construction dates to the year 491 CE, during the Northern Wei dynasty. According to legend, a solitary monk named Liao Ran was the chief architect and builder. With the help of only a few assistants, he is said to have spent years hauling materials up the steep mountainside and carving out the rock. Initially, the temple was held in place by means of support beams, driven deep into the cliffside, which gave it the impression of floating in midair—although pillars were later added for extra support. During the Tang dynasty, a divine hand is said to have safeguarded the temple during a massive storm that threatened to destroy it. Local villagers gathered to pray for the temple, and, miraculously, it survived unscathed.

Perhaps it was not a single divine hand that guided the temple throughout the centuries, but three: Buddhists, Taoists, and Confucianists have each found a home here to retreat into silence and contemplation—symbols from all three religions are present side by side. Since the time of the Wei dynasty, the fortunes of Buddhism, Taoism, and Confucianism have risen and fallen with each ruler, but over time, the three philosophies came to be seen not as rivals, but as complementary. Religious sites helped foster broader acceptance and integration among the people, and, in the case of the Hanging Temple, provided a welcoming stopover to travelers of different faiths. Within the Hanging Temple, statues of Buddha, Laozi, and Confucius stand in harmonious coexistence, inviting visitors to seek spiritual truth through the lens of each tradition, or through a creative merging of the three.

Finally, the temple's natural surroundings make it the perfect location for all three religions. Its setting is seemingly destined for Confucian self-cultivation, the Taoist notion of retreat and connection with nature, and for Buddhist meditation practices—right where heaven and earth meet.

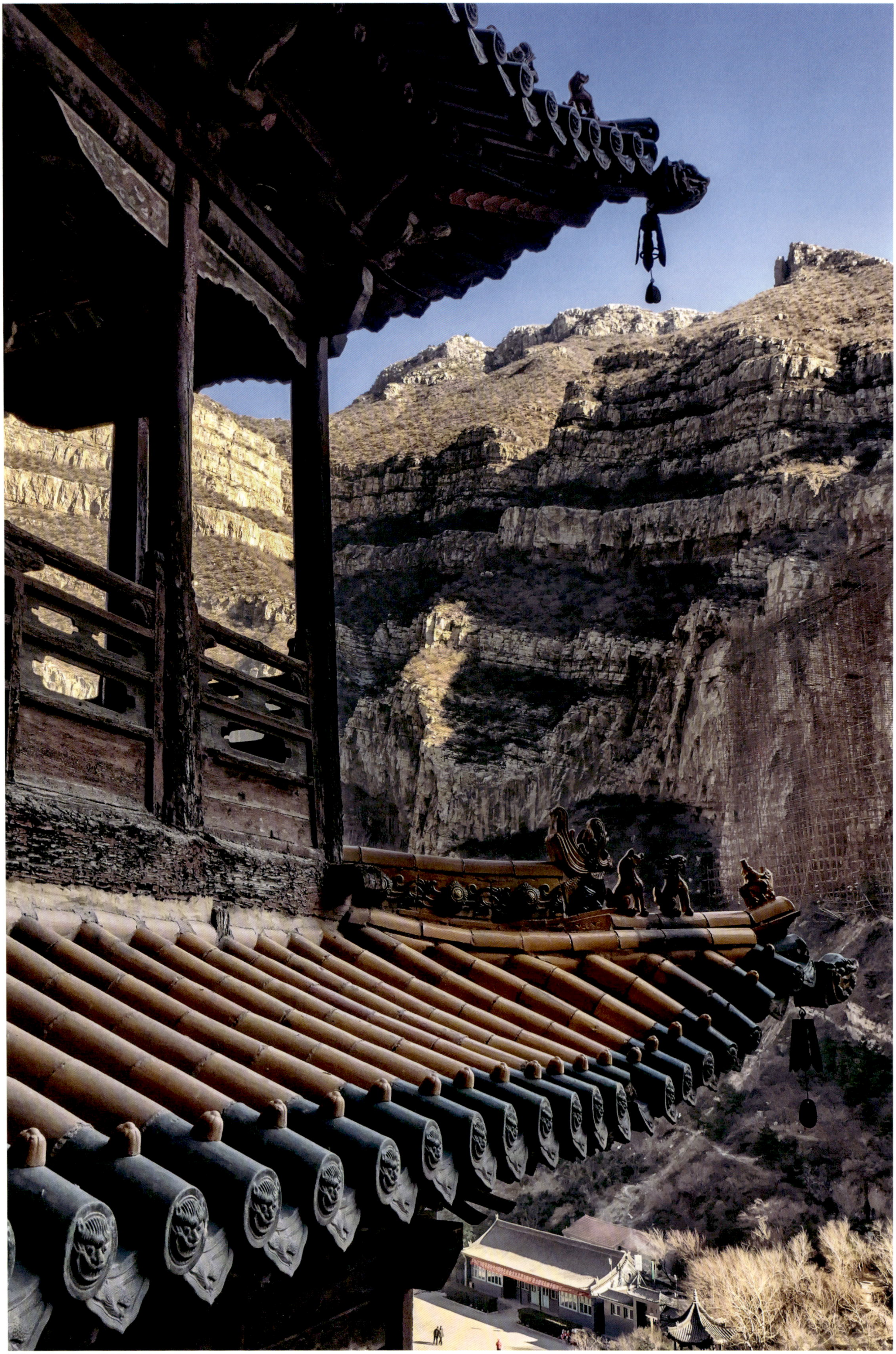

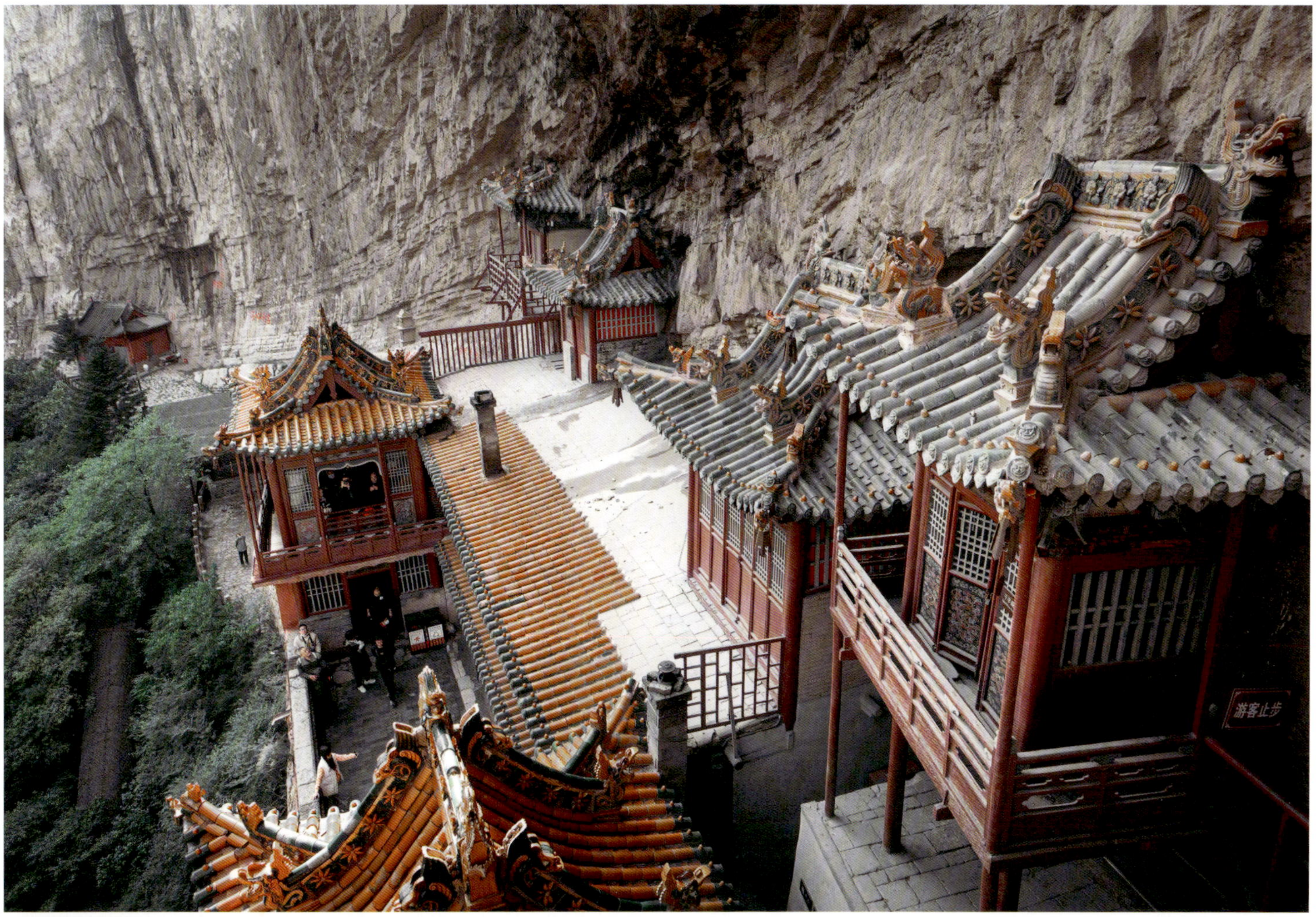

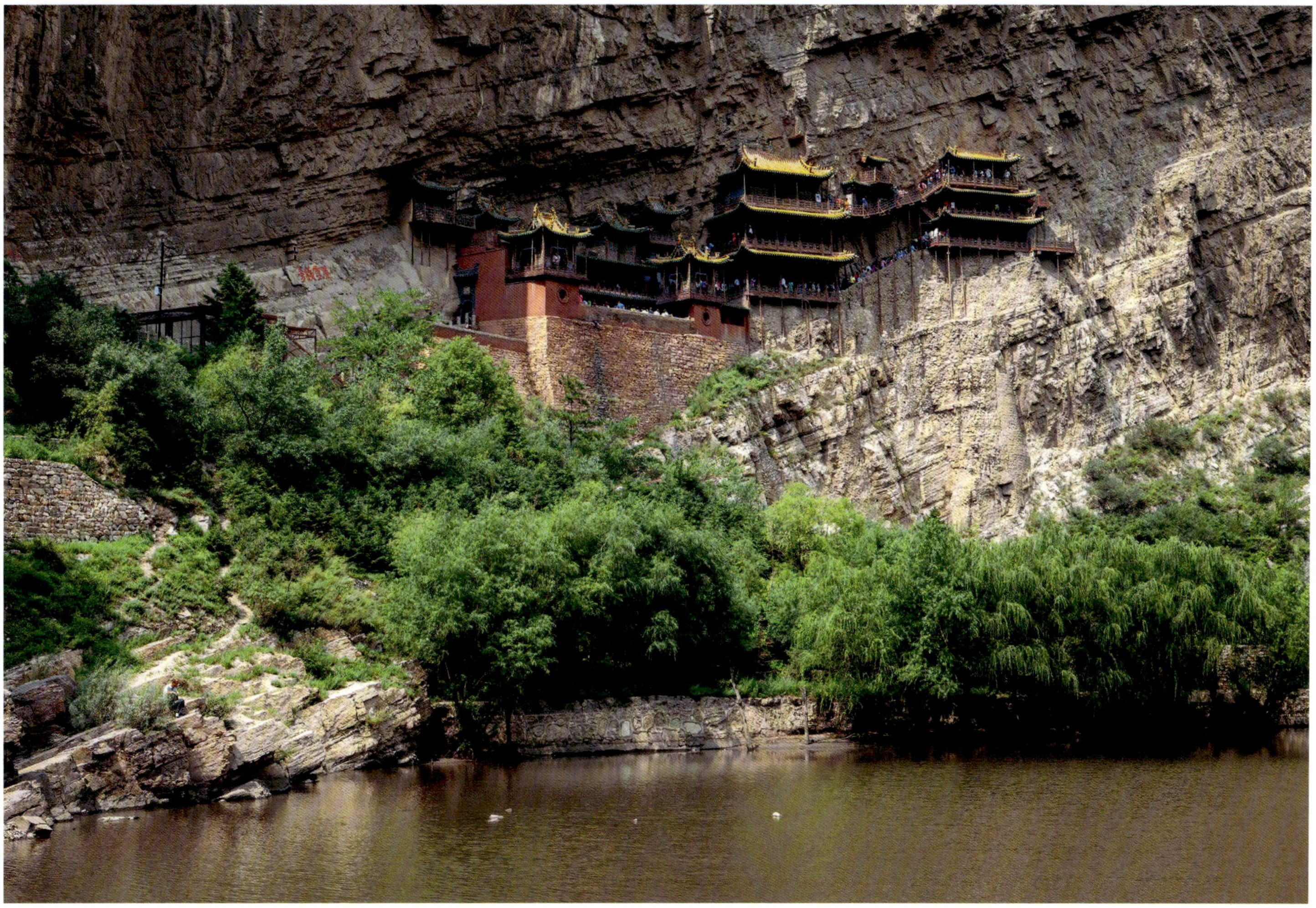

Opposite Natural disasters have left the Hanging Temple unscathed over the centuries.
Top Buddhists, Taoists, and Confucianists come here to find peace in silence.
Bottom The masterful builders of the Hanging Temple aimed to create a place of stillness and seclusion, far removed from worldly temptations.

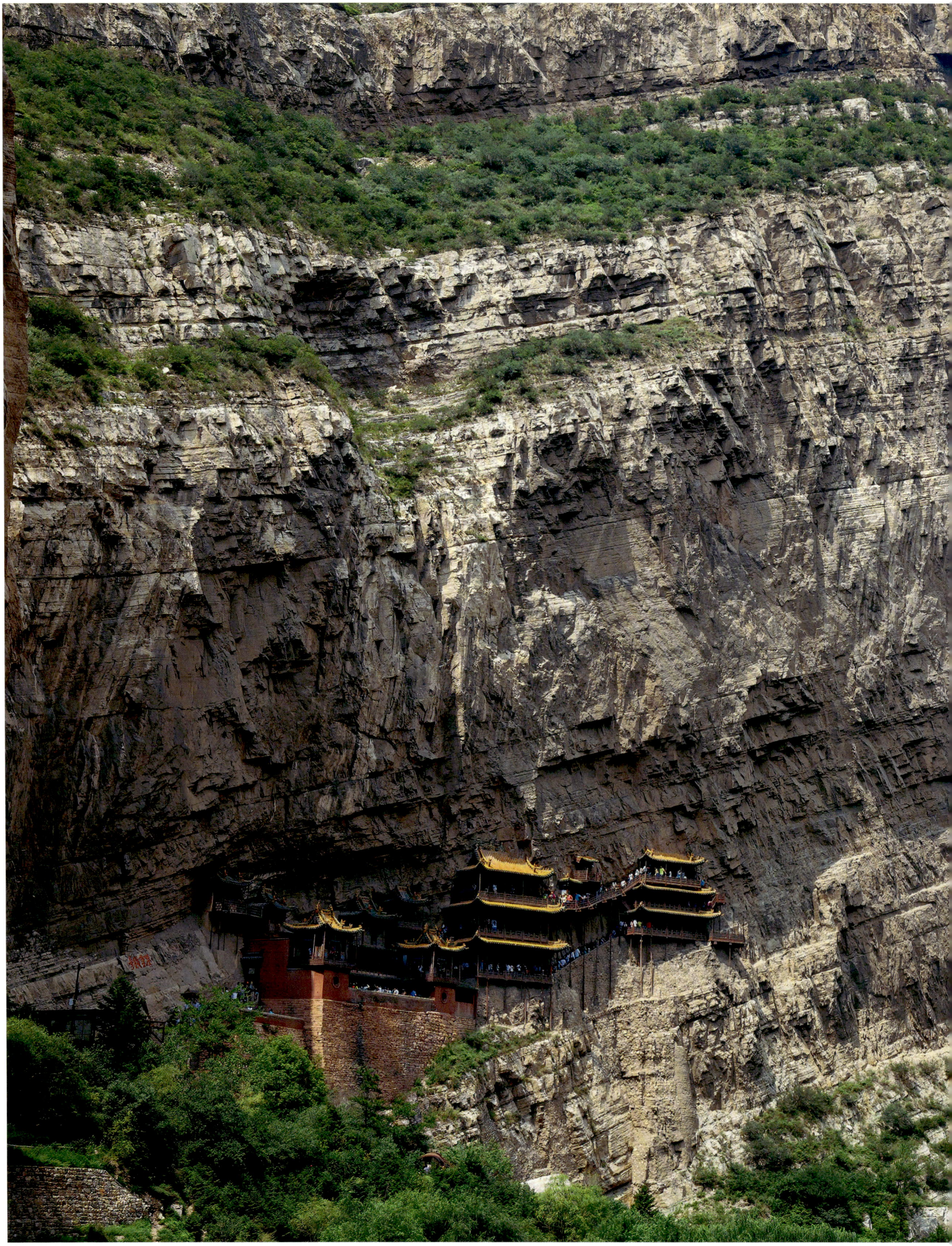

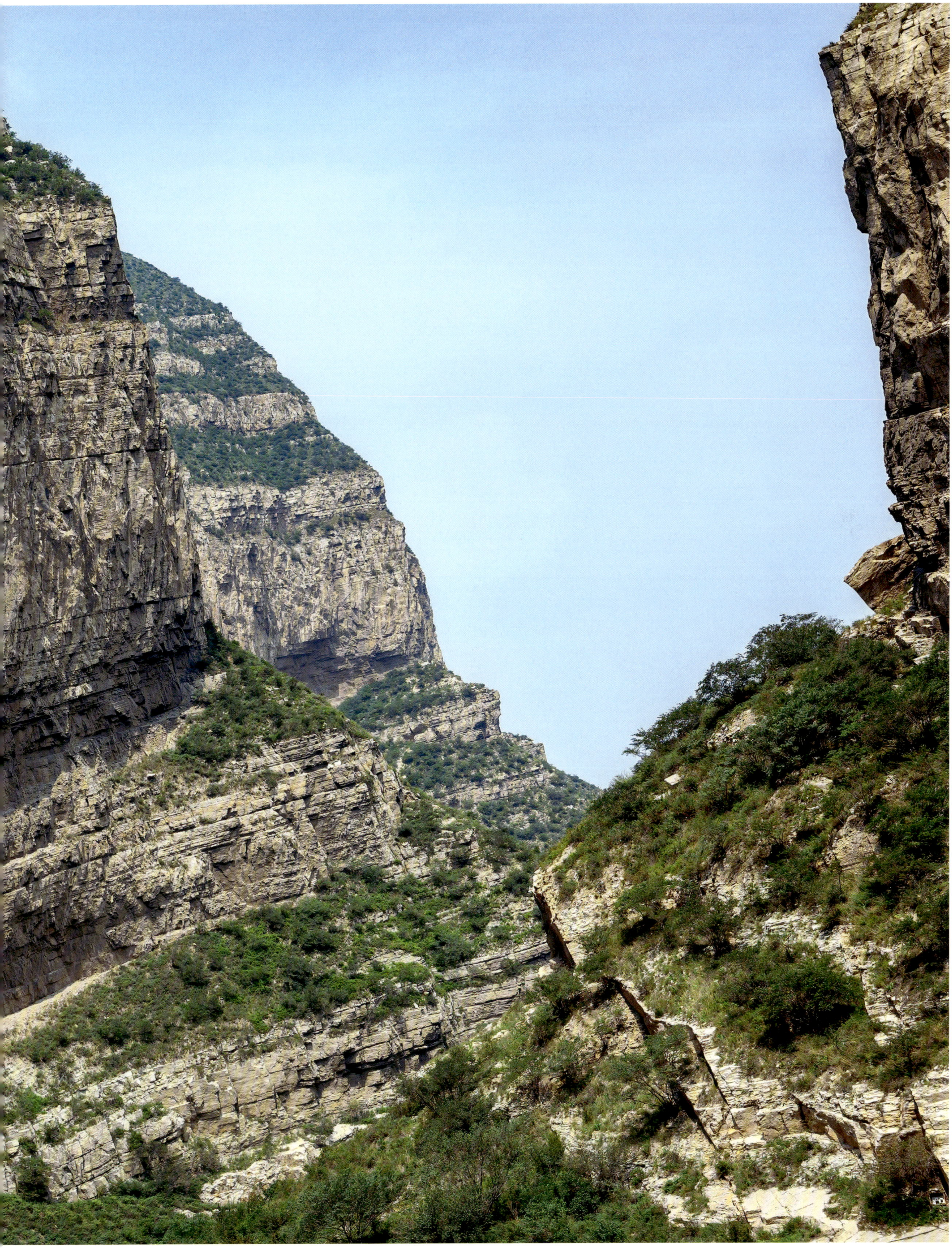

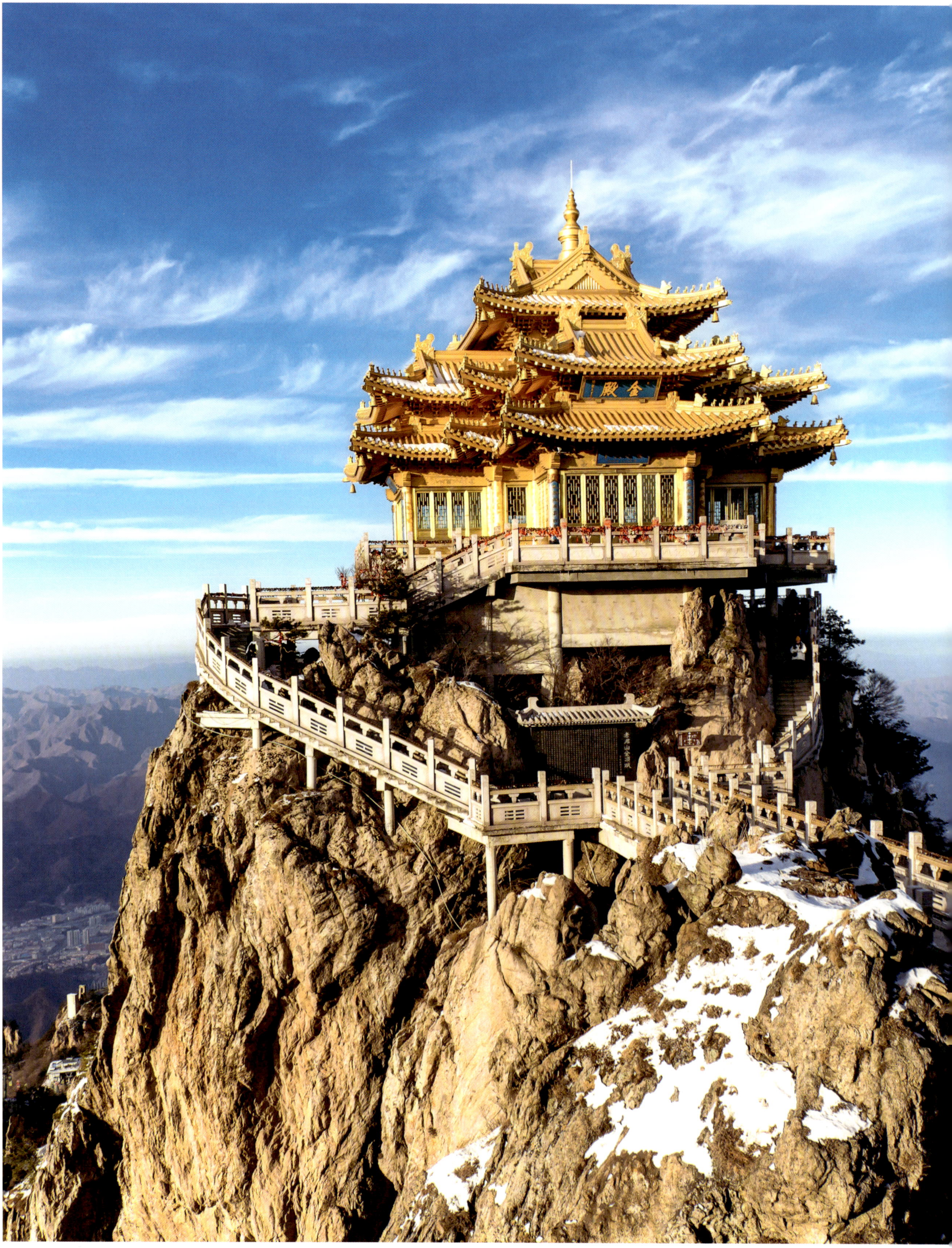
金殿

Temple Complex on Mount Laojun

The Summit of the Tao

Built: 2014 CE (current form), Henan Province, China

Mountains like Laojun are believed to concentrate *Qi* in its purest form, making them powerfully spiritual places for personal growth.

The legendary sage Laozi could scarcely have chosen a more spectacular place for his meditation than Mount Laojun. Here, it is said, he retreated in solitude to meditate and develop the philosophy of Taoism, later captured in his seminal work, the *Tao Te Ching*. To this day, monks and followers study his words to understand the essence of the Tao—the "way" or "principle" underlying all existence.

Visible from afar, the temple complex atop Mount Laojun crowns the Chinese province of Henan. Dating back some 1,200 years—but rebuilt in 2014—the site honors the great sage Laozi and the Taoist faith. Though the structures are relatively new, Mount Laojun has held spiritual significance for thousands of years and is deeply rooted in Taoist tradition.

In Taoism, the Tao reveals itself less in books than in nature, particularly in places of great natural beauty like Mount Laojun—literally, the "Mountain of the Old Master." Mountains, with their giant forms protruding skyward, are, to Taoists, sublime examples of energy transformed into matter. They are places where the cosmic energy of the Tao concentrates most powerfully, offering a setting in which the ultimate aim of Taoist practice—unity with the Tao—can be realized. Over centuries, many Taoist masters and practitioners have retreated to Mount Laojun to nurture their spiritual growth in solitude.

The earliest records of religious structures on Mount Laojun date back to the Tang dynasty (618–907 CE), a period when Taoism flourished under imperial patronage. The construction of the golden temple complex on Mount Laojun is part of a revival of Taoism that began in China in the 1980s. After decades of religious repression, especially during the Cultural Revolution, the Chinese government now promotes the preservation of cultural heritage. As part of this movement, Mount Laojun has been restored as a significant Taoist site. In the spirit of Laozi, these temples invite visitors to rediscover Taoism's profound connection with nature and its ancient teachings—and to perhaps tap into the Tao more deeply.

In Taoism, the Tao reveals itself less in books than in nature, particularly in places of great natural beauty like Mount Laojun—literally, the "Mountain of the Old Master."

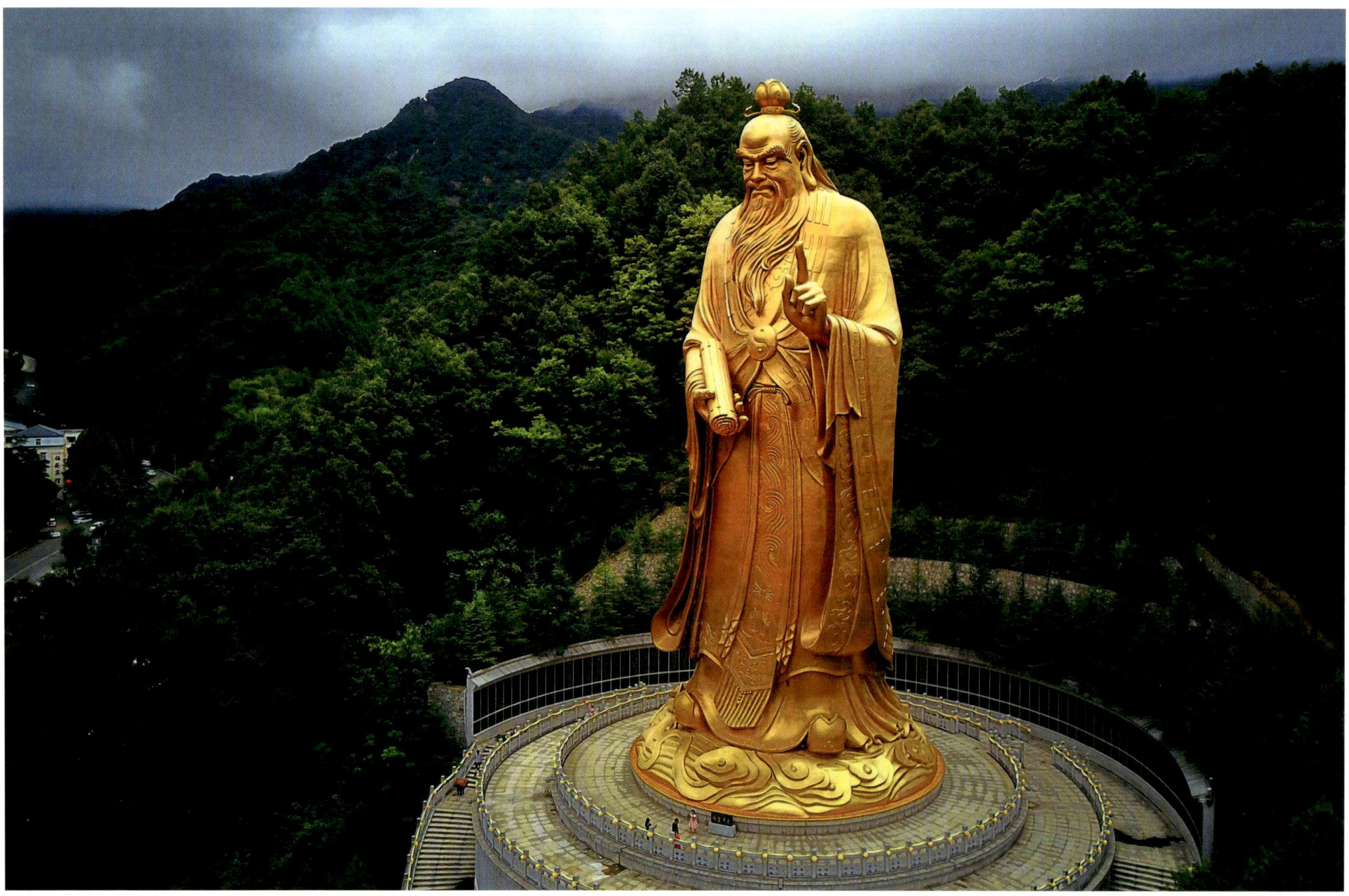

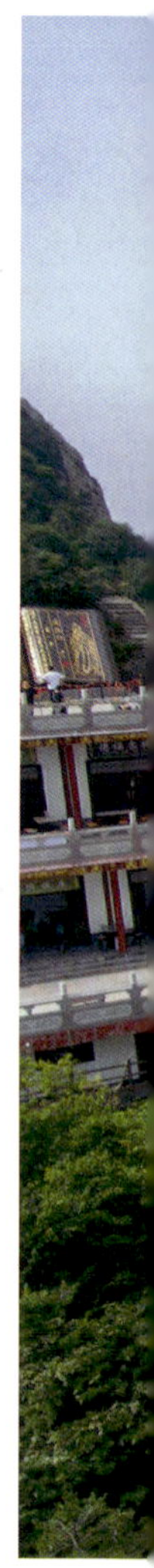

Henan Province, China

Top Mount Laojun is revered as one of the most sacred sites in Taoism.
Bottom left Laozi watches over the place where he developed his teachings.
Bottom right The temple's location symbolizes the steep ascent toward enlightenment.

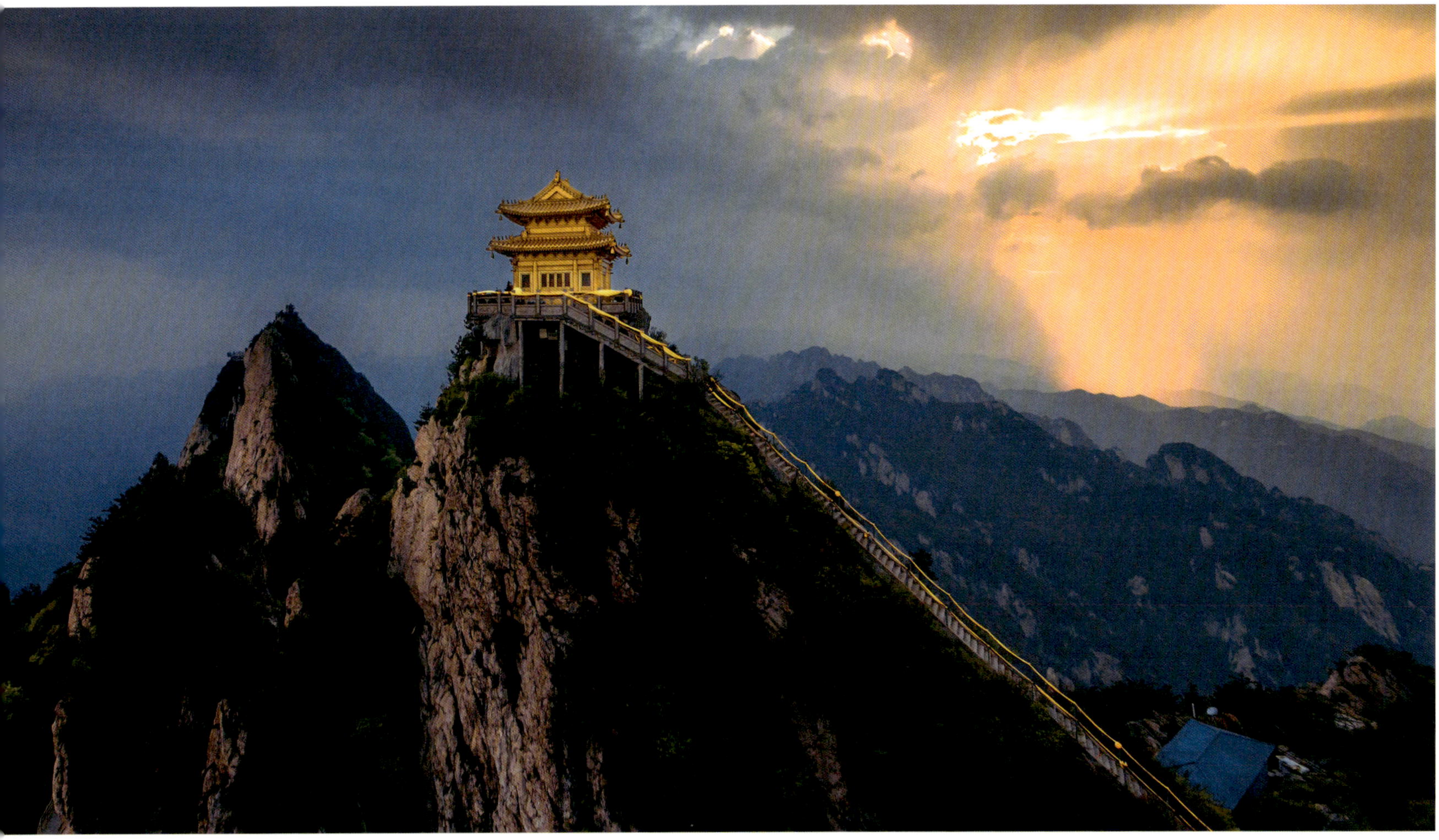

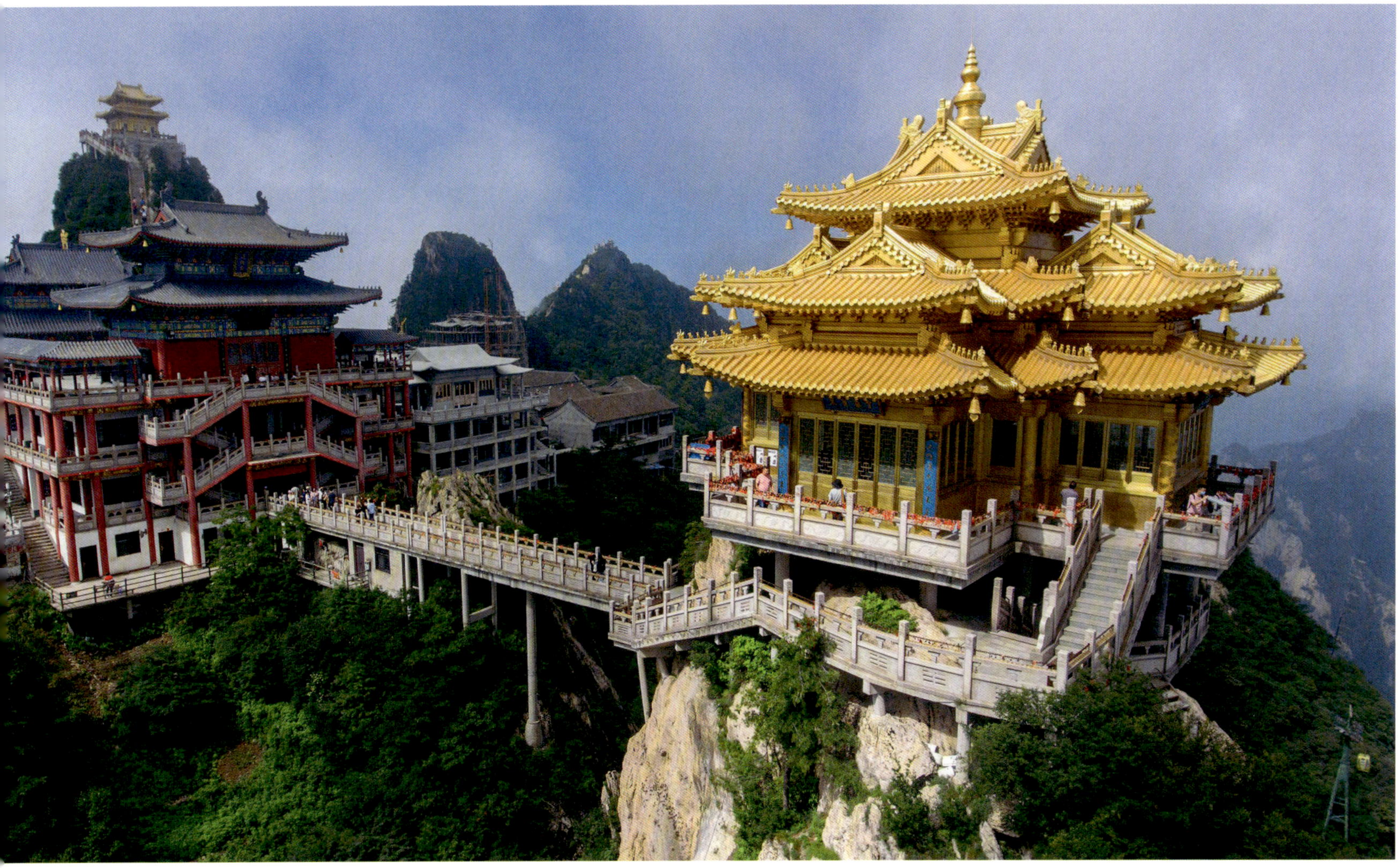

Red Clouds Golden Summit

A Breathtaking Bridge to a Better Future

Built: ca. 1618 CE,
Guizhou Province, China

When the second age of the dharma comes to an end, and morality continues its decline, the future Buddha will appear on this mountain.

Those who float slowly up towards the summit on the cable car, gliding over the UNESCO-protected forests and rugged landscapes, can understand why Fanjingshan is considered a sacred mountain in Vajrayāna Buddhism. Rising dramatically into the sky over the Wuling Mountains in the Chinese province of Guizhou, its highest peak is crowned with two small temples atop a narrow, split rock known poetically as "New Golden Summit," or "Red Clouds Golden Summit." An astounding and sublime site, the western temple is dedicated to Buddha Maitreya—the future Buddha—while the eastern temple is consecrated to Buddha Shakyamuni—the present Buddha.

Buddha Shakyamuni, the historical Siddhartha Gautama and founder of Buddhism, was born around 562 BCE as a prince in Lumbini, present-day Nepal. Leaving palace life behind, he sought to understand the truth of human existence. Tradition holds that he attained enlightenment under the famed Bodhi tree in Bodh Gaya, India, and became known as Buddha Shakyamuni—the "awakened sage of the Shakya clan." After his enlightenment, he taught the Four Noble Truths and the Eightfold Path. In essence, the Four Noble Truths state that life is marked by suffering *(dukkha),* stemming from desire and attachment. However, enlightenment, and an ultimate release from suffering and desire can be attained *(nirvāna)* by following the Eightfold Path—a guide to ethical, noble living that includes correct understanding, intention, speech, action, livelihood, effort, mindfulness, and concentration. To this day, Shakyamuni's teachings form the foundation of Buddhist philosophy.

Buddha Maitreya is the foretold Buddha, the one who will appear in a future era. According to Buddhist thought, we are currently in an age where Shakyamuni's teachings are gradually weakening, and the world finds itself in moral and spiritual decline. This is described as the "end of the teaching," or the "Age of Degeneration." When this decline reaches its nadir, and Shakyamuni's teachings are forgotten, Maitreya, a *bodhisattva,* or enlightened being, will appear to renew the dharma—the teachings of Buddhism—in a way that aligns with the world as it will then exist.

At Fanjingshan, Shakyamuni and Maitreya are depicted together, as in many Buddhist temples, to represent this coming spiritual transition. Crossing the narrow stone bridge between the two temples, one can symbolically enact this passing of the ages. And when the cable car begins its descent, and the majestic Fanjingshan gradually fades from view, the teachings of Shakyamuni, and their insistence on the primacy of the present moment, continue to resonate.

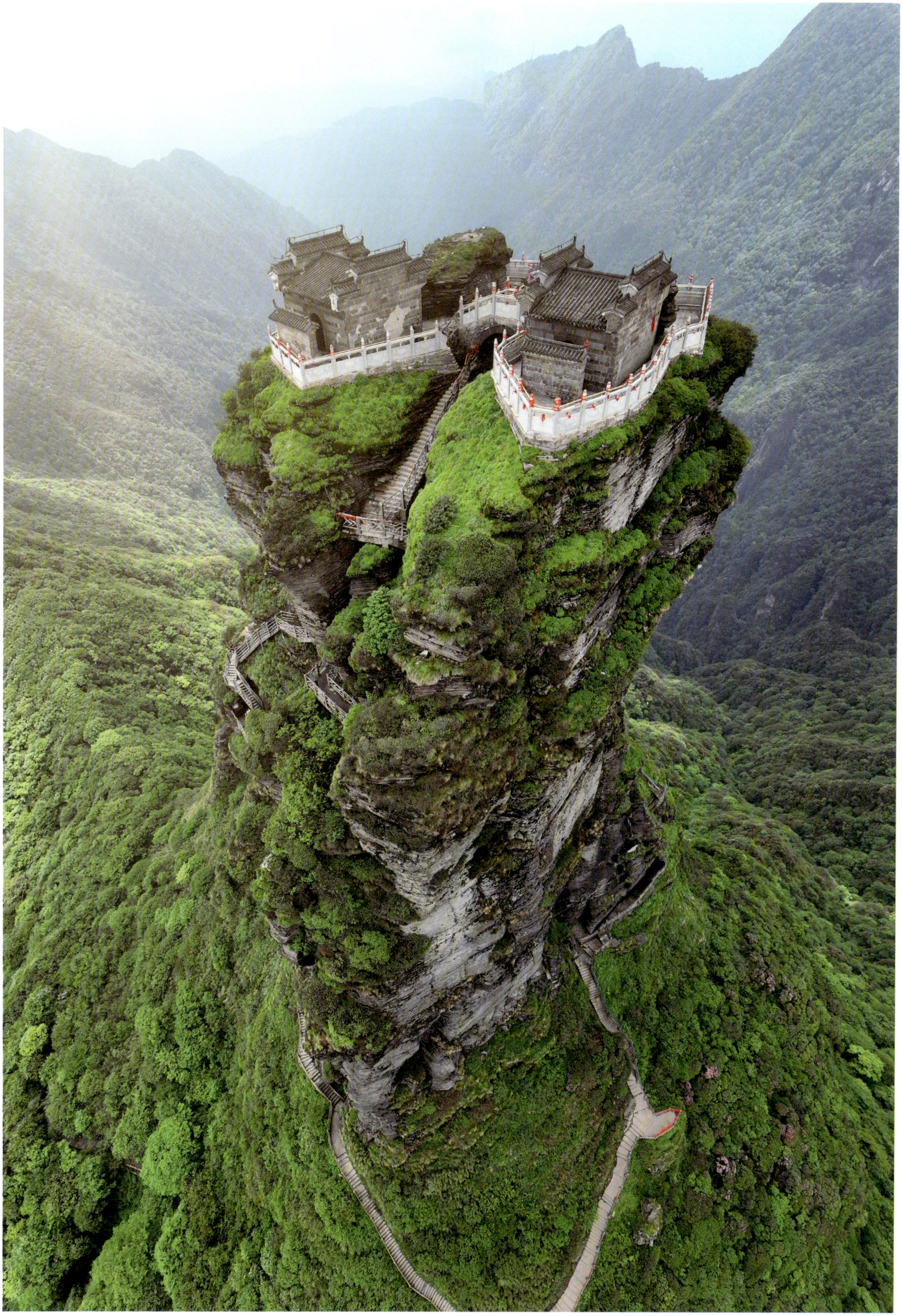

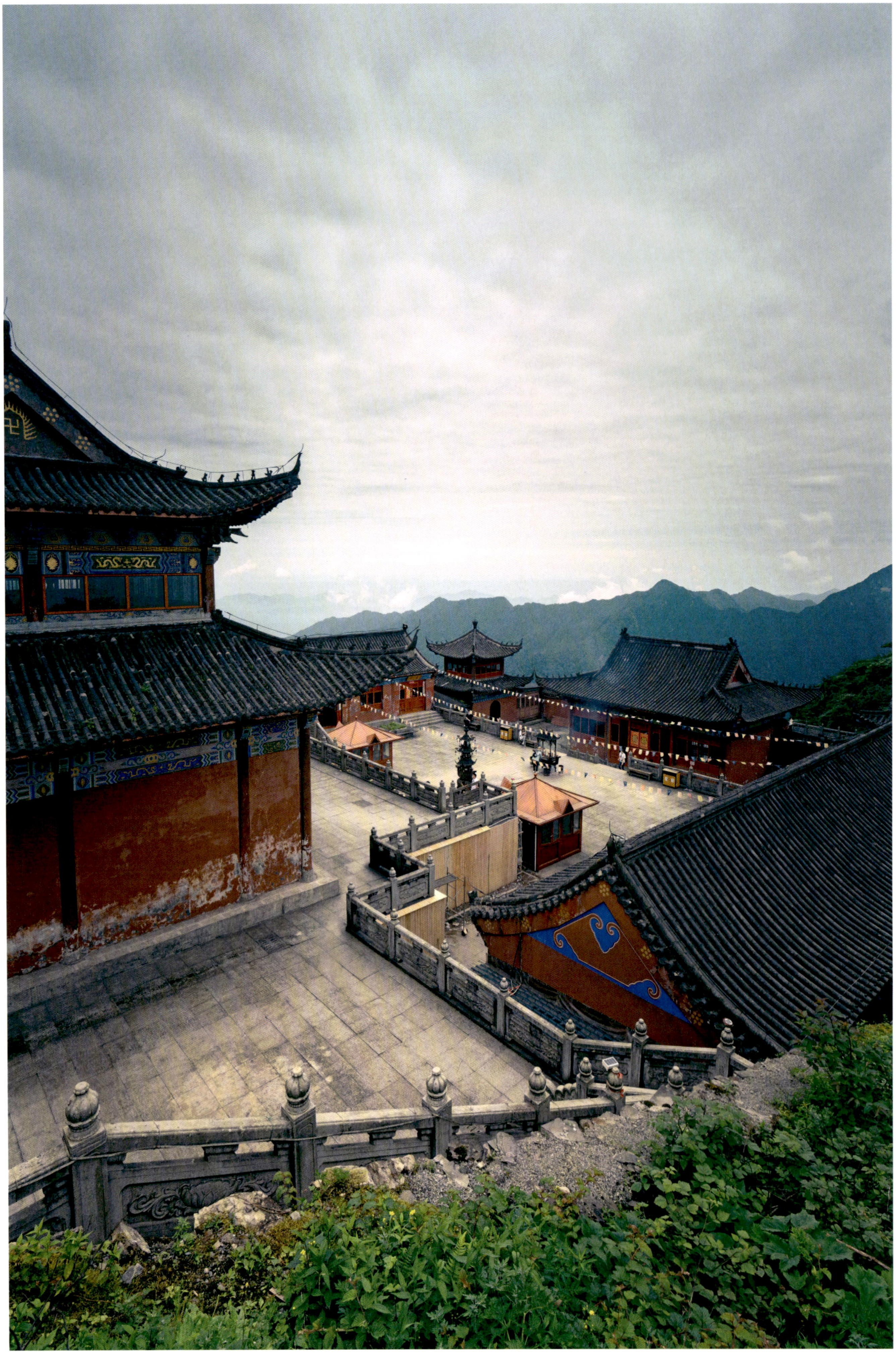

Above Most pilgrims begin their ascent at the Cheng'en Temple, which was rebuilt during the Ming Dynasty. *Opposite* About 8,800 steps lead up to the two temples.

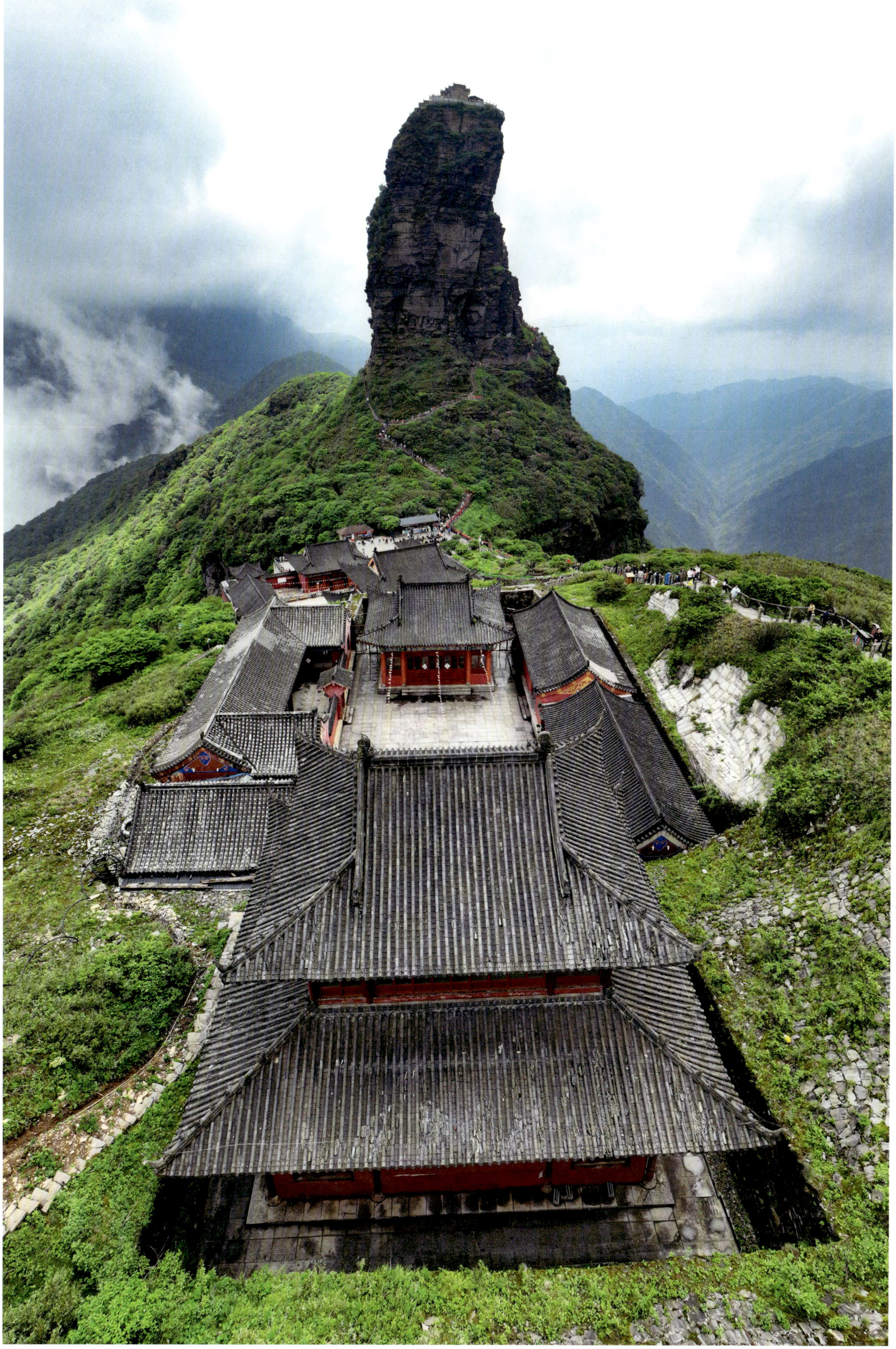

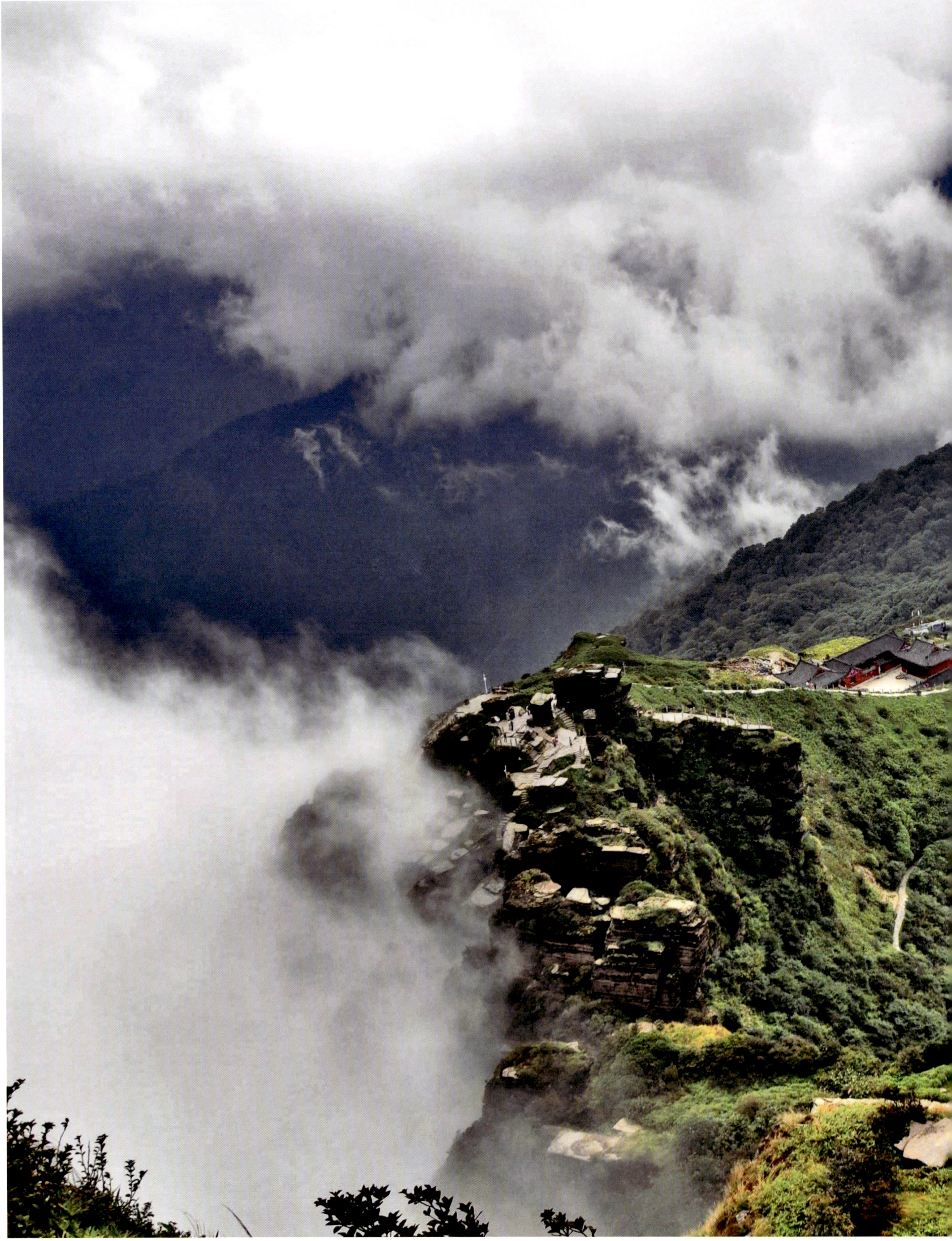

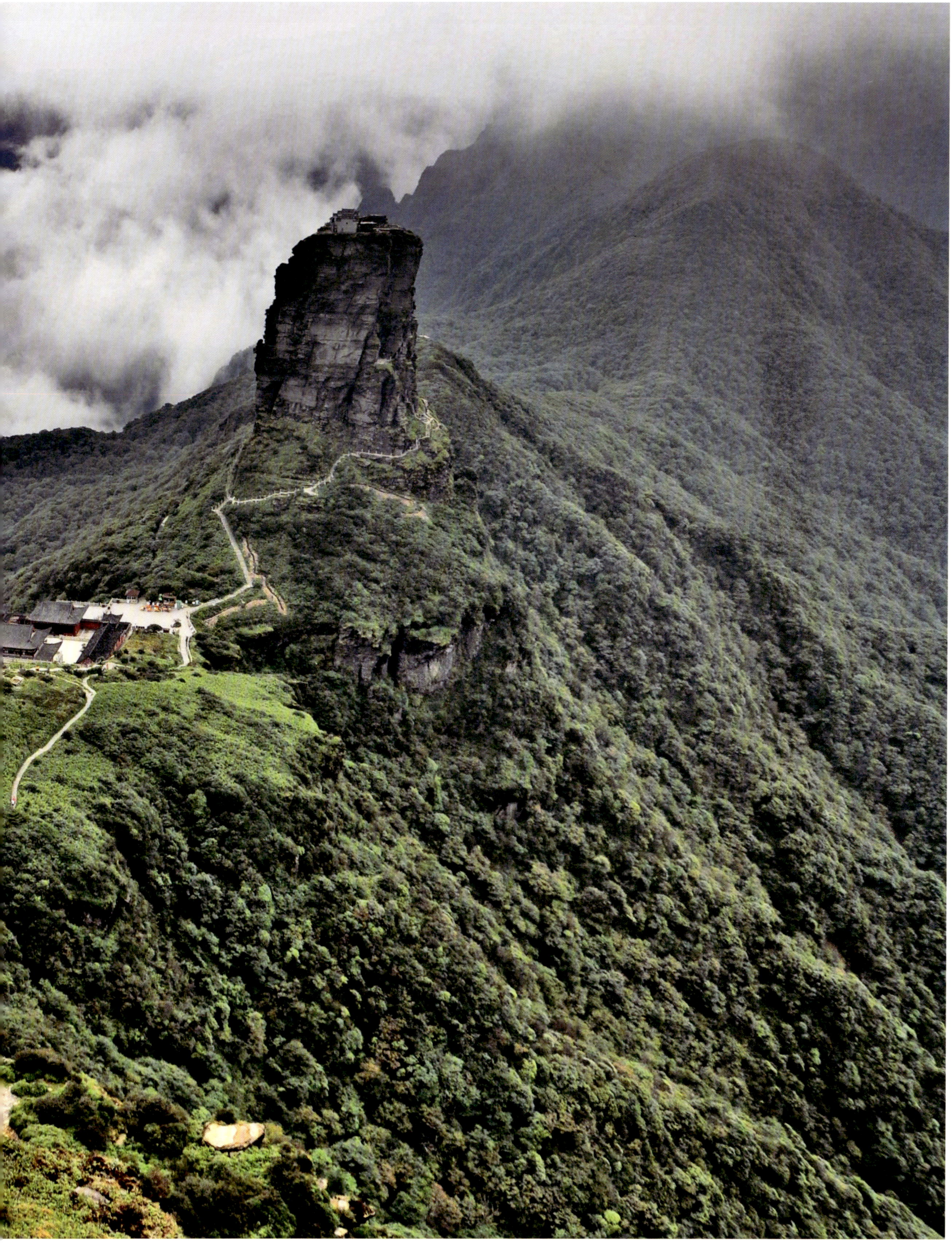

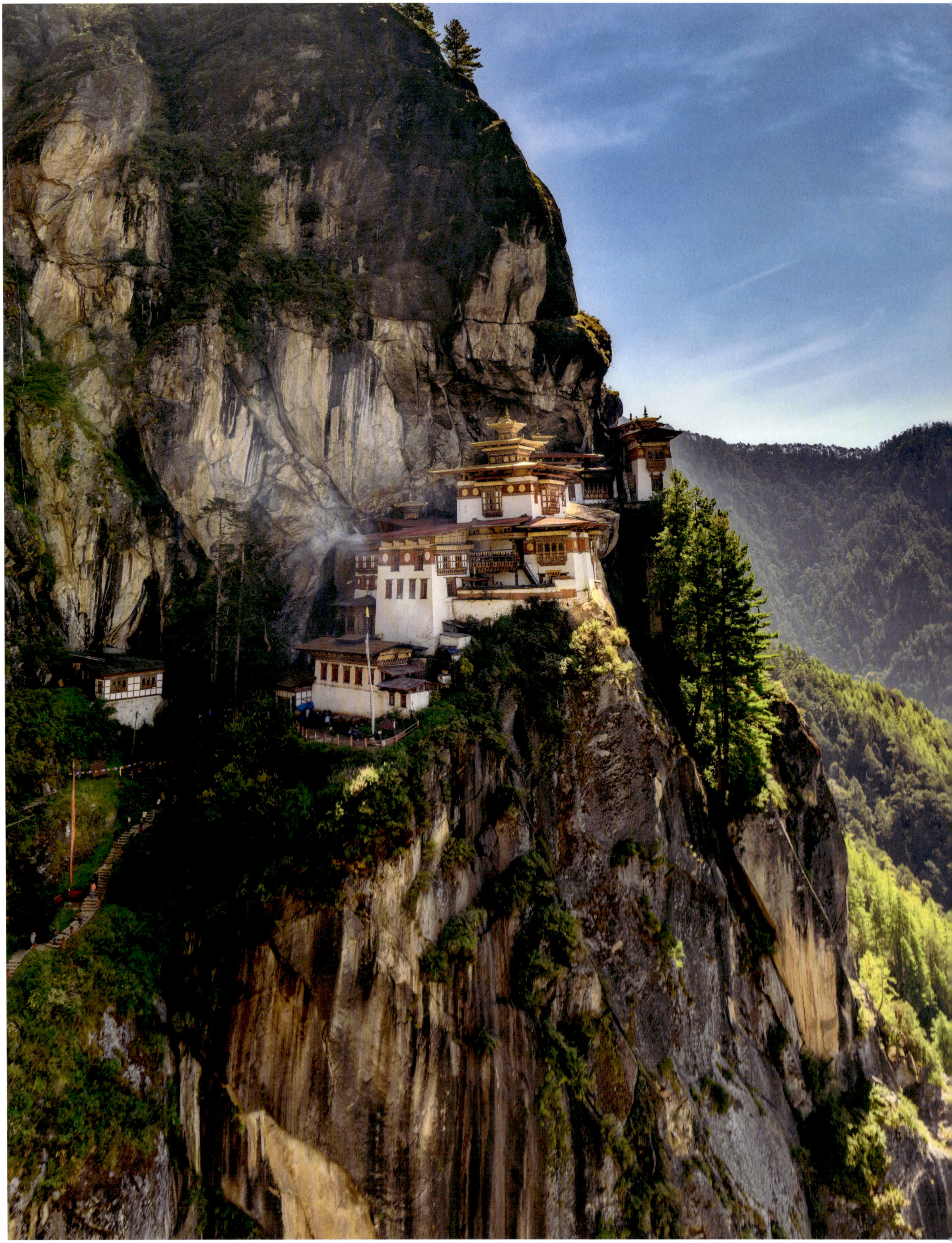

Tiger's Nest

Built: 1692 CE,
Paro Valley, Bhutan

The legend of this Buddhist monastery is as wild and beautiful as the climb to reach it.

Resembling something glimpsed in a dream, Paro Taktsang, a monastery also known by its literal name, "Tiger's Nest," clings to bare rock, 3,000 feet (914 meters) above the Paro Valley. One legend about the monastery's founding is also the story of Buddhism's arrival in Bhutan. According to tradition, the Buddhist master Padmasambhava, or Guru Rinpoche, came to Bhutan in the 8th century to spread Buddhism to the isolated valleys of the Himalayas. His mission was to subdue malevolent spirits and unite the land spiritually. Riding on the back of a tigress—his transformed consort, Yeshe Tsogyal—he flew over the steep cliffs of the Paro Valley and landed at a small cave high in the mountains. Here he meditated, according to some versions, for three months, three weeks, three days, and three hours, and subdued the demons threatening the land. In the following centuries, the cave became an important pilgrimage site for Tibetan saints and other key figures—however, the development of Buddhism in Bhutan was still far from complete.

In the 12th century, representatives of the Drukpa-Kagyü school of Vajrayāna Buddhism established many monasteries across the country. Yet Buddhist traditions in Bhutan remained highly localized, lacking a unified structure and relying primarily on individual communities and their religious leaders. It wasn't until the 17th century that Buddhism in Bhutan truly consolidated, with new political structures based on Buddhist teachings. Fortresses were built, serving as both religious centers and administrative hubs. It was during this period that Gyalse Tenzin Rabgye, an influential cleric, introduced rituals that gradually unified the country, and in honor of Guru Rinpoche, had the Tiger's Nest monastery built around the small cave above the Paro Valley.

The path up is not for the fainthearted. The climb can take two to three hours, leading through dense forests, up steep rocks, and past roaring waterfalls. Halfway up, a teahouse offers a place to rest, as well as the first breathtaking views of the monastery. Upon reaching the top, the phenomenal view over the Paro Valley rewards the weary pilgrim. Guru Rinpoche's cave serves as the spiritual heart of the monastery in its main chapel. The Monks at Paro Taktsang hold daily prayers and rituals here, warmly inviting visitors to participate.

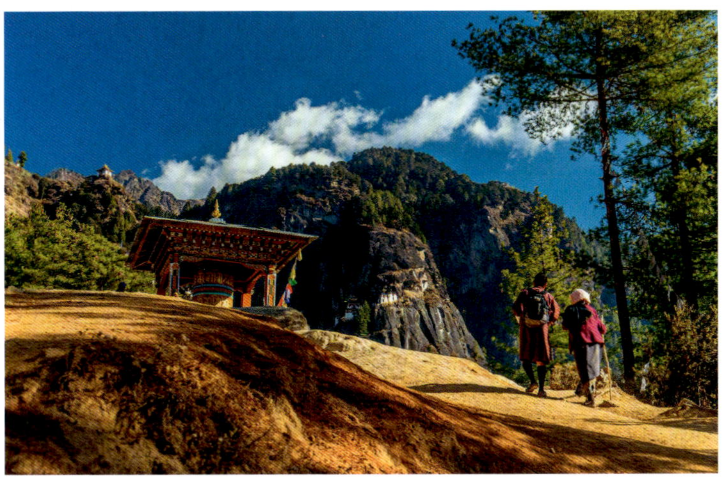

To this day, Bhutan is a Buddhist kingdom, with its ruler also holding the title of "Dragon King." This title grants the king not only political authority but spiritual responsibility. He serves as both protector and promoter of Buddhism, and is believed to embody the moral and ethical values deeply rooted in the religion, such as compassion, wisdom, and service to the common good.

Opposite The ascent to Tiger's Nest is considered a deeply spiritual journey.
Above The trail covers an elevation gain of 2,526 feet (770 meters).

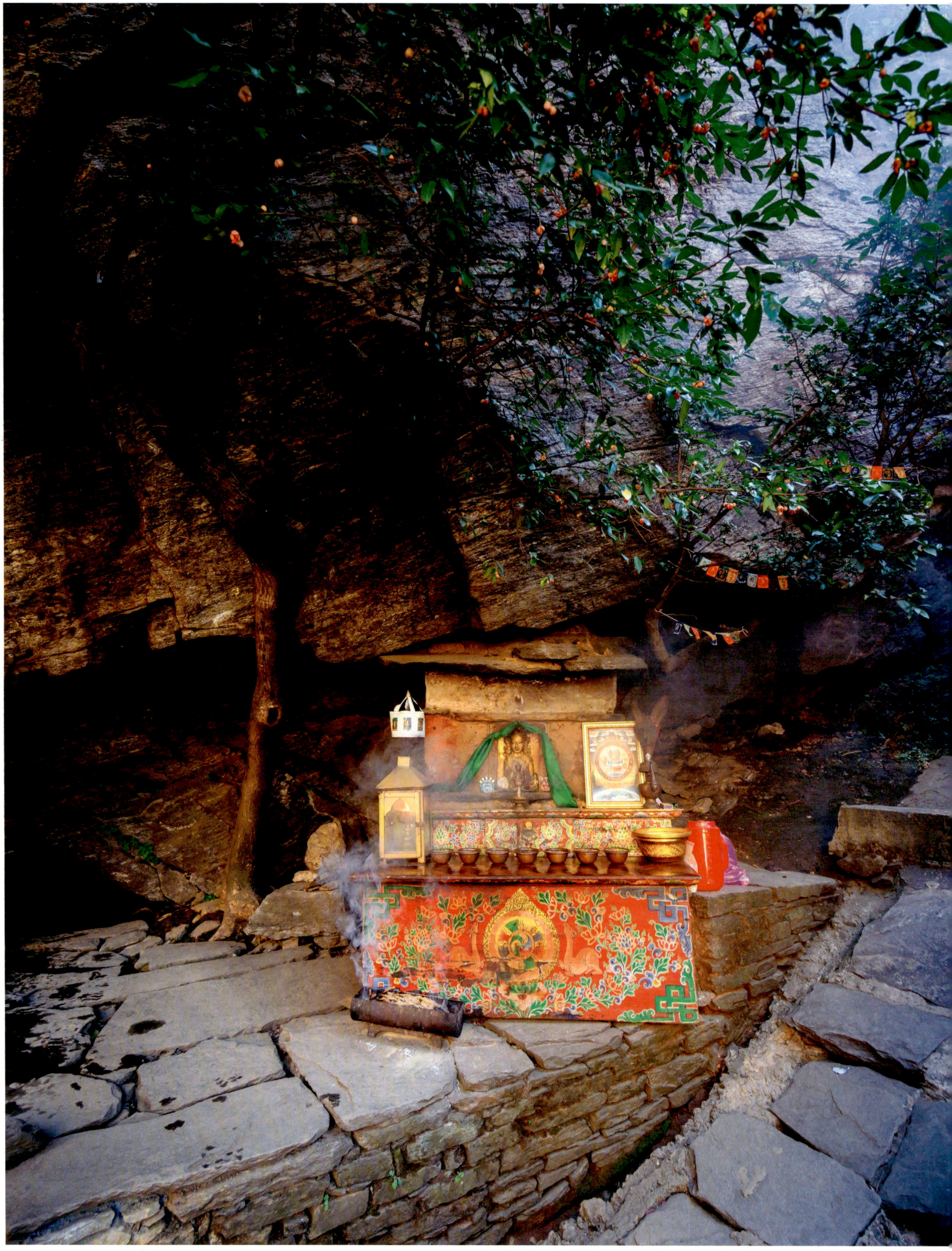

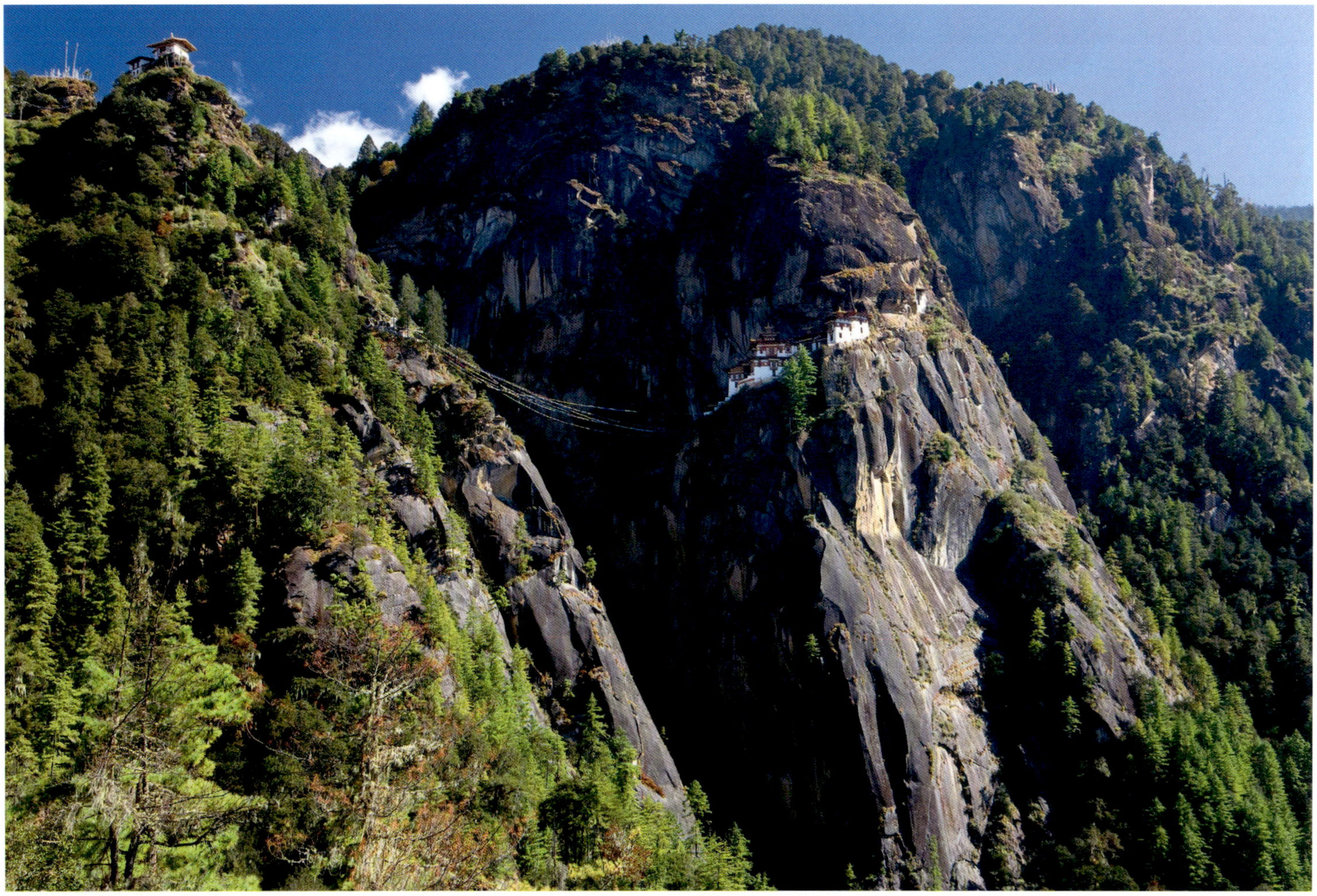

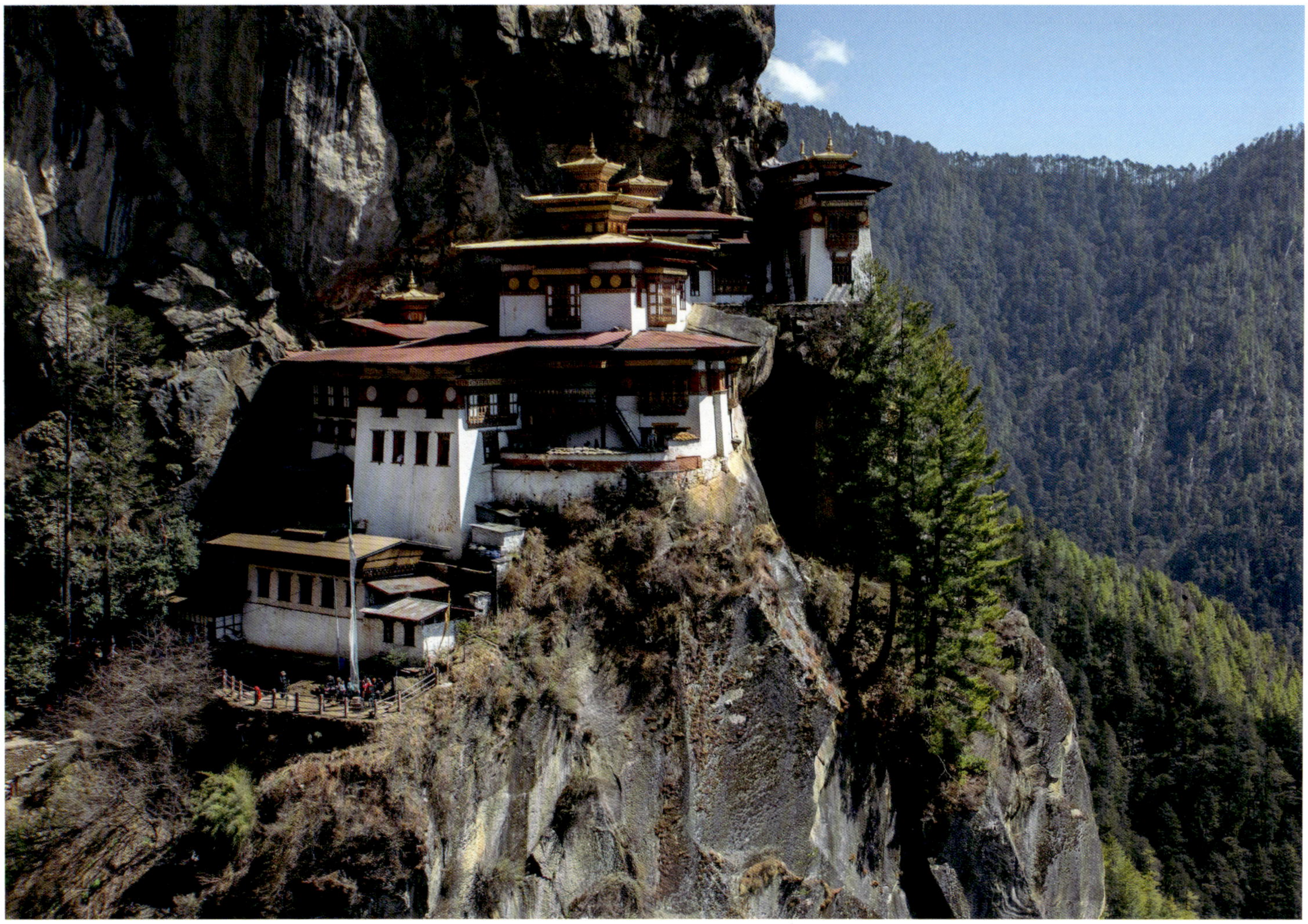

Opposite Small shrines line the long, strenuous path to the monastery.
Top The prayer flags suspended over the abyss provide protection from evil spirits.
Bottom With its whitewashed walls, carved wood, and curved roofs, the monastery is a classic example of Bhutanese architecture.

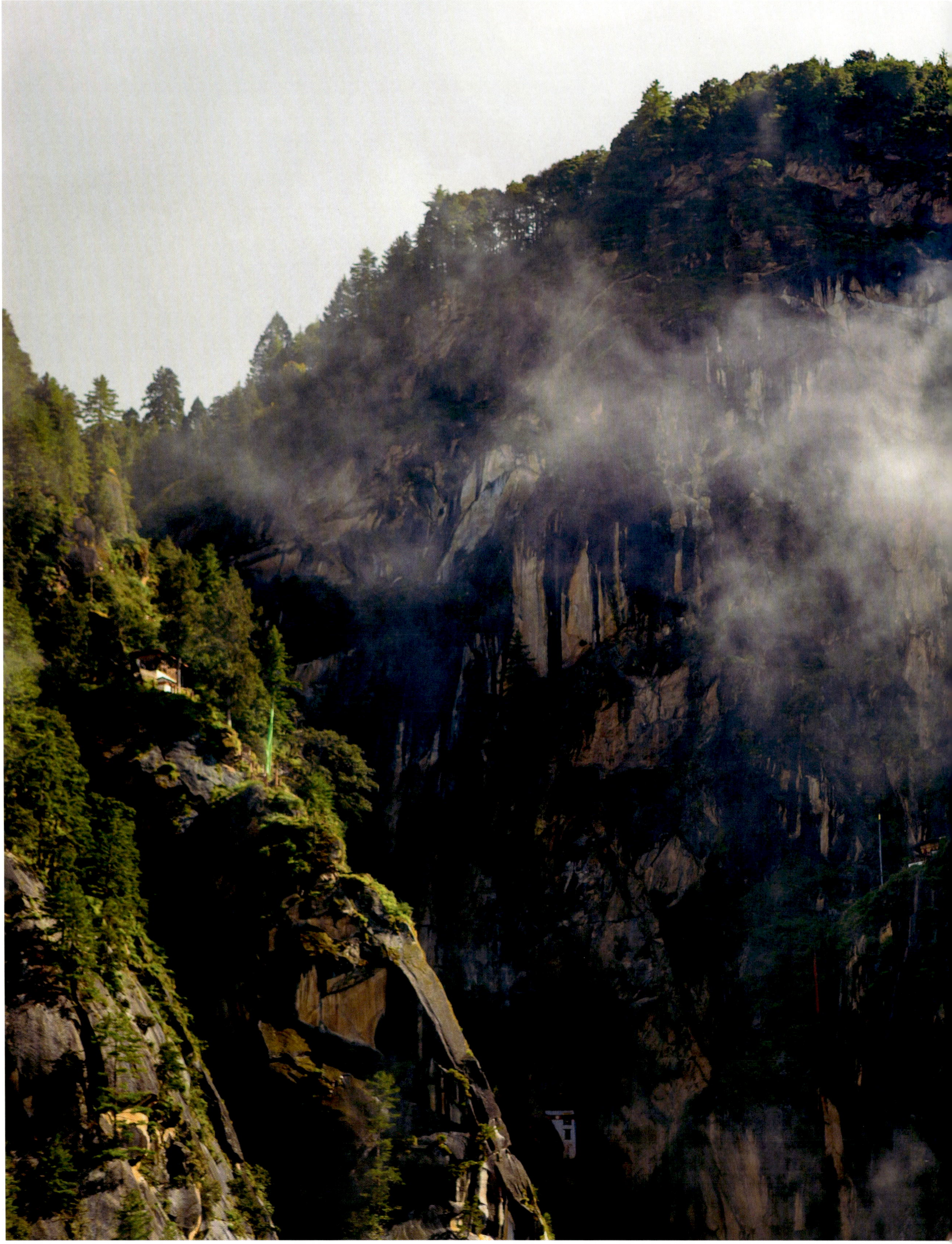

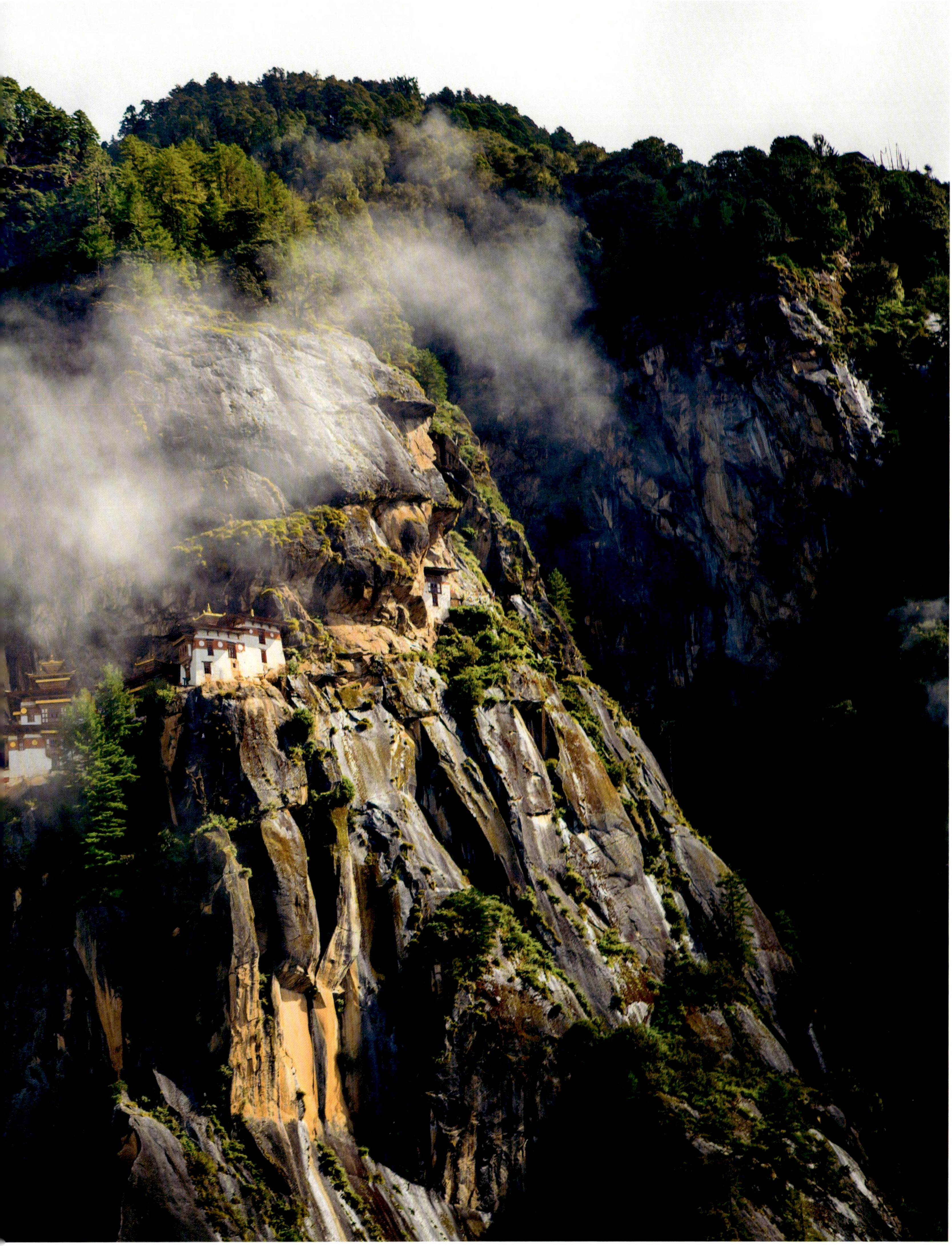

Seokguram Grotto

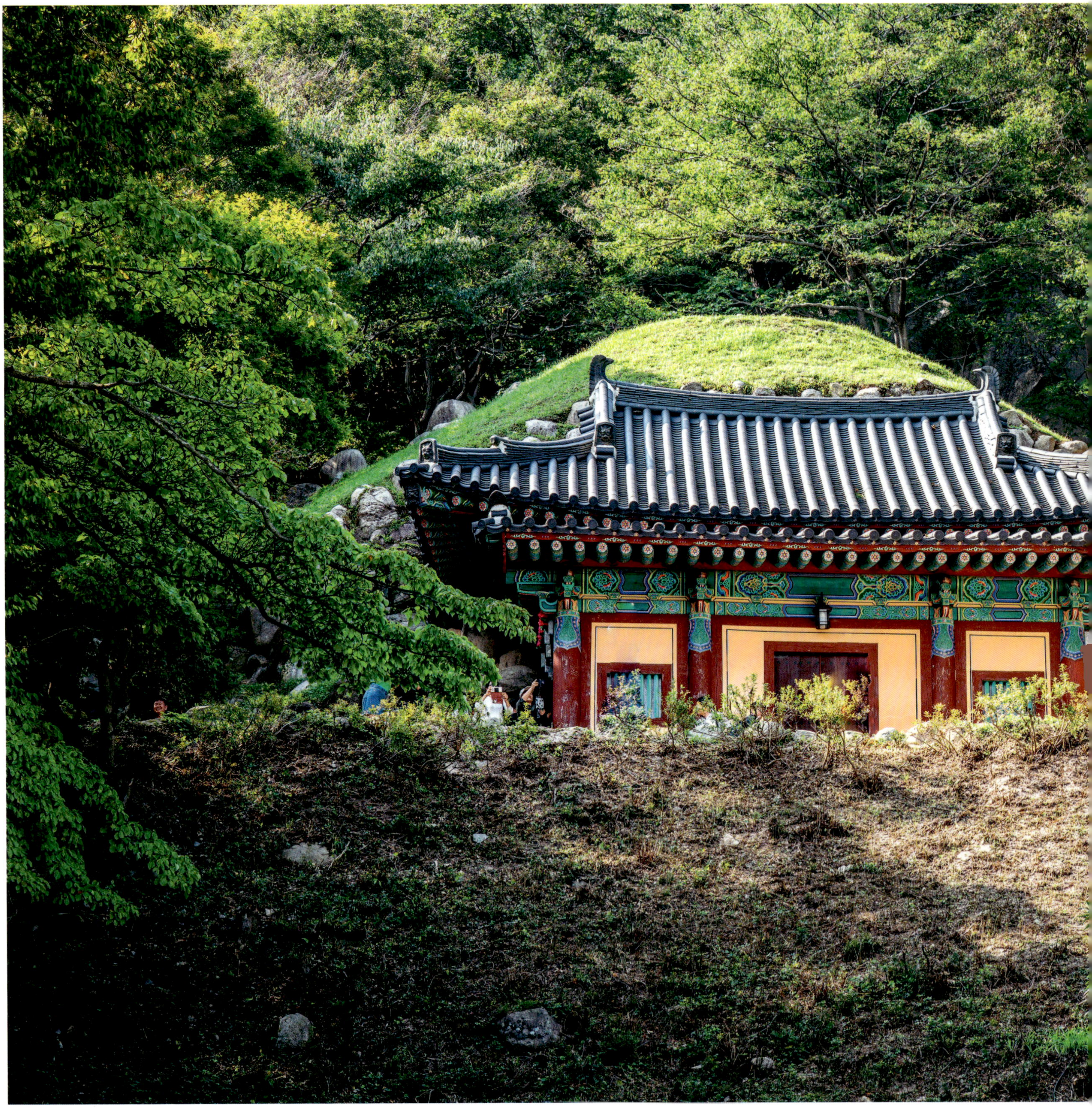

Built: 8th century CE,
Gyeongju, South Korea

Over 1,000 years old, this Buddhist cave temple was created to honor parents from a former life.

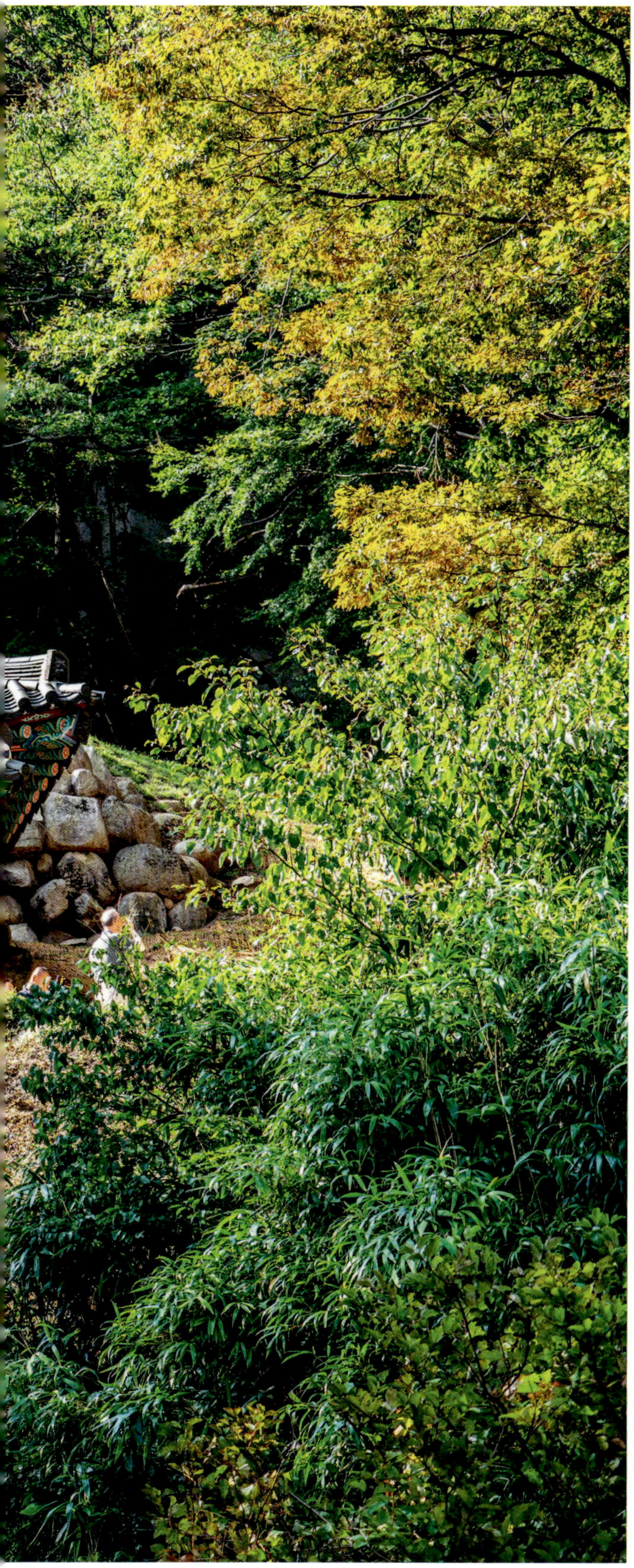

For nearly a millennium, Gyeongju served as the political, cultural, and spiritual heart of the Silla Kingdom, which spanned large parts of what is now South Korea from 57 BCE to 935 CE. Amidst Gyeongju's modern buildings, its ancient burial mounds and temple ruins speak of its rich history. One of its greatest spiritual treasures is the Seokguram Grotto.

Ascending the winding path from Bulguksa Temple on the slopes of Toham Mountain, pilgrims reach the entrance to this sanctuary after about an hour's walk. Here, two Vajrapanis, the mighty bearers of the thunderbolt, greet visitors with stern gazes, reminding them that the journey to enlightenment demands both courage and protection. Just beyond, the Chaturmaharaja, the Four Heavenly Kings, await in the corridor that leads to the central rotunda. These guardians of the cardinal directions usher pilgrims into the sacred stillness of the main chamber. At the center of this circular space sits a massive statue of Buddha upon a lotus pedestal. His eyes are half closed in serene meditation, and his hands form the Bhumisparsha Mudra, the gesture in which he calls upon the Earth to bear witness to his enlightenment. The geometry of the room is masterful—no mortar binds the precisely cut granite slabs, yet the structure has stood steadfast for centuries.

Buddhism first reached the kingdom of Silla in the 4th century, and was declared the state religion 200 years later. Over time, its influence rooted itself deeply in the kingdom's history, architecture, and identity. After unifying the central and southern regions of the Korean Peninsula in the 7th century, the kingdom of Silla entered a cultural golden age, during which countless Buddhist pagodas and temples were built—including Seokguram Grotto and Bulguksa Temple below it. While Bulguksa symbolizes the earthly paradise of Buddha, Seokguram represents the realm of enlightenment. Historical records suggest that both sites were commissioned by an influential minister. He dedicated Bulguksa to his current-life parents, while Seokguram was built, following Buddhist tradition, to honor the parents of his past life. Here between temple and grotto, earthly and spiritual dimensions merge into an inseparable unity, where more is possible than the human eye can perceive.

Back under the open sky, the sounds of the forest seem as though part of a larger harmony. The Buddha's inner peace seems to accompany the moved visitor on their descent back to the worldly life of Gyeongju. It is another step along the path to the self—a step away from the ego and toward a life lived in harmony with the universe.

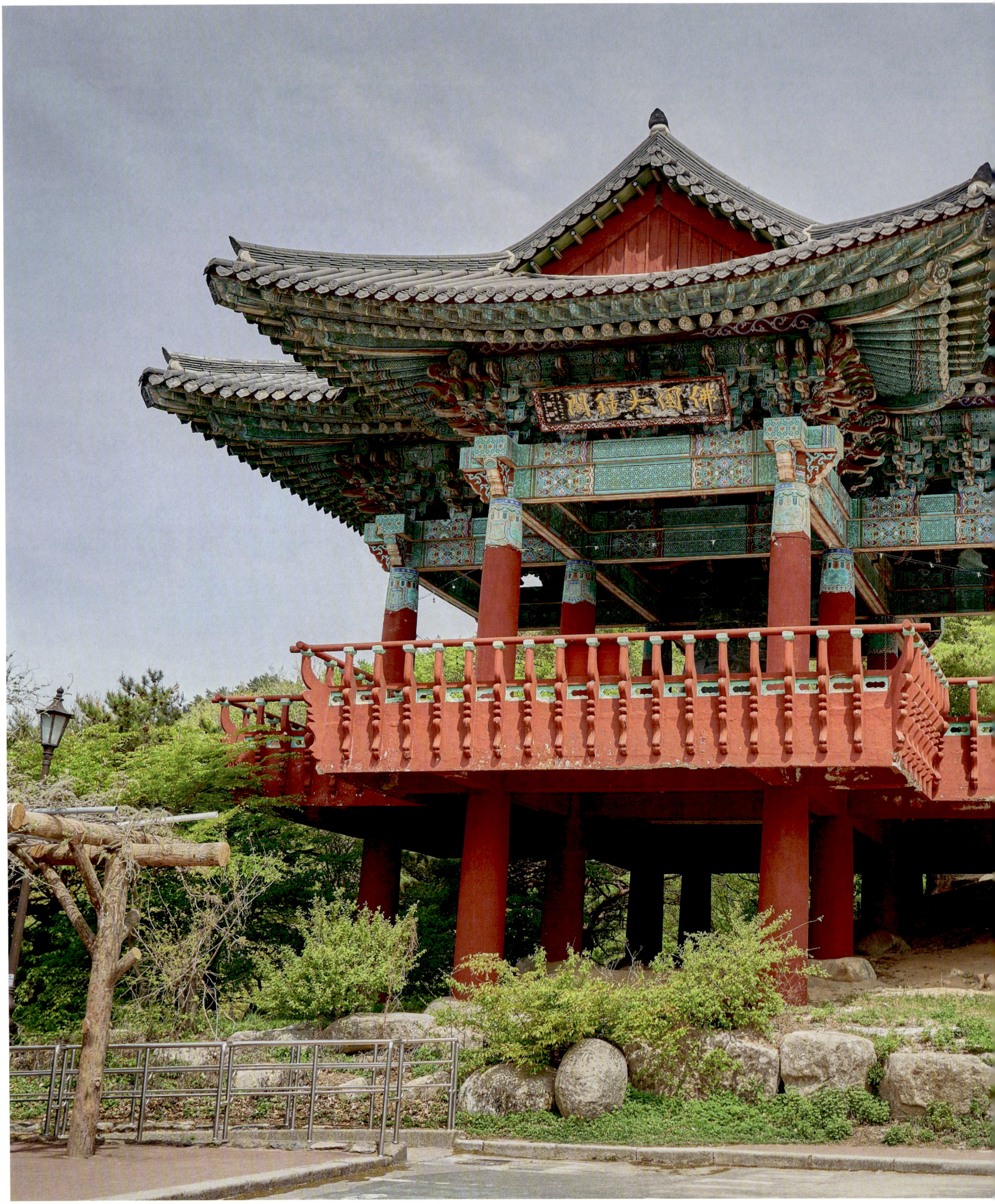

Above The pavilion on the path to the grotto is painted in red and turquoise, with red symbolizing protection and energy, and turquoise representing nature and harmony.

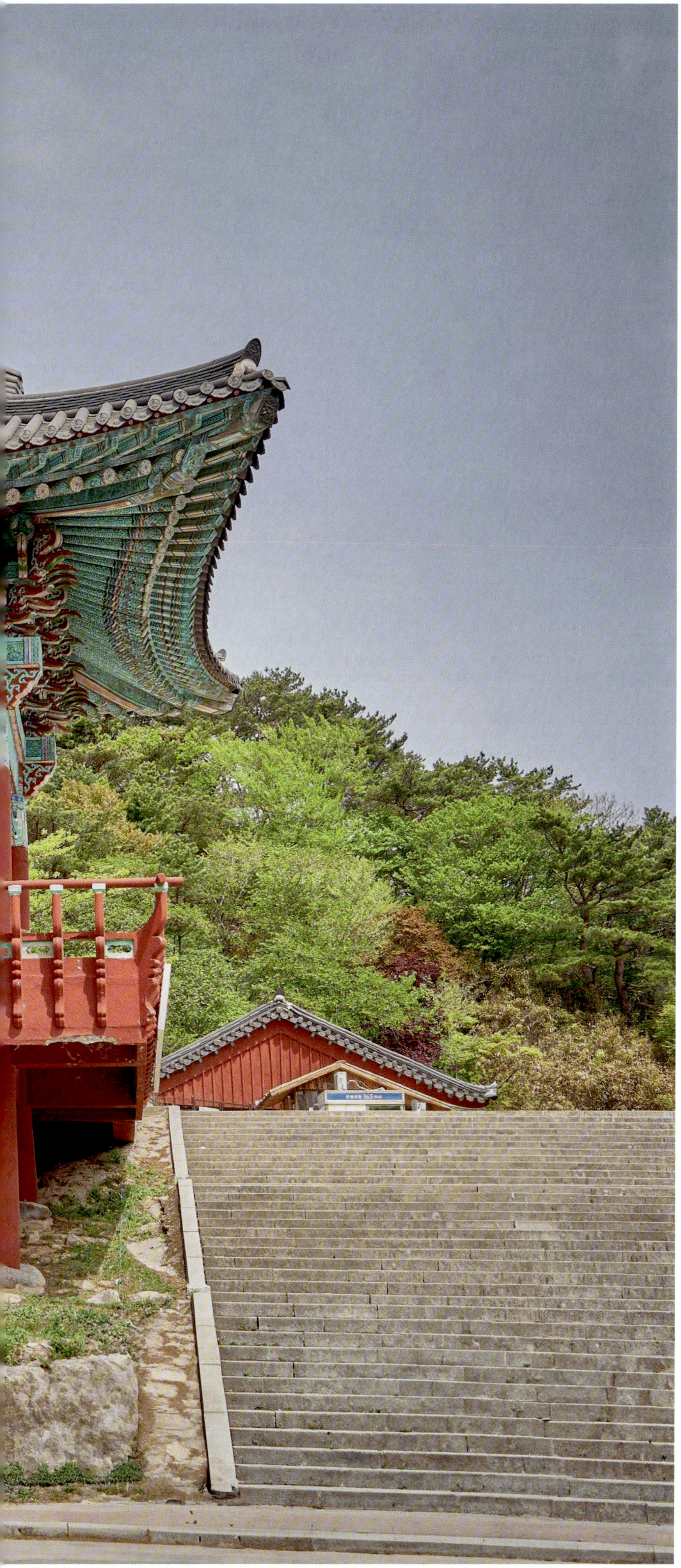

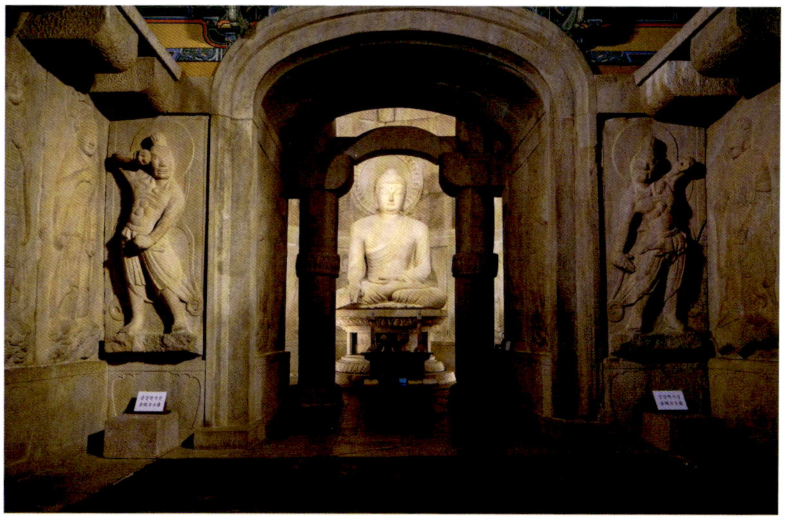

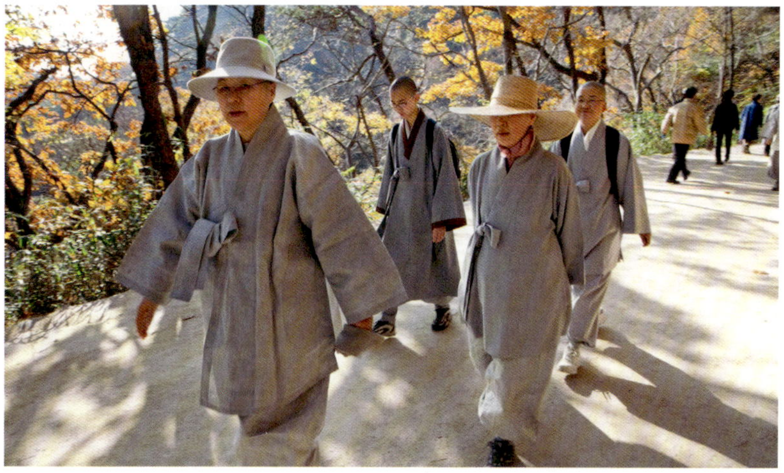

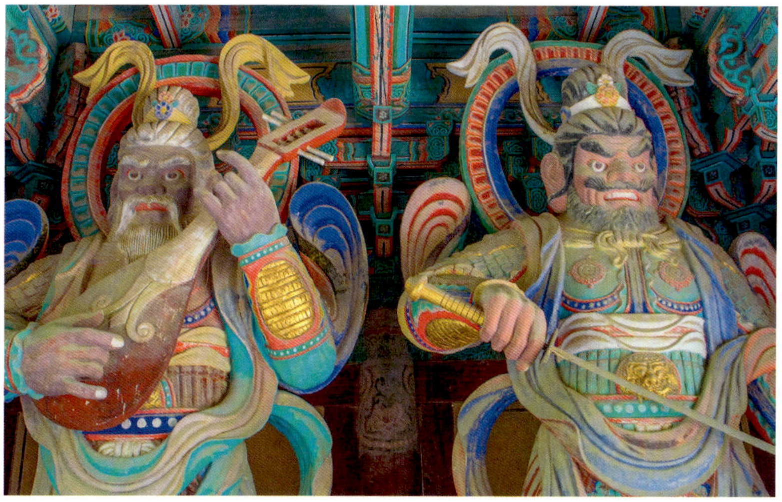

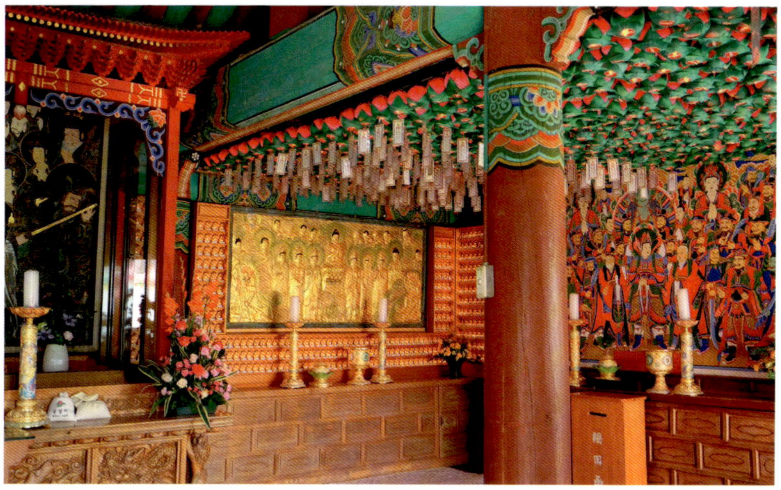

Top The serene aura of the Buddha fills the grotto.
Upper middle Visitors reach the grotto via a winding path.
Lower middle Before entering, one must pass the guardians.
Bottom Inside the sacred grotto, a scene of pure splendor unfolds.

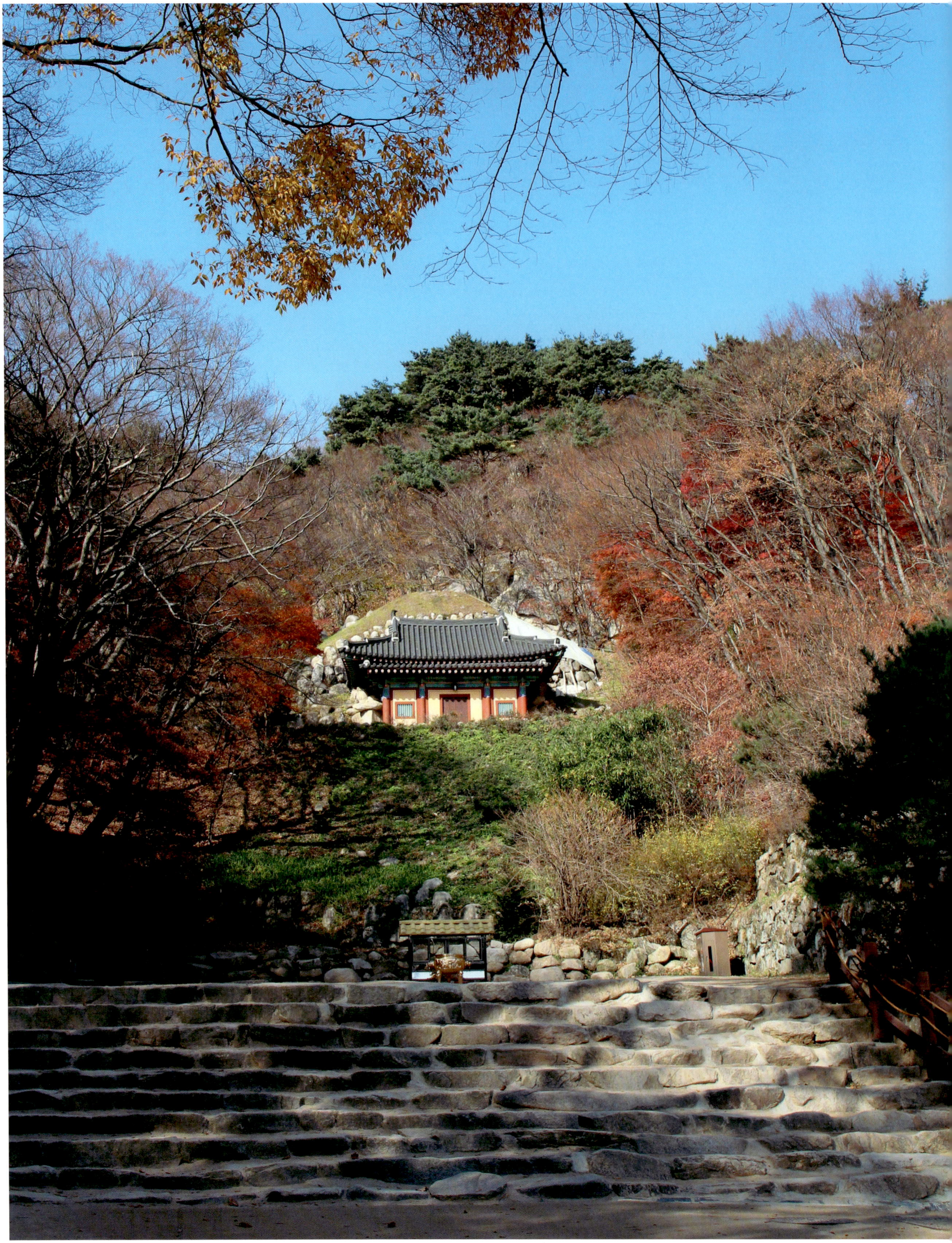

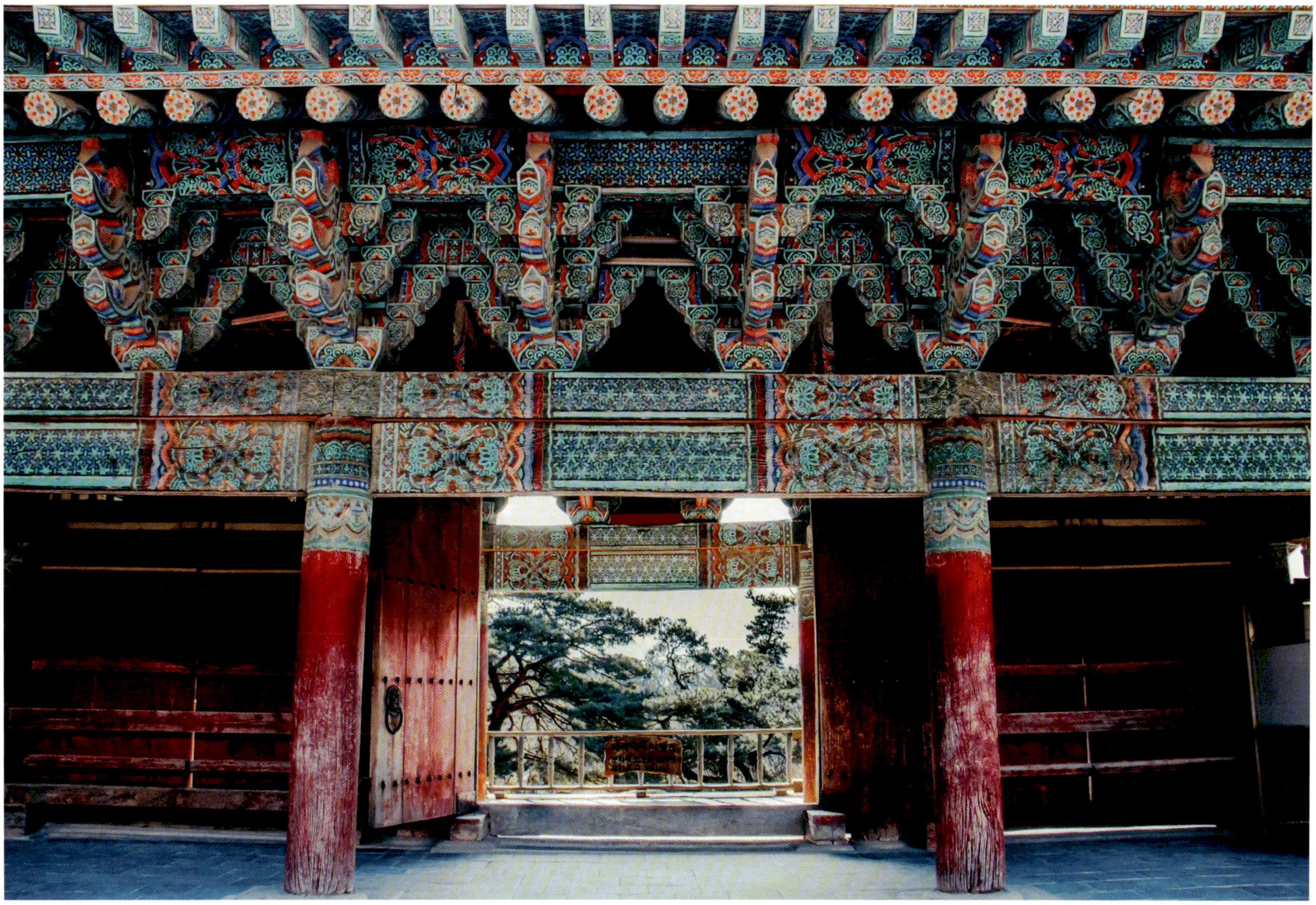

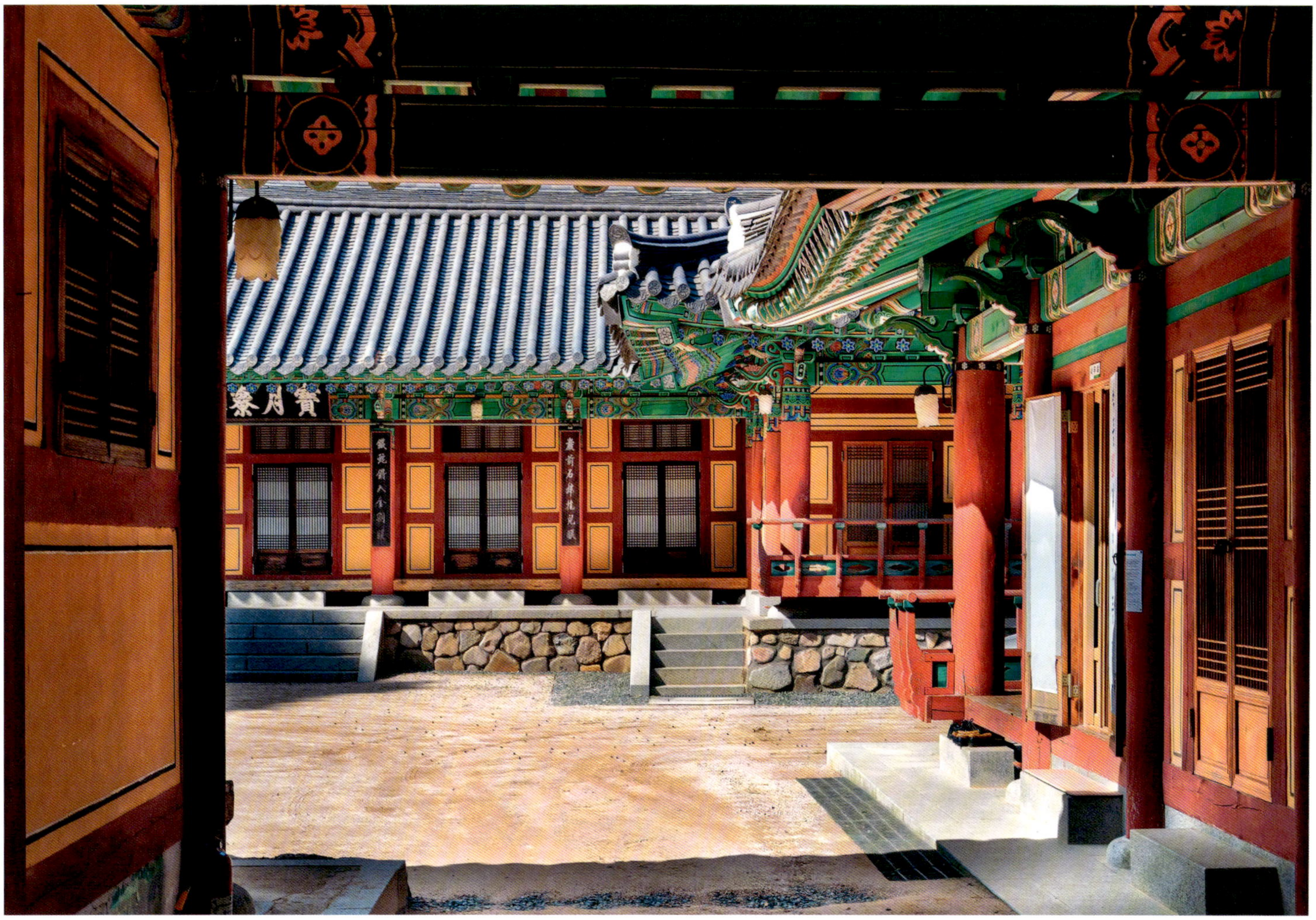

Opposite The elevated location on Toham Mountain symbolizes proximity to the heavens and the ascent to enlightenment, a central theme in Buddhism.
Top Traditional Korean Dancheong painting decorates many areas of the complex.
Bottom The curved roofs showcase the craftsmanship of the Silla era.

Borobudur

In the Three-Tiered Universe

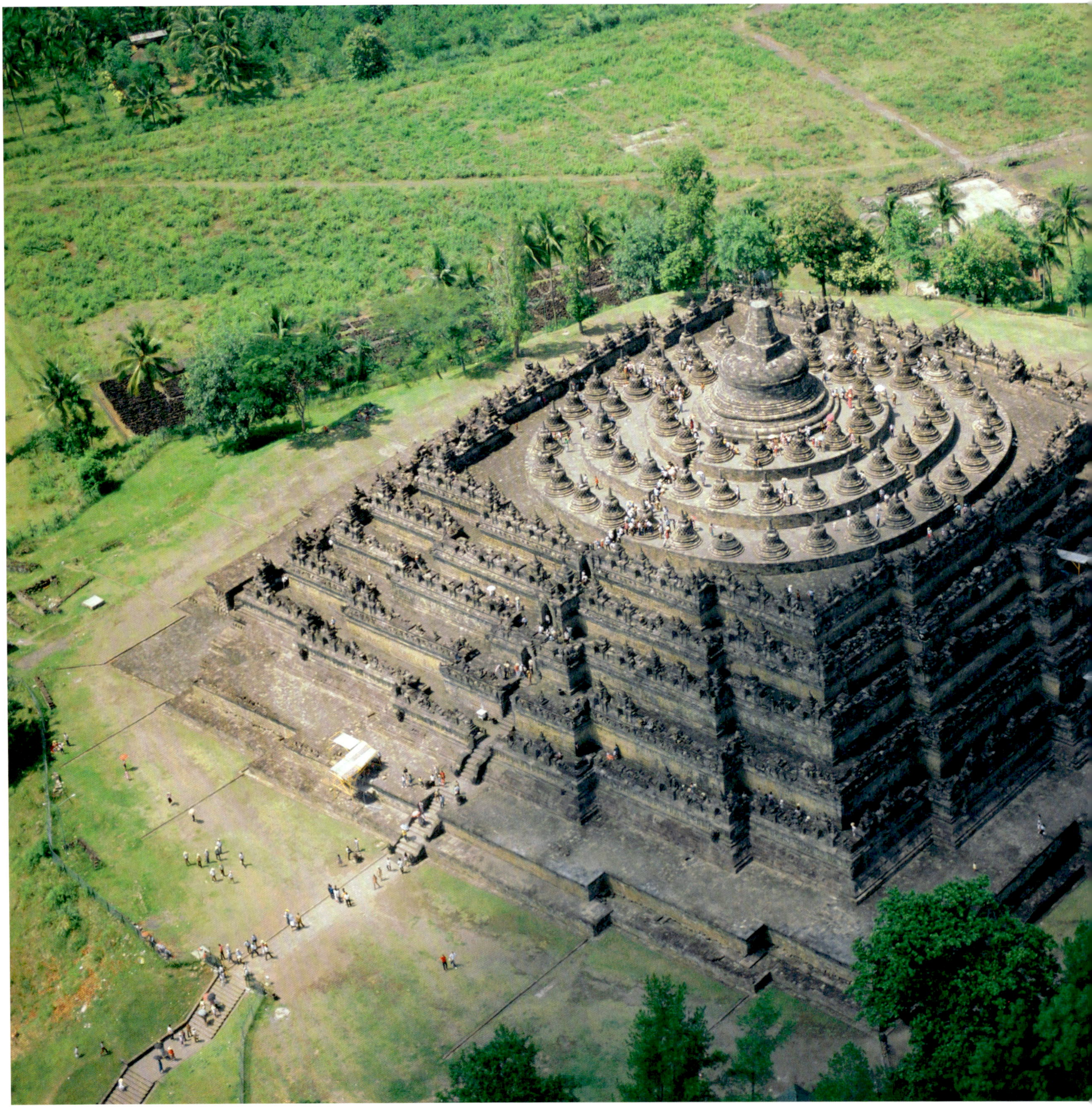

Built: 780 – 850 CE,
Magelang, Indonesia

For centuries, the world's largest Buddhist monument lay hidden beneath volcanic ash and Java's flourishing jungle.

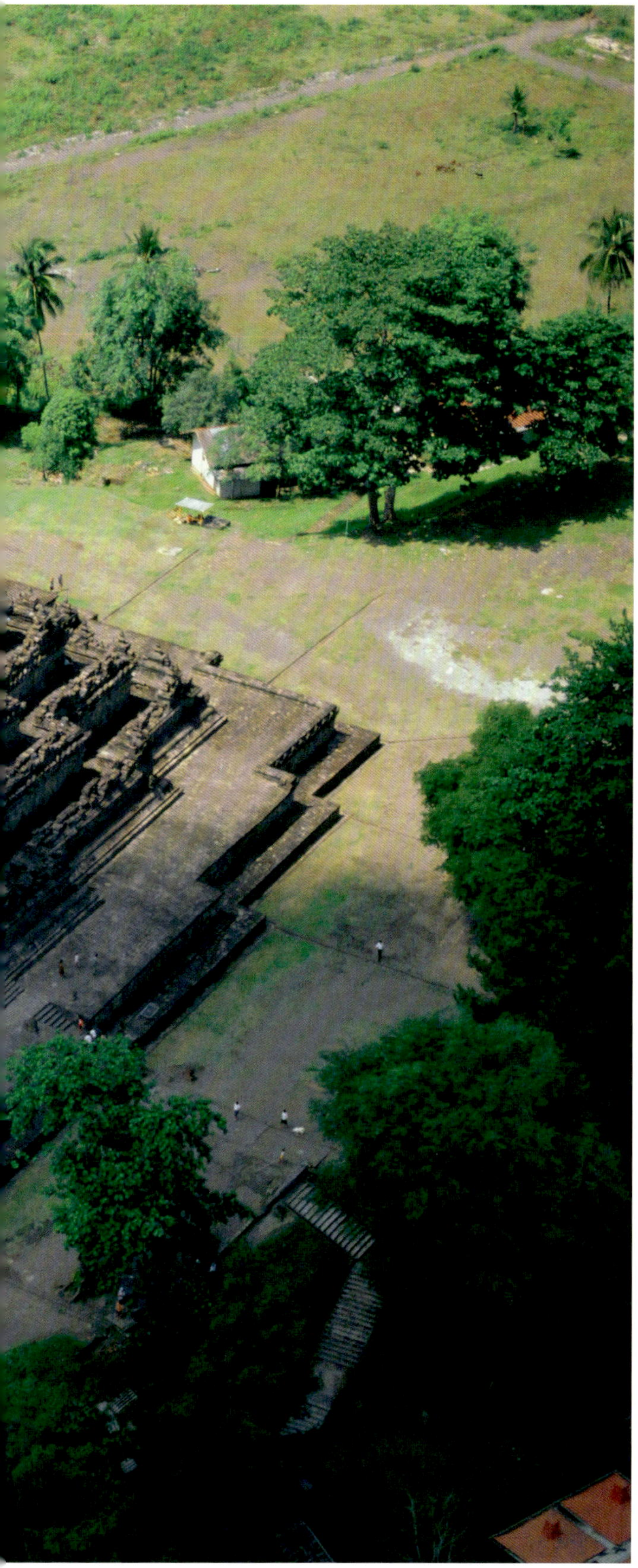

Warm wind brushes your face as small villages and fields of rice blur past—riding a scooter from Yogyakarta to Borobudur immerses you in Java's mystical allure. The scent of freshly cooked food wafts from tiny *warungs,* as the road winds through the island's lush green heart. Finally, it appears between the twin volcanoes of Sindoro-Sumbing and Merbabu-Merapi—the rediscovered temple.

Borobudur is a three-dimensional representation of Buddhist cosmology. Its nine levels invite visitors to embark on a clockwise spiritual journey *(Pradakshina),* beginning in the realm of desire, or *Kamadhatu,* and ending in enlightenment. The temple's base is adorned with richly detailed reliefs illustrating human weaknesses such as greed and sin, as well as the karmic cycle. From there, three square terraces lead into the realm of forms, the *Rupadhatu.* Here, over 1,300 intricate reliefs narrate the life and teachings of Buddha. These levels represent a transitional phase, where one begins to overcome desire but remains bound to physical forms and worldly concepts. The structure culminates in the upper three levels, which are representative of the *Arupadhatu,* or realm of formlessness. These circular platforms are devoid of ornamentation, symbolizing purity and a release from worldly attachments. Within the temple's central dome, 72 perforated bell-shaped *stupas* house meditative Buddha statues, each radiating serenity. At the heart of the temple, symbolizing the ninth level, stands the great central *stupa.* Its emptiness signifies ultimate enlightenment—the unburdened spirit. In this highest spiritual sphere, beyond form and desire, the inner journey concludes.

Although it thrived for several centuries after its construction, by about the 10th century, as Java's political and cultural center shifted eastward, the immense temple complex faded into obscurity. Multiple volcanic eruptions buried it under thick layers of ash, while vegetation overran its terraces. For nearly a millennium, Borobudur lost, but its memory was passed on from generation to generation. In 1814, the British ruler of Java, Sir Thomas Stamford Raffles, heard reports of a hidden monument and dispatched a team to Magelang. Excavations revealed nothing less than the largest Buddhist structure in the world. By 1835, large portions of Borobudur had been cleared, and, in the 20th century, it was restored under UNESCO's guidance.

Today, Borobudur is once again a place of meditation, and a pilgrimage site for seekers from across the globe. Some believe its rediscovery was more than a coincidence—that perhaps, after centuries of oblivion, the temple's reappearance was an effort to guide humanity back toward enlightenment.

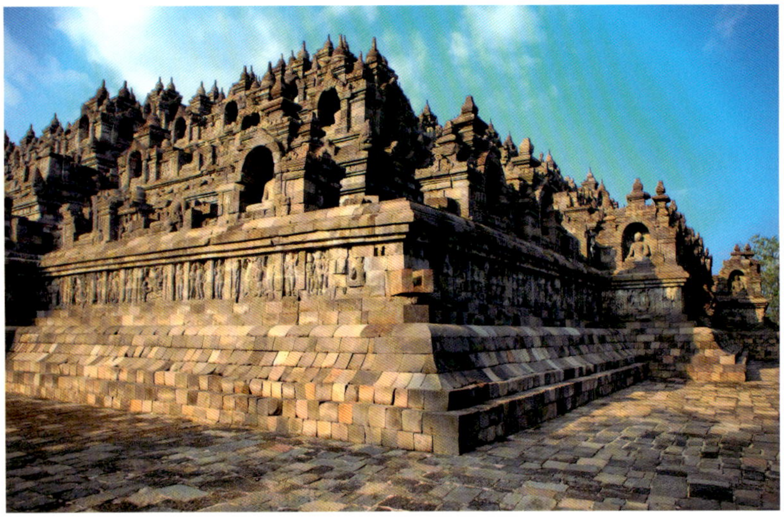

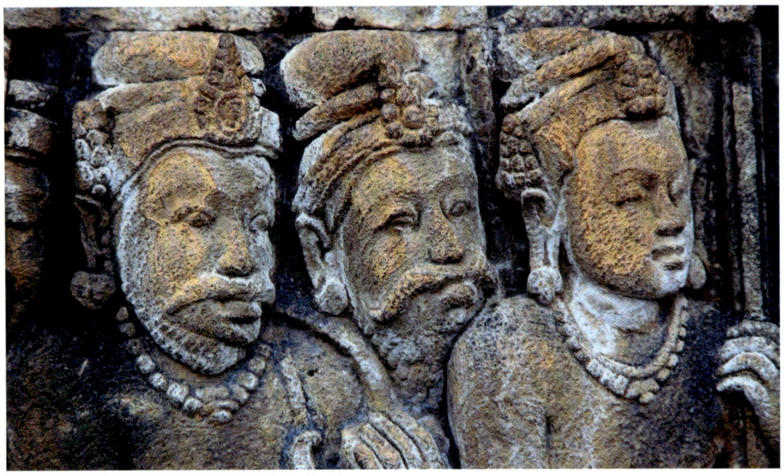

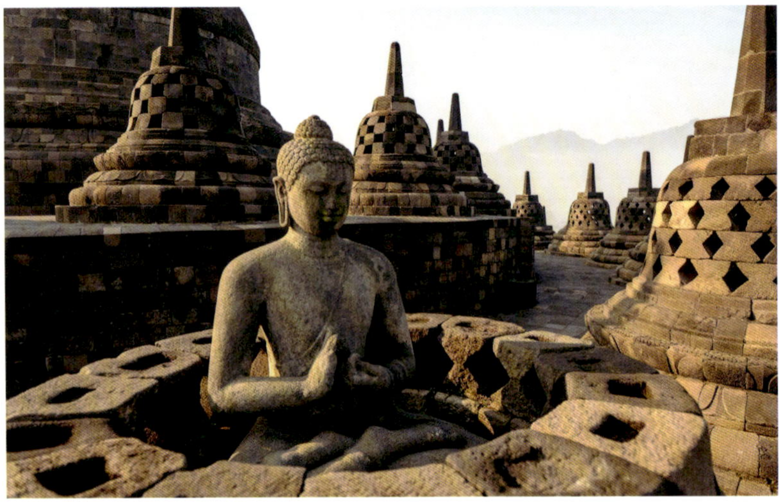

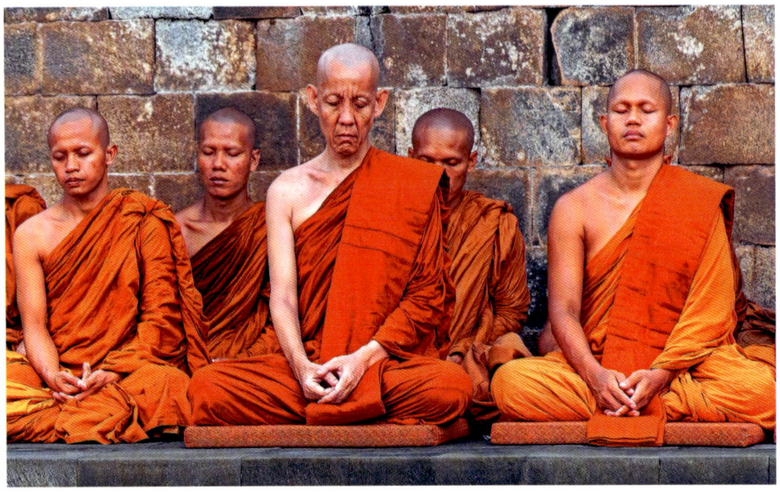

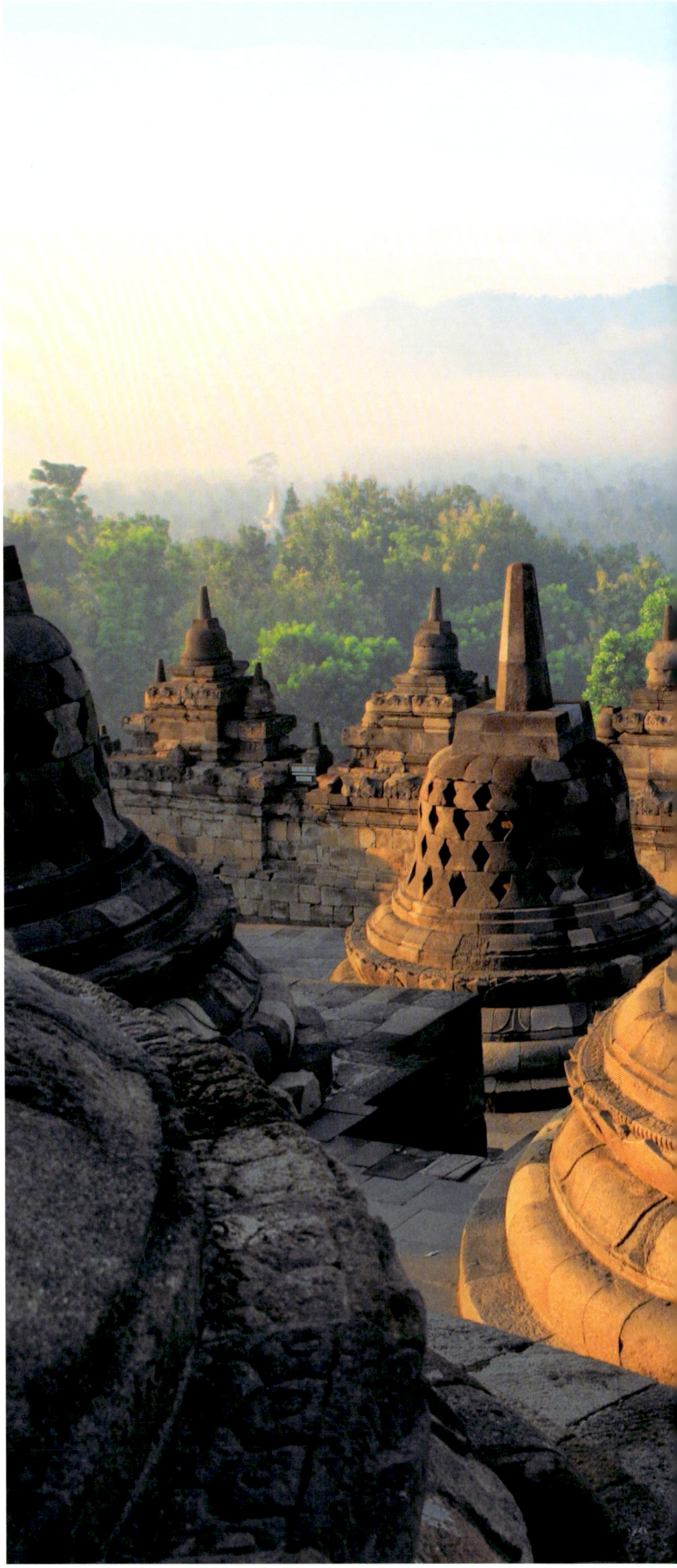

Magelang, Indonesia

Top The steps of Borobudur symbolize the inner spiritual journey.
Upper middle Detailed reliefs tell of spiritual teachings and life in ancient Java.
Lower middle Buddhas showing the "Dharmachakra Mudra" pose.
Bottom To this day, Borobudur serves as an important Buddhist center.

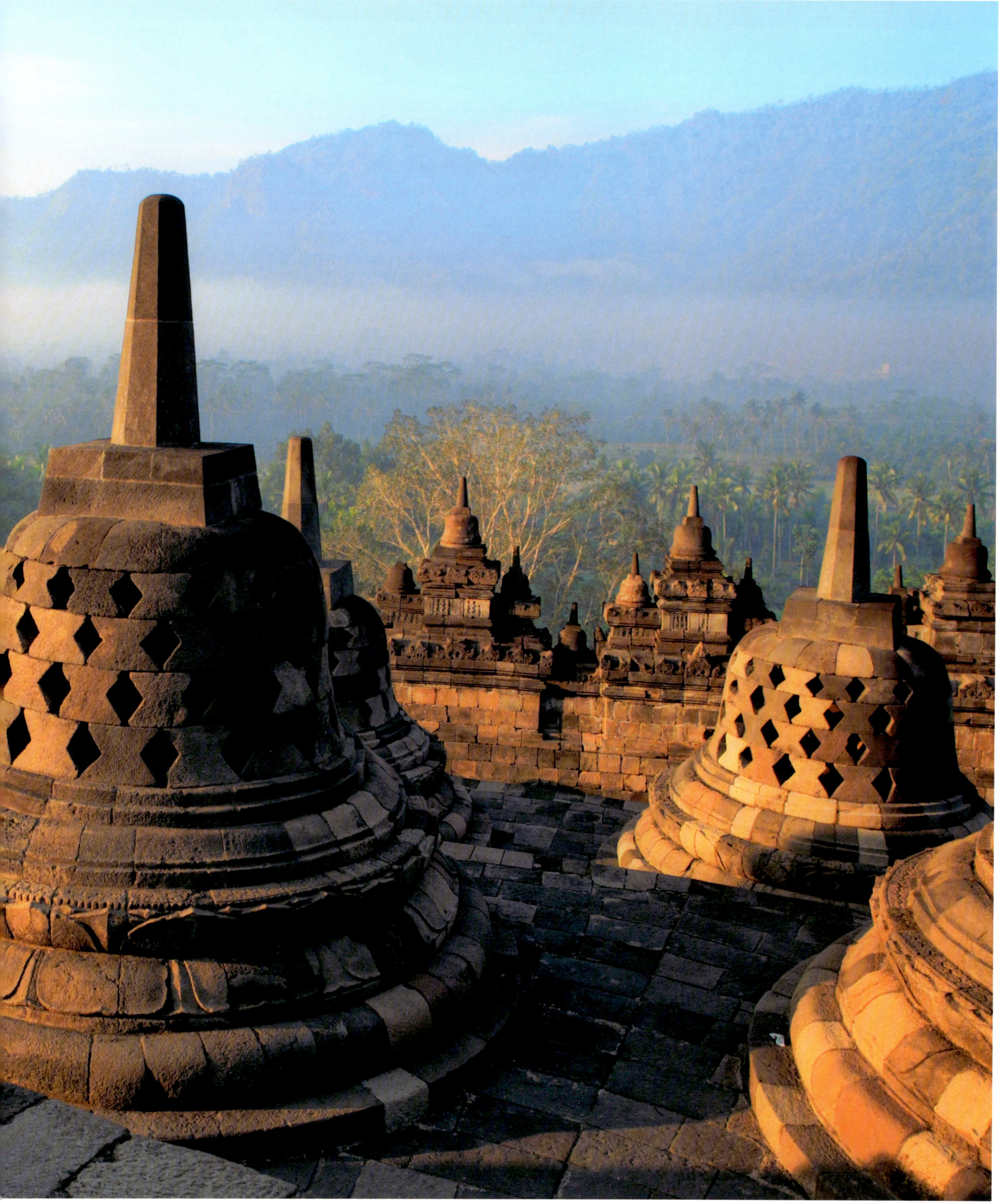

Above Seventy-two small *stupas* are distributed across Borobudur's circular terraces, each containing a seated Buddha statue in a meditative pose.

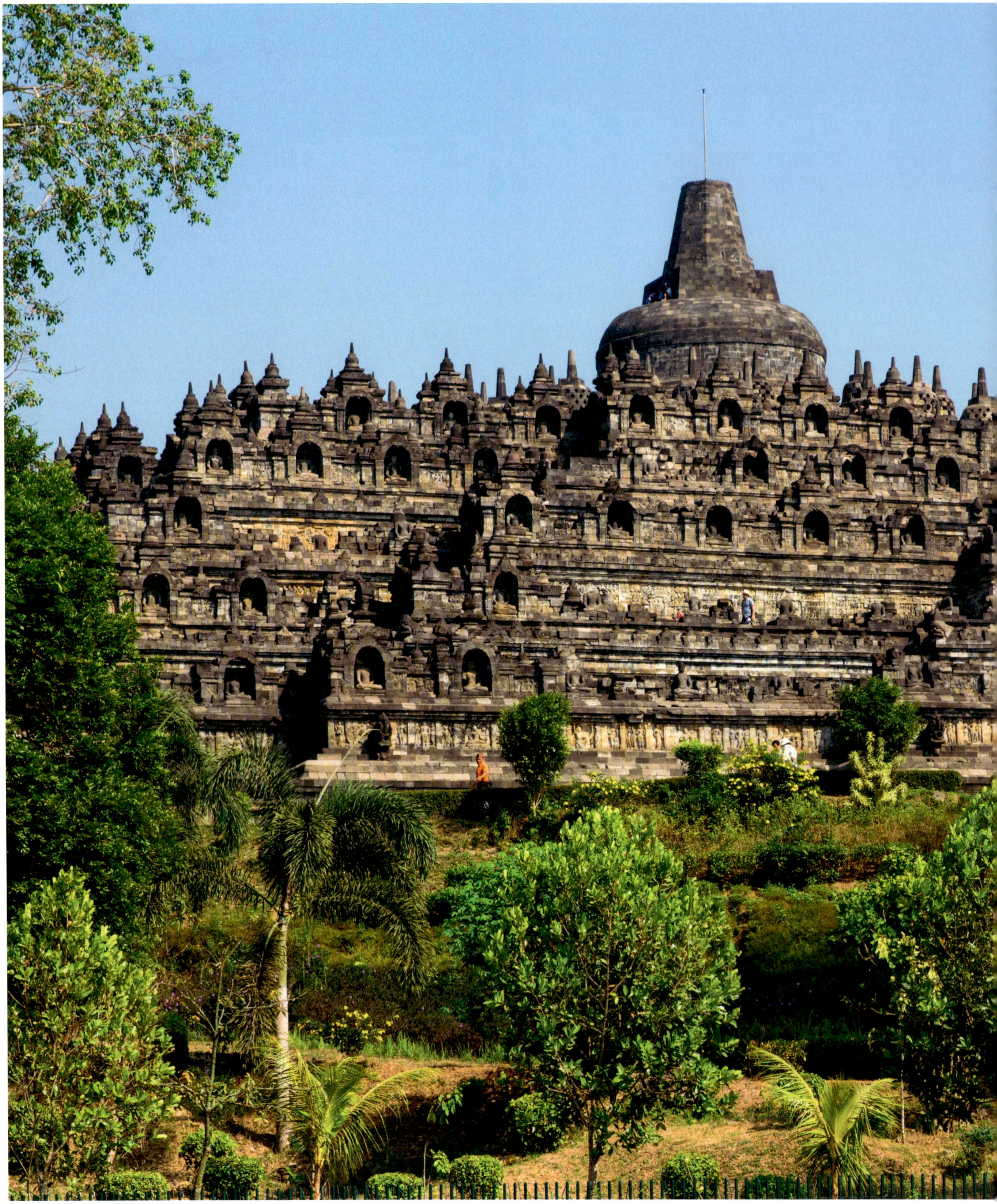

Above The towering central *stupa* of Borobudur represents the attainment of nirvana. It is precisely positioned, connecting both the spiritual and natural worlds.

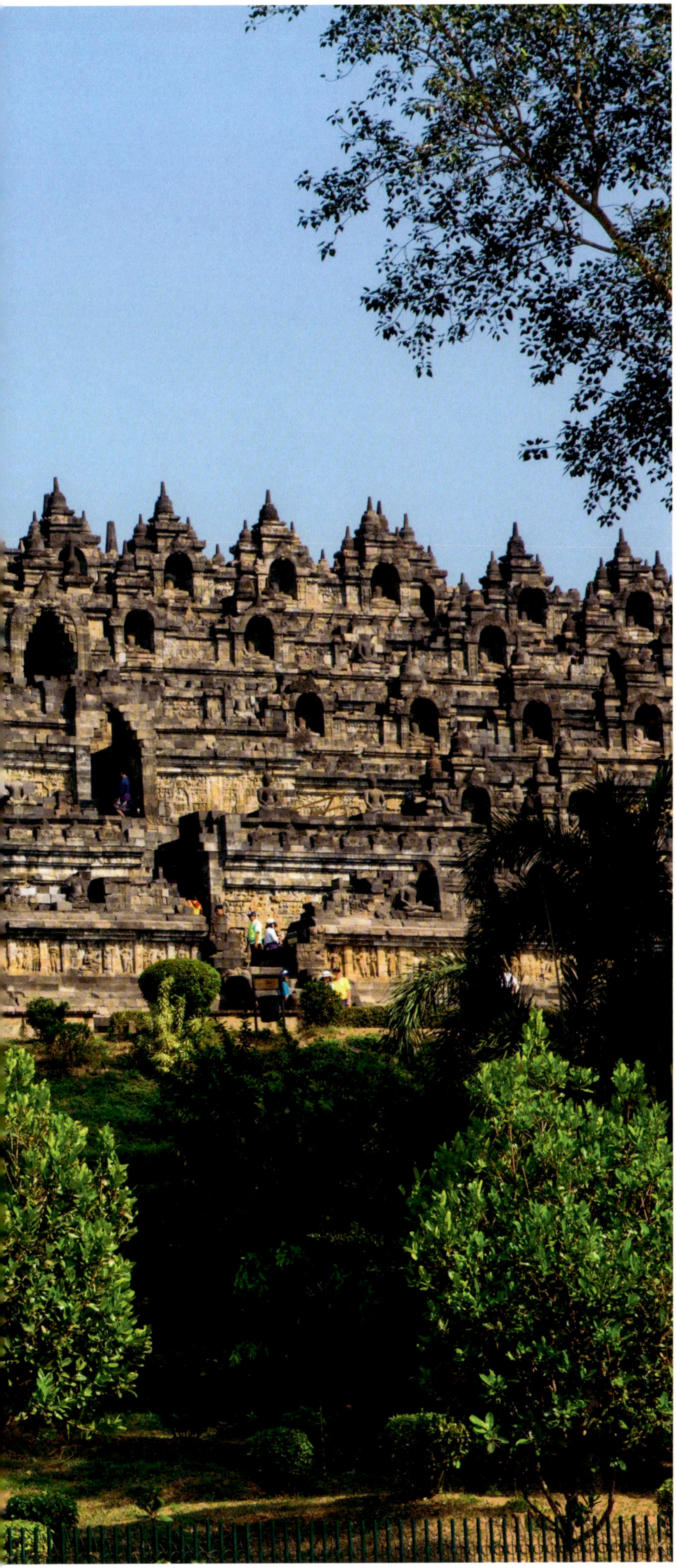

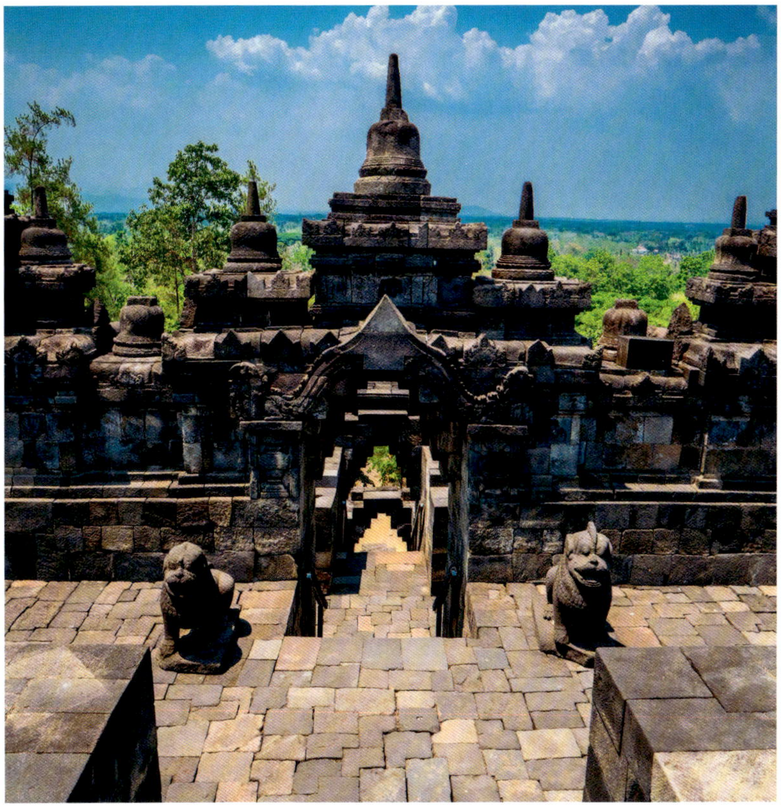

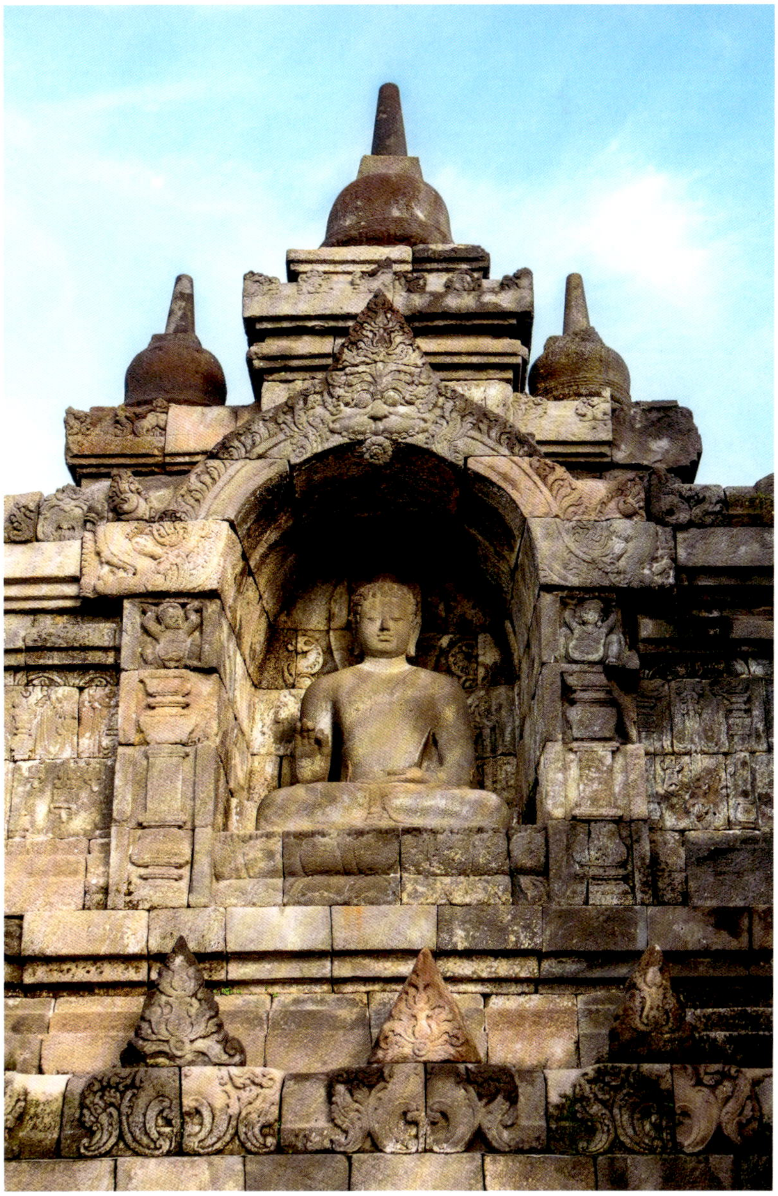

Top Today, Borobudur is a UNESCO World Heritage Site.
Bottom The Buddha's serene gaze radiates enlightenment.

Temples of Bagan

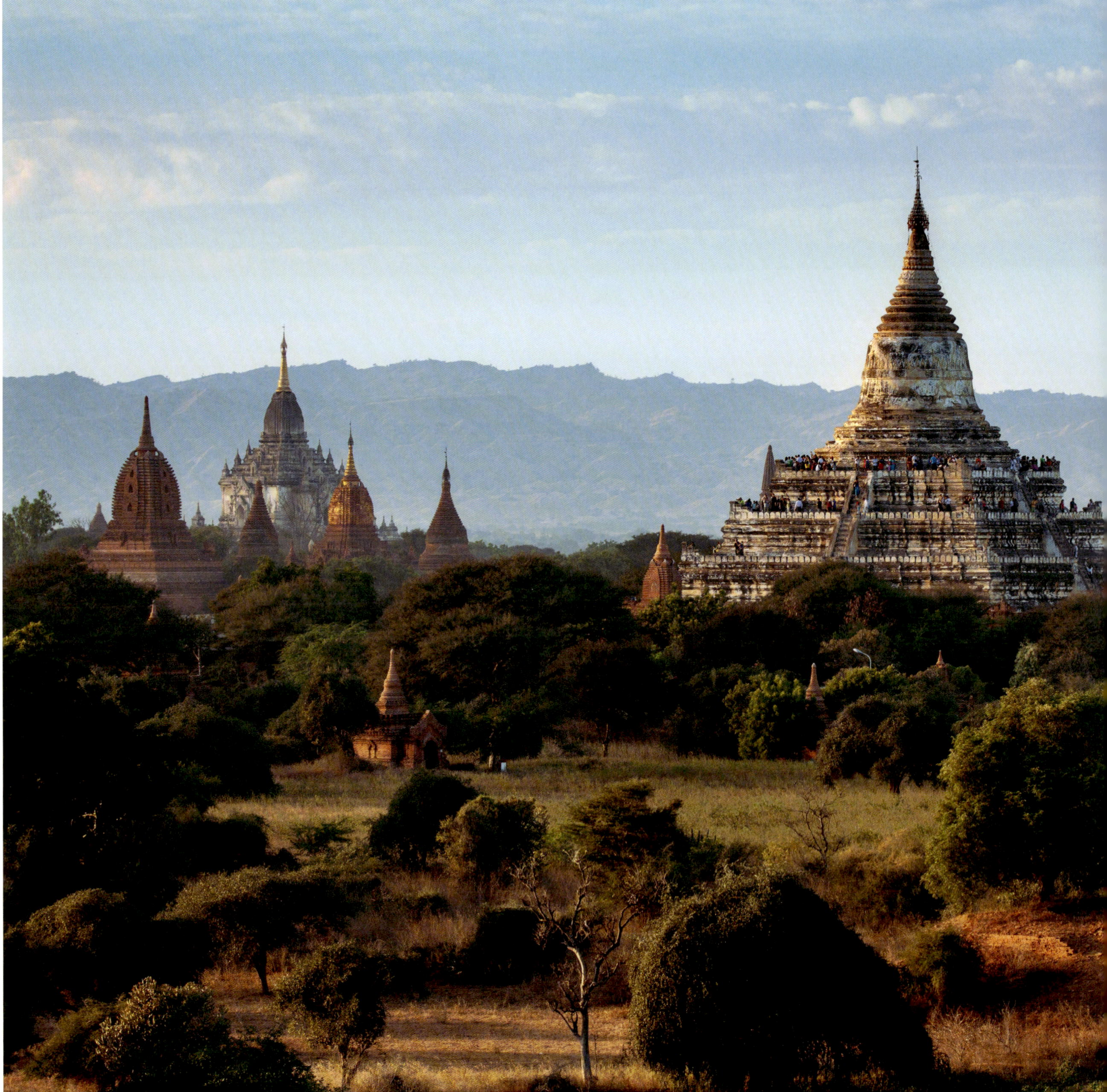

Built: 11th–13th centuries CE, Bagan, Myanmar

A ride over this breathtaking temple landscape offers an unforgettable journey into a world of spiritual architecture.

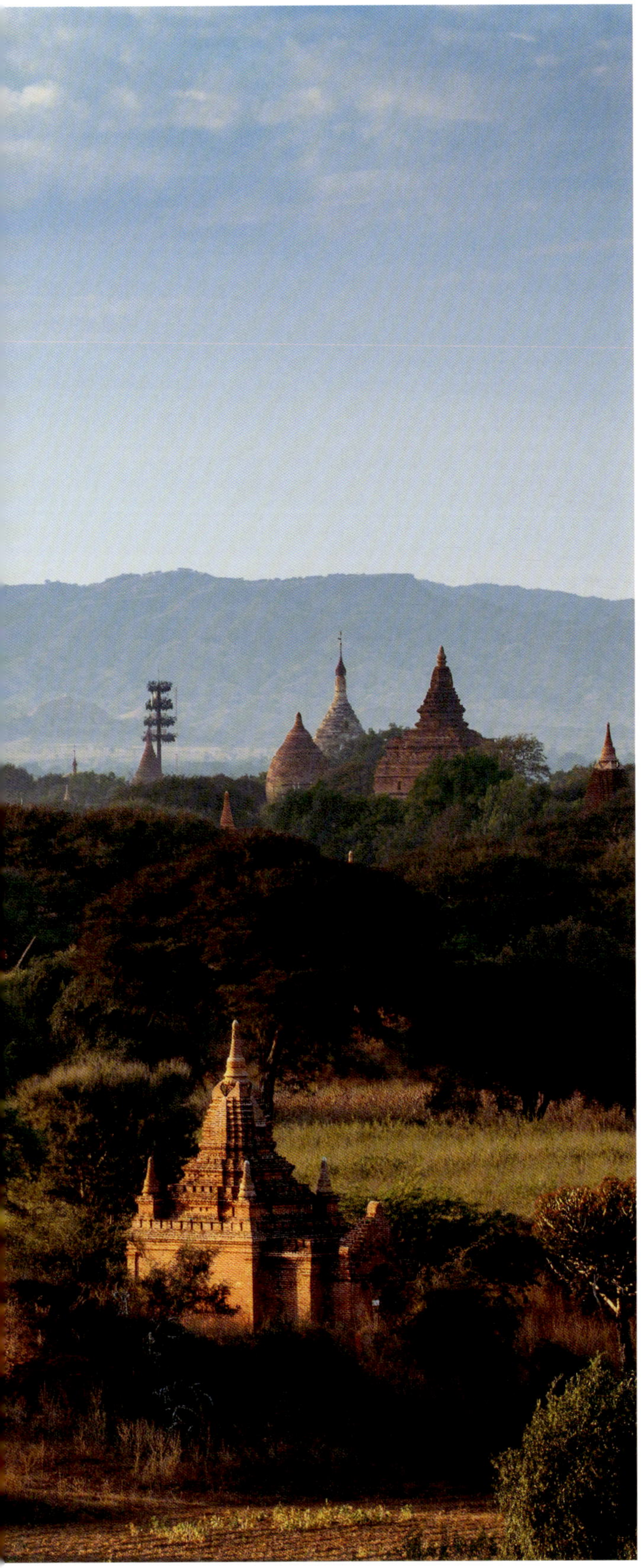

The first light of day pierces the twilight as the flames from the burner fill the massive balloon with hot breath. As the basket lifts off, it jolts slightly, then floats over the mist-shrouded valley of the Ayeyarwady River. With every passing second, the view of Bagan's majestic landscape comes into view.

As if by magic, the silhouettes of over 2,200 temples and pagodas emerge from the mist. The morning sun reflects off the golden dome of the Shwezigon Pagoda, one of Bagan's thousands of highlights. The former capital of the Pagan Kingdom was the heart of an early Buddhist empire between the 9th and 13th centuries. The rulers of that time, followers of Theravāda Buddhism, erected temples and *stupas* at a staggering pace. It is said that more than 10,000 religious structures once stood here, spanning over 38 square miles (100 square kilometers). These temples are testaments to both spiritual commitment and government power. They not only reflect the religious devotion of the kings, but also their ambition to maintain cosmic order. Each temple granted its patron spiritual merit—a kind of karmic benefit—which could also work in reverse, helping one atone for sins. The immense scale of the magnificent, if unfinished, Dhammayangyi Temple offers a striking indication of the remorse its builder might have felt.

The balloon now drifts over the grand Ananda Temple, built in 1091 CE by King Kyansittha. Its perfectly symmetrical architecture and majestic golden spire rise from the surrounding plain, while inside, enormous Buddha statues gaze in the four cardinal directions. Between the temples, the bell-shaped *stupas* symbolize Mount Meru, the sacred mountain at the center of the Buddhist cosmos, considered the axis mundi and central pillar connecting the heavens, earth, and the underworld. Every terrace, every spire, and every ornament is imbued with profound significance. The temples of Bagan have survived both the Mongol invasion in the 13th century and a devastating earthquake in the 20th century, albeit with scars, and to this day, the ancient city is visited by pilgrims from all over the world. From above, casual visitors and devotees can be glimpsed placing flowers and making small offerings to Buddha.

Slowly, the balloon descends, returning back to the earthly realms and gently landing on an open field. What an experience! After the slightly wobbly exit, your feet are once again on solid ground, yet your head and heart remain in the clouds, soaring above the majestic temples of Bagan.

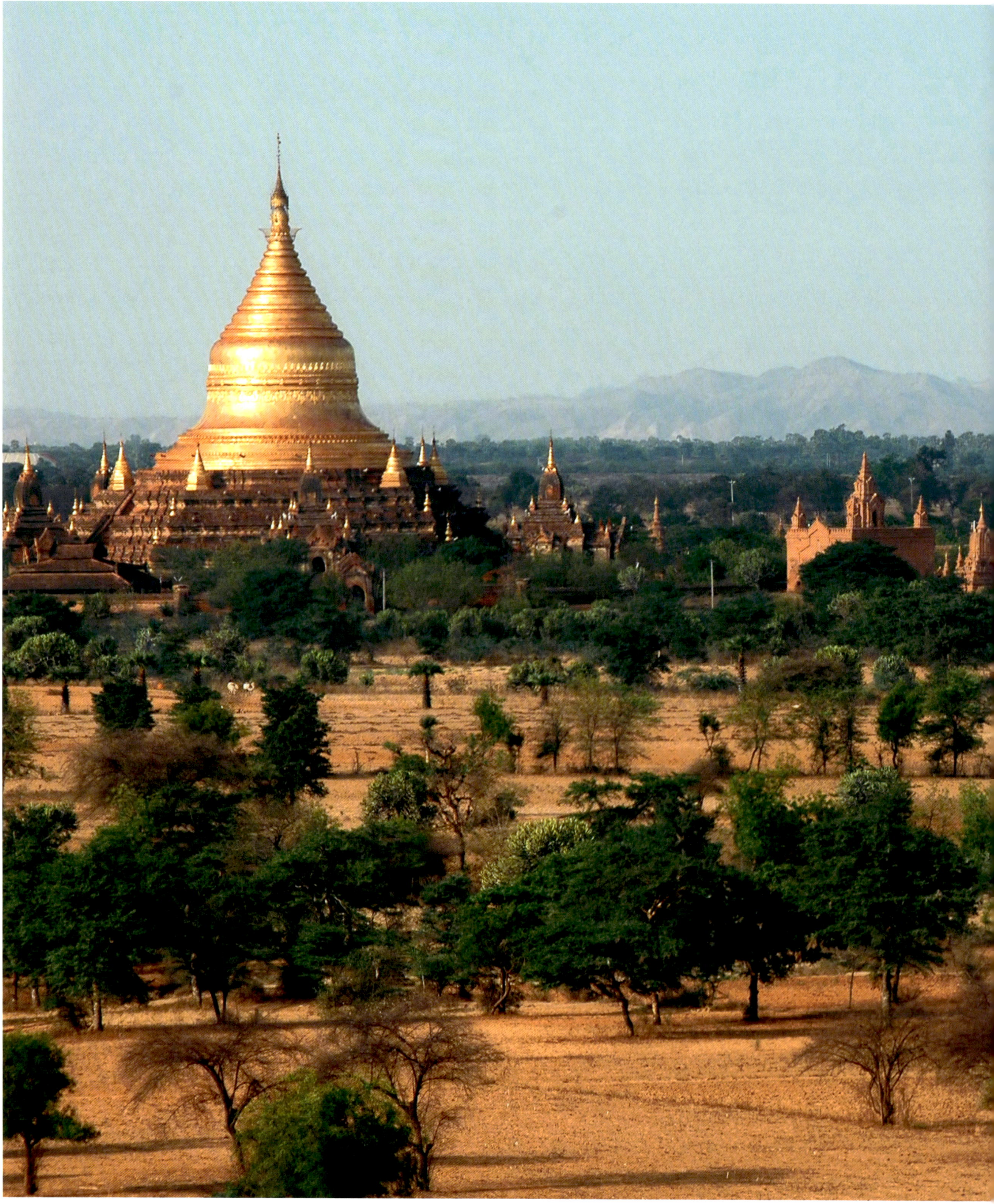

Bagan, Myanmar

Above In 2019, the magnificent Temples of Bagan were declared a UNESCO World Heritage Site. They remain one of Myanmar's most cherished national treasures.

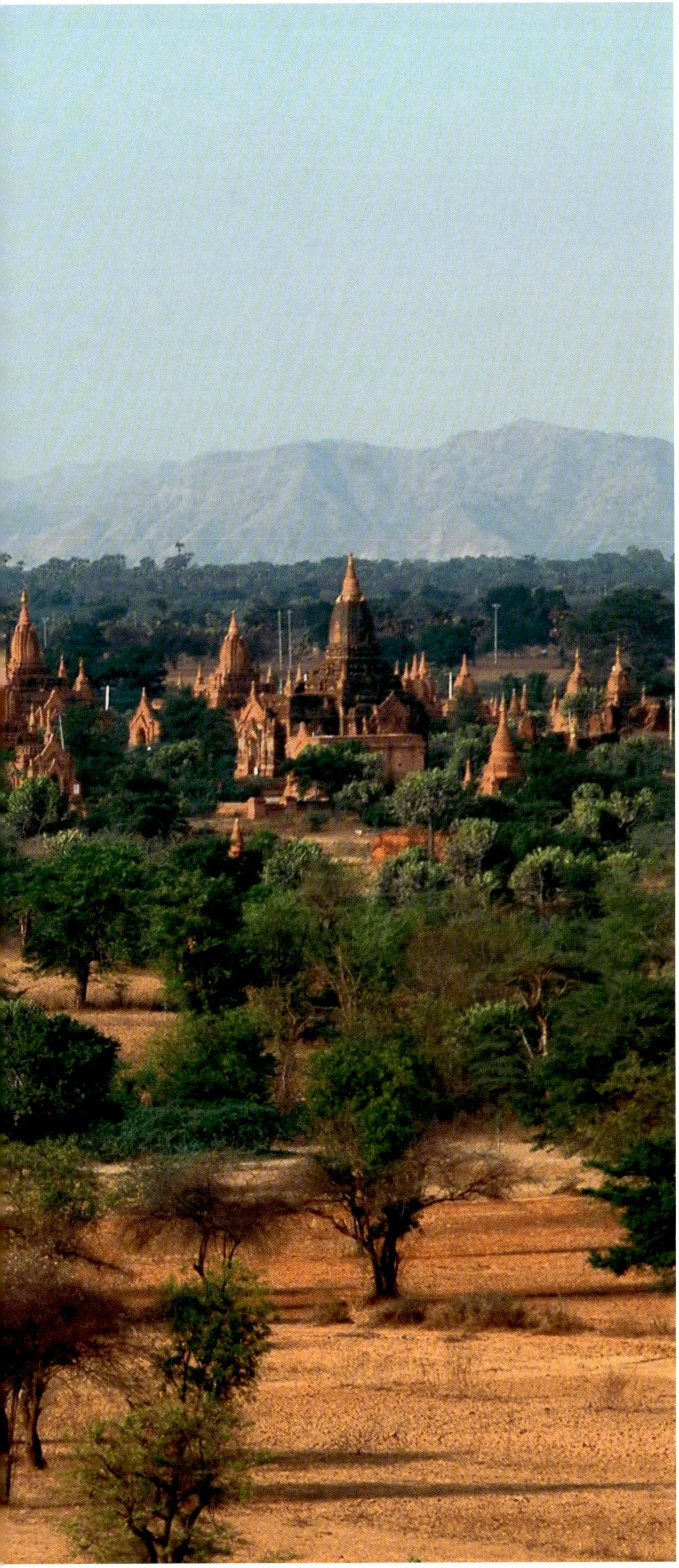

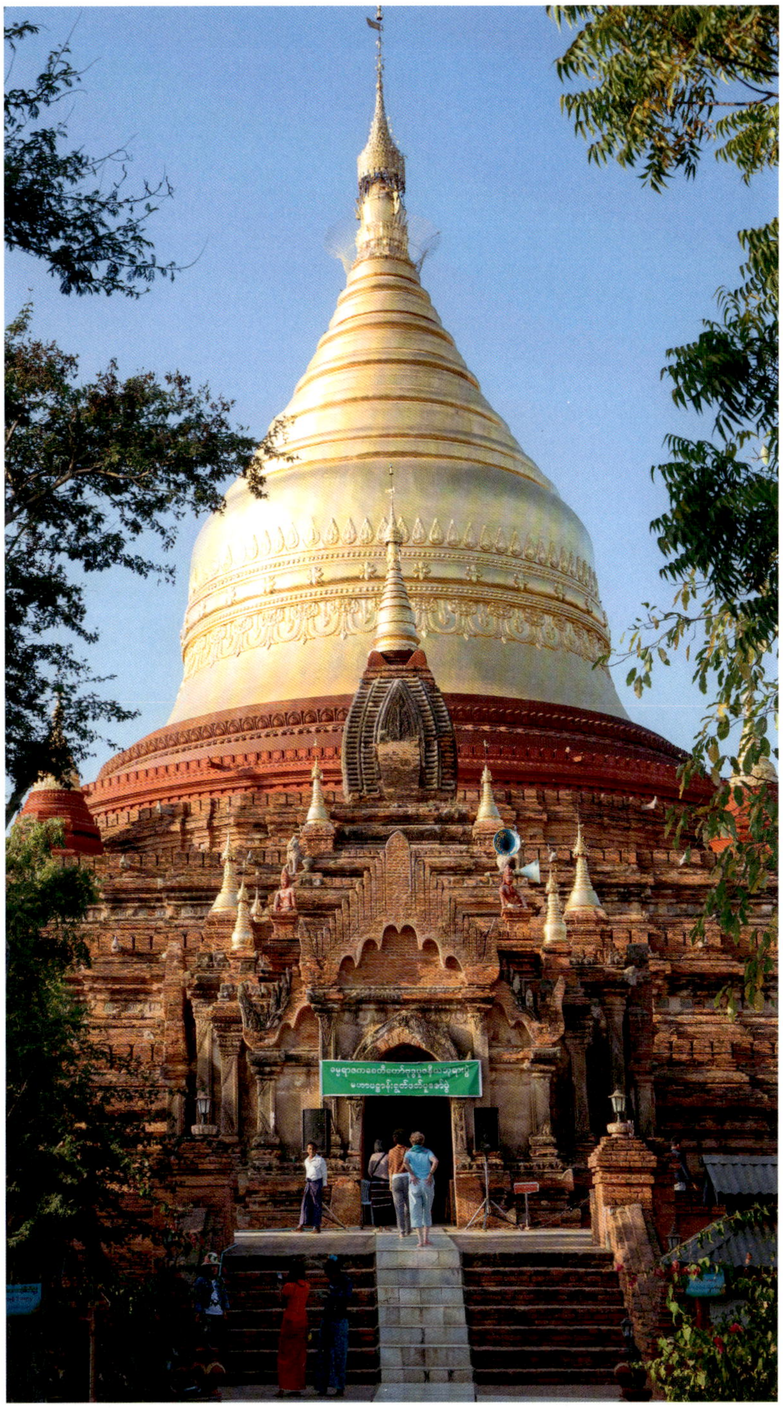

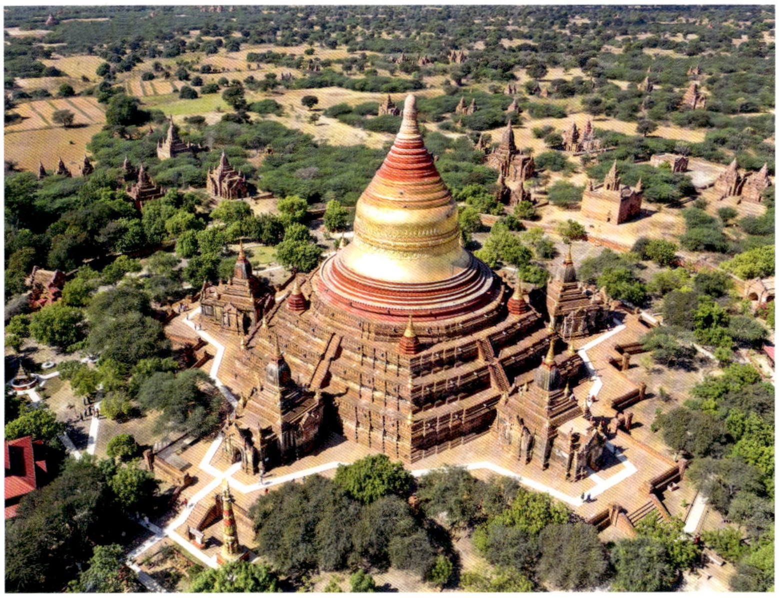

Top The grand Dhammayazika Pagoda, with its distinctive golden dome, is among the most popular highlights of Bagan.
Bottom From a bird's-eye view, the impressive architecture of the pagoda and the full splendor of Bagan is revealed.

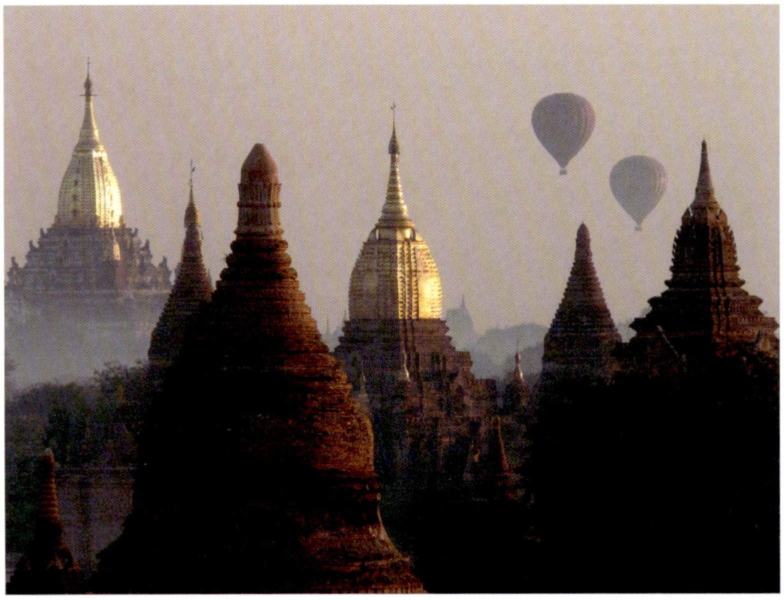

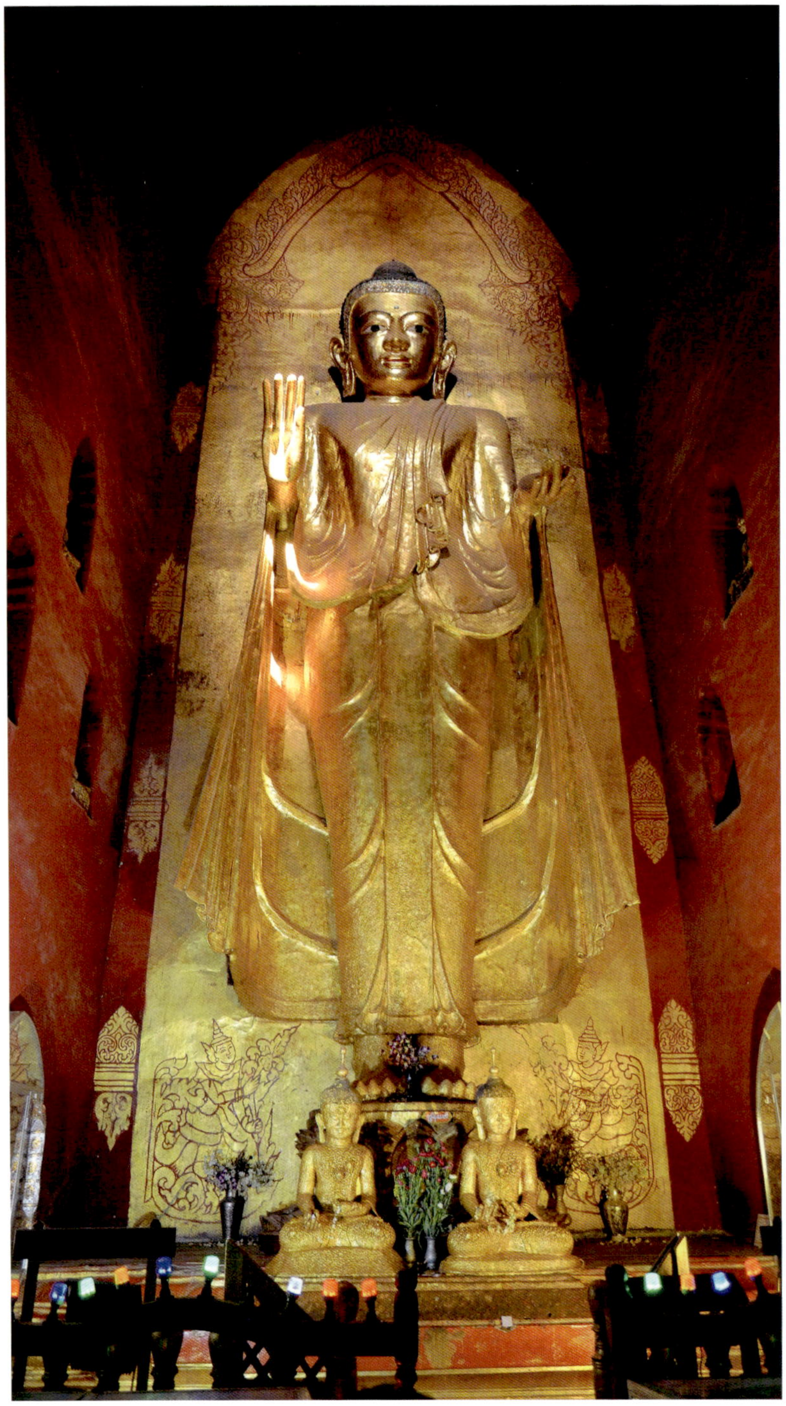

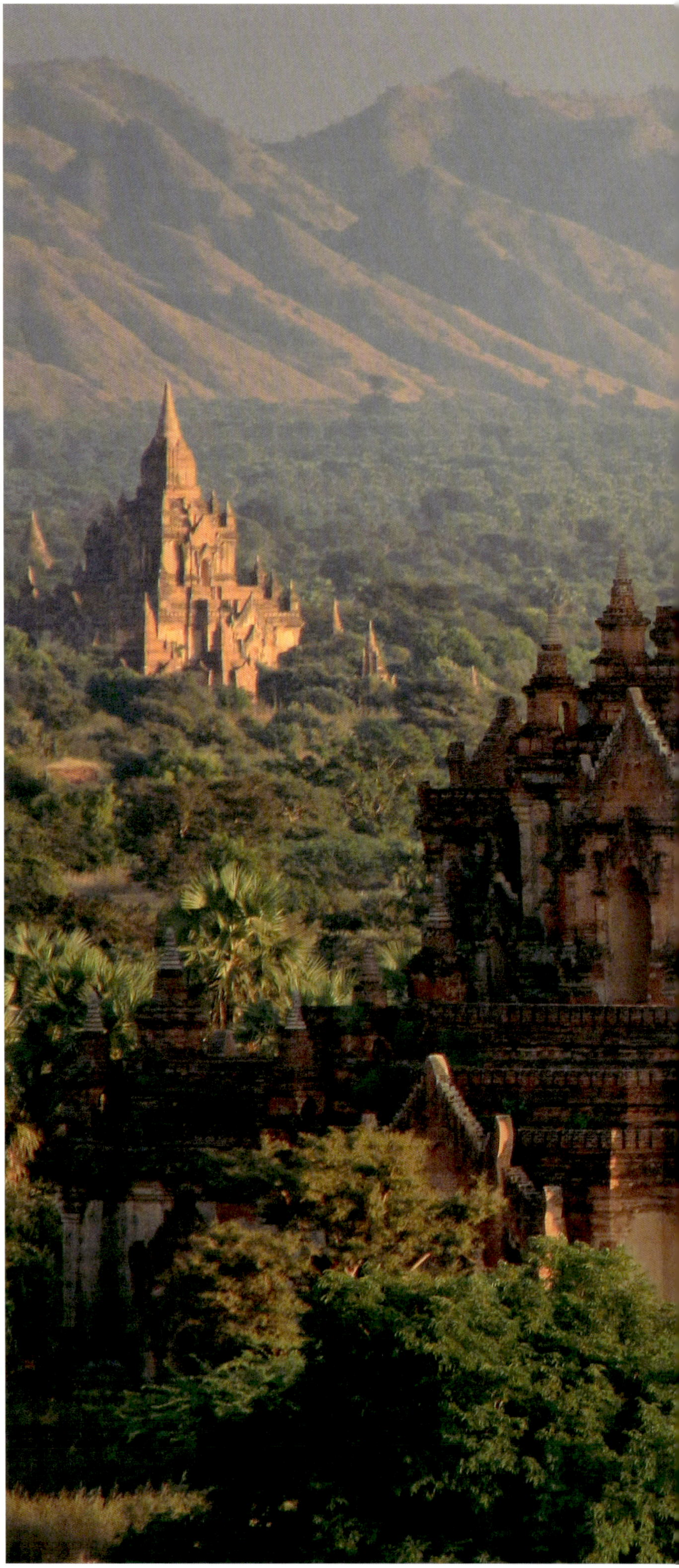

Bagan, Myanmar

Top One of the most popular ways to experience the Temples of Bagan is by hot air balloon.
Bottom Within the Ananda Temple, four standing Buddhas are positioned in accordance with the cardinal directions. The Buddha Gautama, seen here, faces west.

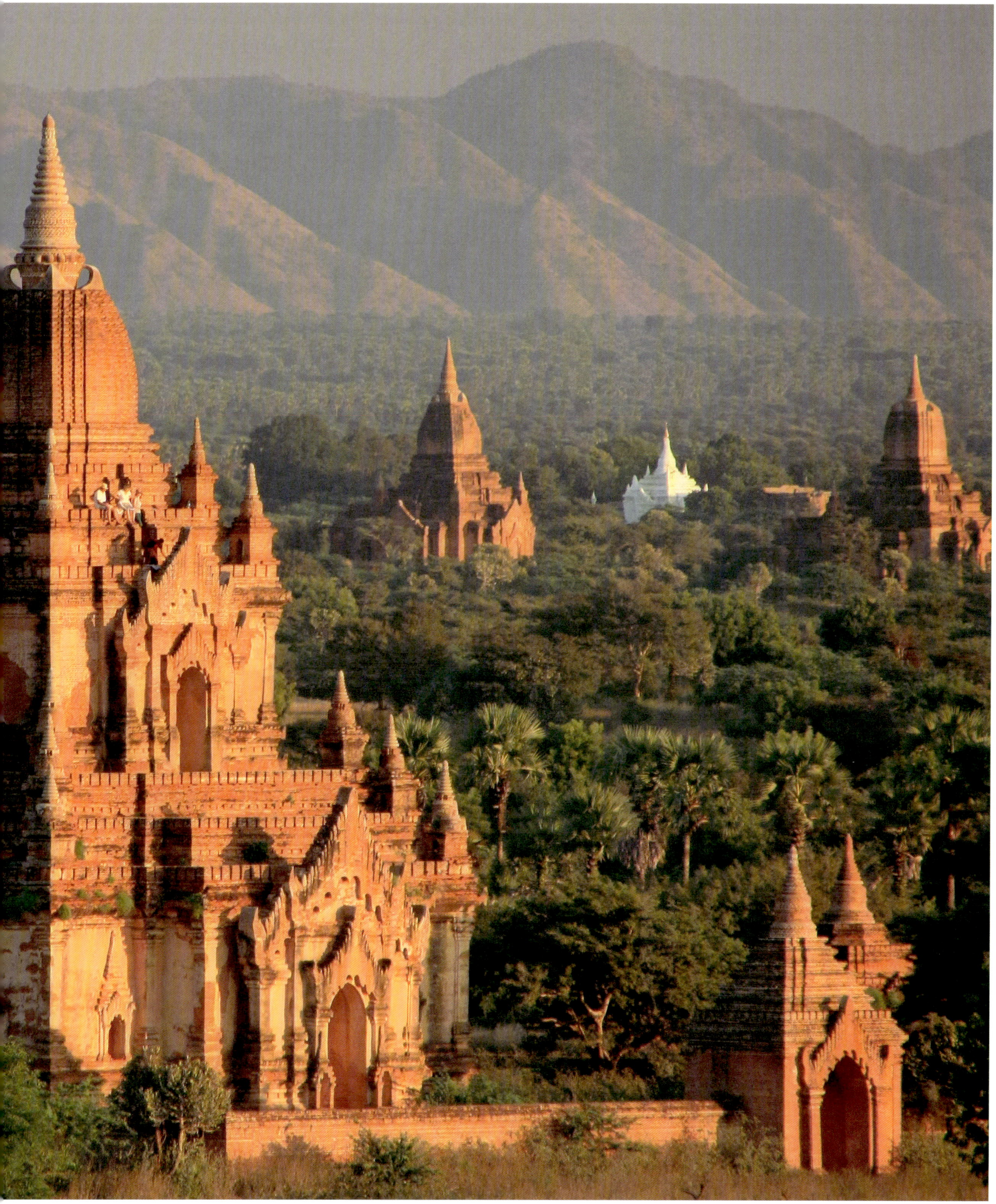

Above Many temples in Bagan, some of which date back to the 11th century, have been meticulously restored after suffering earthquake damage throughout the years.

Shah-i-Zinda

In the City of the Dead

Built: 11th – 15th centuries CE, Samarkand, Uzbekistan

Beneath the adorned domes and intricate mosaics of this necropolis, a king patiently awaits his return.

Samarkand, whose founding likely dates between the 8th and 7th centuries BCE, flourished during the Middle Ages. Caravans traveling along the Silk Road between China and the Mediterranean transformed the city into one of the wealthiest and most beautiful in Asia. Gardens bursting with flowers, serene ponds, and graceful palms were meticulously cultivated. Mosques and mausoleums shimmered with exquisitely crafted tiles.

The necropolis of Shah-i-Zinda, one of the holiest sites in Samarkand, stands as a testament to this splendor, embodying centuries of architectural brilliance. Its delicate mosaics, majolica, and glazed tiles are unparalleled in all of Central Asia. According to legend, the history of Shah-i-Zinda dates back to the 7th century CE, when Qusam ibn Abbas, a cousin of the Prophet Muhammad, came to Samarkand to spread the message of Islam. As the story goes, while deep in prayer, he was beheaded by followers of a fire-worshipping cult. But since a man who dies in God's name cannot truly perish, Qusam ibn Abbas picked up his head, tucked it under his arm, and descended into a sacred well said to lead directly to the gardens of Paradise. It is there, they say, that he lives to this day, and will return when Islam is in peril. The name Shah-i-Zinda, meaning "The Living King," is a tribute to this tale.

His mausoleum is regarded as the spiritual heart of the entire complex. Ornate tiles cloak the magnificent structure in hues of blue, turquoise, and gold. Over the centuries, additional mausoleums were built around it. Paved pathways wind through the artistically adorned tombs, which are graced with geometric patterns, floral motifs, and intricate Arabic calligraphy. Unlike Samarkand's central landmarks—Registan Square or the mausoleum of Tamerlane—Shah-i-Zinda does not reveal its treasures all at once. It is a place that rewards slow and thoughtful exploration, a sanctuary that opens itself only to those willing to engage with its history.

With the dawn of the modern age, Samarkand's significance waned. Trade increasingly shifted to maritime routes, leaving fewer caravans passing through the city. The intellectual heart of the Islamic world also migrated to other regions. The suppression of Islam during the Soviet era pushed Samarkand further into the shadows. Yet for those who wander through the narrow paths of this necropolis today, its silence resonates with the profound faith, pride, and cultural brilliance of a bygone era. Here, in the City of the Dead, that past feels vividly alive—and will even more so, one day, when the Living King returns.

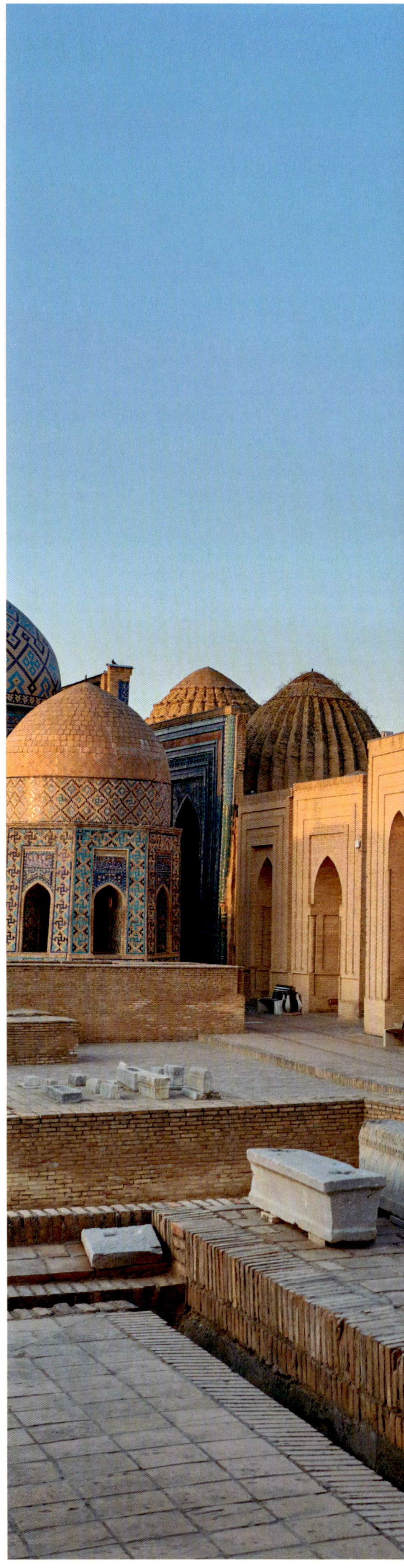

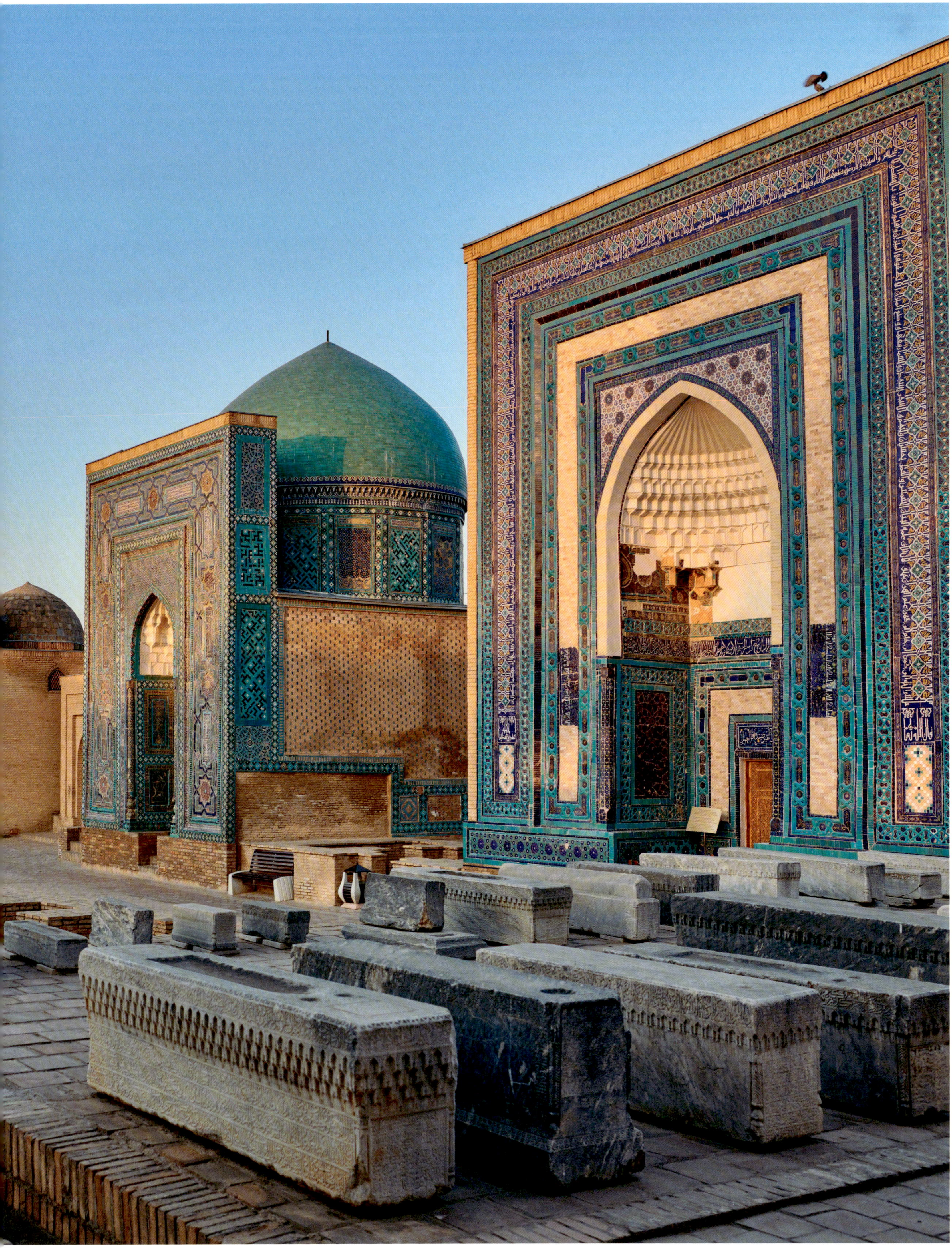

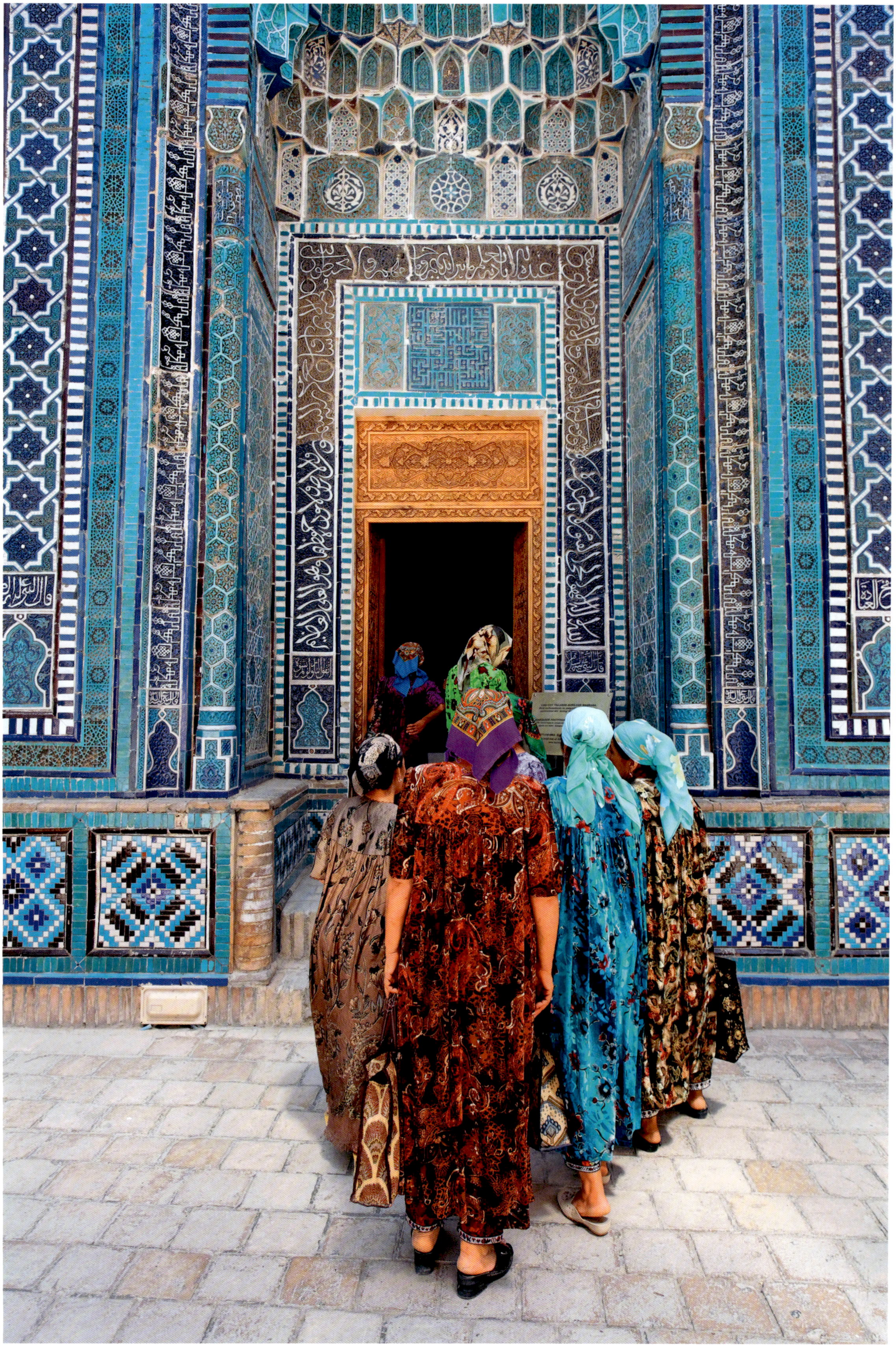

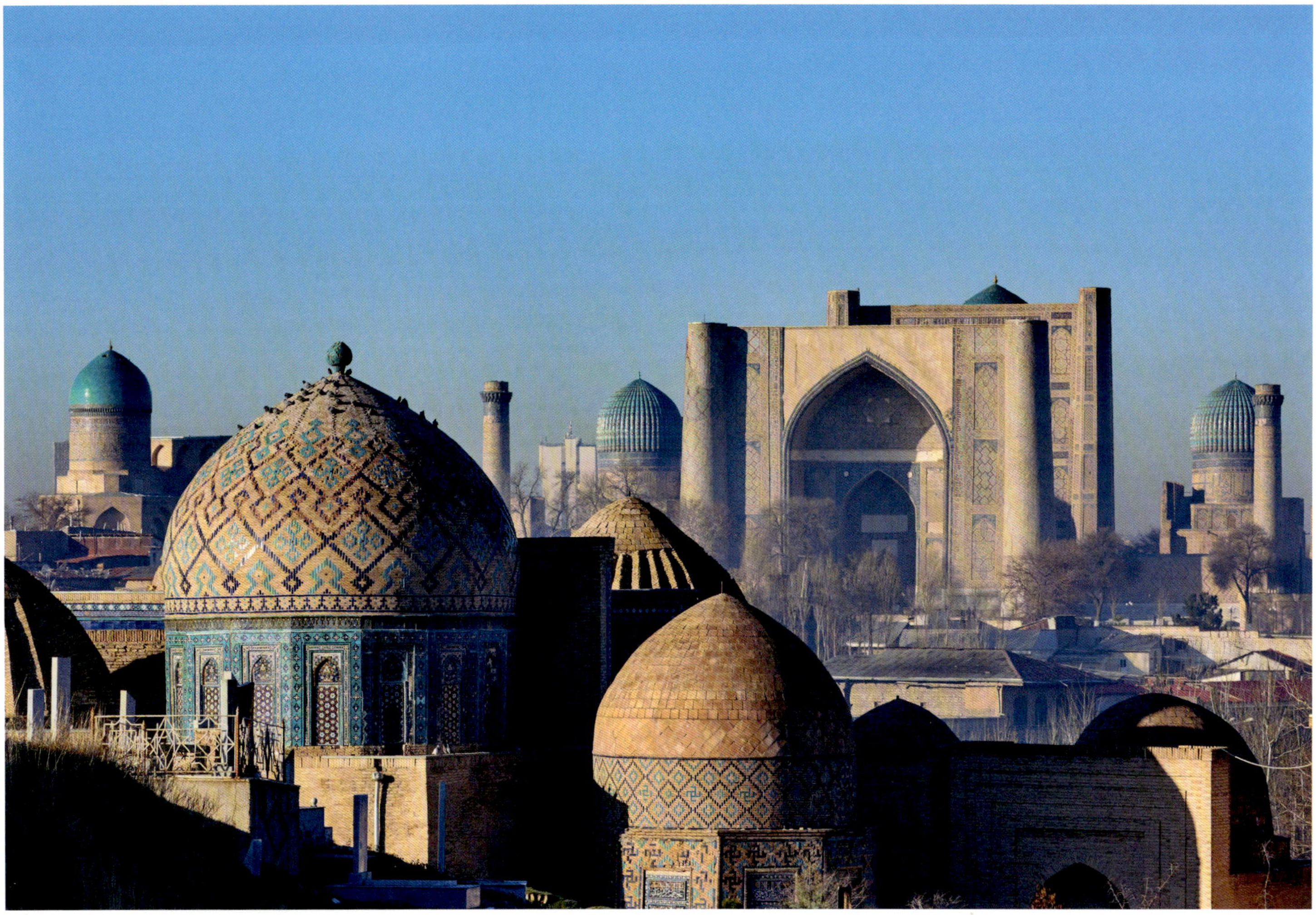

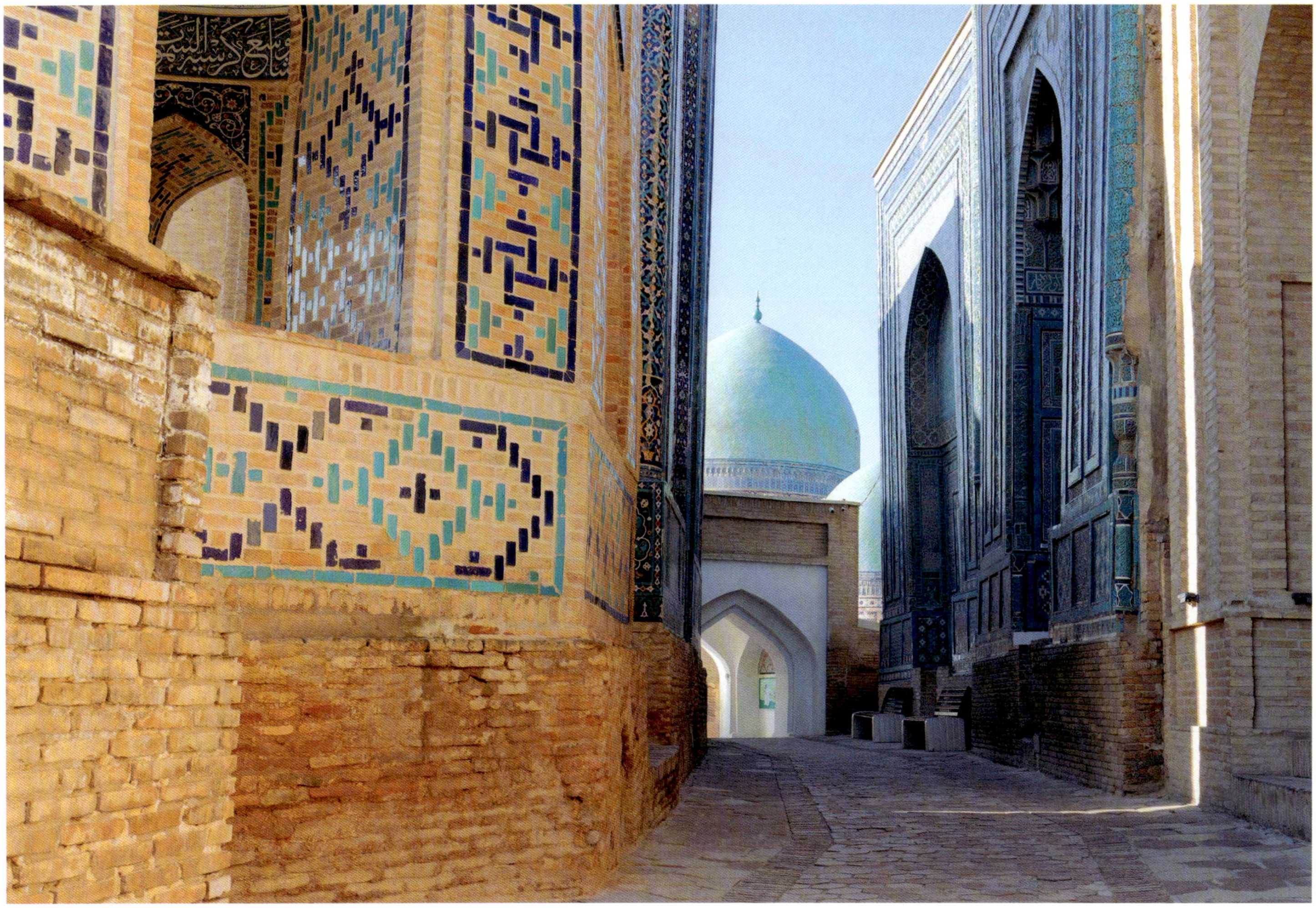

Opposite The mosaics of Shah-i-Zinda are considered prime examples of Timurid art.
Top The intricately designed mausoleums form a harmonious ensemble.
Bottom Around every bend of the necropolis, visitors encounter intricate mosaics, fresh perspectives, and new architectural marvels.

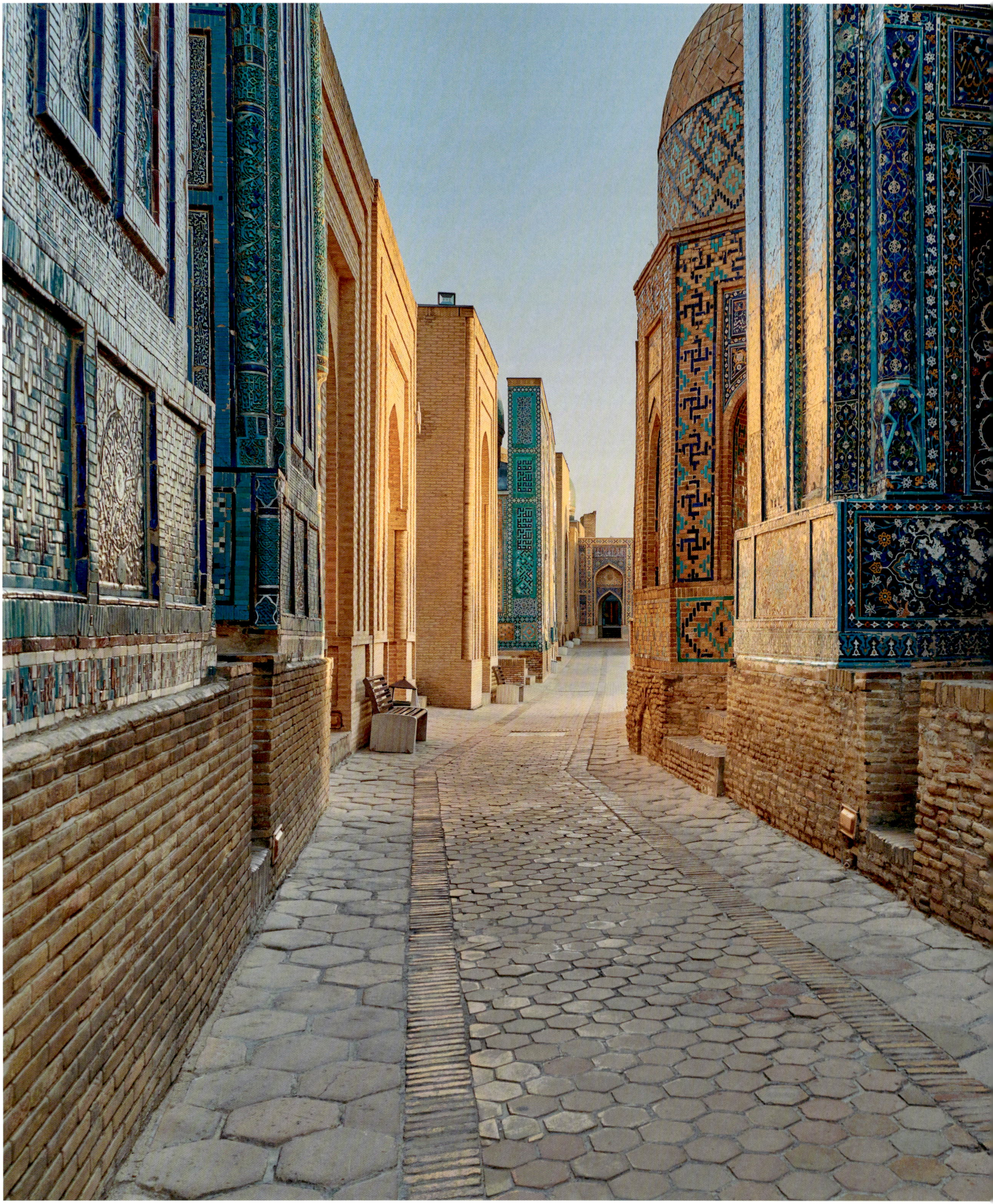

Samarkand, Uzbekistan

Above Shah-i-Zinda remains an important Islamic pilgrimage site to this day. Devout Muslims, particularly those practicing Sufism, visit to seek *baraka*, a blessing of spiritual energy.

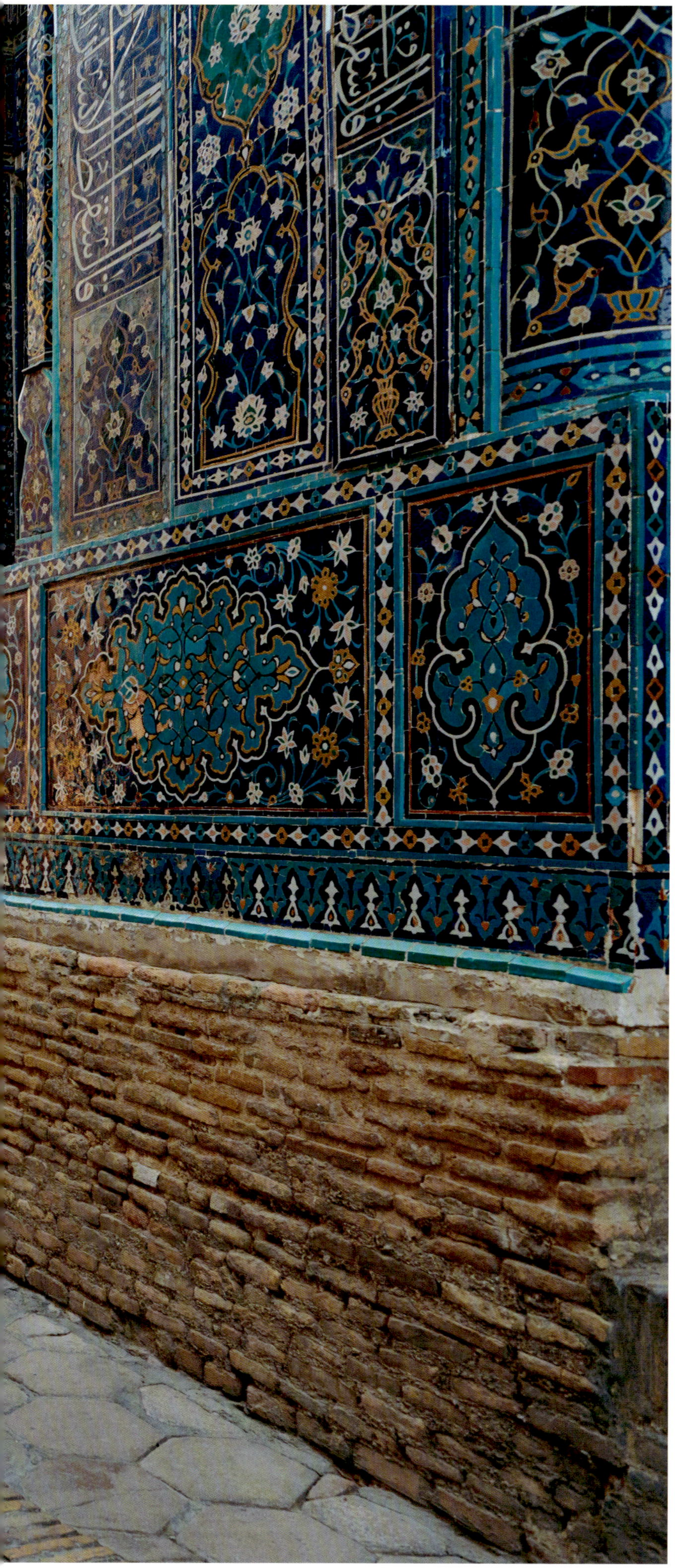
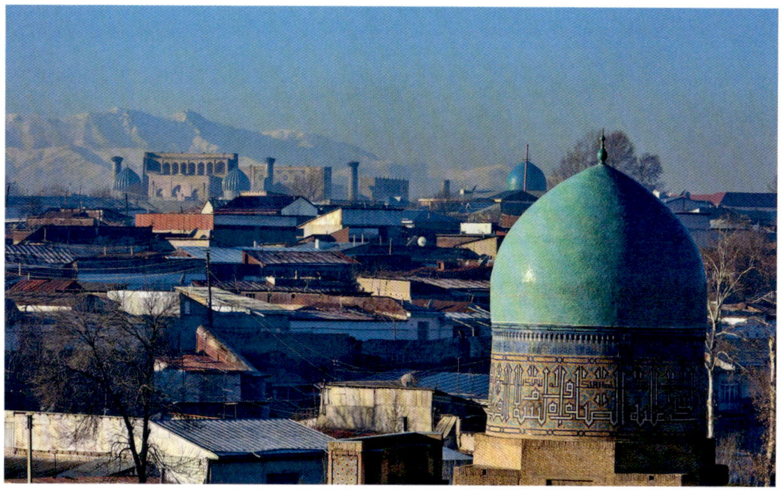
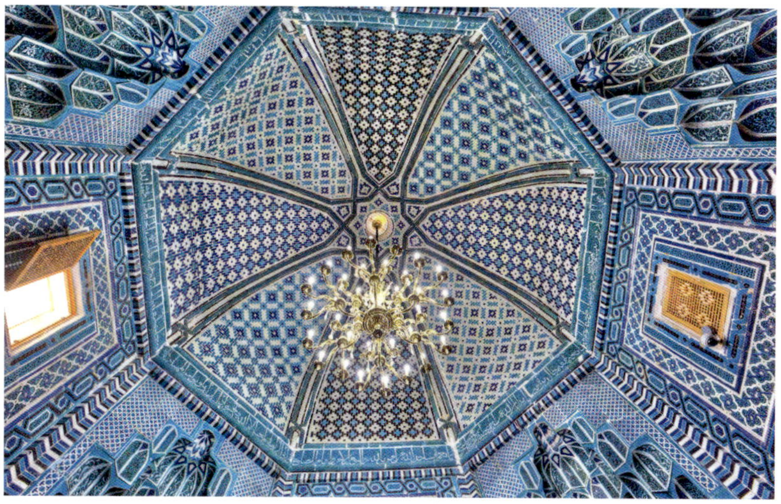
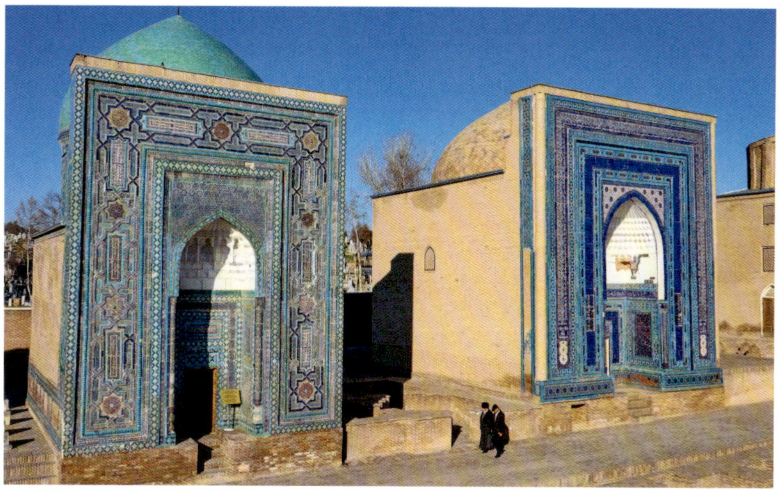
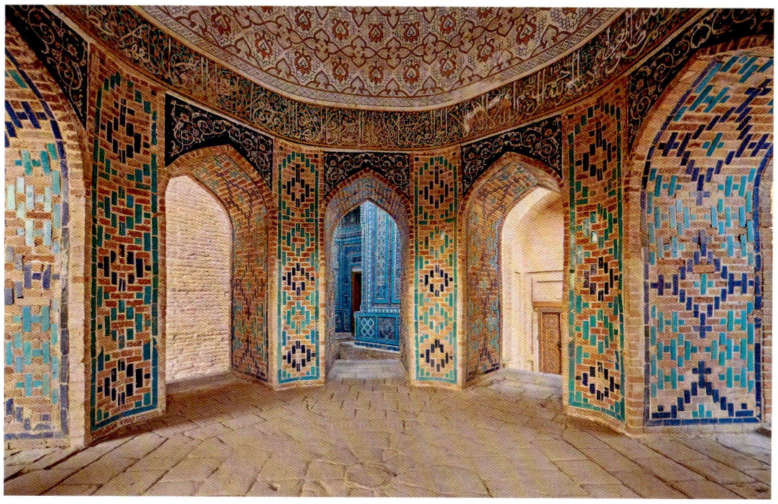

Top Blue and turquoise symbolize the infinite, lofty realms of the sky.
Upper middle Intricate tile patterns also adorn the interiors.
Lower middle Royals, nobles, and dignitaries are buried in the necropolis.
Bottom The calligraphy on the walls often contains blessings.

Architecture of Deep Faith and Complex Identity

Between Indigenous tradition, colonial embellishment, and modern houses of worship lies a rich and dynamic spiritual history.

To understand the collective soul of the Americas, one need only look at its temples. From the impressive pyramids of the Maya to the ornate churches of the colonial era and its modern cathedrals, the sacred architecture of the continent speaks of dramatic upheavals, profound connection to nature, and cultural fusion.

Before the arrival of Europeans, monumental structures formed the heart of Indigenous spirituality. The Maya, Aztecs, and Inca built sacred sites that connected heaven and earth. The Temple of the Great Jaguar, found in the ancient Guatemalan ruin of Tikal (pp. 88 – 91), stands as a fascinating witness to this era, and symbolizes, with its step-pyramid structure, the nine levels of the underworld in Mayan cosmology. From Cerro de la Estrella in Mexico to the Sun Temple Coricancha in Peru, sacred pre-colonial sites like these remain scattered across the continent. In stunning harmony with the natural spaces they inhabit, they quietly hint at the great civilizations that once thrived in the green expanses of the Americas.

With the arrival of Europeans in the 16th century, the spiritual identity of the continent, along with its appearance, underwent a profound transformation. The Catholic Church introduced not only new religious practices but also European architectural aesthetics, which soon merged with the traditions of the Indigenous population. A remarkable example of this fusion is the Sanctuary of Las Lajas in Colombia (pp. 100 – 103). Rising above a gorge that was considered sacred long before it was first trod upon by European feet, this stunning neo-Gothic church is today a place where periods of spiritual history coexist. In Mexico and the Andes, missionaries built similar churches, often, troublingly, on the foundations of Indigenous temples. The Metropolitan Cathedral of Mexico City, constructed on the remains of the Aztec Templo Mayor, and the numerous Baroque churches in Cusco, Peru, are examples of this challenging chapter in history.

In the modern era, migration and urbanization brought about a new phase in the sacred architecture of the Americas. St. Patrick's Cathedral in New York City (pp. 104 – 107), one of the most iconic examples of neo-Gothic architecture in the United States, stands as a reminder of the Irish who immigrated to the city in the 19th and 20th centuries. A spiritual child of old Europe, it has become a haven of faith amid bustling Manhattan. Meanwhile, in Brasília, the decidedly modern capital of Brazil built in the 1950s, Catholicism took on entirely new, surprising forms. Here, the turquoise windows of the Cathedral of Brasília pose refreshing questions, bathing spirituality, quite literally, in a new light.

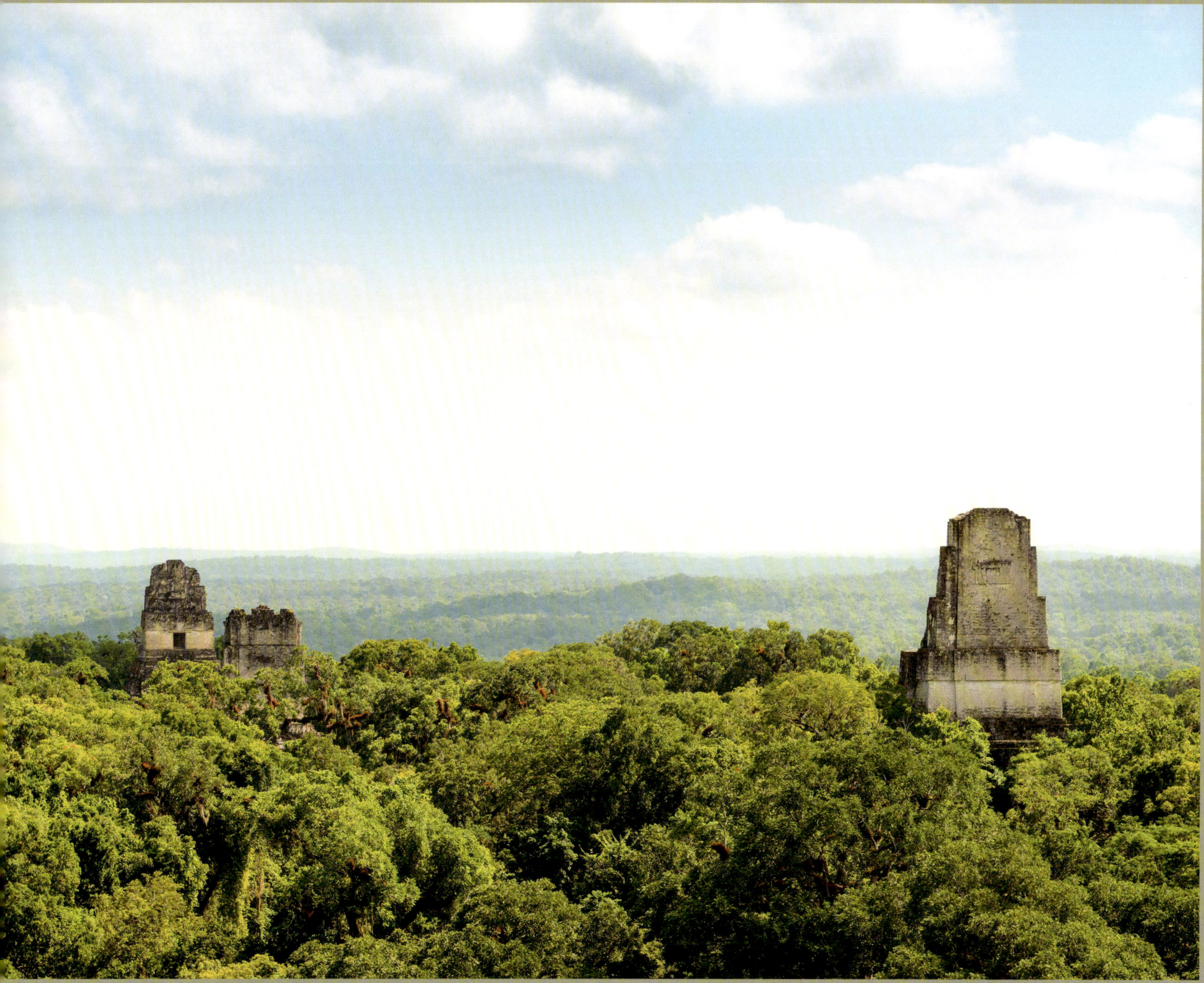

THE AMERICAS

Temple of the Great Jaguar

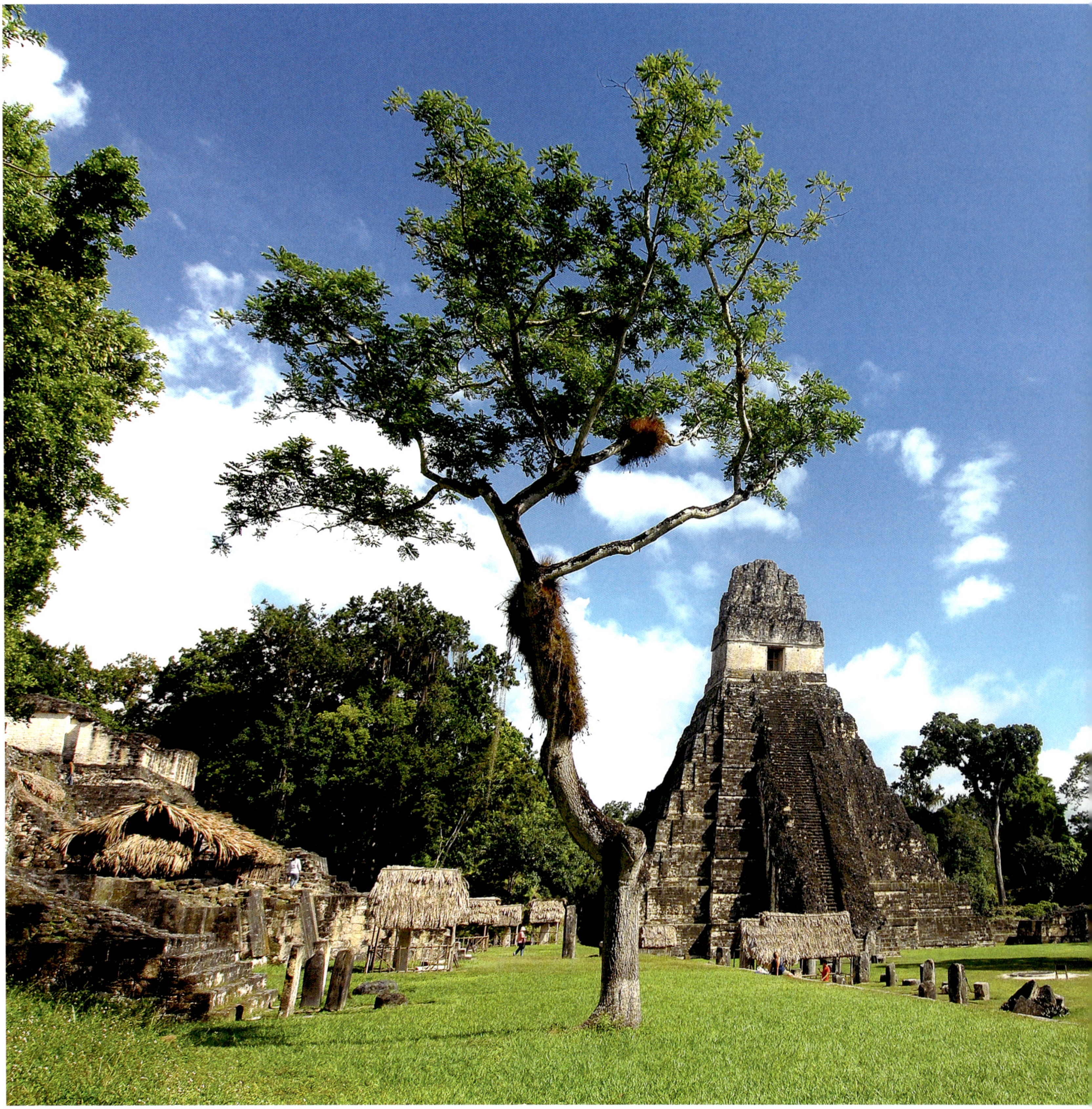

Tikal, Guatemala

Built: 8th century CE,
Tikal, Guatemala

In the Mayan underworld, only the most intrepid souls can endure its many terrors and trials.

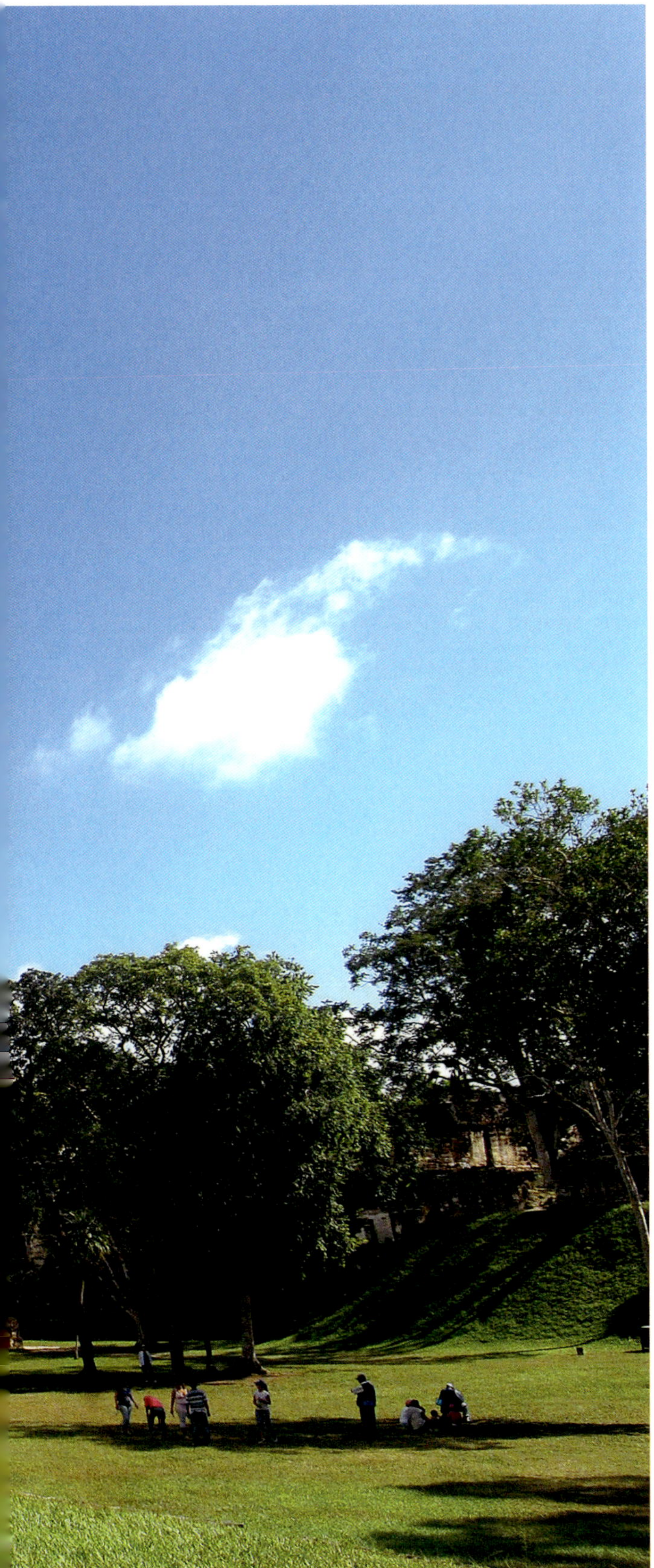

To delve into the history of the Maya is to immerse oneself in a world rich with mythology, symbolism, and great spiritual depth. For the Maya, numbers held profound significance: above the earth, the sky shone with its thirteen levels, while below lay the underworld—Xibalba—with nine. Each of these underworld levels represented a symbolic place where the soul, after death, faced various trials on its spiritual journey. The Temple of the Great Jaguar is a testament to how the Maya translated their cosmological beliefs into architecture. Its nine terraces are believed by many researchers to evoke Xibalba, while the pyramid's steep ascent can be understood as a spiritual path—the uphill journey of the soul in search of enlightenment and peace.

In the Popol Vuh, the sacred book of the K'iche' Maya, the concept of Xibalba is vividly described. Within its pages, the Hero Twins, Hunahpú and Xbalanqué, descend into the underworld. Some of what they encounter is also what the Maya believed awaited the soul after death: it first enters Xibalba through a portal shrouded in darkness and mist. Here, the soul's determination is tested; it must navigate through the dense fog, resisting fear and the terrors of darkness. Next, the soul faces a hall filled with razor-sharp blades and must wade through a river of blood as grotesque creatures reach out to grasp it. Will the soul face its demons with courage? Once it survives this third level, it must navigate another river—this one filled with poisonous pus—followed by a chamber of complete darkness and a place of icy cold. At the seventh, the soul encounters attacking jaguars—powerful deities that moved effortlessly between worlds. Then, the soul faces a swarm of bats symbolizing the forces of chaos and the unconscious. Here, the soul must master its fears to find its way through the darkness. The final and most daunting trial awaits in a chamber filled with glowing coals and flames, through which the soul must pass to be cleansed of all earthly sins. Only a purified soul can endure this ultimate test and cross the threshold to enlightenment or eternal peace.

At the very top of the Temple of the Great Jaguar, a funerary shrine acts as a bridge between the heavens, the earth, and the underworld. Beyond the narrow opening, the structure houses carved wooden lintels—gorgeously ornate works of Mayan art. The temple's deliberate westward orientation aligns it with the setting sun, reflecting the soul's entry into the underworld, and marking the beginning of a new, difficult phase of spiritual existence.

The steep ascent of the Temple of the Jaguar can be understood as a spiritual path—the journey of the soul in search of enlightenment and peace.

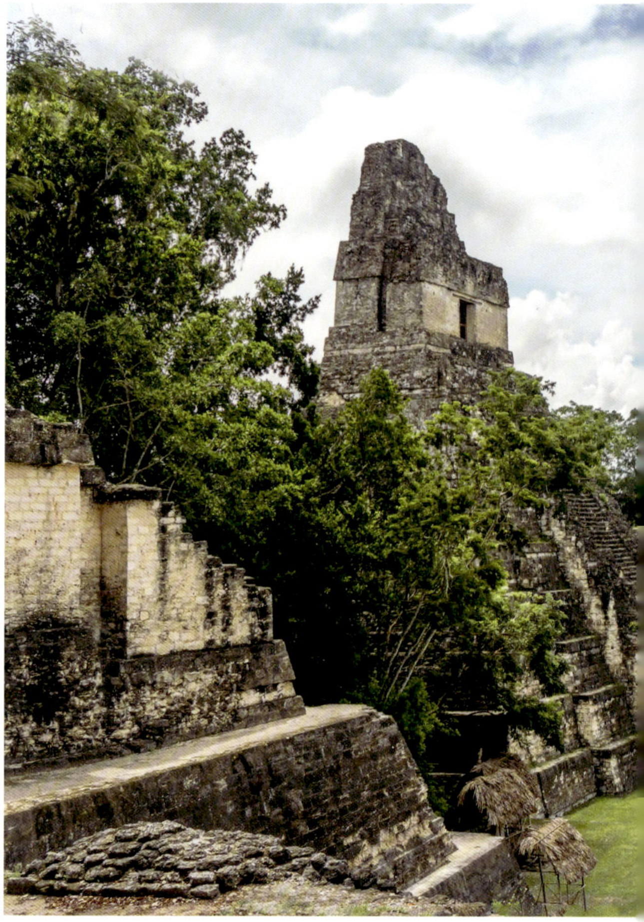

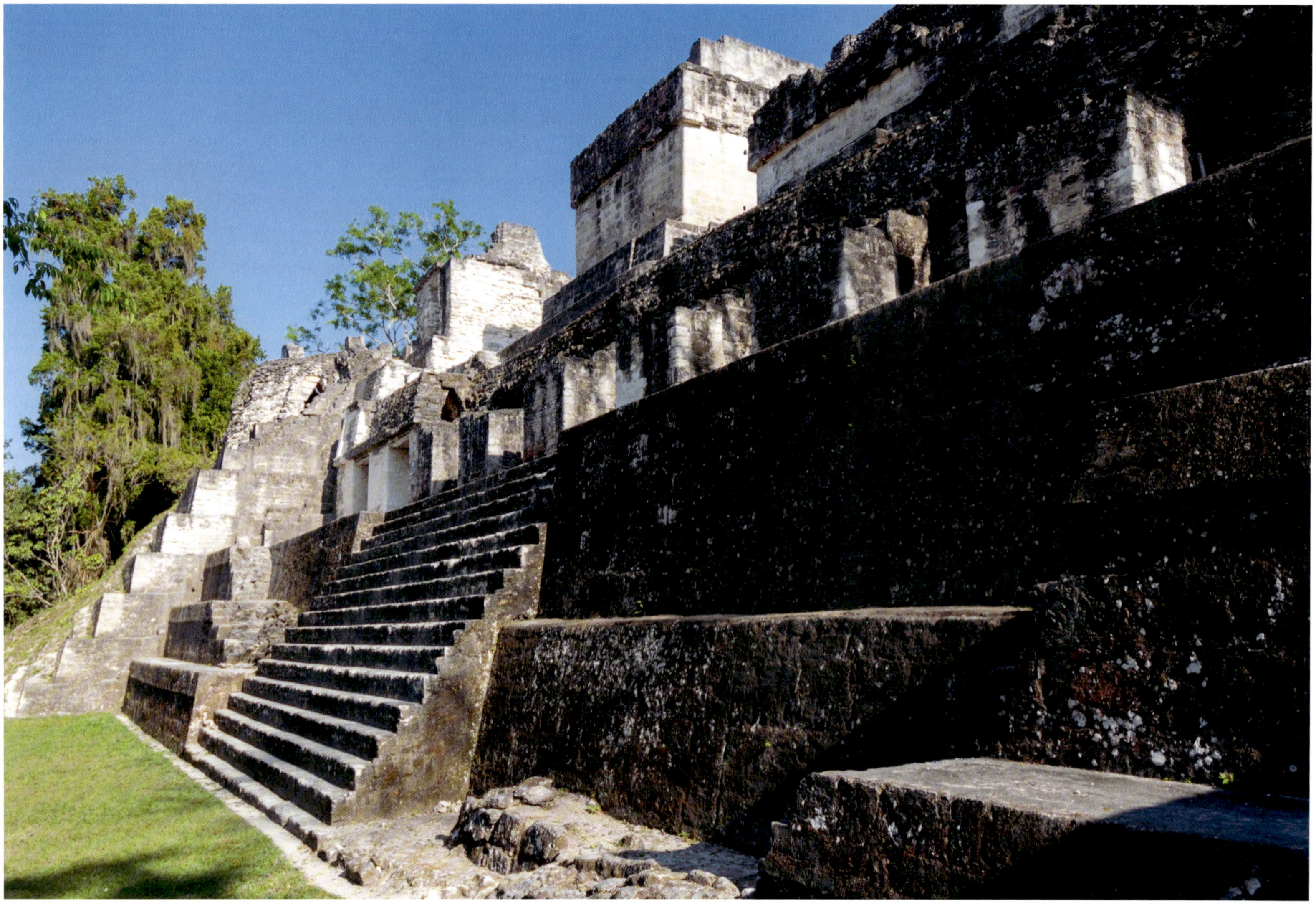

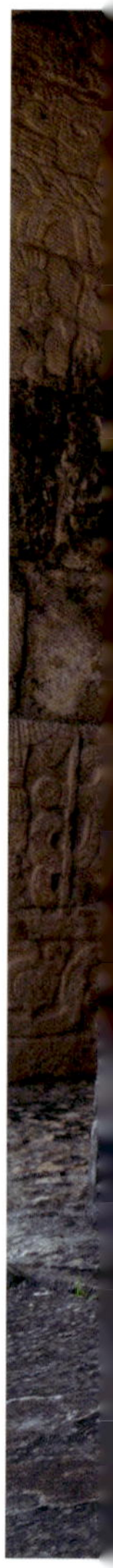

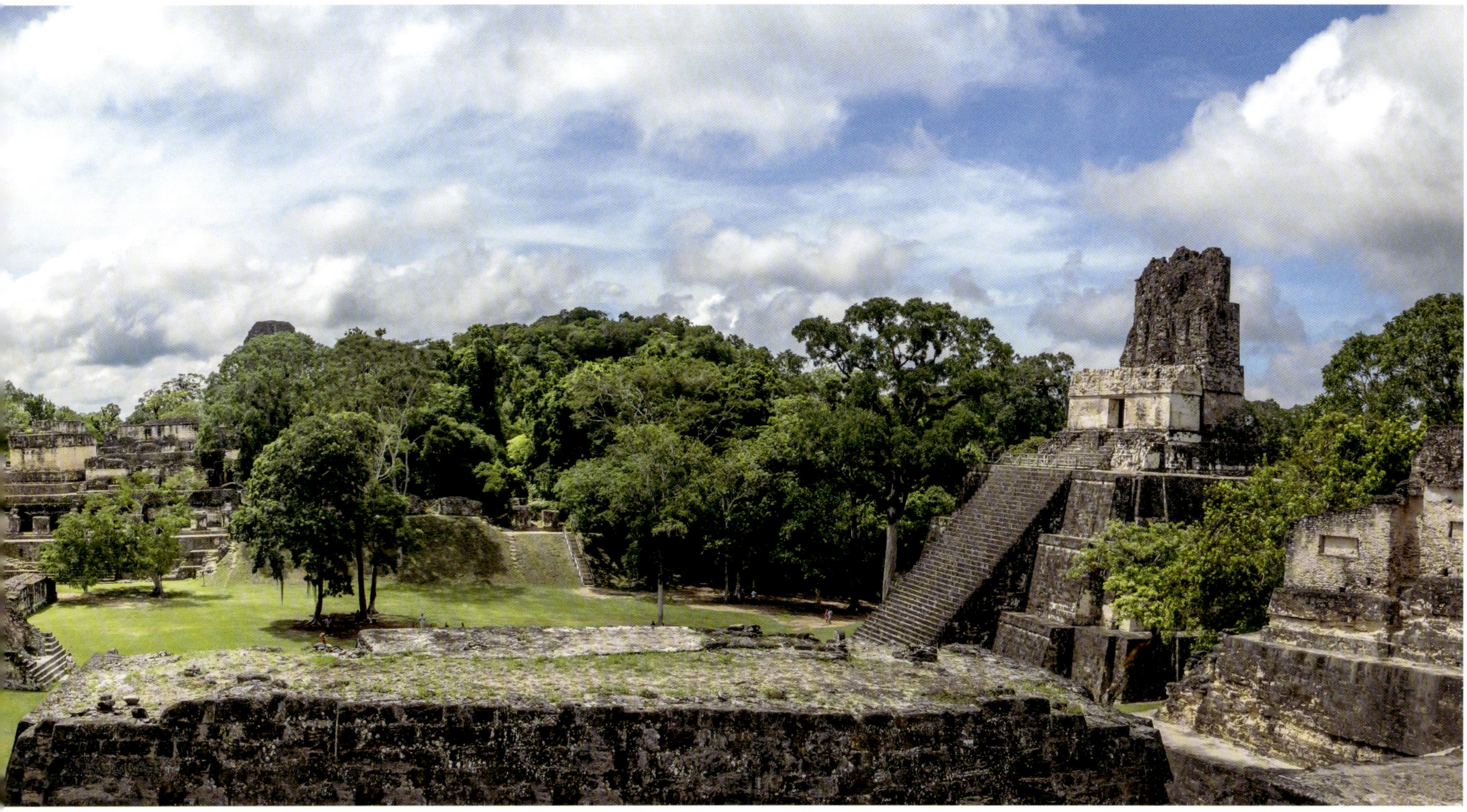

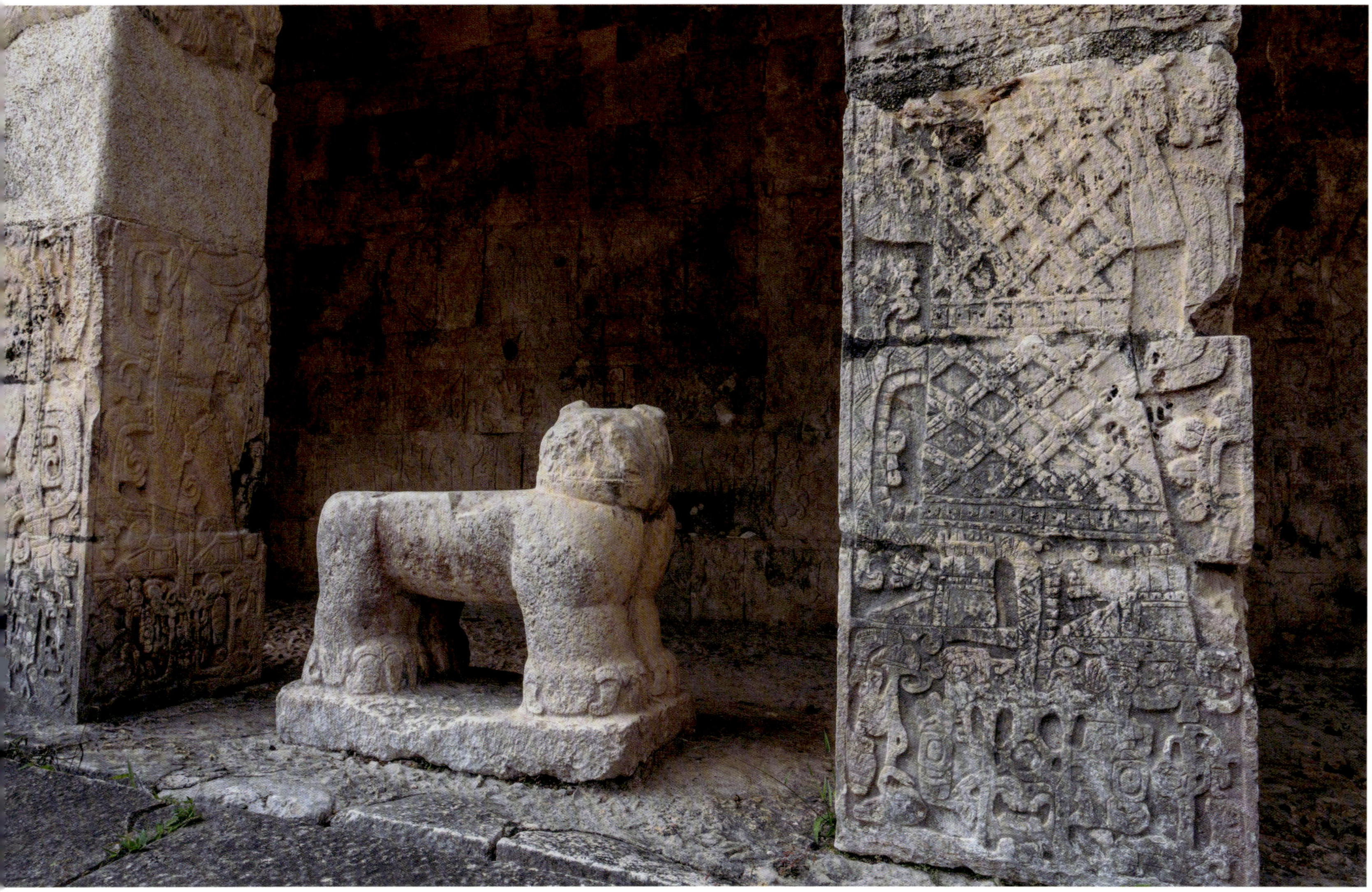

Top The temple rises high above the ancient Maya town of Tikal.
Bottom left Priests likely used the temple to study the movements of the stars.
Bottom right Journeying through the underworld, a soul would encounter jaguars.

Temple of Kukulkán

Pyramid of the Feathered Serpent God

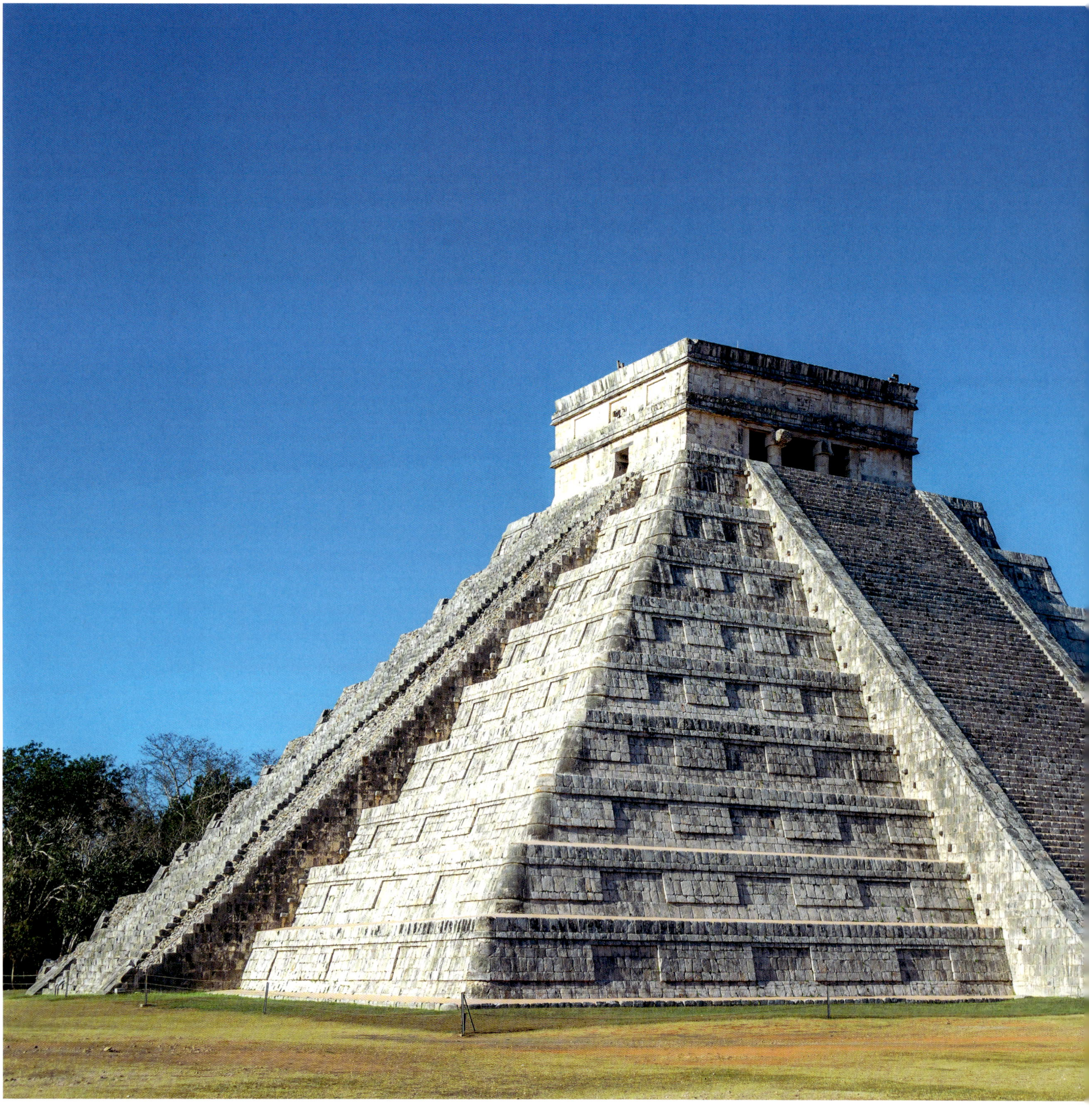

Built: between 800 and 1000 CE,
Chichén Itzá, Mexico

During the equinox, a snake-shaped shadow appears on the steps of this sacred monument.

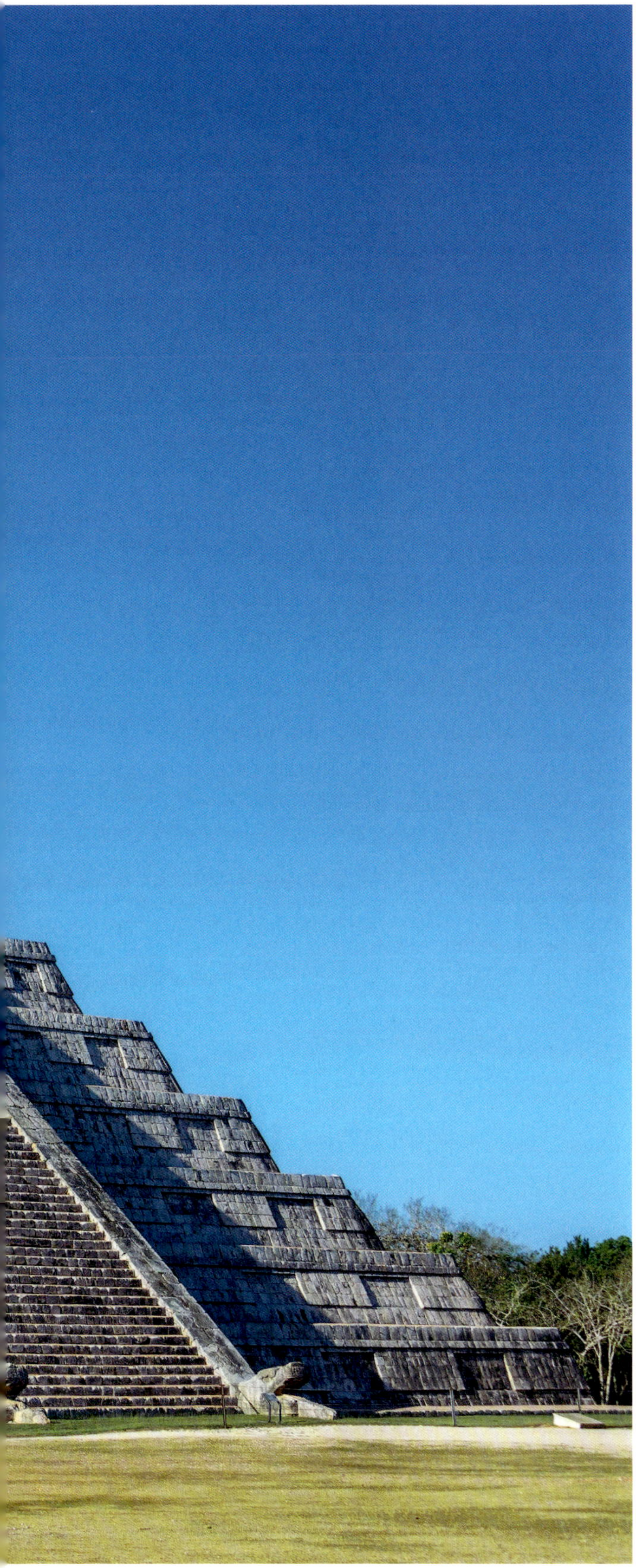

At the heart of the ancient Mayan city of Chichén Itzá stands the Temple of Kukulkán (also known as El Castillo), a witness to an extraordinary era. The 98-foot-tall (30-meter-tall) step pyramid is dedicated to the feathered serpent god Kukulkán, revered by the Maya as a creator deity and embodiment of the elements. A spiritual cousin to the Aztec god Quetzalcóatl, Kukulkán moves through air and land, a mediator between worlds and an important symbol of fertility, war, and life itself.

One of the most impressive features of the Temple of Kukulkán is its function as a precise calendar. The pyramid's four staircases, plus the platform itself on top, add up to 365 steps—one for each day of the year. The temple is aligned in such a way that, near the spring and autumn equinoxes, a remarkable spectacle unfolds: as the sun's rays fall on a corner of the pyramid, the structure casts a shadow in the shape of a serpent. As the sun advances, this "shadow serpent" appears to creep down the side of the northern staircase until it merges with the stone serpent sculpture at the base of the pyramid. This phenomenon is believed to symbolize Kukulkán's descent from the sky, an act which revitalized the land and its people.

The Temple of Kukulkán holds yet another secret. During excavations in the 1930s, archaeologists discovered a second, older pyramid within the temple, dedicated to an earlier deity. Inside this older structure, researchers found a statue of Chac Mool—a reclining warrior figure holding a bowl on its stomach—as well as human remains. These discoveries suggest that, at one time, the temple might have been used for ceremonies where offerings to the gods—possibly of a sacrificial nature—played a central role.

Today, the Temple of Kukulkán is a UNESCO World Heritage Site. Thousands visit Chichén Itzá every year to marvel at the ancient city and its largest pyramid, especially during the shadow display at the equinoxes. In this way, Kukulkán, the feathered serpent, serves as a bridge not only between realms but also between cultures and eras, transmitting the spiritual legacy of the Maya that continues to fascinate the world.

The pyramid consists of a total of 365 steps, divided into four staircases with 91 steps each, plus a final step at the top, completing the cycle.

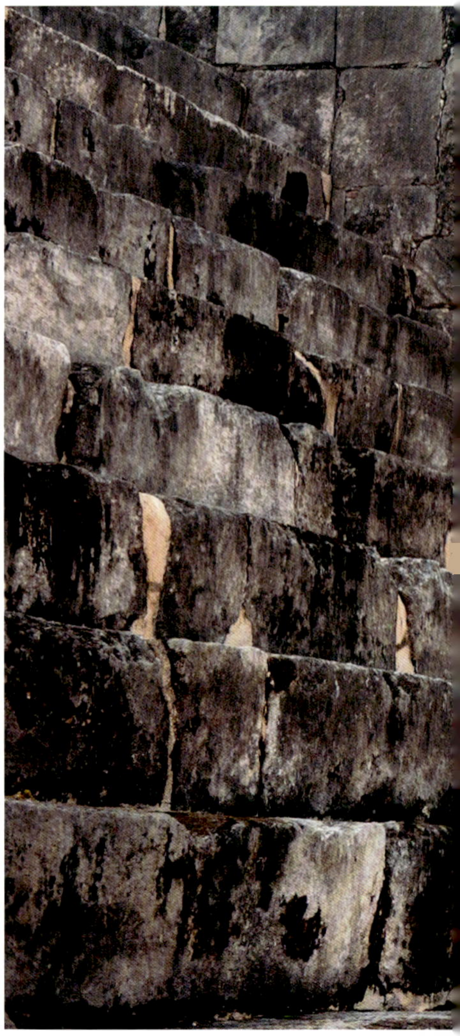

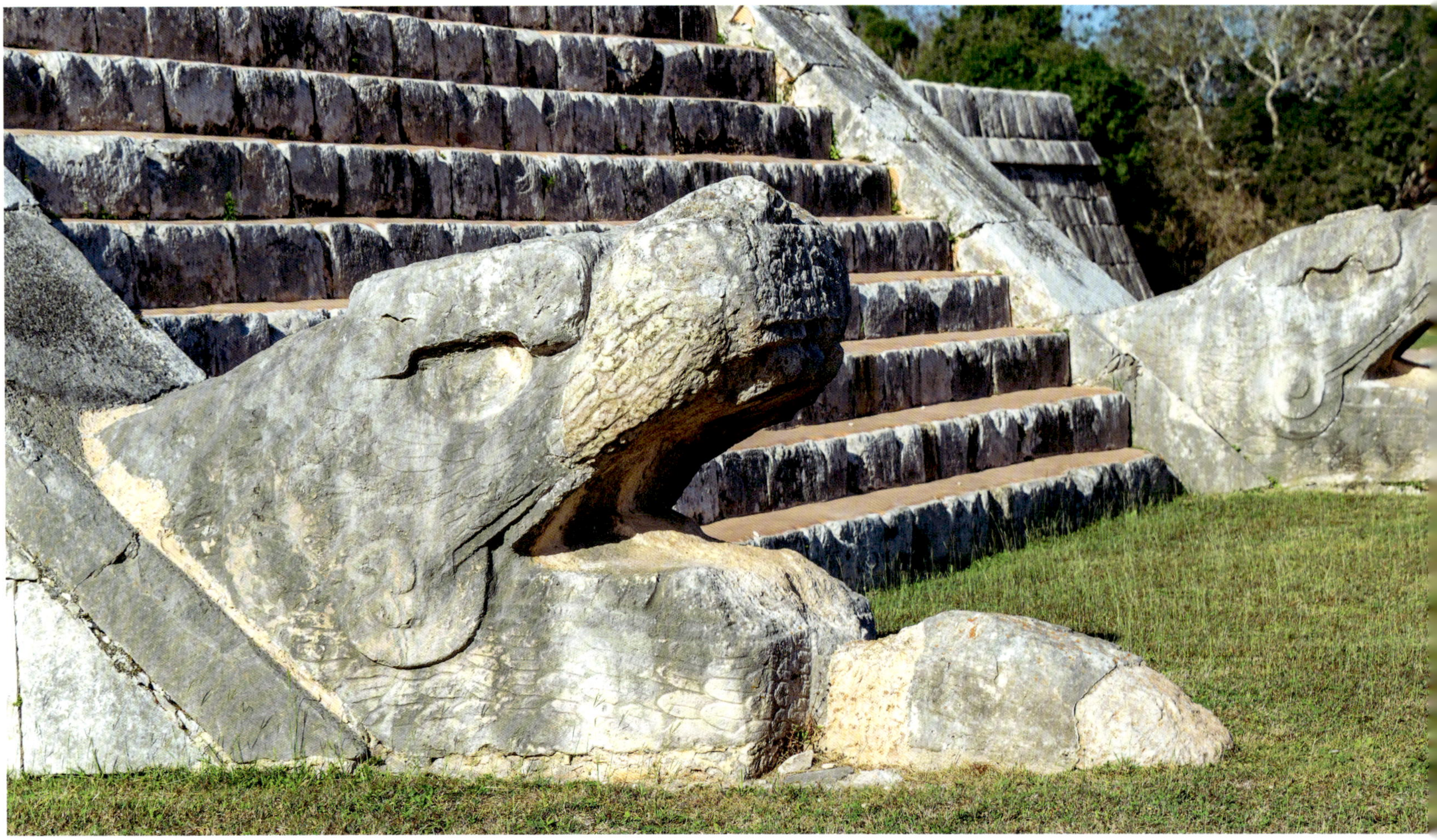

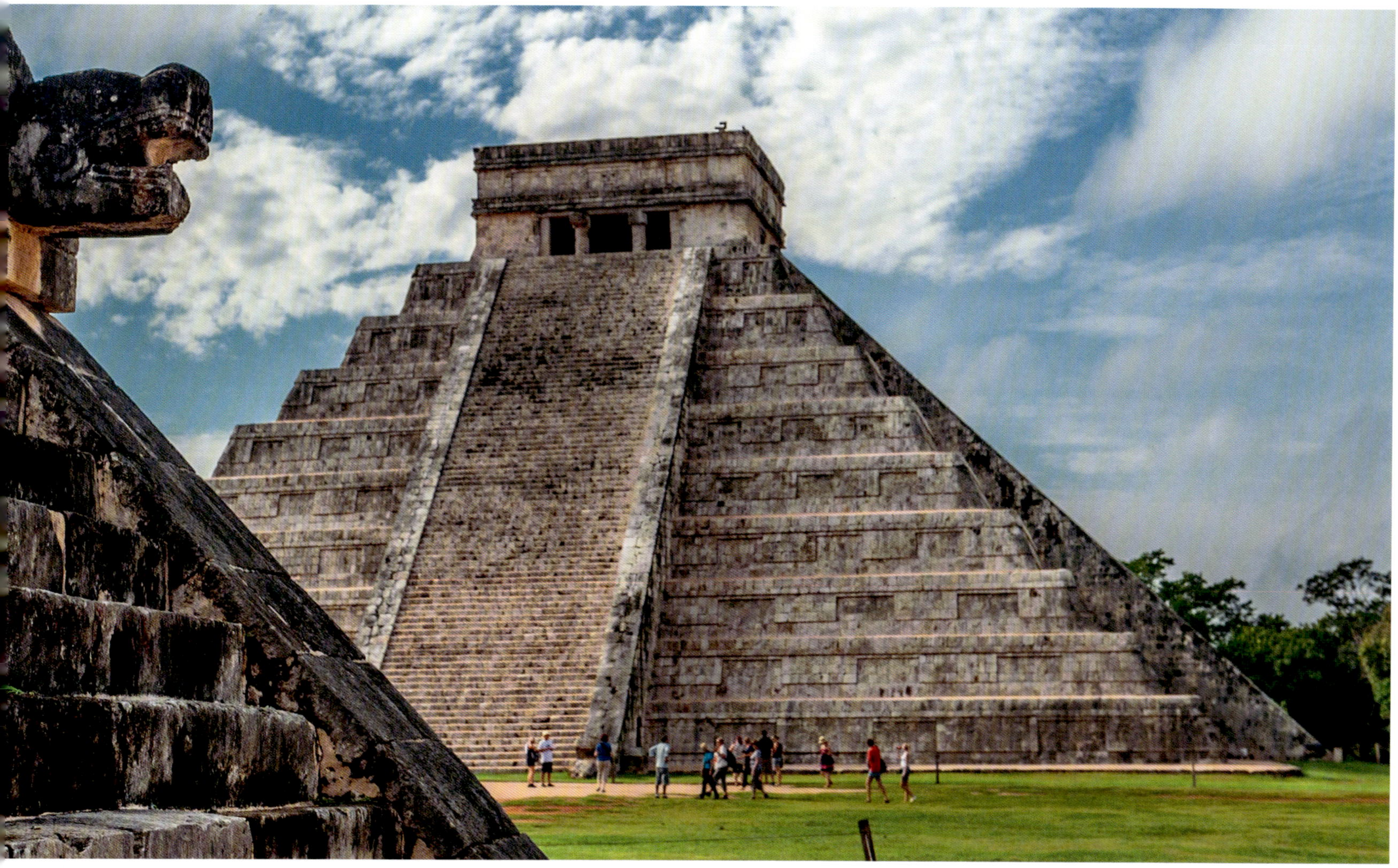

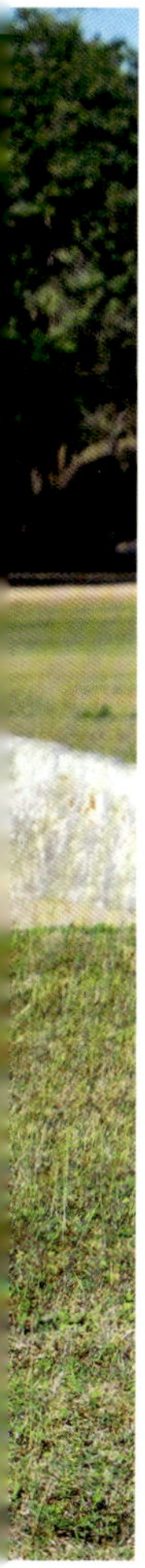

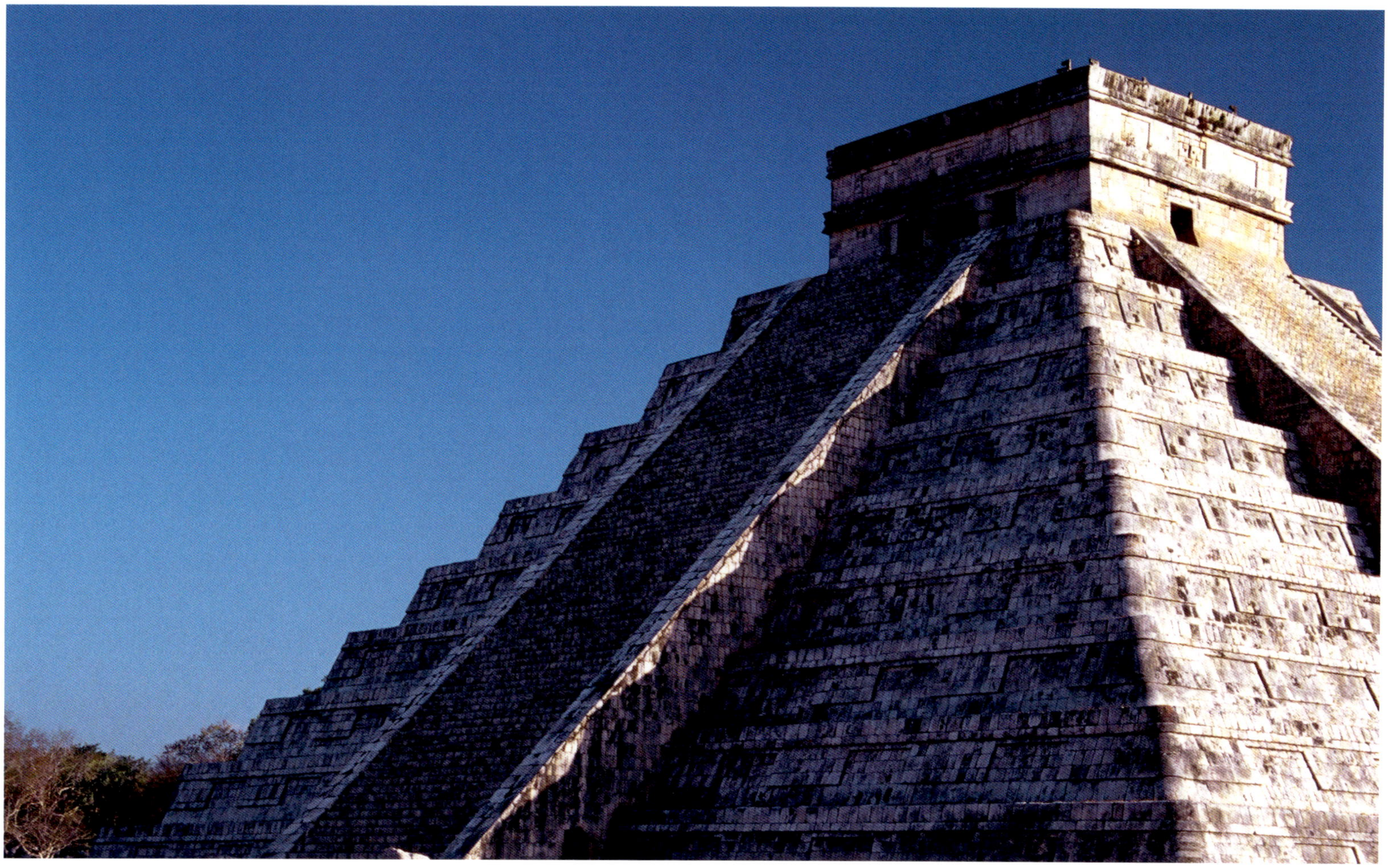

Top Who wants to count? Each stone step is thought to represent a day of the year.
Bottom left The feathered serpent god Kukulkán symbolizes both sky and earth.
Bottom right Slowly, the shadow serpent slithers down the side of the pyramid.

Metropolitan Cathedral of Brasília

A New Blossom

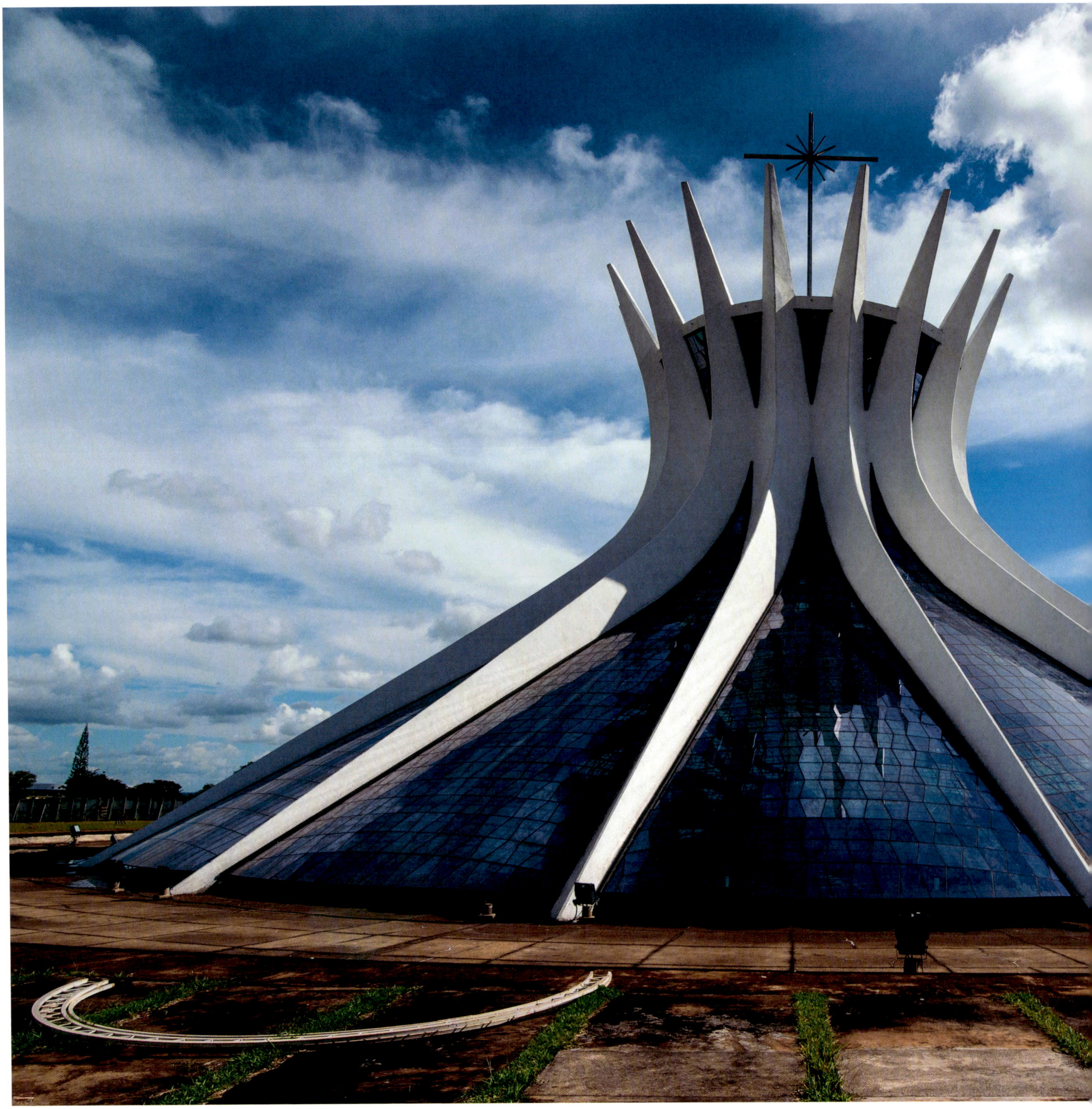

Built: 1958 – 1970 CE,
Brasília, Brazil

Behind the unconventional form of this modernist cathedral lies a familiar idea.

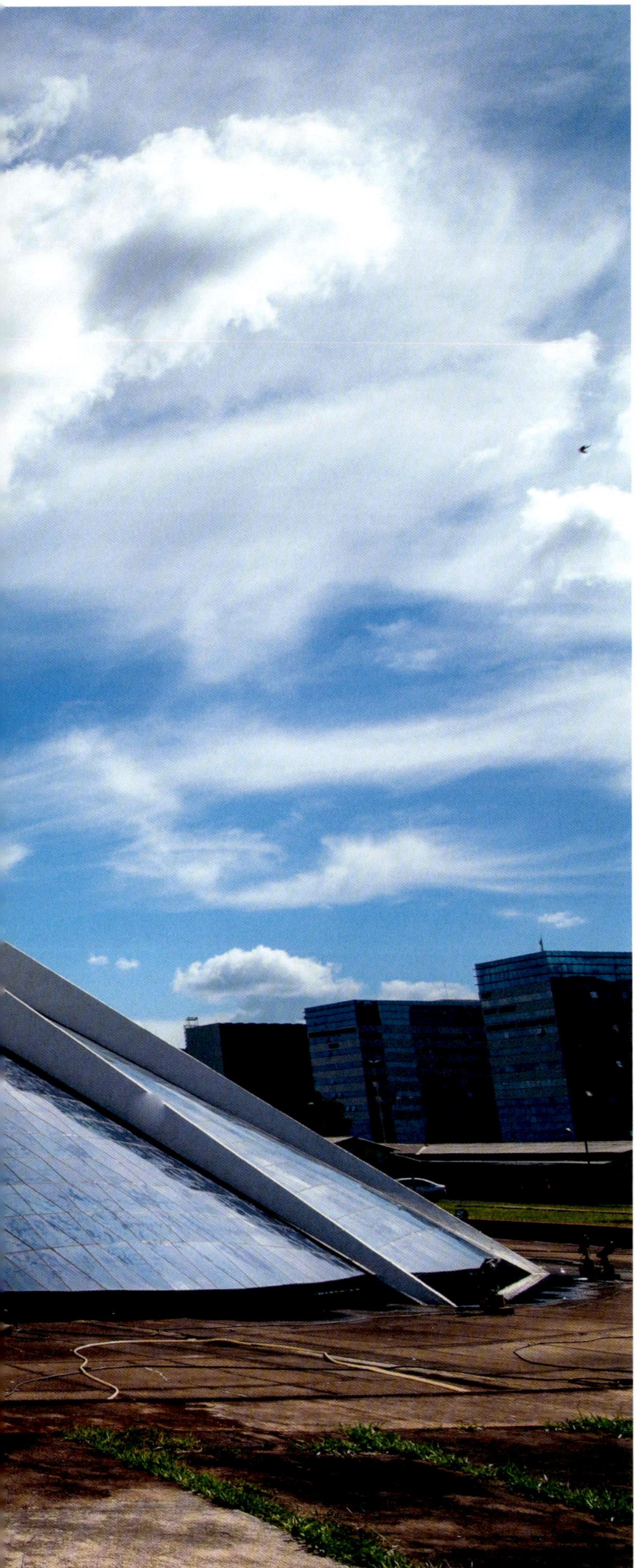

The Cathedral of Brasília is perhaps one of the most renowned works by Oscar Niemeyer, the Brazilian architect celebrated for his visionary approach to form. In the 1950s, Niemeyer designed this modernist house of worship as part of the new capital, Brasilía, a city built to profoundly modernize the country and guide it into the future. Visually, almost nothing about the cathedral resembles the Gothic or baroque churches of past centuries, yet its spiritual core remains the same.

With its 16 curved and pointed concrete columns, the Catedral Metropolitana de Brasília (its Portuguese name) opens up to the sky, as though reaching out to embrace it. Its 230-foot (70-meter) diameter offers ample space for faith, prayer, spiritual searching, and interpretation. Does the cathedral symbolize the crown of thorns Christ is said to have worn? Or is it the ever-open hand of God, reaching out to the believer? Unlike traditional churches, with their large, front-facing portals, this cathedral is accessed through a tunnel-like corridor that suddenly opens into the bright, expansive interior, symbolic perhaps of the sometimes-difficult passage from the earthly to the divine. Impressive beams of light, tinted in shades of blue and green, pour into the cathedral. These vast stained glass windows, which fill the spaces between the pillars, were created by French-Brazilian artist Marianne Peretti. Unlike the windows of traditional cathedrals, which often illustrate biblical stories, the glass in Brasília's cathedral bathes visitors in the light of a more modern and forward-looking faith. Perhaps the blue lines represent the waves of an eternal ocean, or the sky over paradise.

Yet the old figures are not far away: three massive angel sculptures, created by Alfredo Ceschiatti, hover from steel cables at the center of the ceiling. As heavenly messengers, they watch over the prayers of visitors. Behind them, in its elegant simplicity, stands the altar, which, despite its restrained design, serves as the clear heart of the cathedral.

It is perhaps edifying to know that Niemeyer himself was not a religious man. Yet his design reflects a deep respect for spiritual and societal yearnings. He saw the cathedral as part of a manifestation of a new society, one that would identify with values such as openness, freedom, and modernity. Accordingly, the floor plan of the cathedral is designed to make everyone feel welcome—a reflection of Niemeyer's vision for a united, progressive Brazil. His cathedral represents a form of spirituality accessible to all, excluding none. To this day, the Catedral Metropolitana de Brasília challenges traditional notions of sacred architecture while preserving the core tenets of Christianity, a modernist blossom of an ancient faith.

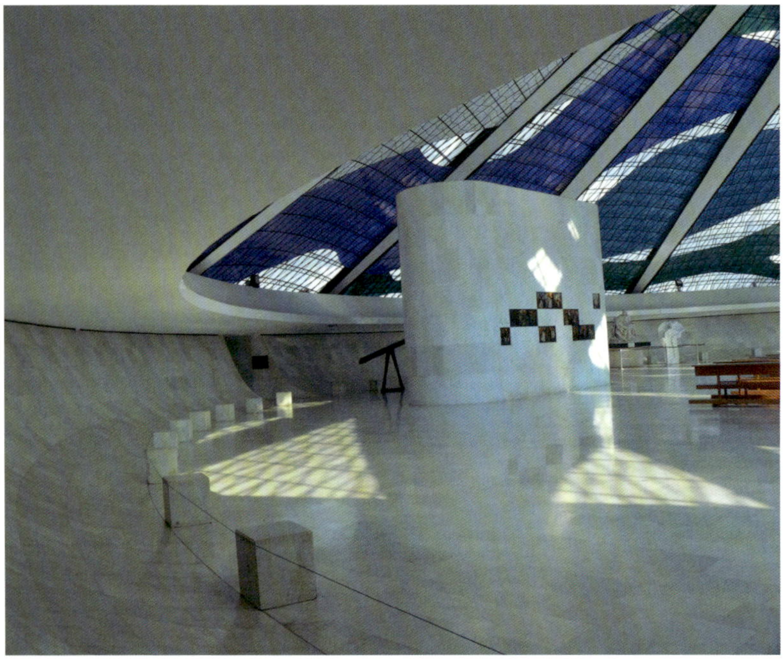

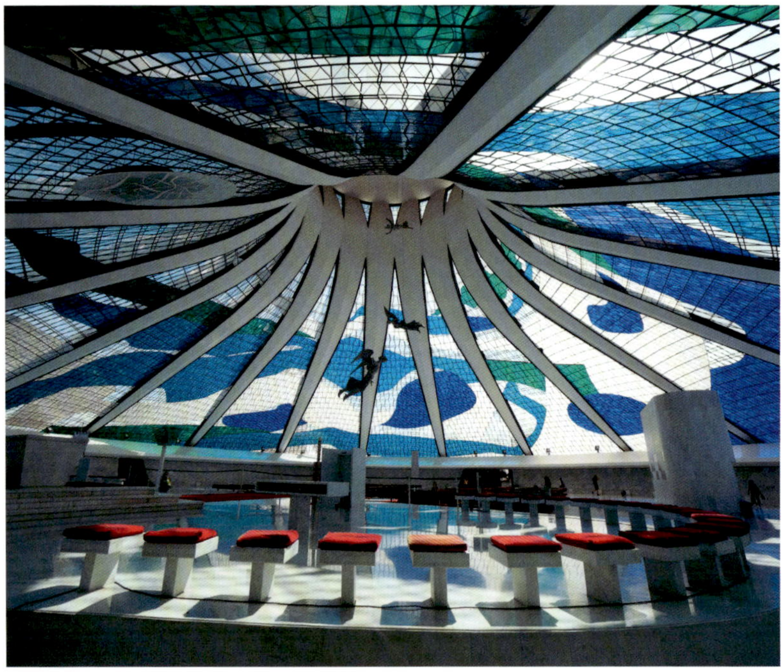

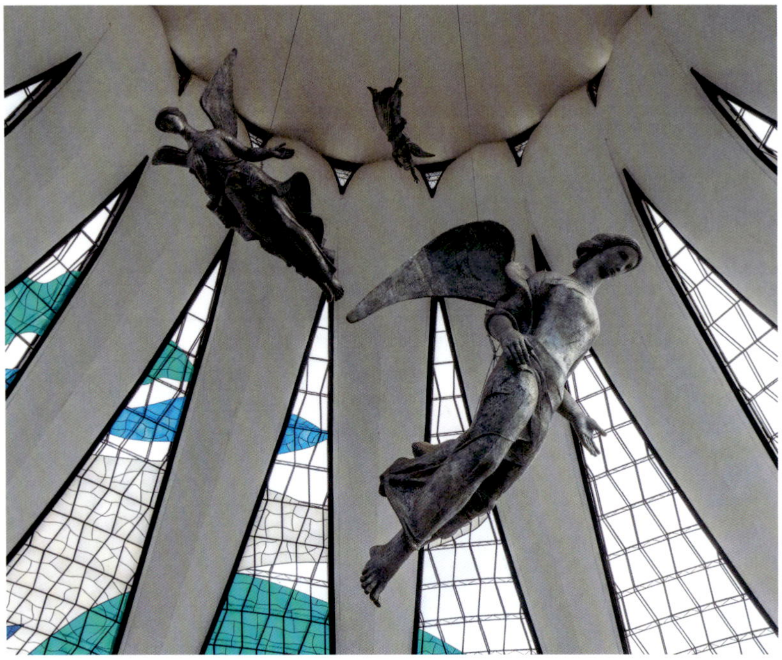

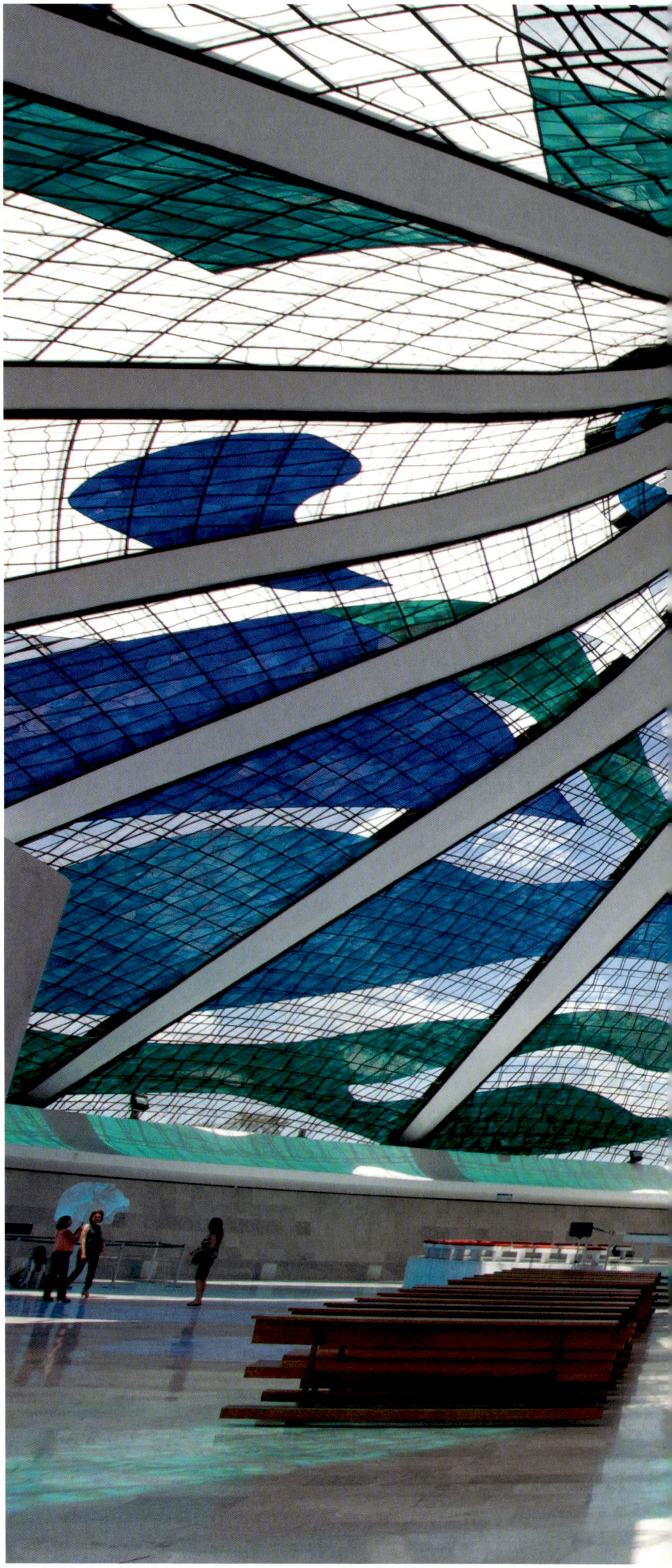

Top The cathedral is dedicated to Nossa Senhora Aparecida, the protector of the poor and needy.
Middle The colorful windows span over 21,000 sq. ft. (2,000 m²).
Bottom The artist responsible for the figures often collaborated with Niemeyer.

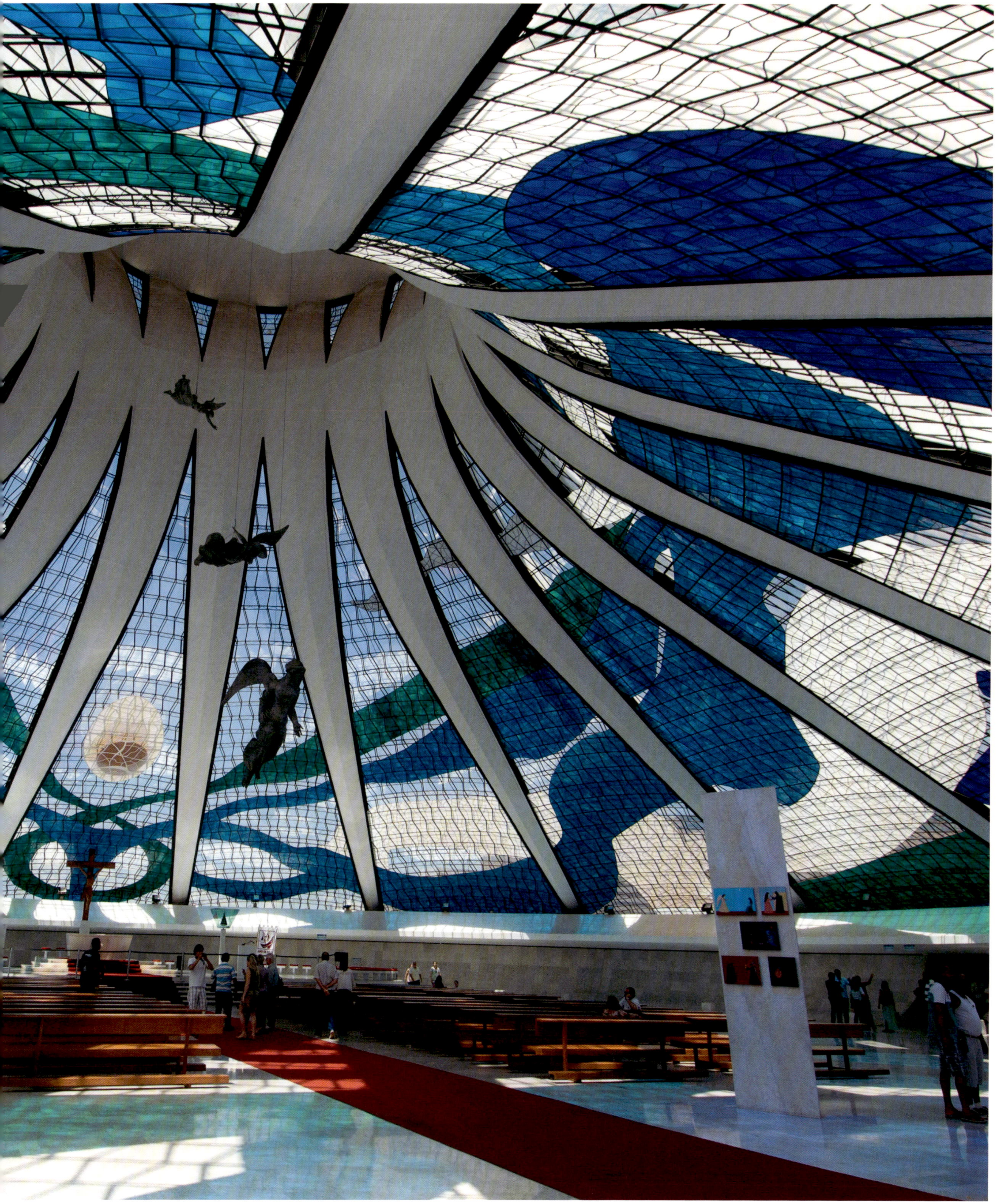

Above The artistic use of reinforced concrete makes possible the extraordinary curvature of the cathedral's arches, whose soaring form creates a dynamic and flowing space.

Sanctuary of Our Lady of the Rosary of Las Lajas

A Marvel Commemorating a Miracle

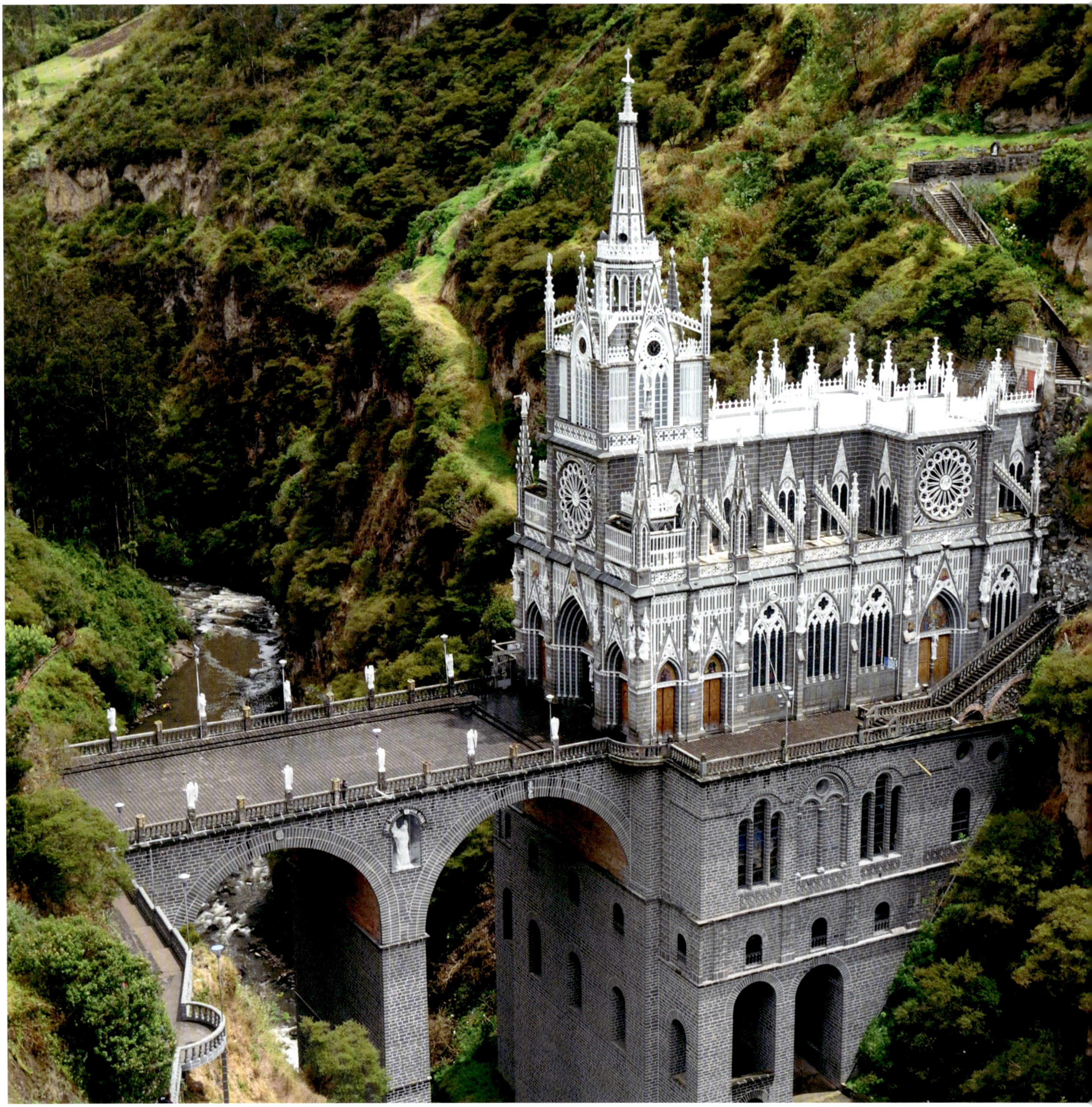

Built: between 1916 and 1949 CE,
Ipiales, Colombia

Amid the Colombian Andes, this sanctuary watches over the mysterious image of the Virgin Mary.

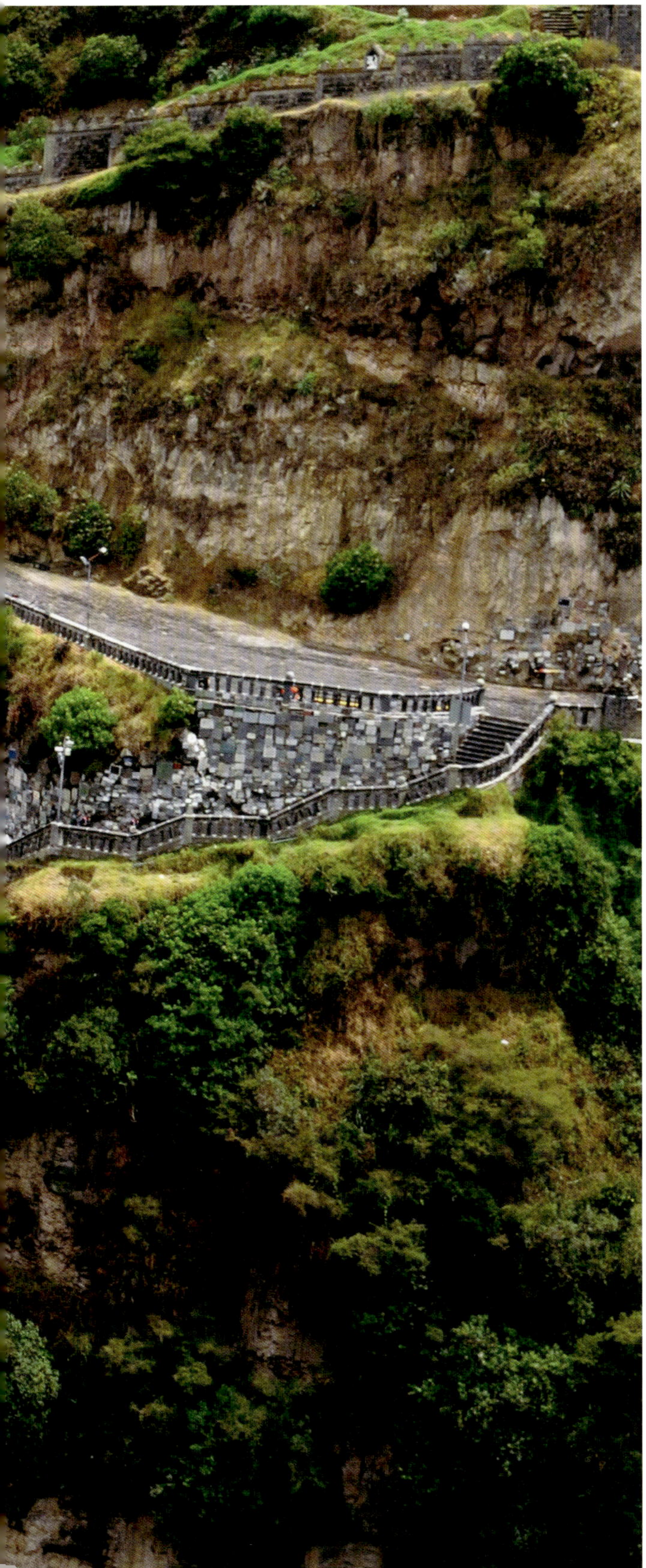

For millennia, the rushing waters of the Río Guáitara have carved their way through the Andes. Some 300 feet (91 meters) above the river, one of the most beautiful and awe-inspiring sanctuaries in Latin America rises—the Santuario de Nuestra Señora del Rosario de las Lajas. With its arches, the sanctuary connects two sides of a dramatic gorge, bridging not only the physical divide but perhaps the earthly and heavenly realms as well.

According to legend, the Virgin Mary appeared here in 1754 on a steep rock wall—a *laja,* as the flat stone slabs of the region are called. One day, a woman named María Mueses de Quiñones was walking through the gorge with her mute daughter Rosita when they were caught in a storm. As they sought refuge among the rocks, little Rosita suddenly exclaimed, "Mama, look! The lady with her little child!" and both mother and child beheld the apparition during a lightning strike. The news of the sighting, as well as Rosita's miraculous healing, spread quickly. Soon after, when the first believers embarked on a nocturnal pilgrimage to the gorge, they themselves witnessed a vision: the Virgin Mary and the Christ child, both surrounded by a radiant glow. This first procession marked the beginning of the pilgrimage route to Las Lajas, and the image of the Virgin and child became a permanent fixture on the rock.

To this day, the image's precise origin remains a mystery. What is particularly striking is that the colors have penetrated deeply into the stone and, despite the adverse conditions—which include the humidity produced by the waterfall and the constant touch of the faithful—have remained unchanged for centuries.

To honor the site of the miracle, and to accommodate the increasing number of pilgrims over the years, larger and larger chapels were constructed. The foundation stone for the current neo-Gothic structure was laid in 1916. The upward-reaching spires, vertical windows, and delicate stone carvings lend the sanctuary an ethereal lightness. Upon entering through the ornate gateway, one is greeted by towering columns, as the sunlight throws colorful patterns on the stone walls. Straight ahead, your gaze falls on the legendary rock wall, where the mysterious image of the Virgin is framed in splendor.

Today, the mountain sanctuary also acts as a symbol of reconciliation between two nations. Although the border between Colombia and Ecuador has been contested throughout history, the veneration of Our Lady of Las Lajas has always united both countries. Here, Colombian and Ecuadorian pilgrims alike direct their prayers to the "Queen of the Andes," high above the thundering waters of the Río Guáitara.

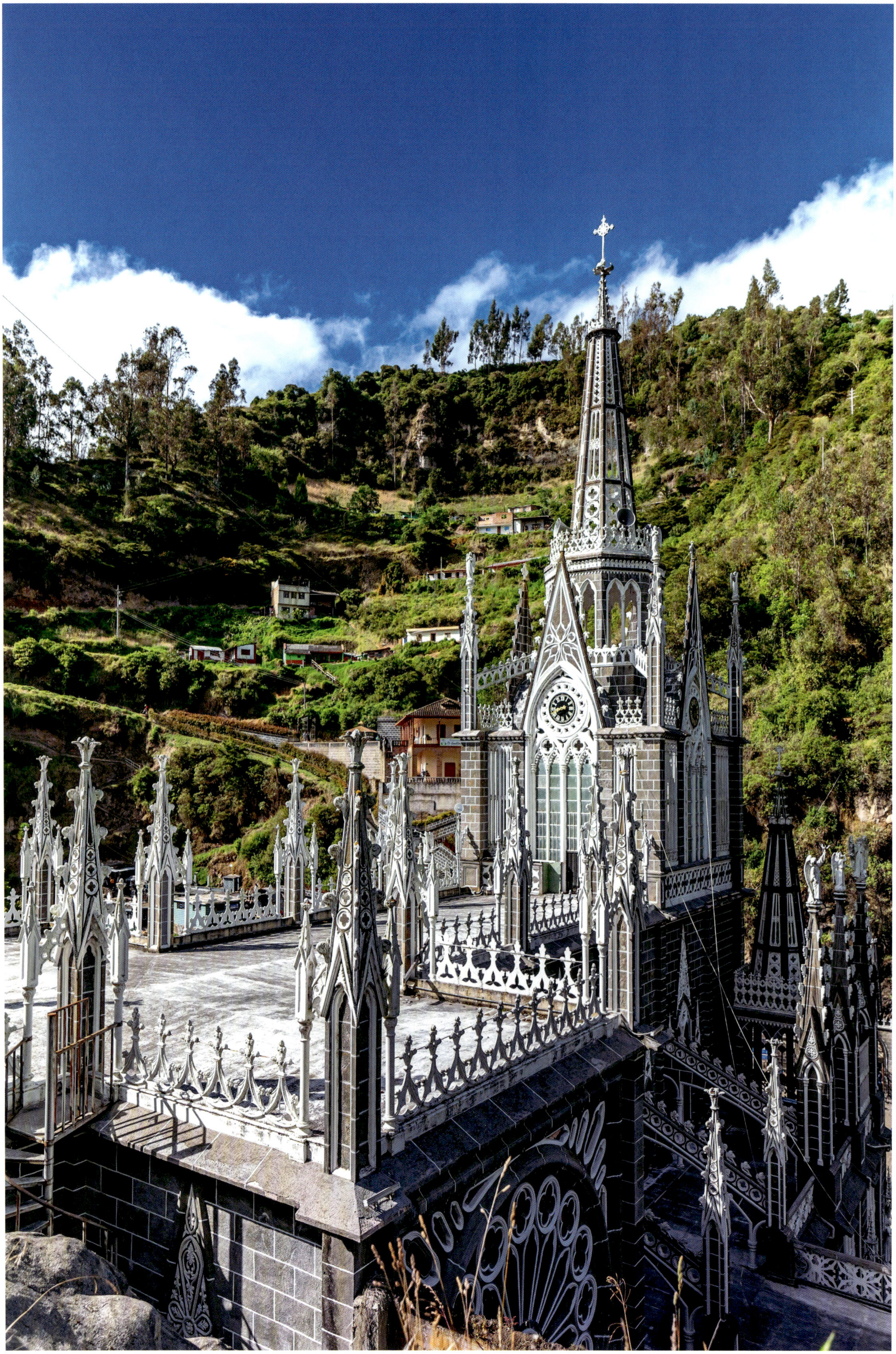

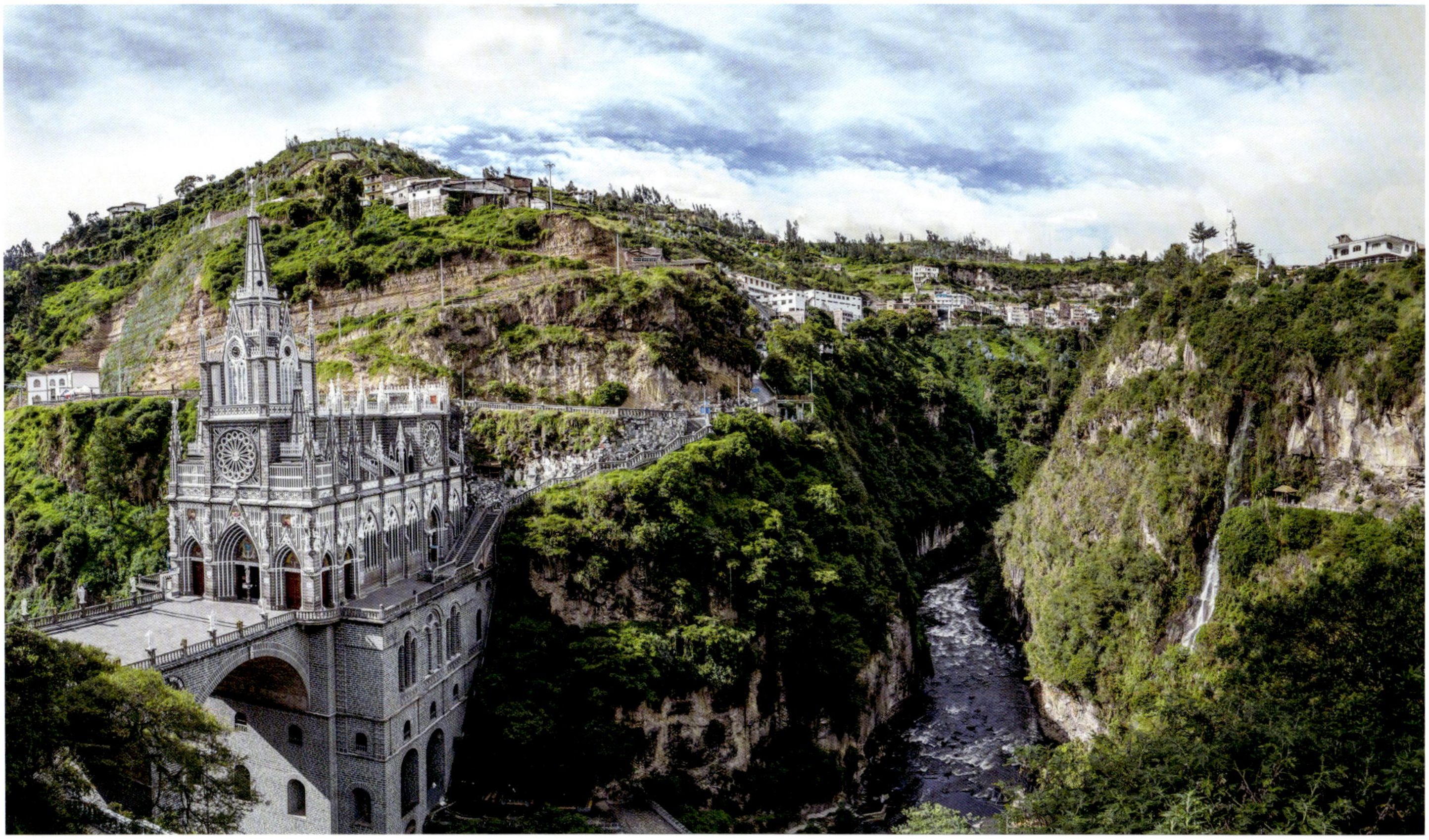

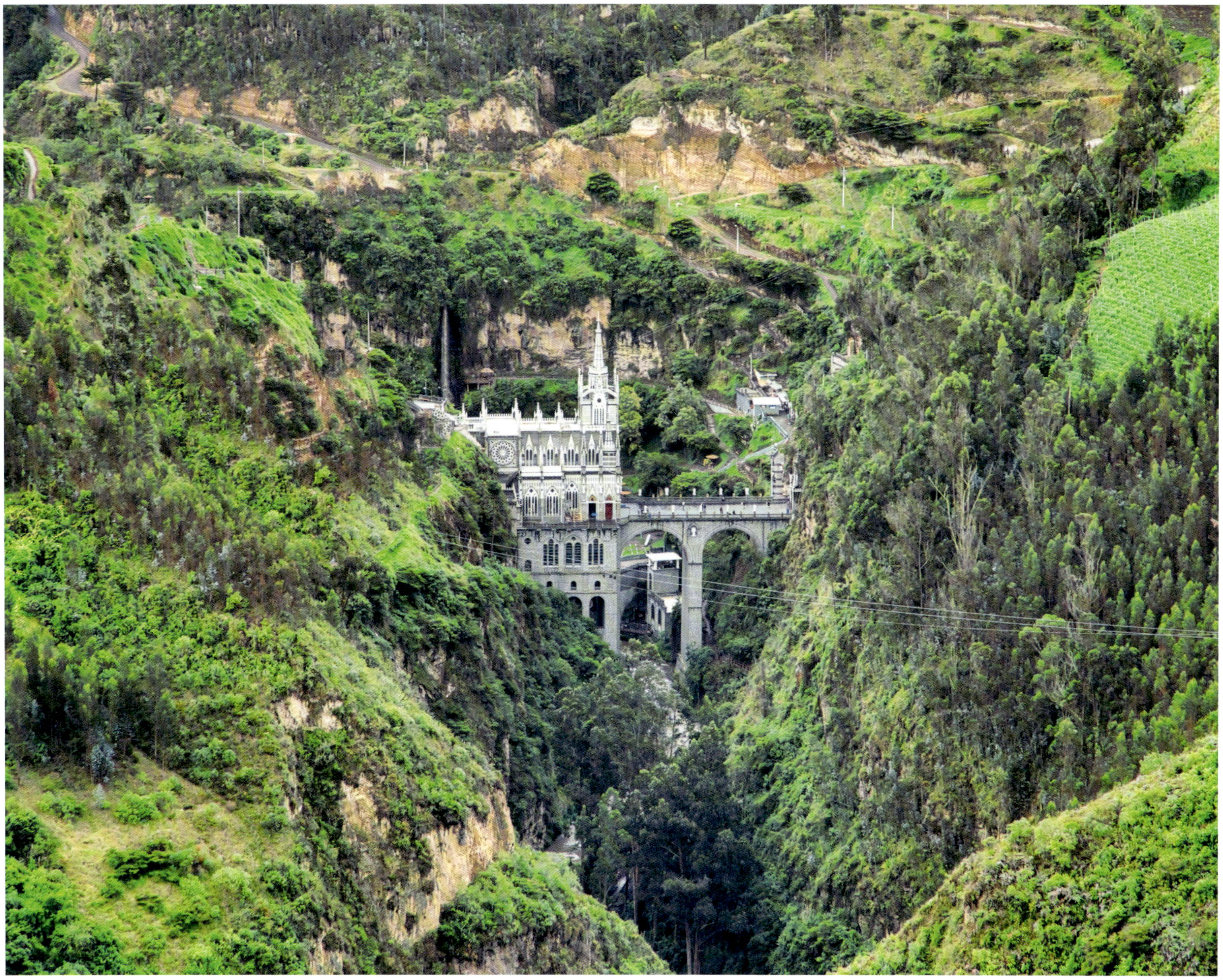

Opposite The delicate neo-Gothic turrets and finials reach toward the heavens.
Top Since 1954, the stunning church has borne the title of a minor basilica.
Bottom For centuries, the area's Indigenous peoples regarded the gorge as sacred.

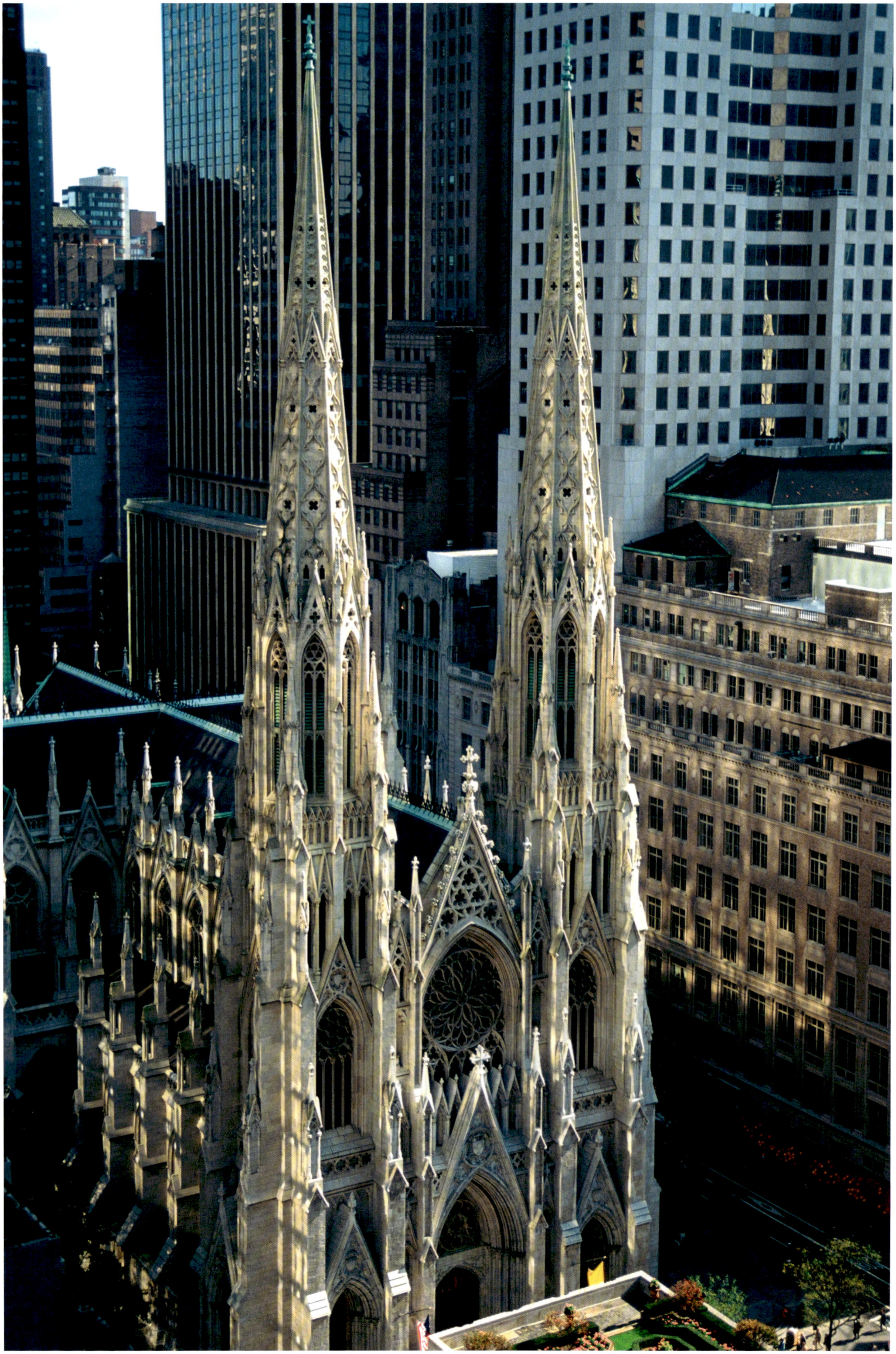

St. Patrick's Cathedral

Finding the Shamrock

Built: 1858 – 1879 CE, renovated and expanded until 1908 CE, New York City, United States

In the heart of Manhattan, a neo-Gothic masterpiece tells the story of a great faith community and its Irish roots.

Surrounded by the posh department stores and trendy boutiques of Fifth Avenue, the venerable St. Patrick's Cathedral feels like an invitation to step away from the chaos of the world.

The American architect James Renwick Jr. designed Saint Patrick's Cathedral in the neo-Gothic style, inspired by the grand European cathedrals of the Middle Ages. Its marble facade is a masterpiece of craftsmanship—delicate pointed arches, richly decorated flying buttresses, and intricately designed gargoyles captivate the amazed gaze. In between, a stunning rose window with intricate stone tracery and vividly colored stained glass takes pride of place, offering a preview of the splendor within. Behind the massive bronze doors, adorned with intricate depictions of saints, lies a majestic scene. In the vast nave framed by towering arches, sunlight dances through stained glass windows, which rank among the most beautiful in North America. Above, a classic ribbed vault spans harmoniously. The journey continues to the high altar and the baldachin towering above it. A masterpiece of neo-Gothic craftsmanship, the ensemble was designed in 1942 by the Boston architectural firm Maginnis & Walsh to perfectly complement the cathedral's style. At the eastern end of the cathedral lies the equally breathtaking Lady Chapel, which was completed in the early 20th century. Beneath magnificent stained glass windows, crafted in England, France, and Germany, visitors are offered a sanctuary within a sanctuary where they might seek intercession from the Virgin Mary.

Manhattan owes this jewel of a church to the persistence of Archbishop "Dagger John" Hughes, who championed the construction of St. Patrick's Cathedral against all odds. Construction was delayed during the Civil War (1861 – 1865) and resumed in 1866, culminating in the cathedral's grand opening in 1879. Its connection to Ireland is unmistakable: St. Patrick, the nation's patron saint and the cathedral's namesake, was a revered figure to the Irish immigrants that made up much of New York's Catholic community. His statue, and the magnificent window in the south transept, tell of his life and work, from converting the Celts to leaving a lasting spiritual legacy.

For those who look closely, the shamrock, St. Patrick's enduring symbol, reveals itself throughout the cathedral. According to legend, he used it to explain the Holy Trinity—Father, Son, and Holy Spirit—to the Irish. Perhaps it also served as a silent blessing for Archbishop Hughes, guiding him in his quest to make this magnificent house of God a reality.

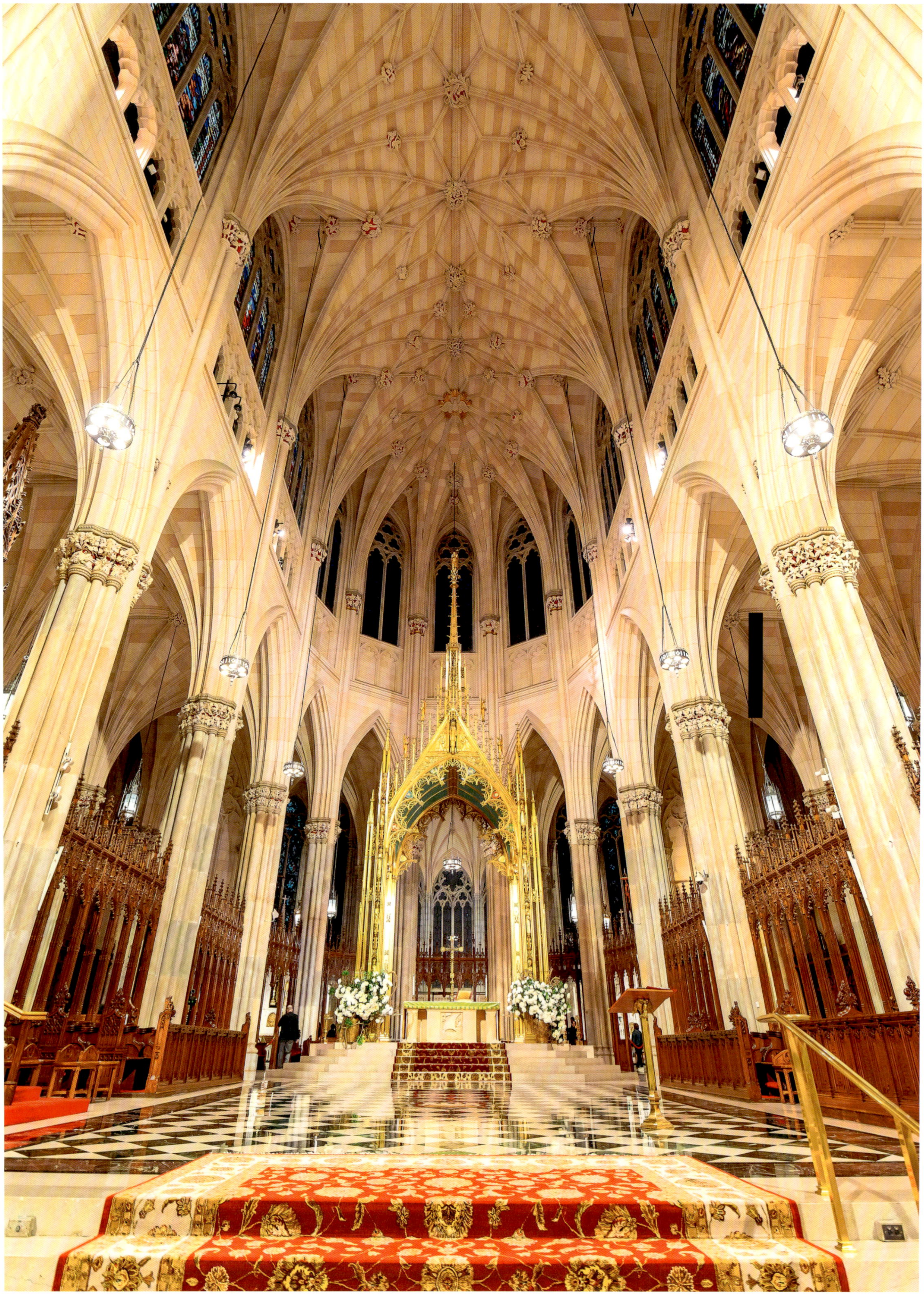

Above Unlike many church altars, the one at St. Patrick's lacks a tabernacle. This reflects a more traditional cathedral design, in which the tabernacle is placed in a separate chapel for pontifical liturgies.

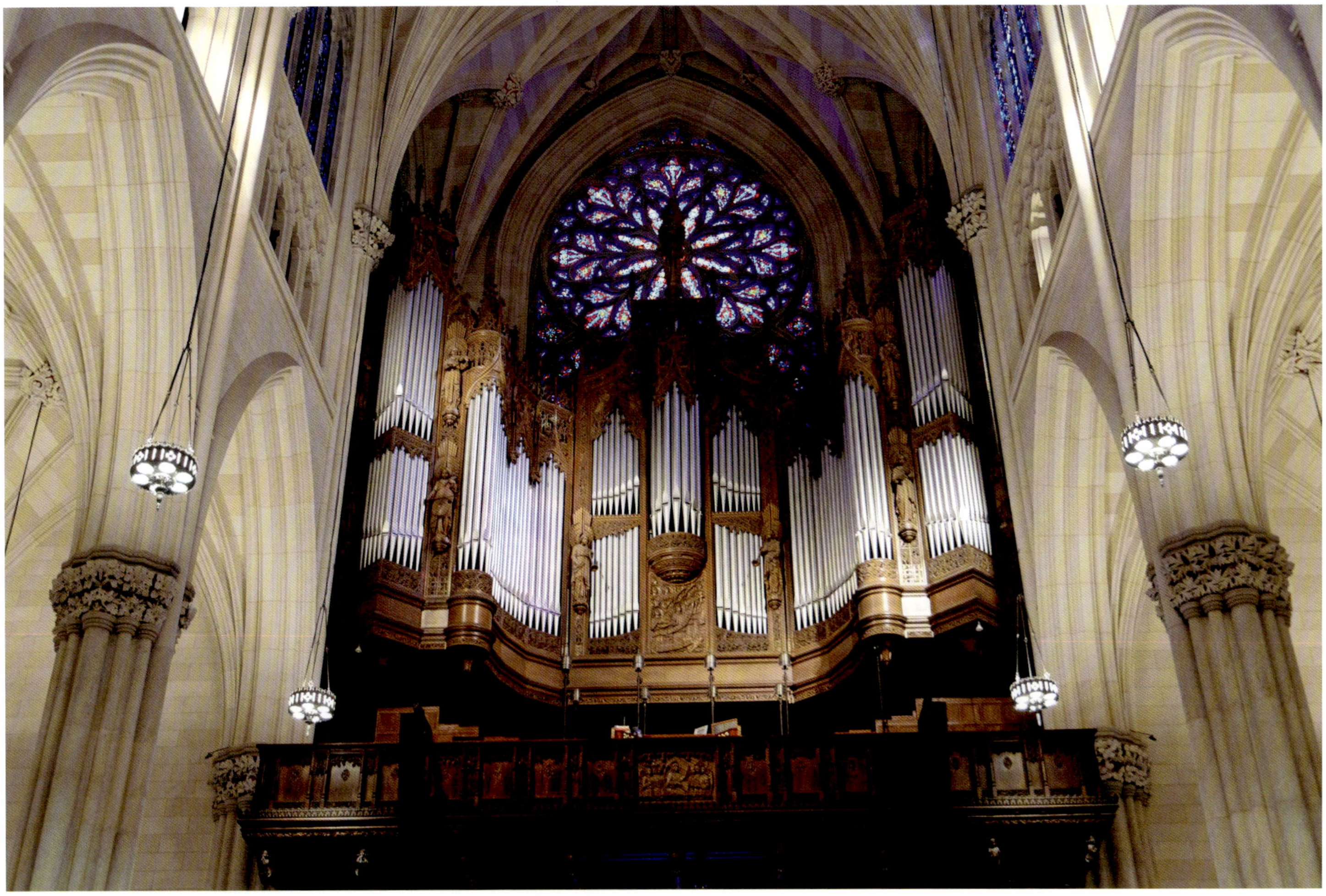

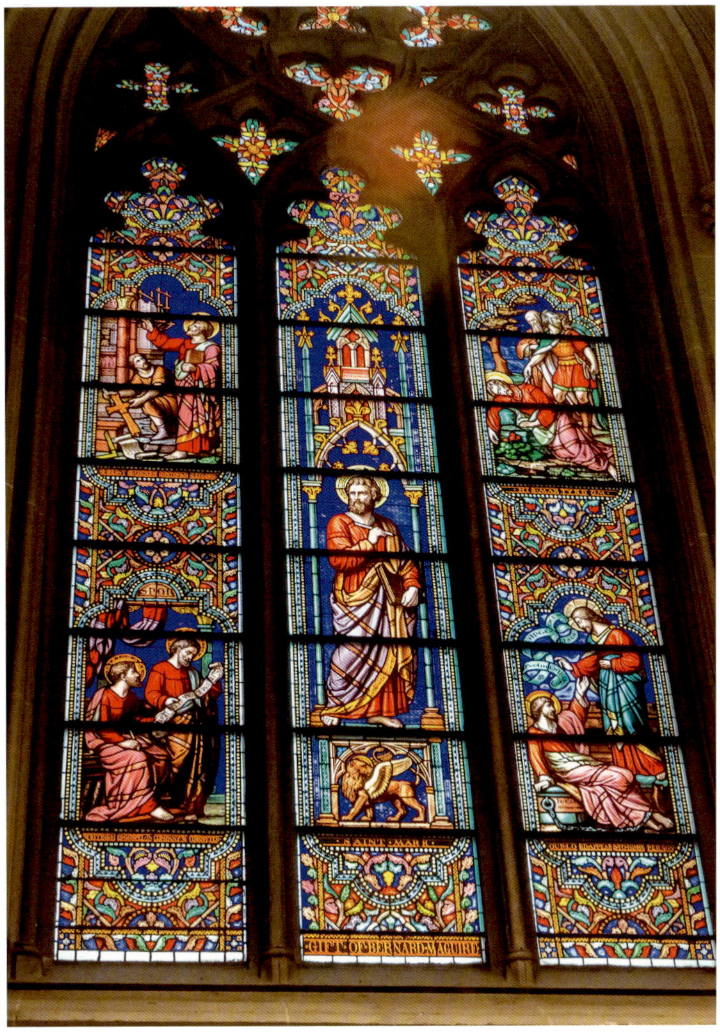

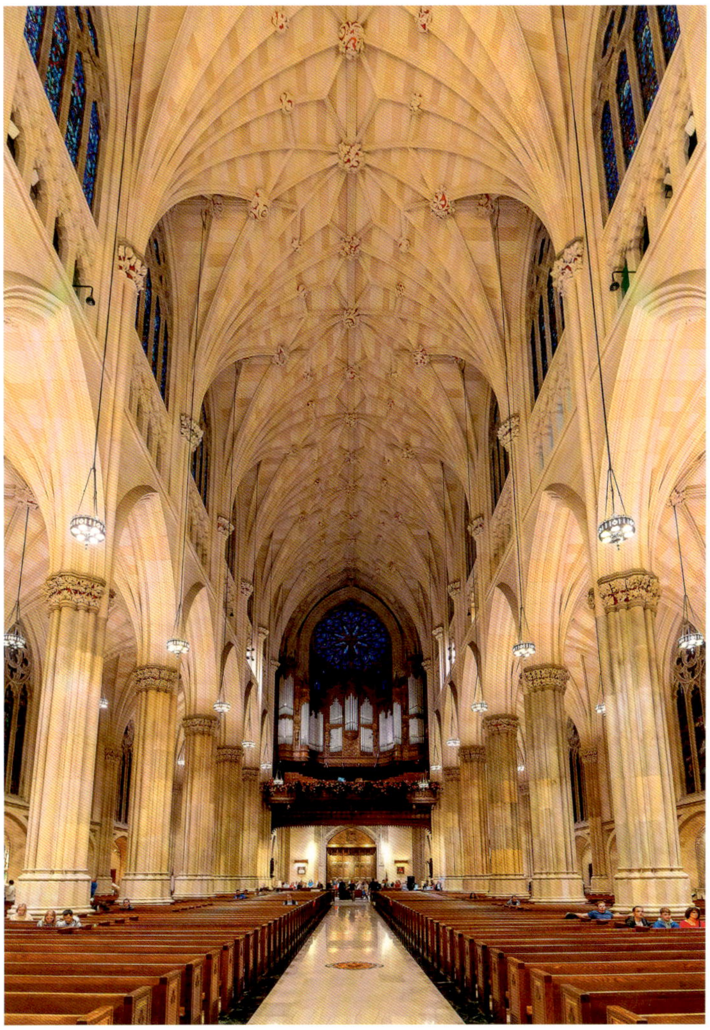

Top The cathedral houses two organs with a total of 9,000 pipes.
Bottom left The stained glass windows depict important biblical figures and scenes.
Bottom right The cathedral was constructed from over 33,000 blocks of white marble.

Machu Picchu

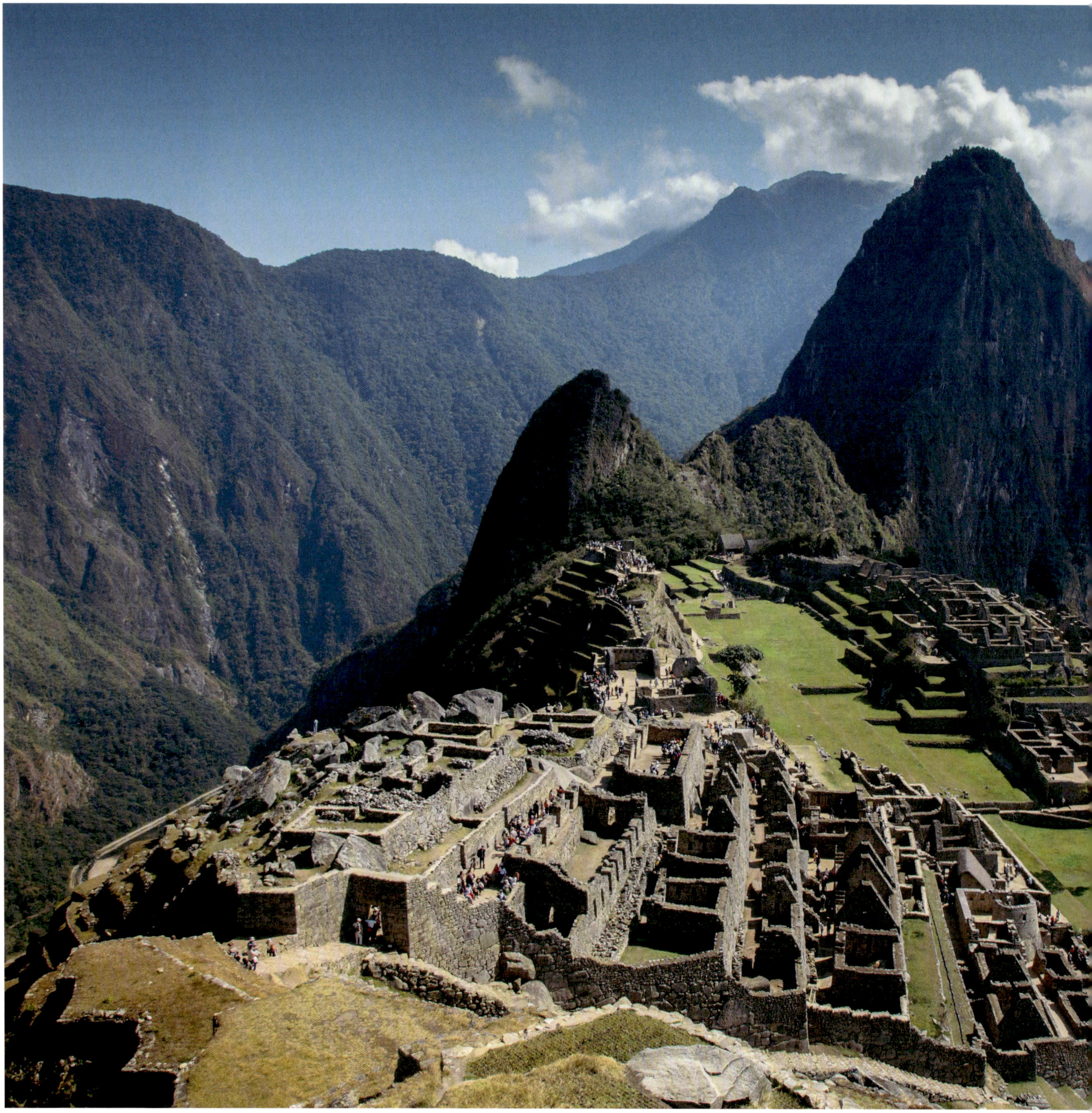

Machu Picchu, Peru

Built: 15th century CE,
Machu Picchu, Peru

High in the Andes, the Inca created a site where one's connection to an awesome and mysterious universe feels almost tangible.

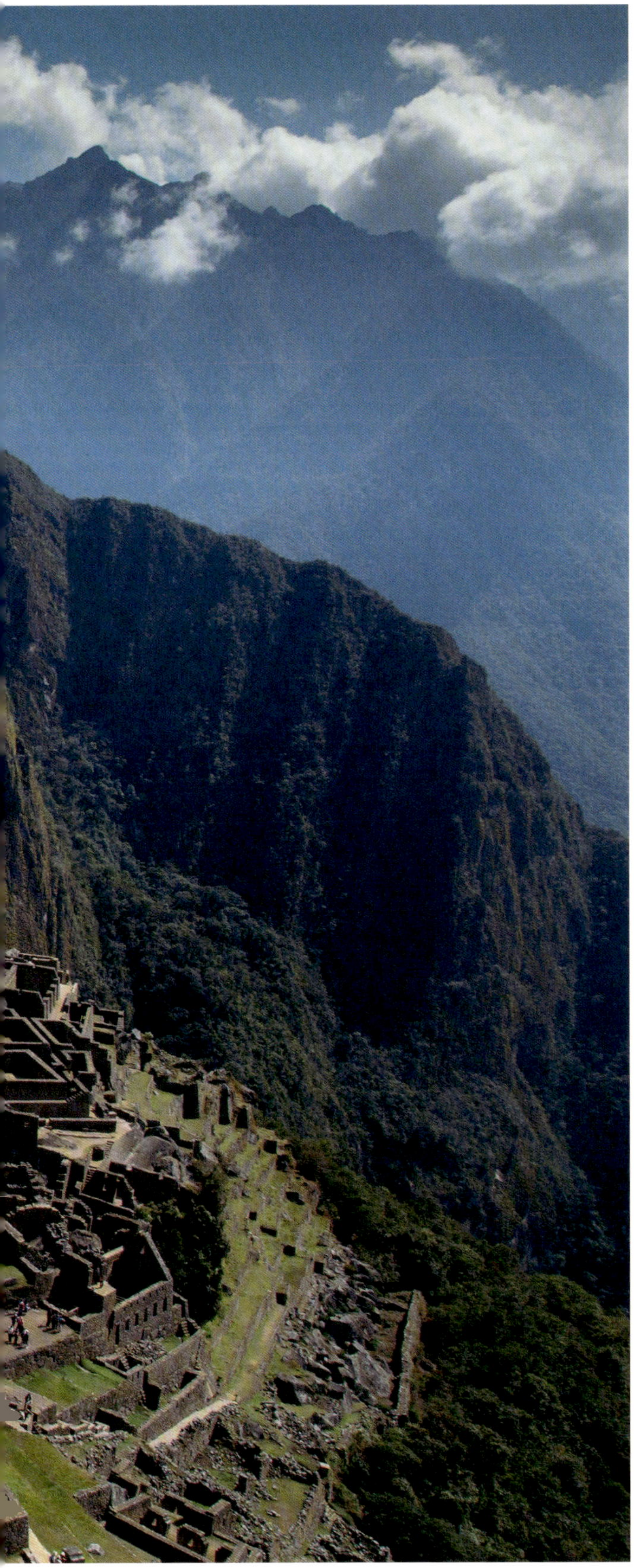

The lyrical words of Pablo Neruda describe the ascent into the mystical world of the Inca: "Then on the ladder of the earth I climbed / through the atrocious thicket of the lost jungles / to you, Macchu Picchu." In *The Heights of Macchu Picchu,* the Chilean poet captured as few others have the feeling that grips the heart when visiting the ruins of this legendary city. Did the Inca, one wonders, hold the key to deeper, more universal truths than we profess to know today?

This thought forces itself upon you as you wander, awestruck, through the Inca city, perched 7,970 feet (2,430 meters) above sea level and surrounded by the rugged peaks of the Andes. Temples and dwellings nestle against the mountain slopes. Steep stairways and grass-covered terraces connect the different levels. On either side rise Huayna Picchu and Machu Picchu—the "young mountain" and the "old mountain" in Quechua—as if guarding the site.

At the heart of Machu Picchu lies the Sacred Plaza, framed by significant temples. The Main Temple, situated on the plaza's northern edge, is widely believed by archaeologists to have been dedicated to the sun god Inti, as it resembles other temples the Inca built in his honor. Next to it stands the Temple of the Three Windows, whose trapezoidal openings gaze out at the surrounding Andes like watchful eyes. These windows may symbolize the three realms of the Inca cosmos: the underworld *(Uku Pacha),* the world of the living or present moment *(Kay Pacha),* and the heavenly realm *(Hanan Pacha).* To the Inca, every action in one realm reverberated through the others, affecting every dimension. Another treasure is the smaller House of the Priest. It is easy to imagine the spiritual leaders of Machu Picchu connecting with the gods here, attuning themselves to the rhythm of the universe. Above the Sacred Plaza stands the Intihuatana, the "place where the sun is tied." This stone served as a sundial and a sacred site for rituals honoring the solstices, the cycles of the earth, and the circle of life.

Pablo Neruda was one of countless visitors whose experience at Machu Picchu profoundly affected them. "Rise up with me, American love," he writes, calling on the Americas to embrace their Indigenous history, their roots, and their ancient wisdom with pride. It is this striking sense of sublime universal connectedness that makes the ancient Inca city so fascinating and mysterious. The mountains around the ruin remain silent—what secrets do they know?

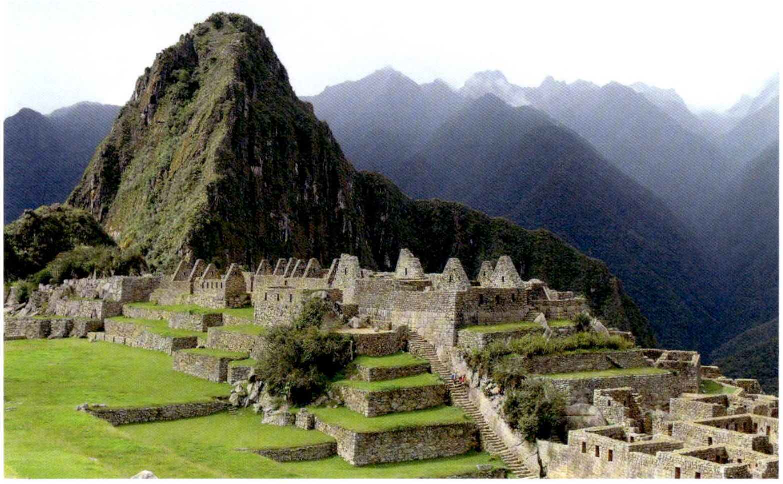

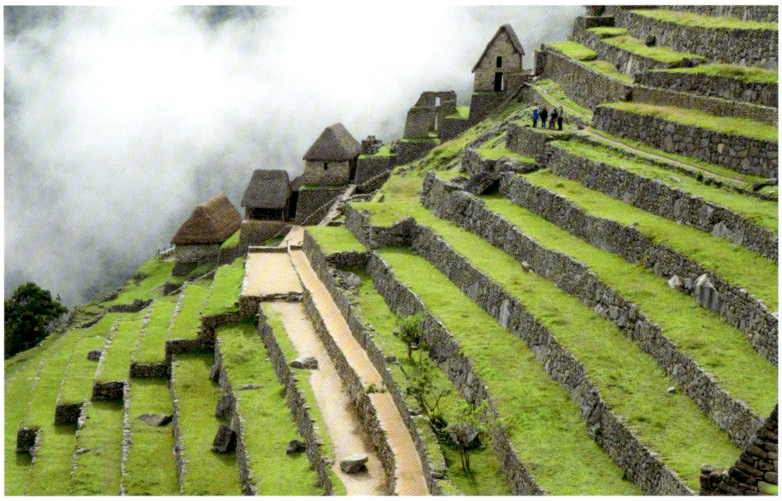

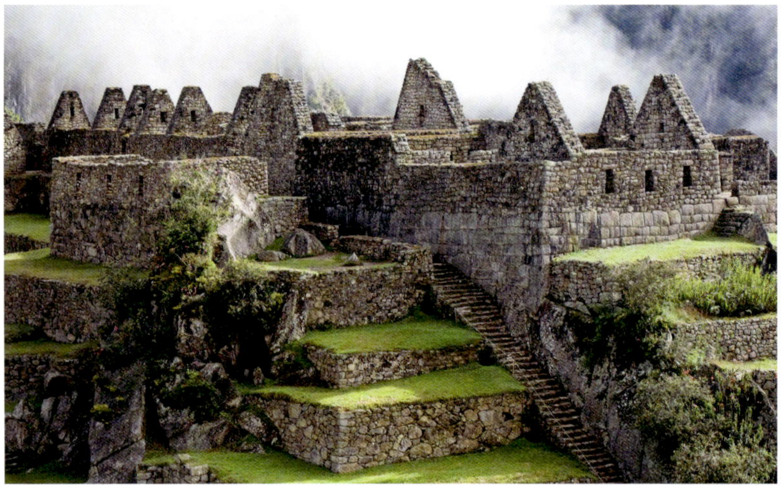

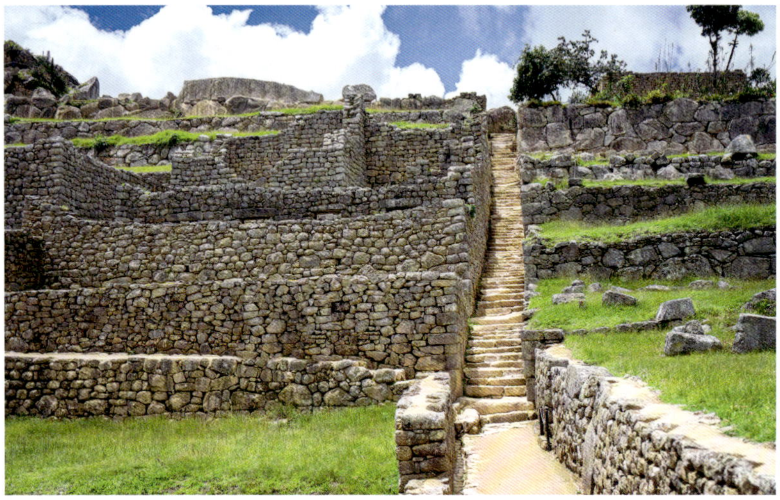

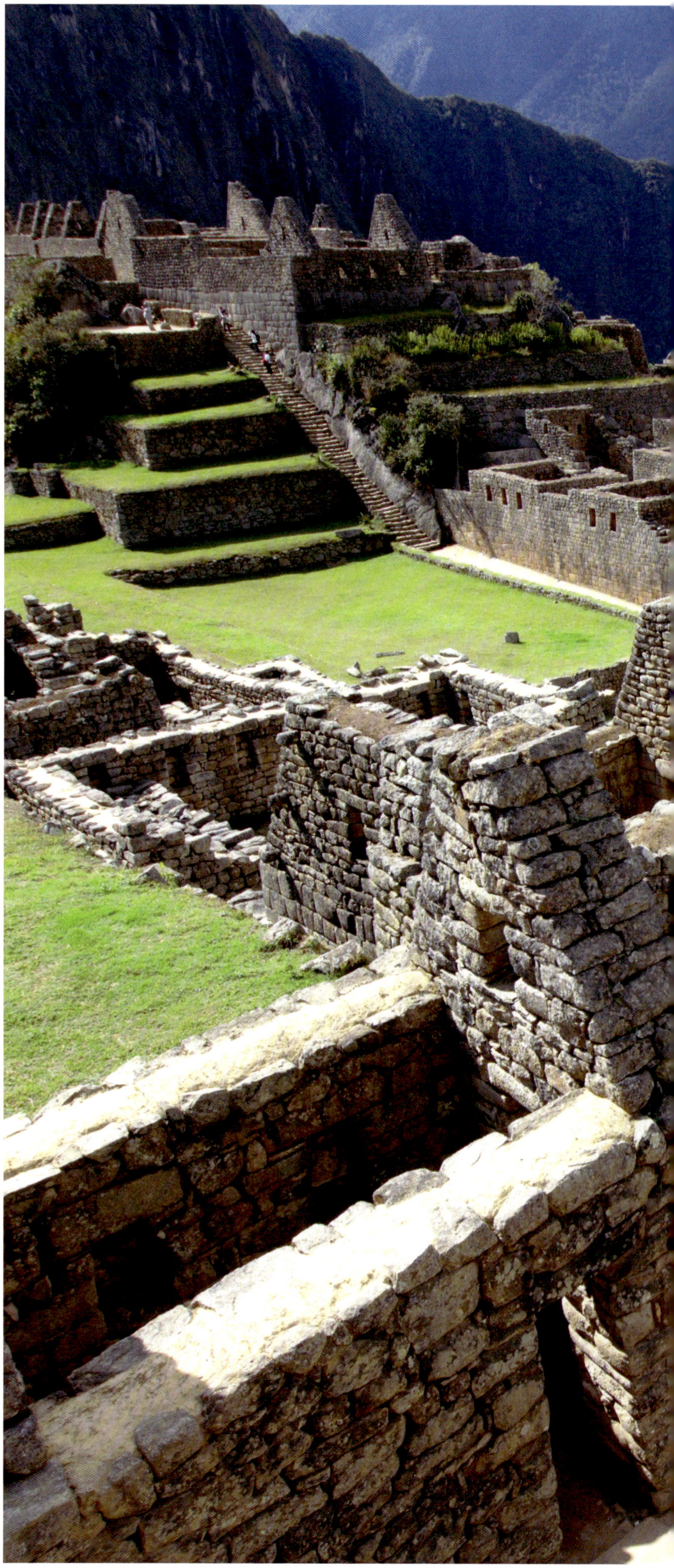

Top Gazing at the ruins of the legendary city, one feels that time has stood still.
Upper middle The terraces around the city were used for agriculture.
Lower middle Around 300 to 500 people lived in Machu Picchu.
Bottom The city was miraculously never discovered during the Spanish conquest.

Machu Picchu, Peru

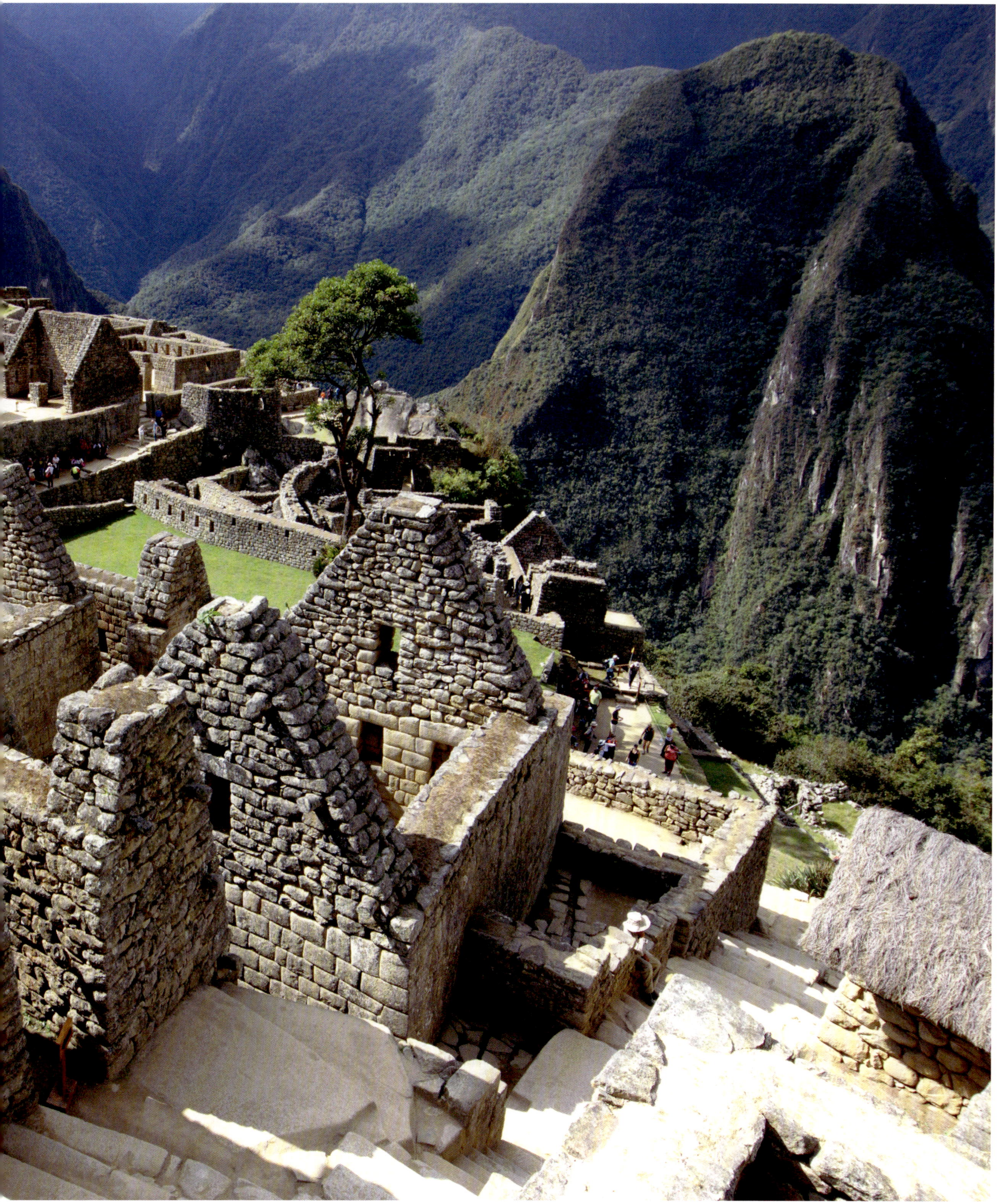

Above Using a specialized construction technique known as *ashlar,* the Inca meticulously joined massive stone blocks, fitting them so tightly together that no mortar was needed.

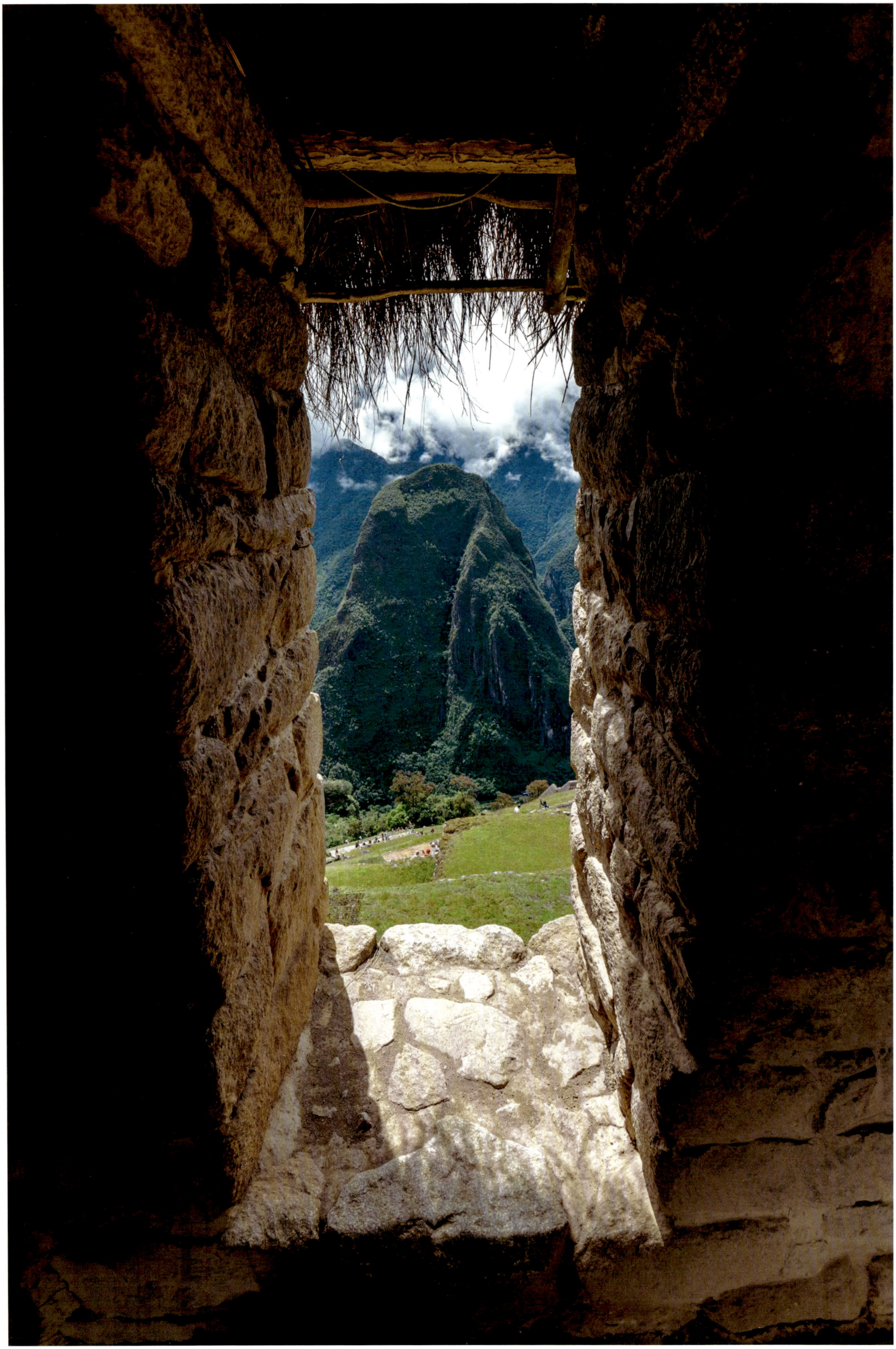

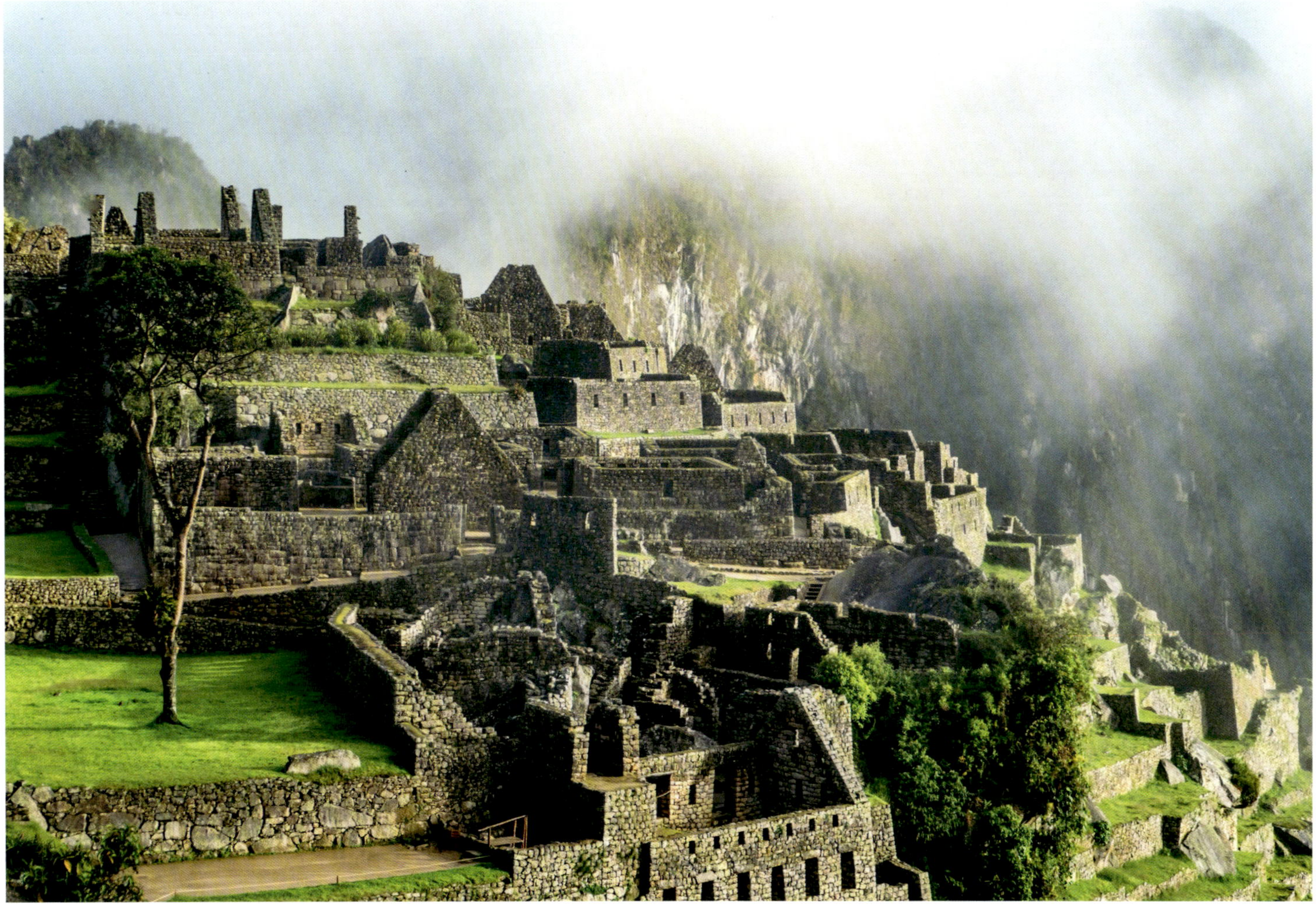

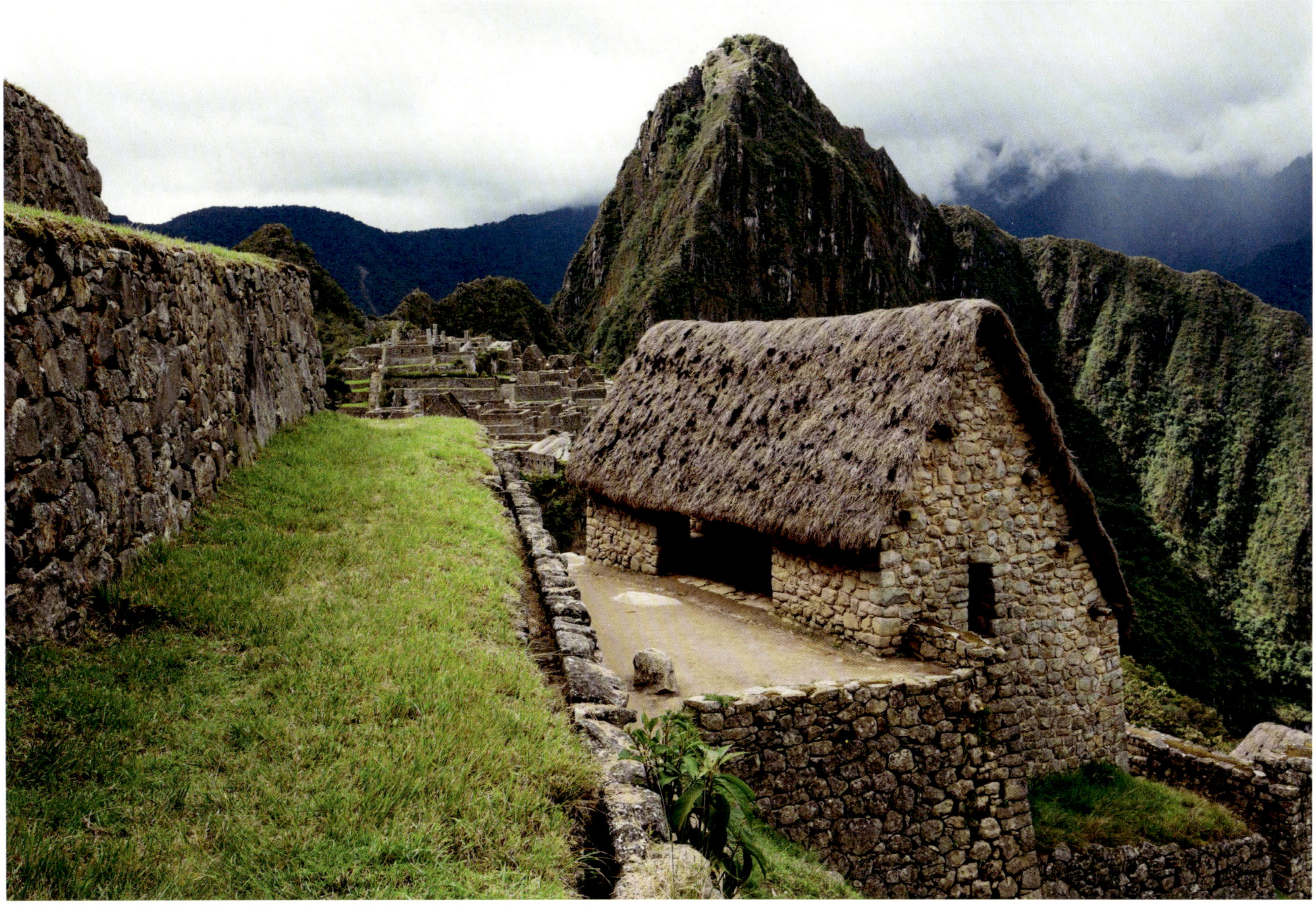

Opposite Machu Picchu was rediscovered in 1911.
Top A sophisticated system of aqueducts and fountains supplied the entire city with fresh water.
Bottom Mostly priests, nobles, and workers lived here.

Moai of Rapa Nui

Backs Against the Sea

Built: 1100 – 1600 CE, Rapa Nui, Chile

How these multi-ton guardians of a forgotten world came to their resting places remains a mystery to this day.

After a five-hour flight from Santiago, Rapa Nui slowly emerges on the horizon. The island lies nearly 2,200 miles (3,540 kilometers) west of the Chilean mainland, in the heart of the South Pacific. In complete isolation, one of the most fascinating civilizations in human history left behind a world-famous legacy: the massive stone *moai* sculptures, which have stood watch over the island for centuries.

Although named Easter Island by the Dutch, the island's Indigenous inhabitants call their land Rapa Nui, a name also given to their people and language. Their ancestors, Polynesian navigators, settled on Rapa Nui between 500 and 900 CE. Over the centuries, various tribes emerged, inhabiting different parts of the island and crafting the legendary *moai* from volcanic stone.

Positioned mostly with their backs to the sea, the statues—believed to be ancestral chiefs—were symbolic of the power of an individual tribe, and were the physical embodiments of divine spirit. In Rapa Nui beliefs, the *moai* channel *mana,* the spiritual energy of their forebears, and stand as intermediaries on the threshold between the visible and invisible worlds. Each statue was carefully placed on an *ahu,* a ceremonial platform where sacred rituals were performed.

By the 19th century, many of the *moai* lay toppled, whether due to inter-tribal warfare or more natural phenomena like earthquakes. The brutal practices of slave traders and imported diseases also took their toll on the Rapa Nui and their culture. In the 20th century, many of the sacred stone figures were re-erected and restored. To their surprise, researchers discovered that the statues were not just heads. The figures had full stone bodies buried underground and were much larger than previously thought, with an average height of 13 feet (4 meters). How these massive statues were transported to their locations remains uncertain. Some theories suggest they were moved using wooden logs, while others propose that they were rocked into position from side to side using ropes.

Today, UNESCO safeguards Rapa Nui. Excavation efforts are ongoing, and new sculptures are still being found. As for the *moai,* they continue to stoically bear witness to it all.

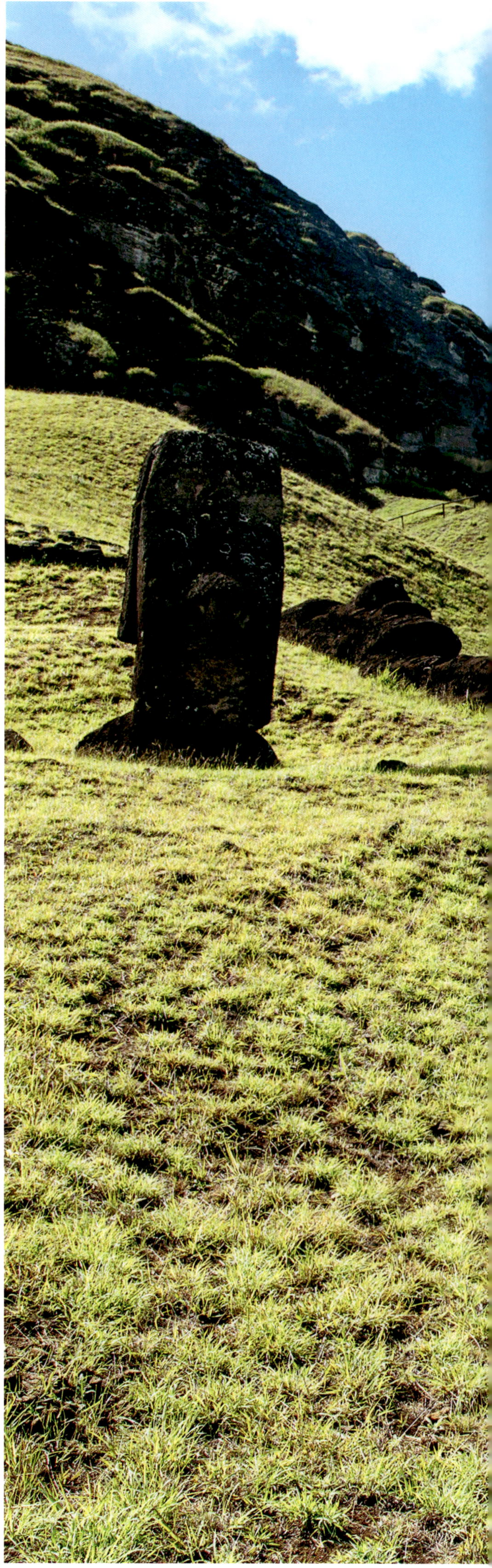

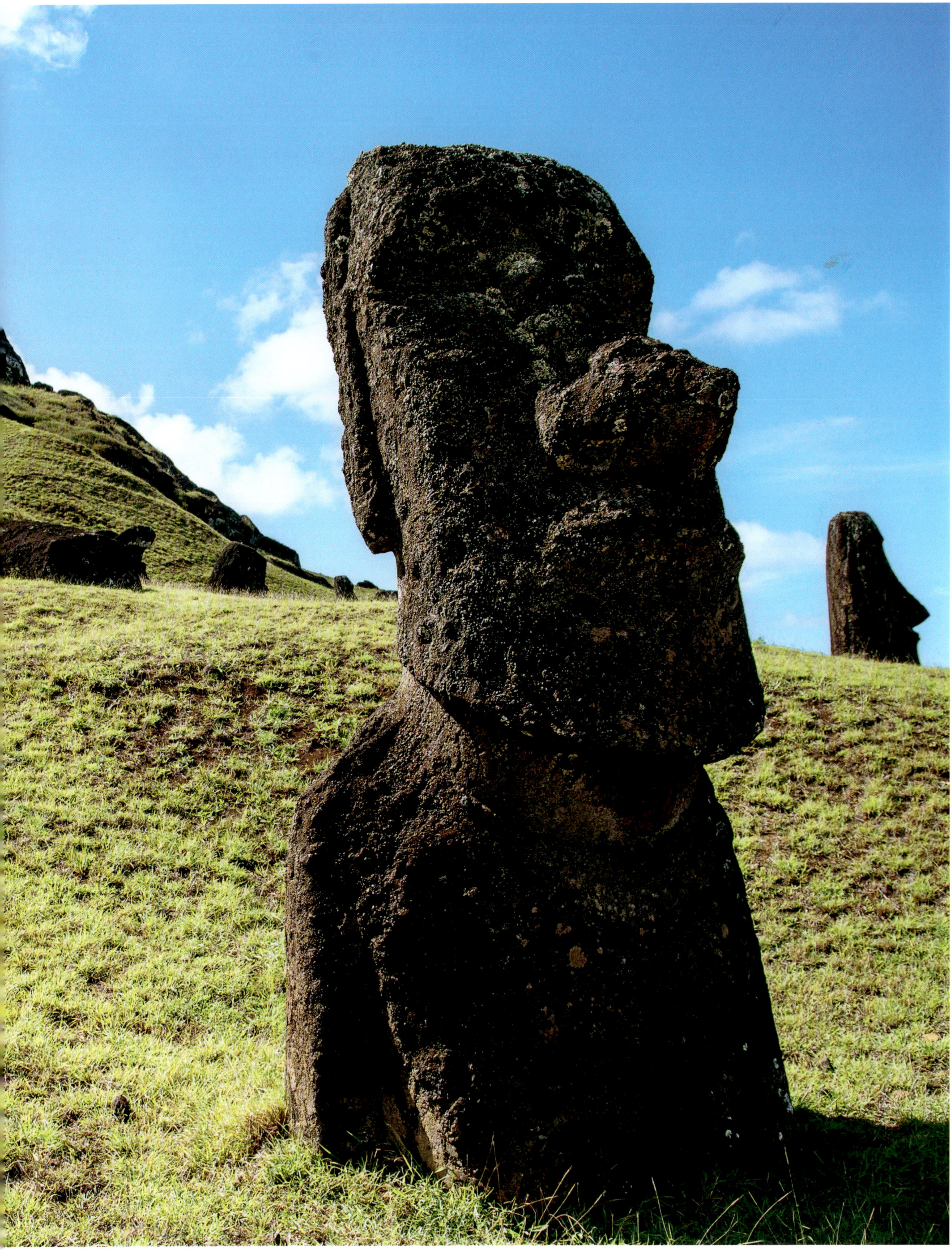

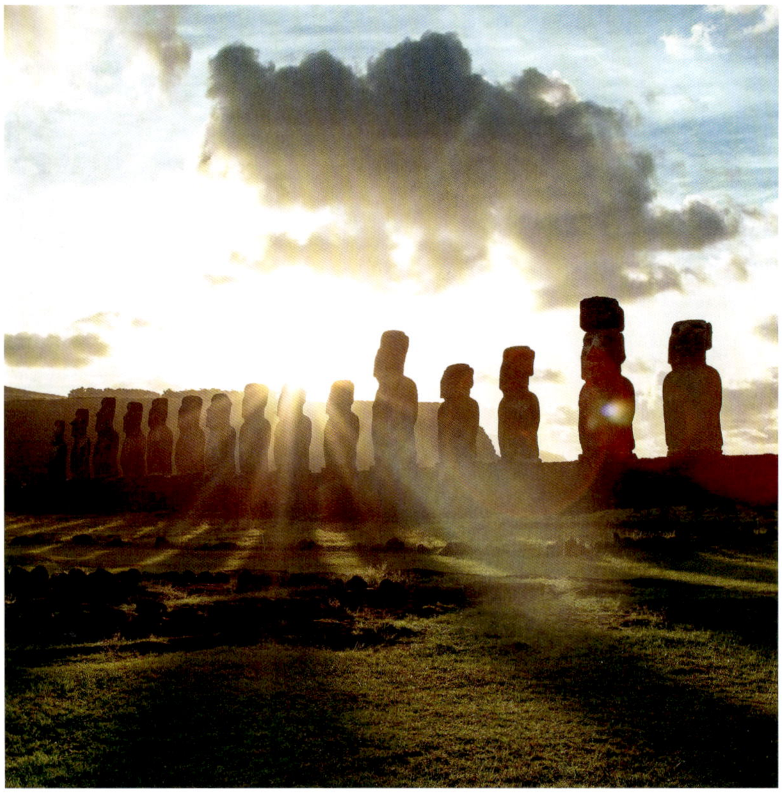

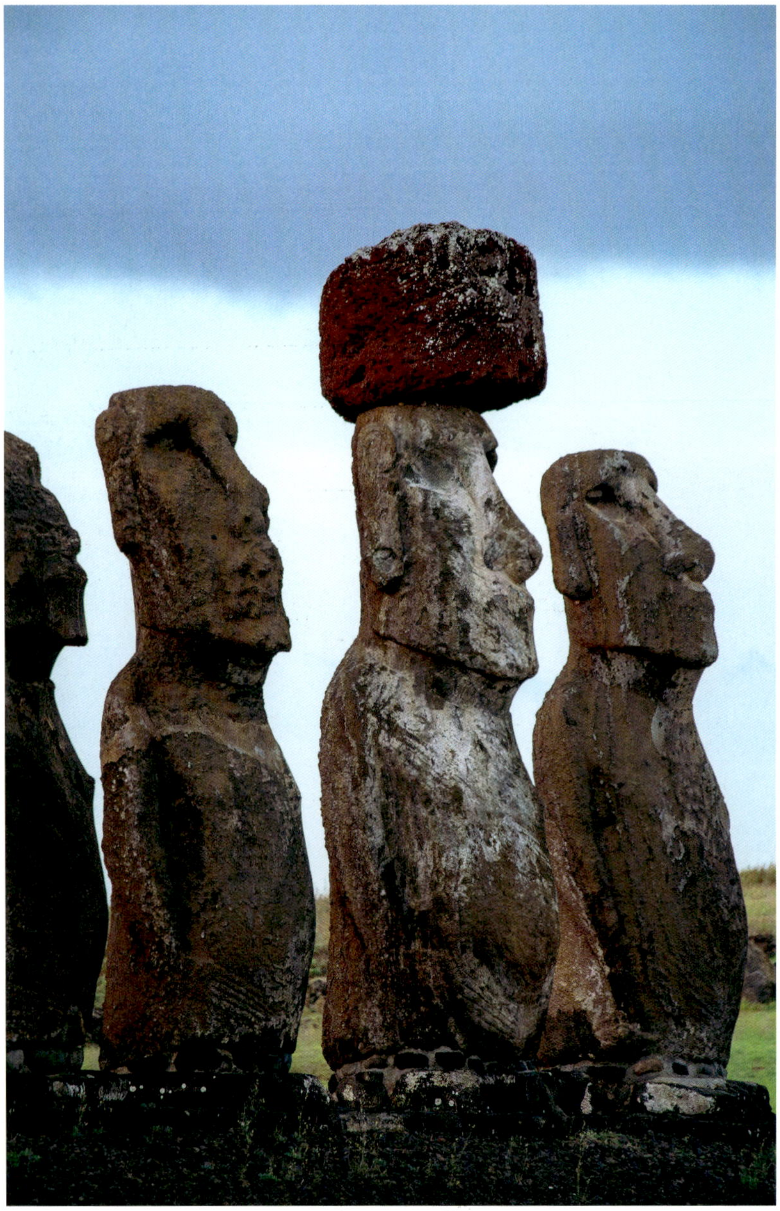

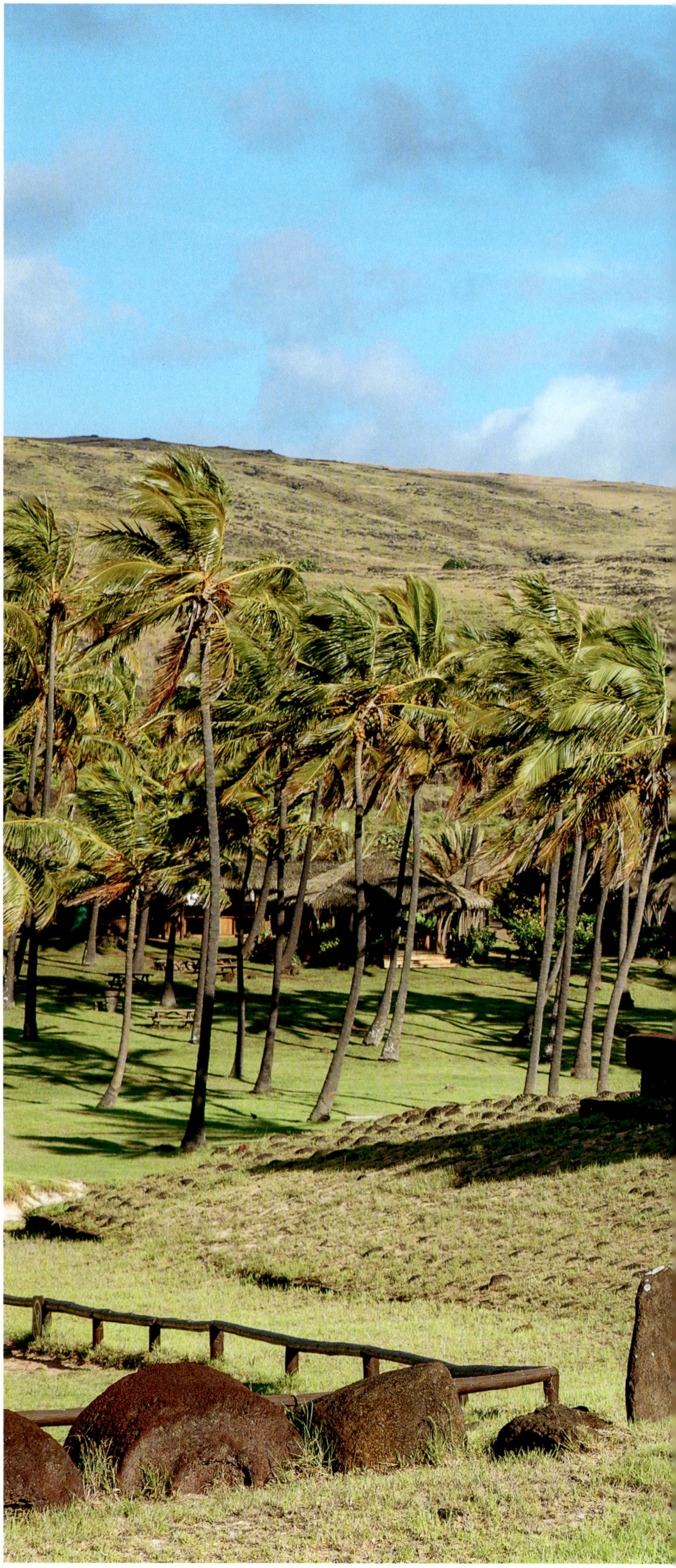

Top Moai come in many forms, varying in size and shape.
Bottom Indigenous rituals followed the cycles of the seasons.

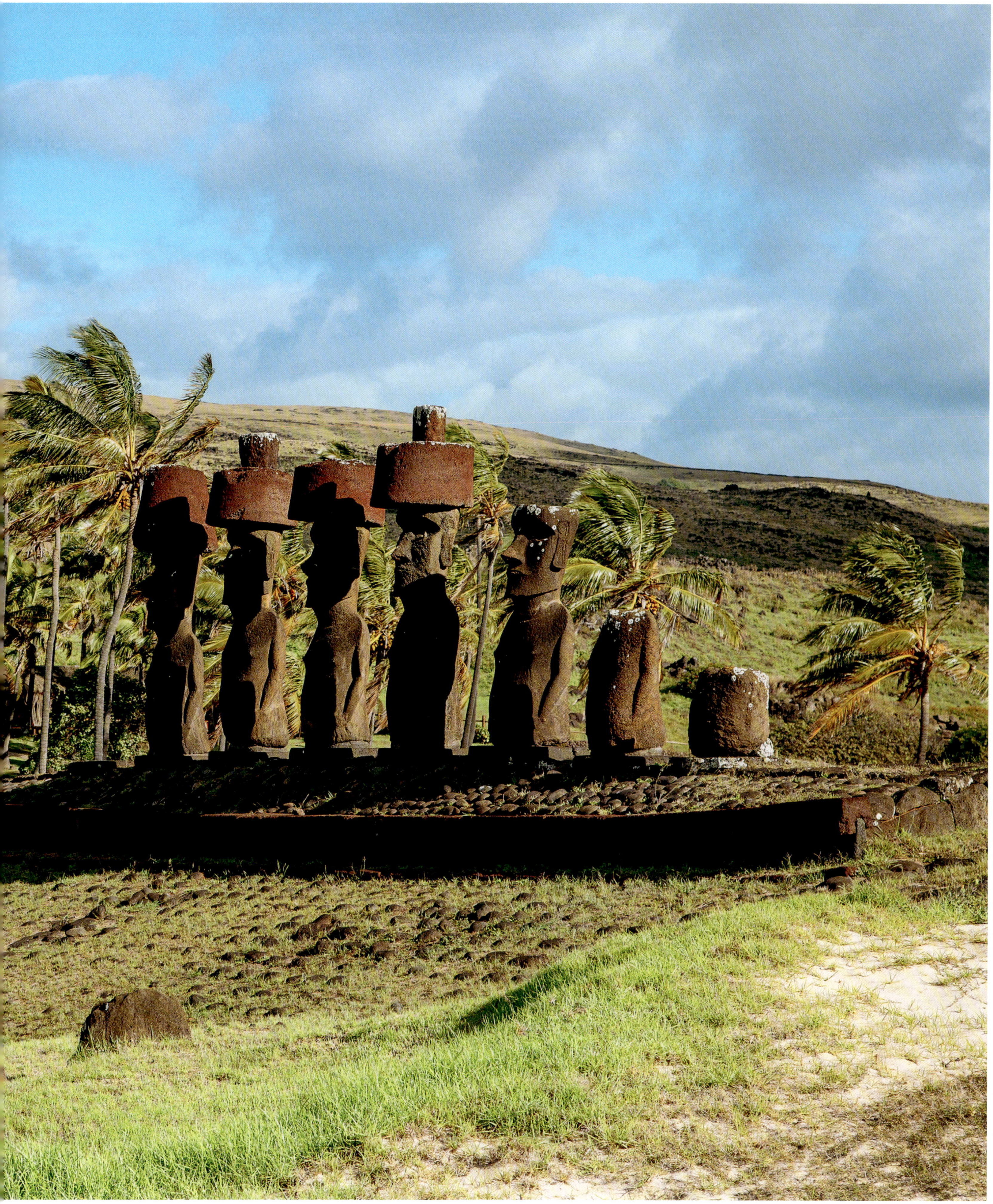

Above The characteristic cylindrical stones, called *pukao*, which some *moai* wear on their heads, were revealed to be special accessories marking particularly significant figures.

Of Megaliths, Cathedrals, and Modernity

Europe's unique mix of pagan, Moorish, and Christian influences has inspired a unique variety of spectacular temples.

From simple stone circles to the majestic cathedrals of the Middle Ages, every era on the European continent has left its mark. Following the age of the megalithic cultures came classical antiquity, with its magnificent temples that served not only as places of worship but as rulers' declarations of divine legitimacy. In Northern Europe, meanwhile, the Norse gods were deeply venerated at natural sites. With the flourishing of Christianity, the spiritual landscape of Europe underwent a profound transformation. The temples of antiquity were sometimes not destroyed but simply retrofitted. A remarkable example is the Pantheon in Rome (pp. 182–185), which became a Catholic church in the 7th century. At the same time, new churches were built, often borrowing from the formal language of antiquity. The design of early Christian basilicas, for instance, was inspired by Roman assembly halls and served as a blueprint for later sacred structures. Simultaneously, Moorish rule in Spain blended Islamic architectural elements with regional traditions.

By the Middle Ages, sacred architecture in Europe reached a new golden age. After the austere and heavy Romanesque style, Gothic architecture revolutionized building design. Churches such as Cologne Cathedral (pp. 160–163) demonstrated what was possible when religious fervor met technical ingenuity. Pointed arches, ribbed vaults, and flying buttresses created luminous, soaring spaces that reached toward the heavens. Stained glass windows, such as rapturous examples found at Chartres Cathedral (pp. 146–149), transformed light into a medium of spiritual experience.

In rural regions, Norse myths often persisted, gradually merging with Christianity. To this day, these myths can be found in the form of protective symbols on church portals or in stone carvings, and they find an architectural homage in the legendary stave churches. With the Renaissance, ancient forms and motifs returned, as can be impressively admired in St. Peter's Basilica in Rome (pp. 186–193). The subsequent baroque period, in turn, brought forth lavishly designed churches. Monumentality, light, and ornamentation merged here into a staging of faith that sought to overwhelm and inspire.

With the secularization and industrialization of the 19th and 20th centuries, Europe's sacred architecture also changed, often adopting a more restrained appearance. Yet some structures, such as Gaudí's Sagrada Família in Barcelona (pp. 136–141), found new and fascinating languages for human spirituality—a spirituality that continues to reinvent itself in its places of worship.

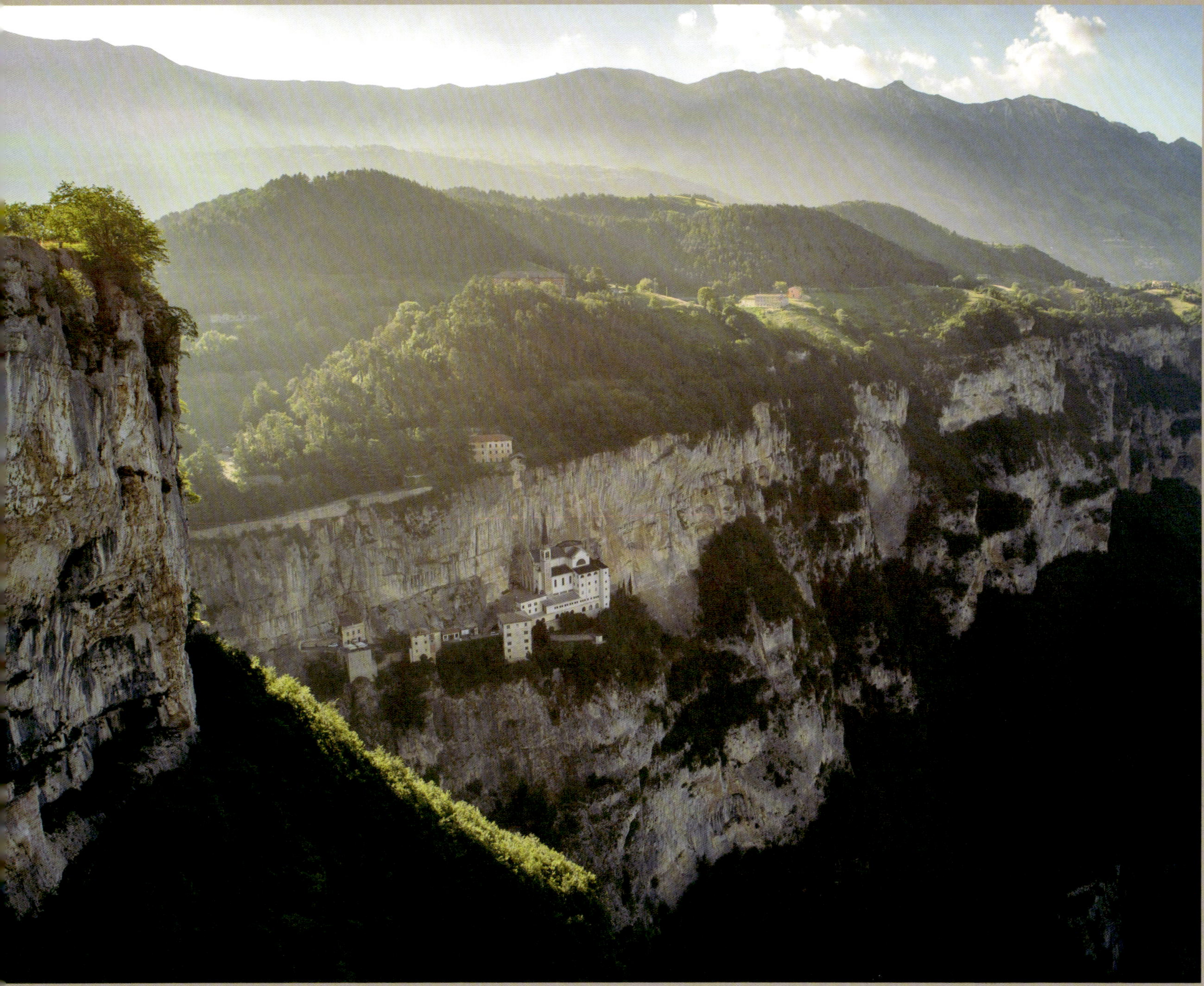

EUROPE

Monasteries of Meteora

Asceticism on High

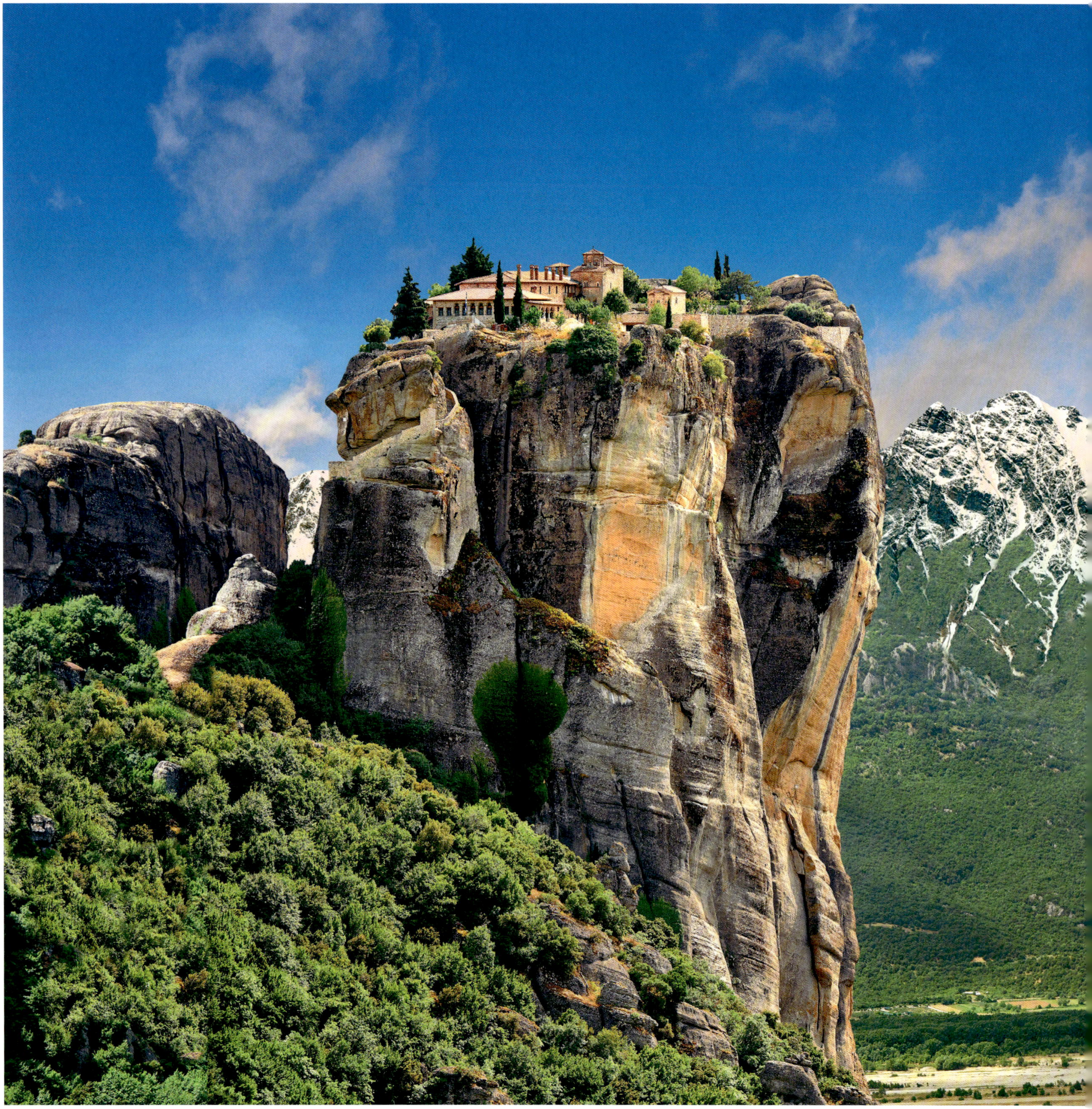

Built: 14th and 16th centuries CE,
Trikala, Greece

Centuries ago, pulleys hauled food, building materials, and even monks up the monastery cliffs.

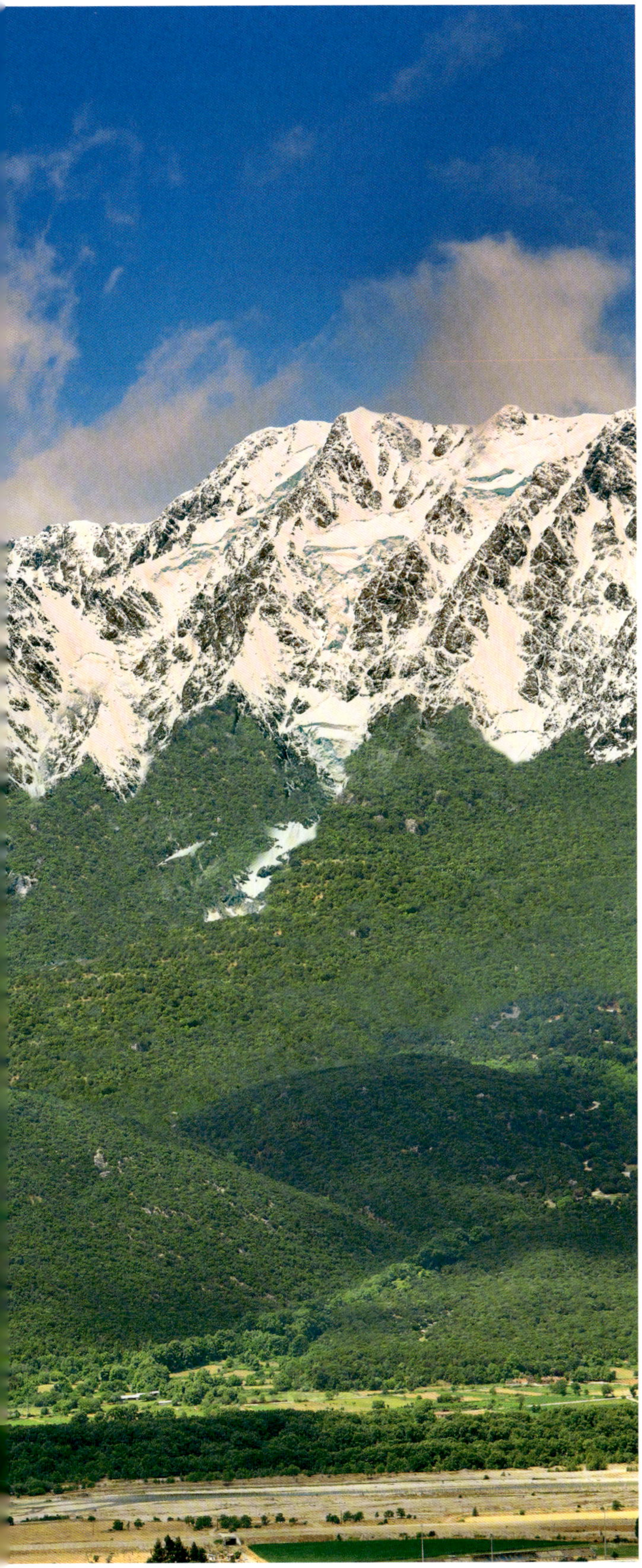

The famous monasteries of Meteora tower high above the vast plains of Thessaly, as if in defiance of everything earthbound. Perched atop dizzying cliffs, some over 1,300 feet (396 meters) tall, they defy both gravity and the imagination. The name says it all: Meteora literally means "suspended in the air."

The history of Meteora dates back to the 9th century, when the first hermits sought solitude in the caves of the sandstone cliffs, carving small cells into the rock to live in complete isolation. However, the true flourishing of Meteora began in the 14th century, as the Byzantine Empire faced increased pressure from the expanding Ottoman Empire. During this turbulent time, Eastern Orthodox monks sought safe refuge—and found it in the almost inaccessible heights of the Meteora cliffs.

Under quite adverse conditions, the monks began constructing the daring monasteries. For decades, they transported building materials, food, and other supplies up the cliffs using primitive pulleys and rope ladders. Even the monks themselves were hauled up the steep rock faces in baskets by their brothers. Deep faith was essential here, given the danger and immense work required. Gradually, narrow staircases and tight paths were carved into the rock, connecting the separate monasteries. These efforts paid off: the cliffs protected them not only from political and military threats, but also from the temptations and distractions of the world below.

Of the original 24 monasteries of Meteora, only 6 remain active today, but they are all the more impressive for it. Among the most famous is the Holy Monastery of Agios Stefanos, or Saint Stephen, a true treasure trove of Byzantine and post-Byzantine art. Its interiors are adorned with precious icons and frescoes depicting the life of Christ, scenes from the Bible, and the martyrdom of the saints. In the central dome of the monastery's church, Christ is depicted as the Almighty, or *Pantokrator,* a common motif in Byzantine churches. Atop the highest cliff sits the Monastery of the Transfiguration of Christ, or Megalo Meteoron, the largest and most important of the Meteora monasteries. Here, visitors can explore the museum, which displays valuable manuscripts, icons, and relics, offering glimpses into the long history of the place and its monastic community.

As richly adorned as the monasteries are, the life within them is notably ascetic. The monks and nuns who reside here continue the legacy of the first hermits, dedicating themselves to prayer, meditation, and the study of scriptures. Their practice preserves the sacred character of Meteora and offers other pilgrims and visitors a truly rarefied experience. Over decades, monks labored to carve narrow stairways into the rock to connect the monastery's various levels, creating altars and niches in the stone.

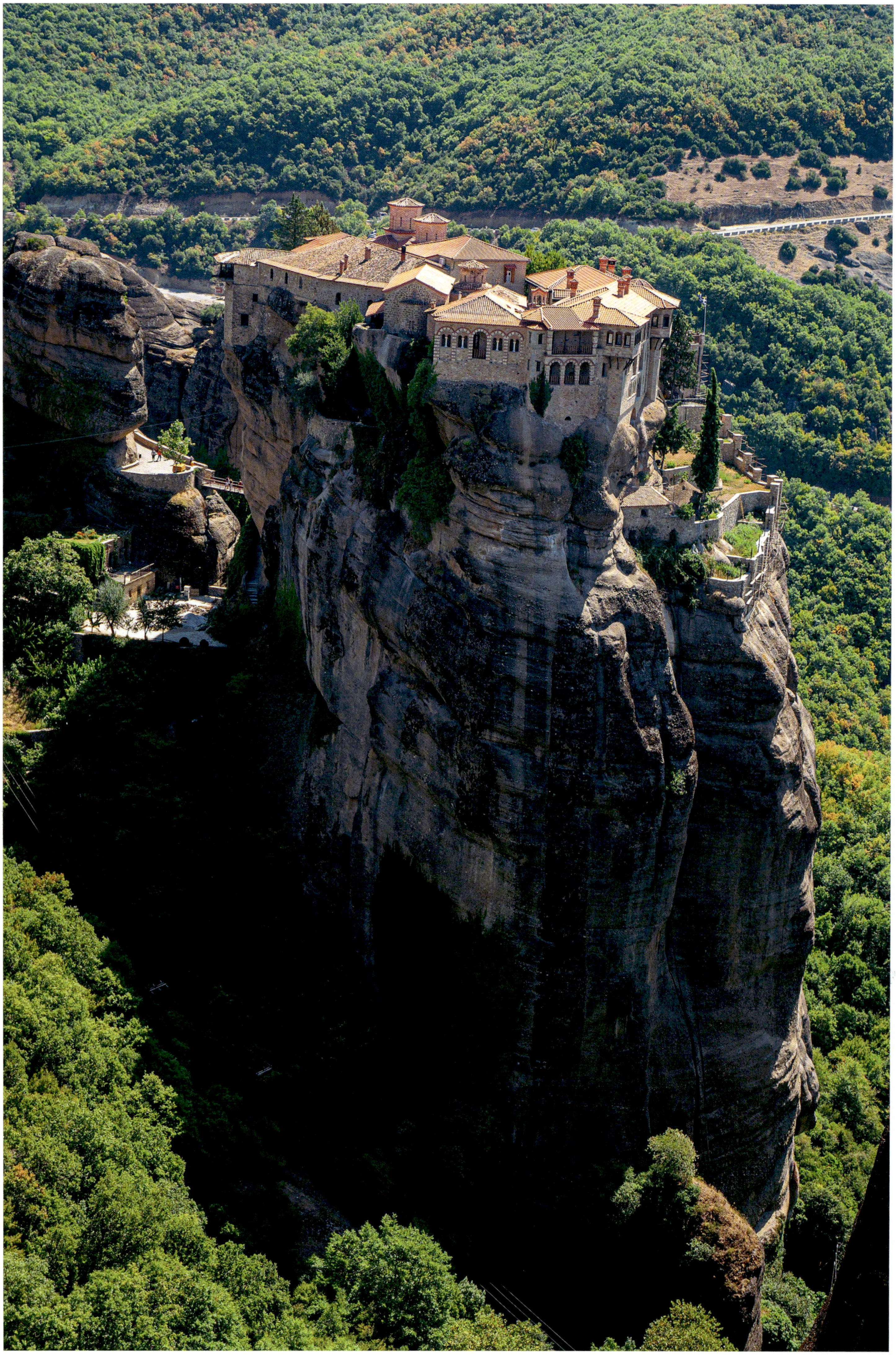

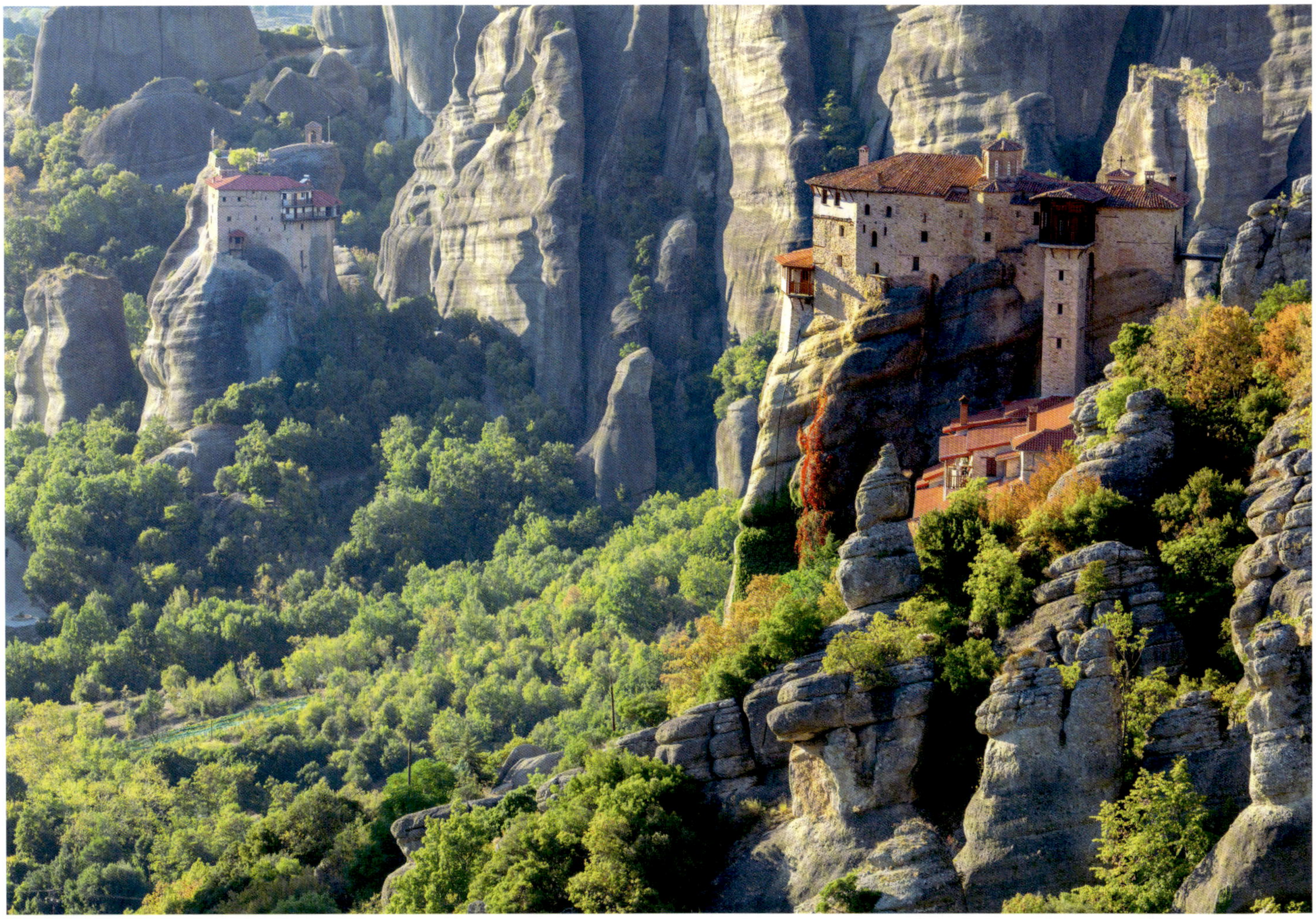

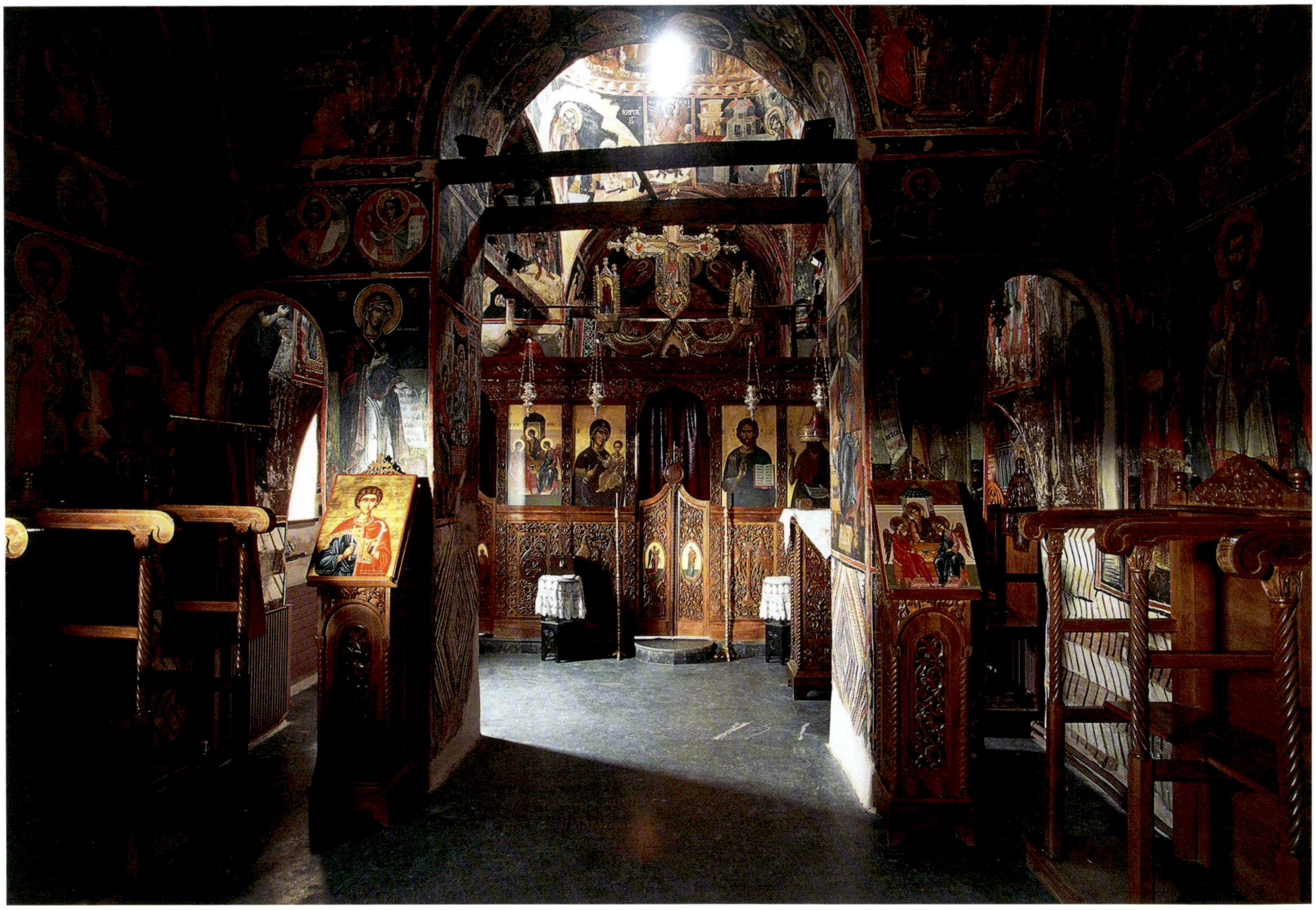

Opposite The legendary monasteries of Meteora are perched on nearly inaccessible cliffs.
Top The temples balance on the outcroppings, and serving as a bridge between heaven and earth.
Bottom The frescoes and icons within the monasteries are considered masterpieces of Byzantine art.

Monastery of Panagia Hozoviotissa

Iconic in the Truest Sense

Built: ca. 9th century CE (current form: 1088 CE), Amorgos, Greece

A surprise from the Holy Land inspired the creation of this cliffside monastery, perched 980 feet (300 meters) above the sea.

A legend begins this way: some 1,200 years ago, the people of Amorgos, a rocky Cycladic island, made an astonishing discovery. A richly adorned icon—more precisely, one half of it—had washed ashore. The Virgin Mary smiled upon the islanders from within the holy image, the Christ Child in her arms—surely a sign from God.

According to this same legend, the icon originally came from St. George of Hozeva, a cliffside monastery in what is now the West Bank of Palestine. During the period of Byzantine Iconoclasm, many Christian artworks were destroyed, and it was during one such siege that a pious woman, in a desperate act to save the icon from destruction, cast it into the sea. Guided by divine protection, it is said, the icon drifted through the Mediterranean, eventually splitting in two before it reached Greece. One part washed ashore on nearby Patmos, while the other found its way to this very coast of Amorgos. Here, the islanders took the icon's arrival as a symbol of divine protection—and an invitation to build a monastery on the sheer cliff above the bay.

The cliffside Monastery of Panagia Hozoviotissa stretches across eight levels, reaching a height of 131 feet (40 meters) and a width of only 16 feet (5 meters). Over decades, monks labored to carve narrow stairways and passages into the rock to connect the monastery's various structures, creating small altars and niches in the stone. The thick stone walls were designed to block the intense sunlight while also shielding the monastery's residents from attacks. Those were turbulent times, and pirates largely destroyed the original monastery, but it was rebuilt in its present form in 1088. The whitewashed walls, characteristic of Cycladic architecture, stand out sharply from the rock face even as they beautifully complement it. From the monastery's small windows, there's an endless view of the deep-blue Aegean Sea, perfectly reflective of the spiritual beauty of the site.

Inside, the icon of Panagia Hozoviotissa rests in a place of honor. For centuries, pilgrims have made the demanding ascent to pray before this image of the Virgin, seeking protection and healing. Today, in the monastery's austere rooms and small chapels, a handful of monks continue to preserve the ancient Orthodox traditions. Part of this legacy is the annual feast celebrating the Presentation of Mary on November 21, drawing pilgrims from all over the world. With solemn processions and prayers, they pay homage to the Virgin Mary, giving thanks for the protection she has given the small island since her miraculous journey from the Holy Land some 1,200 years ago.

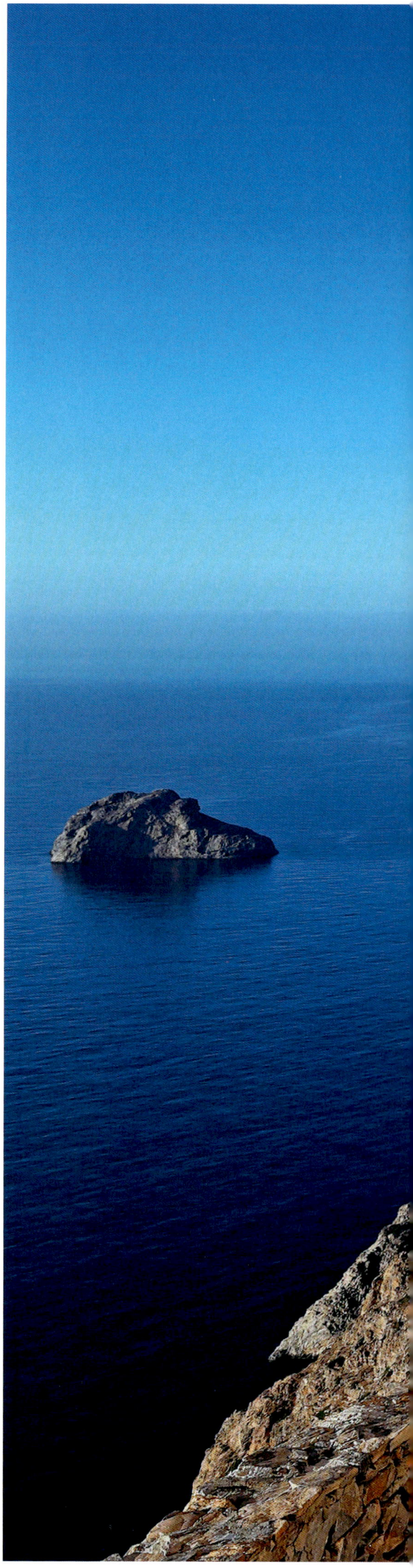

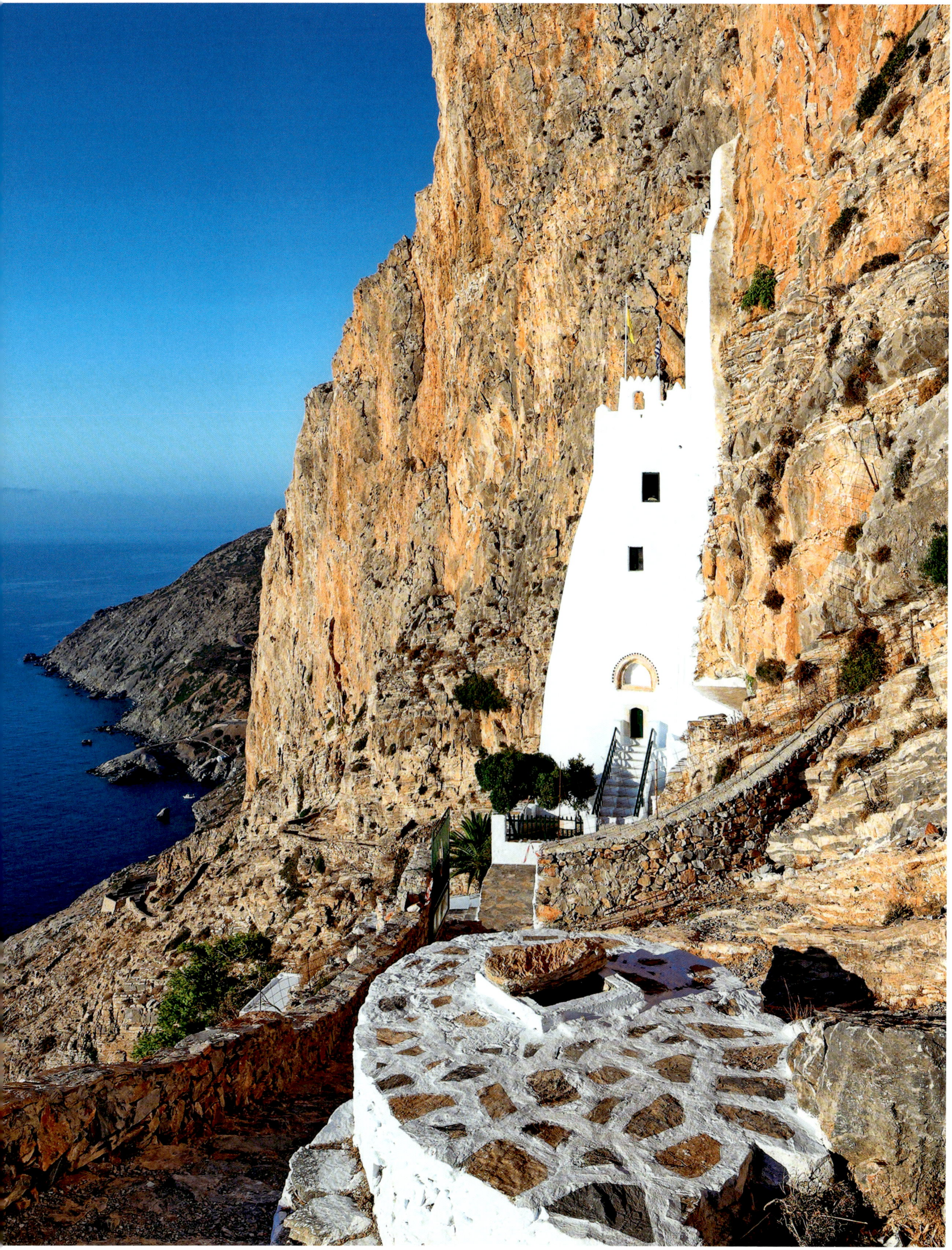

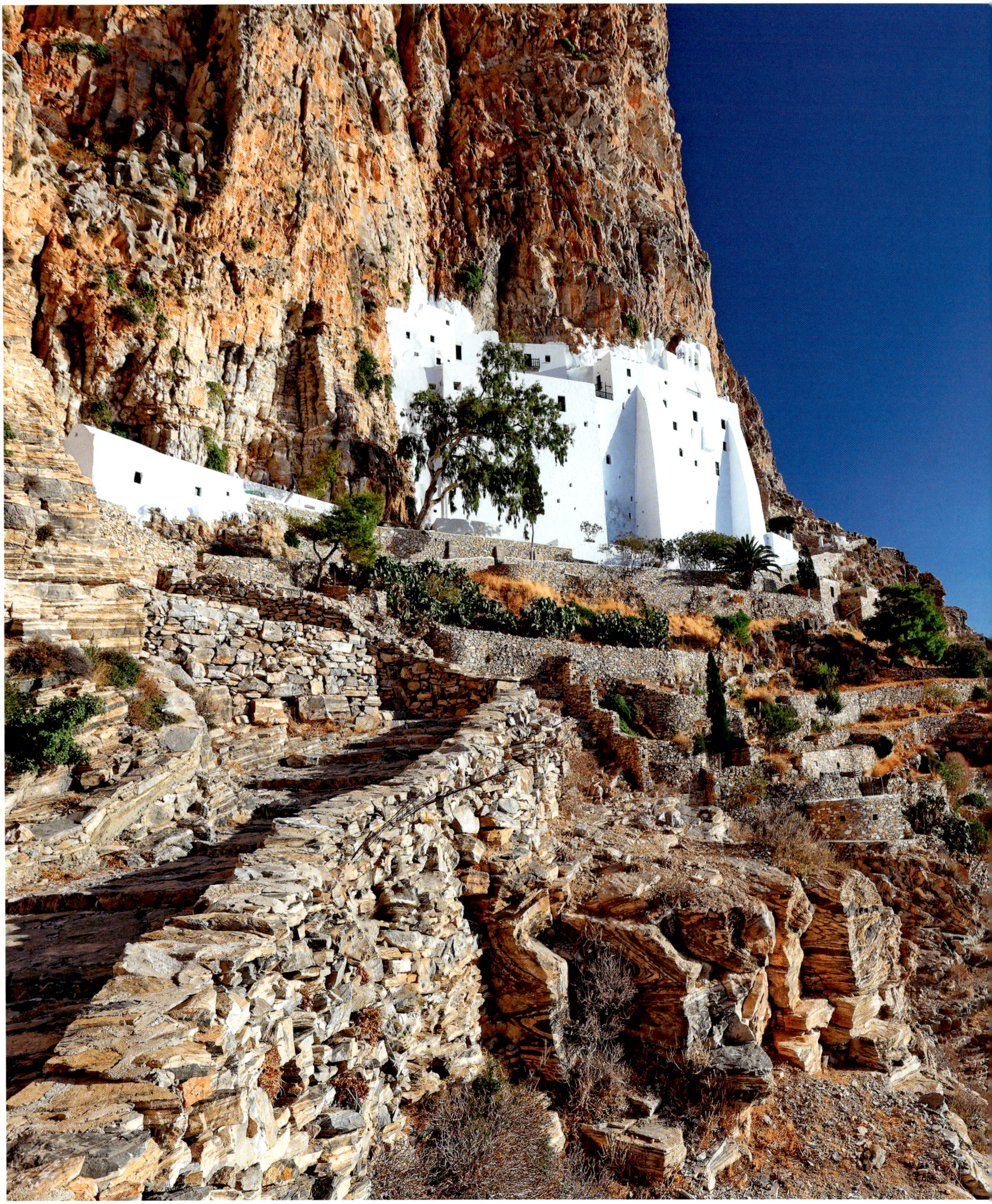

Above Nearly 1,000 feet (300 meters) above the sea, the Monastery of Panagia Hozoviotissa clings to the steep cliffs of Amorgos, and is accessible only via a small staircase winding through the rock.

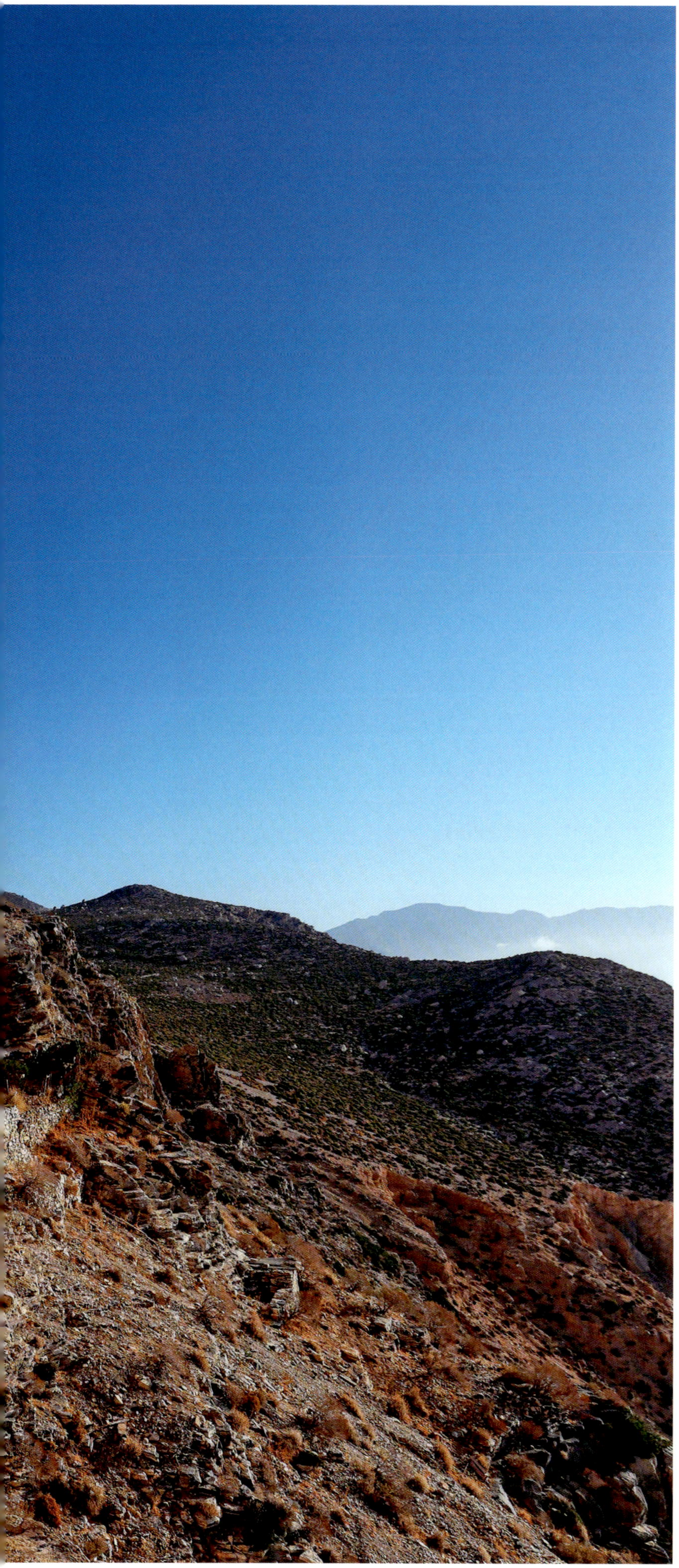

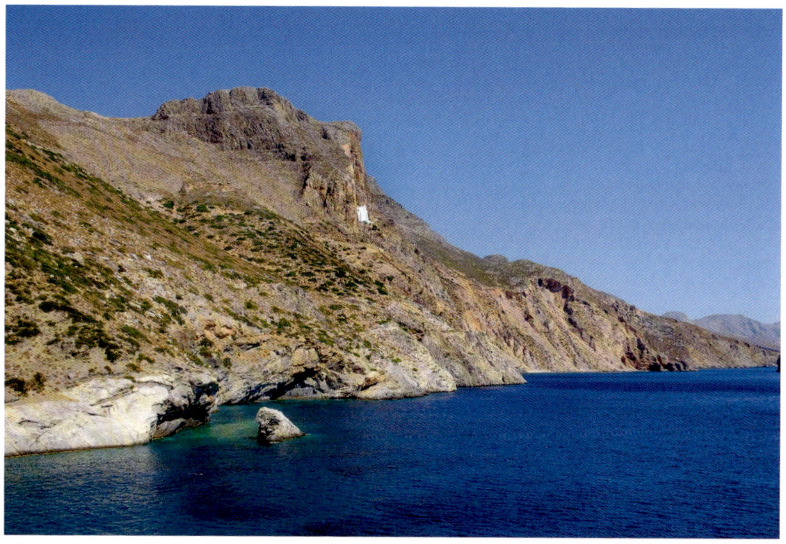

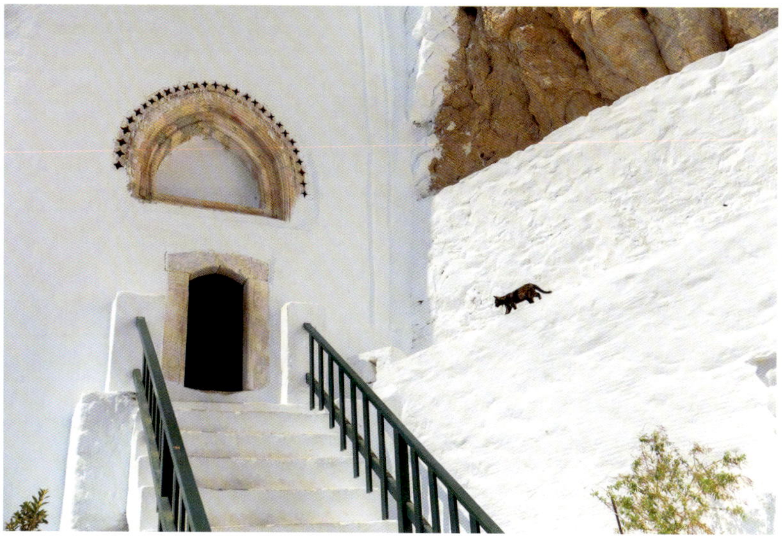

Over decades, monks labored to carve narrow stairways into the rock to connect the monastery's various levels, creating altars and niches in the stone.

Top The monastery's sea view is absolutely breathtaking.
Bottom It's hard to believe, but until its confiscation in 1952, the monastery was one of the wealthiest in Greece.

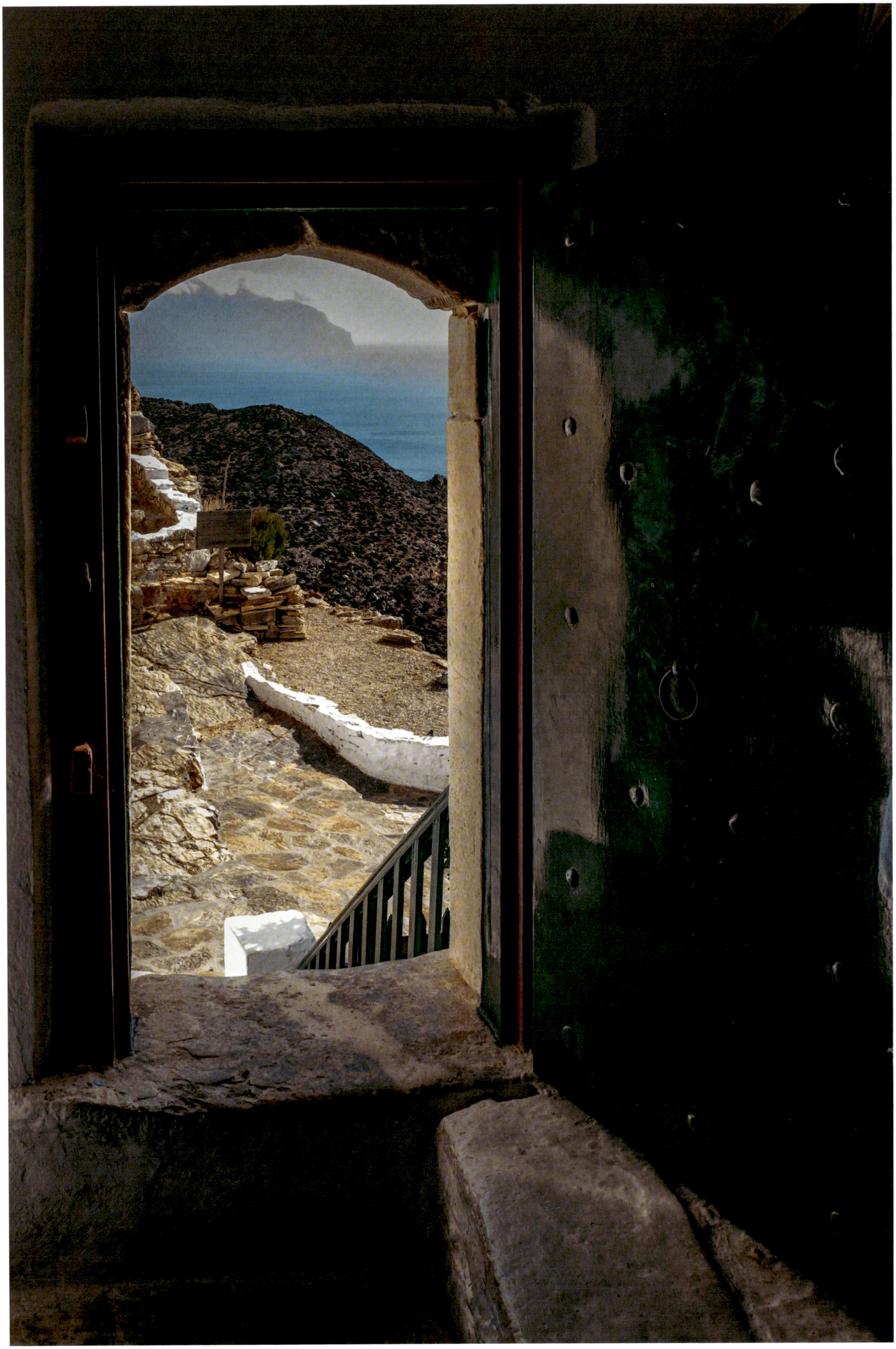

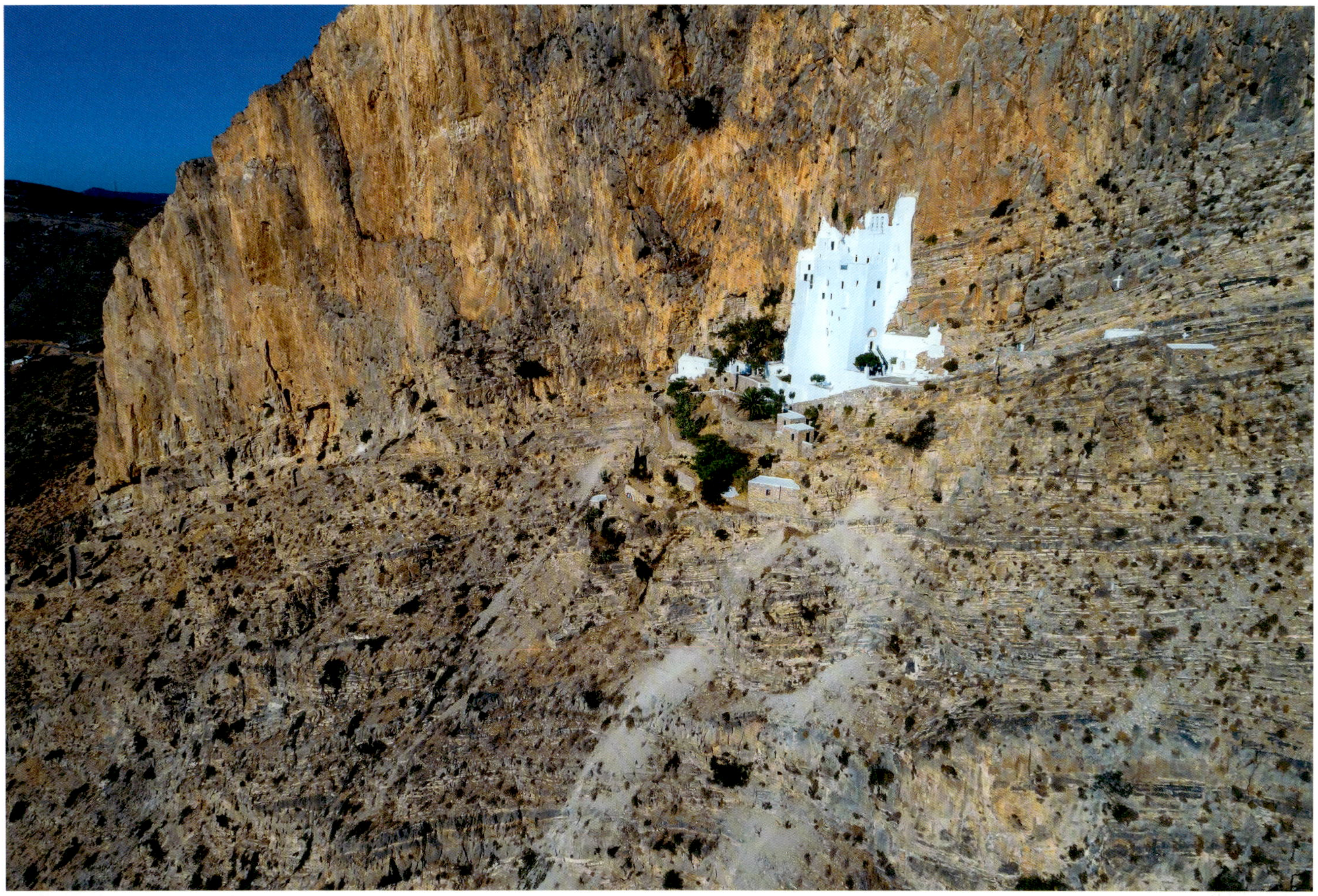

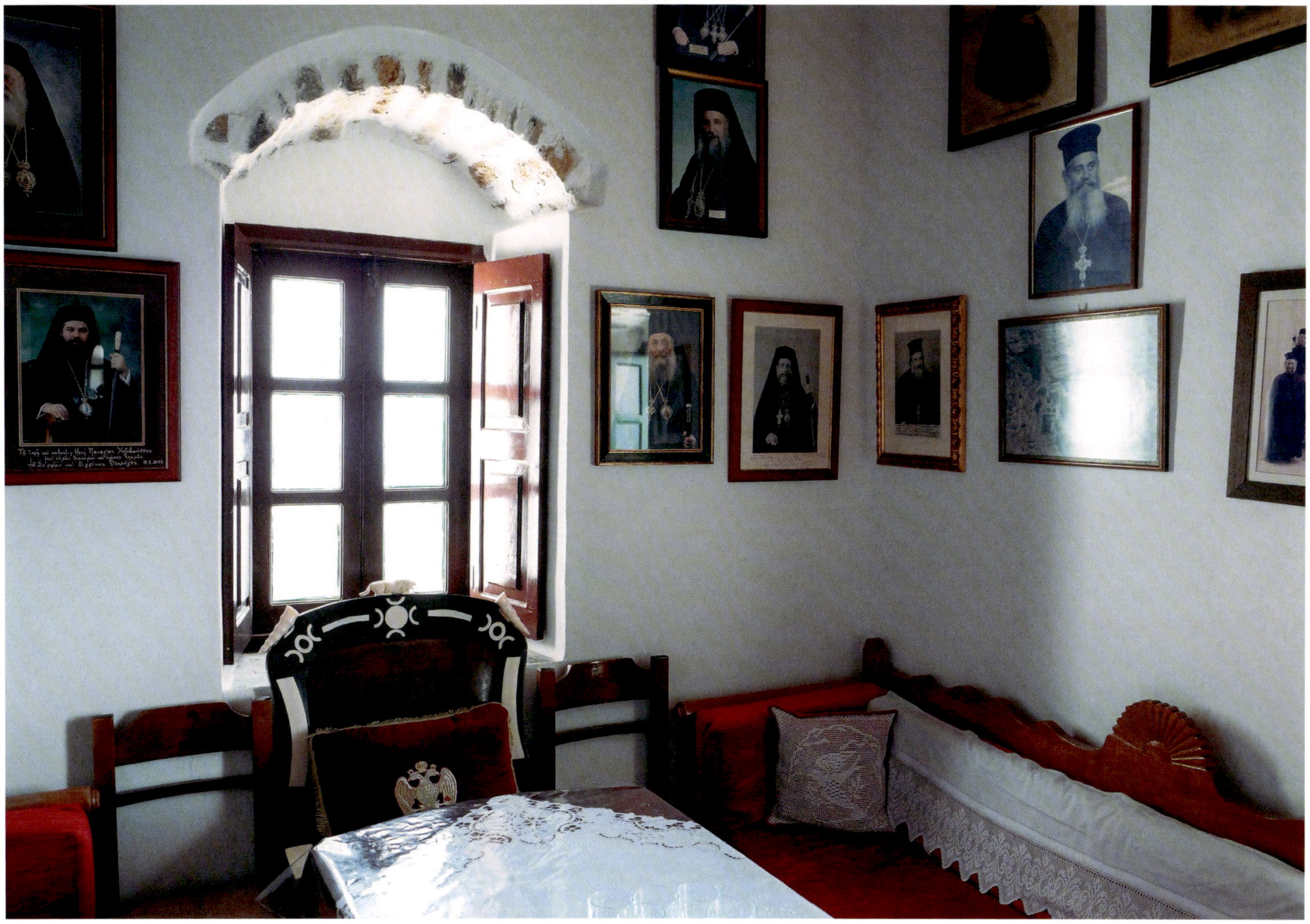

Opposite The small monastery is regarded as one of Greece's most captivating.
Top A few monks live here, preserving the ancient Orthodox tradition.
Bottom For centuries, Orthodox priests have safeguarded the monastery in the cliffs. Their memory is revered in this humble chamber.

Hagia Sophia

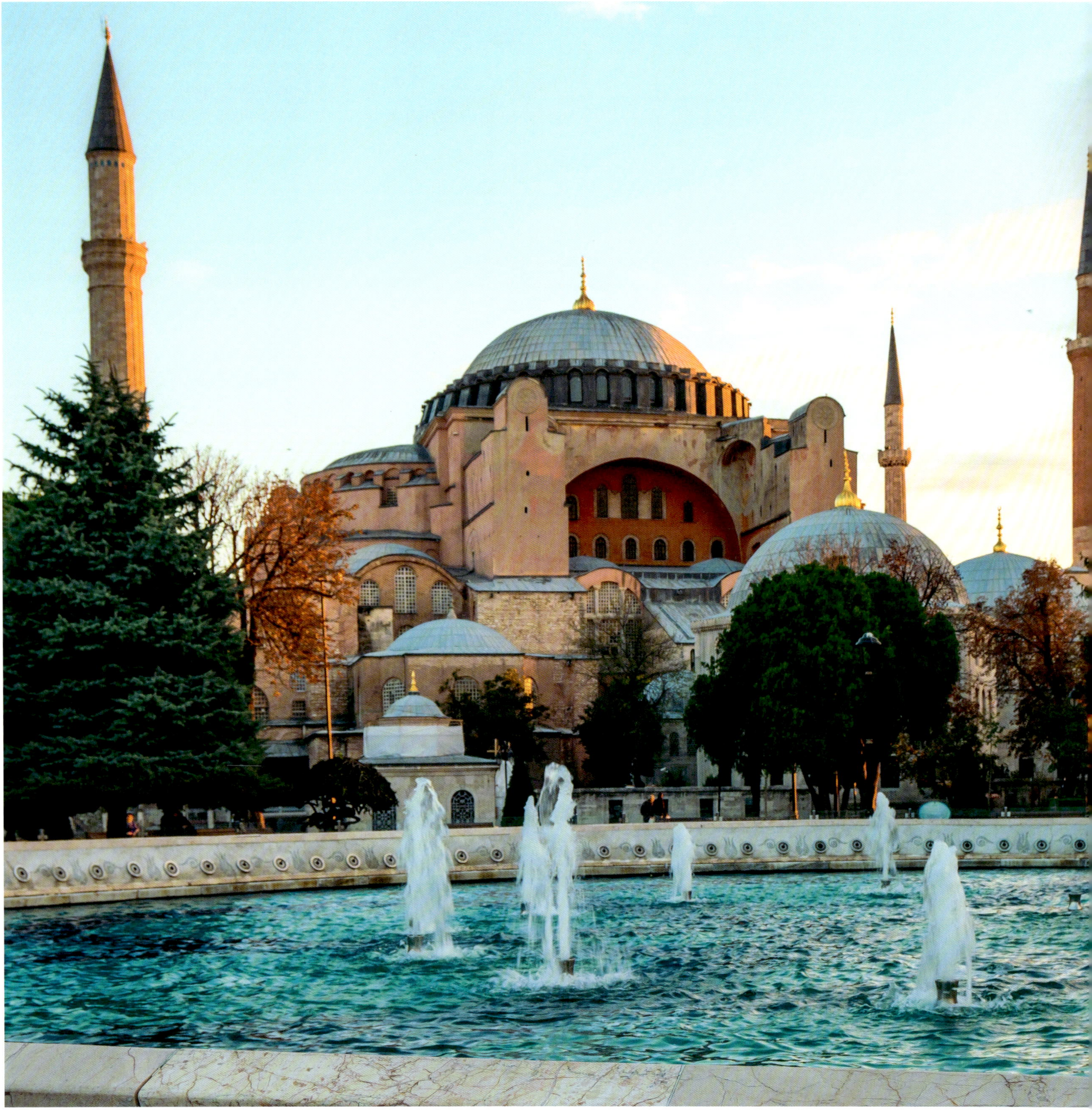

Built: between 532 and 537 CE, Istanbul, Turkey

The spiritual journey of this magnificent temple spans Christianity, Islam, and secularism.

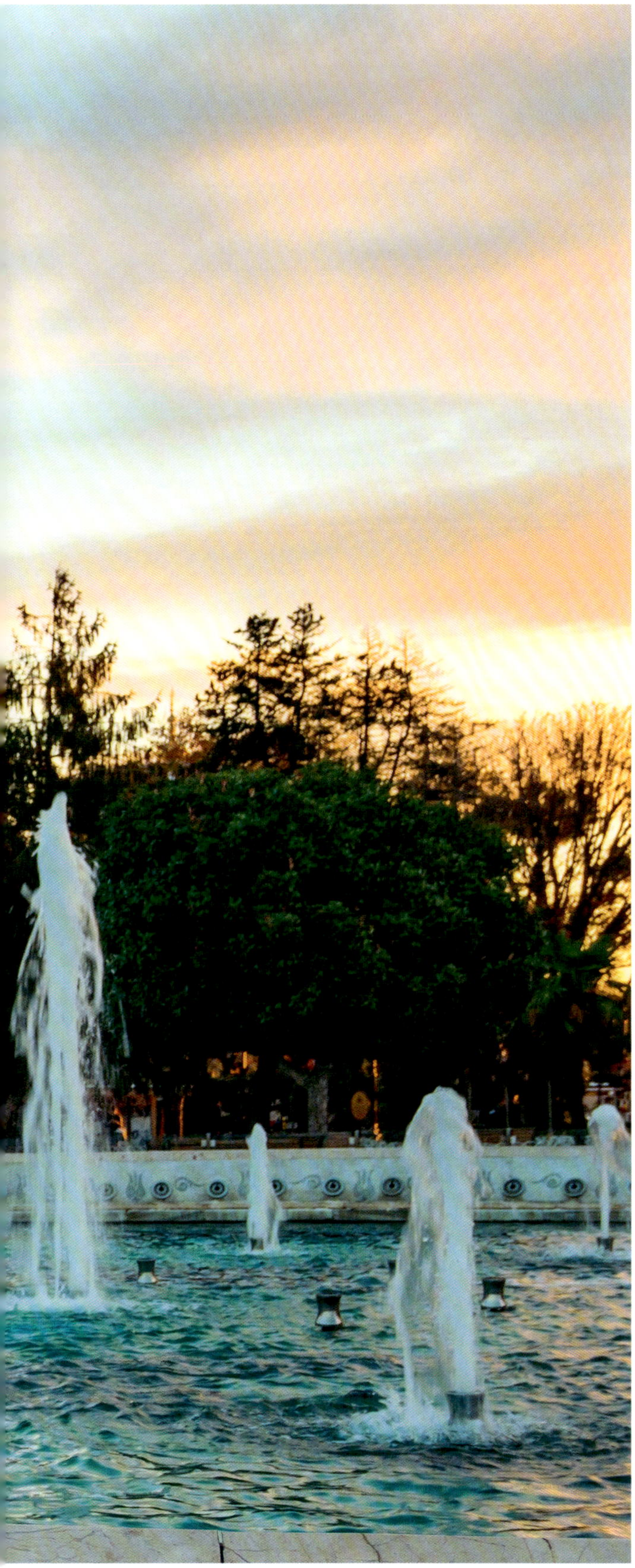

Perhaps its adaptability has secured the Hagia Sophia a special place in the world's heart. For nearly 1,500 years, its monumental dome has defined the skyline of what is now the Turkish city of Istanbul. Its name—"holy wisdom" in Greek—is fitting: Christian, Islamic, and secular thought have all found, at various times, a haven within its walls.

The site was previously home to two earlier churches of the Byzantine Christian tradition before Justinian I, in the 6th century, decided to build the world's largest cathedral in Constantinople. Following the destruction wrought by the Nika riots in 532 CE, he ordered the demolition of the existing structures and commissioned mathematicians Anthemius of Tralles and Isidore of Miletus to design a house of worship that would embody the power and glory of the empire. After just five years of construction, the Hagia Sophia was inaugurated in 537 CE. "Solomon, I have surpassed you!" Emperor Justinian is said to have proclaimed upon its completion. Larger and more ornate than Solomon's Temple referenced in the Old Testament, Justinian's cathedral would stand as the heart of Christianity for nearly a thousand years.

When Constantinople was conquered by the Ottomans in 1453, Sultan Mehmed II transformed the Hagia Sophia into a mosque, removing the bells and altar and plastering over many mosaics and frescoes. A pulpit and a *mihrab*, a prayer niche facing Mecca, were integrated into the building to adapt it for Islamic worship. While the structure of the Hagia Sophia remained largely intact, the Ottomans also added four minarets, whose presence still shapes Istanbul's skyline today.

After the fall of the Ottoman Empire and the establishment of the modern Republic of Turkey in 1923, Turkey's first president, Mustafa Kemal Atatürk, declared that the Hagia Sophia should become a symbol of the secular state. In 1935, the building reopened as a museum, allowing the world to admire layers of religious history all in one place. The architecture of the Hagia Sophia influenced religious construction for centuries—many Byzantine and Islamic structures, including the famous Sultan Ahmed Mosque, borrowed key stylistic elements, with the most iconic being the temple's elegant, sky-augmenting dome. Since 2020, the Hagia Sophia has returned to Islam, and once again serves as a mosque. It is a place of living faith, yet remains open to visitors who wish to stand at the crossroads of history and two major religions.

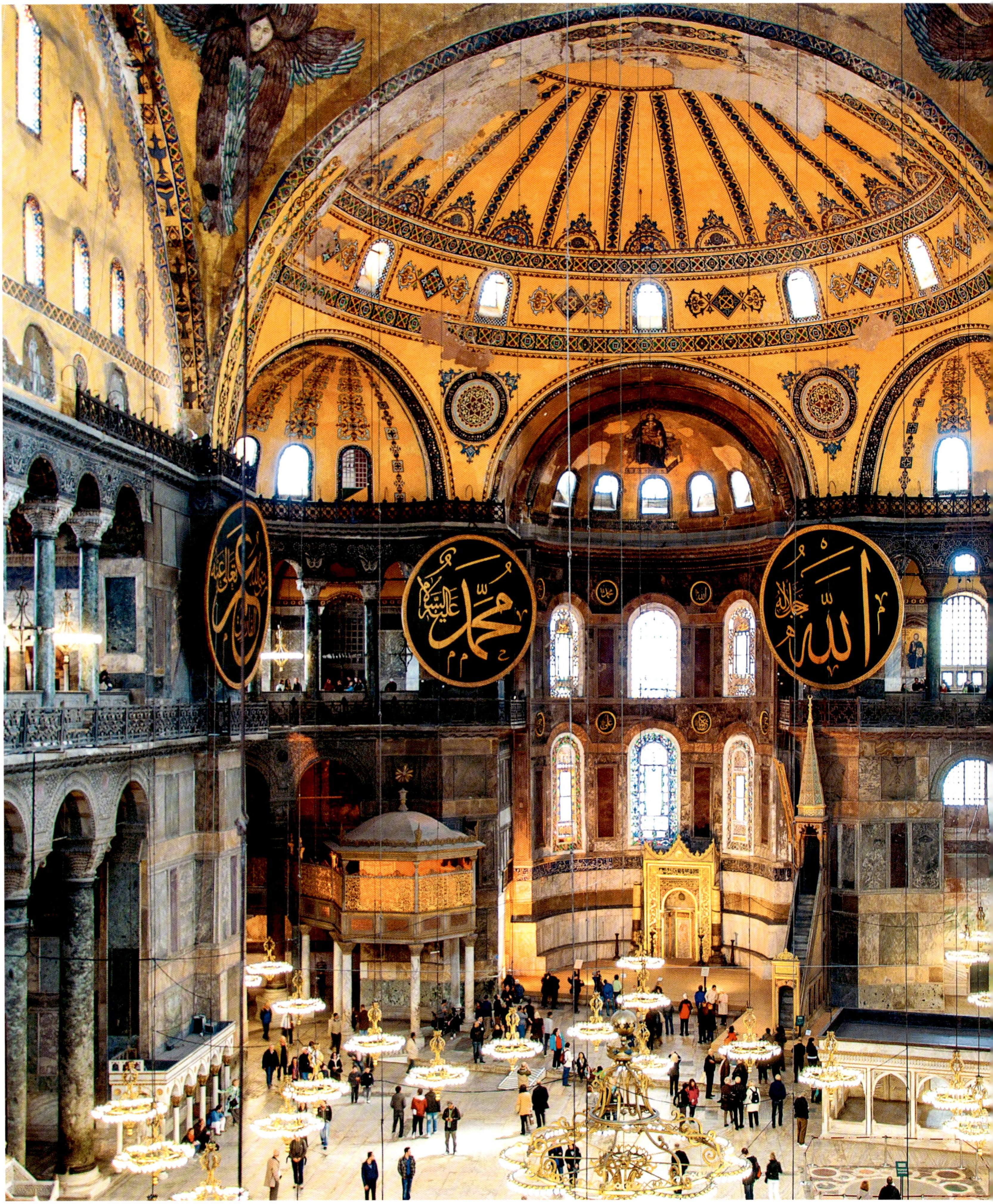

Above Massive columns of various types of marble support the Hagia Sophia. Its mosaics and Islamic calligraphy beautifully blend Byzantine and Ottoman history.

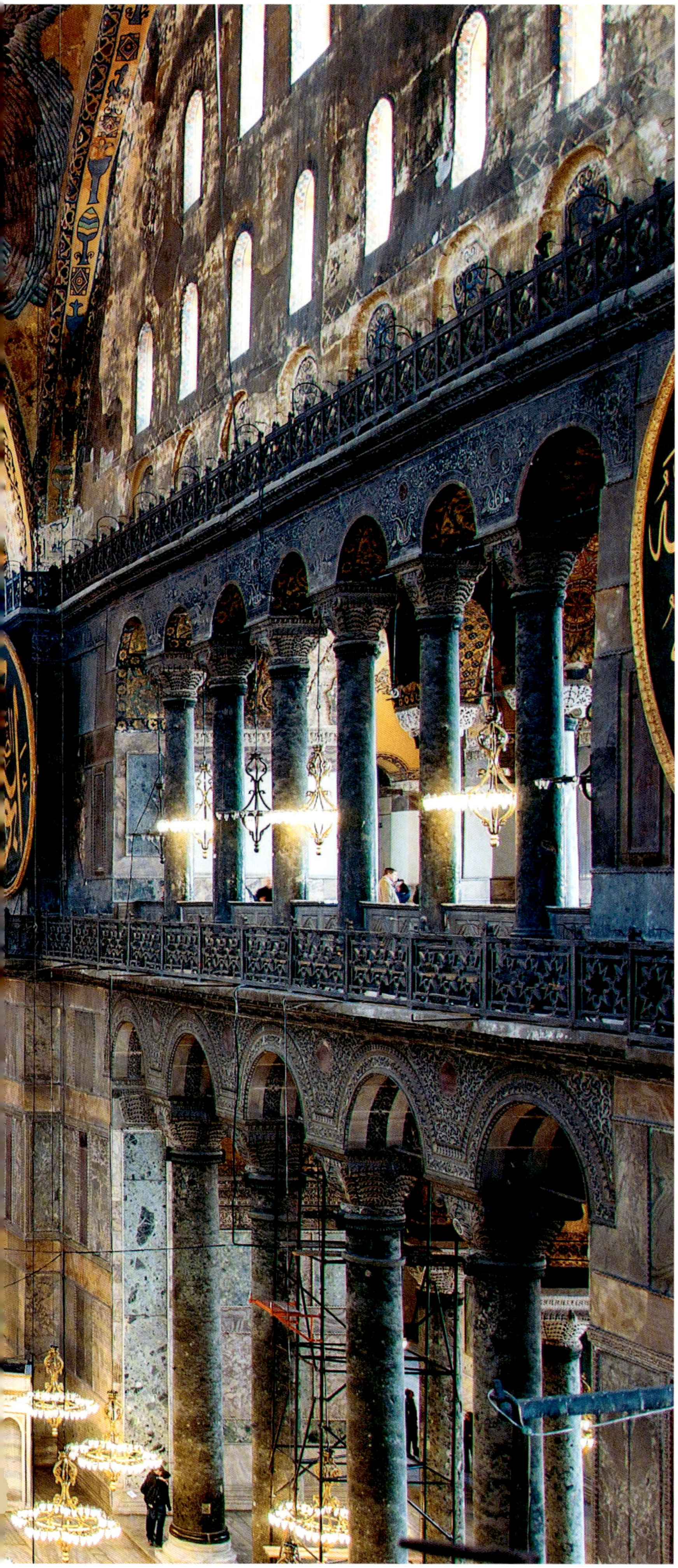

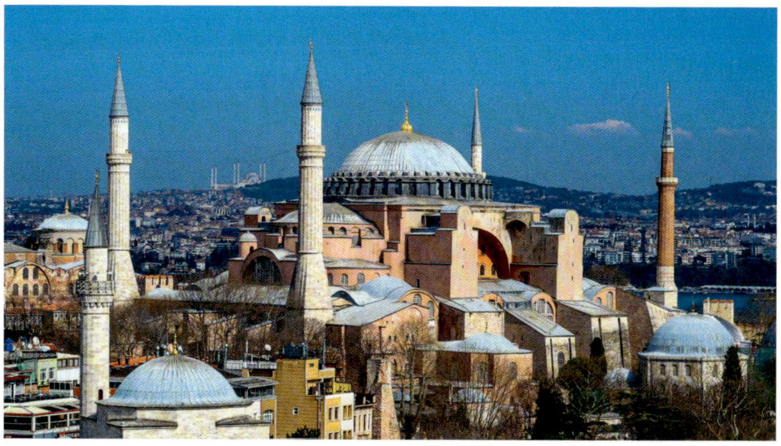

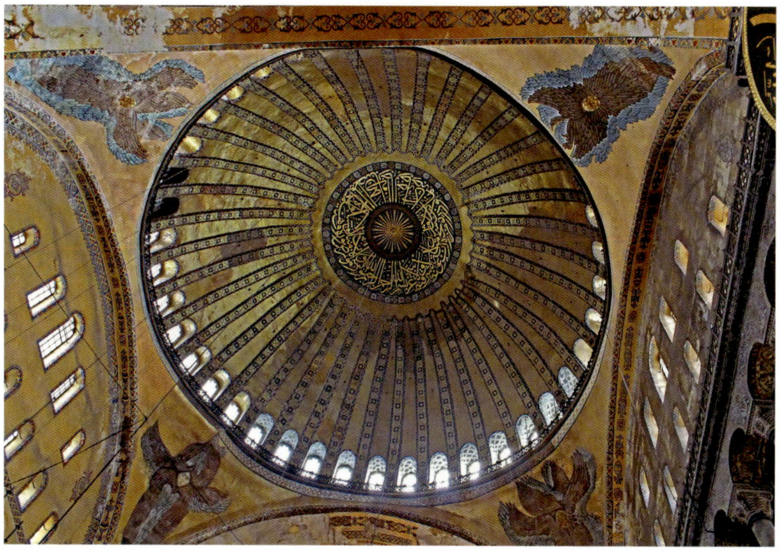

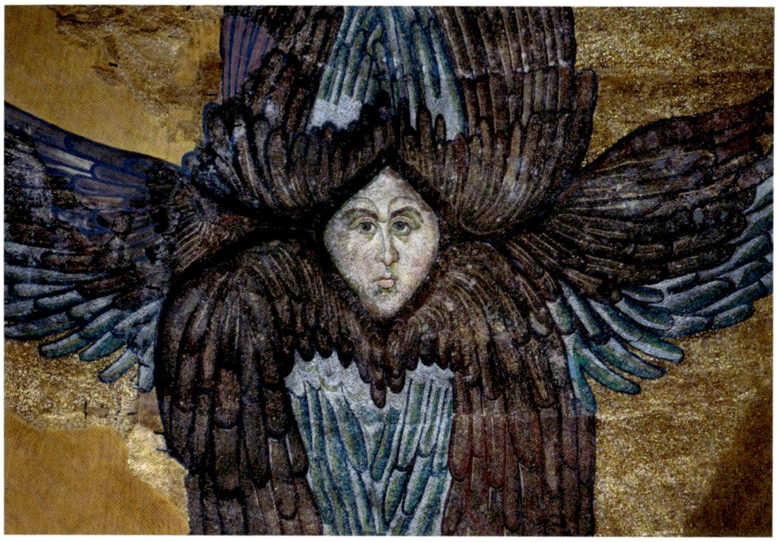

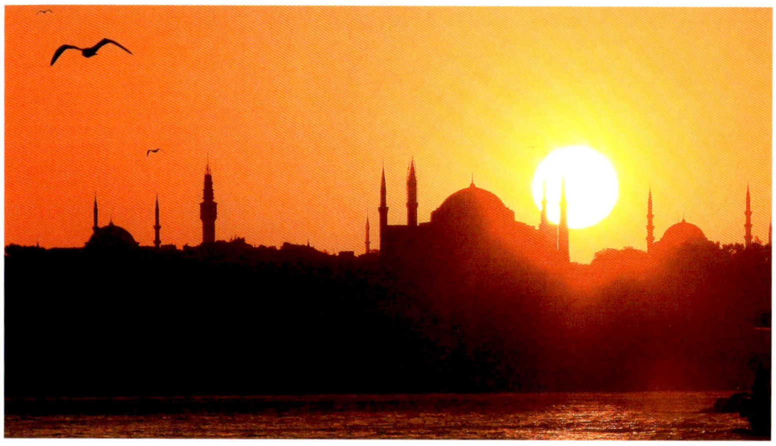

Top In 2020, the Hagia Sophia shed its secular identity and once again became a mosque.
Upper middle The golden dome reaches a height of 180 feet (55 meters).
Lower middle The Seraphim mosaic is a Byzantine masterpiece.
Bottom The Ottoman minarets were added in the 15th century.

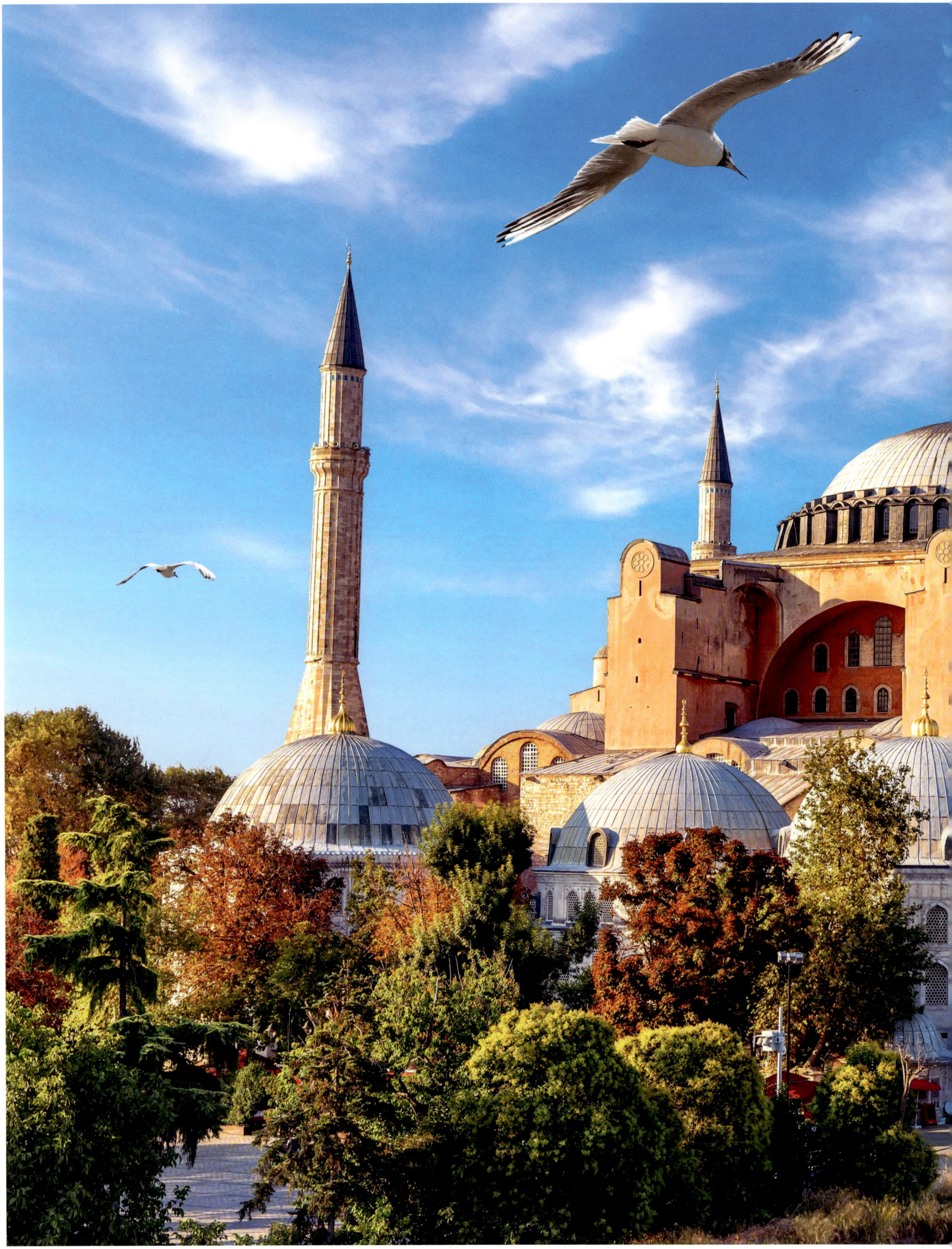

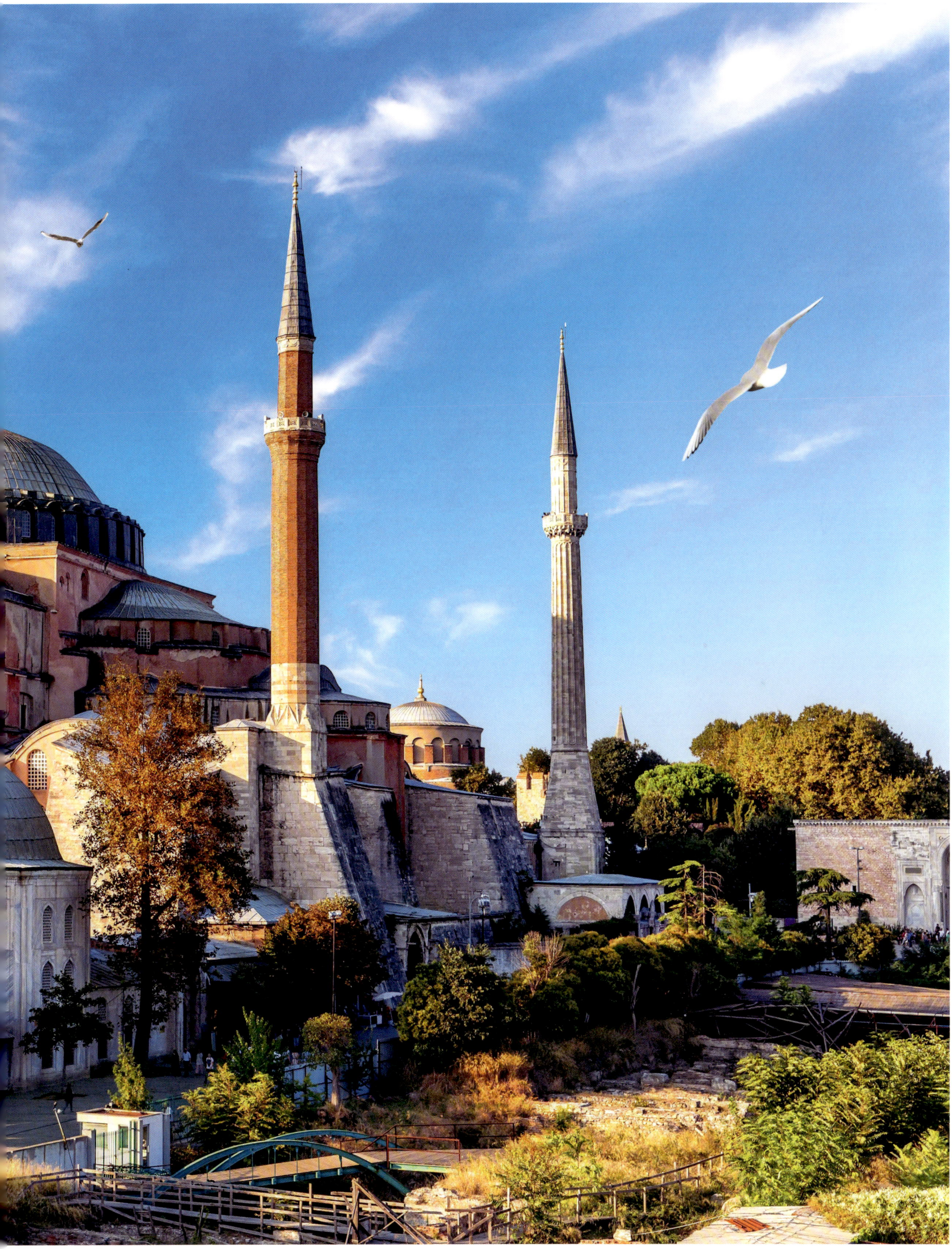

Sagrada Família

Built: between 1882 CE and today, Barcelona, Spain

The main patron of this extraordinary cathedral is, fortunately, in no hurry.

Like a dream vividly captured in stone, the Basílica de la Sagrada Família rises from the heart of Barcelona. Alongside depictions of biblical events, motifs of twisting vines, stars, and flowers are carved into its majestic towers and facades.

And just like the saga of humanity that began long ago, the story of this church continues to unfold: to this day, it remains unfinished. After construction began in 1882, Catalonian architect Antoni Gaudí took over the project just a year later, and it became his life's work. He envisioned a temple to unite architecture, nature, and faith in perfect harmony. He knew well that he would not live to see the Sagrada Família completed. "My client is not in a hurry," he once remarked, referring to the infinite patience of the divine. When Gaudí tragically died in 1926, only a small portion of the basilica had been completed.

His design for the exteriors of the Sagrada Família is imbued with overt symbolism. The three main facades represent the life, suffering, and eternal glory of Jesus. *The Façana del Naixement,* the nativity facade celebrating Christ's birth, is the only one Gaudí saw completed. In stark contrast, with its harsh, angular figures, the *Façana de la Passió* depicts Christ's suffering, sacrifice on the cross, and resurrection. Once finished, the *Façana de la Glòria,* which will encircle the main entrance, will portray Heaven and Hell, the Last Judgment, and the Ascension of Christ, offering a vision of eternal life.

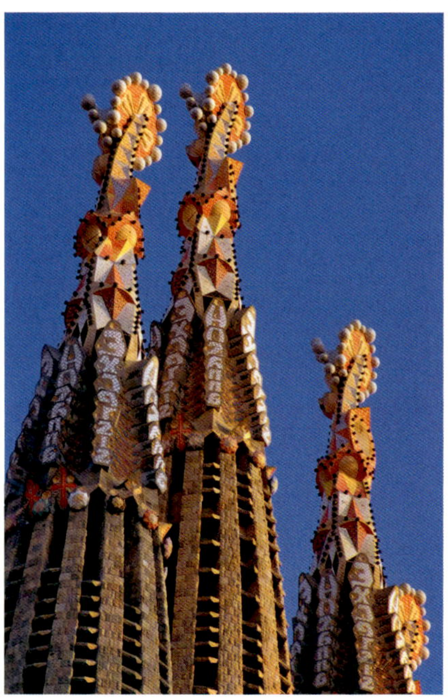

During the Spanish Civil War, Gaudí's workshop was set ablaze, destroying many of his original plans and models. Yet, like the city itself, the basilica rose from the ashes. Architects and craftsmen have spent decades reconstructing Gaudí's vision from the surviving fragments, and even today, more than a century after the construction began, they continue working to bring his vision to life—a task funded by private donations and ticket sales from millions of visitors every year.

Inside the basilica, worshippers and visitors wander awestruck through the sanctified halls, where columns rise like the strong trees of a protective forest. Sunlight streams through the colorful stained glass windows, flooding the church's interior with a thousand colors. The inspiration that guided Antoni Gaudí must have been divine, one might conclude. In 2026, precisely 100 years after the architect's death, the Sagrada Família is set to be completed, save for a few finishing touches. The planned celebrations will be crowned by a 55-foot-tall (17-meter-tall) cross atop the central tower, reflecting the sun by day and illuminating the city by night—a fulfillment of Gaudí's illumined vision.

Left Once completed, the Sagrada Família will feature 18 towers.
Opposite Gothic elements meet Catalan modernism.

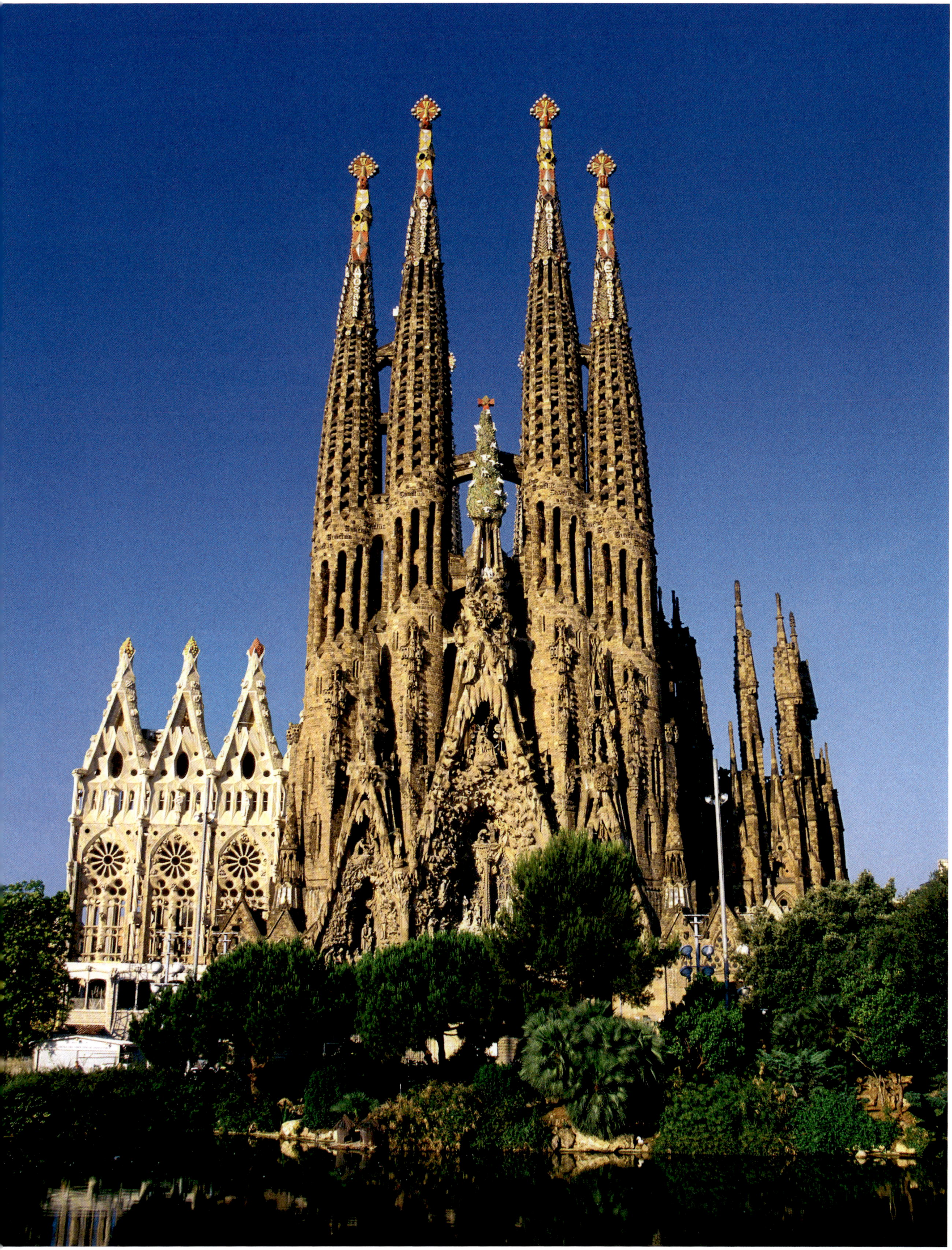

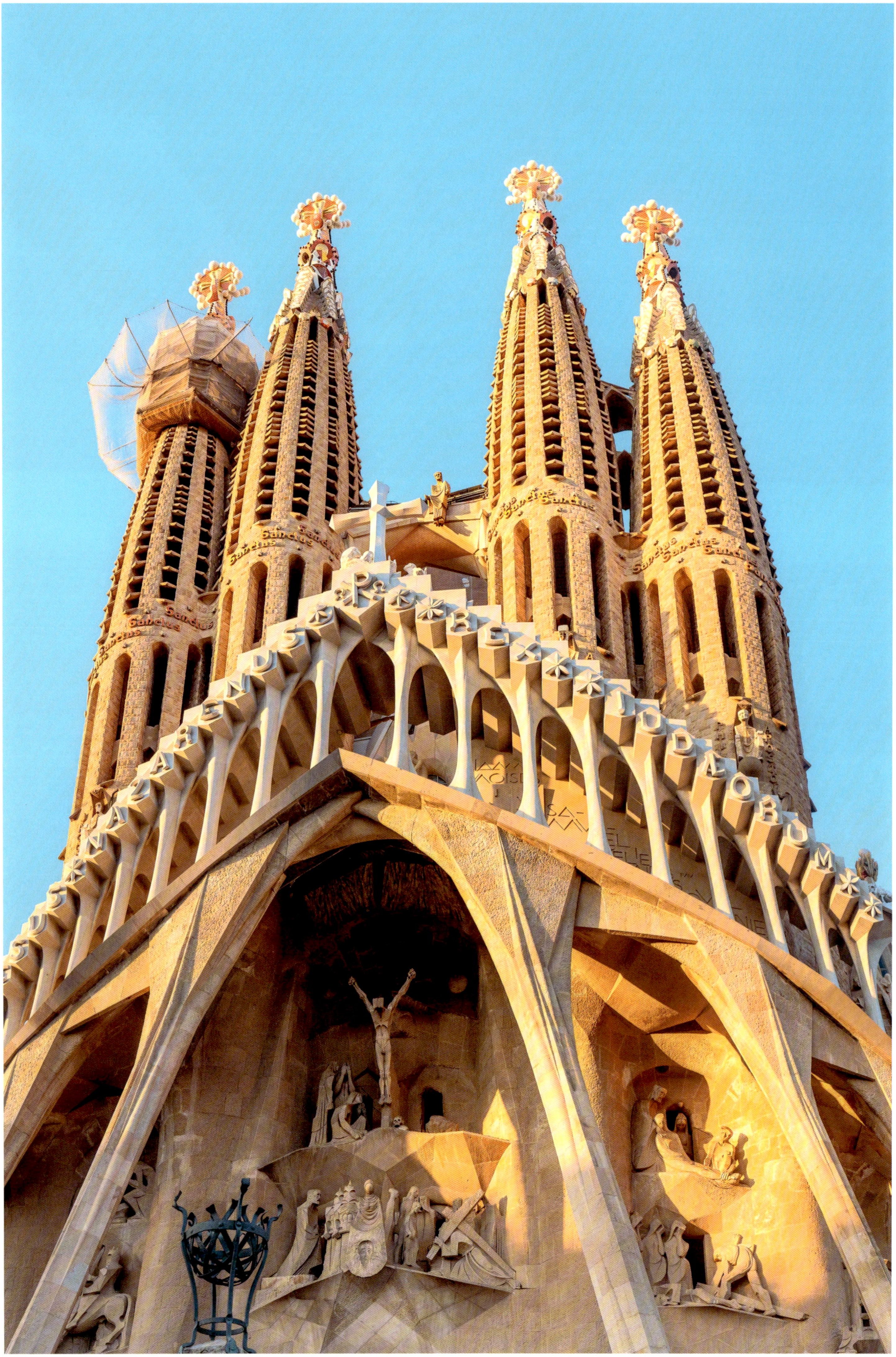

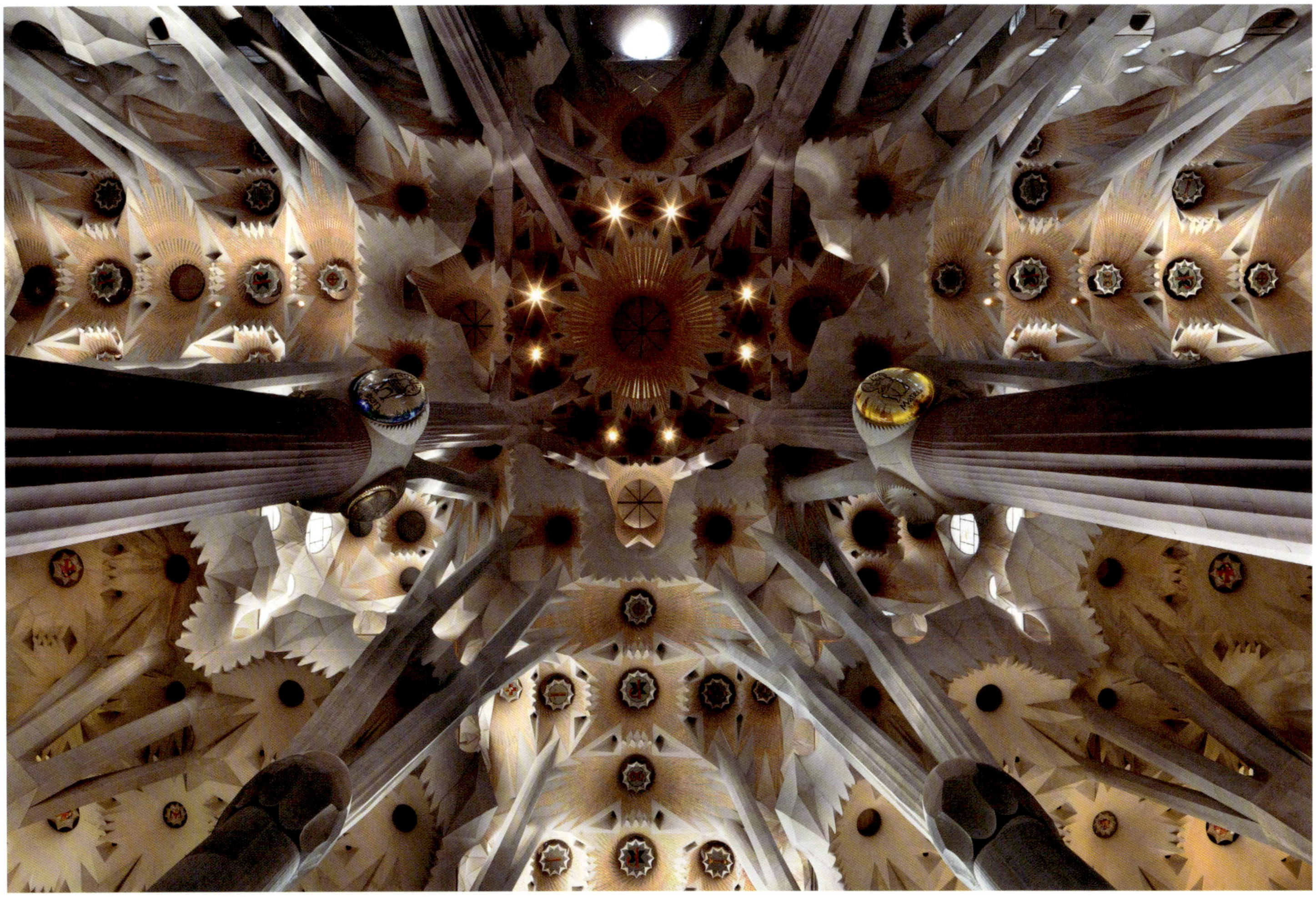

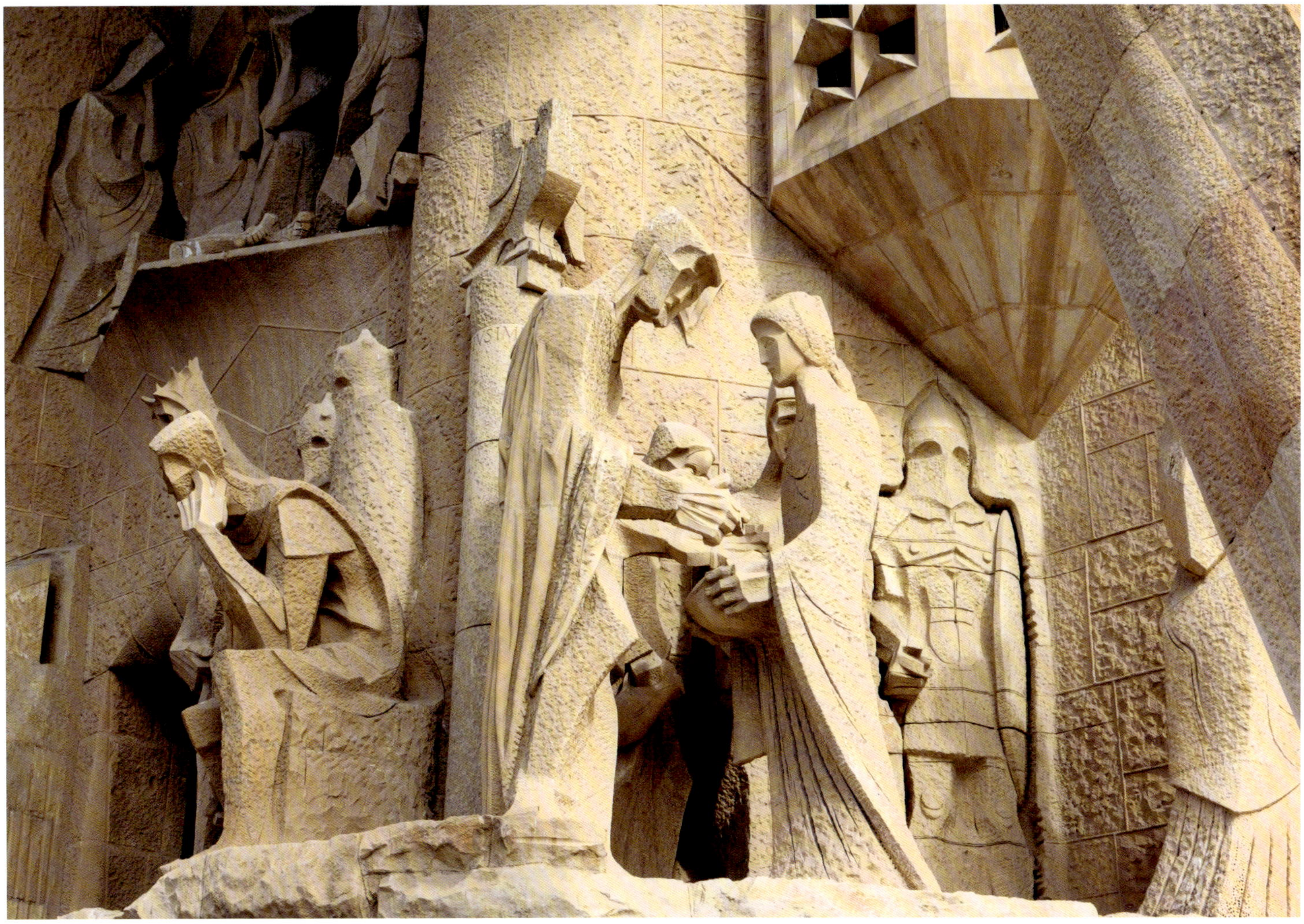

Opposite The striking organic forms that comprise the structure are inspired by nature.
Top The columns inside resemble tree trunks that branch out as they rise.
Bottom The starkly designed Passion Facade is oriented toward the west, allowing the light of the setting sun to accentuate its dramatic depictions.

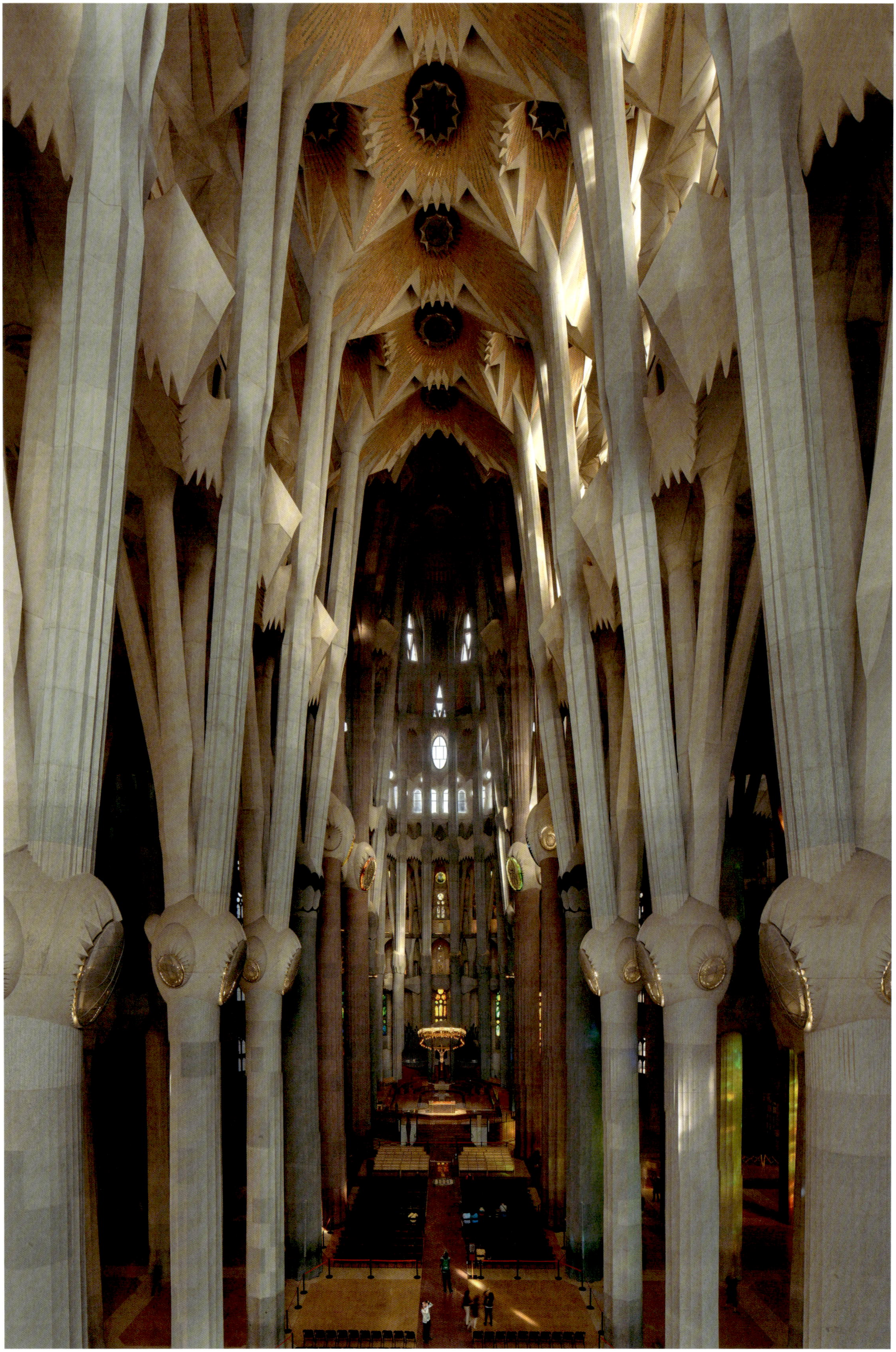

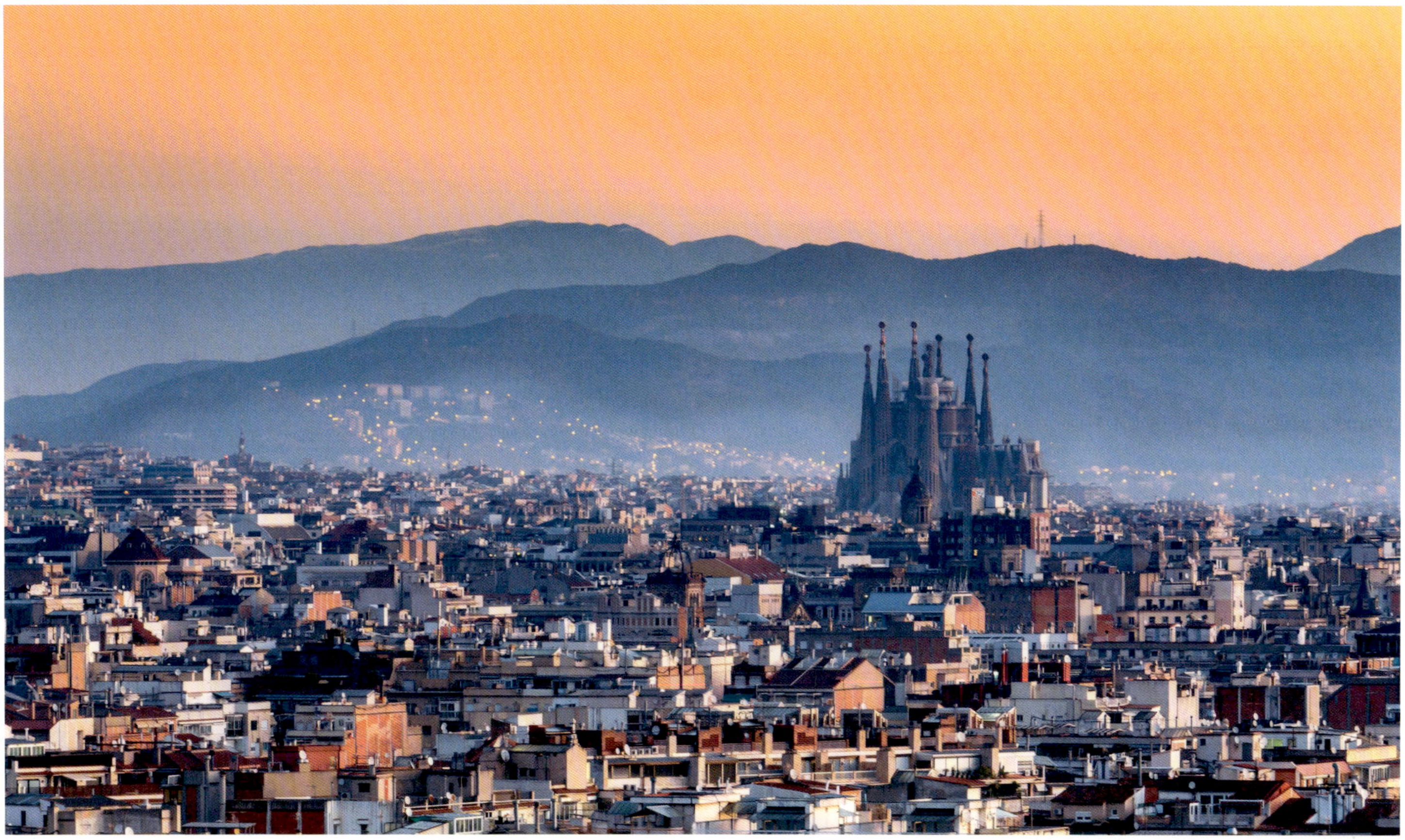

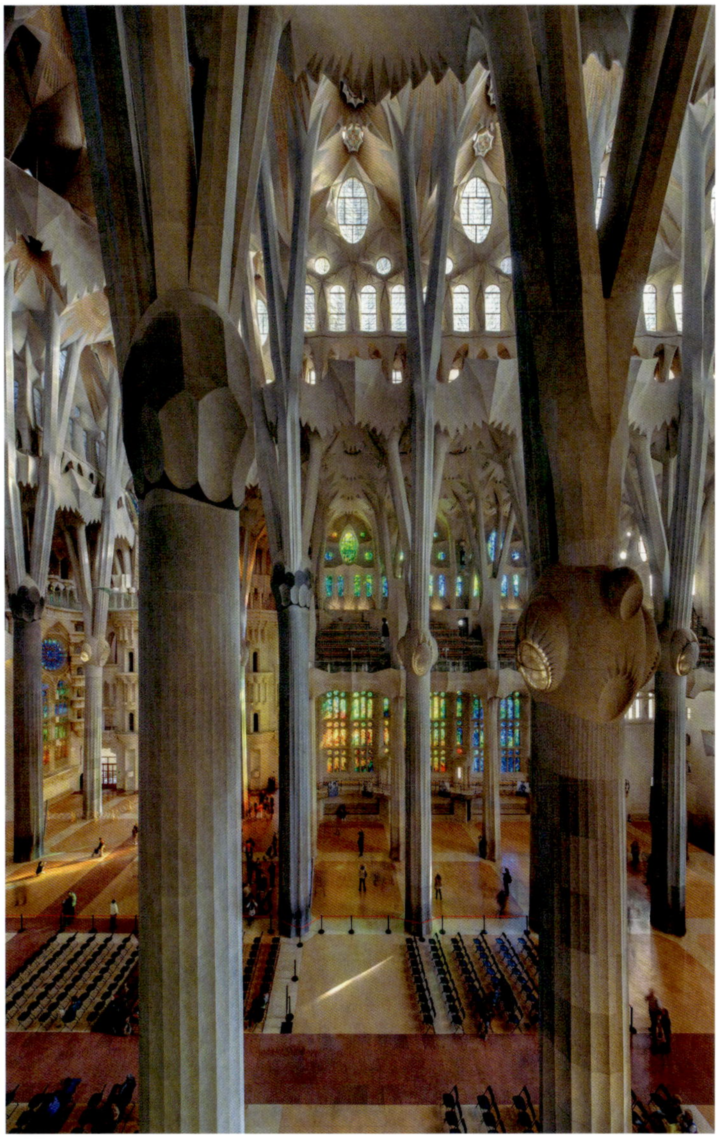

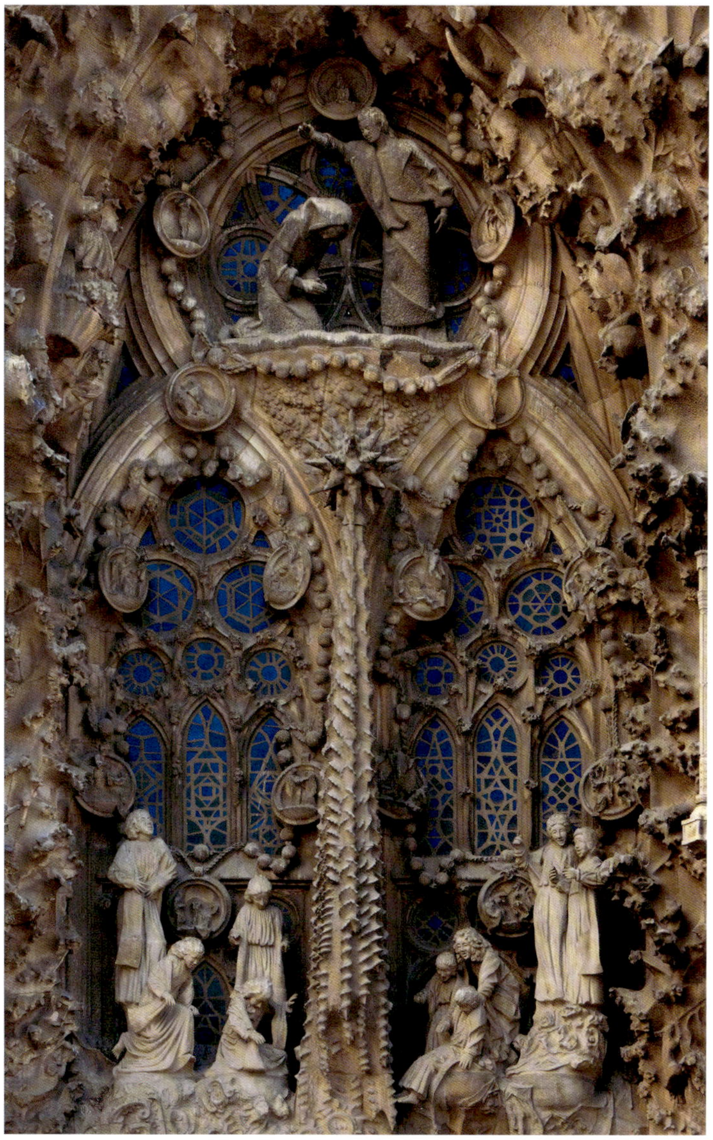

Opposite In the nave, the natural character of the church becomes particularly evident.
Top The Sagrada Família towers prominently over the Catalan capital.
Bottom left The stained glass windows fill the church with colorful plays of light.
Bottom right The Nativity Facade fully embodies Gaudí's vision.

Milan Cathedral

Looking Out Over All

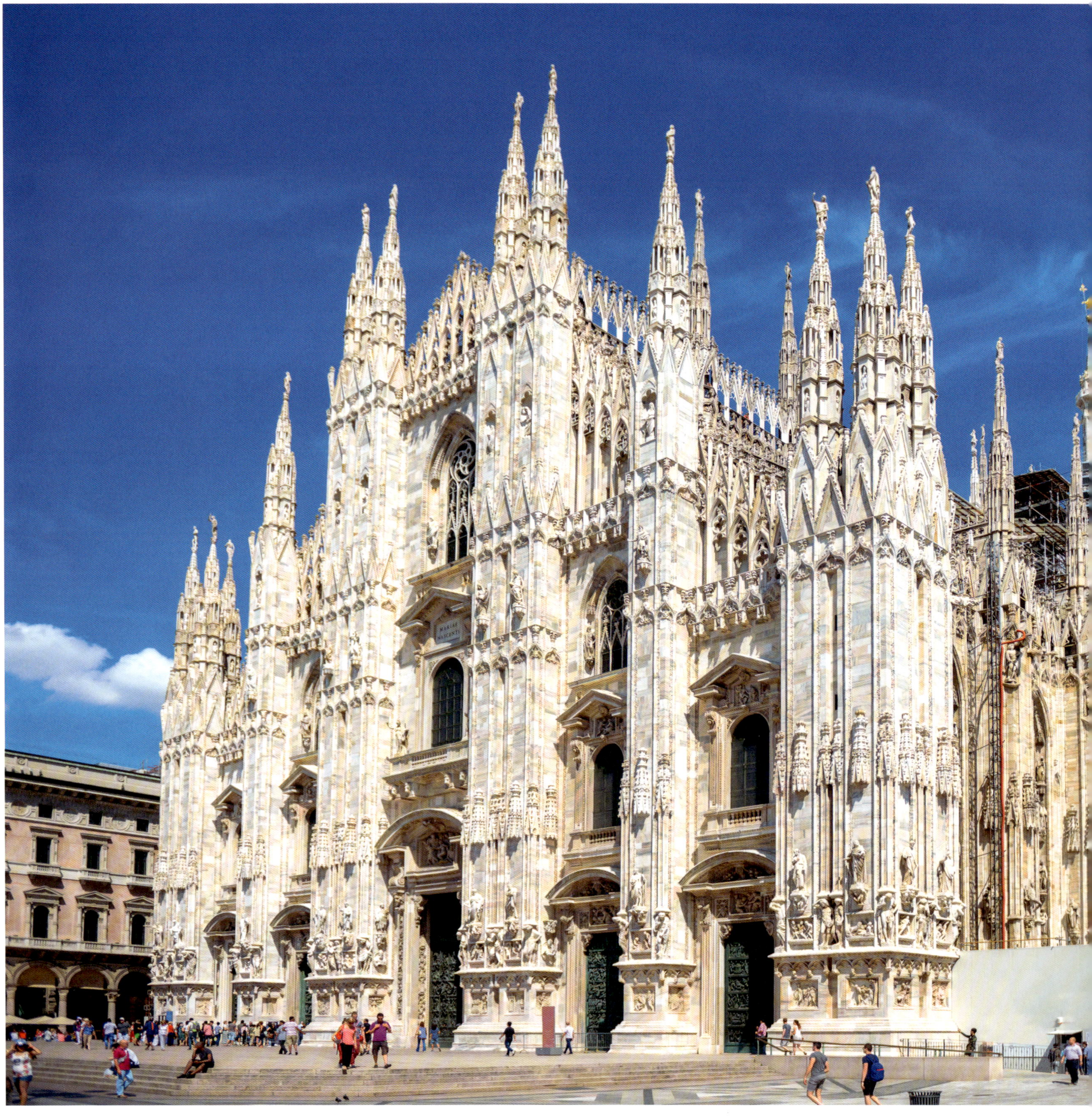

Built: 1386 – 1965 CE,
Milan, Italy

For a staggering 600 years, Catholic Milan toiled to construct a resplendent house of worship in honor of the city's patron saint.

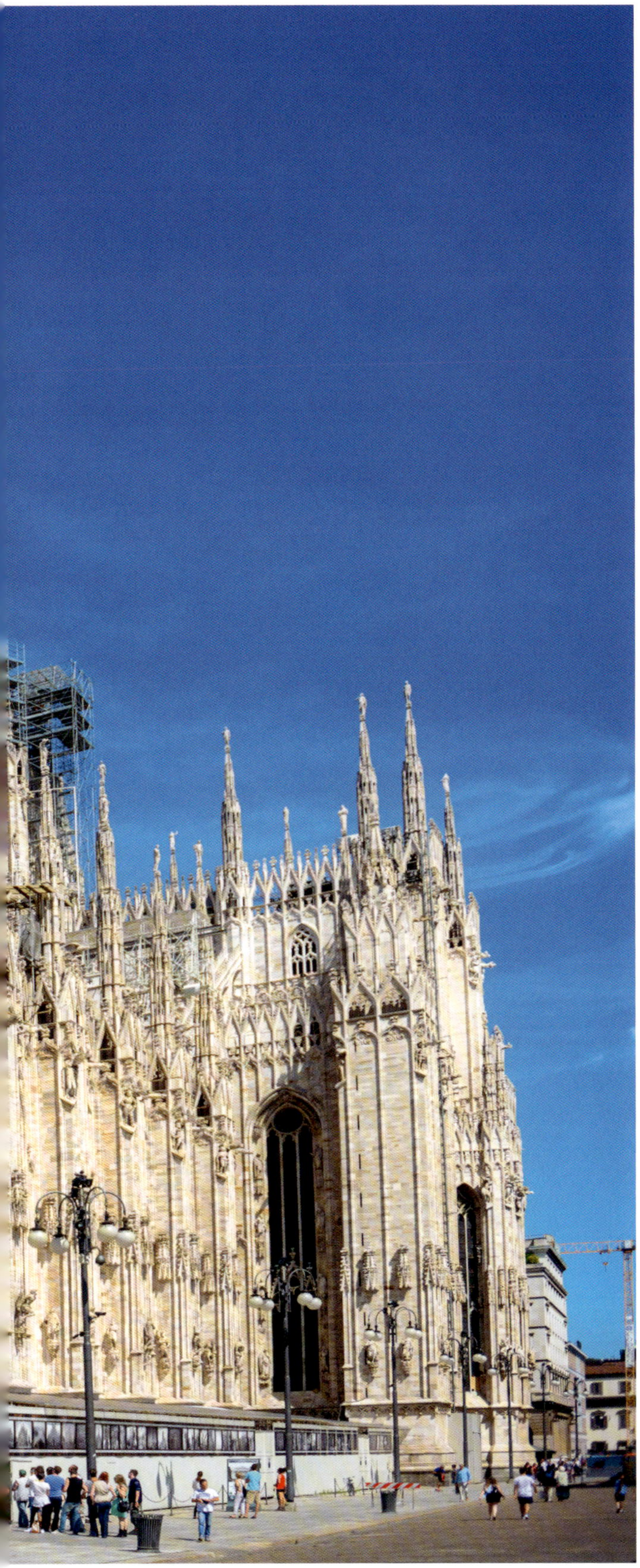

In 1386, Gian Galeazzo Visconti, Duke of Milan, laid the foundation stone for one of the most ambitious architectural undertakings of the late Middle Ages: the Duomo di Milano, or Milan Cathedral, dedicated to the birth of the Virgin Mary, the city's protector. Legend has it that the cathedral was built as an act of gratitude to the Milanese who endured the rule of Gian Galeazzo's powerful uncle, Bernabò Visconti. Another tale tells of a haunting dream in which Gian Galeazzo was visited by the Devil, prompting him to pledge the construction of a magnificent church as an act of atonement.

The project dwarfed all previous architectural efforts of its time. The cathedral was to serve not only as a spiritual center but as a symbol of Milan's prestige and the glory of its rulers. The entire city was called to contribute: the duke arranged for a marble quarry in Candoglia to supply the stone, wealthy citizens provided financial support, and common folk transported materials to the building site.

The construction of the cathedral was marked by immense technical and design challenges. From the outset, the church's scale—a five-aisled interior with a footprint of nearly 126,000 square feet (11,700 square meters)—was extraordinary. Its intricate structure demanded advanced engineering, drawing architects and craftsmen from across Europe. The initial design envisioned a cathedral in the form of a Latin cross, and its choir area, built in the Gothic style, is among the oldest surviving parts of the structure. The two sacristies and the elaborately designed windows also date back to this early phase. These windows, especially those in the apse, rank among the most stunning examples of Gothic stained glass in Italy.

The construction would end up spanning six centuries. In the 15th century, Renaissance luminaries Leonardo da Vinci and Donato Bramante submitted models for the cathedral's cupola design. In the early 19th century, Napoleon Bonaparte ordered the completion of the cathedral's facade to coincide with his coronation as King of Italy. Five generations later, on Italy's national holiday Epifania in 1965, the last portal of the cathedral was inaugurated, marking the official completion of the building.

From atop the cathedral today, the statue of the Virgin Mary gazes benevolently upon her city. Affectionately called the Madonnina by the people of Milan, the statue watches over all earthly and spiritual matters below. And while tradition once forbade any building from rising higher than the statue, modern skyscrapers now surpass it—though each carries a small replica of the Madonnina to preserve the city's symbolic heritage.

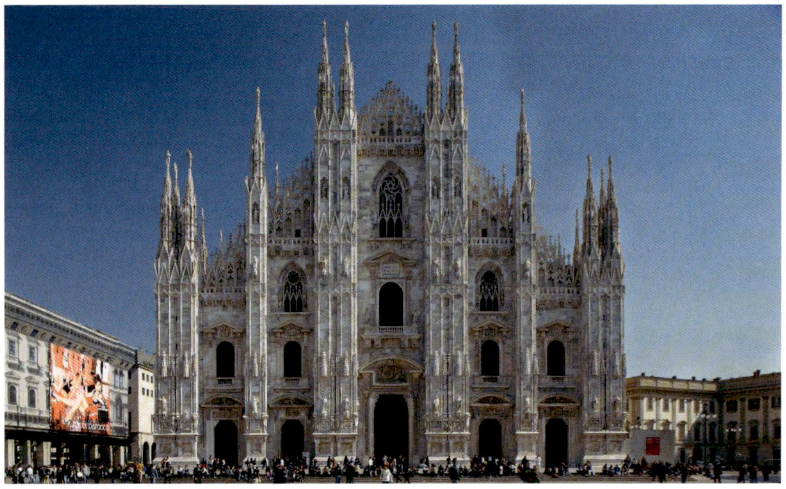

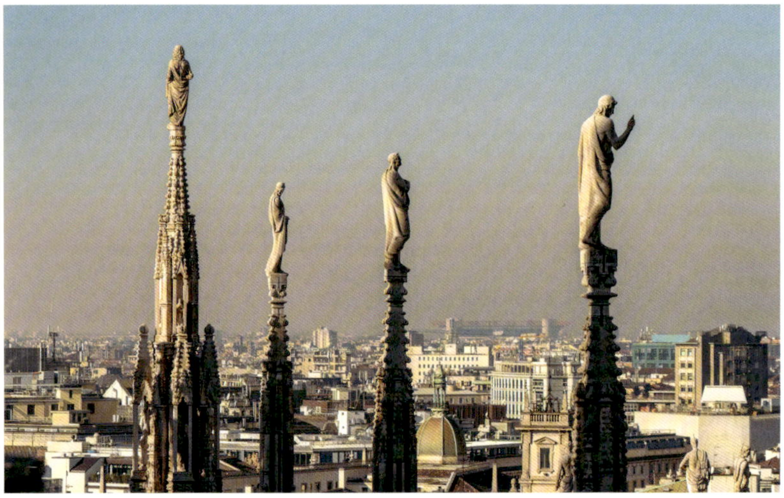

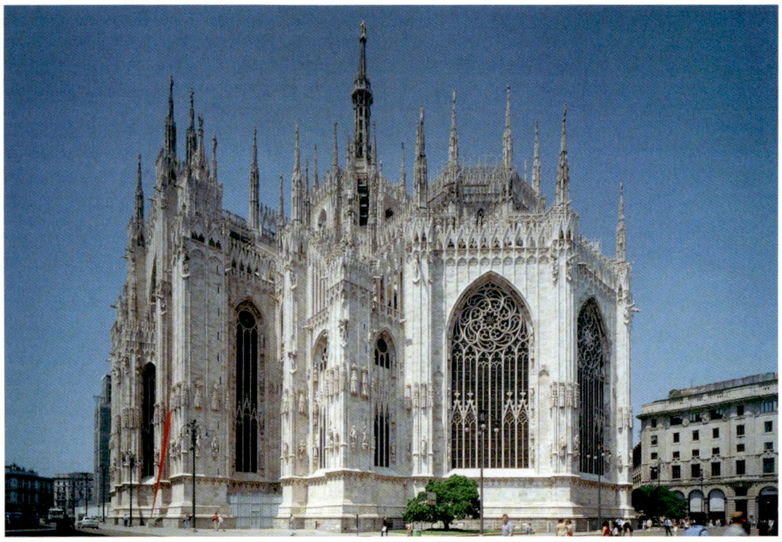

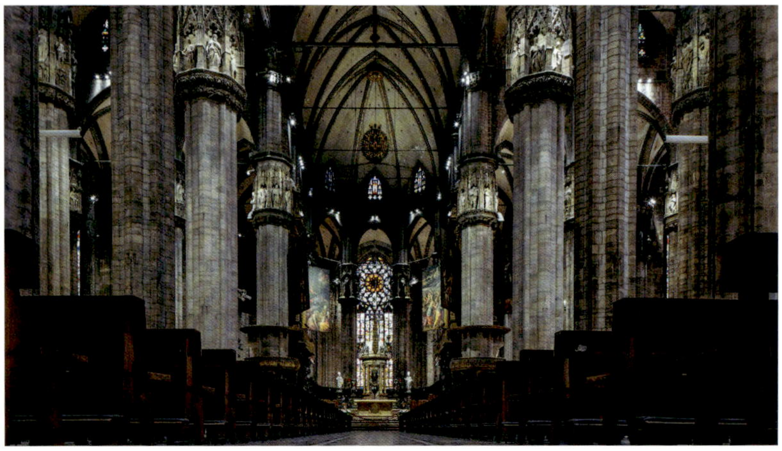

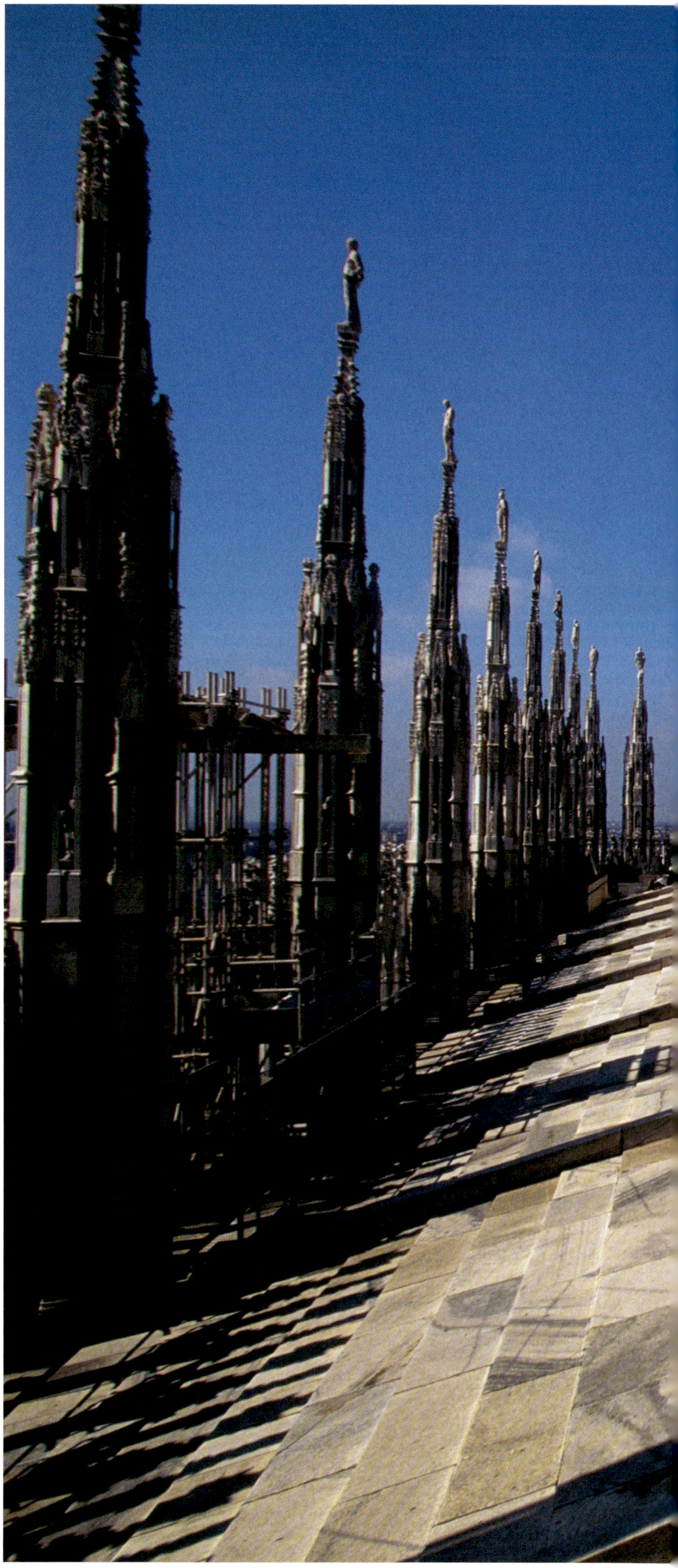

Top The cathedral ranks among the world's largest churches.
Upper middle The statues reflect a belief in divine providence.
Lower middle The iconic Madonnina perches atop the highest spire.
Bottom The relic of the Holy Nail rests above the main altar.

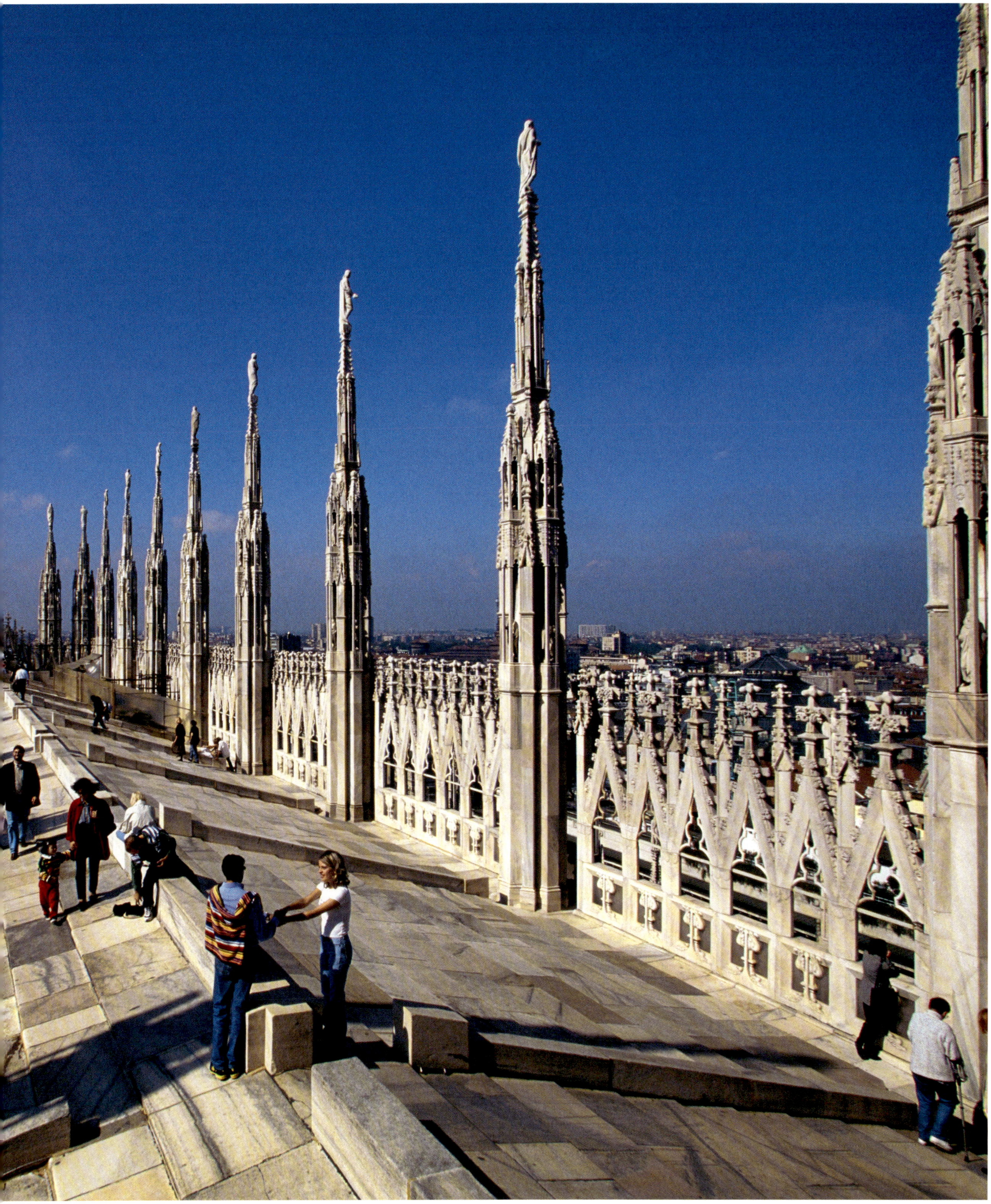

Above The cathedral's 135 marble spires, adorned with over 3,400 statues, are a defining feature of its Gothic architecture. You can get an up-close view of them by visiting the roof.

Chartres Cathedral

Gothic Perfection

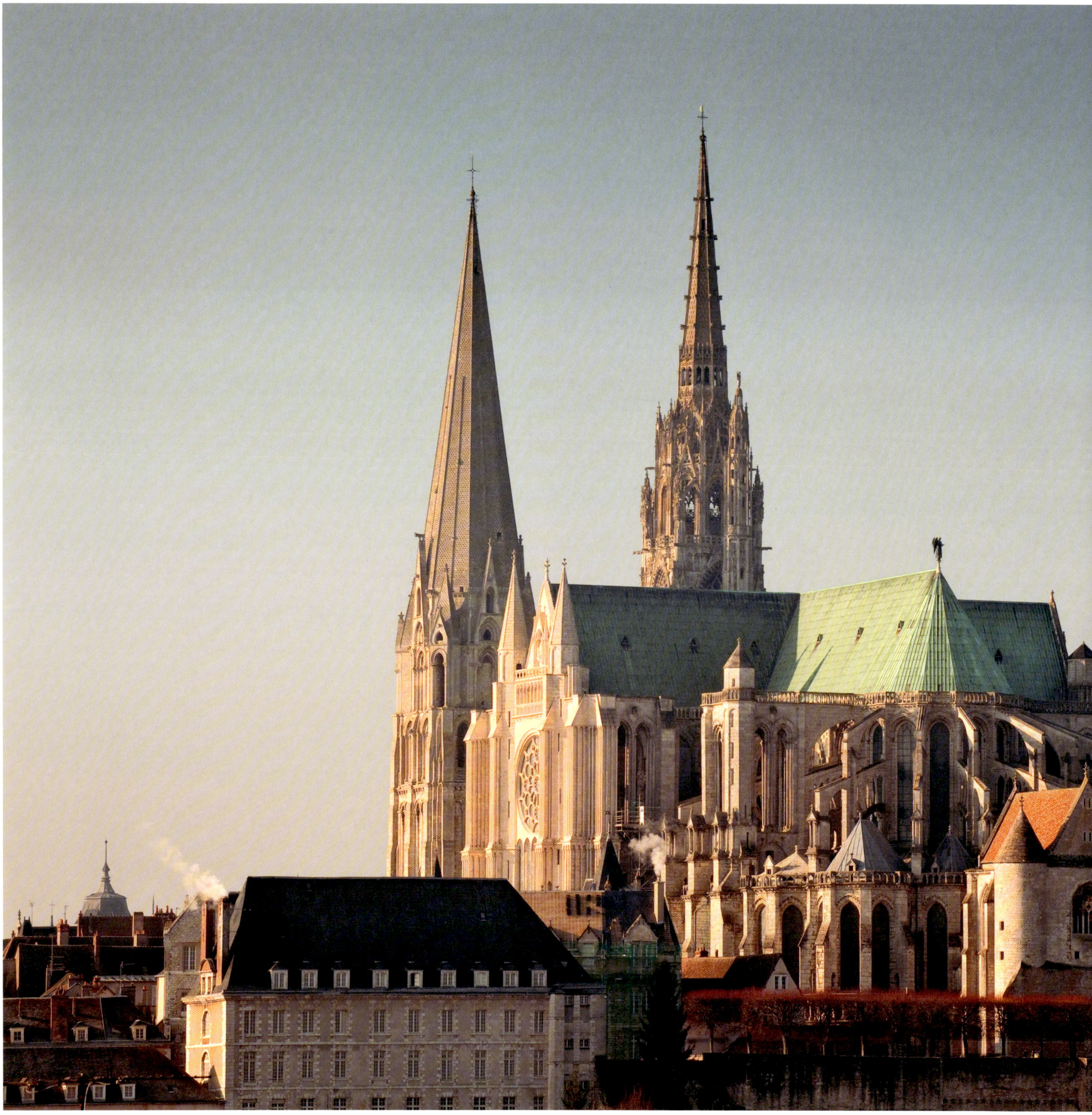

Chartres, France

Built: 1145 – 1220 CE,
Chartres, France

Within this cathedral lies one of Christianity's most precious relics, miraculously preserved from a devastating fire.

La Cathédrale Notre-Dame de Chartres is often called "the ultimate Gothic cathedral"—so impeccable is its architecture, so profound its spiritual significance, and so exquisite its artistry. Standing in the heart of the city of Chartres, about 50 miles (80 kilometers) southwest of Paris, it is one of the most important and best-preserved Gothic cathedrals in Europe.

The cathedral's history is inextricably tied to a fire in 1194 that destroyed much of the site's original Romanesque church. Yet the reconstruction began almost immediately, and the new cathedral was completed in just 30 years, a feat rarely achieved in medieval construction. This rapid pace allowed the entire structure to be built in a cohesive style, making it a model of High Gothic architecture.

One of the cathedral's most striking features is its collection of 176 stained glass windows, among the most vivid and best preserved in the world, and a unique showcase of medieval glass artistry. These windows depict biblical scenes, saints, allegorical figures, and the Last Judgement, offering medieval worshippers a vision of Christianity's past and future, and a visual experience that is at once literal, highly metaphorical, and deeply mysterious. The most renowned is the Blue Virgin window *(Notre-Dame de la Belle Verrière),* a radiant image in glowing red and cobalt blue of the Virgin Mary seated on a throne, holding the Christ Child.

Entering through the Royal Portal, visitors join the ranks of countless others who have made the pilgrimage throughout the centuries, drawn primarily by one of Christianity's most treasured relics: the silken *Sancta Camisia,* or "Holy Tunic" believed to have been worn by the Virgin Mary at the birth of Christ. This relic, venerated in Chartres since the 9th century, survived the 1194 fire unharmed, and was enshrined in the newly built cathedral. The journey to its resting place in the Saint-Cœur de Marie Chapel leads over a labyrinth laid in the cathedral's stone floor. Here, believers can undertake a miniature pilgrimage: as they follow the path full of twists and turns, they are encouraged to meditate on death and eternal life.

After losing oneself in the depths of the labyrinth, the intricately crafted shrine holding the *Sancta Camisia* beckons. Pilgrims and visitors stand before it in reverence, bathed in the soft light of the chapel. Colorful rays pour through the cathedral's magnificent stained glass windows, casting hues upon their praying hands and enraptured faces. In such moments, no place seems more fitting for the veneration of this most sacred relic.

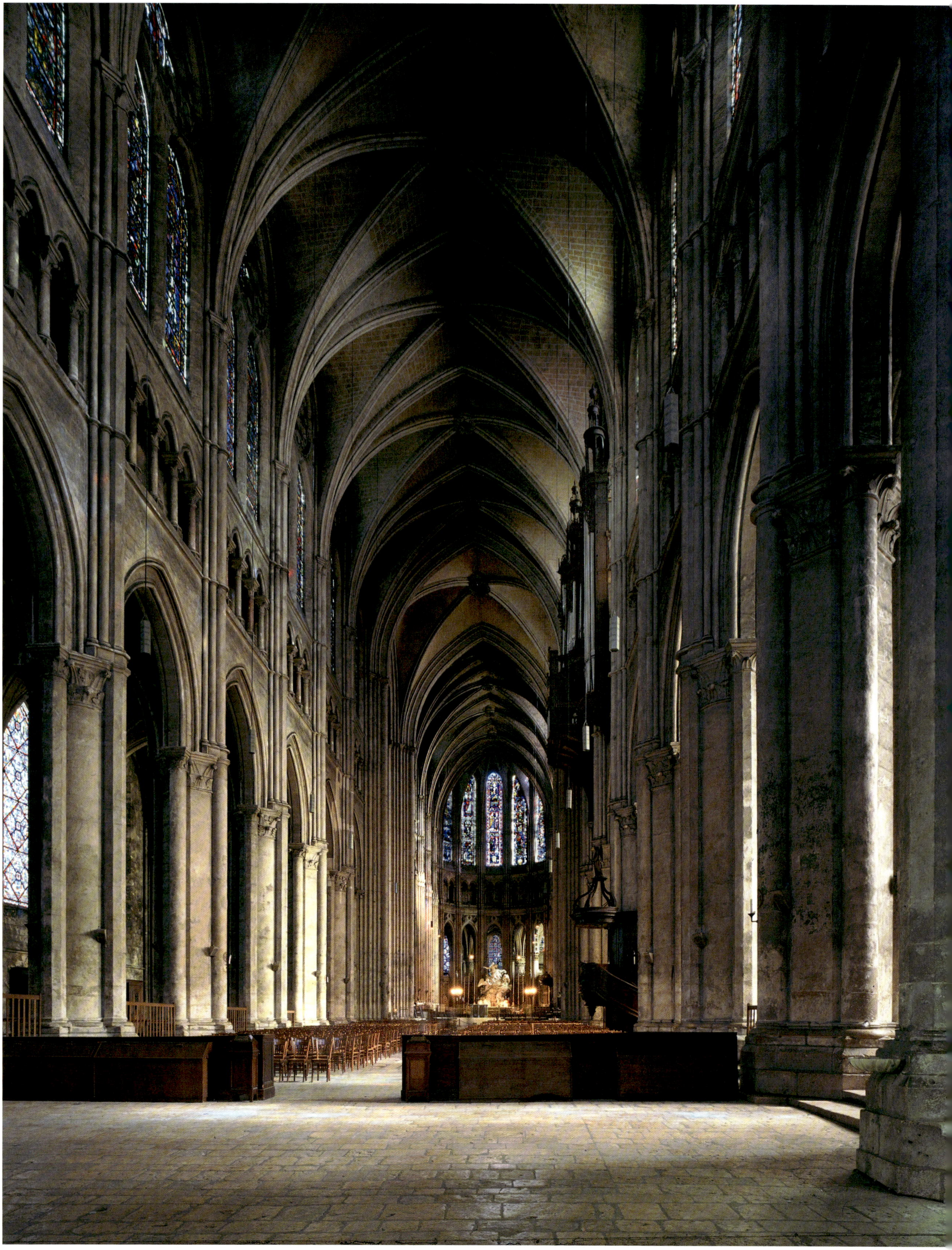

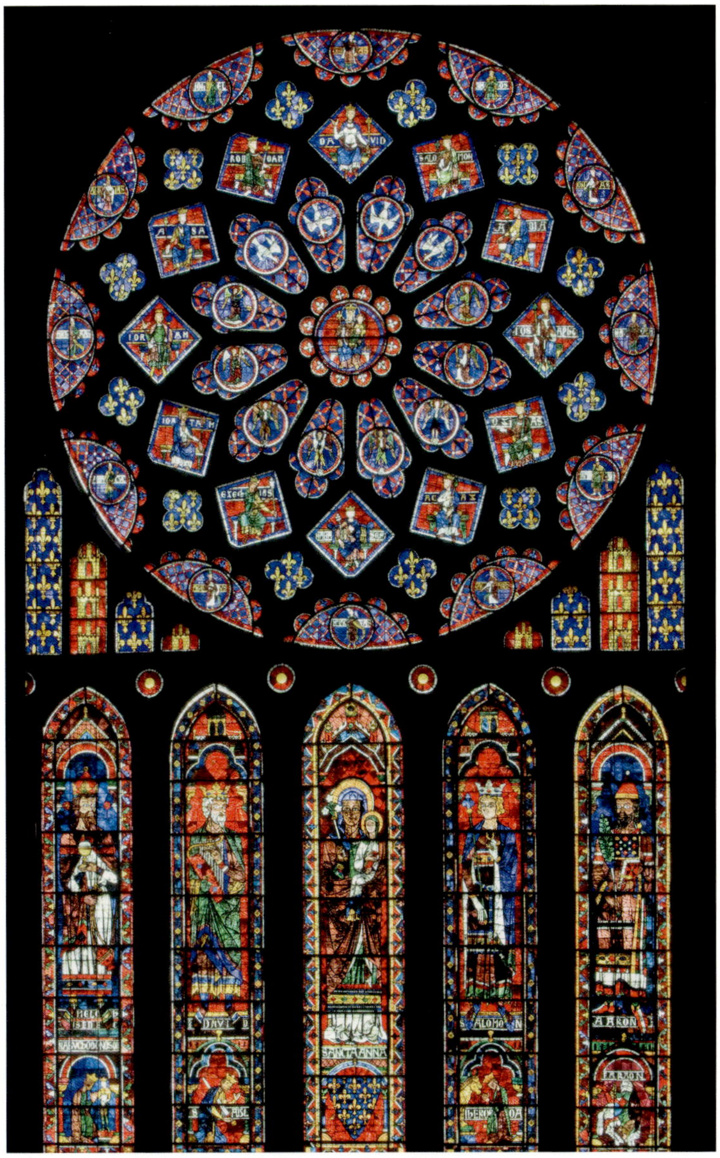

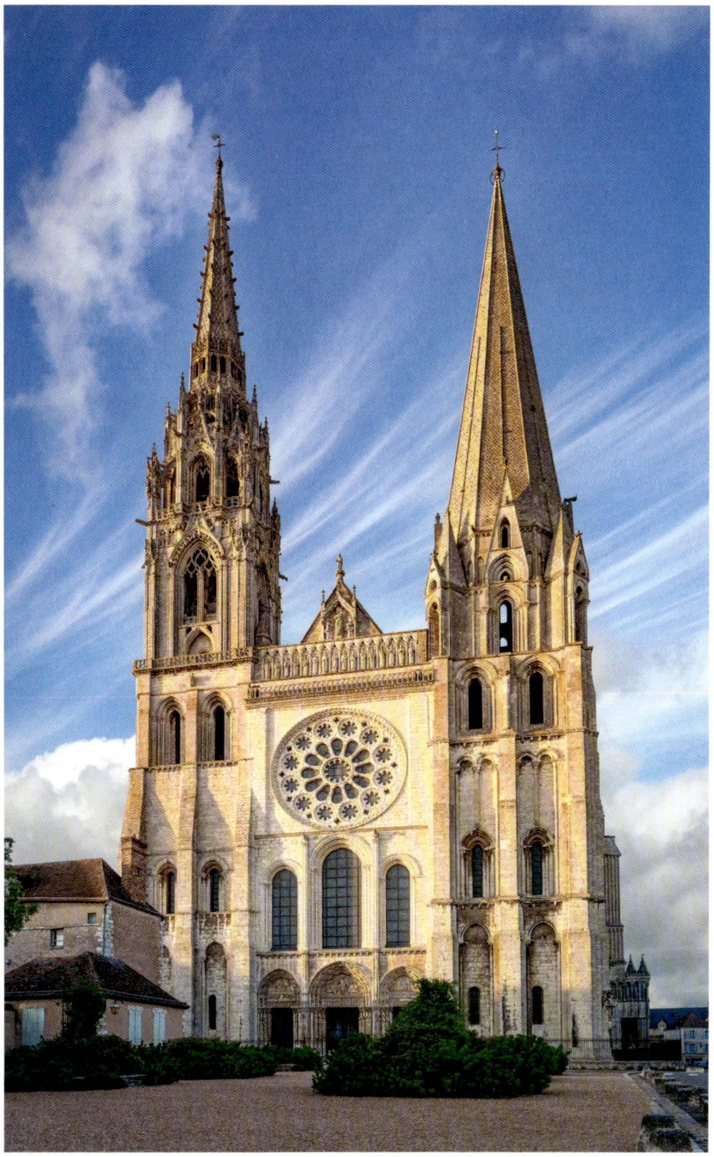

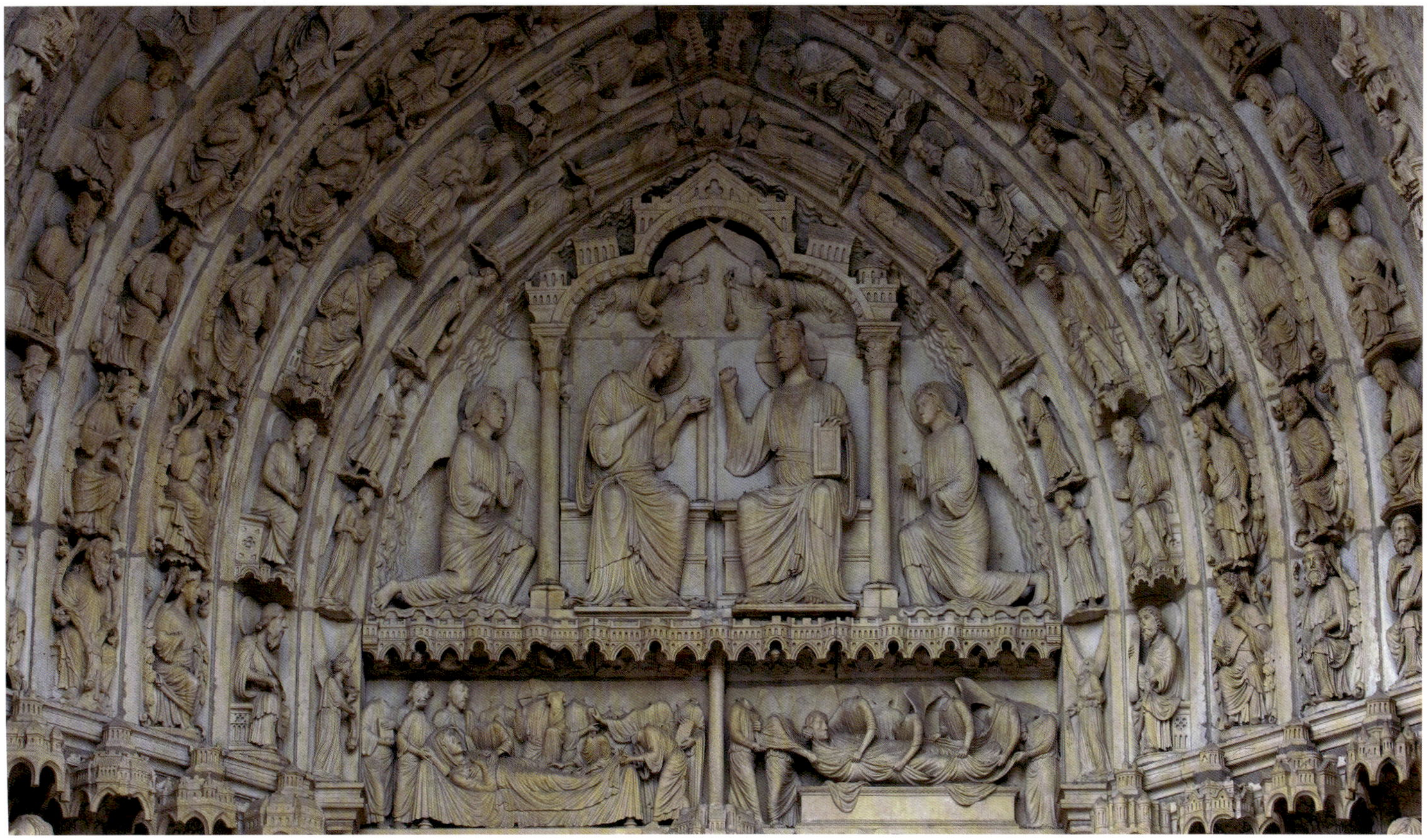

Opposite The wide nave was made possible by the then-innovative use of the flying buttress.
Top left The colorful stained glass windows narrate multiple biblical stories.
Top right The heights of the towers differ by a total of 32 feet (10 meters).
Bottom The North Portal combines Romanesque and early Gothic elements.

Mont-Saint-Michel Abbey

Built on a Vision

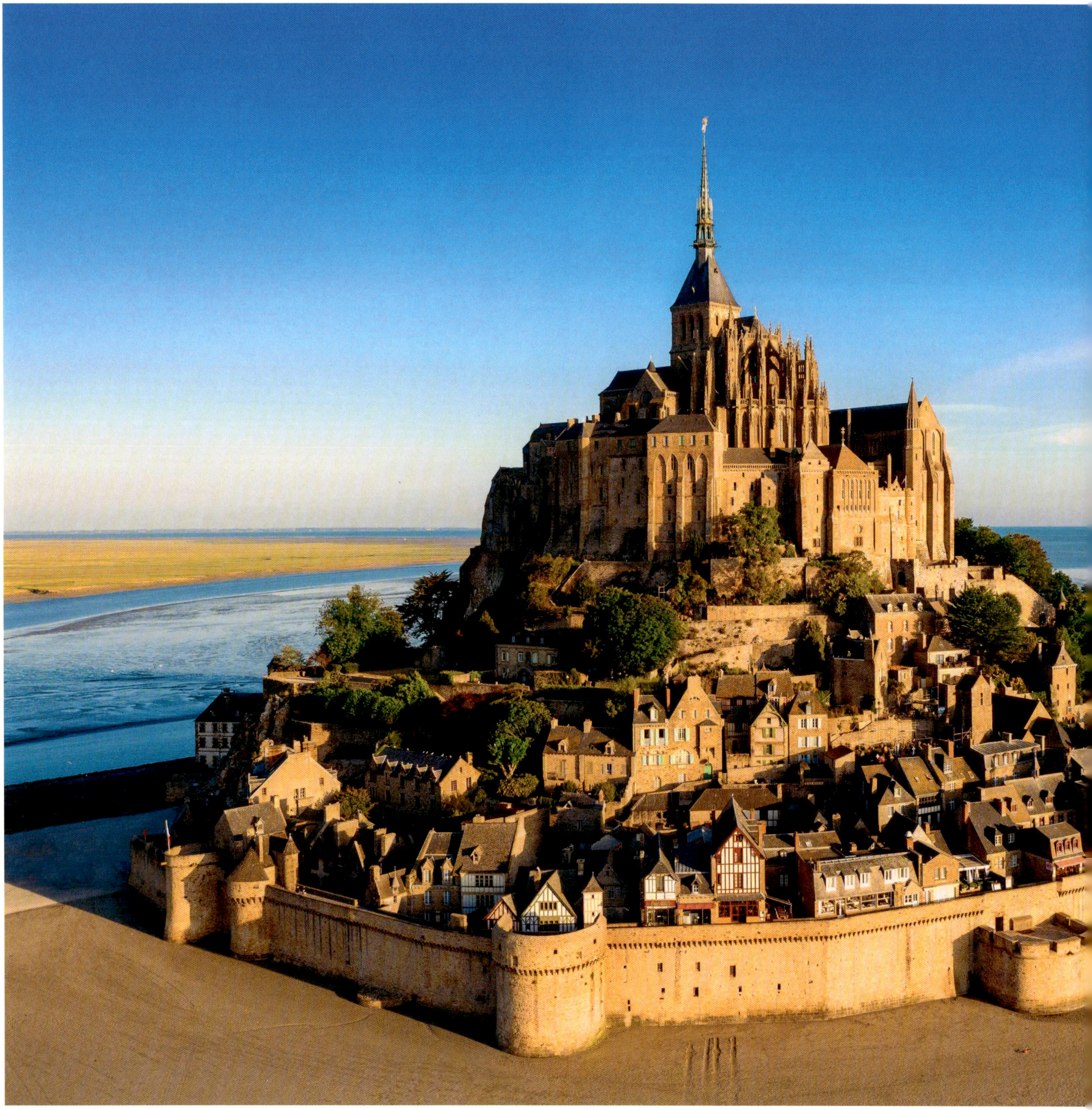

Built: 8th century CE onward, Normandy, France

When the tide rises around this legendary monastic island, it appears completely separated from the earthly world.

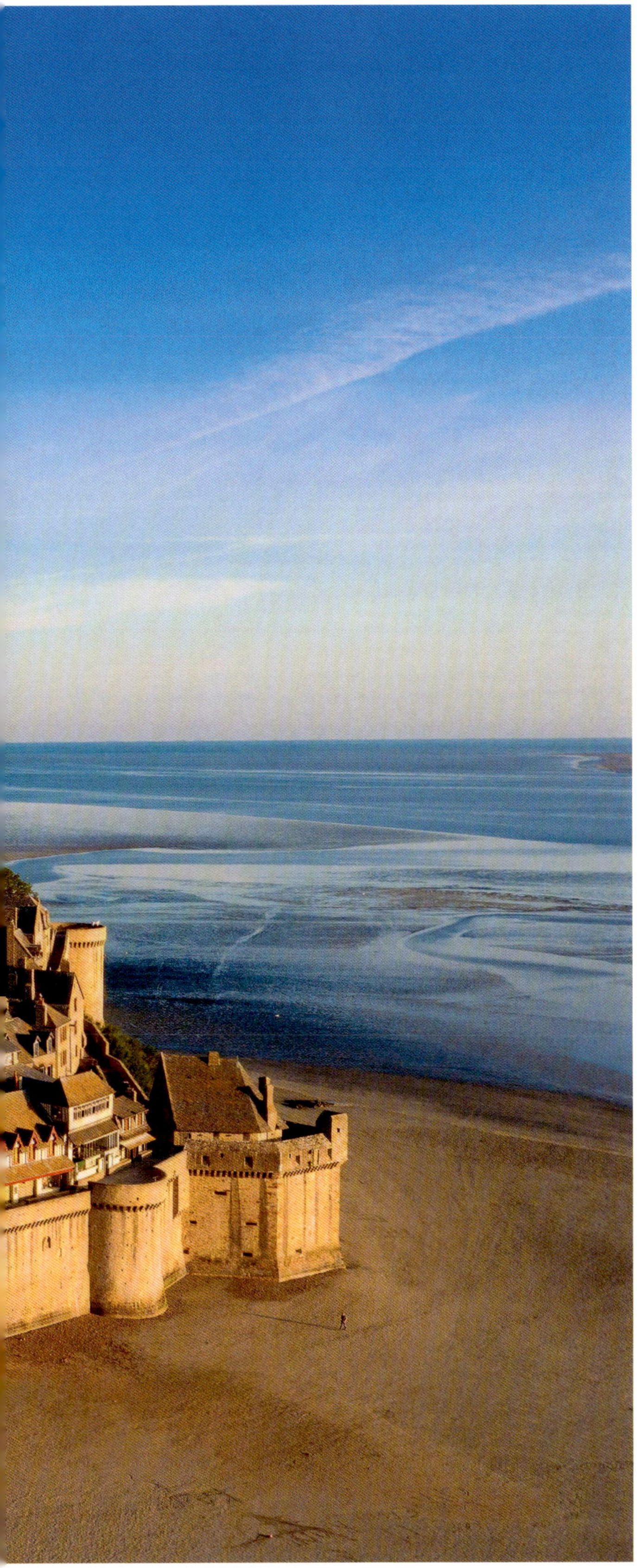

"Mont-Saint-Michel is to France what the Great Pyramid is to Egypt," wrote Victor Hugo, the renowned French writer and poet. When he visited the site in June 1836, he was so captivated by its beauty that he described it as "truly the most beautiful place in the world." Could it be mere coincidence that this monumental abbey owes its very existence to a vision?

According to legend, the Archangel Michael appeared to Bishop Aubert of Avranches, instructing him to build a church on the rocky mount then known as Mont-Tombe. Initially, Aubert ignored the vision, until the archangel emphatically reinforced his command by placing a burning finger on the bishop's skull. Thus, in the early 8th century, the construction of a small church began, which over the centuries grew into the mighty abbey we see today.

Its architecture follows the natural contours of the rock. Over time, additional terraces, stairways, and labyrinthine rooms were added. Sections from the 10th century, such as the crypt, were built in the Romanesque style, but in the 13th century, numerous Gothic buildings were erected, including the famous *La Merveille ("The Marvel")*, a three-story monastic complex with finely crafted cloisters, and the Knights' Hall with a sensational view over the bay. A more recent addition is the golden statue of Archangel Michael, which has crowned the top of the abbey church since 1897. With wings outstretched and sword raised, he watches over Mont-Saint-Michel Abbey, ready to defend the abbey against demonic forces and the encroaching tides.

When the tide is low, the rocky monastery can be reached on foot via the exposed seabed. At high tide, however, the way is completely submerged, and the land is transformed into a majestic island. In the Bay of Saint-Michel, the water rises to great heights particularly quickly—historically, pilgrims risked being caught off guard by the rushing waters as they made their way across the seabed. This twice-daily transformation also contributed to Mont-Saint-Michel Abbey's security, making the site an impregnable fortress during the Middle Ages. During the Hundred Years' War, for example, it withstood several sieges by the English and became a symbol of French resistance.

In addition to being a UNESCO World Heritage Site and one of France's most visited tourist attractions, the abbey remains a vibrant pilgrimage site and is home to a small community of brothers and sisters of the Fraternités Monastiques de Jérusalem. They safeguard Mont-Saint-Michel Abbey—the realized vision of the Archangel Michael's command, one that continues to captivate visitors to this day.

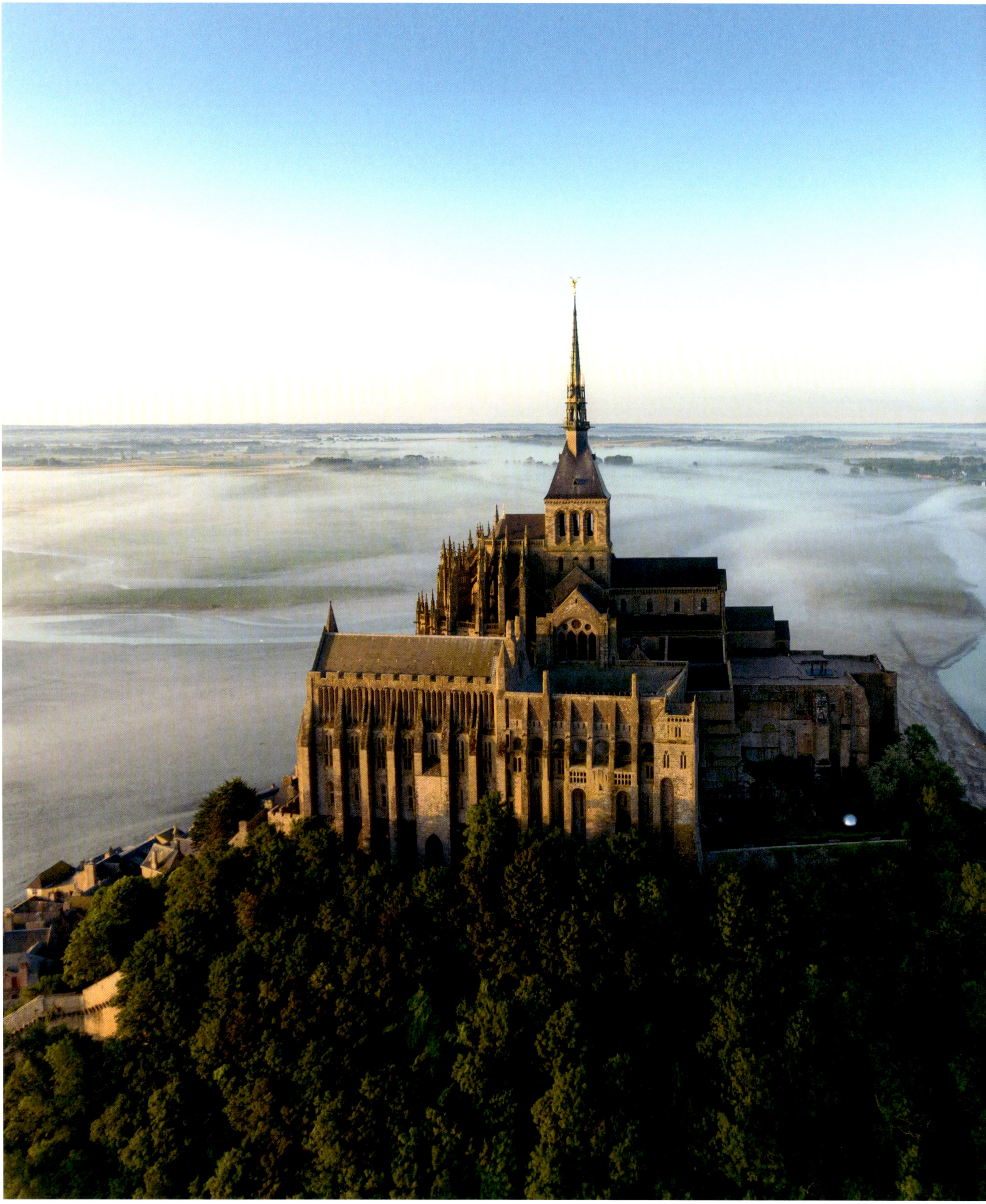

Normandy, France

Above The breathtaking Gothic architecture of Mont-Saint-Michel Abbey rises above the expansive bay, showcasing its historical significance as both a religious sanctuary and a military stronghold.

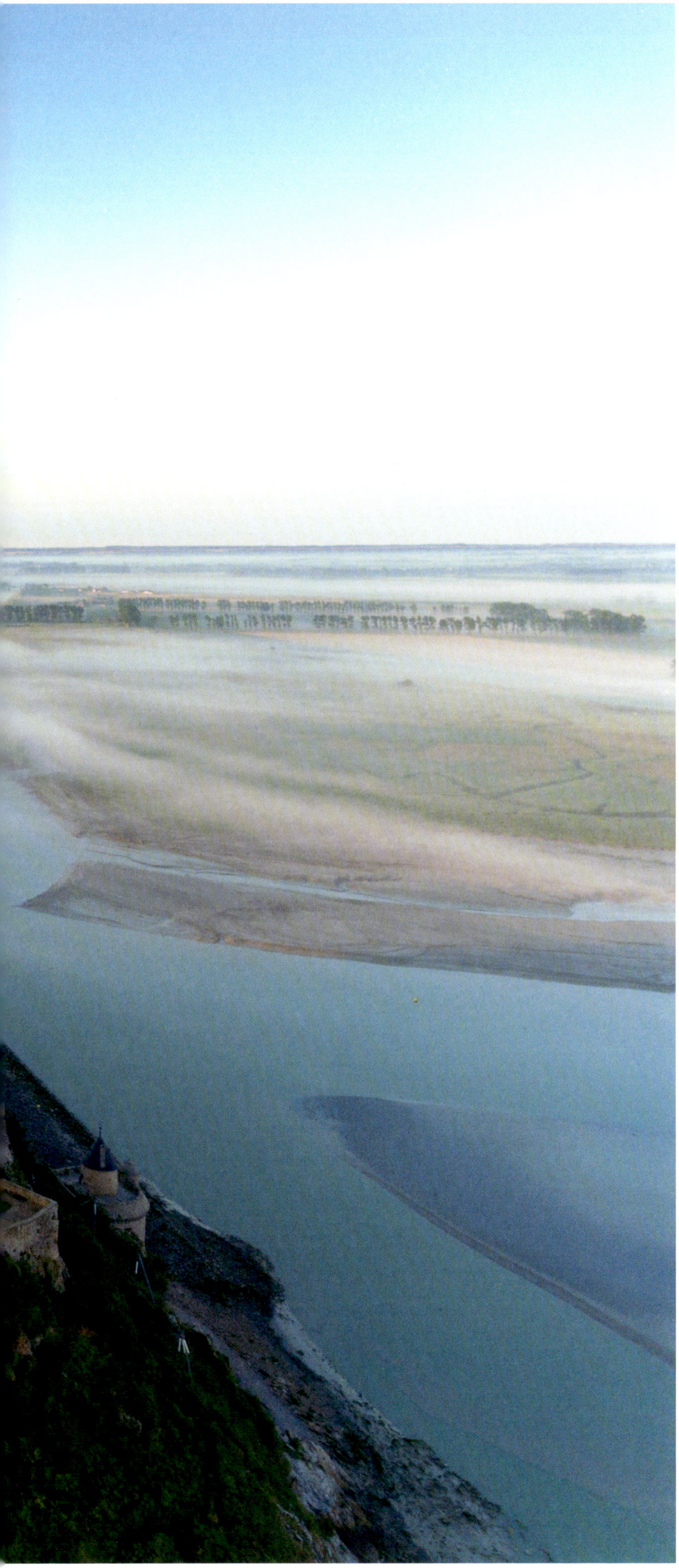

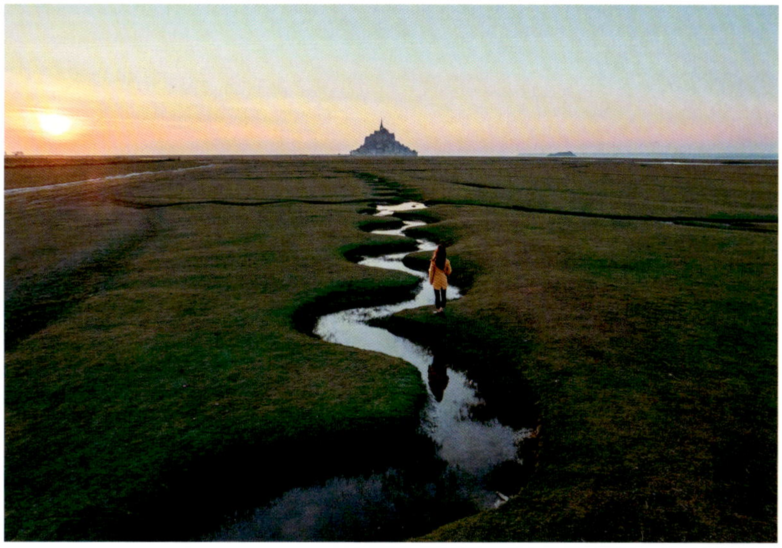

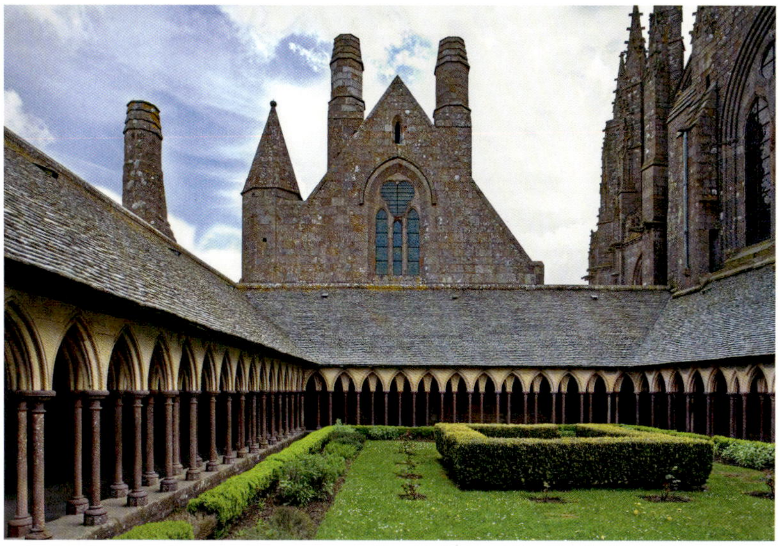

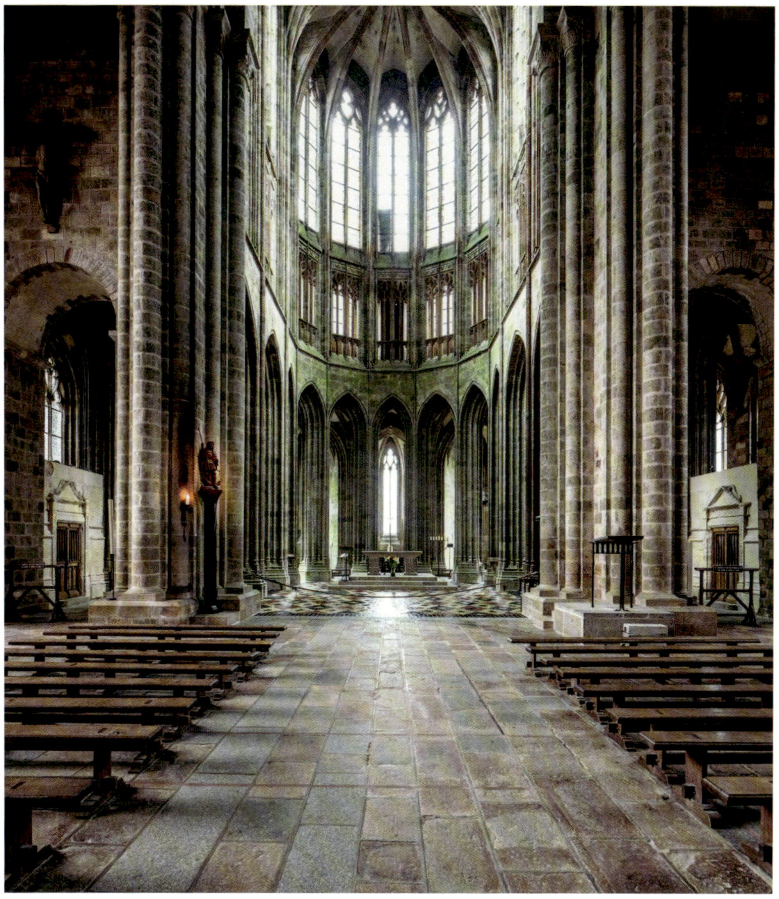

Top From a distance, the monastery island, home to just 40 residents, is a mesmerizing sight.
Middle The medieval cloister provides a serene space for reflection.
Bottom The Gothic abbey church inspires awe with its soaring beauty.

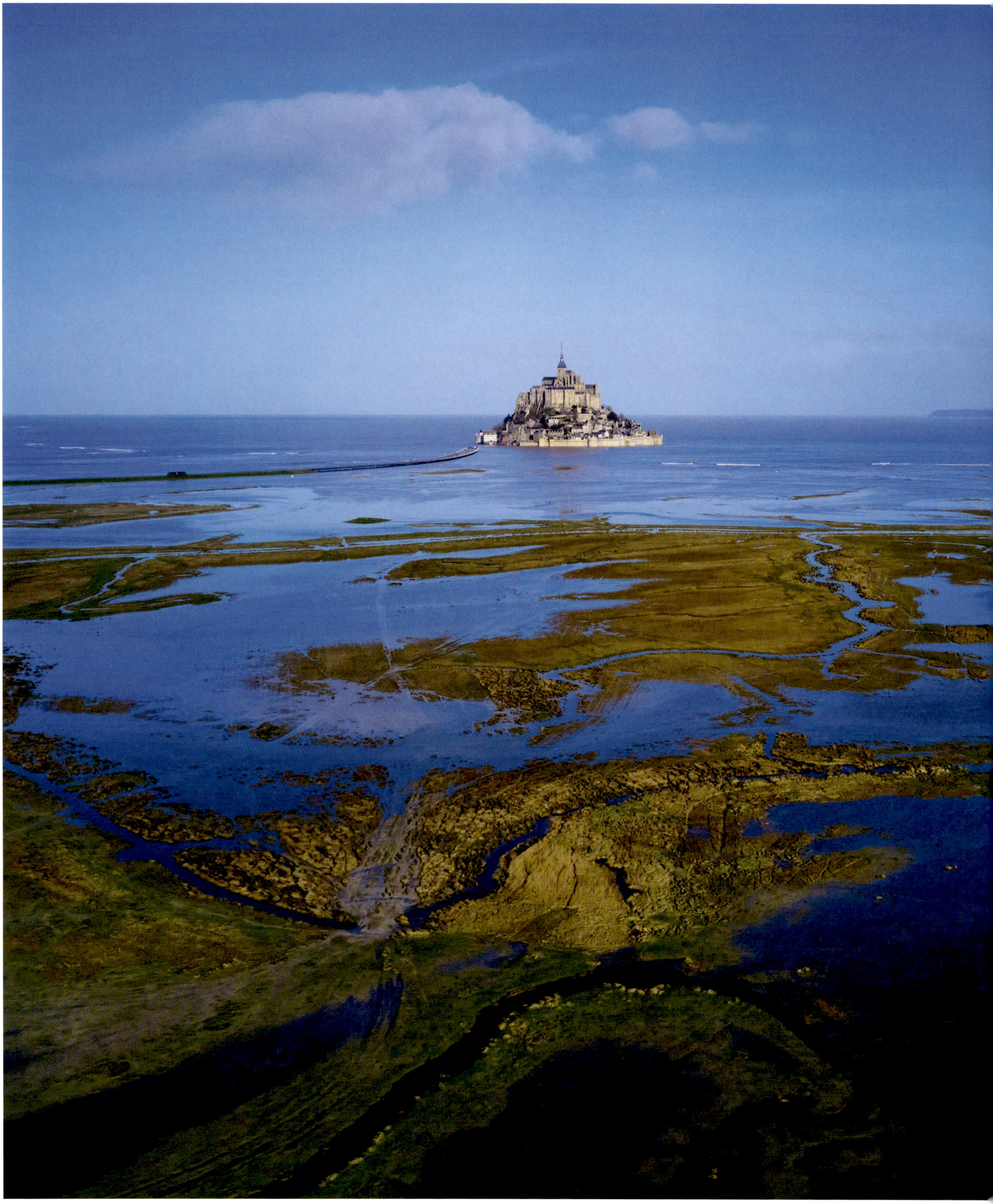

Normandy, France

Above In the Bay of Mont-Saint-Michel, tides can rise as high as 45 feet (14 meters). The bay's shallow depth, combined with powerful tidal forces, produces some of the highest tides in Europe.

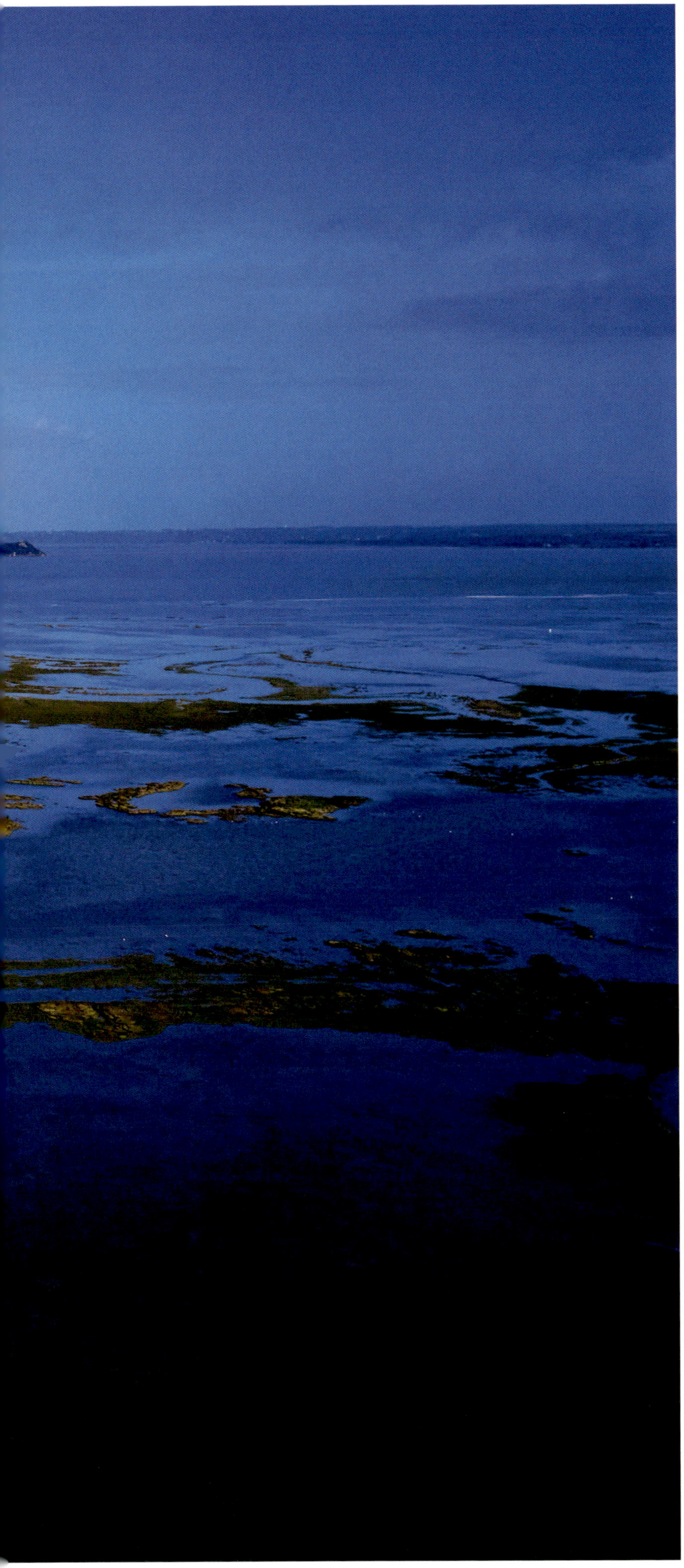

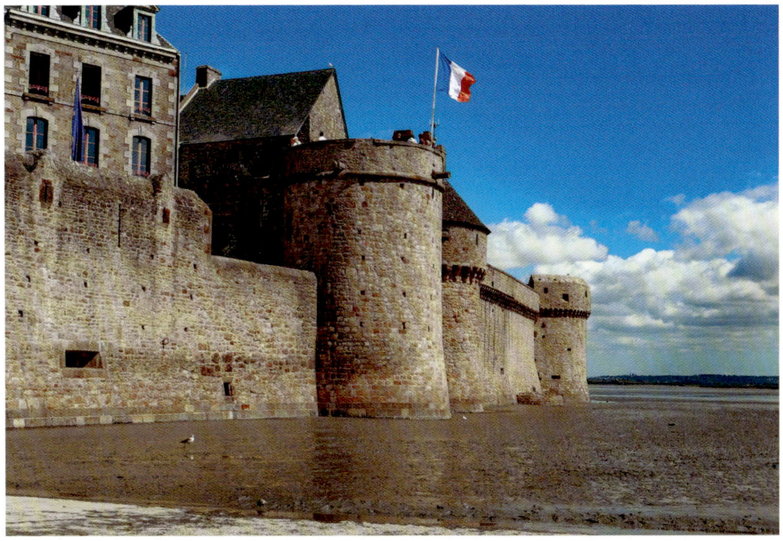

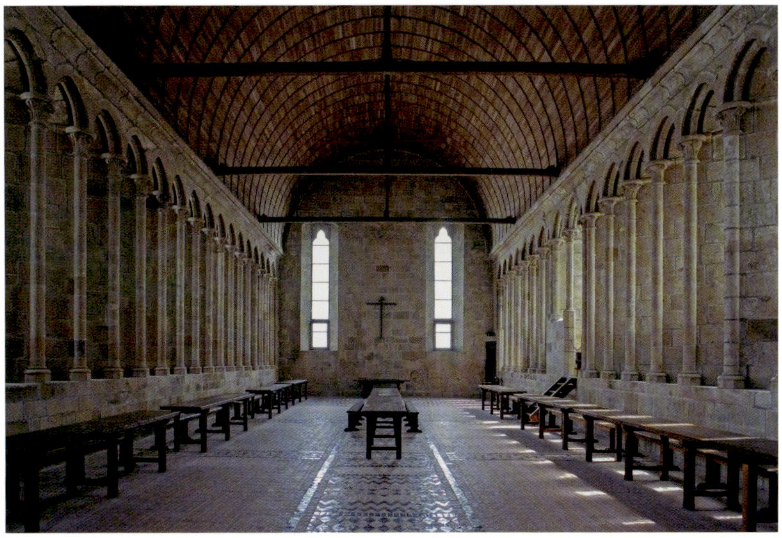

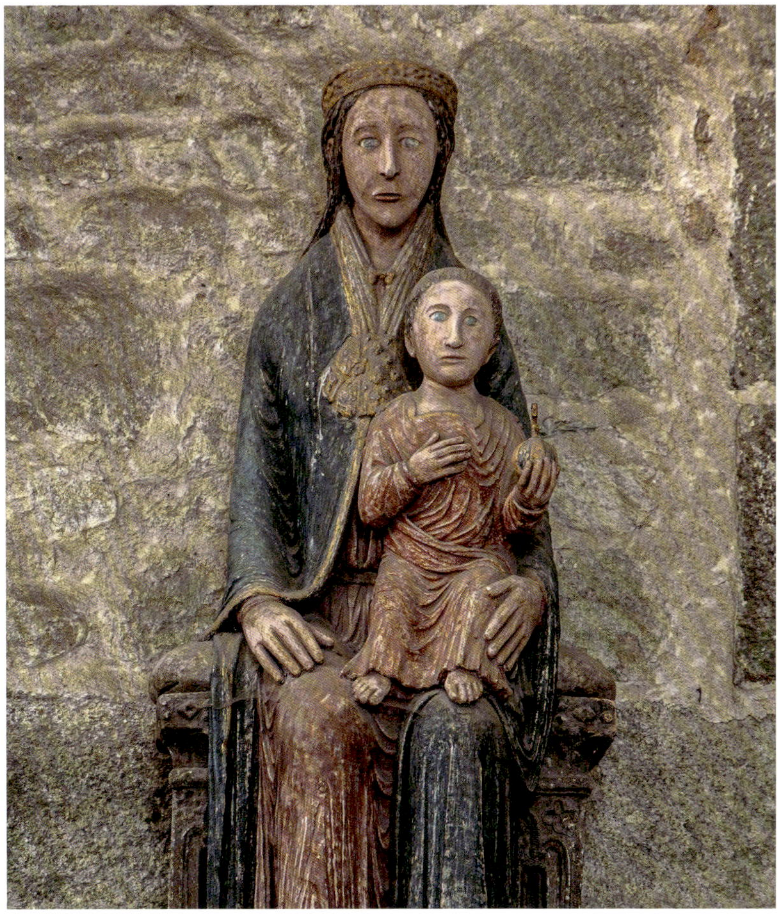

Top During the French Revolution, Mont-Saint-Michel Abbey was secularized and repurposed as a prison.
Middle In the 19th century, monks returned to restore spiritual life on the island.
Bottom The statue of the *Vierge à l'Enfant* gazes gently down upon visitors.

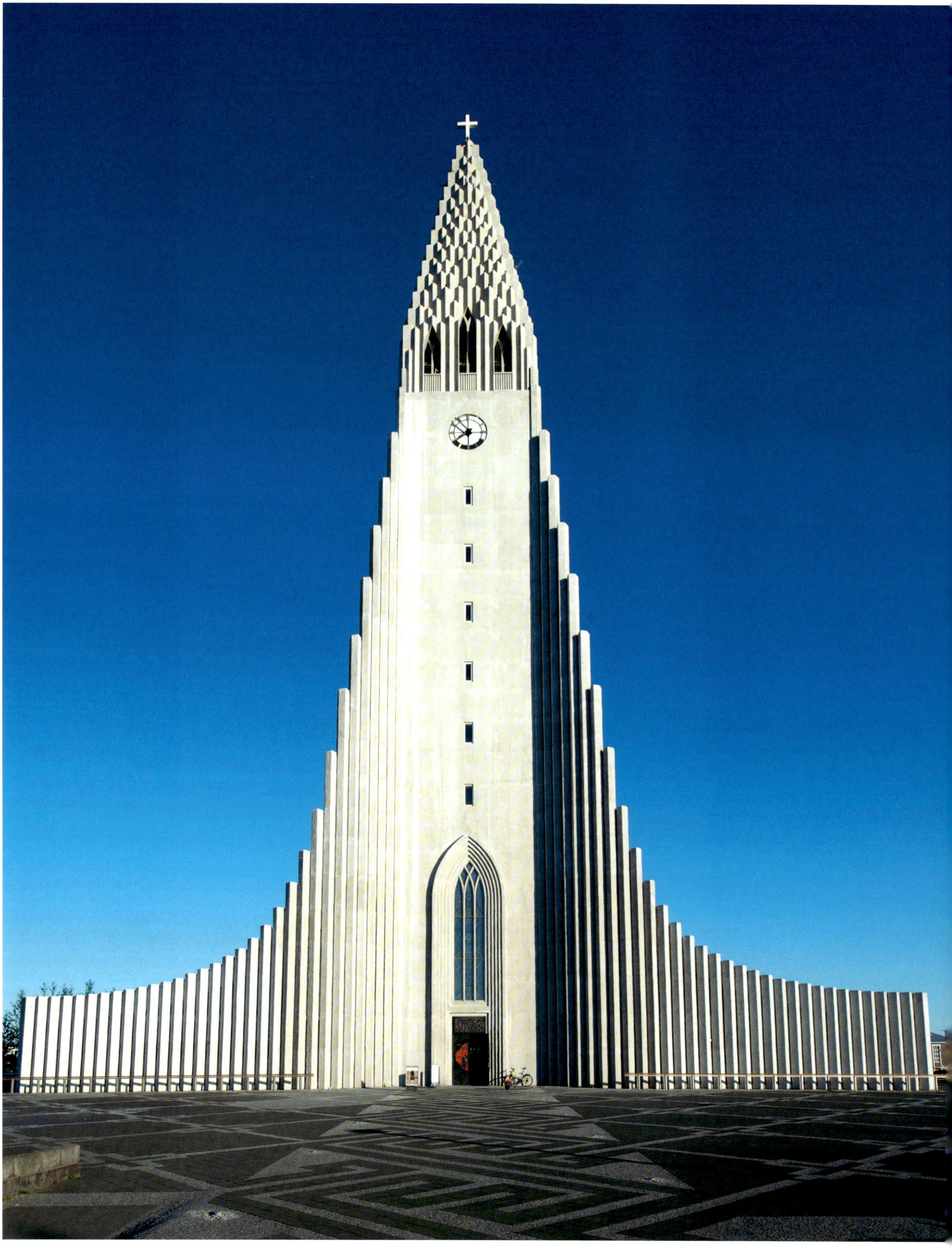

Hallgrímskirkja

A Testament to Raw Nature

Built: 1945 – 1986 CE,
Reykjavík, Iceland

After a volcanic eruption, lava cools into hexagonal columns, and it's just this kind of natural phenomenon that helped inspire a modern refuge in Reykjavík.

Like a monumental basalt-rock formation, Hallgrímskirkja rises into the sky over Iceland's capital, Reykjavík. No building in Iceland has ever taken so long to complete, nor divided the nation so profoundly. The Icelandic state architect, Guðjón Samúelsson, was commissioned for its design and first presented plans for the new church in 1937. Samúelsson had previously designed plans for the University's main building, the National Theater, and the Lutheran church of Akureyri. But this time, he sought more than mere functionality; he wanted to capture the very essence of Iceland in stone. His muse was the rugged beauty of the island itself—its mountains and glaciers, its volcanoes and solidified lava formations—yet the design was also the product of an intense, personal vision.

Its location, Skólavörðuholt hill, had been selected long before. Here, in the rapidly growing eastern part of the capital, the new church was meant to serve as a visible center for Reykjavík. While some Icelanders were captivated by the architect's bold vision, others yearned for a more traditional church structure. Nevertheless, Samúelsson's vision prevailed, and in 1945, the decades-long construction began. In 1948, the first small chapel held services in the lower level, in what is now the choir area. Nearly 30 years later, the tower and side wings, with an additional chapel, were completed. Finally, in 1986, Reykjavík's bicentennial year, the nave was ceremoniously consecrated.

The church's namesake, Hallgrímur Pétursson (1614 – 1674), was a Lutheran pastor and poet whose 50 *Passiusálmar,* or "Passion Hymns," have been read, memorized, sung, and revered by generations of Icelanders. His works found purchase in a country that adopted Christianity in the year 1000, and as a result profoundly shaped the island's spiritual life. Even today, over half of Iceland's Christian population belongs to the Evangelical Lutheran National Church, where faith is uniquely intertwined with the natural world, which is often seen as an expression of divine creation. Elements of folk beliefs, such as belief in *huldufólk*—hidden beings and elves—remain widespread, and peacefully coexist with Christian faith in a way rarely found in other Lutheran churches.

The resemblance of Hallgrímskirkja to Iceland's basalt columns may therefore also be read in a spiritual light. Basalt columns are formed after a volcanic eruption, when lava cools slowly and fractures into characteristic hexagonal shapes. Powerful and unwavering, they stand as a testament to a living earth—a necessary complement, perhaps, to a living faith.

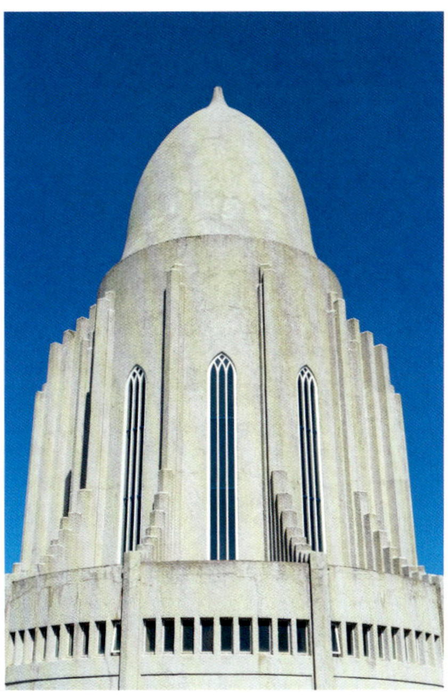

Opposite The magnificent Hallgrímskirkja towers above Reykjavík.
Above The bell-shaped rear evokes traditional church architecture.

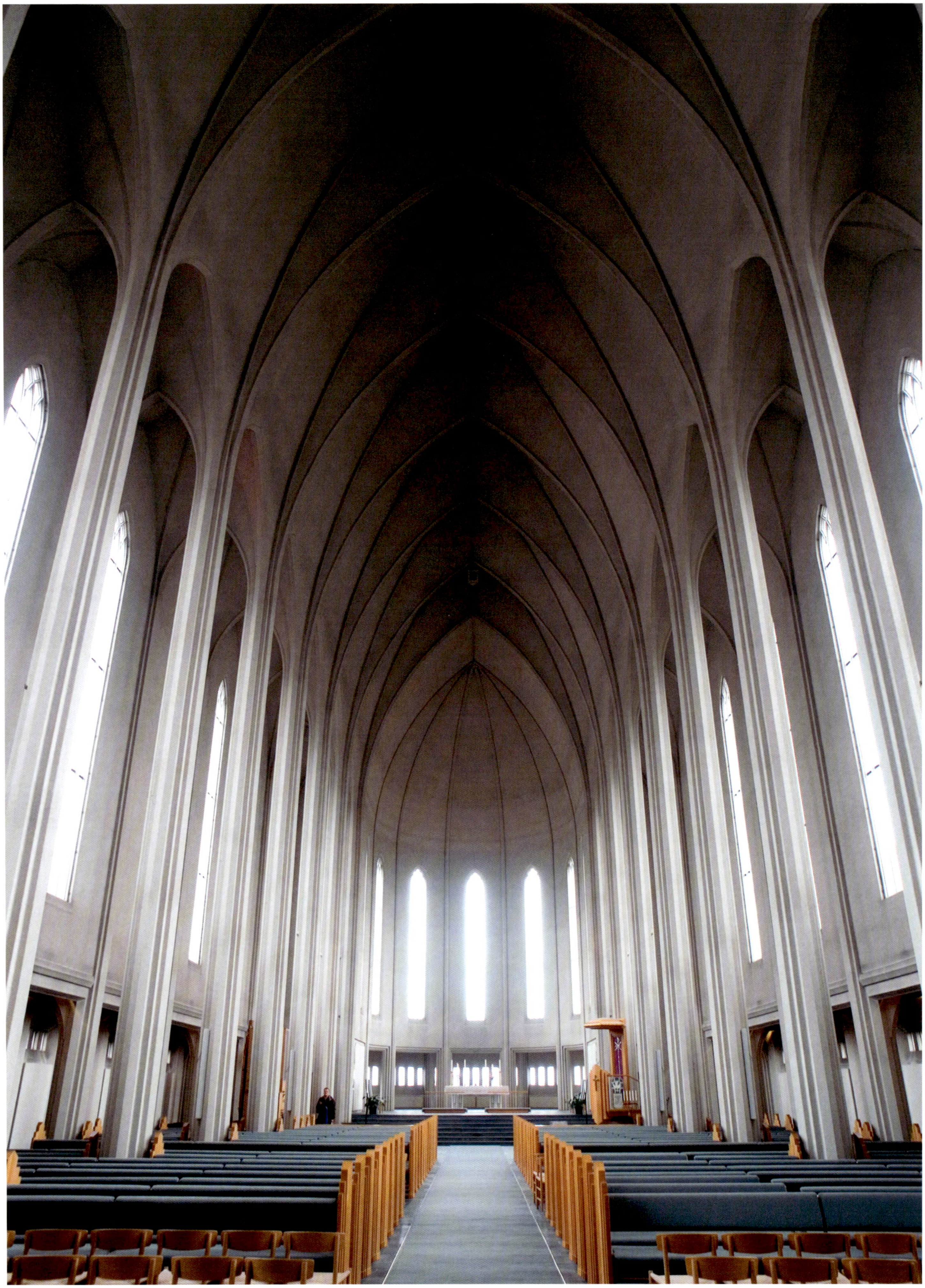

Above The interior is characterized by its serene, minimalist design, which reflects the simplicity of the Icelandic landscape while also offering exceptional acoustics due to its expansive architecture.

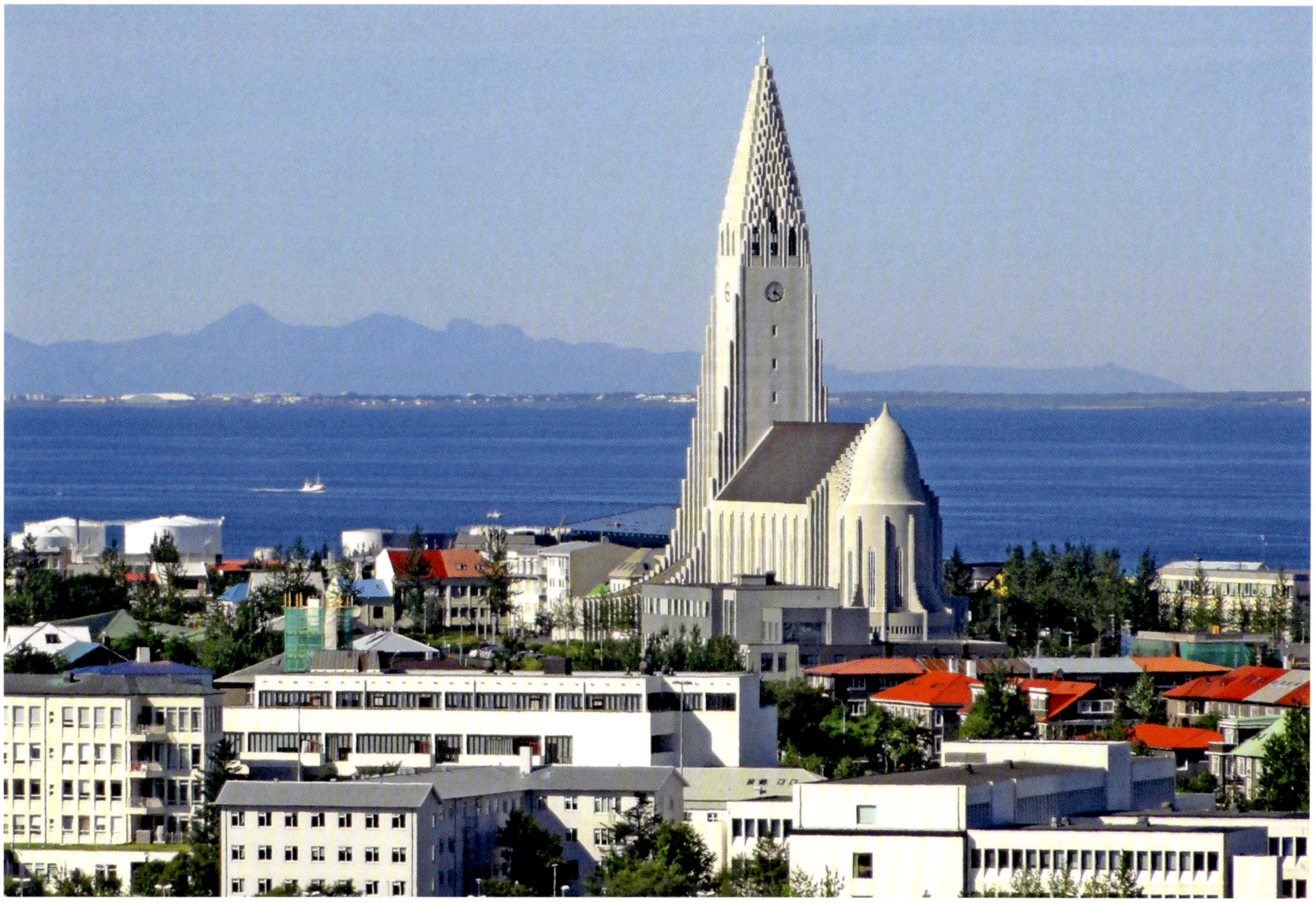

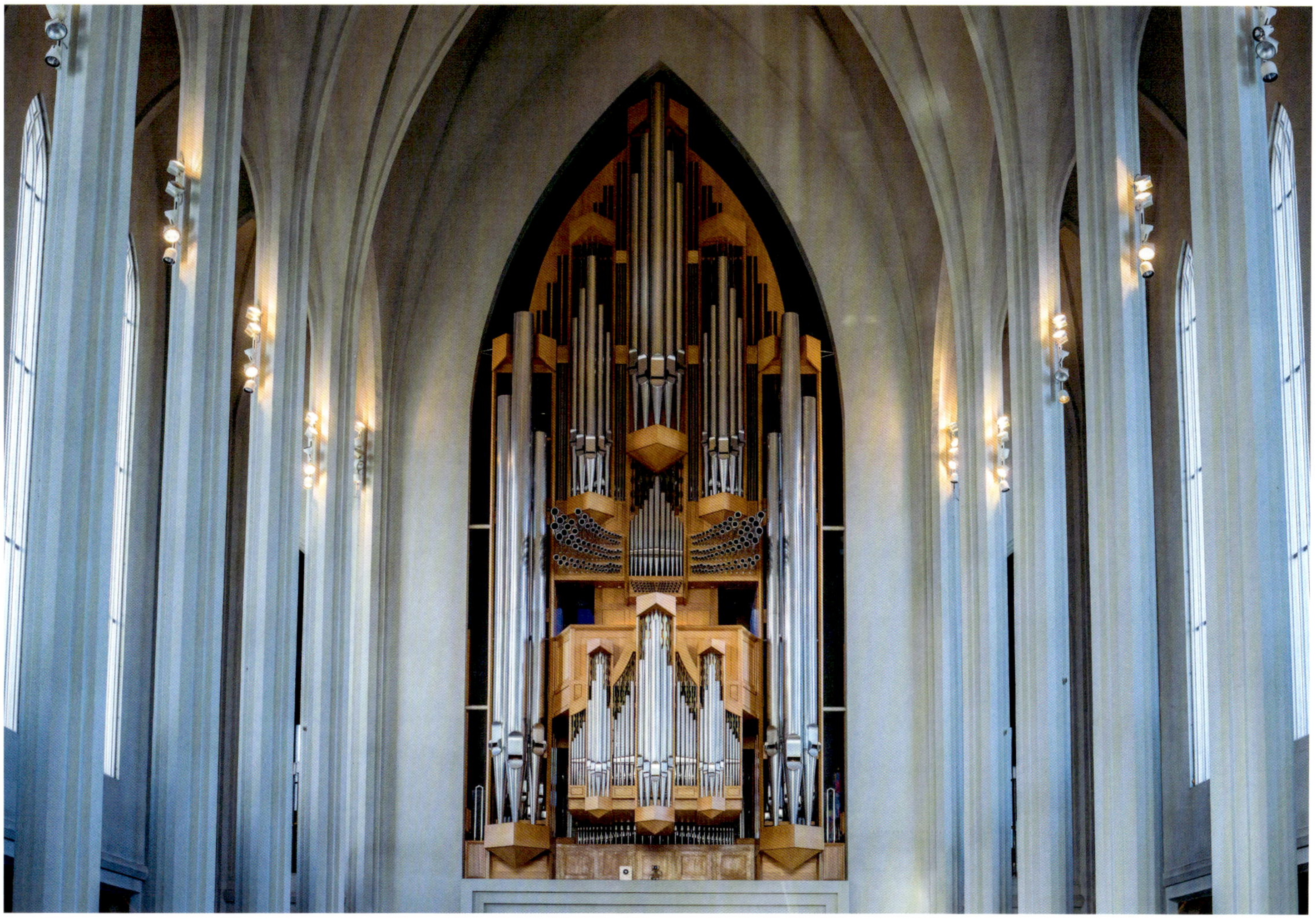

Top The Hallgrímskirkja stands as a striking landmark, dominating the skyline of Iceland's capital.
Bottom The magnificent German organ, with 72 registers and 5,275 pipes, was installed in the 1990s.

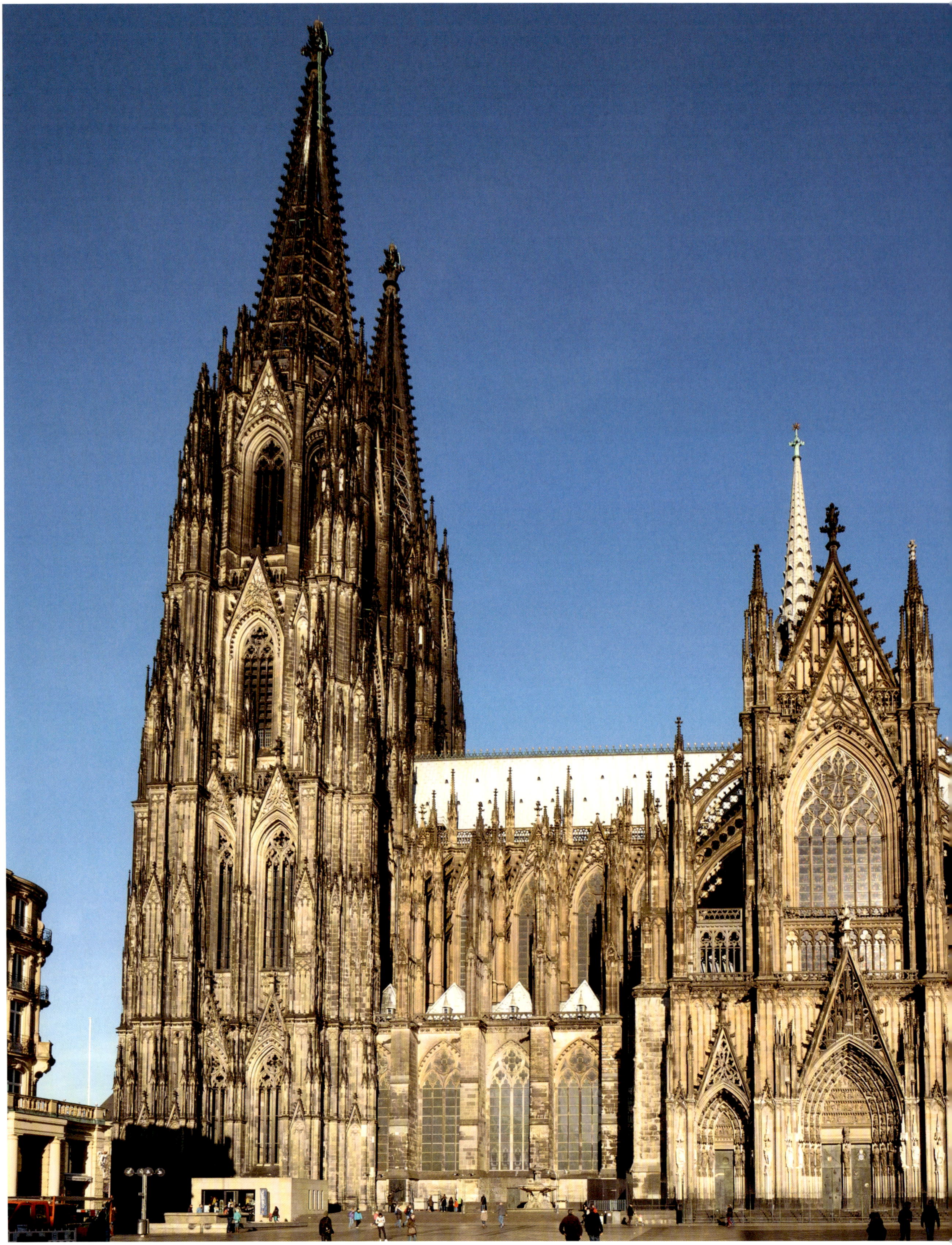

Cologne Cathedral

Of Emperors and Kings

Built: 1248 – 1880 CE, Cologne, Germany

A campaign against Milan set in motion a series of events that culminated in the construction of this awe-inspiring cathedral.

In 1162, after the Holy Roman Emperor Frederick Barbarossa vanquished the Italian city of Milan, he claimed a priceless treasure from the Basilica di Sant'Eustorgio: the relics of the Three Wise Men. In an era when relics held both profound religious and political weight, possessing them signified both imperial authority and divine favor.

The relics arrived in Cologne two years later, a flourishing trade city on the Rhine, forever altering its destiny. To honor and house these relics, work began on the Shrine of the Three Kings—an opulent, golden reliquary adorned with gemstones and intricate reliefs, crafted over many decades. Pilgrims from every corner of Europe began journeying to the city, and the idea of a cathedral worthy of such relics grew ever more vivid.

Inspired by the grand Gothic cathedrals of France, the builders commissioned by the archbishop envisioned an unparalleled sanctuary centered around the Shrine of the Three Kings. Lavish donations from the nobility and local communities fueled the construction efforts, yet the project demanded more than human imagination—it demanded lifetimes of commitment. For centuries, architects and stonemasons labored over the cathedral's rise. Wars, plagues, and financial hardships ultimately led to a halt in construction during the 16th century. For over 300 years, Cologne Cathedral stood as an unfinished Gothic relic on the Rhine—a slumbering giant, guarding the Shrine of the Three Kings within an incomplete choir.

Not until the 19th century, amid a European revival of Gothic architecture, did the vision of the medieval builders come to life again. German Romanticism and its quest for national unity reignited interest in Cologne Cathedral, and upon its completion in 1880, it rose as the tallest building in the world, a source of pride for the newly unified German Empire.

Today, visitors who pass through the main entrance of the cathedral find the Shrine of the Three Kings in the high choir, the eastern part of the cathedral, behind the main altar and facing the rising sun. Standing at 59 inches (150 centimeters) tall and 87 inches (220 centimeters) wide, the shrine is the largest reliquary of the Western Middle Ages. Its golden reliefs narrate scenes from the birth and adoration of Jesus, his baptism, the Annunciation to the shepherds, and the Crucifixion. Towering above, the cathedral's spires and flying buttresses form a suitably majestic backdrop for the earthly remains of the Magi.

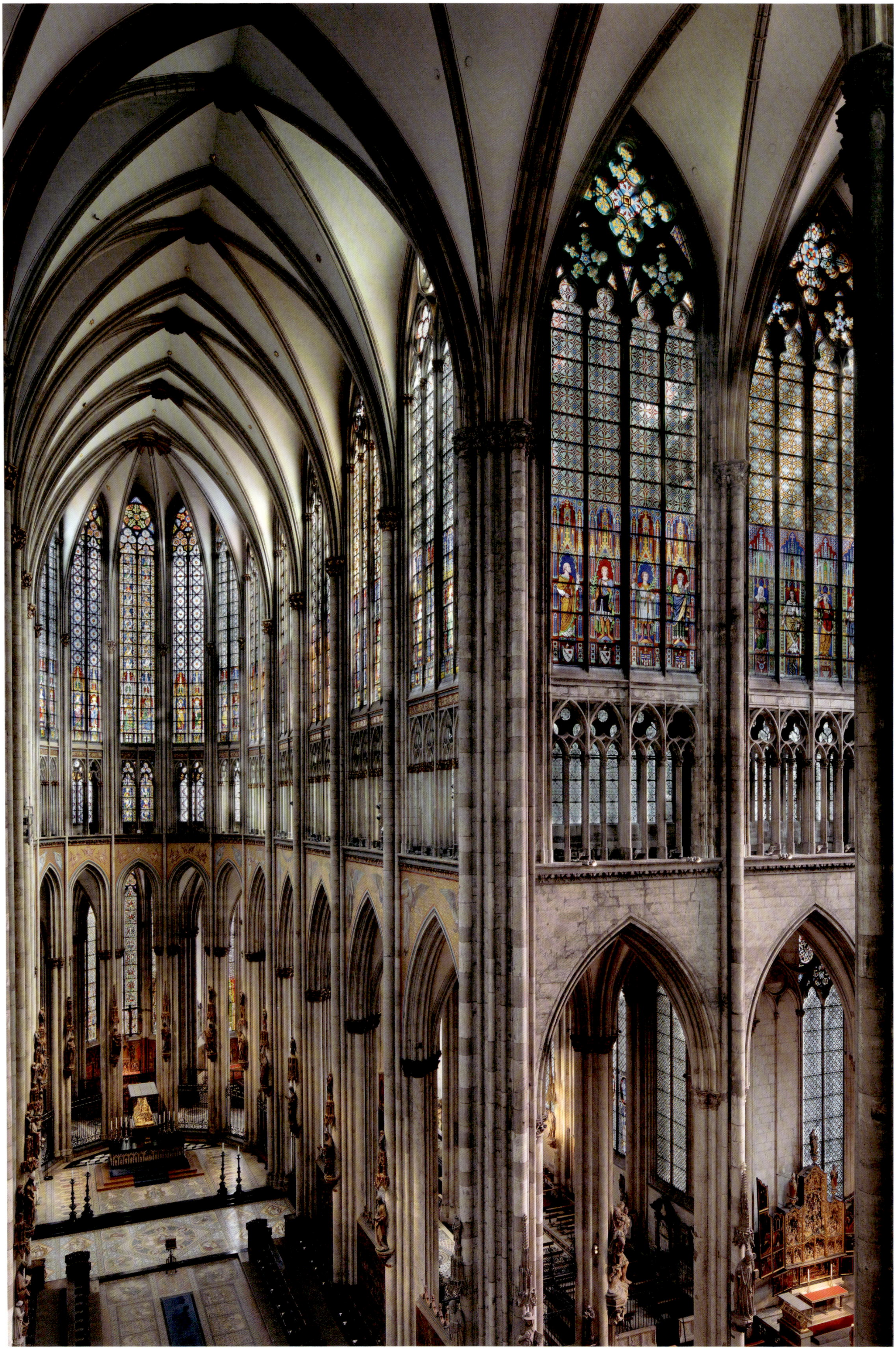

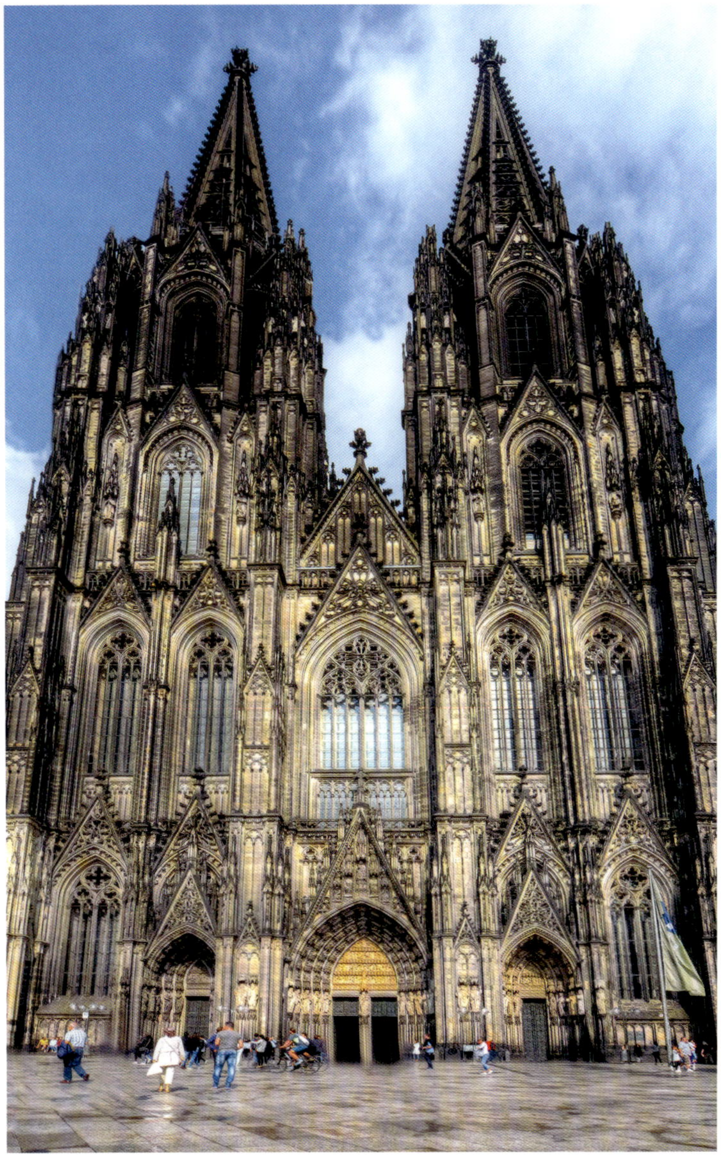

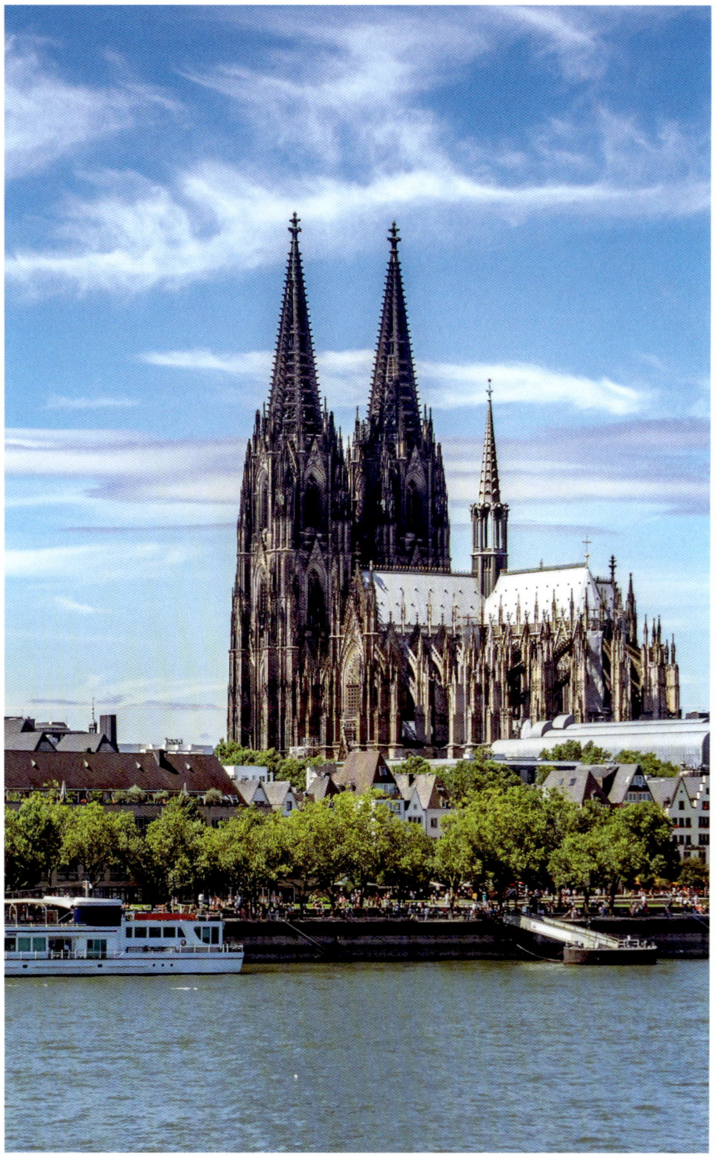

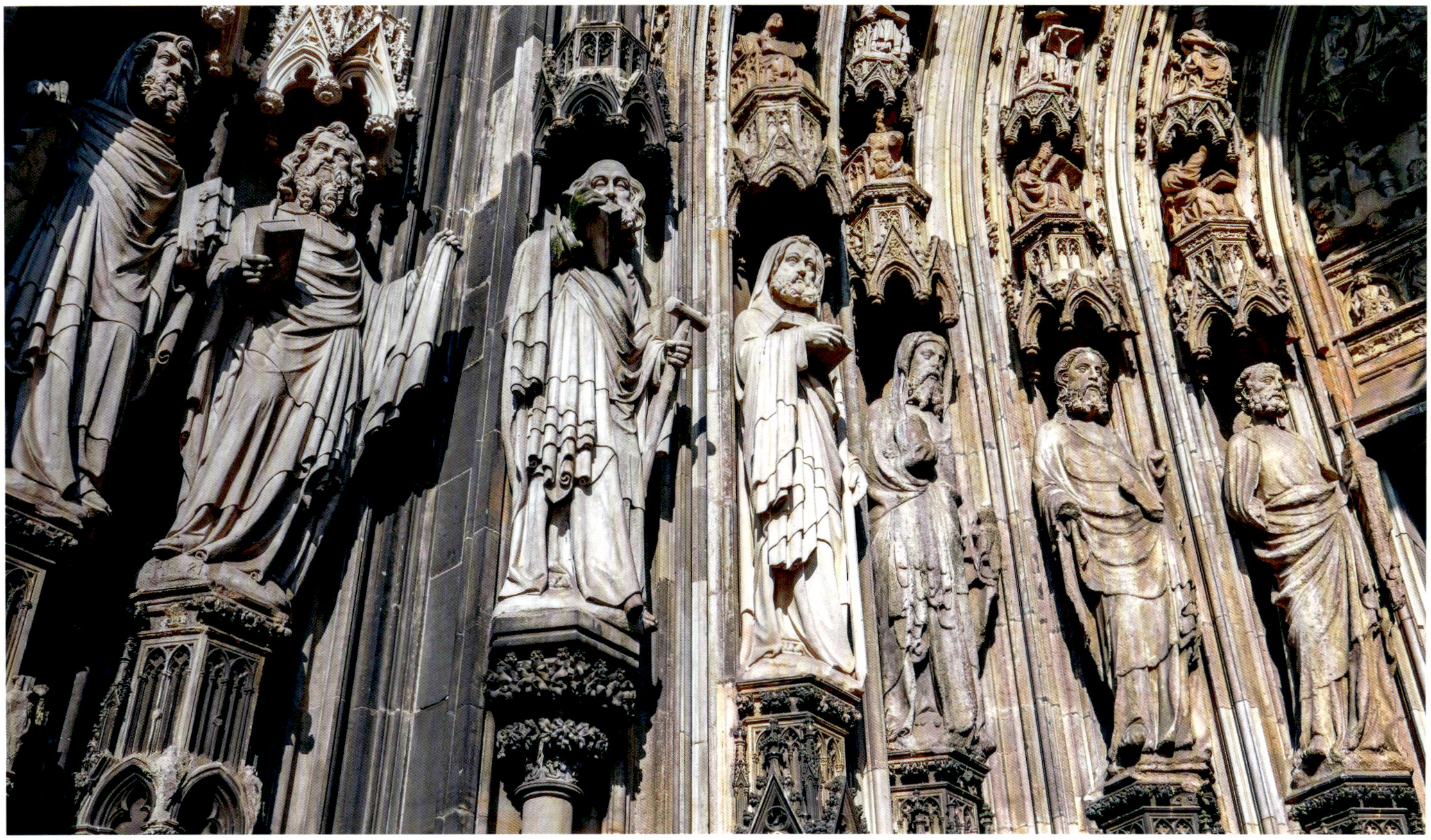

Opposite At over 141 feet (43 meters) high, the Gothic nave is the tallest in Germany.
Top left Cologne Cathedral remains among the world's tallest churches.
Top right The twin Gothic towers reach nearly 525 feet (160 meters) high.
Bottom Visitors enter the cathedral under the watchful eyes of the saints.

St. Basil's Cathedral

Domes Above Red Square

Built: 1555 – 1561 CE, Moscow, Russia

As colorful and varied as the towers of this cathedral may appear, their numerological symbolism is remarkably deliberate.

For some, its continued existence is sheer luck; for others, the fact of St. Basil's endurance through the centuries is proof of divine protection. After narrowly escaping destruction by Napoleon's troops, it was saved again in 1936 by Konstantin Baranovsky, a brave architect who, so the story goes, defied Stalin's orders and locked himself inside this unique place of worship to prevent its demolition.

Today, Red Square is unimaginable without the presence of St. Basil's—the cathedral was built in the 16th century following Ivan the Terrible's victory over the Khanate of Kazan. Legend has it that the Tsar had the two architects blinded after the cathedral's completion so they could never again create anything as magnificent.

Standing near the Moskva River, the church paints vibrant colors across Moscow's sky. Beneath the fantastically strange and ornate onion domes, the eight original freestanding chapels surround the main church. The cathedral's floor plan is as impressive as it is symbolic. Every axis and diagonal is arranged in groups of three to honor the Holy Trinity. Together, they form the shape of an eight-pointed star, a number, in the Christian tradition, symbolic of Christ's resurrection. Each part of the cathedral tells its own story. The central church is dedicated to the Feast of the Intercession of the Virgin Mary, known in the Orthodox tradition as the Pokrov feast, celebrated on October 1—one day before Kazan was finally conquered. Its green-and-gold dome rises majestically above the others, which glow in radiant shades of red, blue, and gold, each honoring saints and feast days significant in the Russian Orthodox tradition.

Among the saints venerated here is St. Basil, whose name soon eclipsed the cathedral's official title, "Cathedral of the Intercession of the Most Holy Theotokos on the Moat." St. Basil, venerated as a holy fool, was revered for his radical humility, courage, and unwavering faith—so much so that even Ivan the Terrible followed his advice. Basil died in the same year as the victory over Kazan, and the tenth chapel, added later at the northeastern corner of the cathedral, is dedicated to him. From there, he continues to watch over Moscow as the city's patron saint.

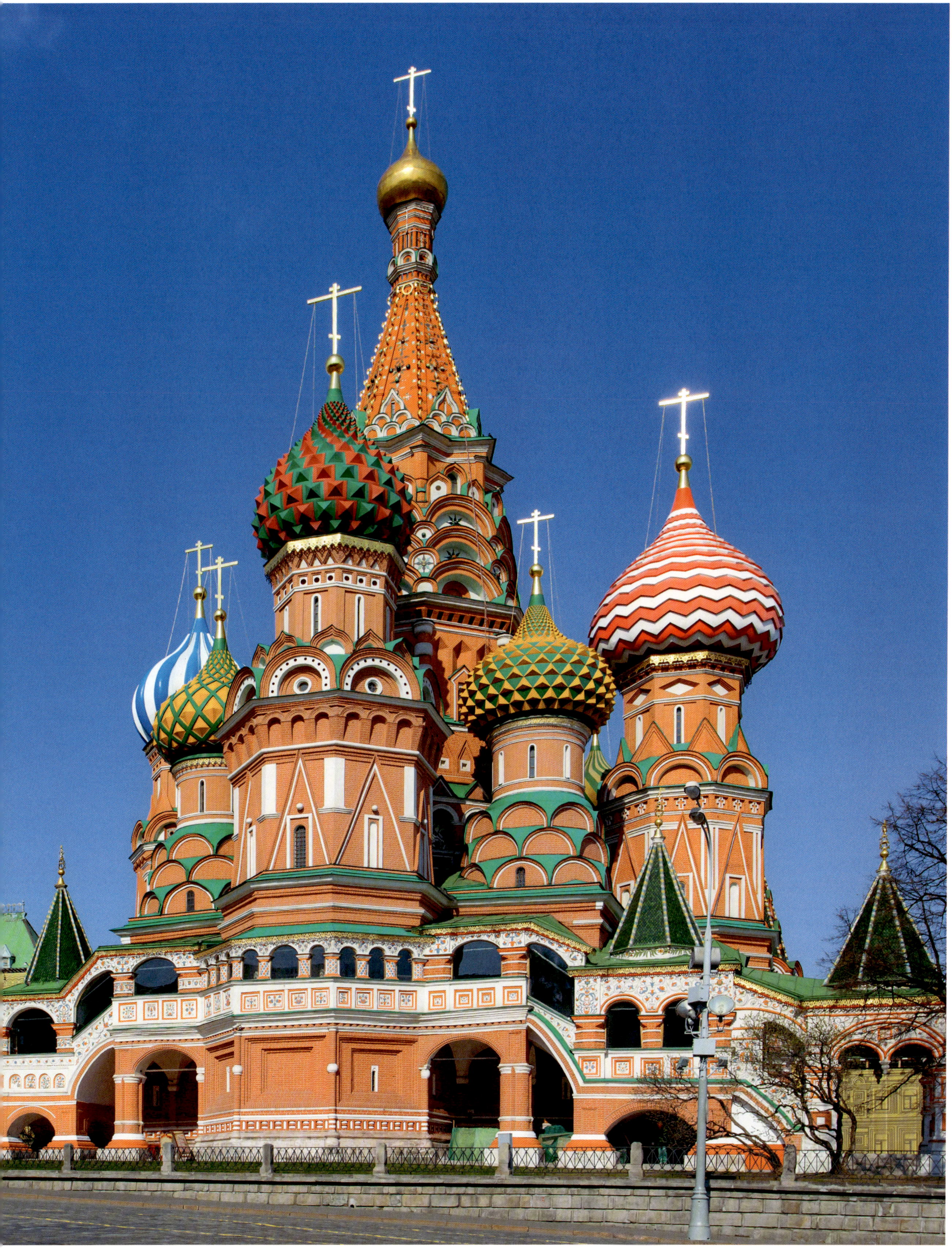

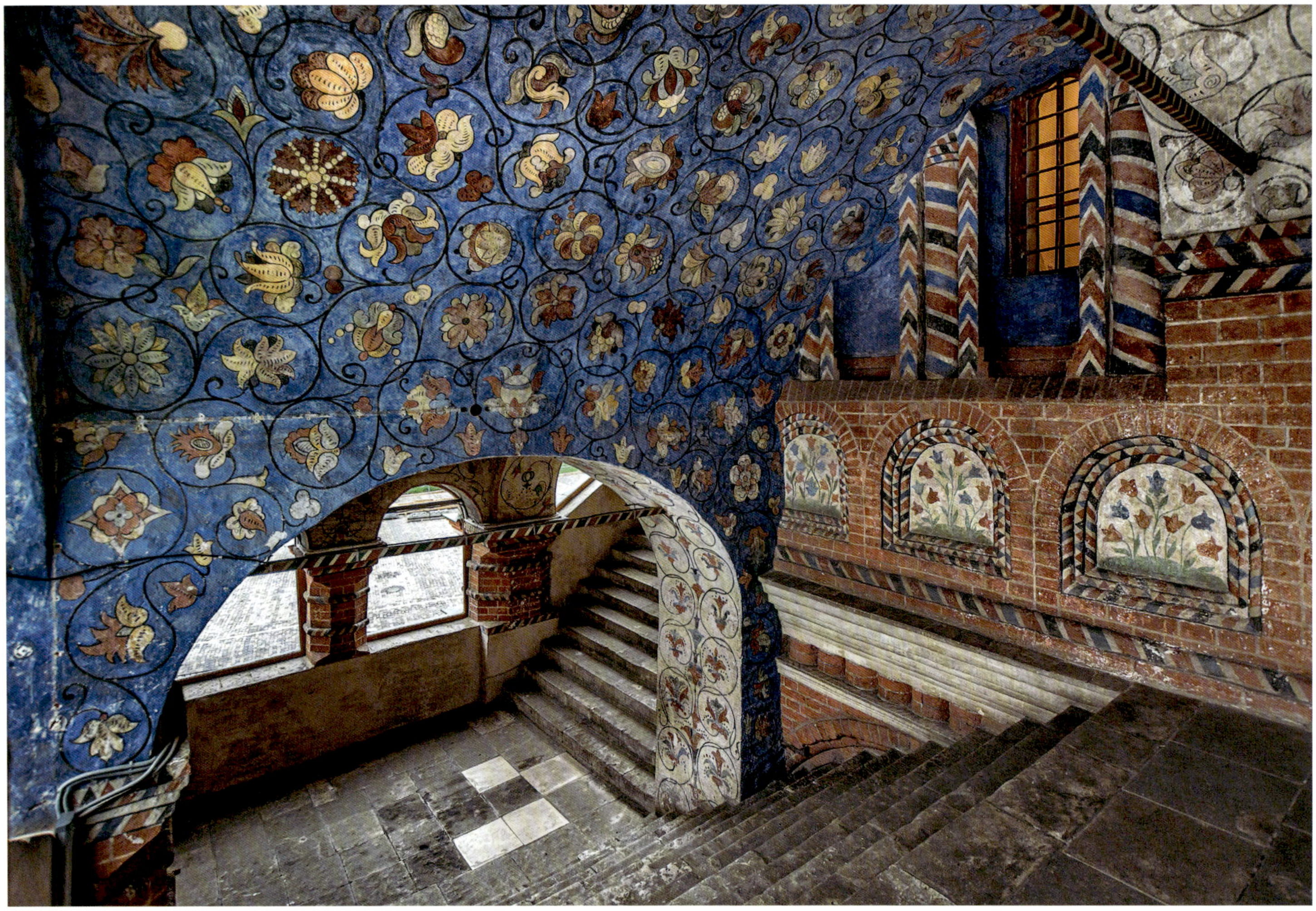

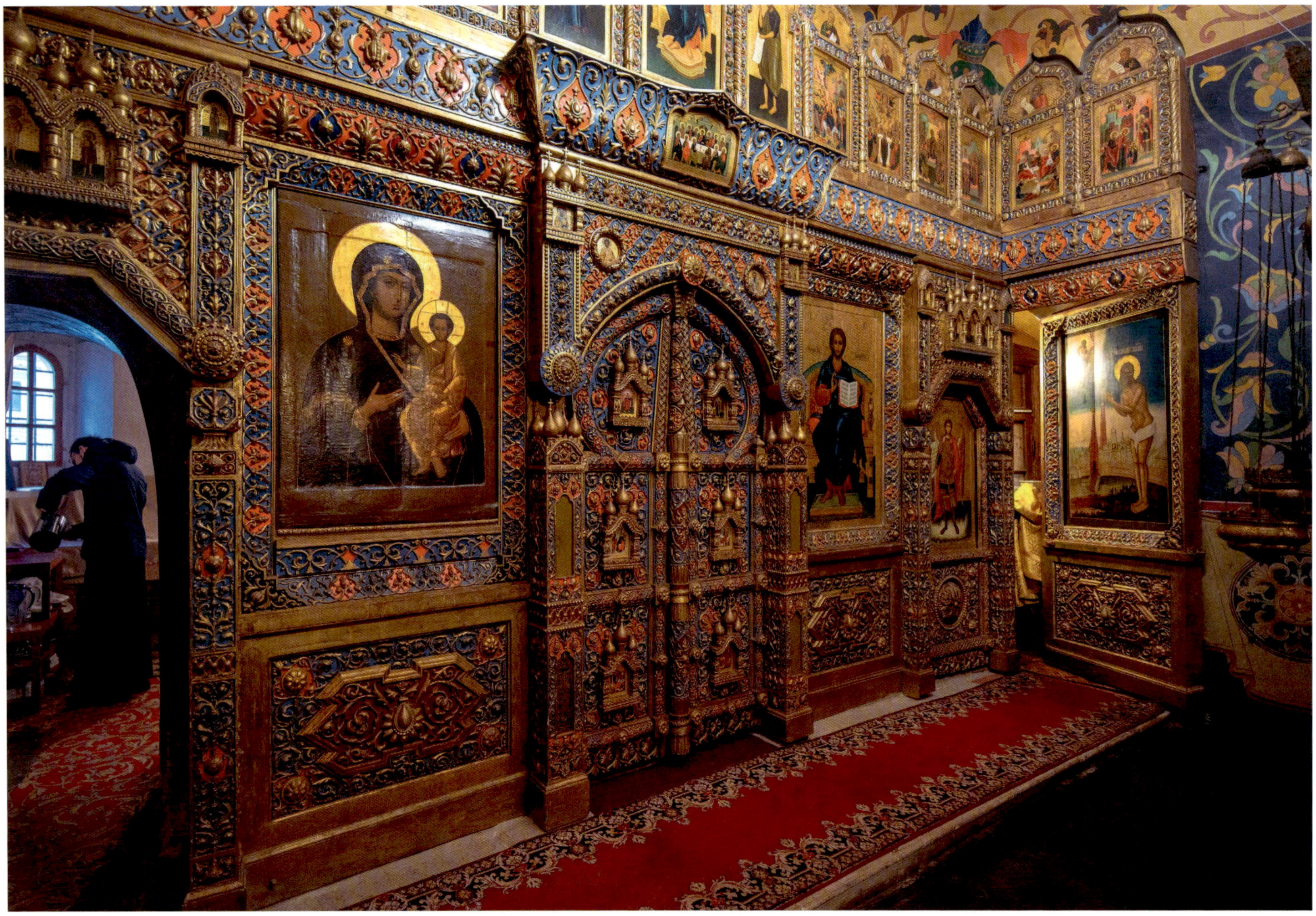

Top St. Basil's Cathedral owes its popular name to St. Basil the Blessed, whose tomb lies inside. *Bottom* The interior of the cathedral is as richly adorned as its colorful domes.

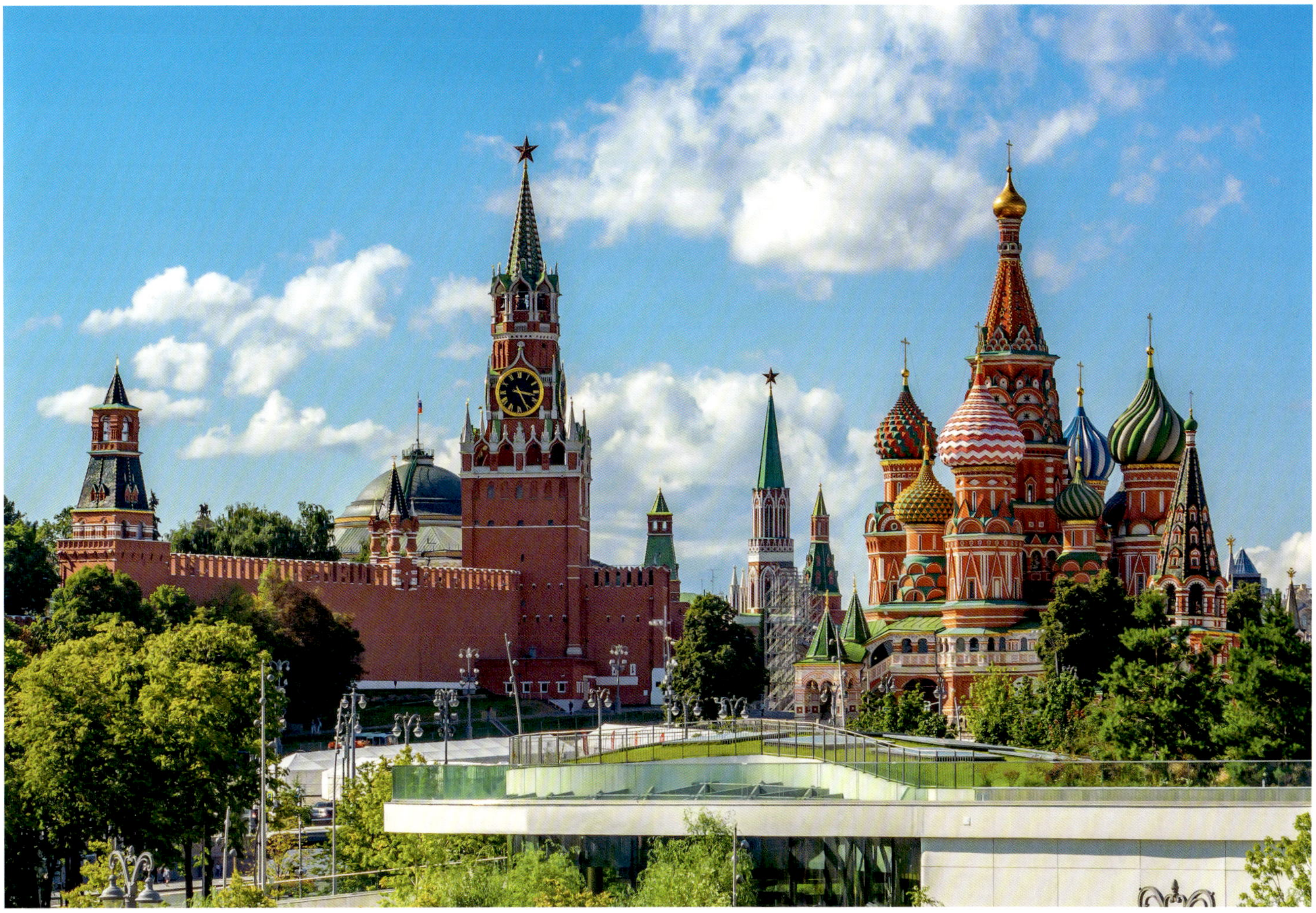

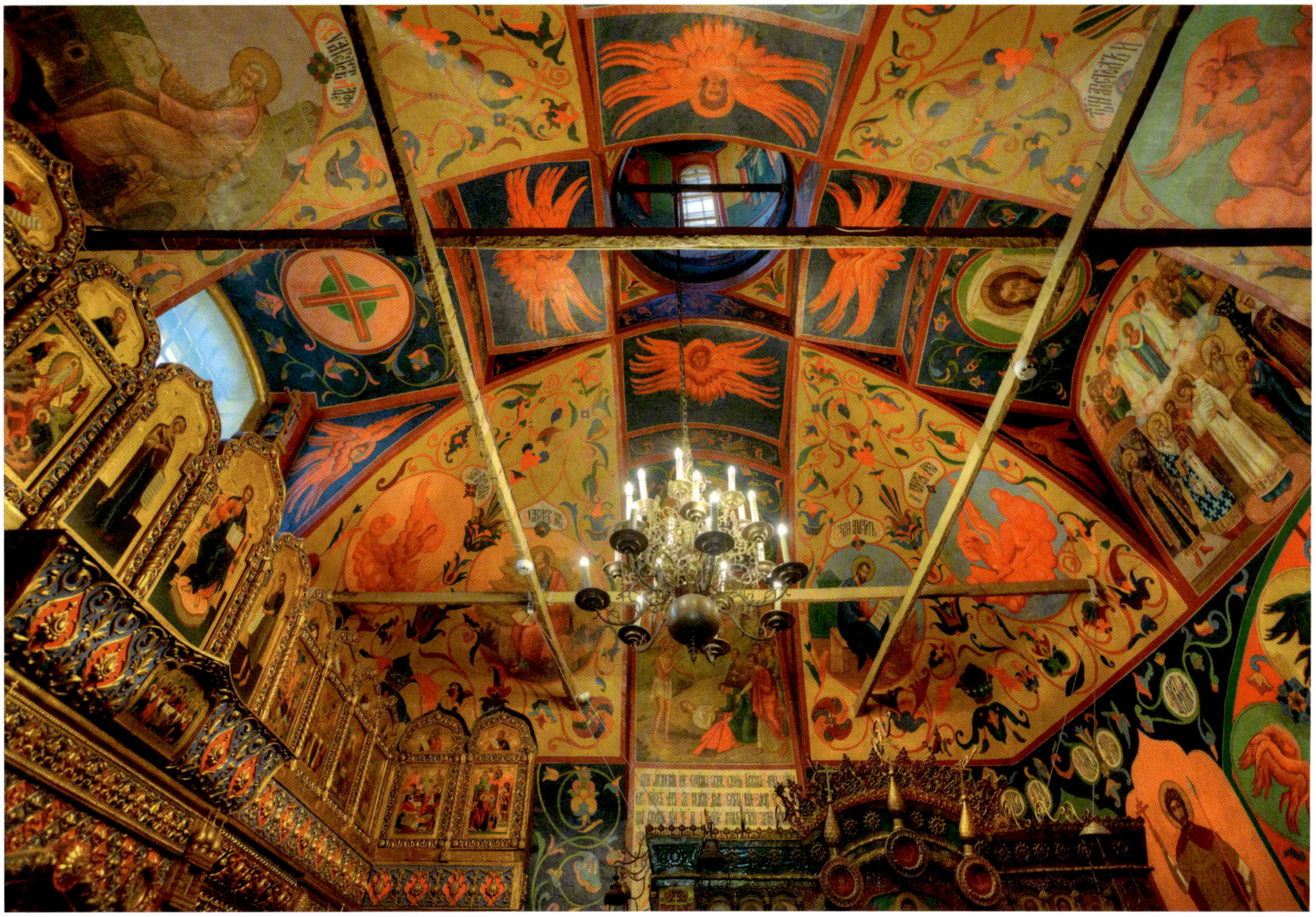

Top Originally, the domes had a simpler design. The now-iconic onion domes were added only in 1586. *Bottom* The priceless ceiling paintings depict various saints and floral patterns.

Borgund Stave Church

A Testament to a Turning Point

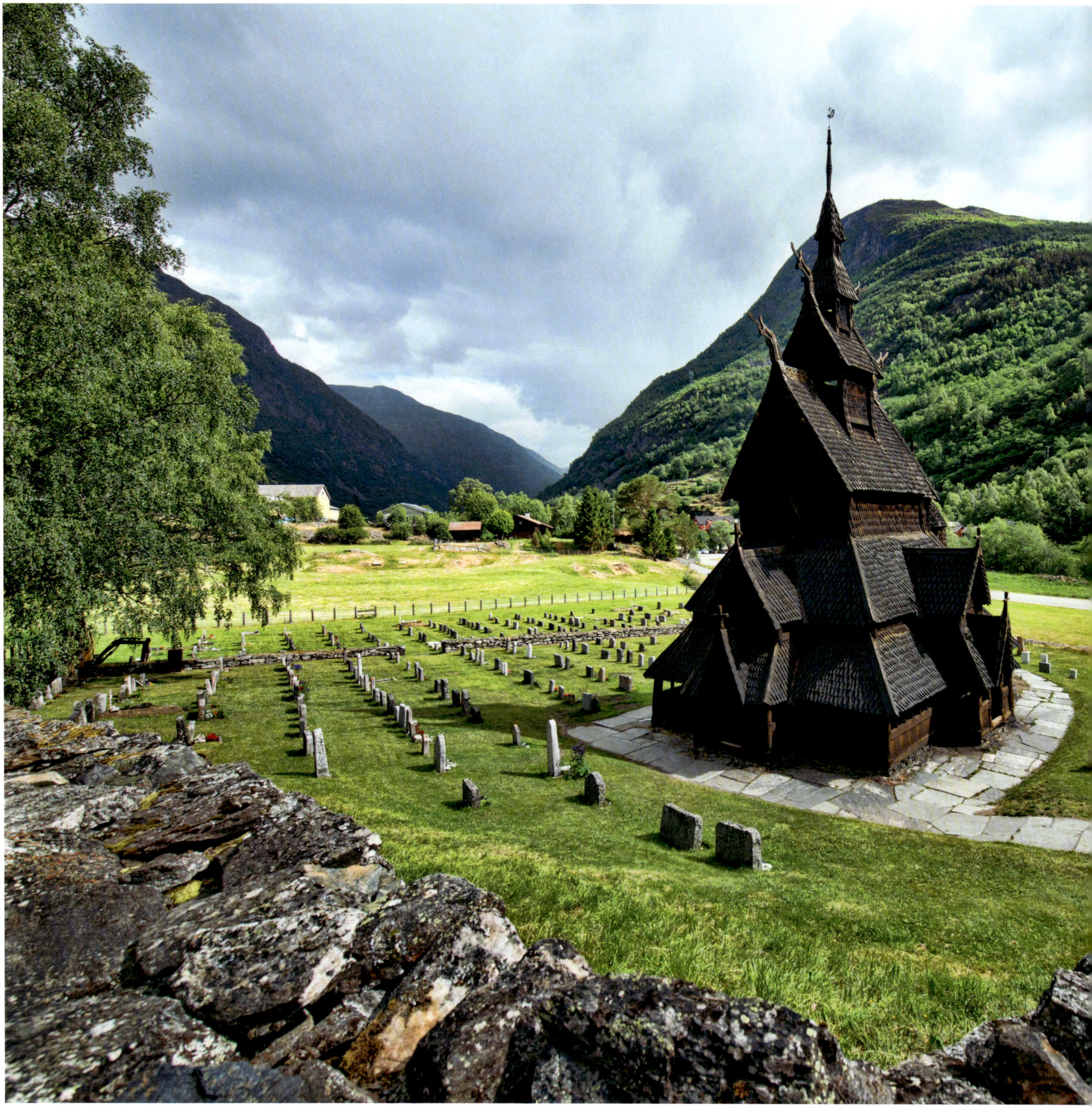

Built: ca. 1180 CE,
Borgund, Norway

Although Christianity supplanted them, the Norse gods have never completely vanished from the country's collective memory.

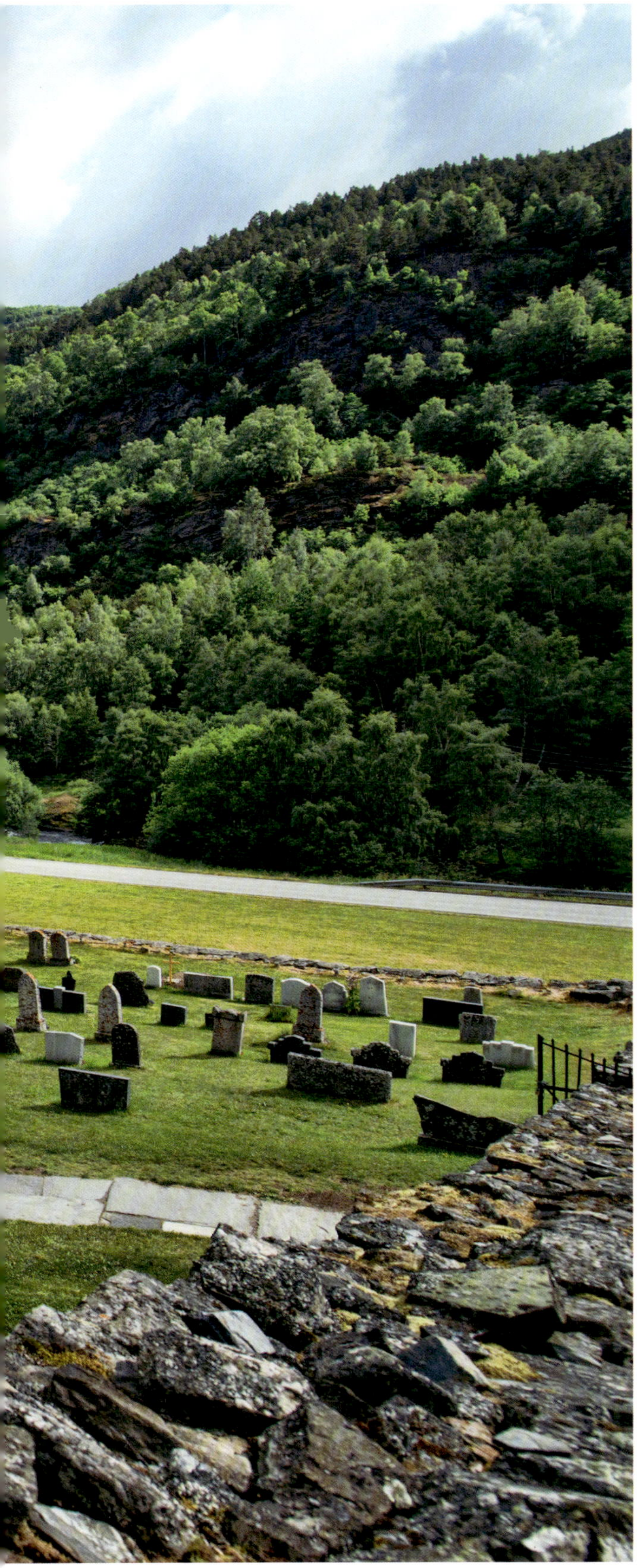

Few structures capture the period between the old Viking culture and the rise of Christianity in Scandinavia as vividly as the Borgund Stave Church. Even as late as the 10th century, parts of Norway were still deeply rooted in pagan traditions and Norse mythology. The spread of Christianity, however, was rapid, driven primarily by Nordic rulers who sought to consolidate their power by unifying the many clans and regions under a centralized faith. This transformation was often accompanied by violence. Over the following centuries, numerous churches were erected directly atop destroyed pagan sacred sites. While Borgund Stave Church has not been definitively proven to be one of them, its construction marked the arrival of Christianity in the remote Lærdal Valley.

Yet the old, beloved customs quietly seeped back into the culture. Elements of pagan festivals began to shape Christian celebrations. Christmas, for example, was merged with the traditional winter solstice festival, and Easter adopted pagan fertility symbols, which explains why Europe and many other parts of the world celebrate the resurrection of Jesus with eggs and rabbits to this day.

Aspects of this kind of religious syncretism are beautifully evident in Borgund Stave Church. Its visually startling, tiered roofs are adorned with dragon heads—traditional Viking symbols likely intended to ward off evil spirits. The church's interior is simple, yet profoundly atmospheric. The wooden pillars bear carvings of animal motifs that echo Norse myths and deities. Dark wooden walls and small, round windows create an intimate, almost fairy-tale ambiance. It is easy to imagine medieval worshippers seated on heavy wooden benches in the dim light, whispering tentative first prayers to a new God.

Around 900 stave churches were built during the Middle Ages, of which only 28 remain today. The term "stave church" derives from the unique construction method, where upright wooden posts, known as staves, form the structural framework. Borgund Stave Church is considered the best preserved and most authentic of them all. Layers of pitch and tar have shielded it from Norway's harsh weather, ensuring its survival.

Today, Borgund Stave Church is no longer used for regular worship. Instead, it serves as a museum, a significant cultural landmark, and a popular tourist attraction. Above all, it stands as a reminder of the Norse gods, who may have lost the battle against the new faith but continue to live on—in architecture, in legends, and in the untamed spirit of Norway itself.

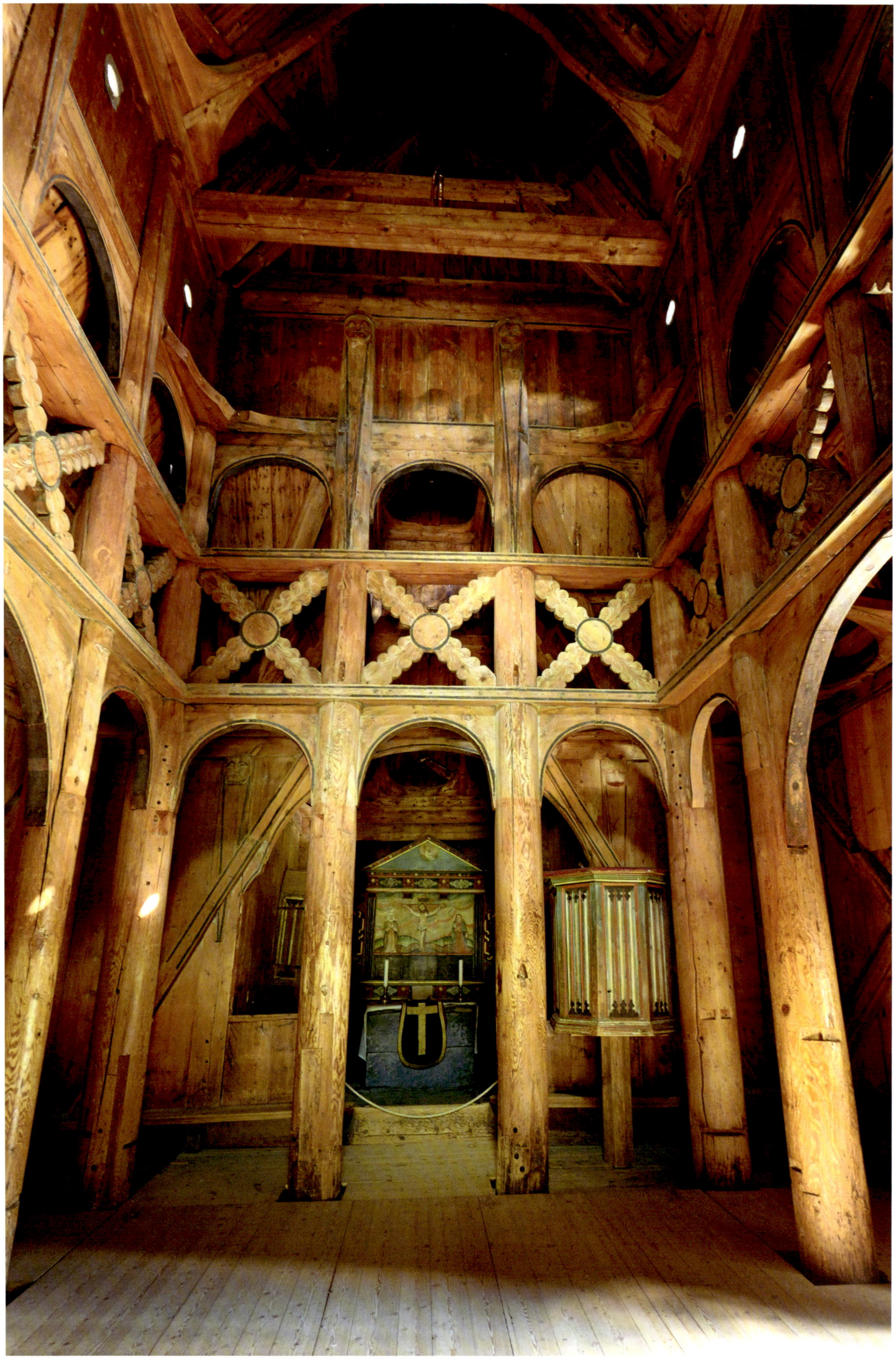

Borgund, Norway

Above Dendrochronological studies reveal that the timber for this mystical church was felled during the winter of 1180/81, later crafted into this masterpiece of syncretic architecture.

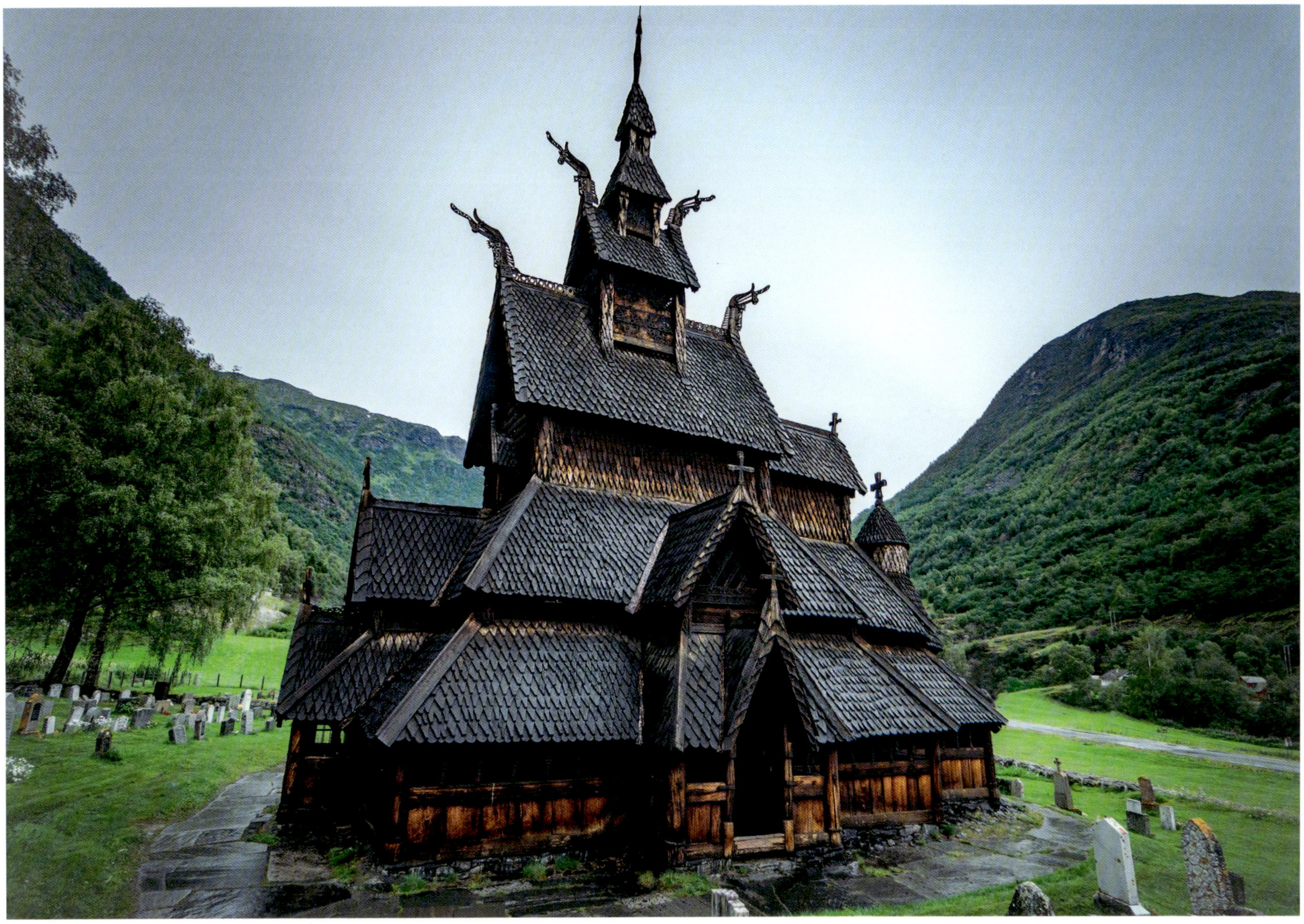

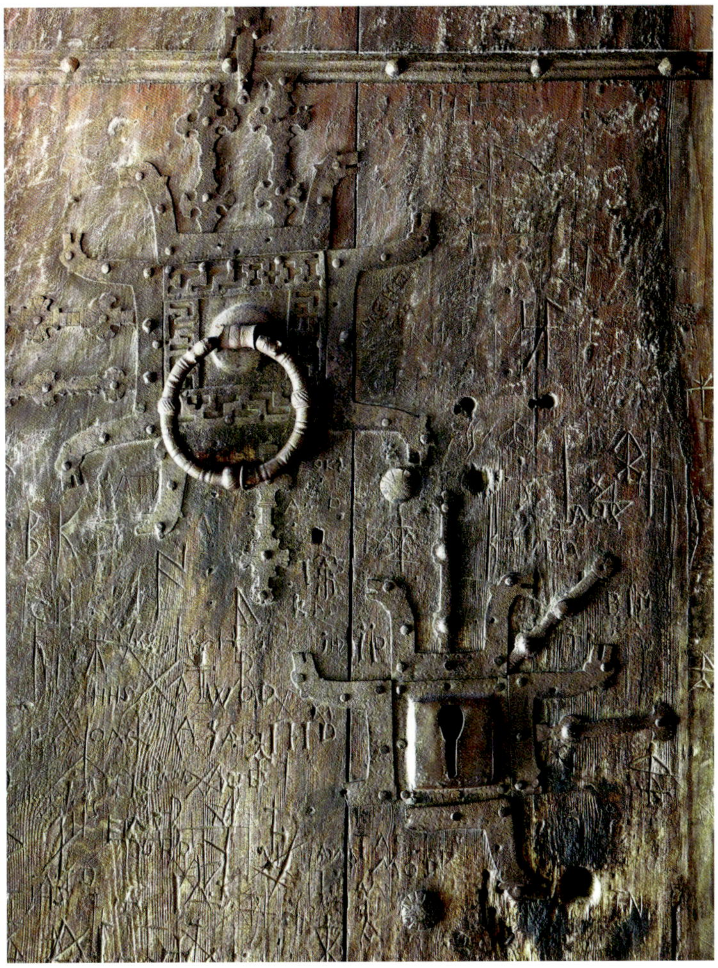

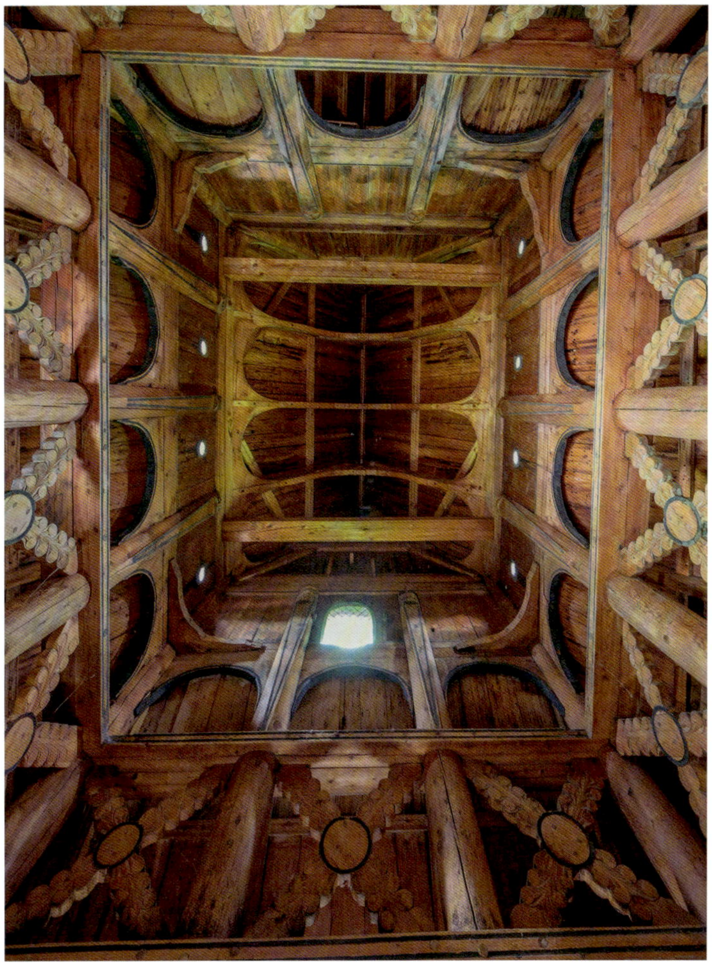

Top The church is a blend of Norse and Christian architecture.
Bottom left The runic inscriptions are like medieval graffiti.
Bottom right Borgund Stave Church is one of Norway's most important cultural sites.

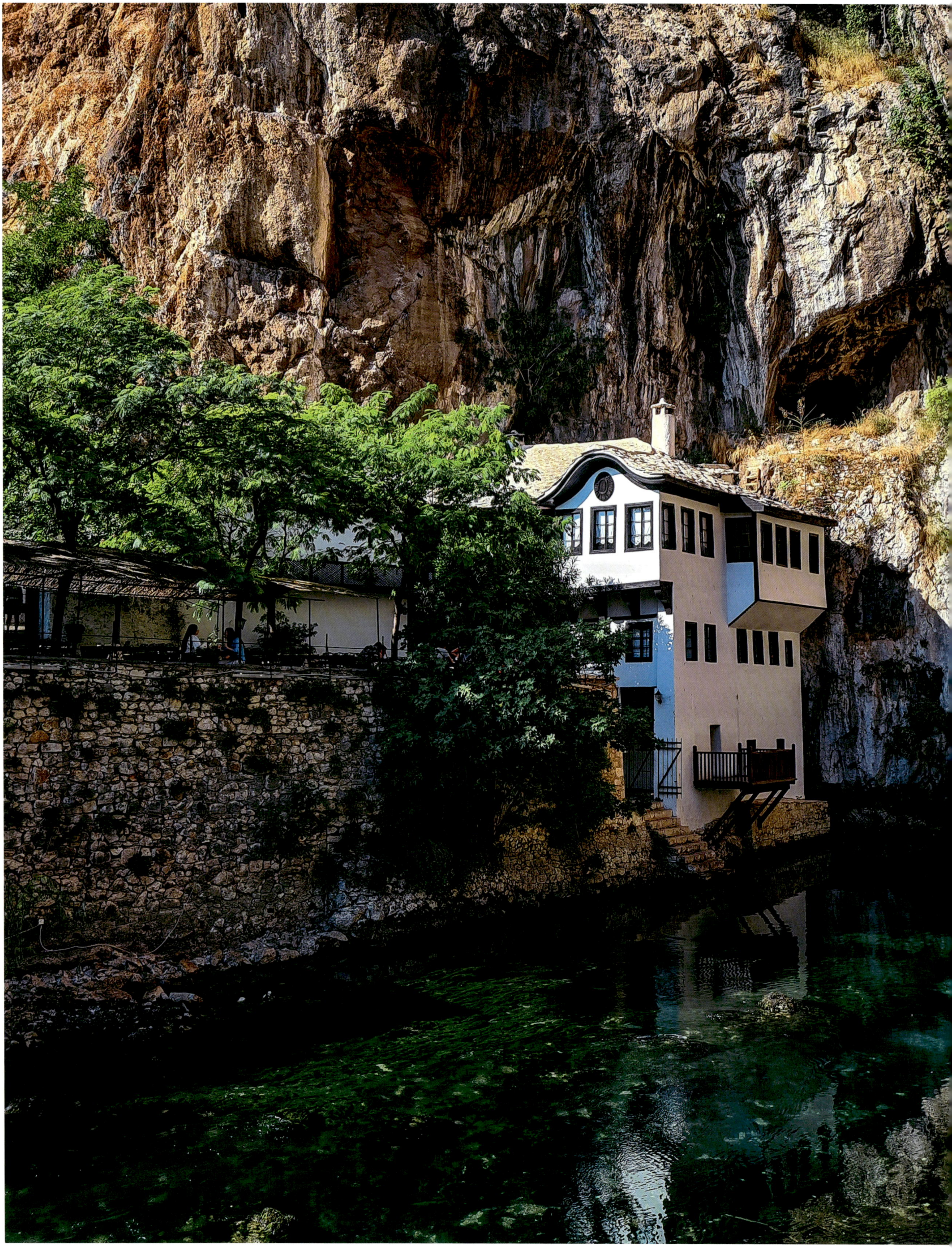

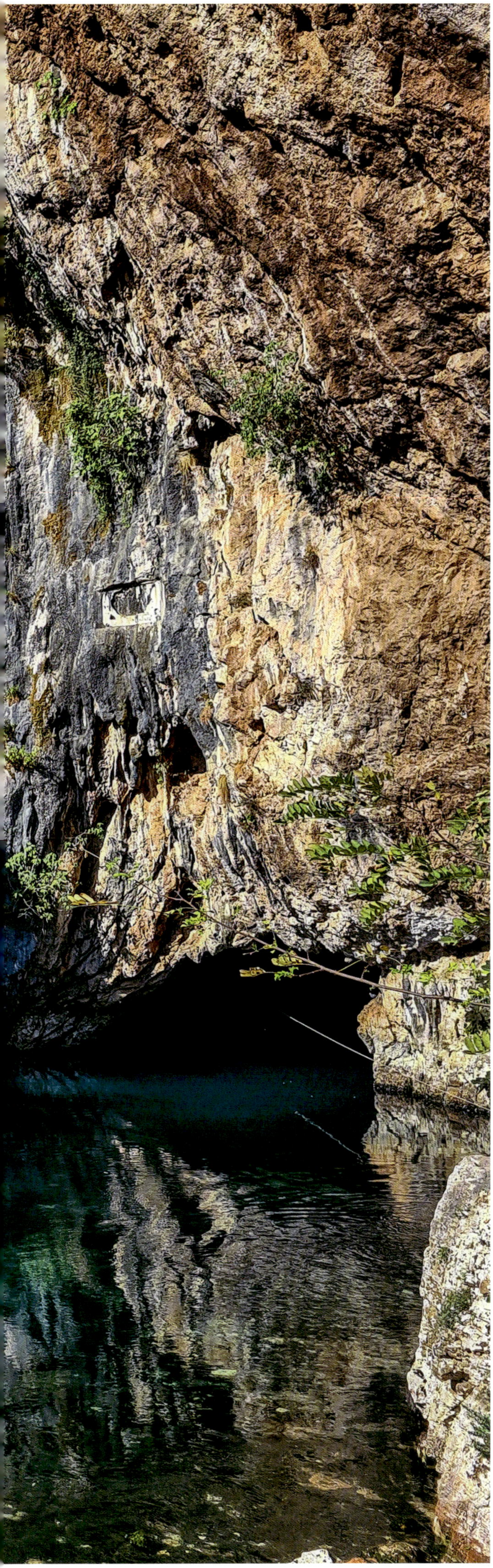

Blagaj Tekke

At the Source of Holiness

Built: 16th century CE, restored several times since,
Blagaj, Bosnia and Herzegovina

Since late antiquity, these waters have witnessed countless believers in various states of prayer.

Like a splendid painting come to life, the dervish monastery of Blagaj Tekke rests at the foot of a towering cliff, nestled by the sacred source of the Buna River. Its gray stone walls and small white balconies reflect in the turquoise water below. From cracks in the walls and crevices in the rock, green leaves and small bushes sprout, adding to the serene beauty. For centuries, this magical place has drawn seekers of spiritual enlightenment.

Blagaj Tekke was built in the 16th century by the Bektashi dervishes, a mystical Sufi brotherhood, and the monastery's architecture is a harmonious blend of simplicity and symbolism. The central prayer room, the Semahana, invites visitors to a state of inner contemplation. Wooden balconies and intricately decorated window frames showcase the period's Ottoman craftsmanship. Even before the Tekke's construction, this site was considered sacred. The Bogomils, a Christian sect of the Middle Ages, had once erected a sanctuary here. Archaeological excavations further reveal that the Buna River's source had been used for religious ceremonies since late antiquity.

Yet the centuries have left their marks: landslides, wars, and political upheavals repeatedly brought destruction to the monastery. Each time, however, it was lovingly restored and often enriched with new stylistic elements. Turkish baroque features, such as the oval roof above the entrance facade and the elaborately decorated ceilings, were added during later renovations. In its most recent restoration phases, the Tekke was outfitted with facilities like the *musafirhana,* or guesthouse, which offered hospitality to wandering dervishes and travelers, in keeping with the brotherhood's traditions.

Today, no dervishes live permanently at the Tekke. Nevertheless, it remains a vibrant center of spiritual practice. *Dhikr* ceremonies are held three times a week, where worshippers chant the names of God in rhythmic recitation. Accompanied by drums and special breathing techniques, participants enter a state of deep focus and spiritual ecstasy. During Mawlid, an annual festival celebrating the Prophet Muhammad's birthday, hundreds of worshippers gather at the Tekke to pray, perform *dhikr,* and celebrate the spiritual traditions of this holy place.

For those who wish to visit, the Tekke's doors remain wide open. Here, at the source of the Buna, the mysteries of Sufism seem almost tangible, framed by the breathtaking natural beauty of this small corner of Eastern Europe.

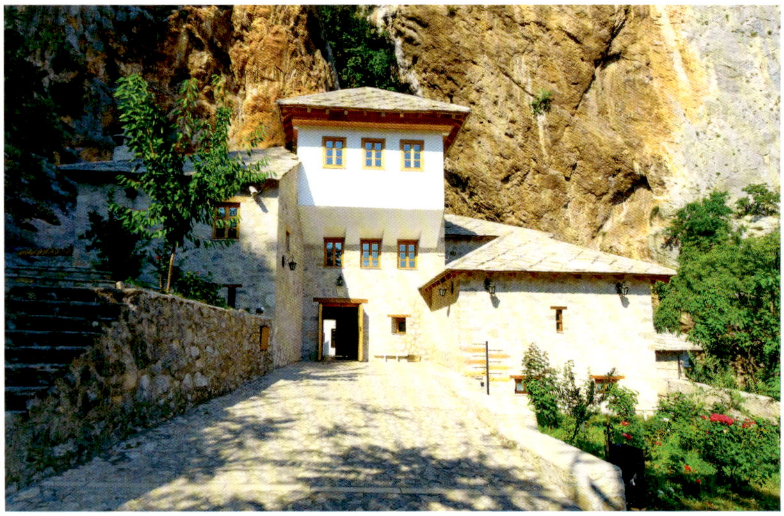

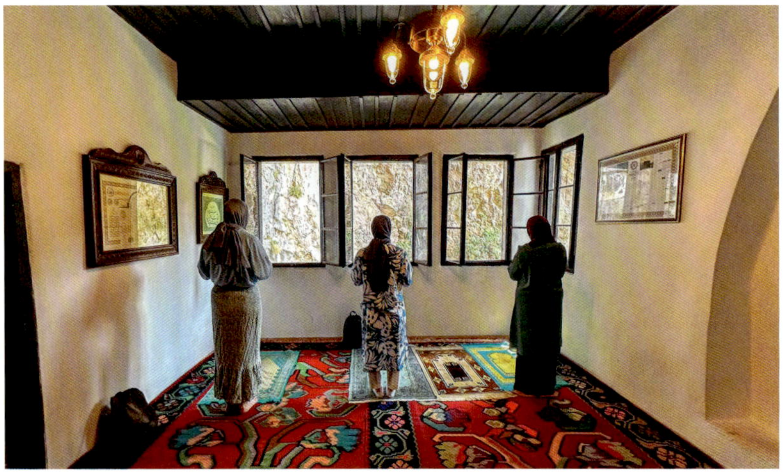

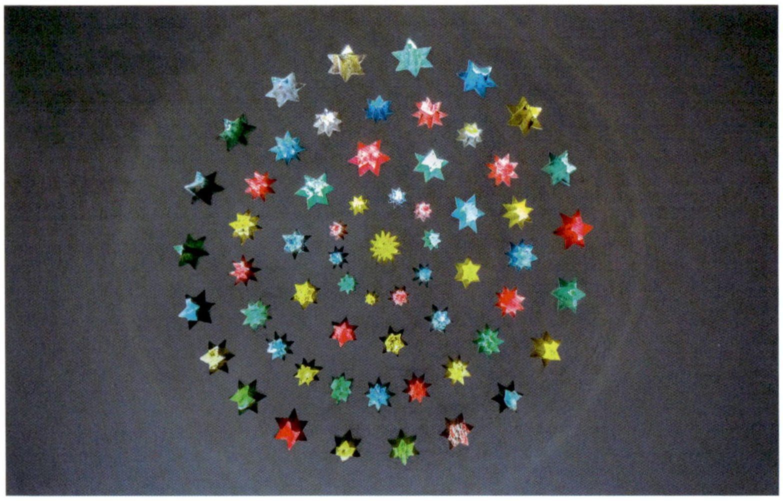

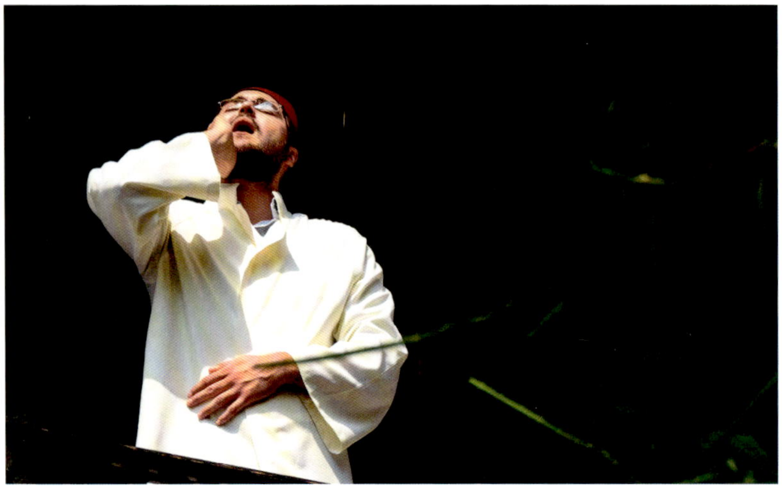

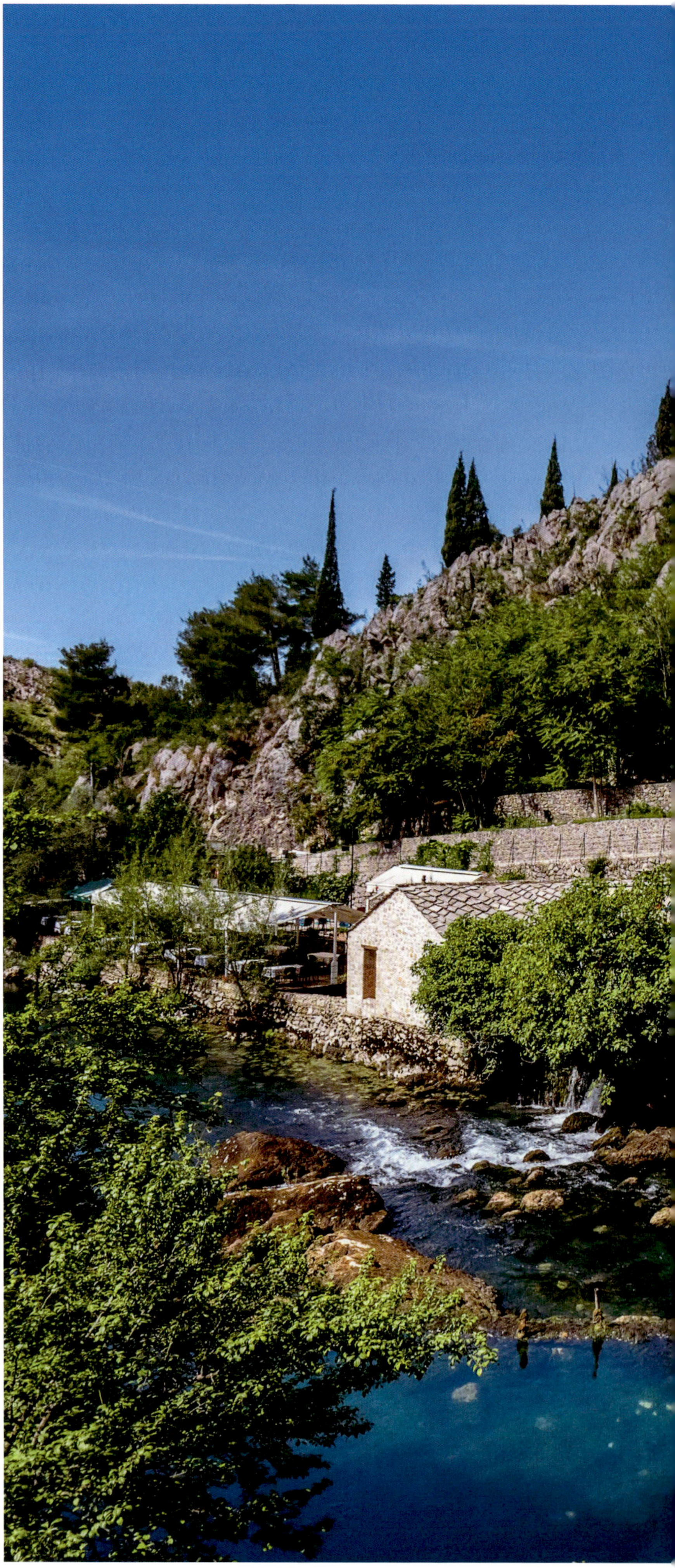

Blagaj, Bosnia and Herzegovina

Top The word *tekke* means a place of retreat or asylum.
Upper middle In May, worshippers celebrate the Prophet's birthday.
Lower middle Sunlight streams through the star-shaped glass.
Bottom A modern revival of the dervish traditions began in the 1970s.

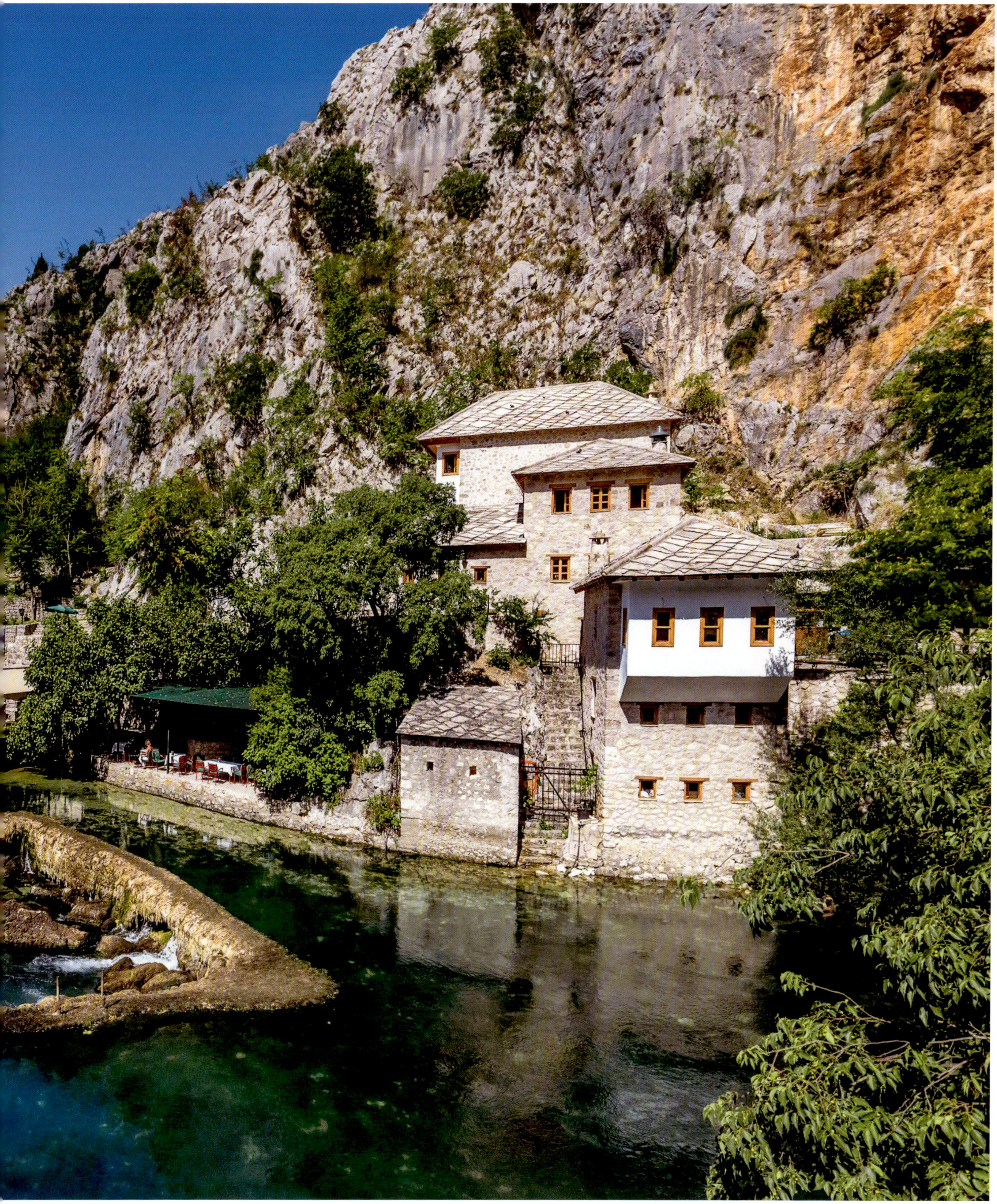

Above Blagaj Tekke houses the *türbe*, or tomb, of the 13th-century mystical dervish Sarı Saltuk. His legacy is intertwined with the spread of Islam and Sufism in the Balkans and Anatolia.

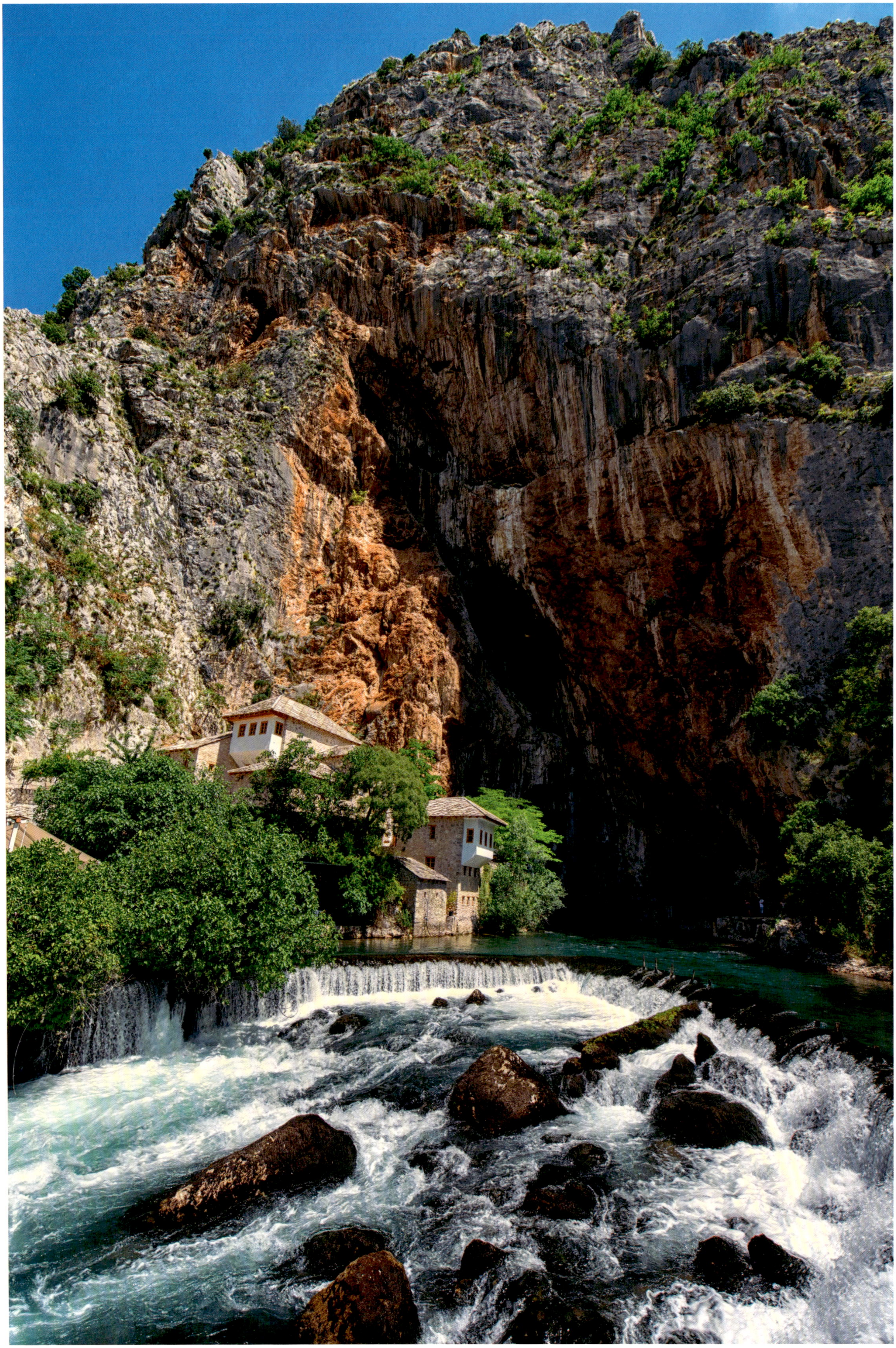

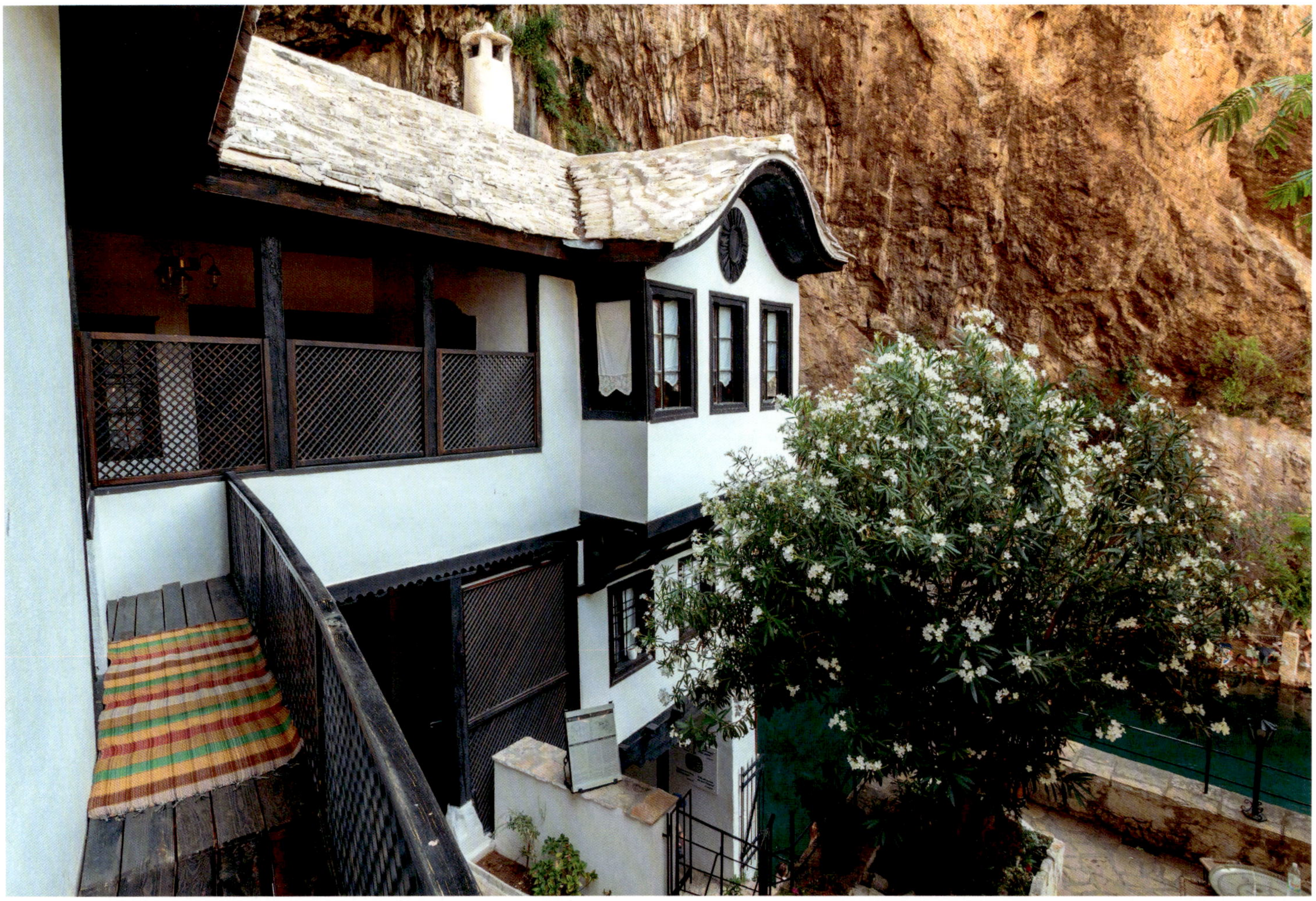

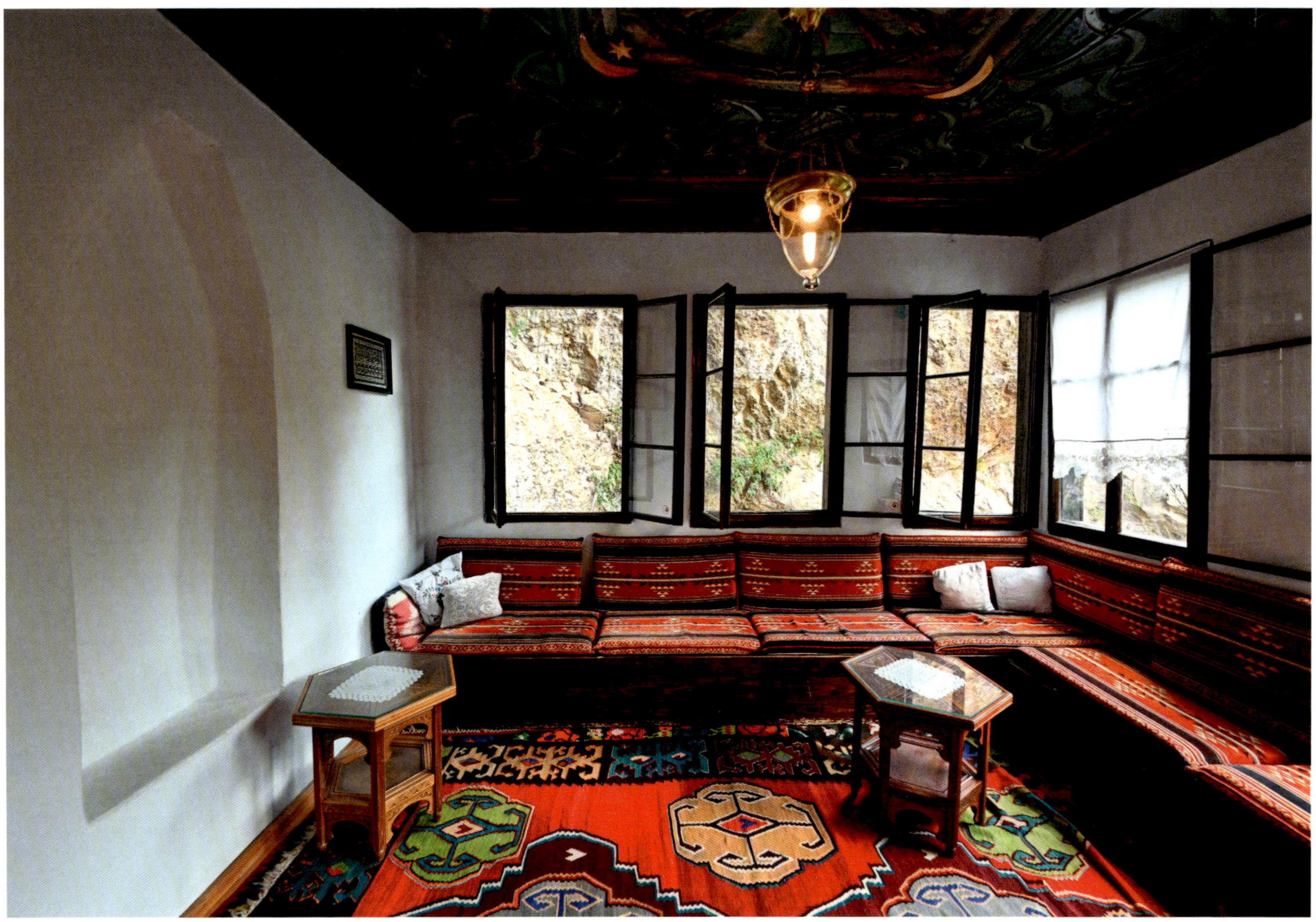

Opposite The source of the Buna River has been considered sacred since late antiquity.
Top A steep cliff rises above the monastery.
Bottom Many Sufi artifacts are safely preserved here.

Sanctuary of Madonna della Corona

Pilgrim's Solace

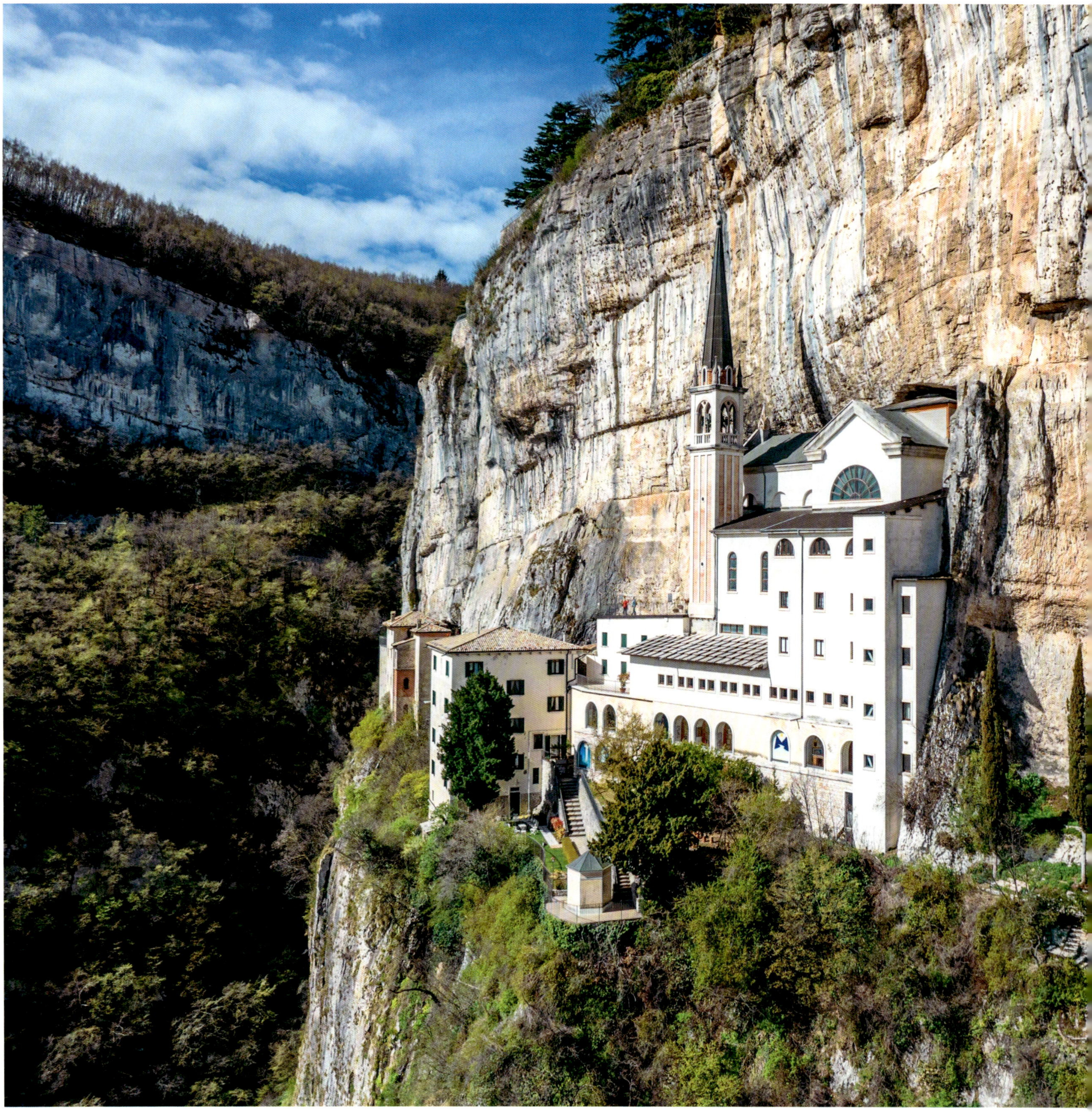

Built: 1530 CE (current form: 1974 – 1978 CE), Spiazzi, Italy

The pilgrimage route to this sanctuary is filled with challenging stretches, the Stations of the Cross, and breathtaking views.

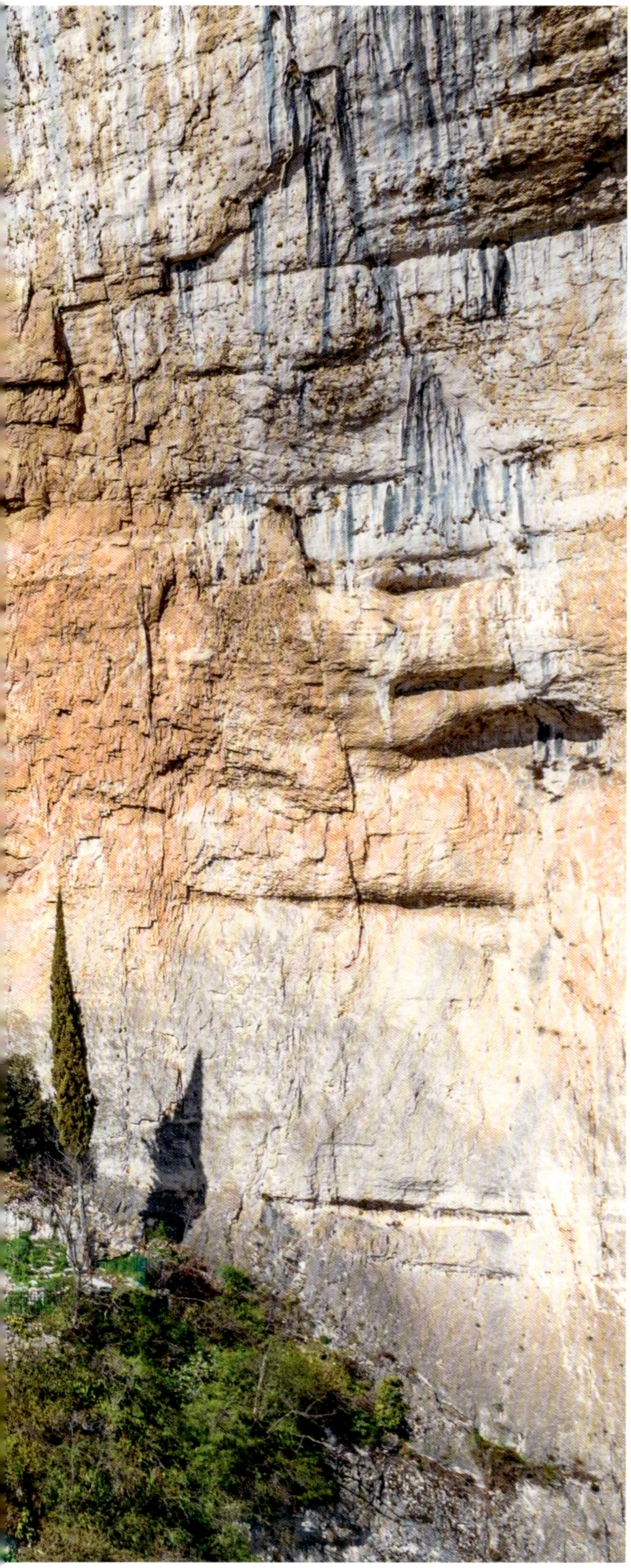

High above the rushing waters of the river Adige, the Santuary of Madonna della Corona clings dramatically to the sheer cliffs of Monte Baldo. Here, east of Lake Garda, pilgrims have sought inner peace and spiritual solace for centuries, entreating the Madonna for her intercession. All around, their prayers drift through the dense green forests of the Veneto region en route to their audience.

To fully embrace the pilgrimage experience, one begins the steep ascent to the sanctuary in the village of Brentino. Though the path is narrow and dizzying in places, the roughly two-hour hike is more than worth the effort. Around every bend, spectacular vistas unfold; behind each switchback lies another spectacular surprise. Along the way, physical markers offer solemn reminders of Christ's journey to the Cross. At the Grotta della Madonna, a sacred cave along the trail, pilgrims know they are close. Just a few more hairpin turns and the full splendor of the sanctuary reveals itself. Majestically, its Gothic facade of pale marble rises against the rugged cliffs. From the forecourt of the sanctuary, the view sweeps far across the verdant valley below.

At that moment, it's easy to believe the legend. In 1522, angels are said to have carried the statue of the Madonna della Corona here from Rhodes, to save it from destruction. Although a handful of hermits had lived on the remote slopes of Monte Baldo as early as the 11th century, and a small chapel was built in the 13th century, this breathtaking location became a site of pilgrimage after word of the miraculous delivery spread. The church evolved over the centuries, expanding and modernizing until the 1970s, when much of the old church was dismantled and then rebuilt in its current form. Inside, the bare rock of Monte Baldo forms the left wall of the church, a natural contrast to its Gothic elements. The restrained use of decoration draws the eye to the high altar cut from marble. Above it, nestled in a small rocky niche, stands the sanctuary's emotional centerpiece: the statue of the Madonna della Corona and her crucified son. Intricately designed windows let in soft, diffused light, while the glow of candles lit by supplicants flickers from the small side chapels.

The church is particularly popular with the faithful during the feast of the Assumption of Mary. For those unable—or unwilling—to undertake the steep climb from Brentino, there's an alternative: park in the nearby village of Spiazzi and take the short, well-paved footpath to the sanctuary. Ultimately, it's not the distances trod by one's feet, but the faith in one's heart that determines the journey.

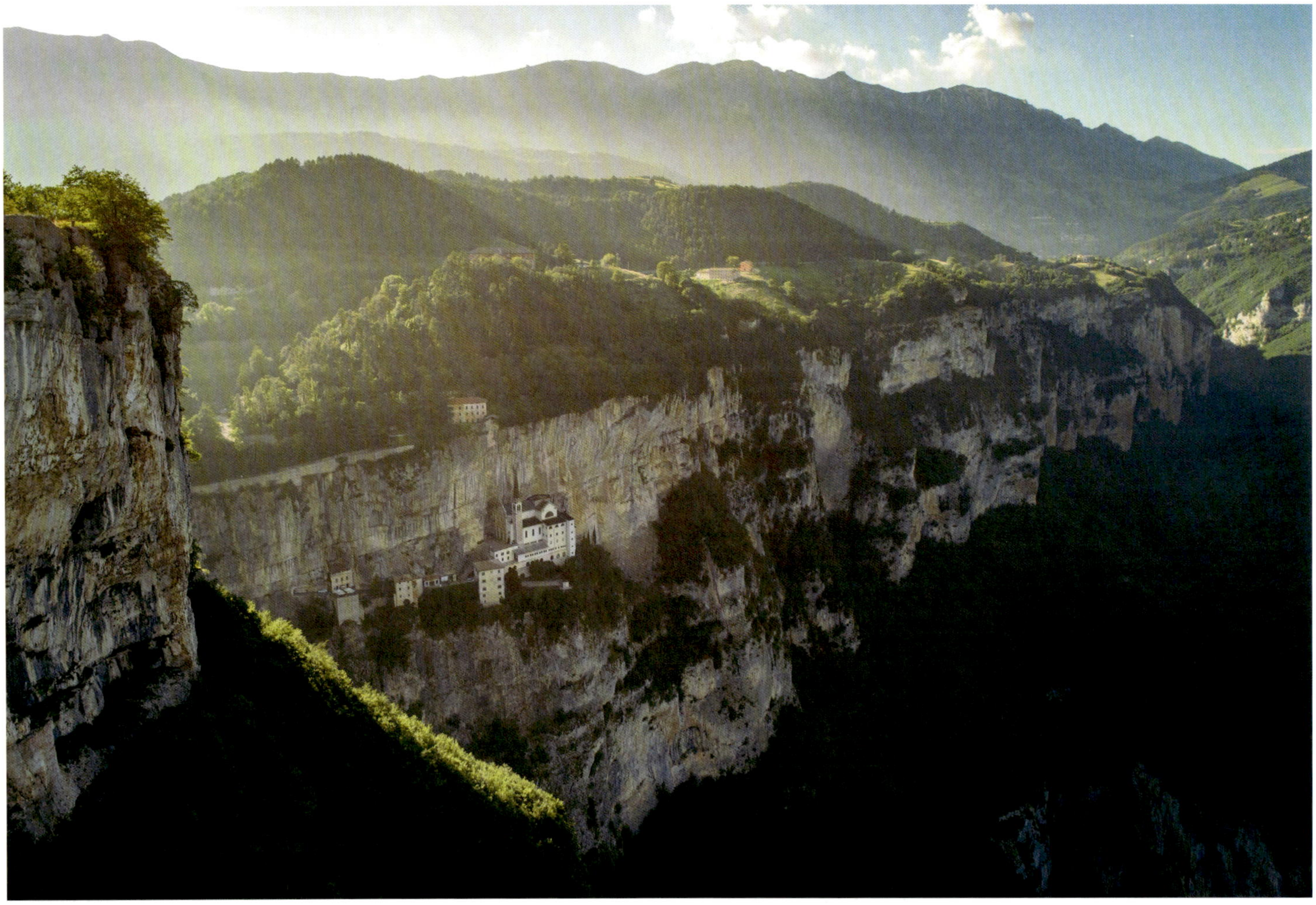

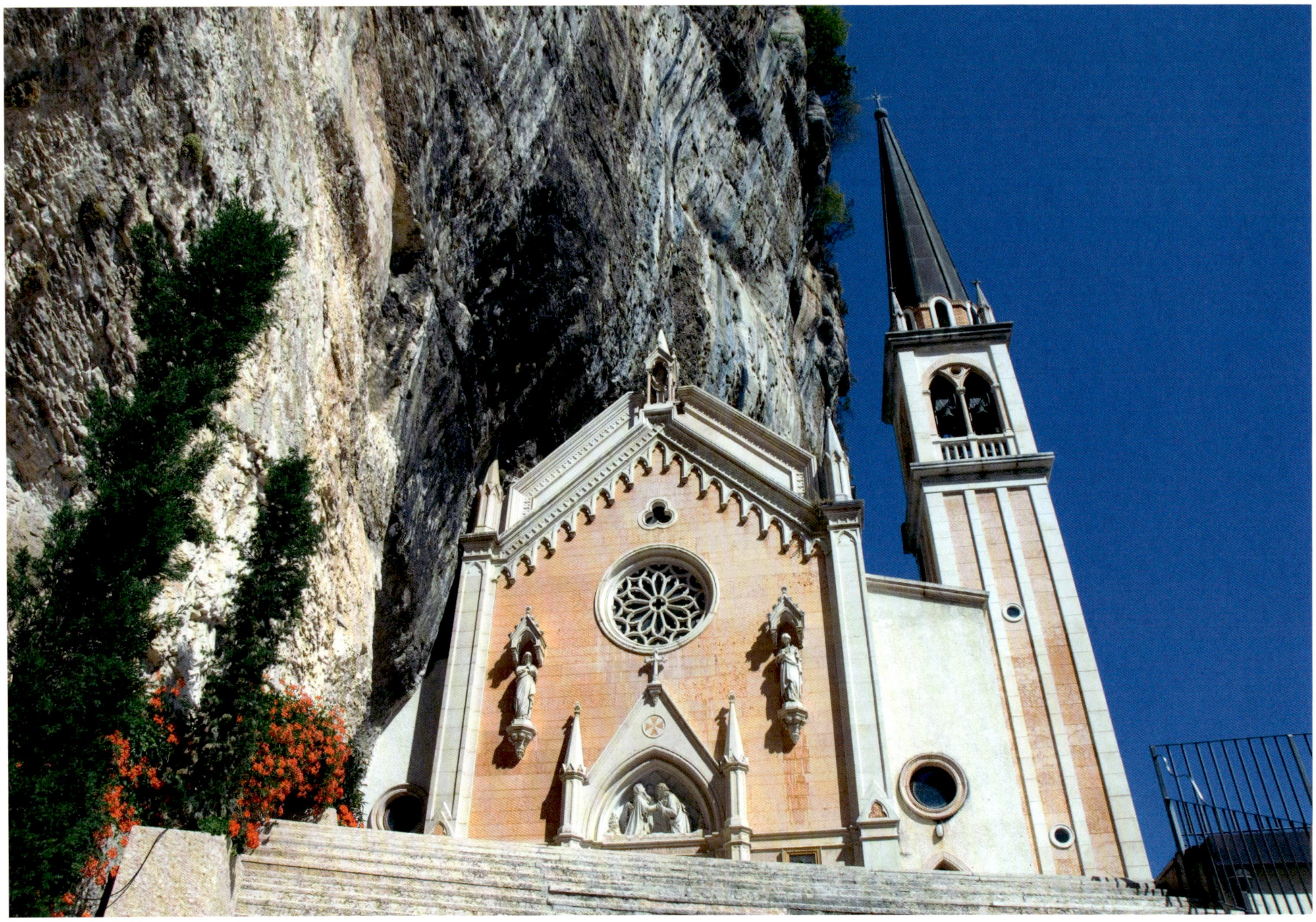

Top The traditional way to the sanctuary winds through dense forests and along rocky precipices. *Bottom* The final steps of the pilgrimage route lead up steep stairs—you're almost there!

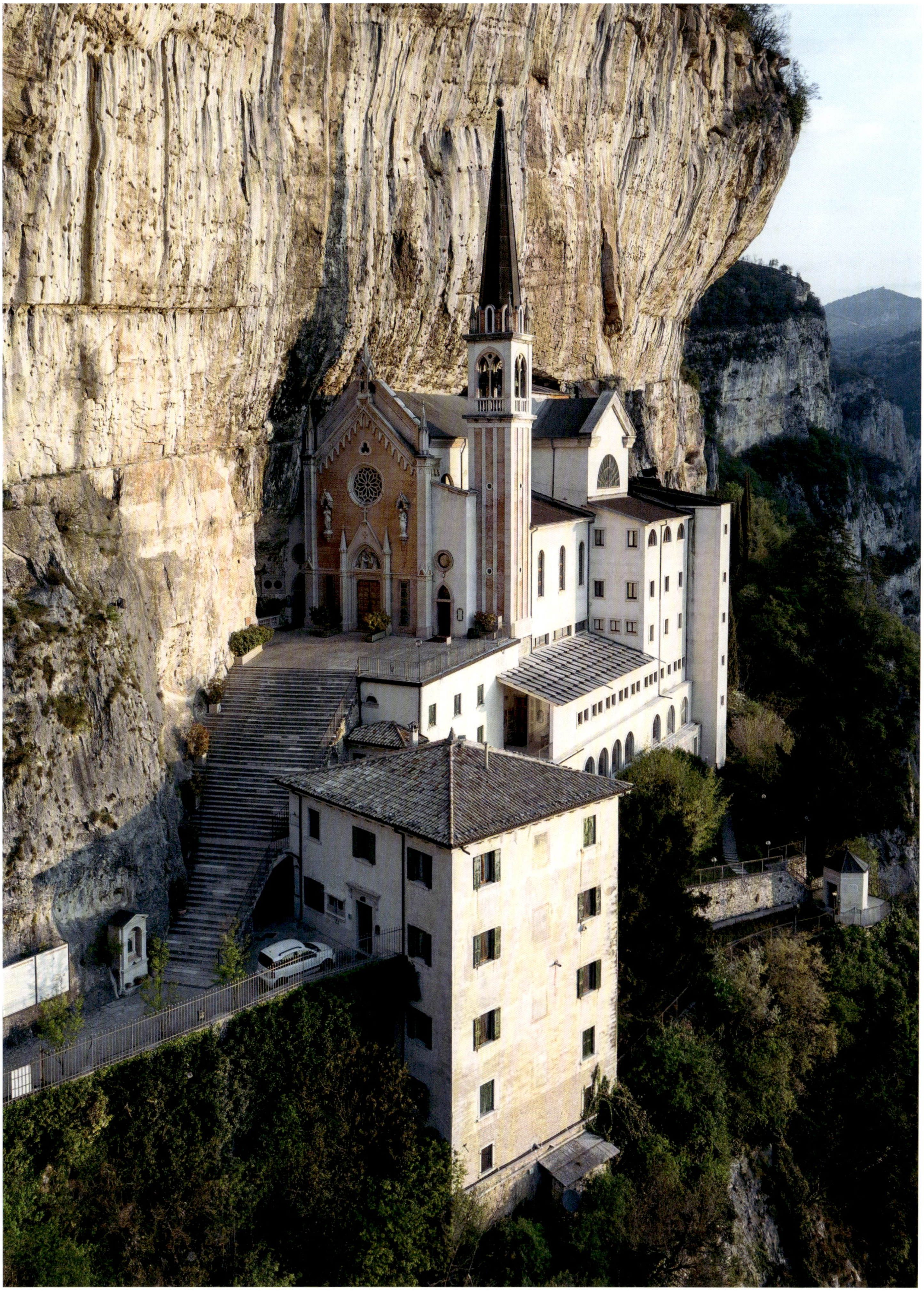

Above The Sanctuary of Madonna della Corona combines elements of Gothic, Lombard Renaissance, and baroque styles, which form a unique and harmonious ensemble.

Pantheon

Under the Gaze of Many Gods

Built: ca. 27 BCE – 126 CE, Rome, Italy

Before the advent of Christianity, a pantheon of Roman gods guided the fate of the Eternal City.

Let us imagine a Roman scene in the early Common Era: in the dim light of the Pantheon, the city's grand and imposing temple, statues of the most important Roman deities gaze down upon mortals from seven niches. The gods are Jupiter, Juno, Neptune, Venus, Mars, Apollo, and Mercury—a divine team offering guidance and aid to the Romans in both everyday matters and spiritual concerns. They reigned in the Pantheon, a name derived from the Greek *pan* (all) and *theos* (gods).

When Romans entered the Pantheon, they stepped into a sacred space where the mortal and divine coexisted. Jupiter, the all-powerful father, was called upon for justice and protection, while Juno safeguarded marriage and childbirth. Neptune, god of the seas and horses, was a natural choice for sailors and charioteers, and Venus, goddess of love and fertility, offered her favor to those seeking passion or prosperity. Mars, embodying war and discipline, held special significance for soldiers preparing for battle, while Apollo inspired artists, healers, and seekers of wisdom with his light and knowledge. Mercury, the fleet-footed messenger, was the patron of commerce and safe travels, vital in a city as dynamic as Rome.

The gods' presence would have been felt not only in the statues—it was embodied in the very design of the structure. Chief among its wonders was the awe-inspiring dome, one of the most iconic architectural achievements of the ancient world. With both the inner diameter of the dome and the height to the oculus measuring 142 feet (43 meters), the dome forms a perfect sphere, a feat of engineering that remained unmatched for over a millennium. Constructed using Roman concrete, the dome's composition was carefully calibrated to manage its immense weight. Heavier stones like travertine were used at the base, transitioning to tufa and brick in the middle layers, and culminating in lightweight pumice at the top. This clever gradation ensured stability and longevity, preventing collapse under the structure's massive weight.

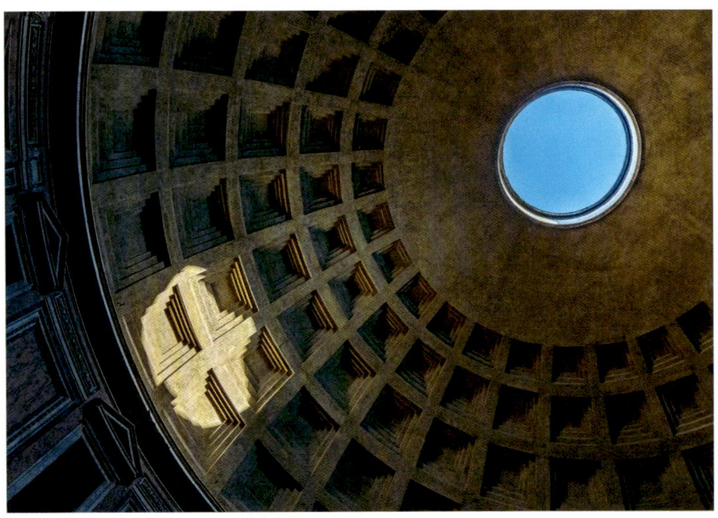

At the dome's center lies the iconic oculus, a circular aperture 30 feet (9 meters) wide. By opening the apex of the dome, the oculus relieves structural pressure while flooding the space with natural light. Its dual purpose is both practical and symbolic: it stabilizes the dome and creates a striking connection to the heavens above.

This connection, of course, has evolved over time. In 609 CE, the Pantheon was converted into a Catholic church, officially named Santa Maria ad Martyres. Yet the gods of ancient Rome loom large in the recesses of the Pantheon and in our contemporary imaginings of the place—silent reminders of how faith transforms and endures, even in the Eternal City.

Left The Pantheon is renowned for its dome featuring a central oculus.
Opposite In our era, the Pantheon hosts regular Catholic masses.

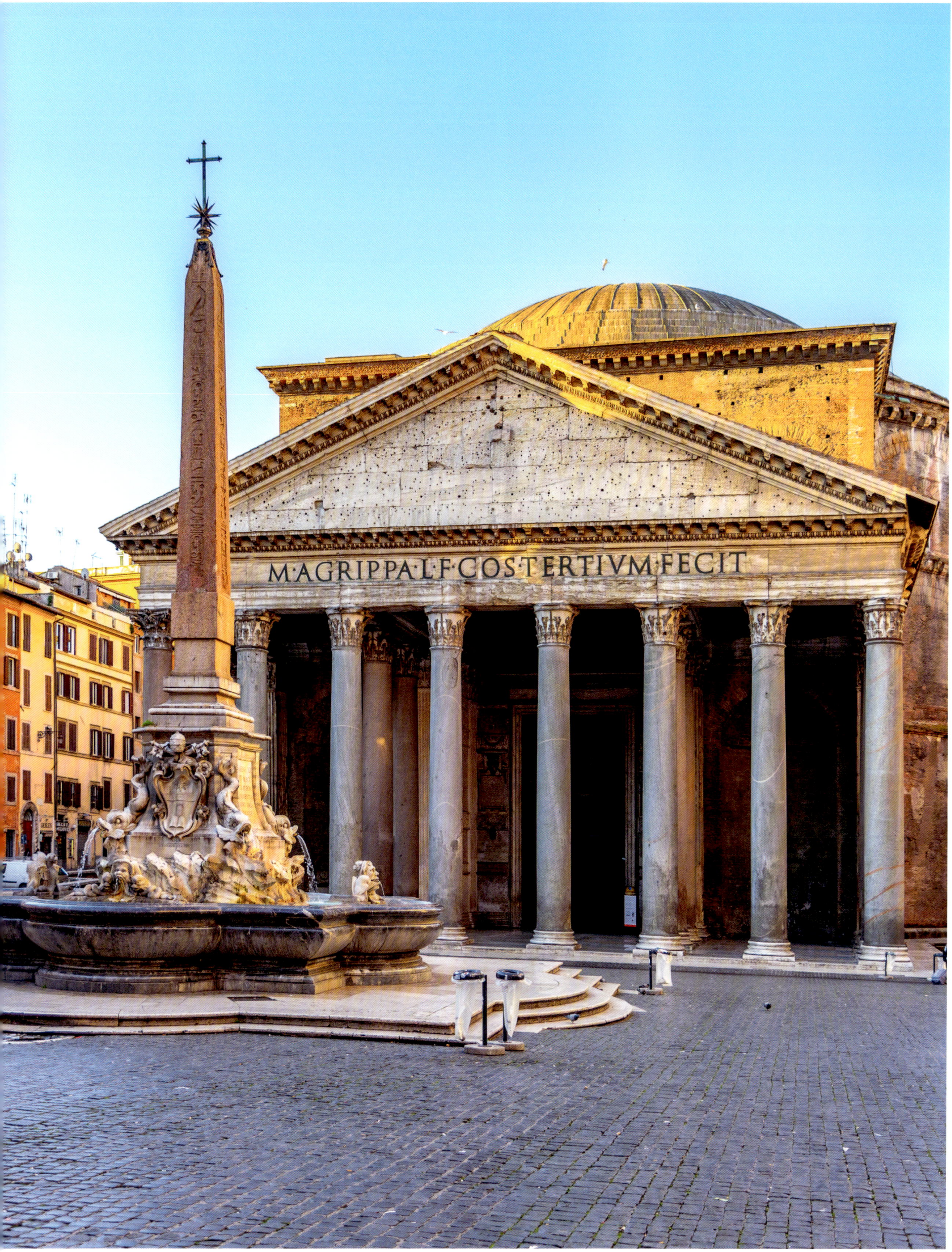
M·AGRIPPA·L·F·COS·TERTIVM·FECIT

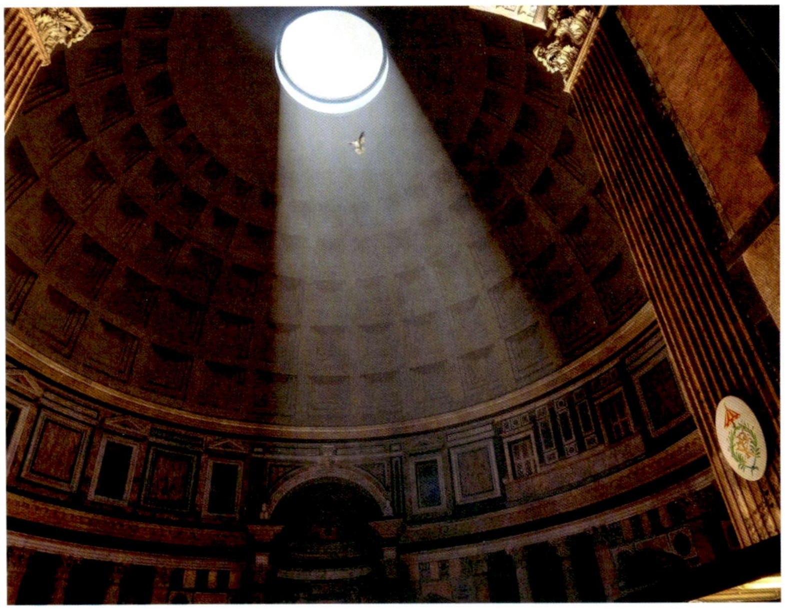

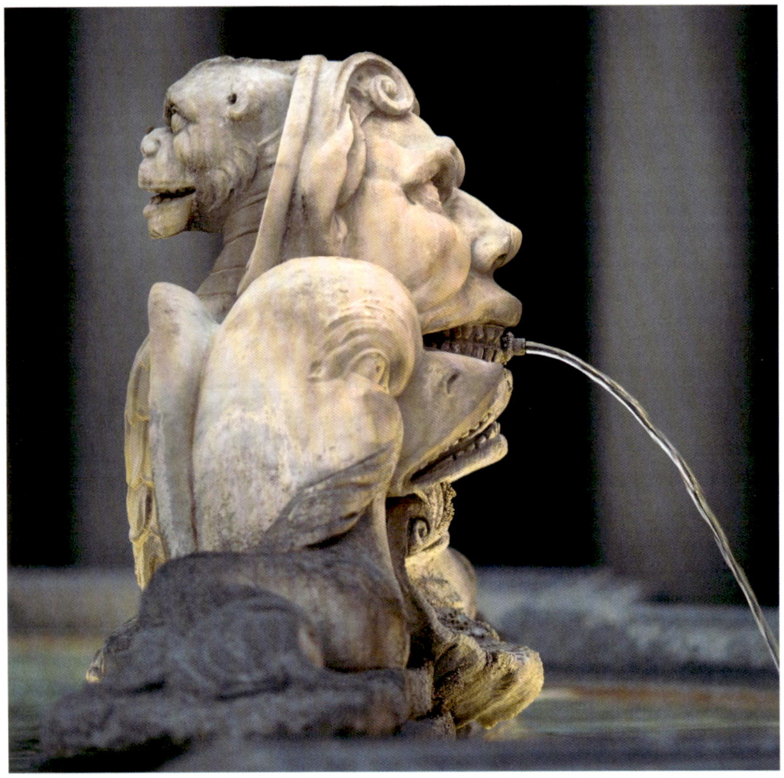

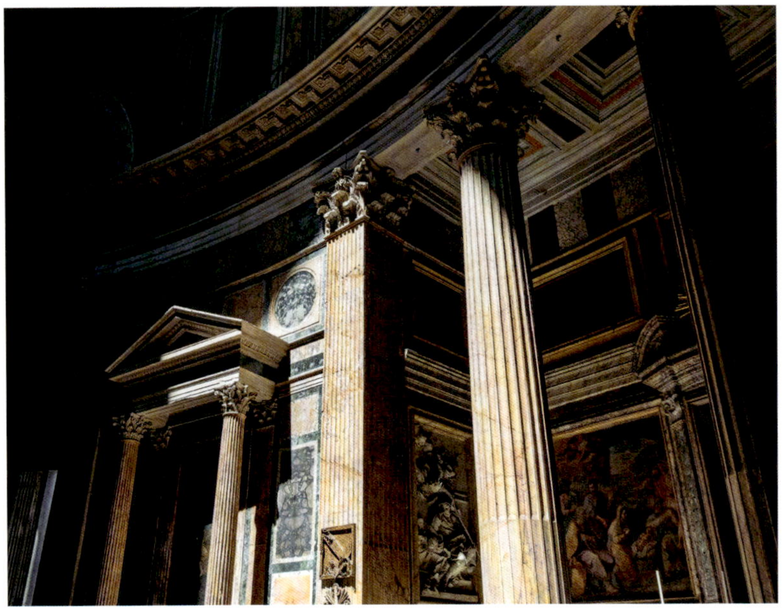

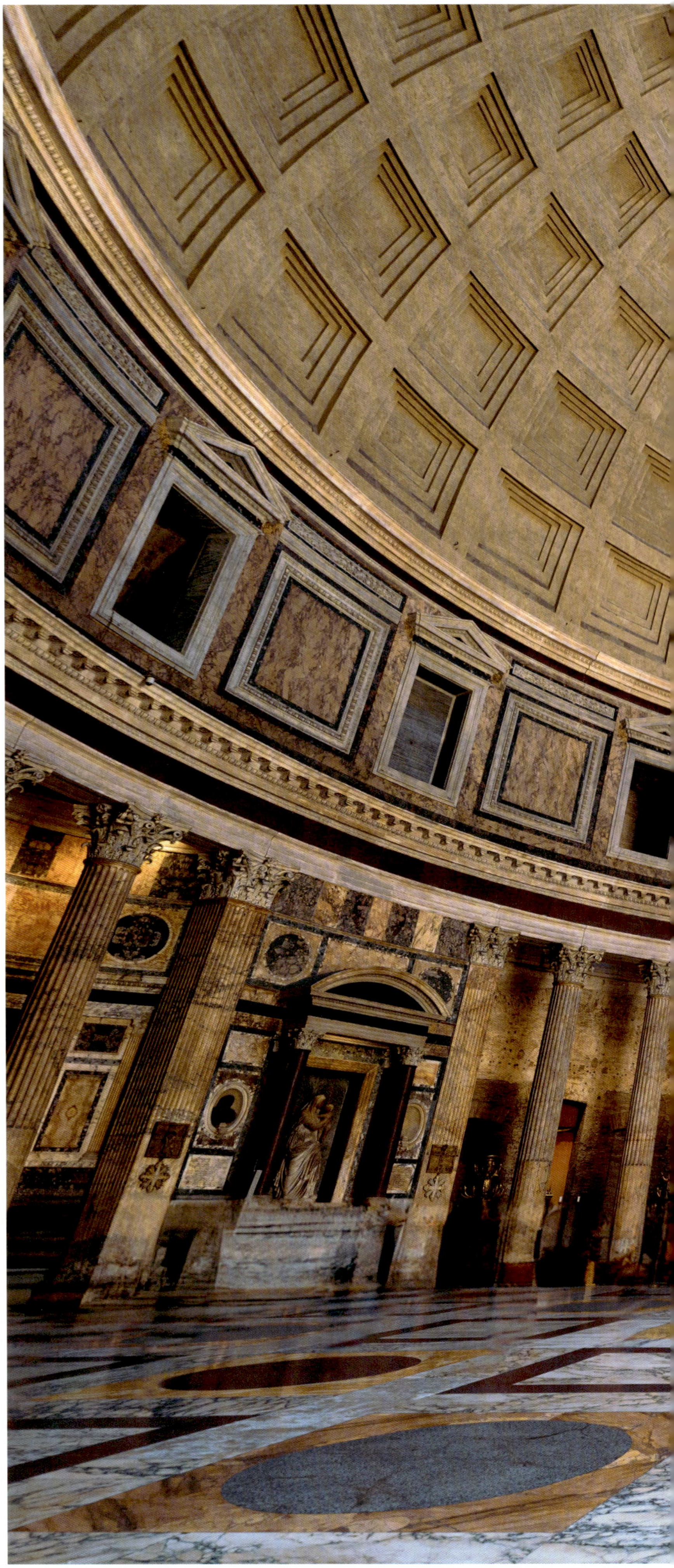

Top The oculus reduces the dome's weight by removing material from a less critical point, enhancing stability.
Middle The beautiful Fontana del Pantheon was built in 1575.
Bottom The Corinthian columns and capitals reveal Greek influence.

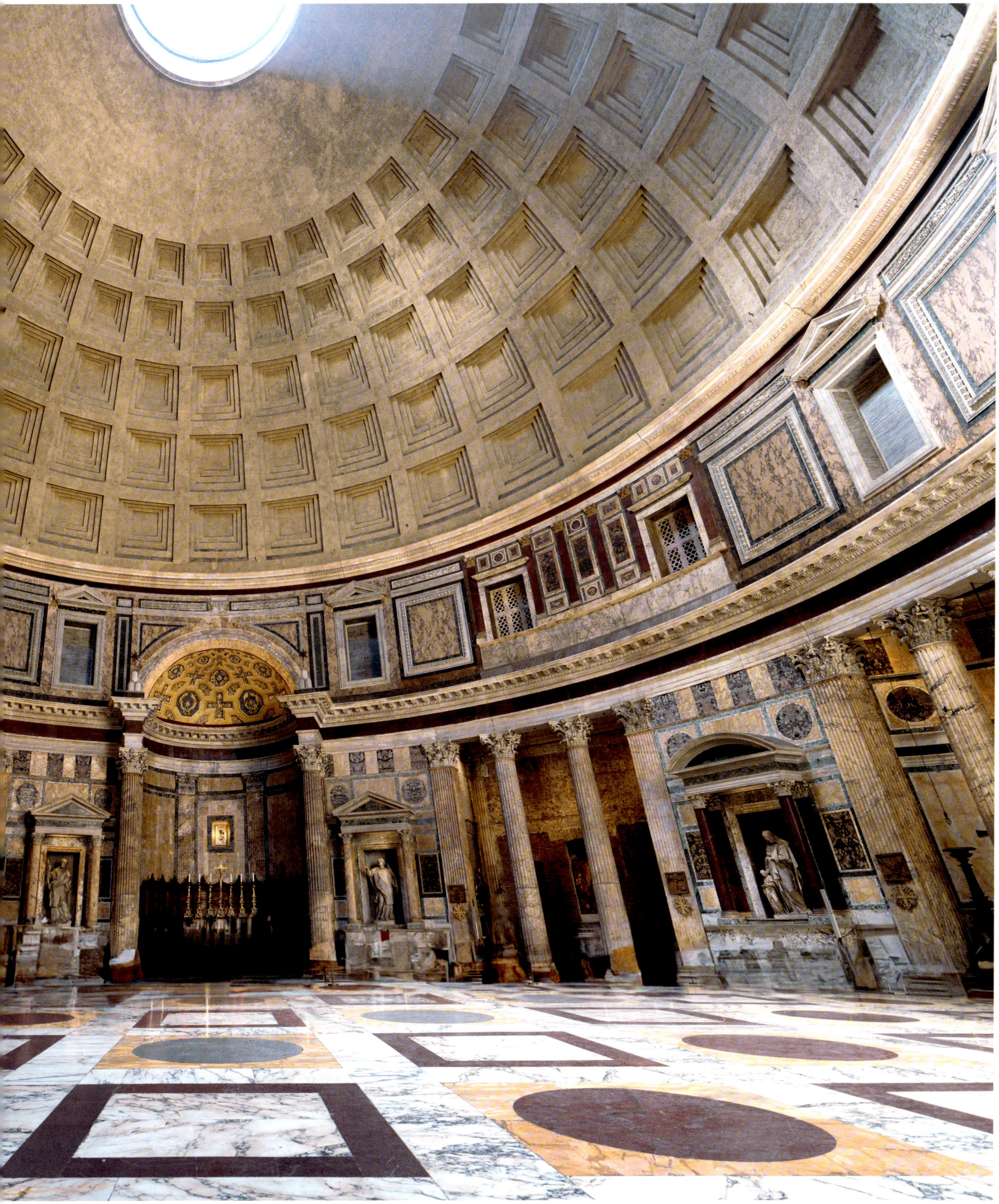

Above The dome's perfect symmetry showcases the Romans' advanced construction techniques.

St. Peter's Basilica

Power, Pilgrimage, and Piety

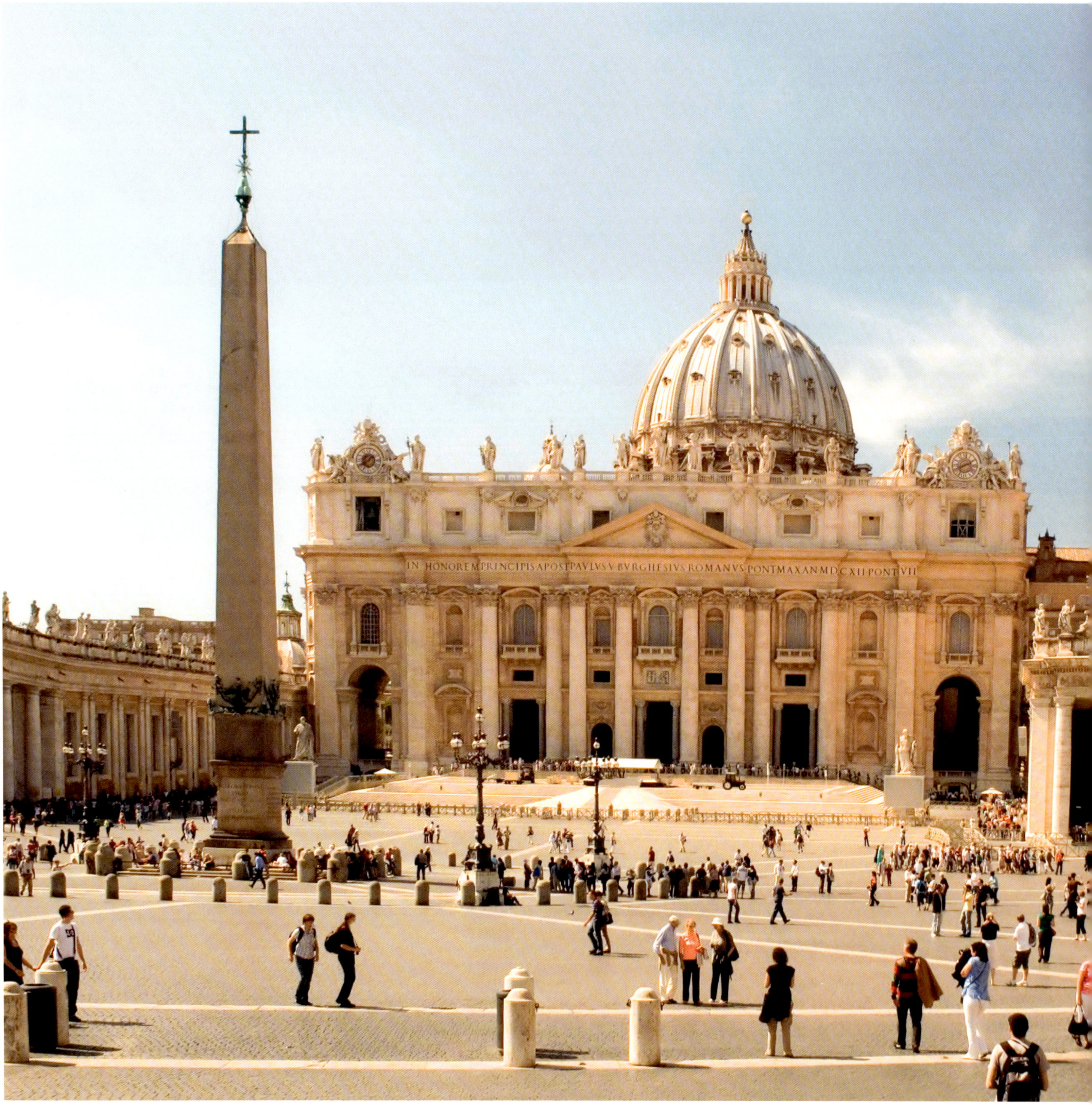

Built: 4th century CE (current form: 1626 CE), Vatican City

As the fulfillment of a holy promise, this basilica is built upon both a literal and figurative rock.

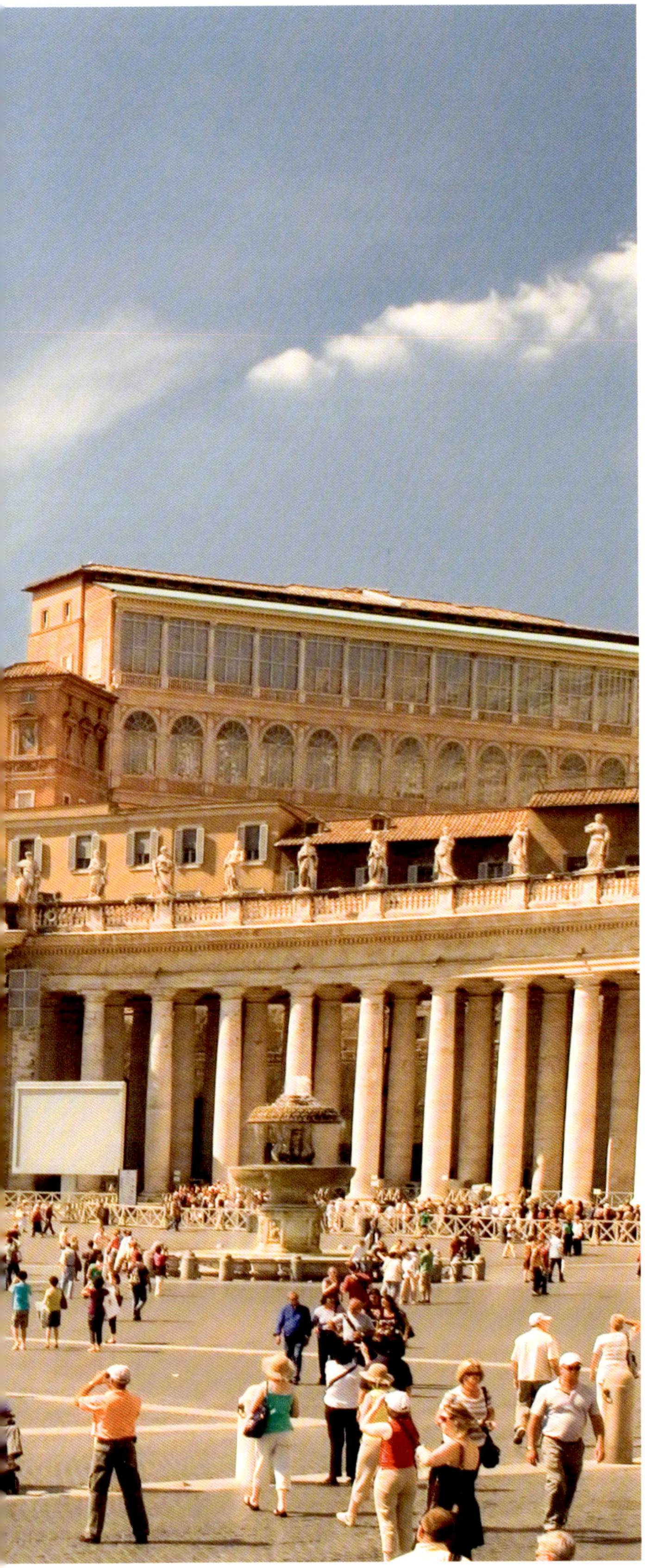

The famous words Jesus spoke to Peter—"You are Peter, and on this rock I will build my church"—find their most impressive realization in the heart of the Eternal City. Indeed, St. Peter's Basilica was first constructed in the 4th century over the tomb of the Apostle Peter. By the 16th century, the original had fallen into such disrepair that Pope Julius II decided to replace it with the new, spectacular basilica that stands today.

St. Peter's is a masterpiece of renaissance and baroque architecture and remains the largest church in the Christian world. Upon entering St. Peter's Square, visitors are awestruck by the giant colonnade, encircling them, according to the architect Bernini, like the "motherly arms" of the Catholic church. The interior is just as overwhelming: beyond the grand entrance doors, a breathtaking silence reigns, broken only by the murmurs of pilgrims. The scent of incense drifts among the imposing columns, and to the left and right of the nave, niches and chapels invite quiet reflection. Michelangelo's *Pietà*, half-hidden in a side chapel, exerts a magnetic pull. There, in the soft light, rests the poignant depiction of Mary holding the lifeless Christ in her arms. It is a moment of intimacy and sorrow, frozen in marble. People linger before the statue—some kneel, while others shed tears, moved by its powerful emotion.

Moving further into the basilica, the focal point is the tomb of Saint Peter, majestically crowned by Bernini's baldachin. Cherubs, coats of arms, and foliage adorn the monument, while the carefully crafted play of light and shadow brings the baroque canopy to life. And then, gazing upward, one encounters the basilica's astonishing dome. Standing beneath its oculus, surrounded by the ornate paintings and golden embellishments, many feel a sense of reverence. At the center of the dome, the inscription in Latin reads: *Tu es Petrus, et super hanc petram aedificabo ecclesiam meam*—"You are Peter, and on this rock I will build my church."

Back in St. Peter's Square, the eye travels over the magnificent baroque facade of the basilica. Directly above the main portal lies the Loggia delle Benedizioni. Here, the Pope delivers the *Urbi et Orbi* blessing to the faithful, traditionally on Easter, Christmas Day, and following the election of a new Pope. From here, hundreds of blessings have been bestowed upon Rome (*Urbi*—to the city) and the entire world (*Orbi*—to the world) over the centuries. In this way, St. Peter's Basilica offers steadfast support, guidance, and grace to the faithful—a proverbial rock in an ever-changing world.

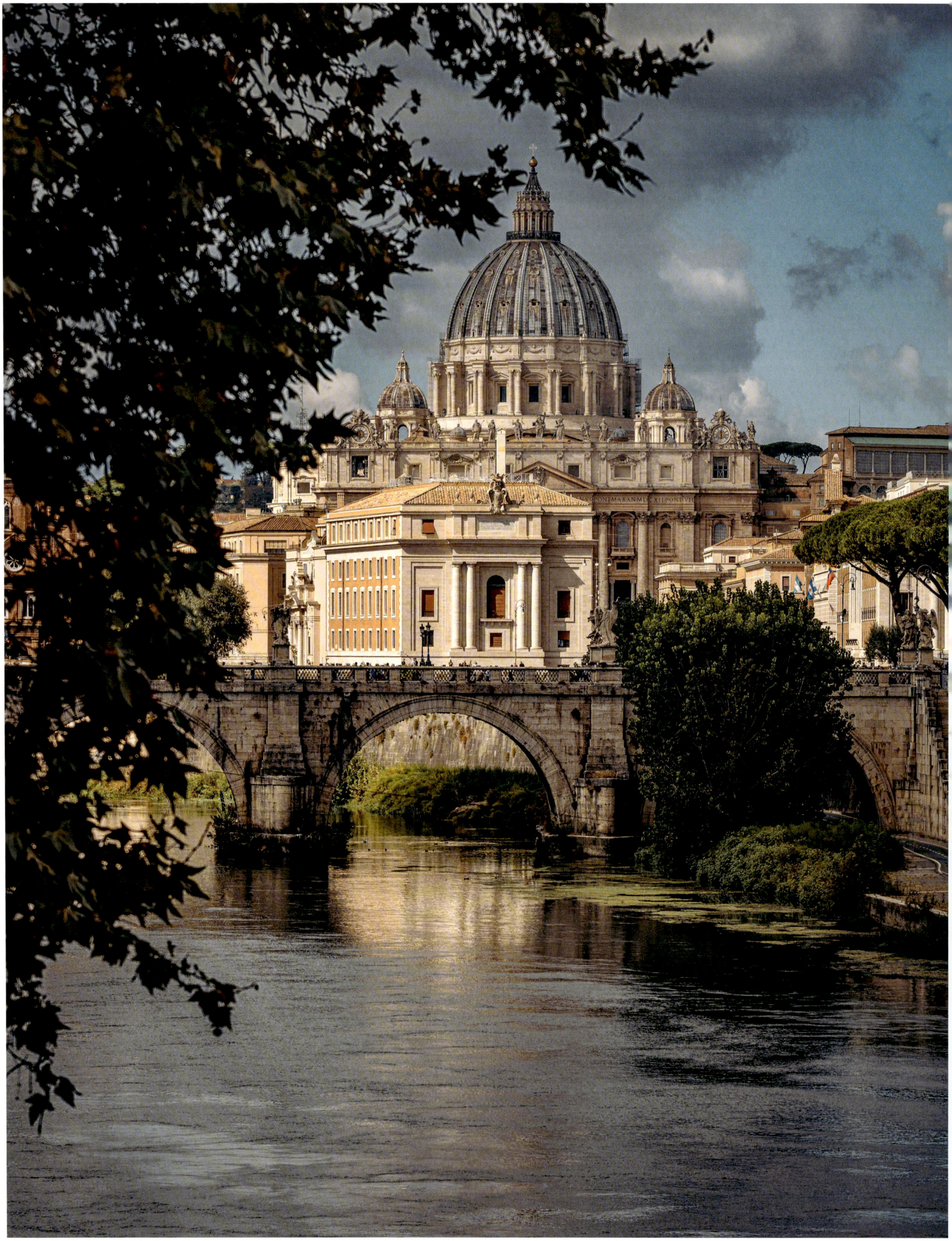

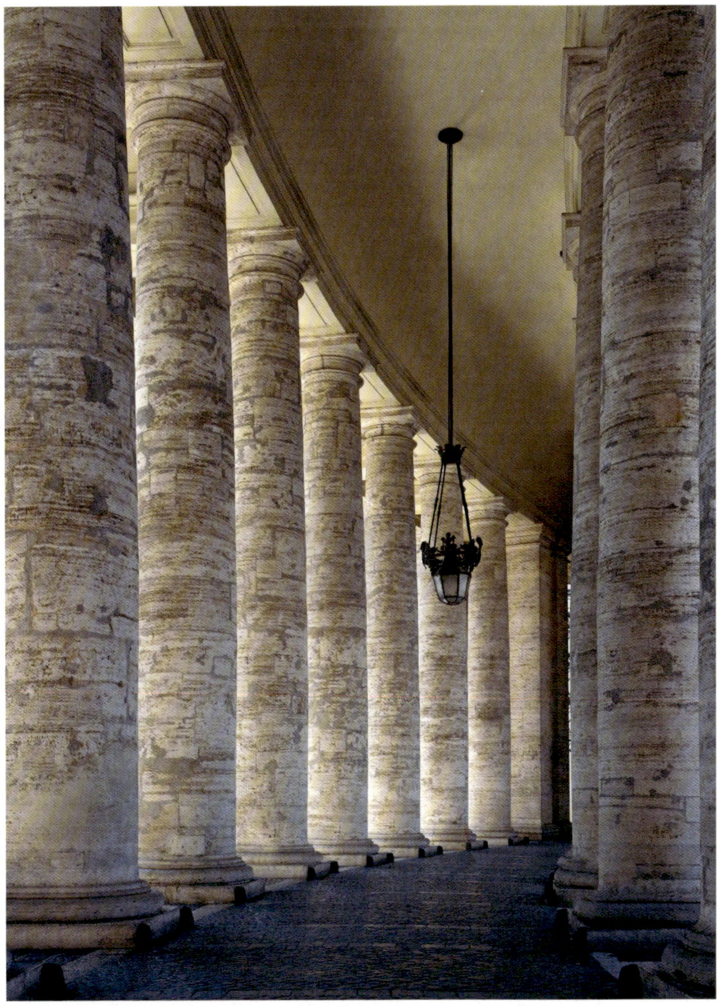

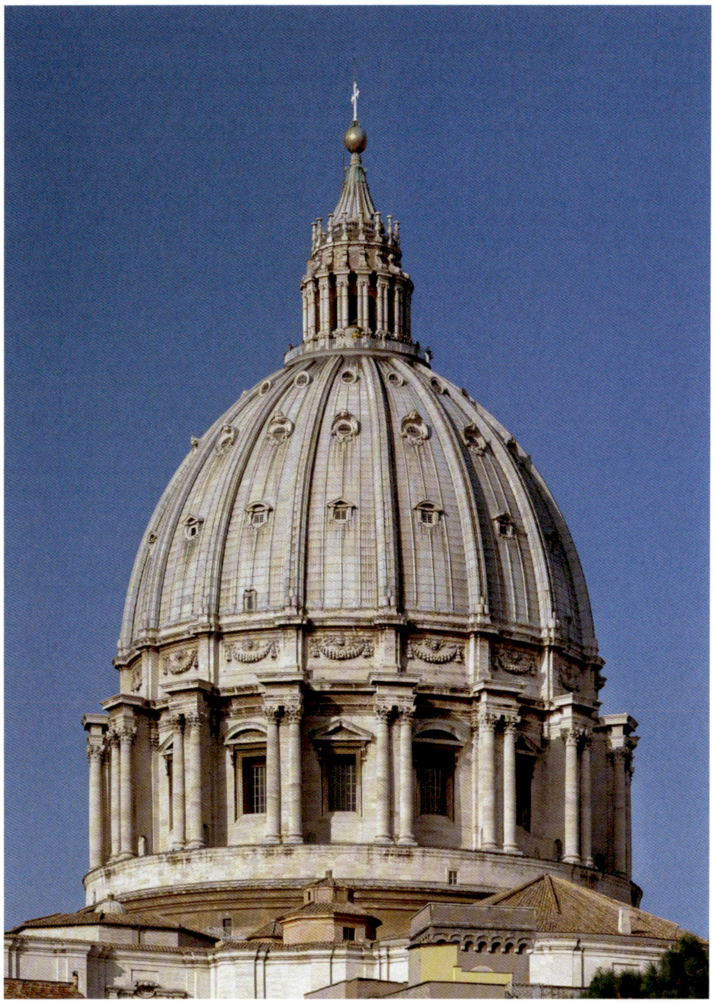

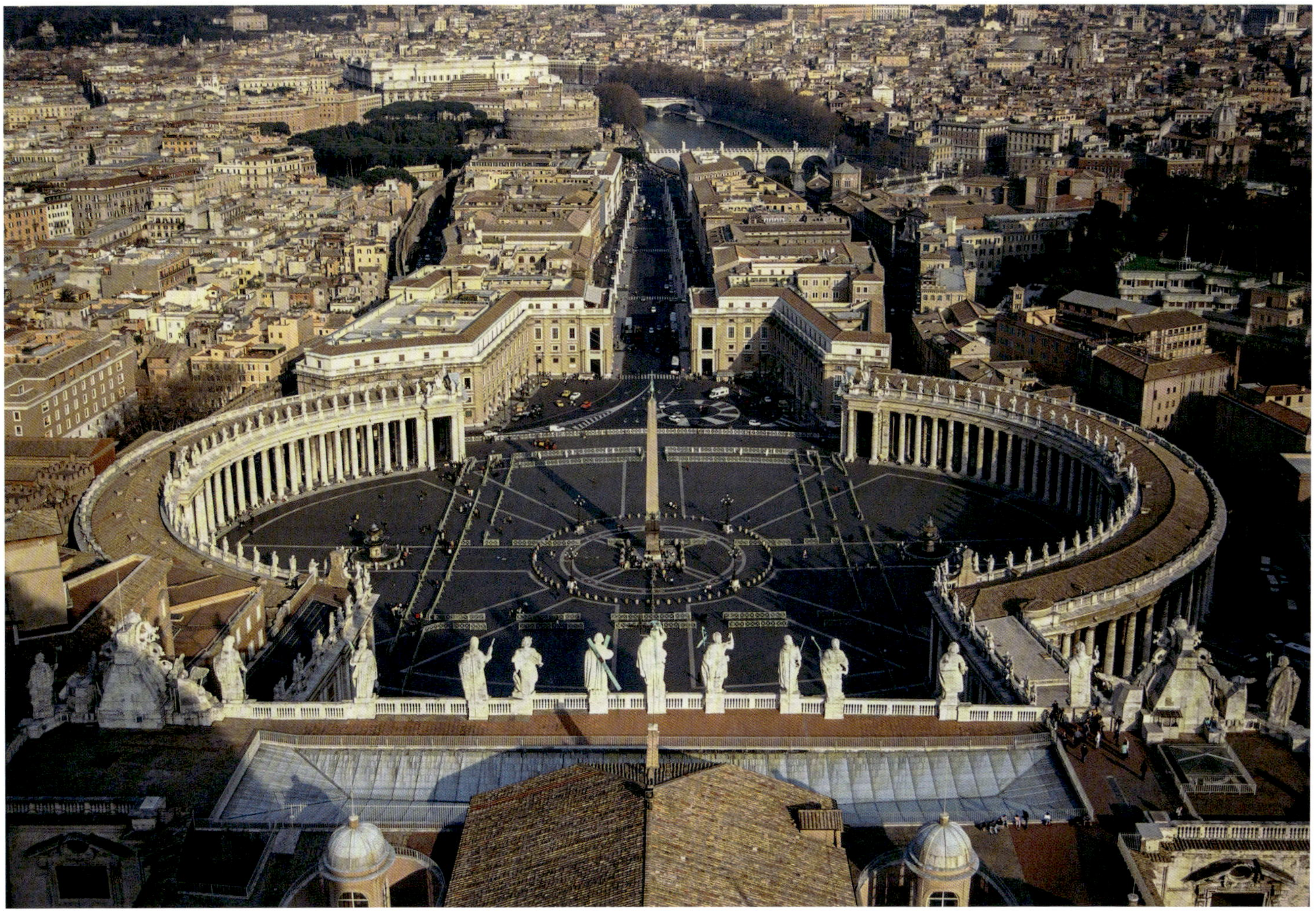

Opposite From the banks of the Tiber, it is only a short distance to Vatican City.
Top left St. Peter's Basilica is the central sanctuary of Catholicism.
Top right The basilica's dome reaches a height of 446 feet (136 meters).
Bottom The obelisk serves as the visual focal point of St. Peter's Square.

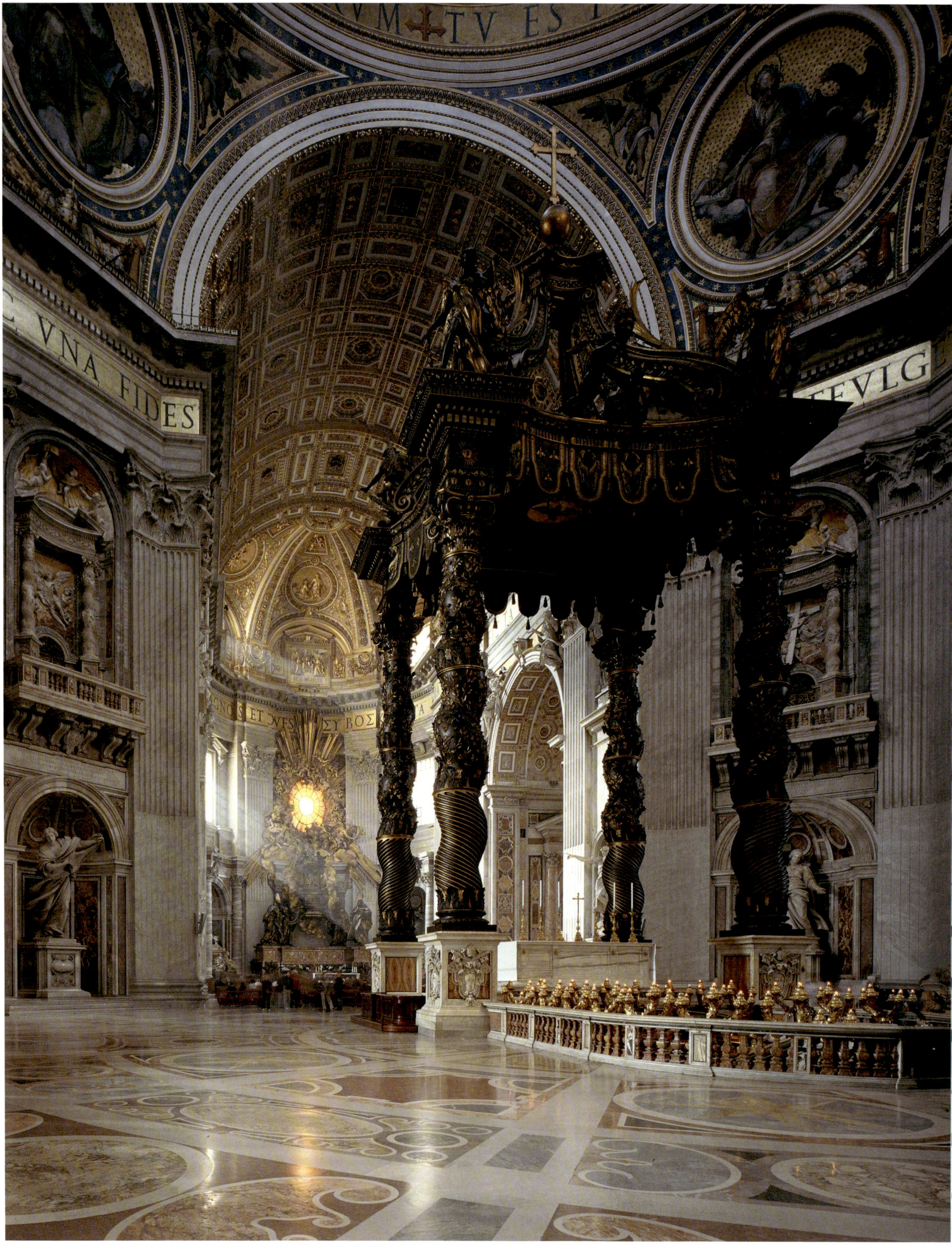
VM TV ES
VNA FIDES
EFVLG

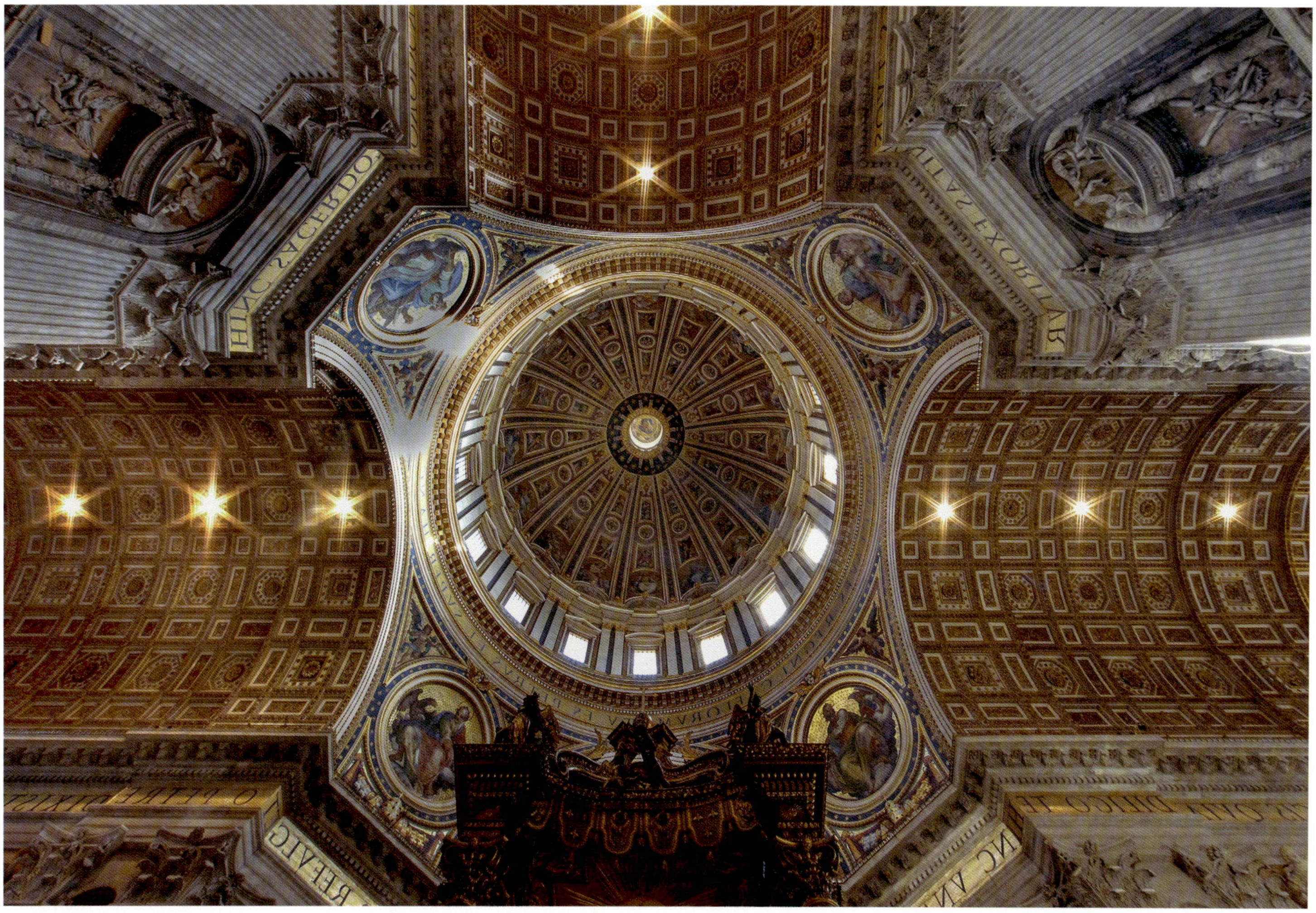

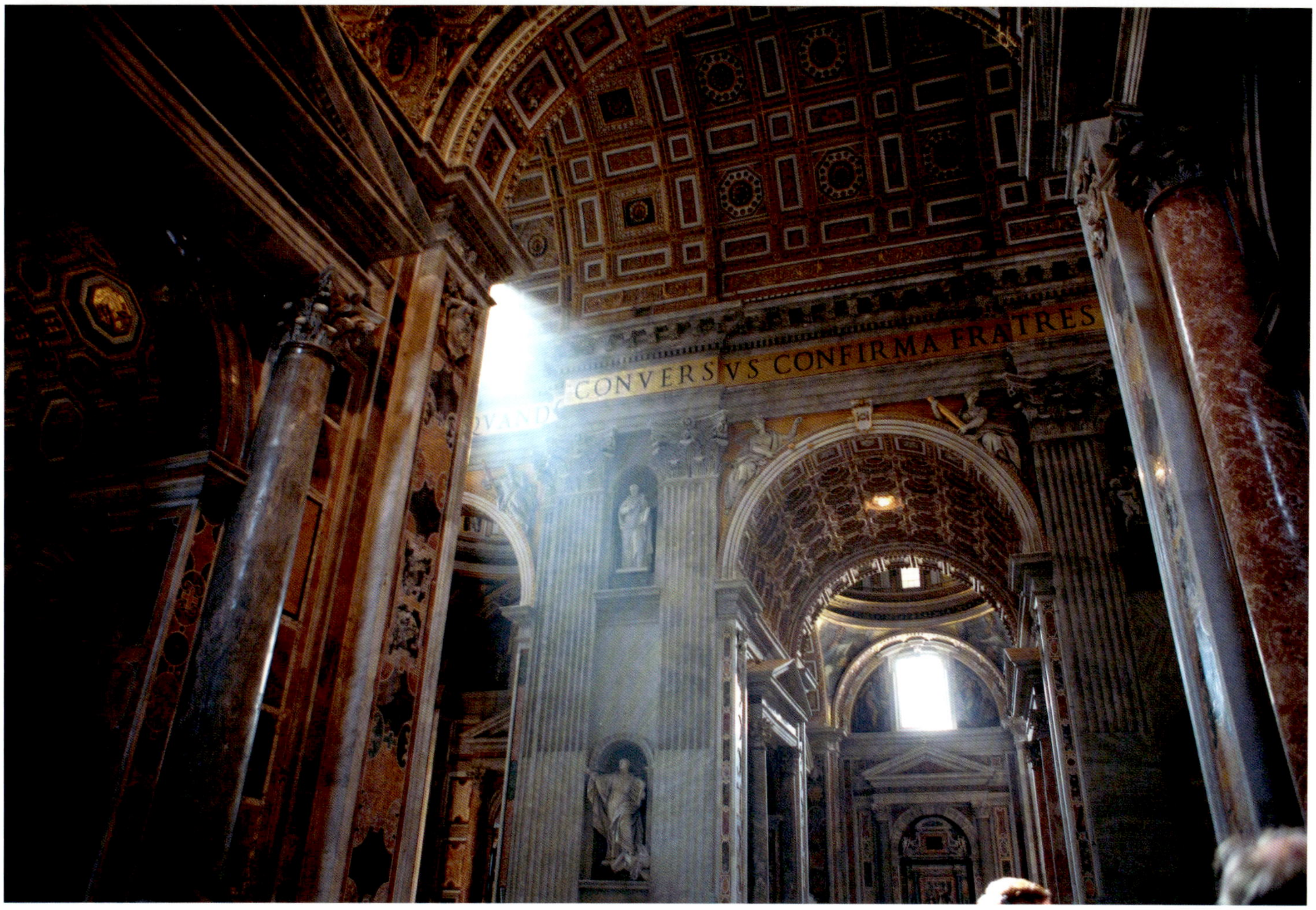

Opposite Bernini's baldachin was erected above the tomb of Saint Peter.
Top The dome's structure was inspired by Rome's Pantheon.
Bottom The basilica is a masterpiece of Renaissance and baroque art.

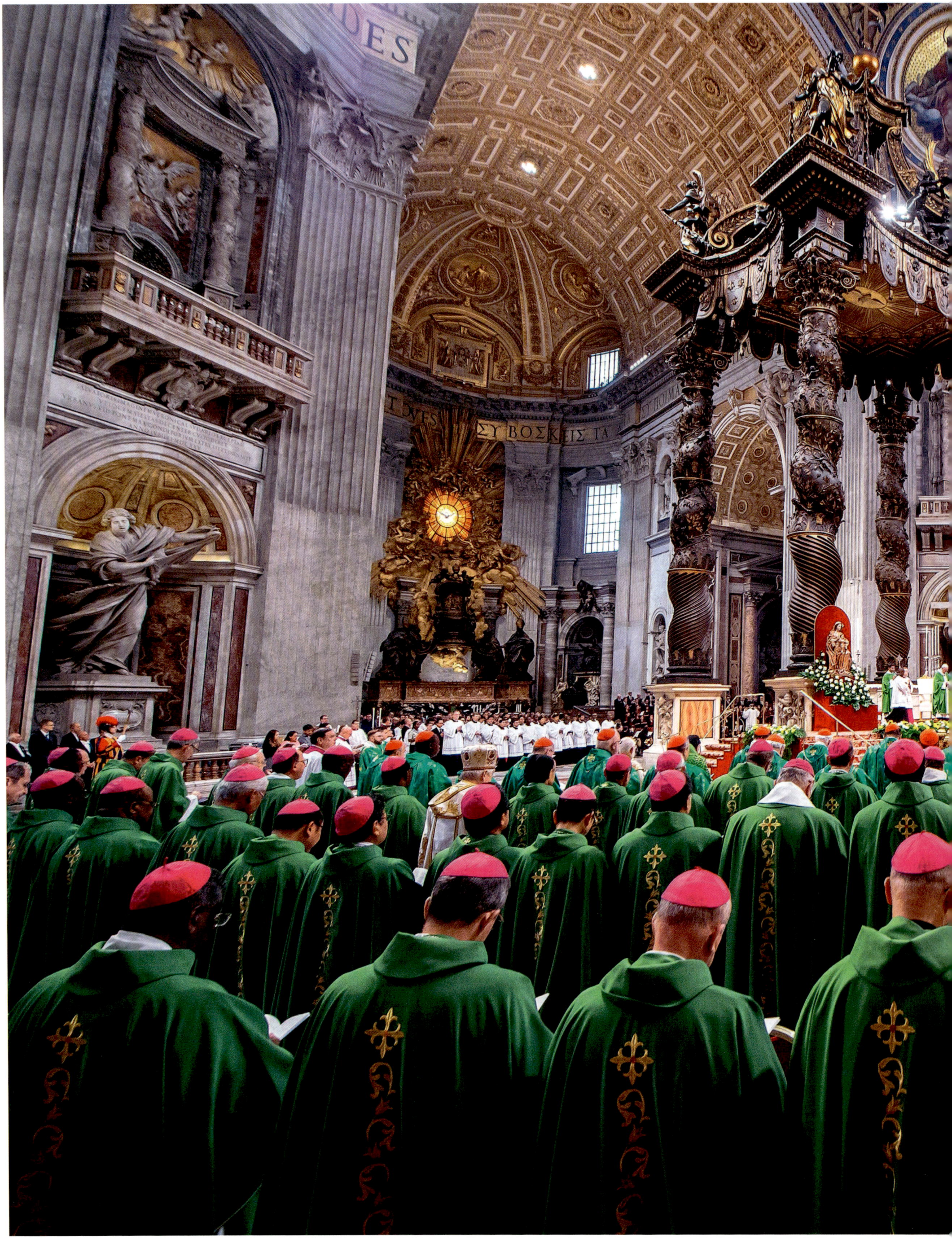

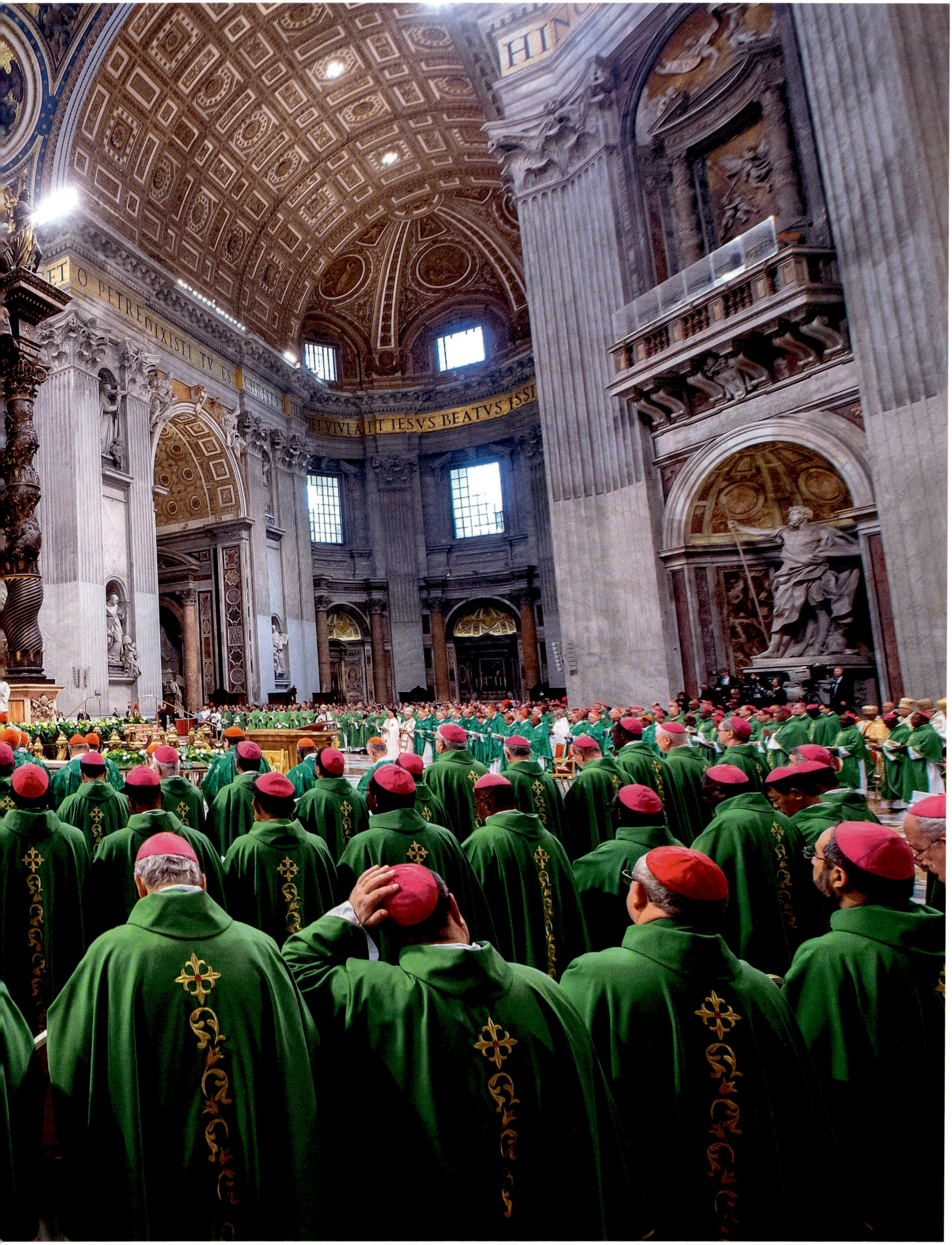

The Cradle of Humanity and Monotheism

Between the vast continent of Africa and the Middle East region, faith has continuously shaped history and architecture.

It seems only fitting that these two regions share the Sinai Peninsula. Politically part of Egypt but geographically belonging to Asia, the Sinai serves as a natural bridge between Africa and the Middle East. The Romans, Crusaders, and Ottomans used the Sinai Peninsula as a gateway to Africa, while Christian missionaries traveled across it along ancient trade routes. Above all, however, the Sinai plays a central role in the narratives of the three monotheistic religions. It was here that Moses received the Ten Commandments (Judaism and Christianity); it was also here that the prophet Musa received the Tablets of Revelation from God (Islam).

All three religions are interwoven in Jerusalem, the spiritual heart of the Middle East. Here stand some of the holiest sites in the world: the Western Wall (Judaism), the Church of the Holy Sepulchre (Christianity), and the Dome of the Rock (Islam). Yet, beyond Jerusalem, the Middle East weaves a rich tapestry of spiritual sites and ancient artifacts. In Iran, traces of Zoroastrianism can be found at Naqsh-e Rostam, where the supreme god Ahura Mazda watches over the rock-cut tombs (pp. 264–267). In Jordan, long before the emergence of Christianity and Islam, the Nabataeans carved the legendary city of Petra and its magnificent temple, Al-Khazneh (pp. 242–249), from the red stone of the desert.

On the opposite side of the Red Sea, an incredible diversity of polytheistic and animistic belief systems flourished for millennia. From the mighty gods of ancient Egypt to the Indigenous Berber religions of North Africa, from the ritual nature worship of East Africa to the trance dances of the San and Khoi in the Kalahari—the continent was alive with spiritual expression. Beginning in the 1st century CE, Christianity spread into ever-wider parts of Africa, though by the 7th century CE, it was displaced in many regions by the expansion of Islam. A notable exception is Ethiopia, where the Ethiopian Orthodox faith endures to this day, embodied by the awe-inspiring rock-hewn churches of Lalibela (pp. 230–235). Islam, in turn, left its mark in the form of resplendent mosques like the Great Mosque of Djenné in Mali (pp. 202–205) and in religious schools like the magnificent Bou Inania Madrasa in Morocco (pp. 206–211).

Across Africa, many ancient spiritual traditions have survived conquest, colonialism, and missionary efforts, enduring as syncretic practices that combine Christian and Islamic elements with traditional beliefs. From Sudan to Zanzibar, from Morocco to Namibia, they form the bedrock of the continent's cultural diversity—a continent that stands not only as the cradle of humanity but also as an inexhaustible source of spiritual inspiration.

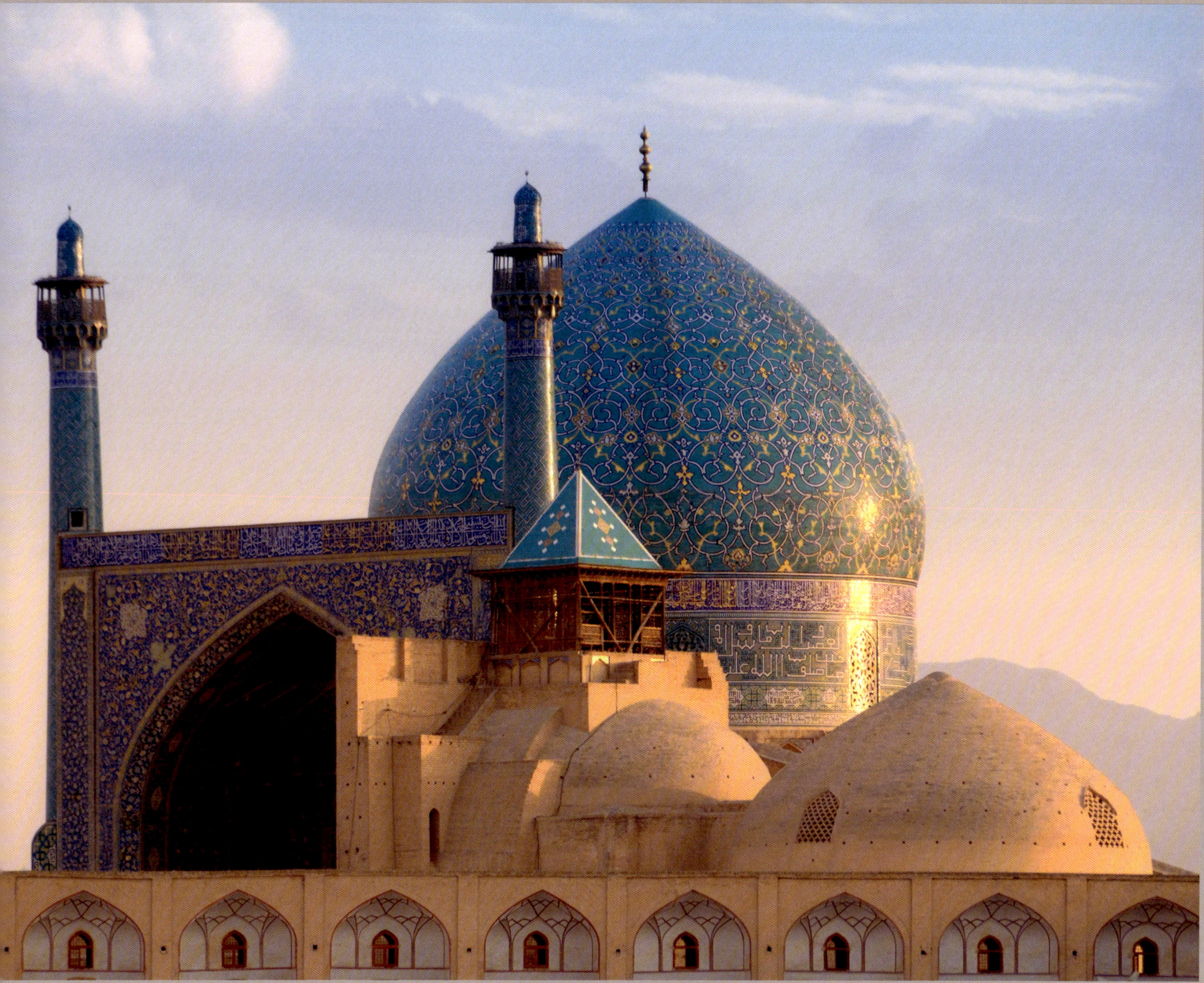

AFRICA AND THE MIDDLE EAST

Great Mosque of Touba

A Vision under the Baobab

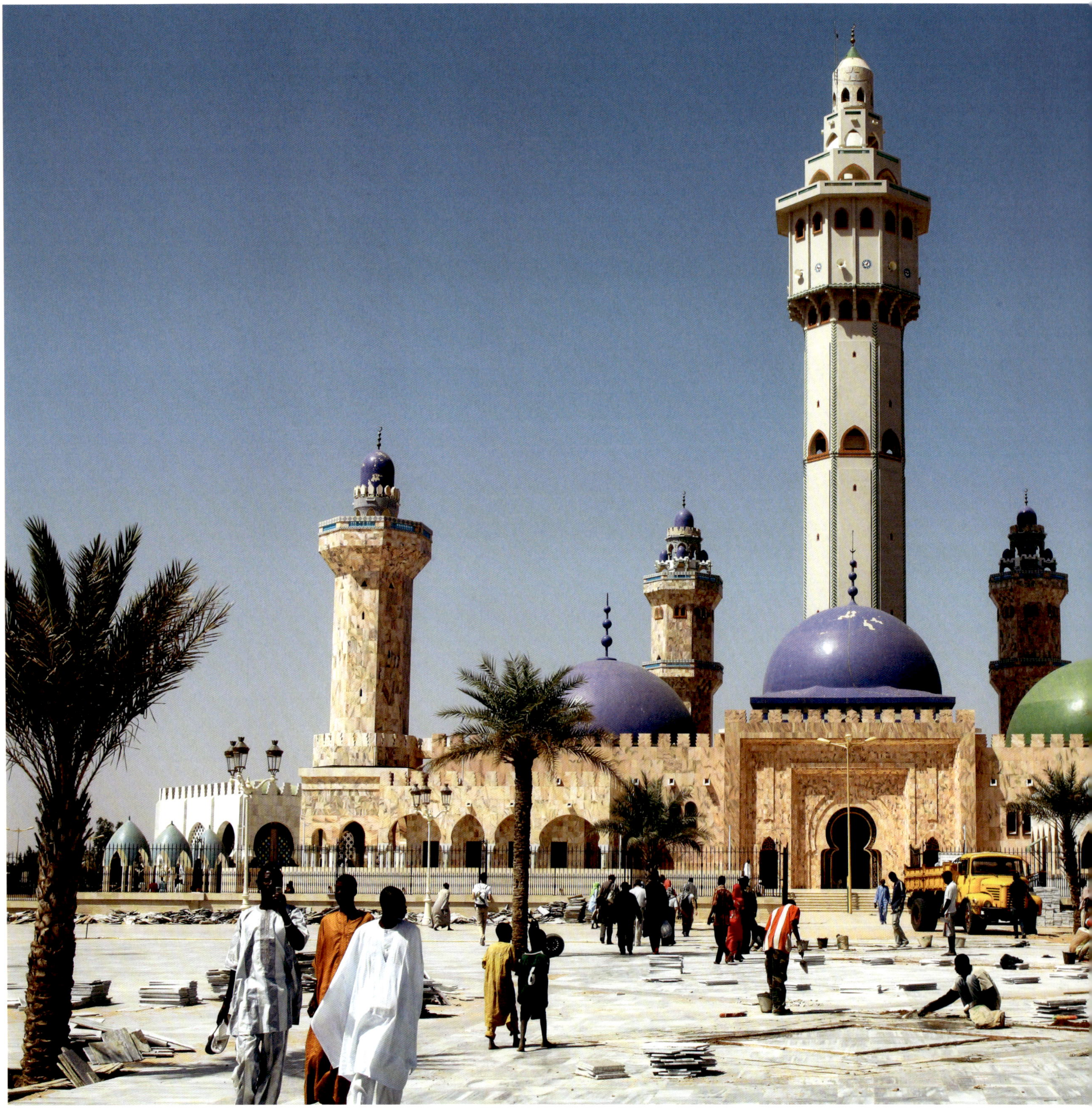

Built: 1932 – 1963 CE,
Touba, Senegal

What began as a small Sufi movement within Sunni Islam is now embraced by almost half of Senegal's population.

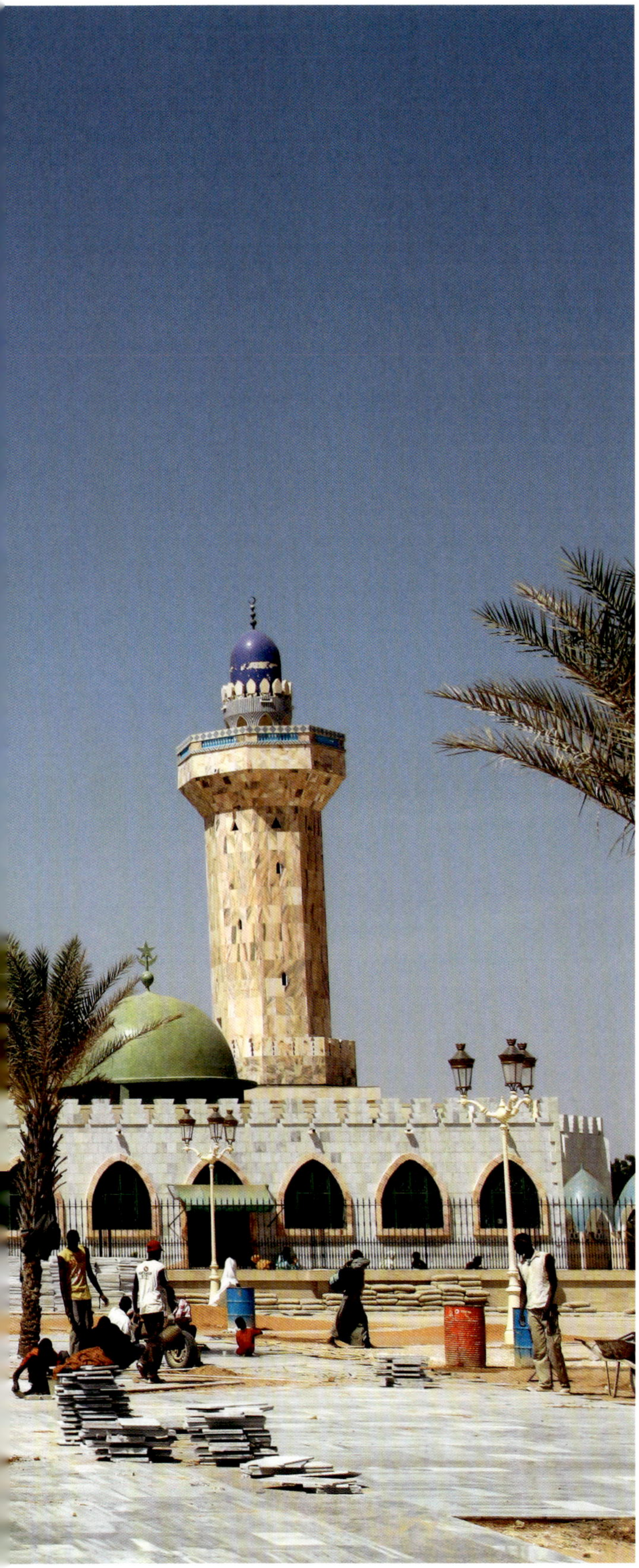

Touba, surrounded by the dry savannah and the mighty baobab trees of central Senegal, is to millions of Mourides what Bodh Gaya is to Buddhists, the Western Wall to Jews, or Mecca to Muslims. Here, Amadou Bamba, the founder of Mouridism, received a divine vision in the desert. Beneath a baobab tree, the *marabout* (Arabic for one who retreats to a place of devotion) envisioned a spiritual sanctuary for peace and communion with God—and in 1887, he founded Touba.

The spiritual heart of the city is the Great Mosque, with its five minarets representing the five pillars of Islam: *Shahada* (declaration of faith), *Salat* (prayer), *Zakat* (almsgiving), *Sawm* (fasting during Ramadan), and *Hajj* (pilgrimage to Mecca), which Mourides also undertake. Beneath these minarets lie the beautifully crafted domes that span the grand interior of the mosque. Intricate mosaics come together in Islamic patterns and motifs, while Quranic verses and the wisdom of the Prophet Muhammad adorn the walls and ceilings. Alongside these inscriptions, the teachings of Amadou Bamba are also displayed.

Bamba founded his Sufi movement within Sunni Islam, during a period when Senegal was under French colonial rule. He chose peaceful resistance through faith, education, and labor, and taught patience, devotion, and self-respect. Many of his followers regard him as a *mujaddid,* a renewer of Islam. His philosophy has shaped the spiritual identity of Touba and Senegal as a whole: today, Mourides make up between 30 and 40 percent of Senegal's population, with a growing diaspora in European and North American cities like Paris and New York, where communities establish a *Keur Serigne Touba* (Residence of the Master of Touba) to provide a home for their faith.

Once a year, an estimated 3 to 5 million believers gather in Touba to celebrate the Grand Magal, held on the 18th day of the Islamic month of Safar and celebrating Bamba's life and spiritual teachings. The highlight of this pilgrimage is a visit to Amadou Bamba's golden mausoleum inside the mosque. During these days, Touba's streets transform into a vibrant mosaic: stalls offer intricately crafted prayer beads, books of Bamba's writings, and aromatic *café Touba*—a special blend of roasted coffee and pepper—and local families prepare generous meals to share with friends and strangers alike. In peace and unity, those gathered in Touba live their faith and draw closer to God, just as their spiritual father envisioned under the baobab tree over a century ago.

At the Great Mosque of Touba, gorgeous mosaics complement intricate patterns and motifs, while Quranic verses and the wisdom of the Prophet Muhammad adorn the walls and ceilings.

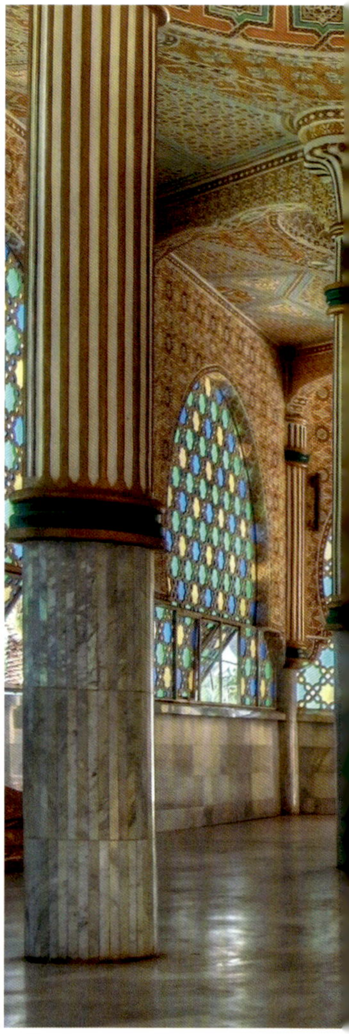

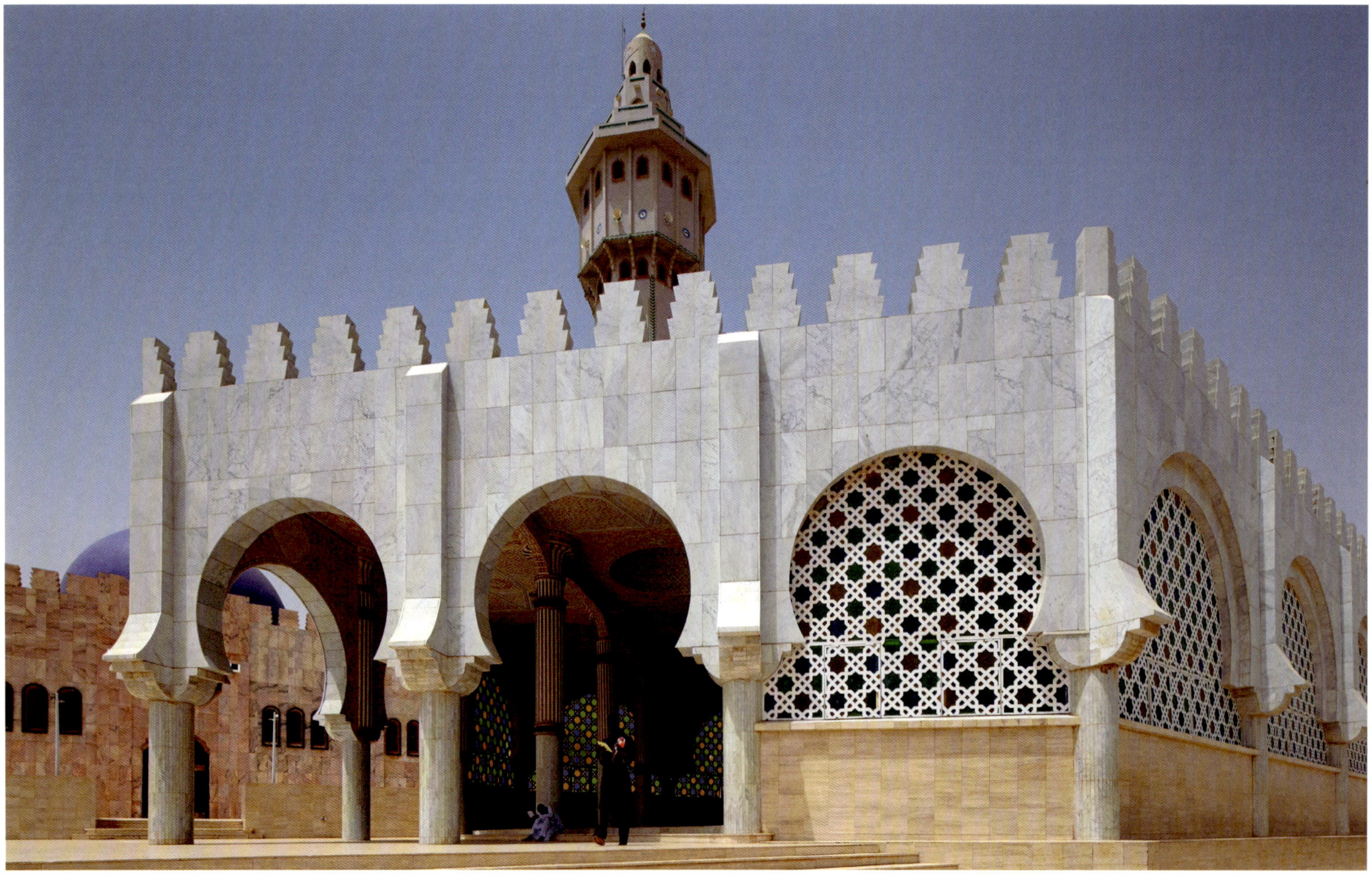

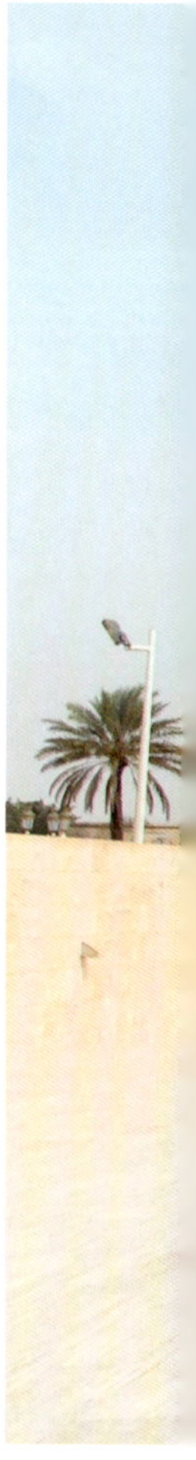

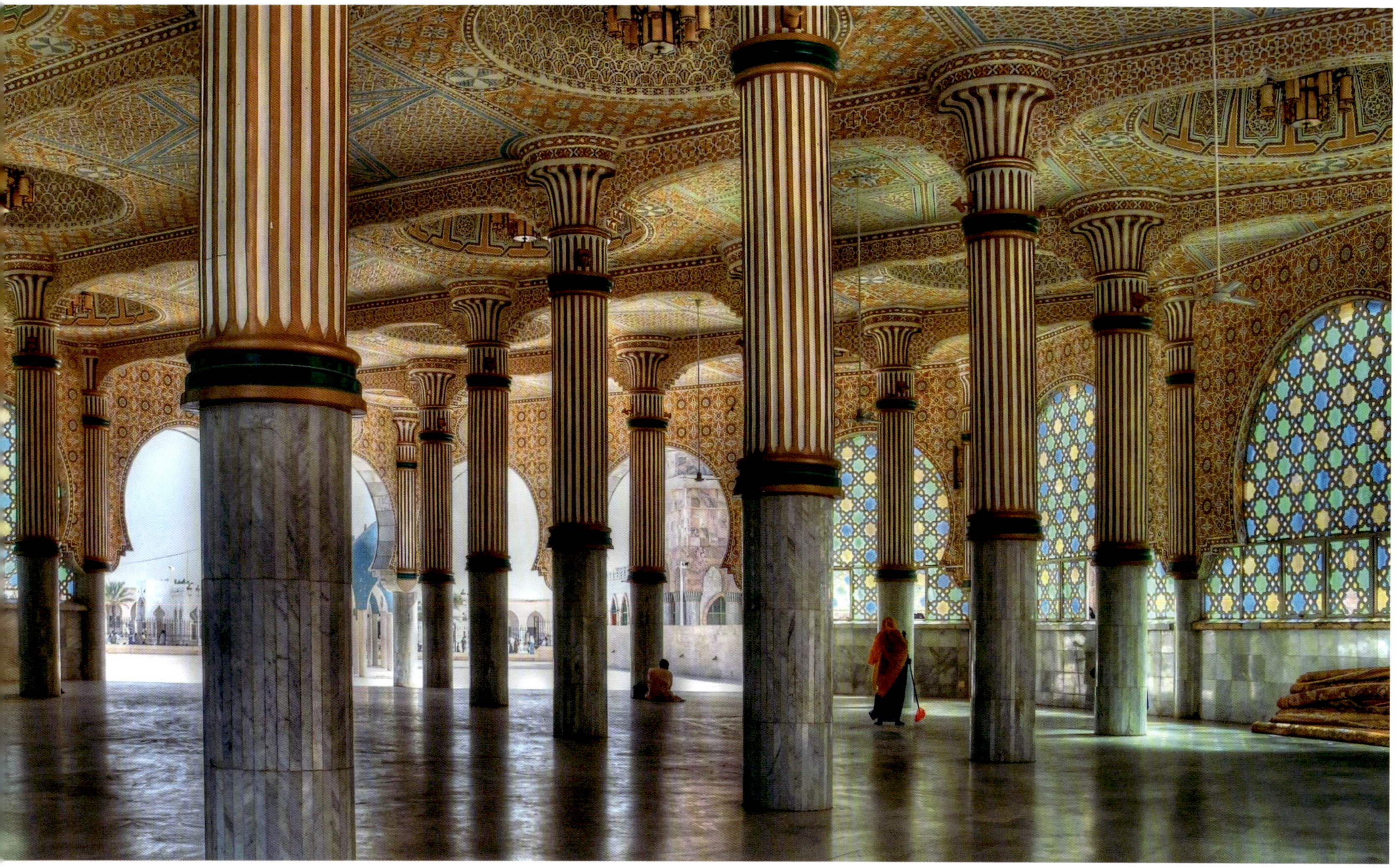

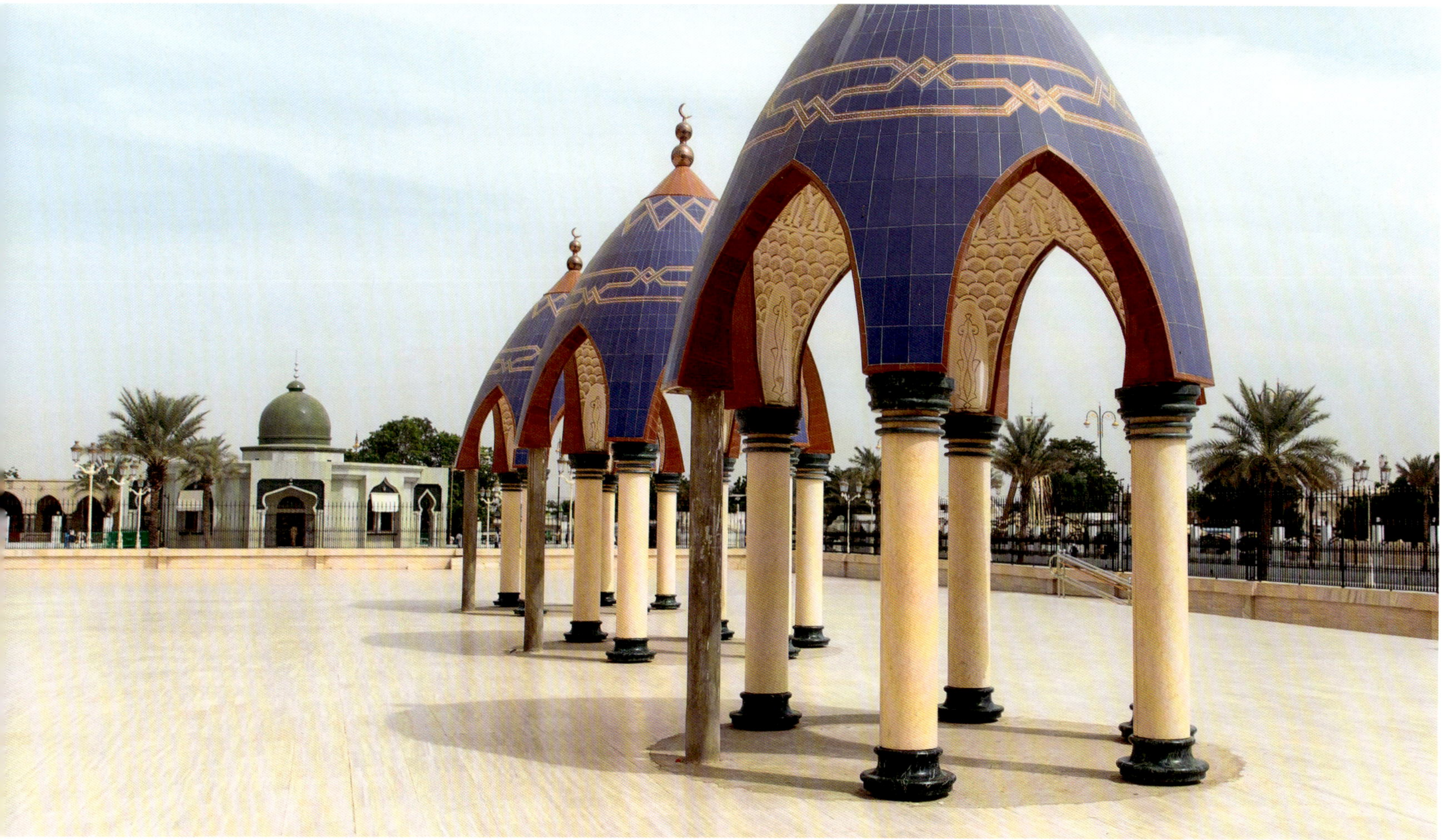

Top The interior of the Great Mosque is as breathtaking as its exterior.
Bottom left Touba and its mosque are the spiritual home of the Mourides.
Bottom right The vast forecourt of the mosque prepares the visitor for prayer.

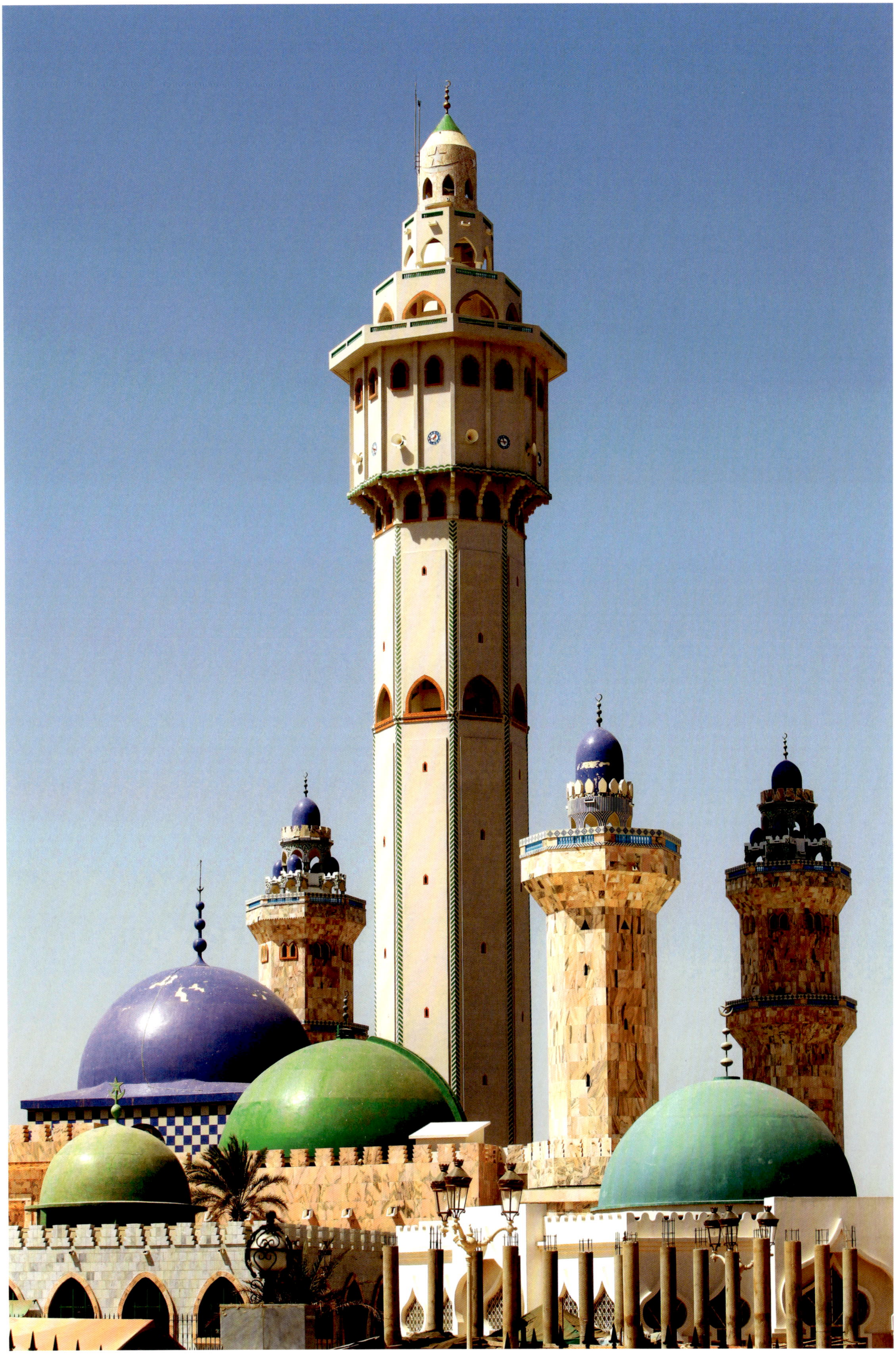

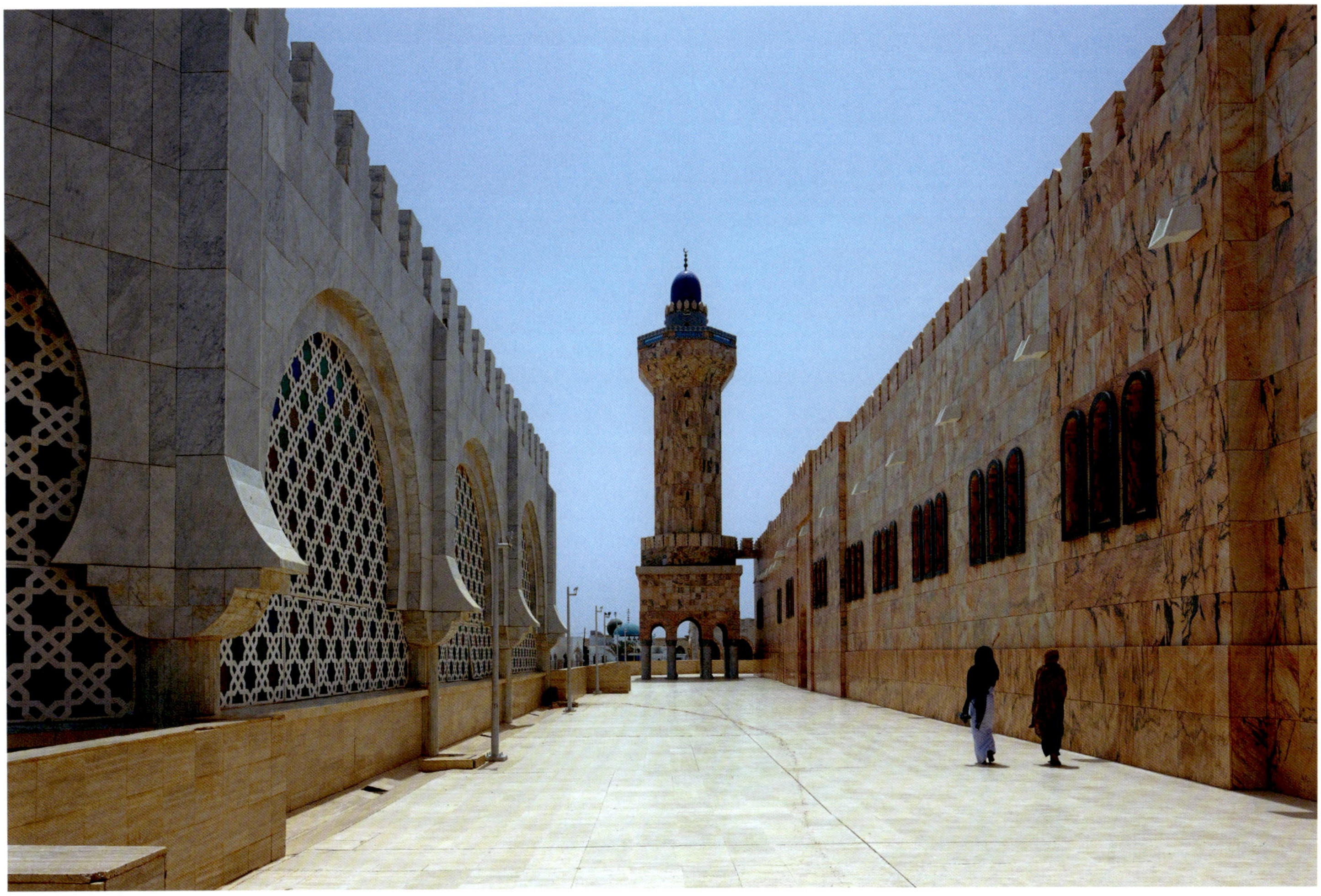

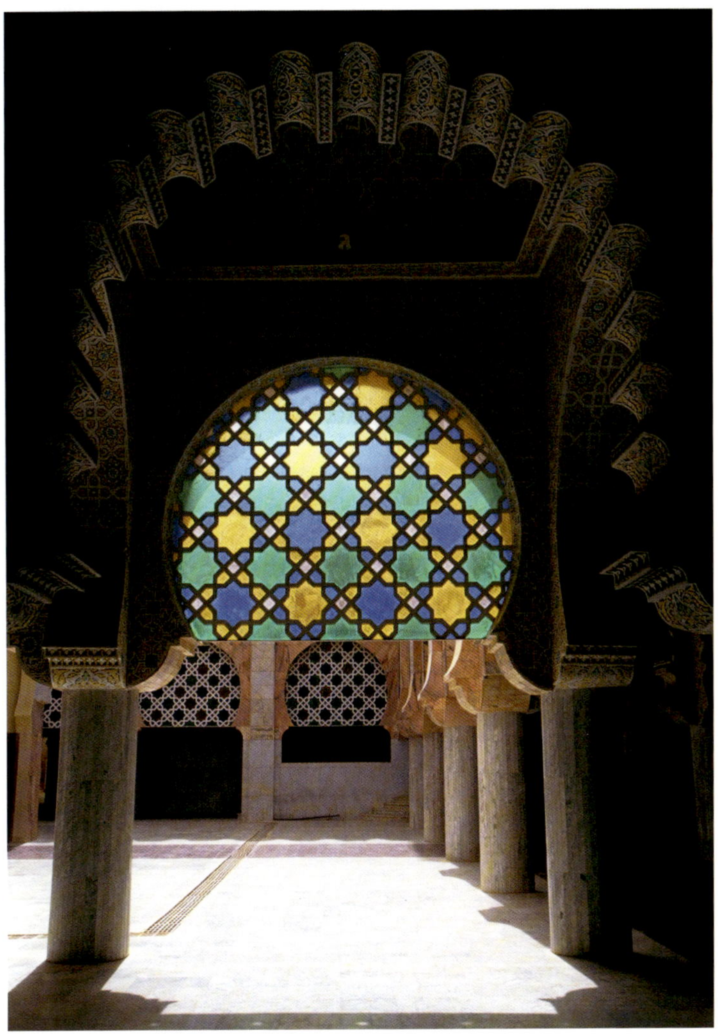

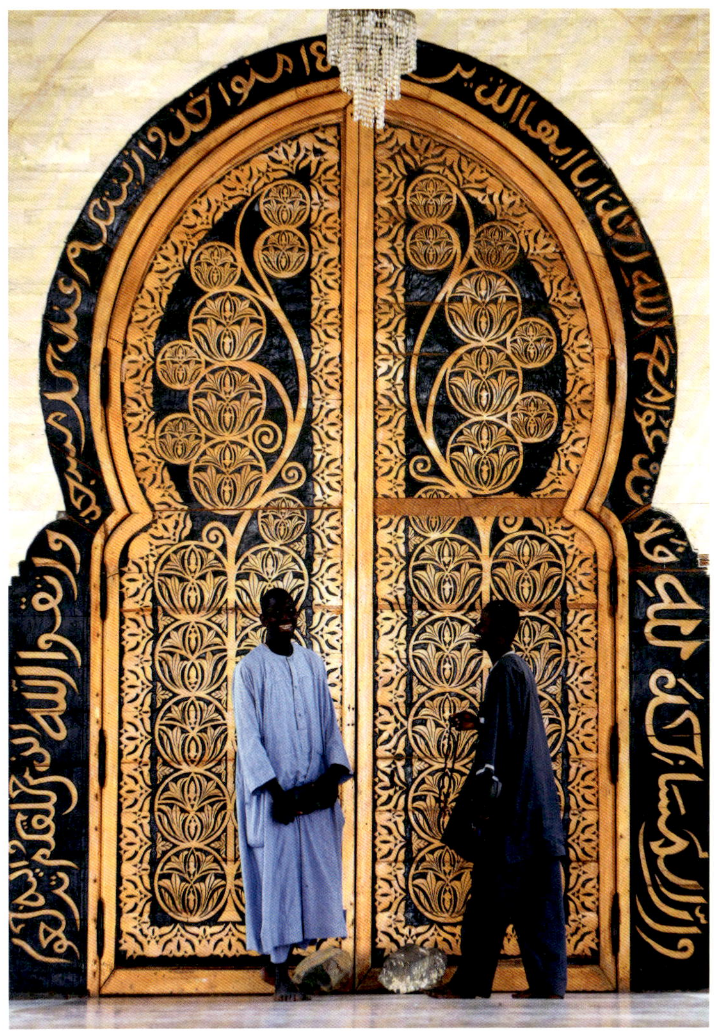

Opposite The central minaret, called "Lamp Fall," is 285 feet (87 meters) high.
Top The smaller minarets are characterized by their purple domes.
Bottom left Kaleidoscopic patterns adorn the windows and walls.
Bottom right The entrance is framed by delicate golden calligraphy.

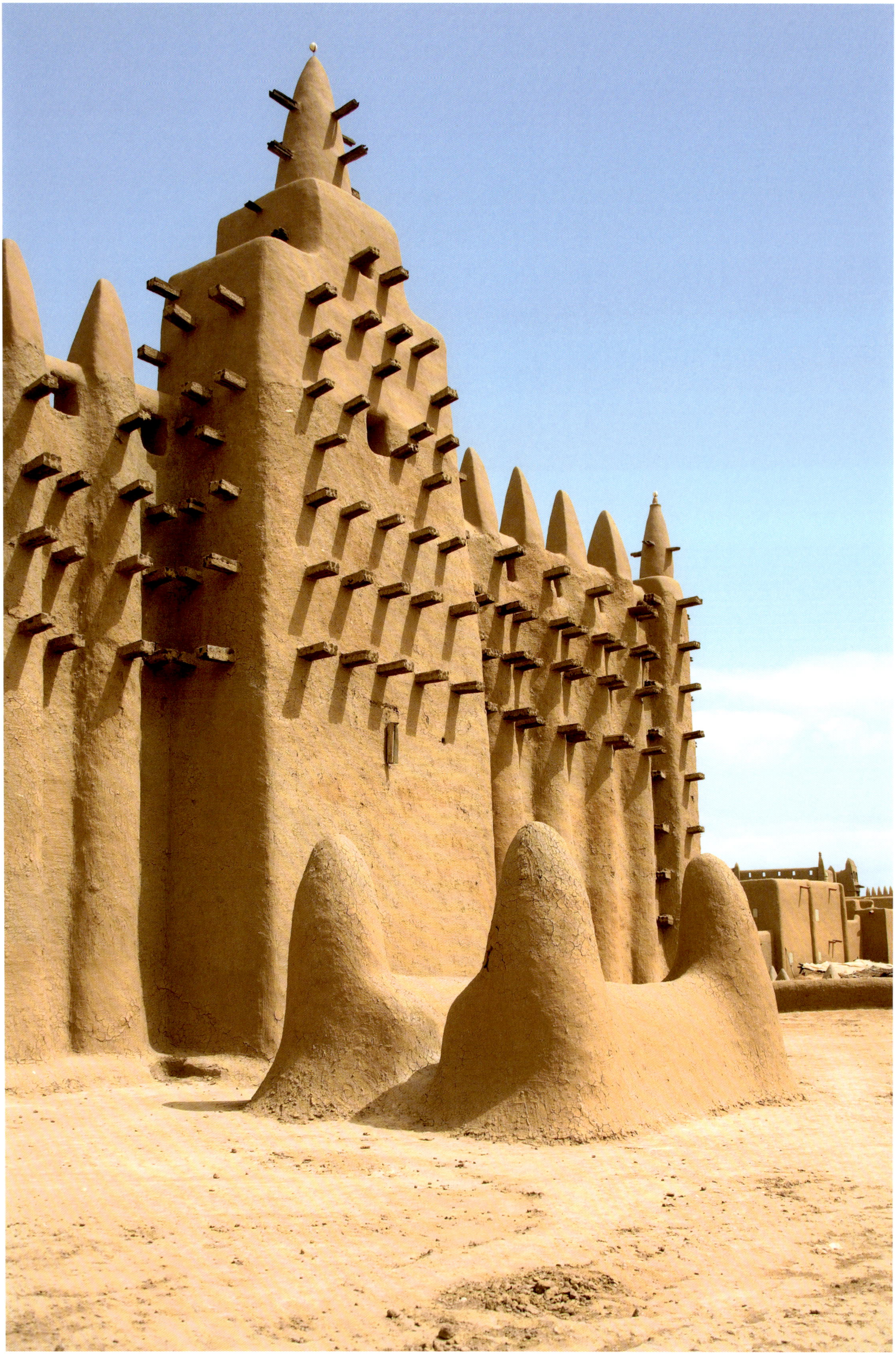

Great Mosque of Djenné

Built: 13th century CE, Djenné, Mali

The preservation of this spectacular house of worship is the work of a deeply dedicated community.

In central Mali, on a floodplain between the Bani River and the mighty Niger, stands a unique monument made of clay: the Great Mosque of Djenné. As the largest mud-brick building in the world, it stands as a masterpiece of the Sudano-Sahelian style and a significant symbol of Islamic history in West Africa.

The mosque is, in every sense, a living building. Each year after the rainyseason, a unique tradition takes place to ensure its preservation: the Crépissage. On this day, the people of Djenné gather to replaster the mosque with *banco*—a mixture of clay, rice straw, and water—repairing the weathered and eroded areas. Drums and songs accompany the faithful as they work, reinforcing not just the mosque but also the bonds of their community.

The tradition likely dates back to the mosque's reconstruction in 1907, but the original temple was built in the 13th century by King Koi Konboro, the first Muslim ruler of Djenné. Before the arrival of Islam, the region practiced animist religions, as was common in many parts of West Africa. In the ensuing centuries, when the Mali Empire gave way to the Songhai, and the region was subjected to invasion and occupation, Djenné lost much of its political and economic significance, and the mosque's upkeep was neglected. By the 19th century, it was largely in ruins.

In 1907, under French colonial administration, the mosque was reconstructed in its present form, closely following the original, 13th-century design. The symmetrical facade is dominated by three prominent minarets. Thick vertical buttresses reinforce the exterior walls, adding structural stability. Wooden beams, known as *toron,* are embedded in the walls, serving both as architectural feature and scaffolding for the annual Crépissage. Inside, the mosque remains pleasantly cool, thanks to the breathable, moisture-regulating clay walls—a blessing for the faithful who gather for Friday prayers and for Islamic holidays like Eid al-Fitr and Eid al-Adha. In addition to worship, the mosque serves as a center for Quranic education and religious studies, especially for younger members of the community. To preserve the mosque's spiritual significance, tourists are strictly prohibited from entering.

Since 1988, along with Djenné's "old towns," the Great Mosque of Djenné has been designated a UNESCO World Heritage Site. Its walls tell the story of a living faith, one that is joyfully reaffirmed and renewed each year.

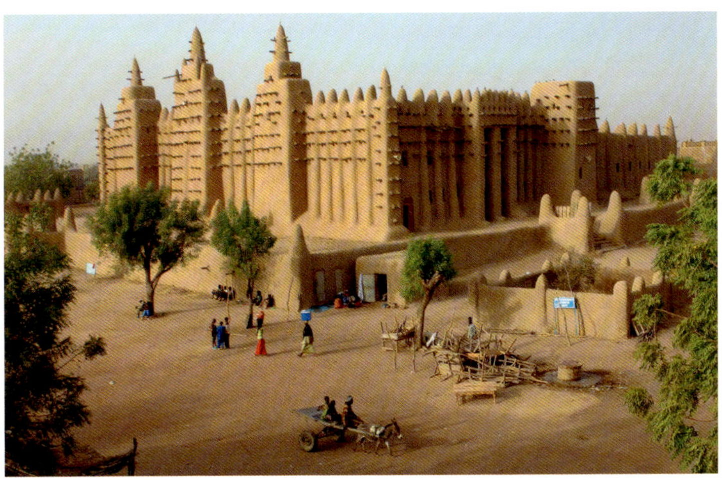

Opposite The mosque was designated a UNESCO World Heritage Site in 1988.
Above It stands in the heart of Djenné's protected Old Town, whose structures are built mostly of earthen bricks.

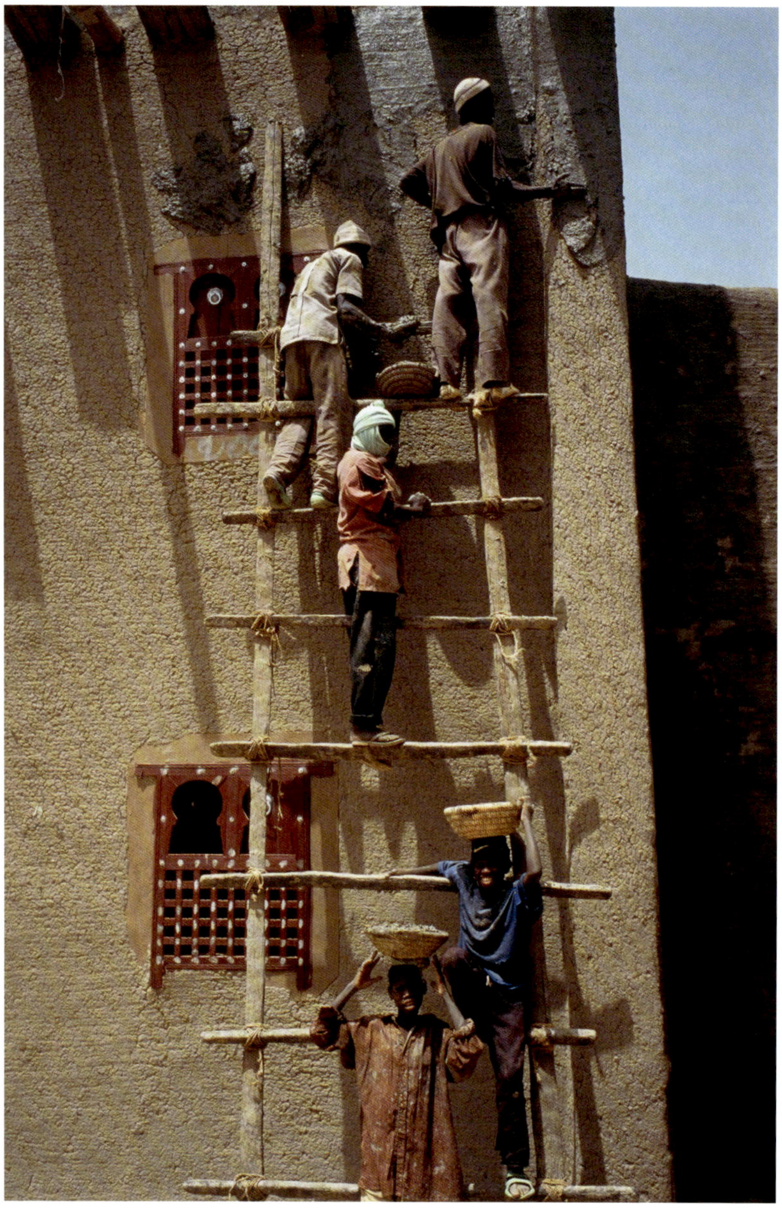

Drums and songs accompany the faithful as they work, reinforcing not just the mosque but also the bonds of their community.

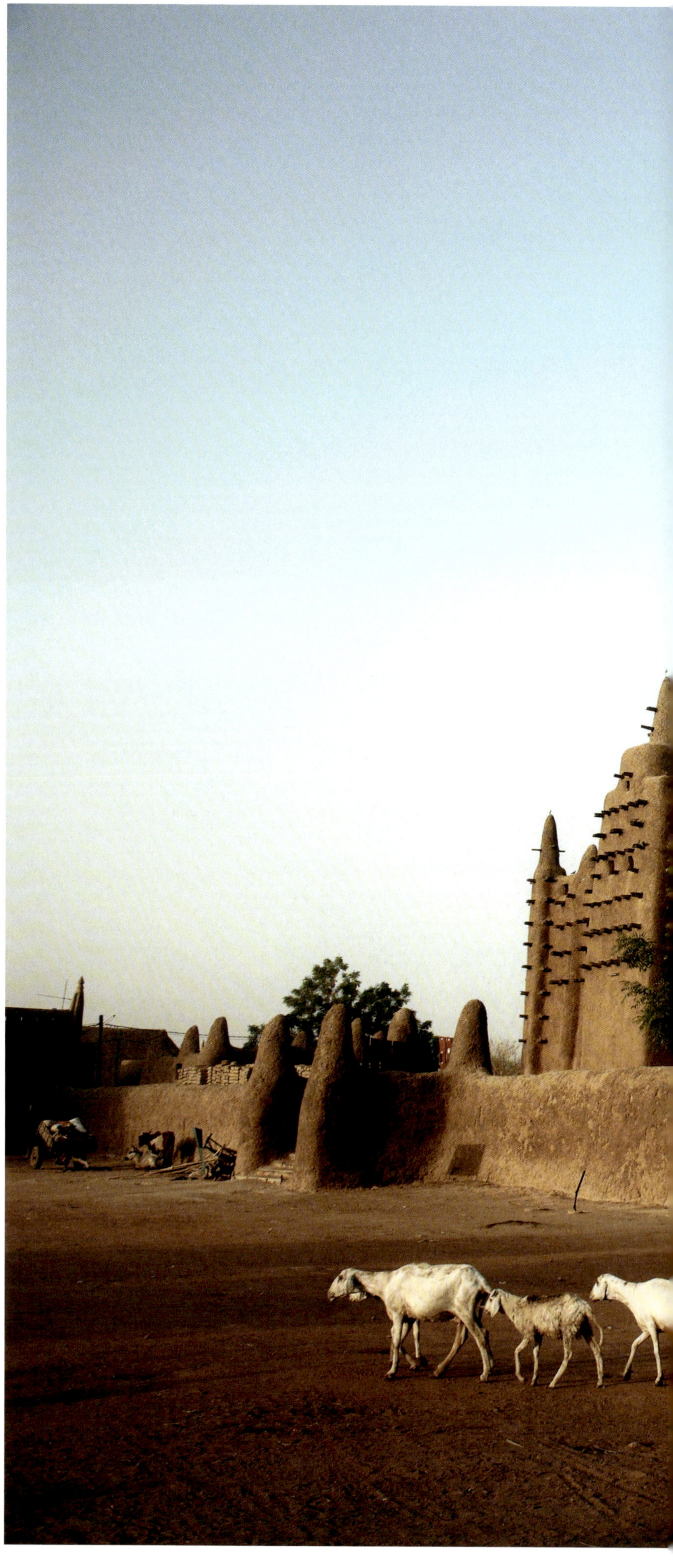

Left Every year, the people of Djenné unite for the Crépissage, renewing the mosque with *banco* and preserving its unique heritage.

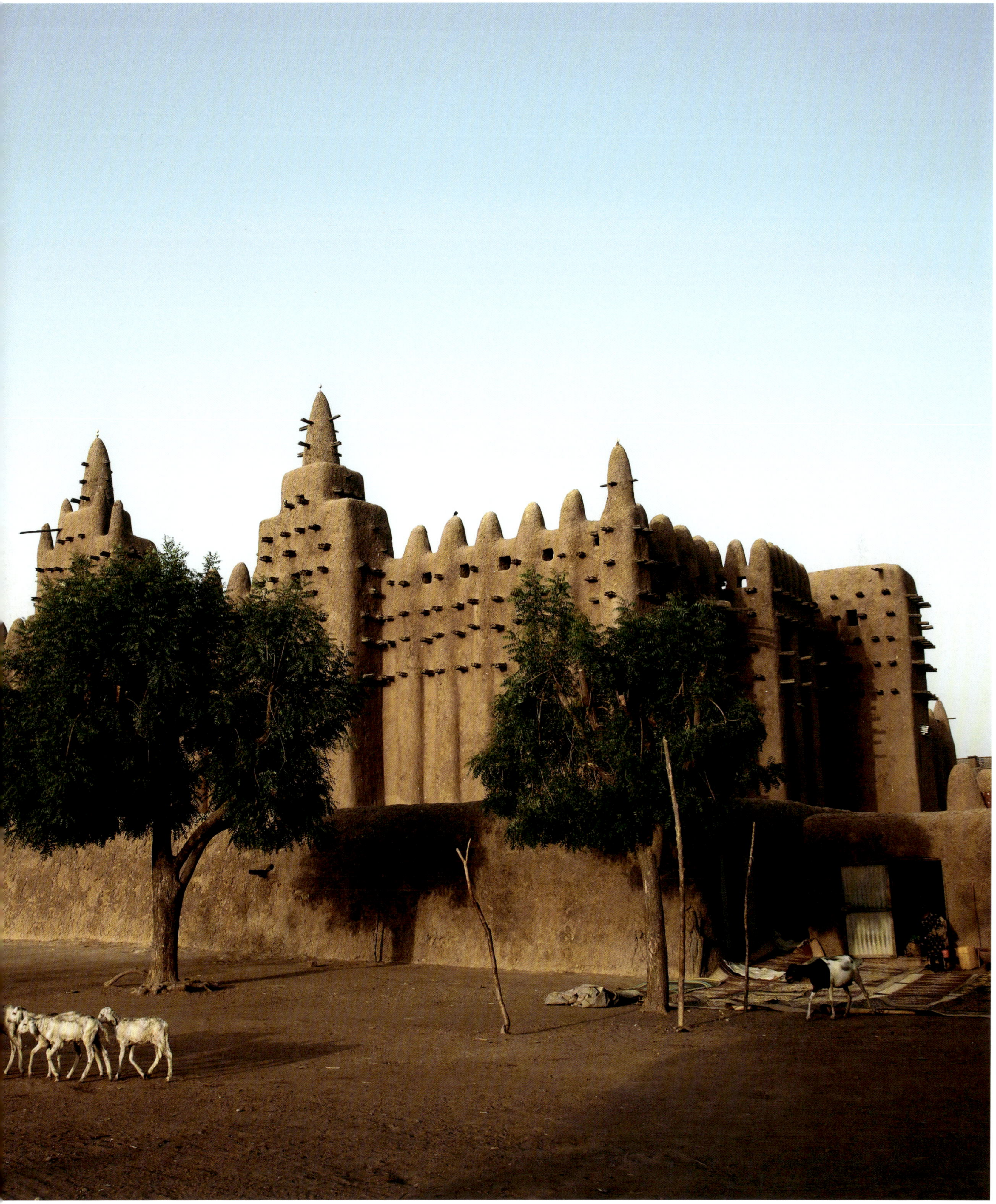

Above Some of the mosque's walls are up to three feet (one meter) thick, providing both stability and natural cooling, a testament to the functionality of traditional Sahelian architecture.

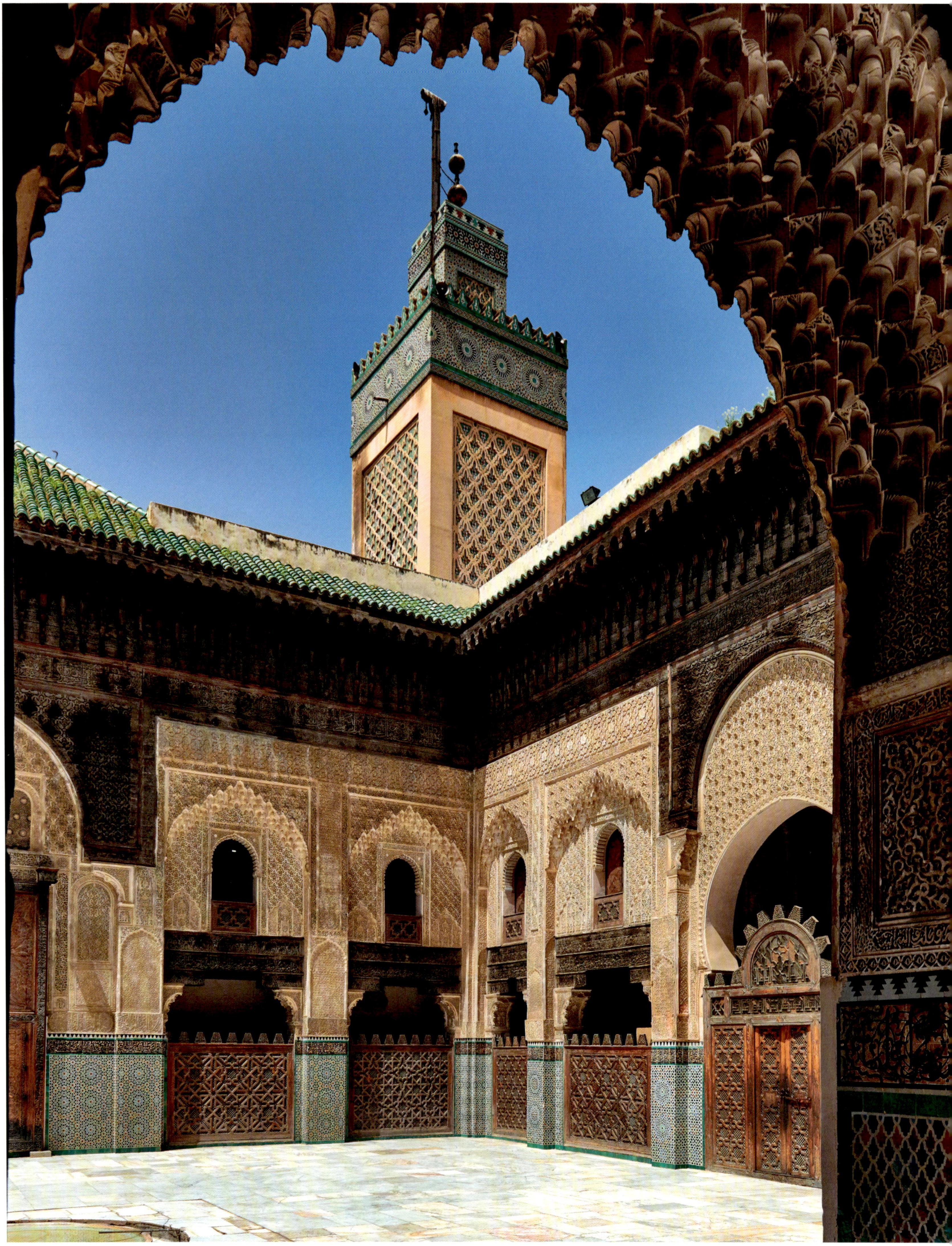

Bou Inania Madrasa

In the Temple of Knowledge

Built: 1350 – 1357 CE,
Fes, Morocco

Where young scholars once studied medicine, poetry, and the Quran, visitors today learn about a world that is often hidden from view.

Anyone wandering through Fes's storied old town will eventually find themselves standing before the massive door of the Bou Inania Madrasa, one of Morocco's most impressive religious colleges. Beyond the door, time seems to stand still, and the bustling energy of the medina gives way to an atmosphere of reverent silence.

At the center of the intricately designed courtyard, a round fountain gently ripples. The air here feels cooler than outside on the dusty streets. Delicate *mashrabiya* screens and smooth *zellij* tiles decorate the walls, their vibrant colors and geometric patterns bearing witness to the artistic mastery of 14th-century craftsmen. Every step reveals new details: fine Arabic inscriptions from the Quran, intricately carved wooden elements forming complex stars and rosettes, and filigree stucco where light and shadow play against one another. Behind the arcades, narrow corridors lead to the former living quarters of the students. It is easy to imagine how the young scholars immersed themselves in their studies in these small spaces, surrounded by the spiritual atmosphere of this extraordinary place. The rooms are simple, almost austere—a striking contrast to the richly decorated courtyard that served as a space for community and reflection.

Eventually, the path leads to the attached mosque, the spiritual heart of the madrasa. High coffered ceilings of the finest cedarwood span the intricately crafted arches and slender columns of onyx marble. At the center of the prayer hall lies the richly decorated mihrab, traditionally oriented toward Mecca. The hall's intricate decoration was as exceptional as the very presence of the mosque. Most madrasas were typically equipped with functional prayer rooms for their students, yet the mosque at the Bou Inania Madrasa was congregational, holding services for the wider community. This distinction gave the facility a particularly prominent status as a religious college of its time. And contrary to what is often assumed, madrasas taught far more than just the Quran. Language and literature, poetry and prose, and scientific subjects such as astronomy, mathematics, medicine, and geography were also on the curriculum. Students here received a broad education rooted in the spiritual convictions of Islam.

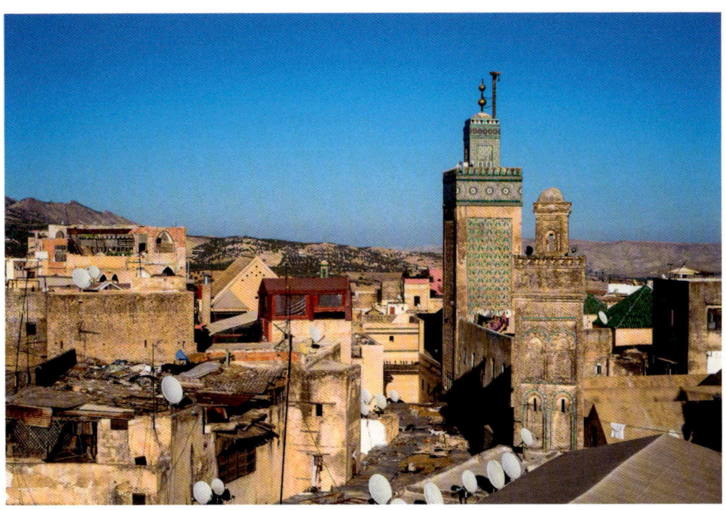

Today, the Bou Inania Madrasa is one of the few religious buildings in Morocco open to non-Muslims. Fortunately, this allows visitors from all over the world to become students here, immersing themselves in a society where knowledge, art, architecture, aesthetics, and spirituality form a harmonious whole.

Opposite The minaret is a rare feature for a madrasa.
Above The madrasa is one of the best-preserved of its kind in Morocco.

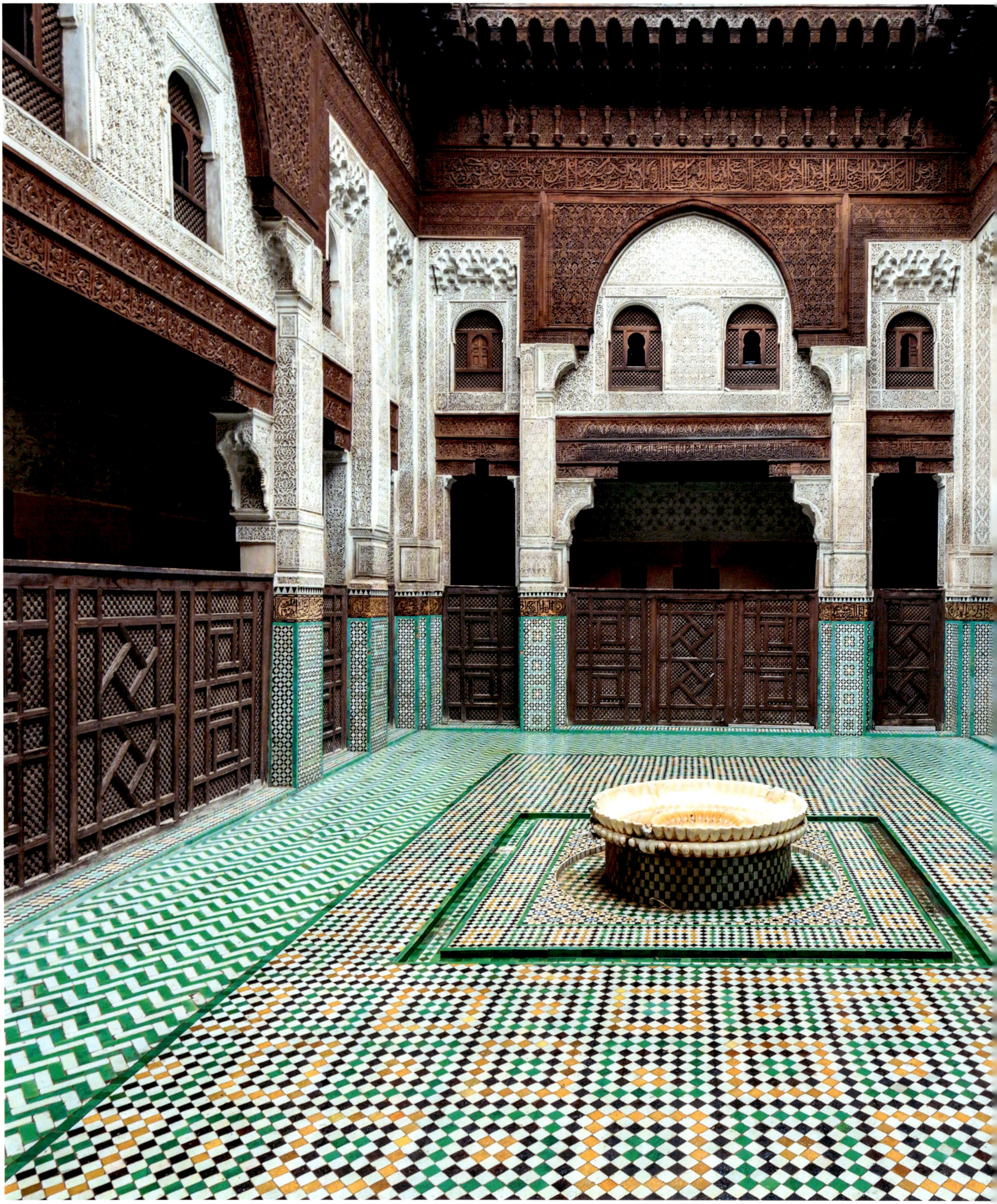

Above The Bou Inania Madrasa is a literal textbook of Islamic architecture, with its arches, mosaics, symbols, and ornaments reflecting a detailed spiritual and cosmological logic.

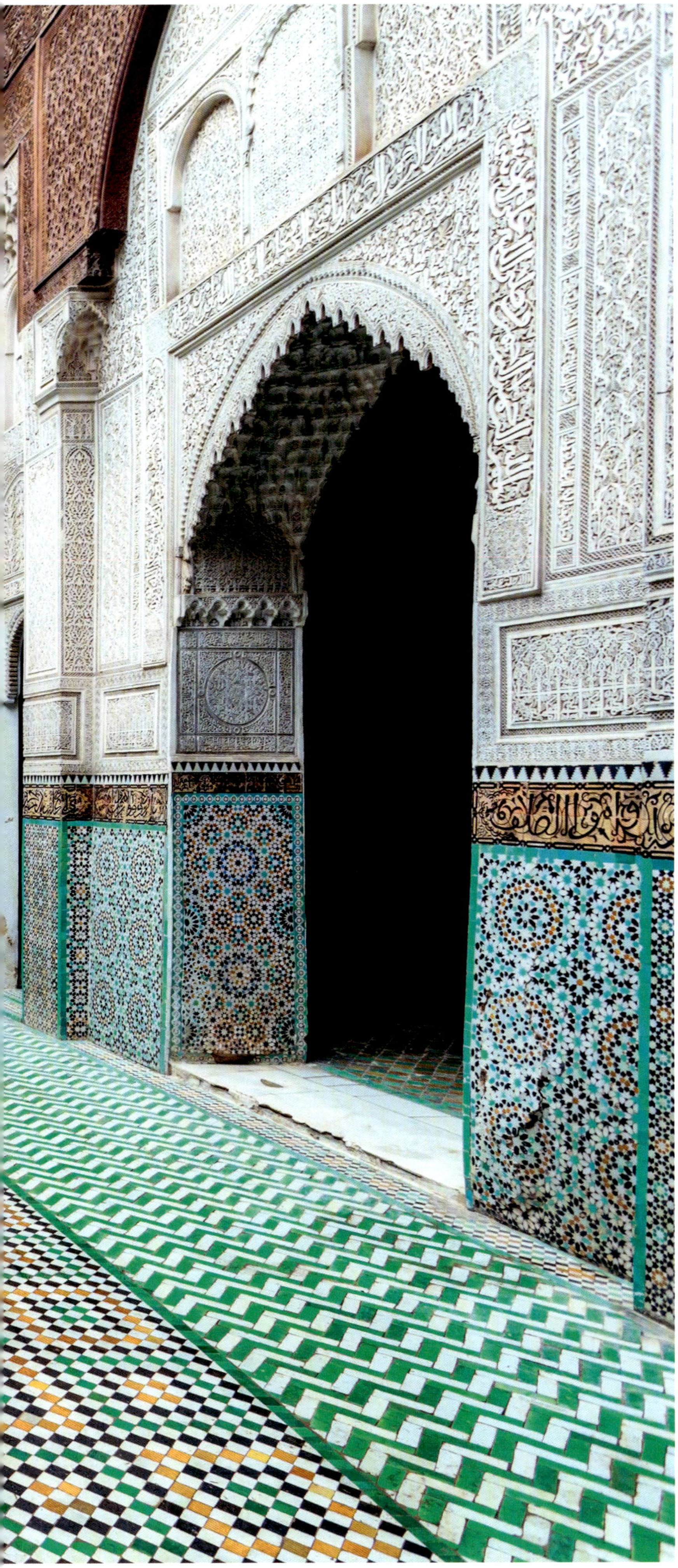

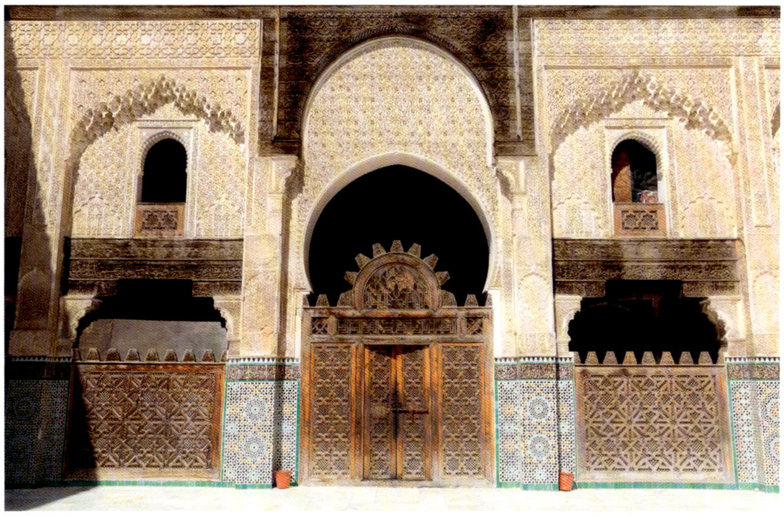

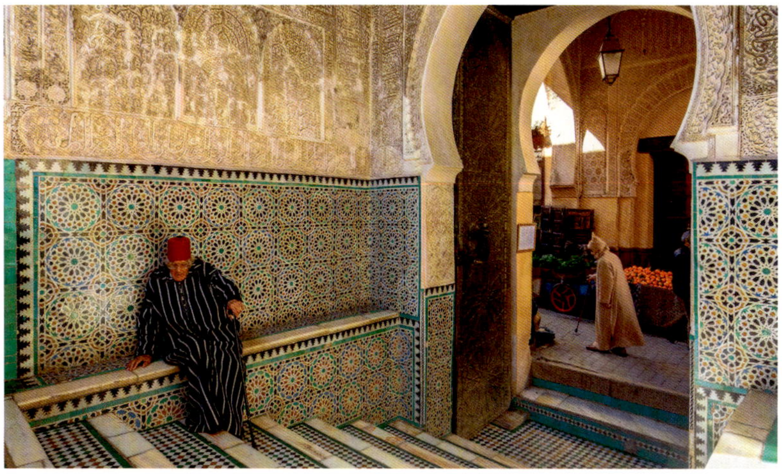

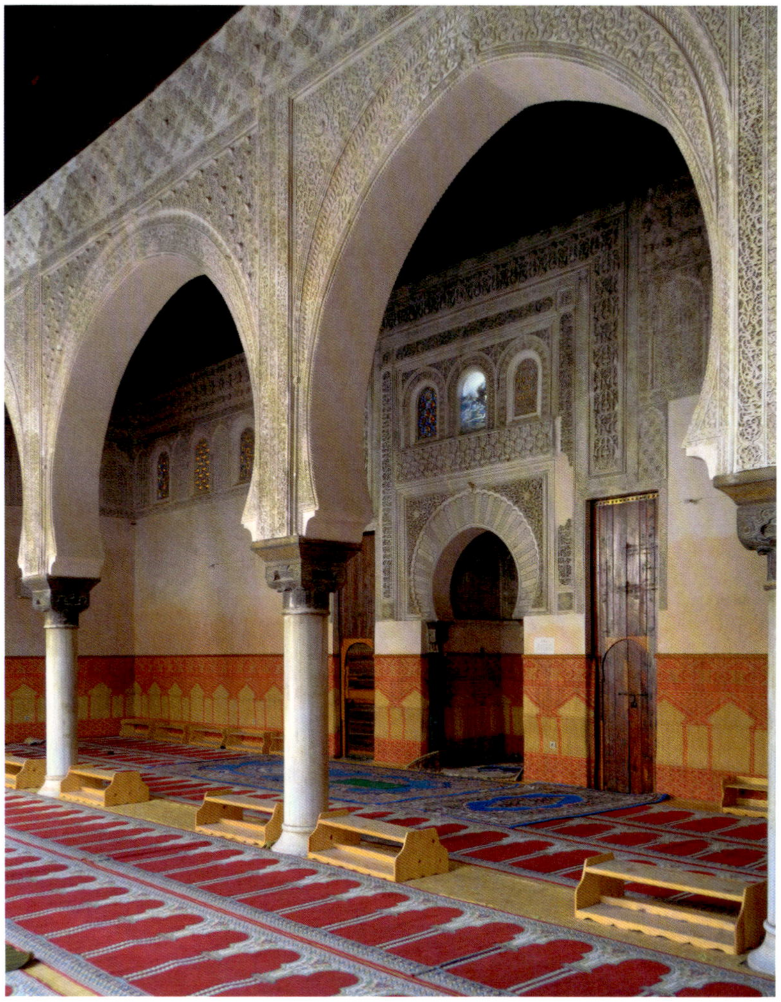

Top The arches are often horseshoe-shaped or slightly pointed.
Middle These forms are typical of Islamic architecture.
Bottom Their precise symmetry pays homage to the Islamic emphasis on God's unity *(Tawhid)*, as everything stems from perfect order.

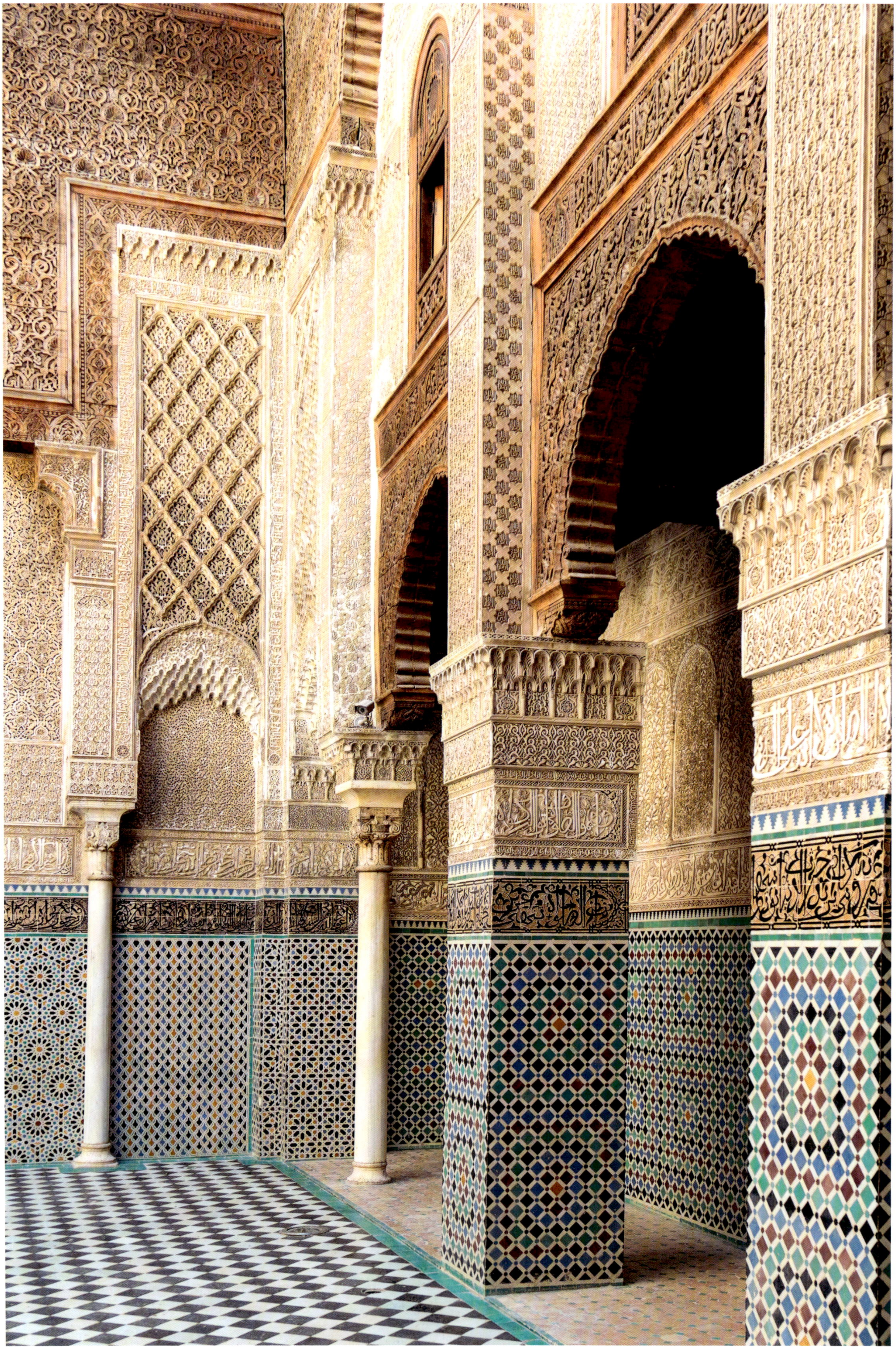

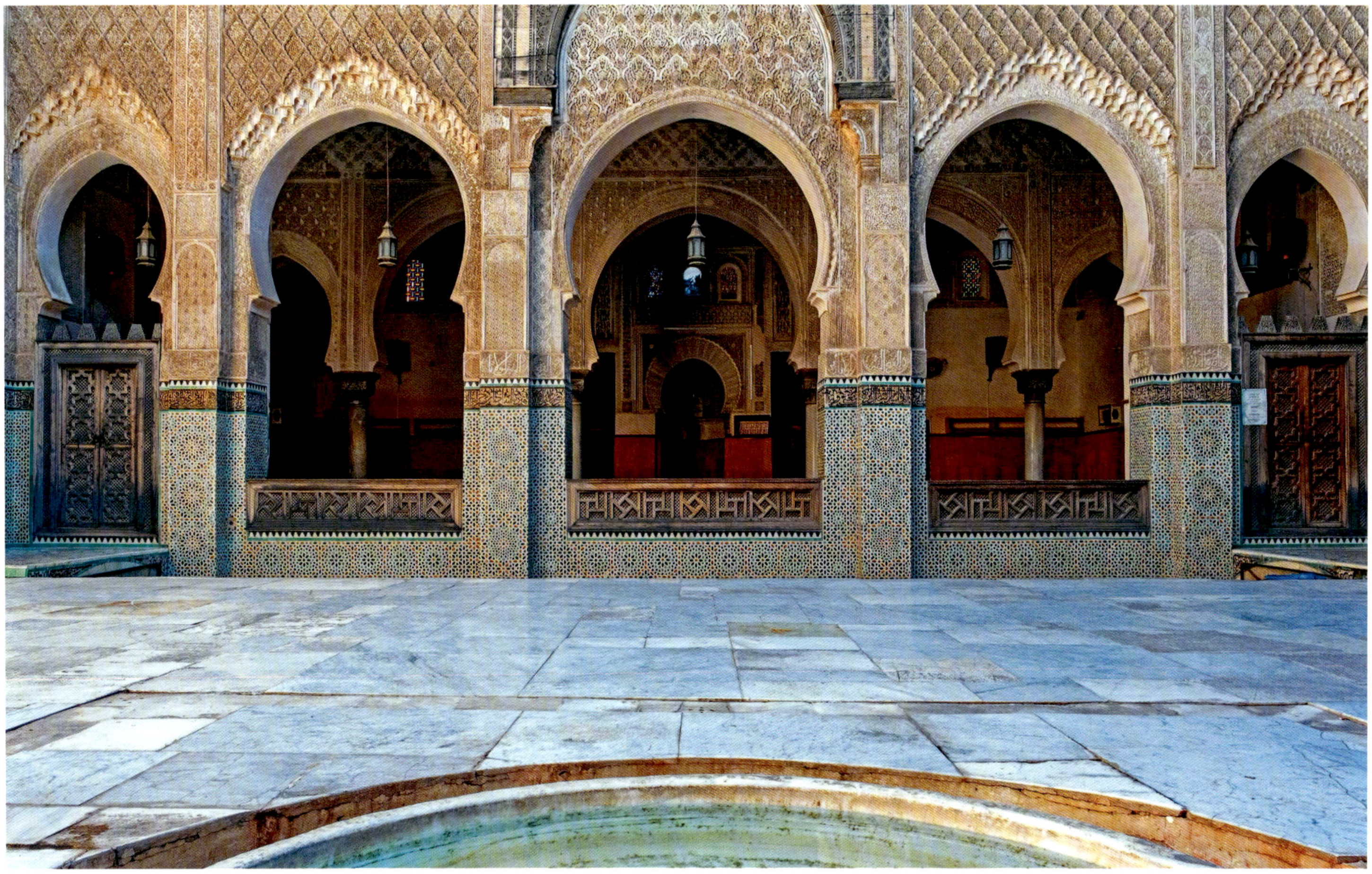

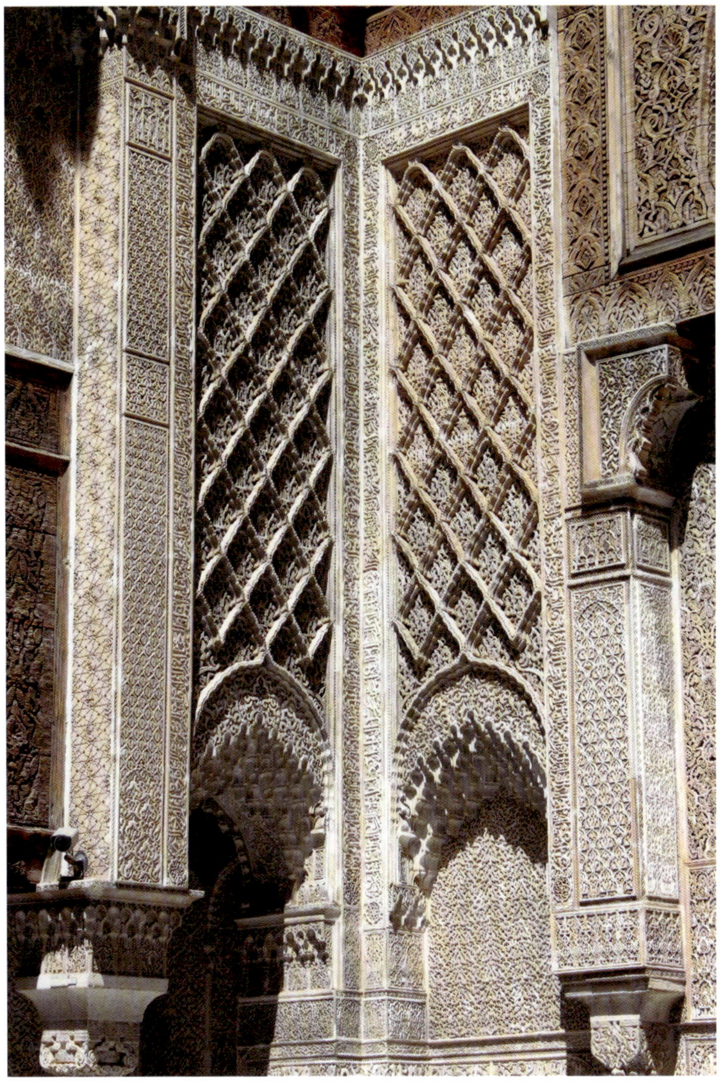

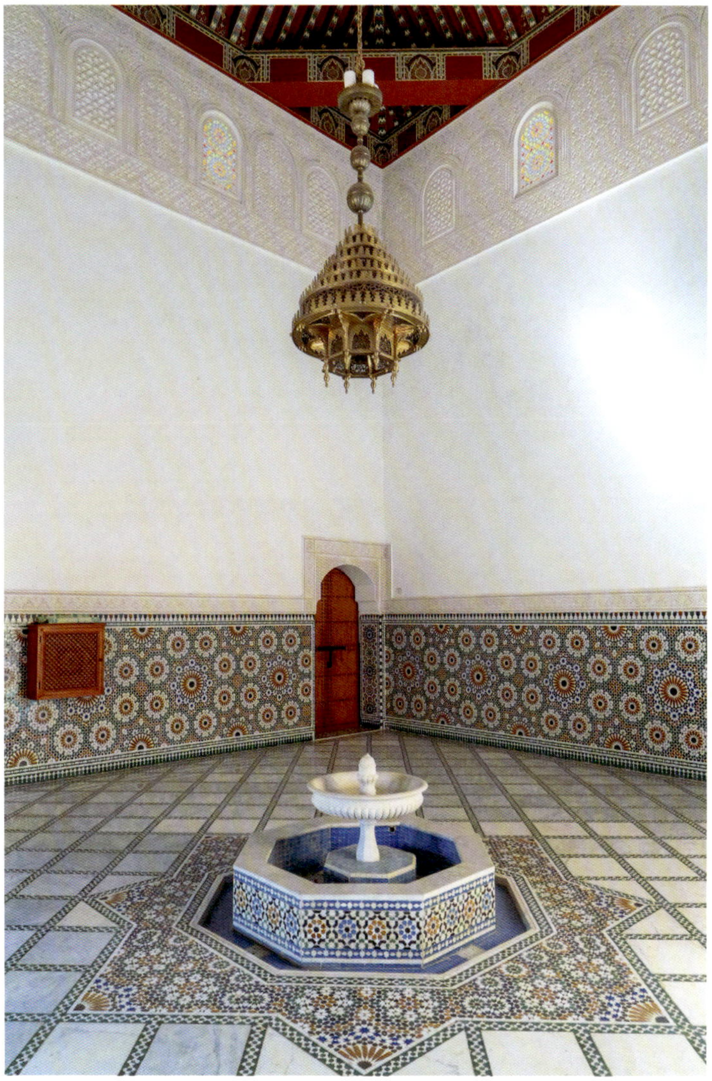

Opposite Various verses from the Quran are integrated into the decoration.
Top Islamic art avoids depicting beings, focusing on abstract and geometric designs.
Bottom left Many patterns in the carvings and mosaics feature stars and octagons.
Bottom right The floral patterns symbolize the eternal paradise (*Jannah*) in Islam.

Temple of Philae

A Temple's Rebirth

Built: 4th century BCE – 3rd century CE,
Agilkia Island, Egypt

In subtle ways, the recent history of this sanctuary mirrors the immortal myth of the ancient deities Isis and Osiris.

In ancient Egypt, for those seeking Isis's favor, no pilgrimage site held greater significance than Philae. Generations journeyed to the temple complex on the Nile, bearing offerings and prayers. To this day, the Temple of Isis, the largest sanctuary at Philae, embodies the essence of ancient Egypt like few others. Its walls and columns are adorned with intricate reliefs recounting the myth of Isis and Osiris—a dazzling saga of love, betrayal, death, and rebirth.

Osiris, it is said, ruled Egypt with a wise and divine hand. Harvests were abundant, and cities flourished. By his side stood his wife Isis, goddess of magic, love, and devotion. But their happiness was not to last. Seth, Osiris's envious brother, hatched a sinister plot. He lured Osiris into a trap, sealed him alive in a coffin, and cast it into the Nile. Grieving her lost husband, Isis embarked on a desperate quest. She finally found the coffin and opened it to discover Osiris's intact body. But Seth stole it, dismembered it into 14 pieces, and scattered them across Egypt (one burial place was at Philae). Yet Isis's love was stronger still. She retrieved the parts of her husband, reassembled him, and briefly brought him back to life to conceive their son, Horus. The gods then made Osiris ruler of the underworld, as he could no longer dwell among the living. Horus grew into a formidable warrior, avenging his father in countless battles against Seth. Despite Horus's strength, Seth was never fully defeated. Ultimately, a tribunal of gods determined the feud's outcome, and the majority favored Horus, granting him the kingship of Egypt. Order triumphed over chaos.

To this day, amulets bearing the "Eye of Horus" are worn in Egypt as protection against the evil eye. They are widely available at souvenir stalls near the jetty where boats depart for the Temple of Philae. Since the late 1970s, these boats have traveled not to Philae Island—where the temple initially stood—but to Agilkia Island, about 1,600 feet (500 meters) upstream, where the temple complex was relocated. The construction of the Aswan High Dam in the 1960s had caused the river's water level to rise dramatically, forming Lake Nasser and threatening to submerge the temples. With international support, the complex was painstakingly dismantled and rebuilt on higher ground. Since then, the temple complex of Philae has stood safe from the floods and under UNESCO's protection. And who knows? Perhaps the goddess Isis herself lent a hand to this spectacular rescue mission—after all, she had once before, and with great effort, restored something precious and brought it back to life.

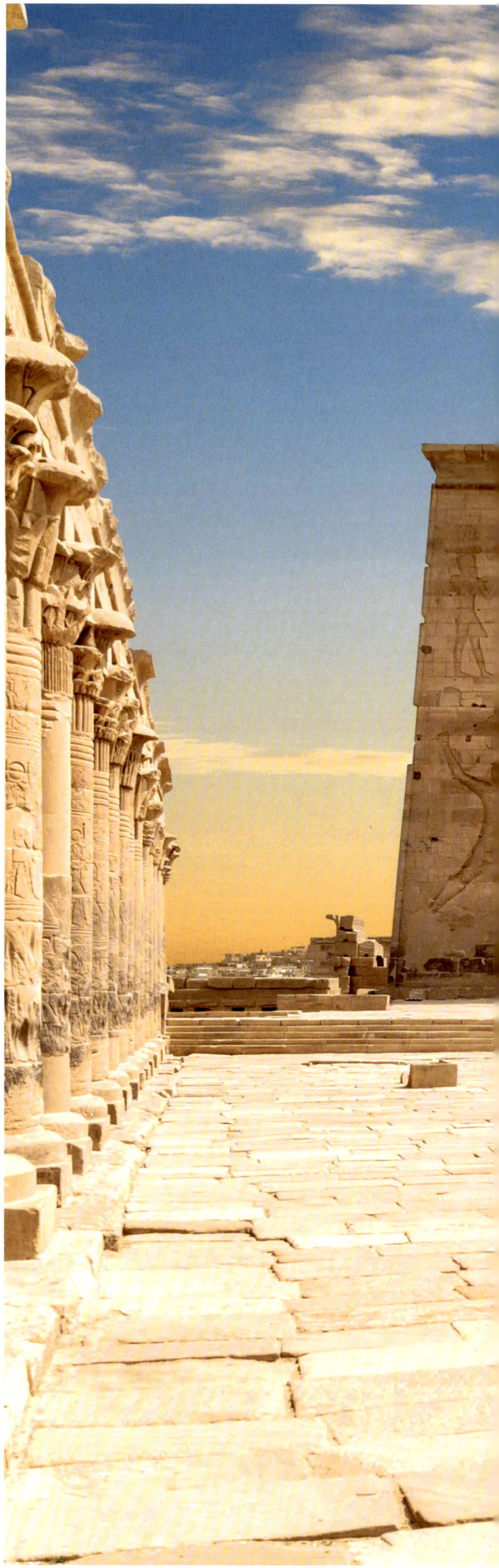

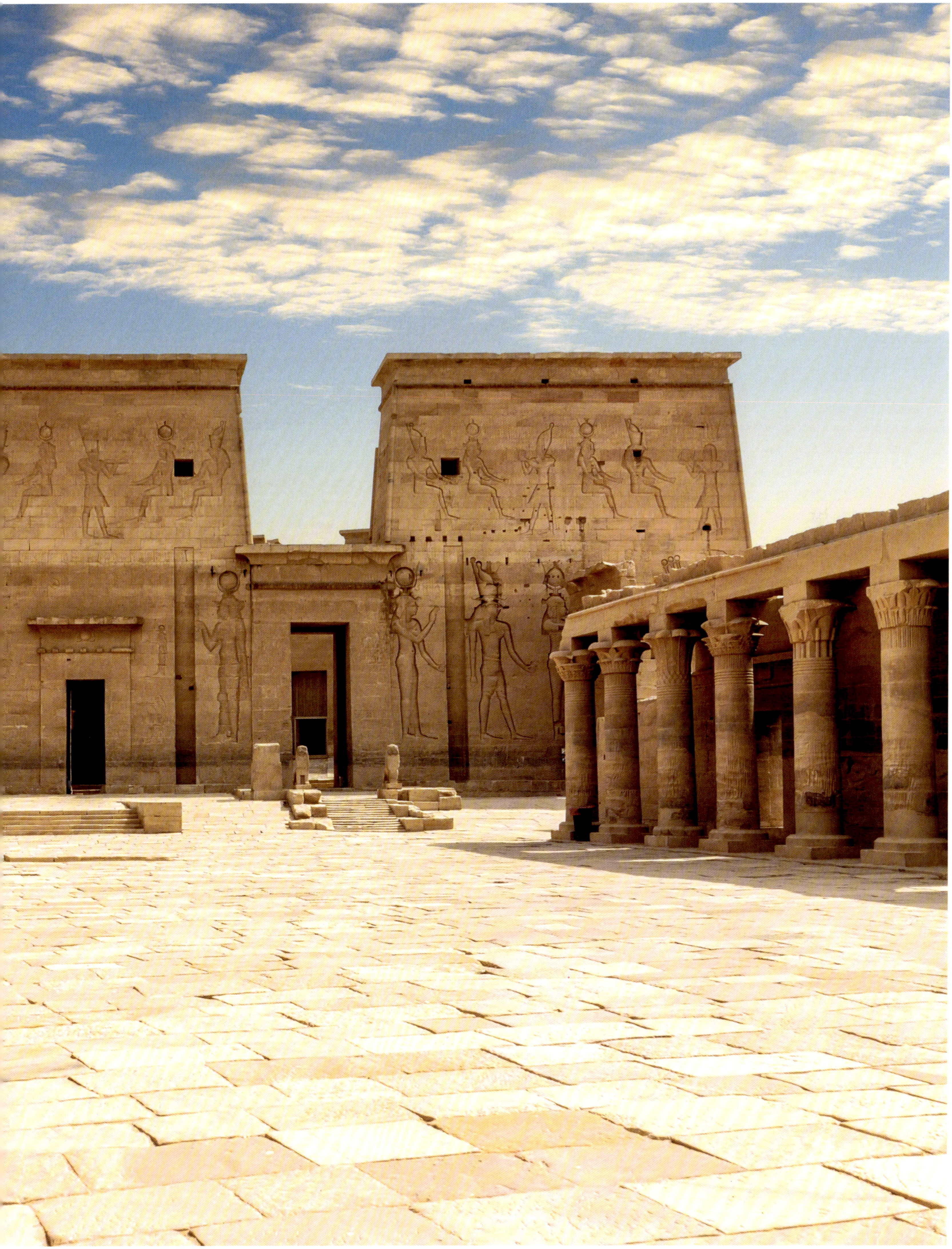

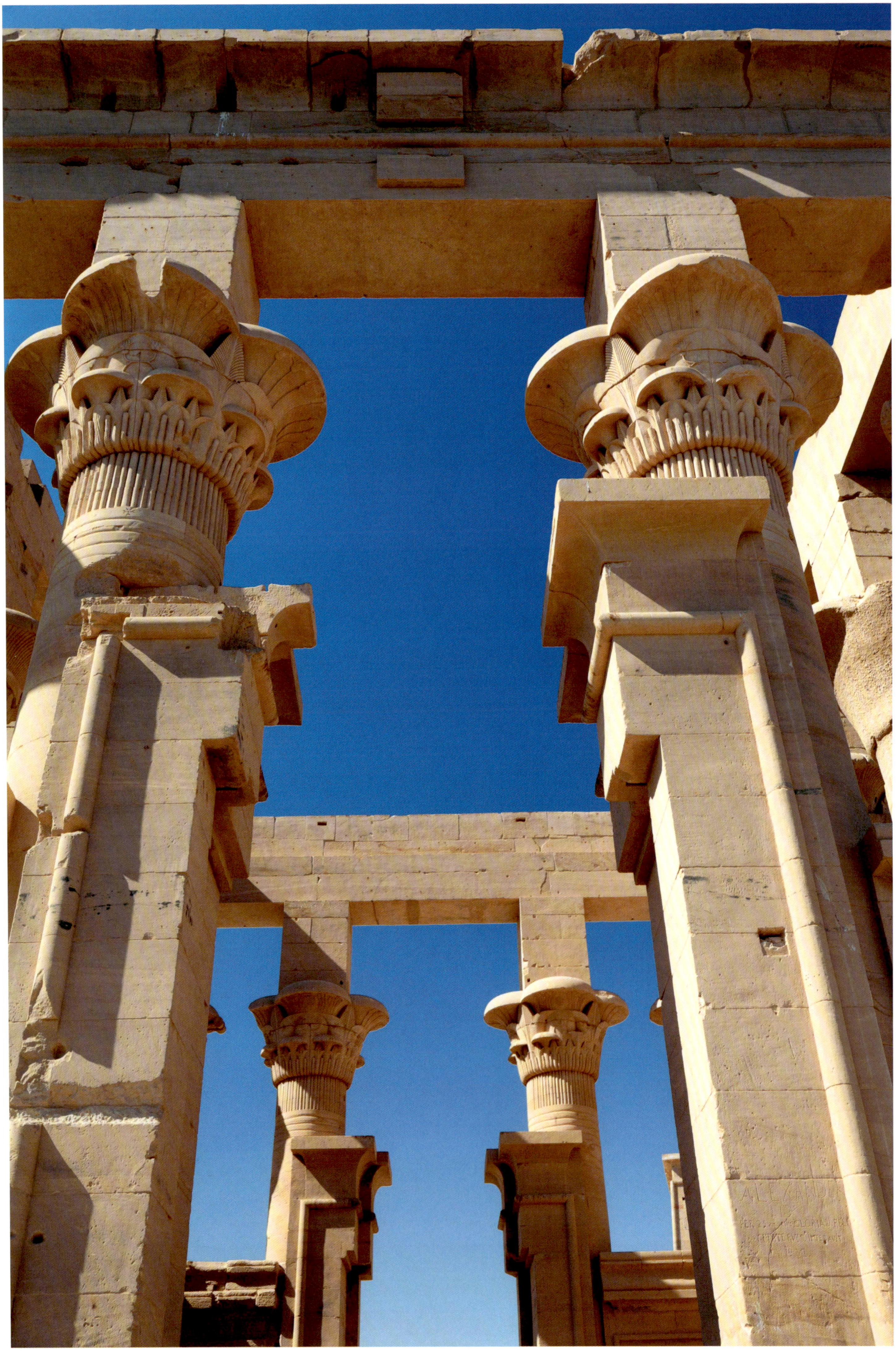

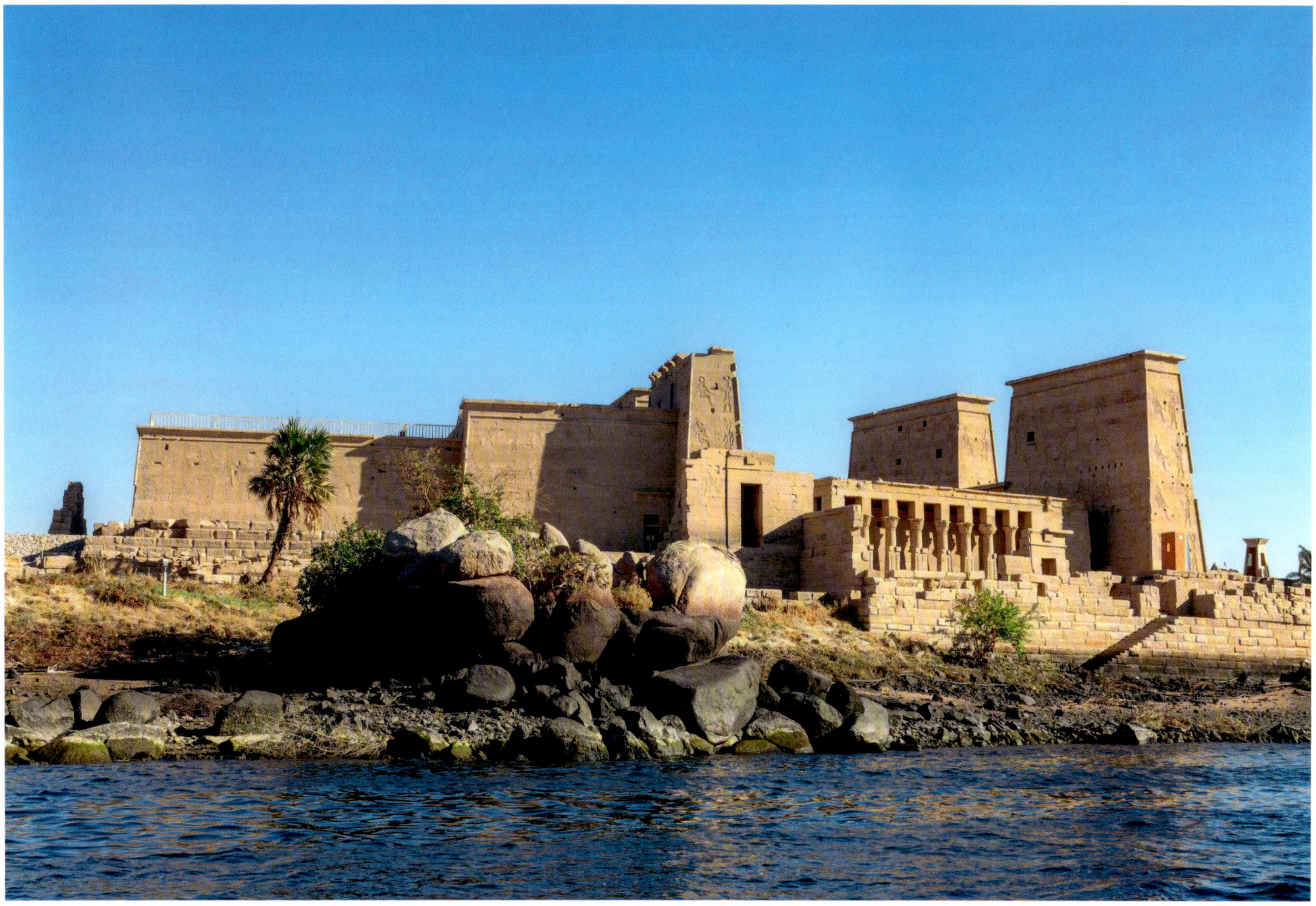

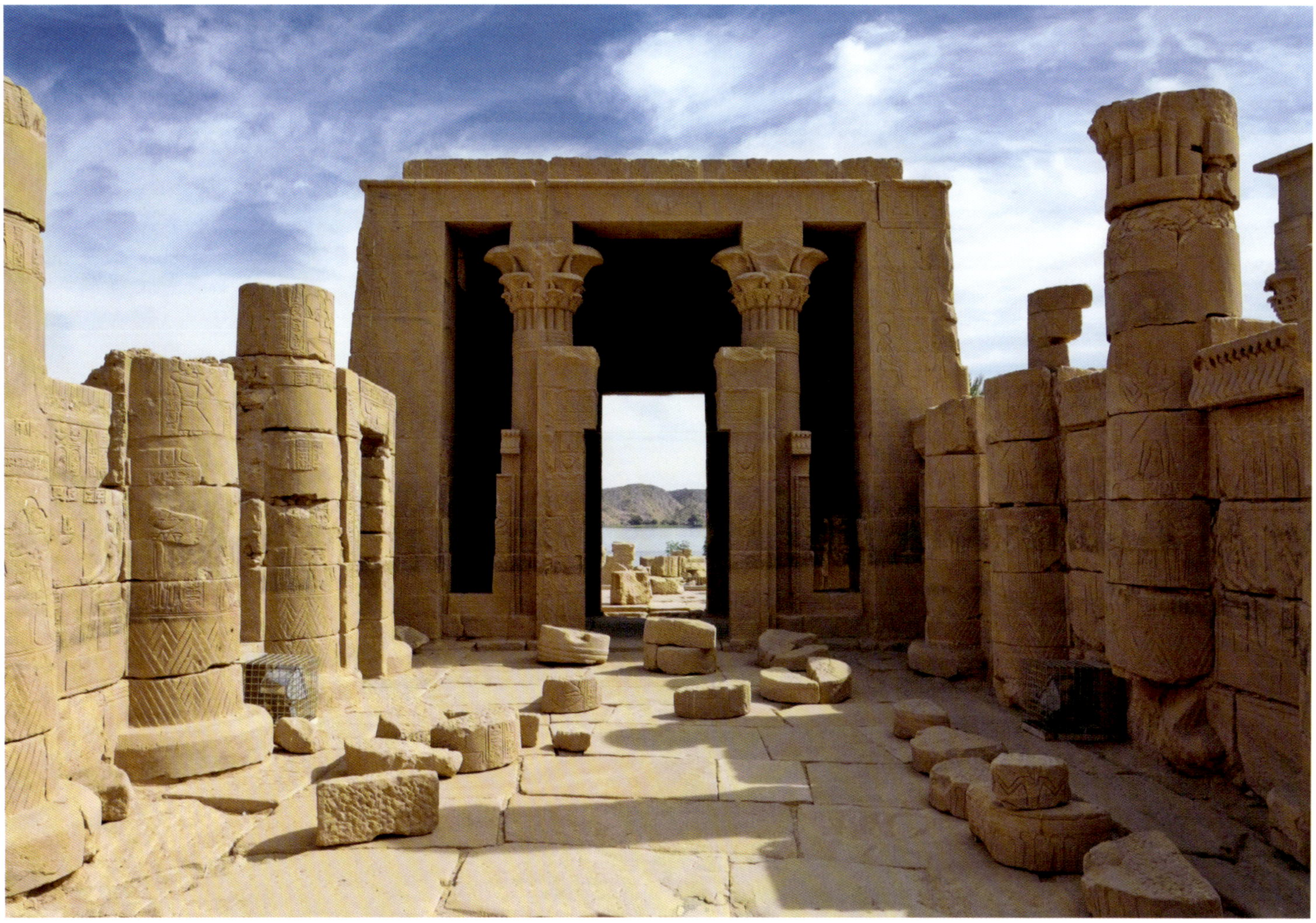

Opposite The myth of Isis and Osiris symbolizes the ancient concept of order and chaos.
Top The Ptolemaic rulers fused Egyptian and Hellenistic styles.
Bottom The Temples of Philae are part of a UNESCO World Heritage Site that also includes Abu Simbel.

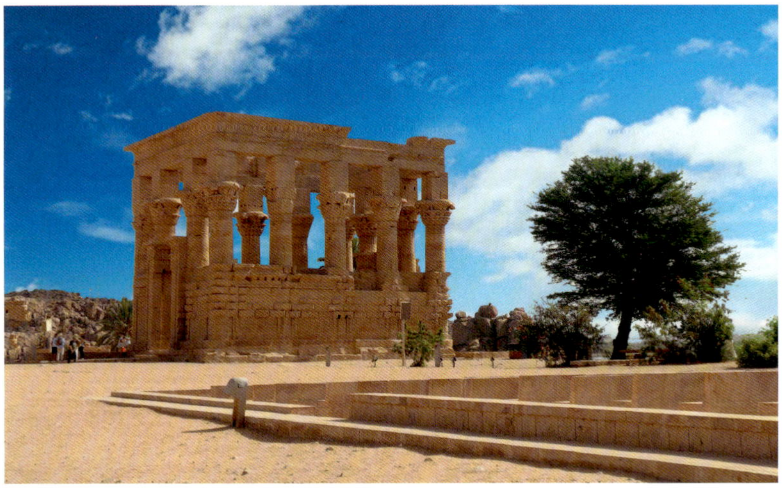

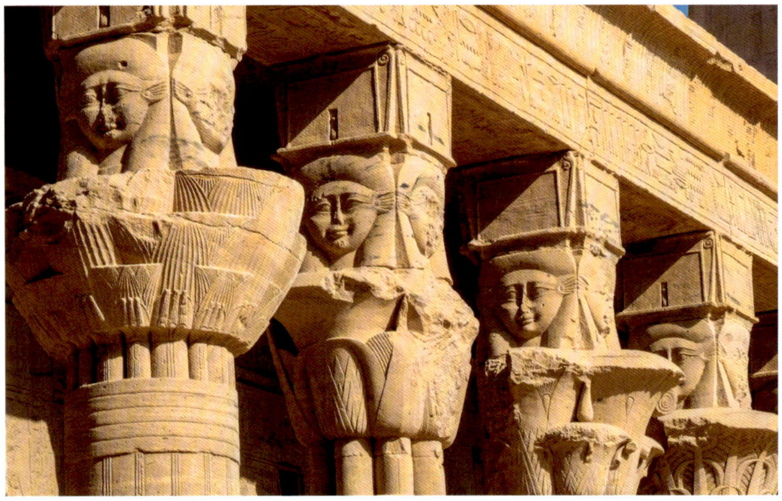

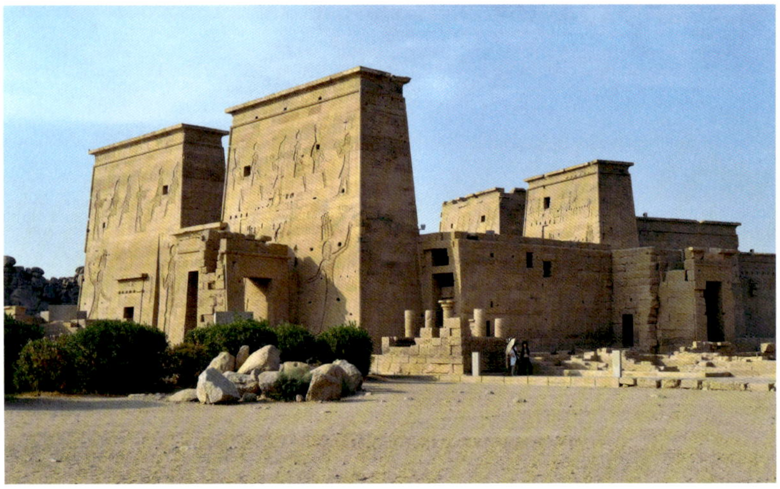

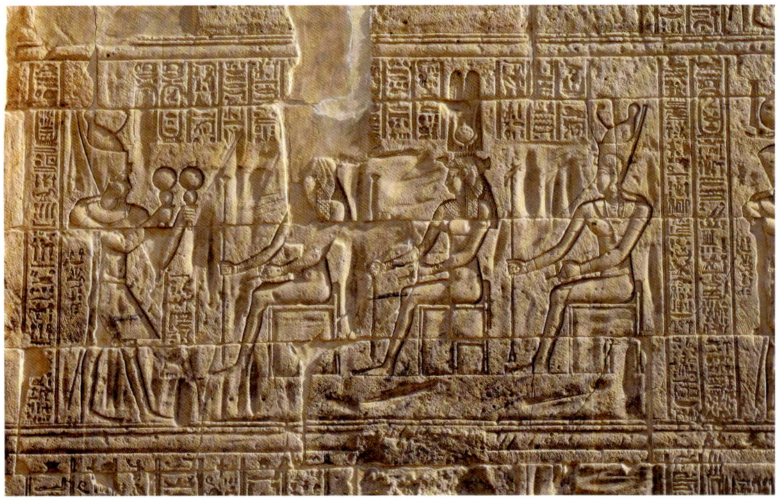

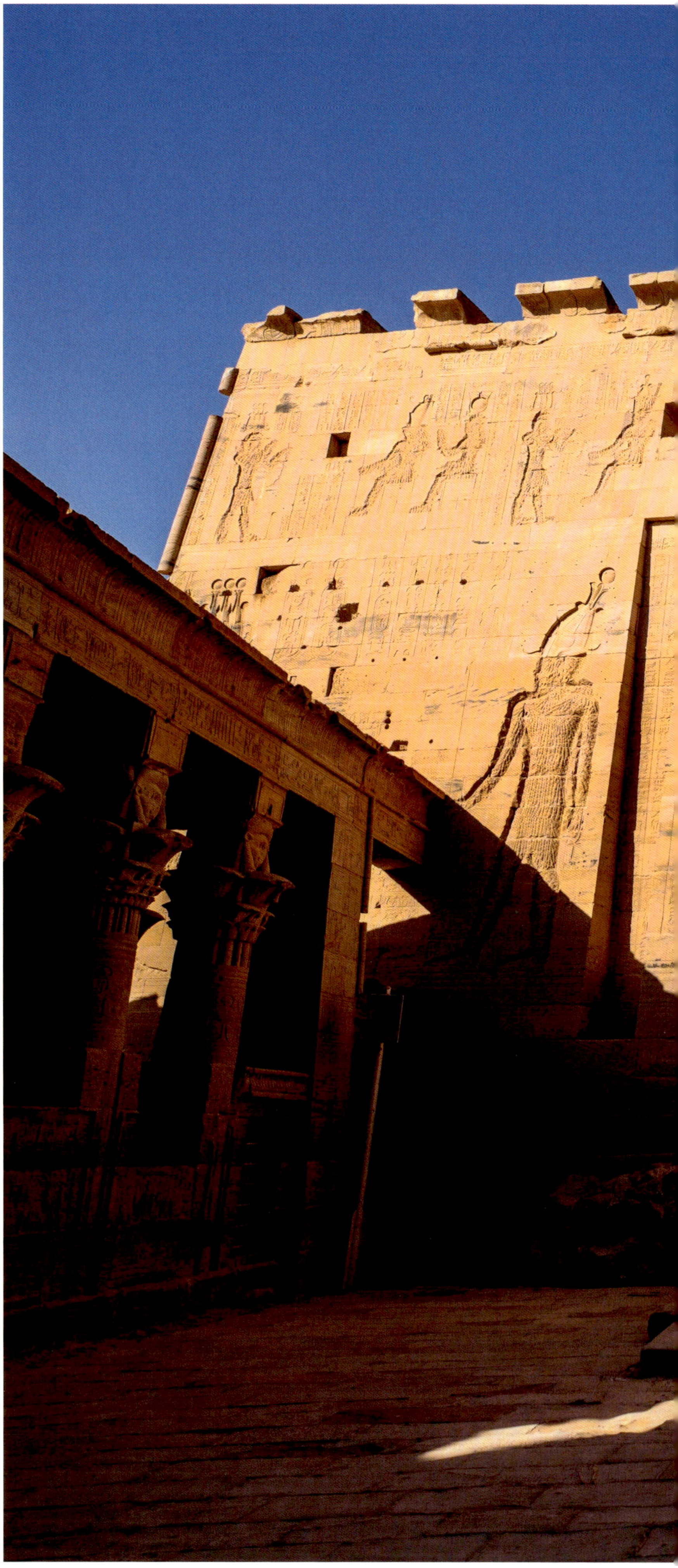

Top The Kiosk of Trajan dates to the Roman Imperial period.
Upper middle Intricately carved details can be found throughout.
Lower middle The temple complex also includes small shrines.
Bottom Hundreds of reliefs depict ancient Egyptian myths.

Agilkia Island, Egypt

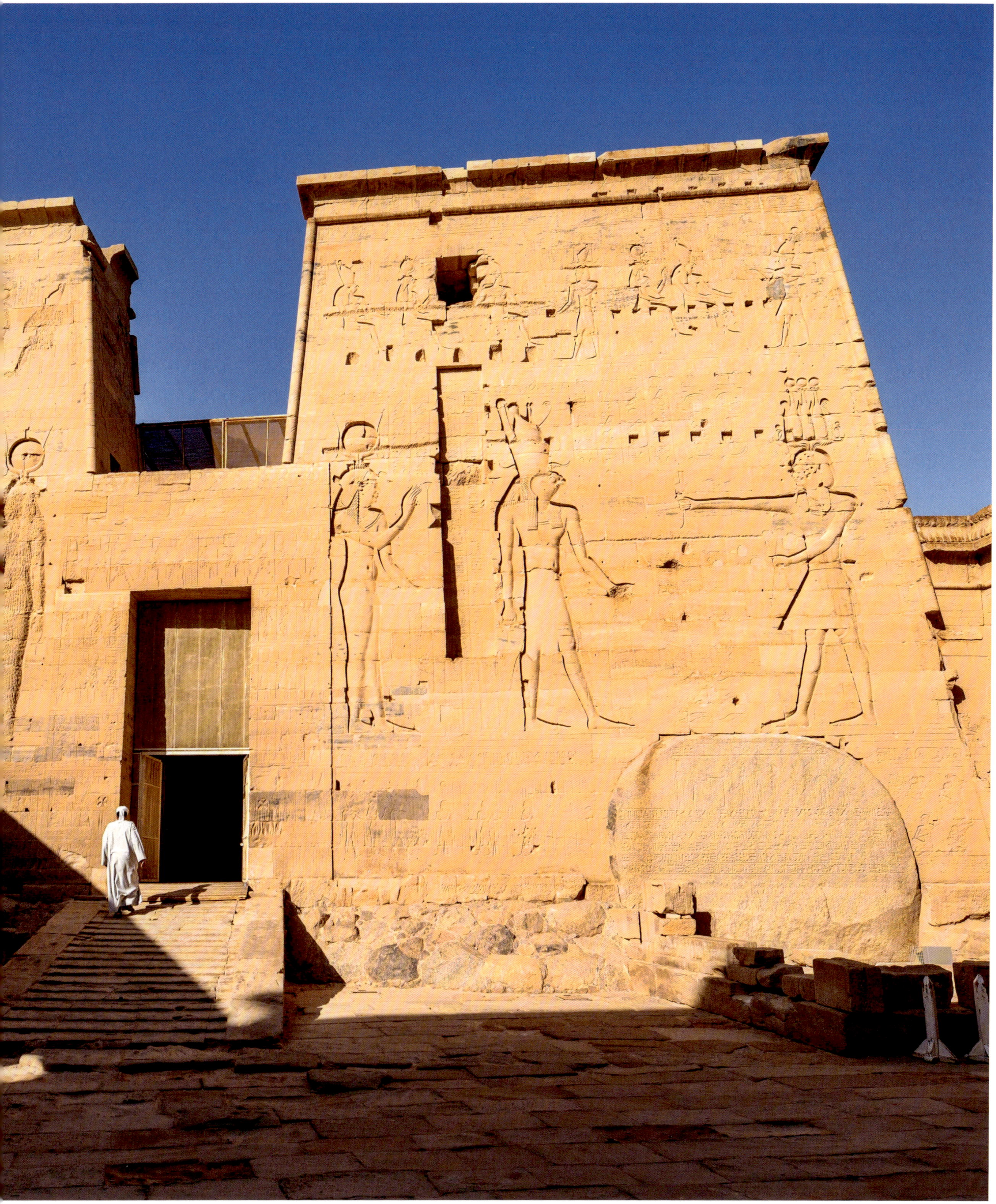

Above Philae was one of the last active centers of ancient Egyptian religion. The temples remained in use until the 6th century CE, when they were converted into a Christian church.

Stone Circles of Senegambia

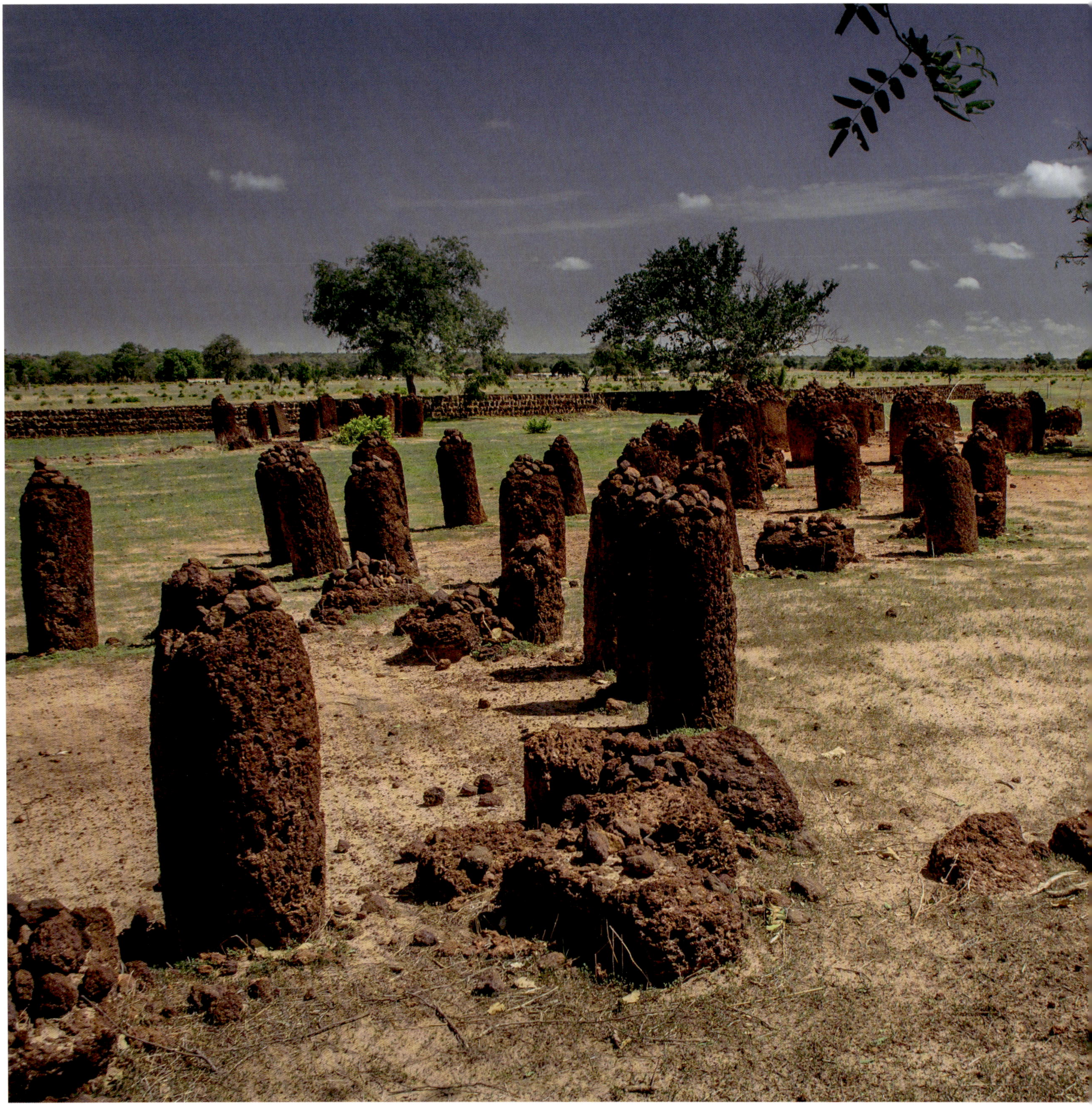

Built: 300 BCE – 1600 CE,
Senegal and Gambia

The early societies of this West African region did not see death as a final state but rather as a passage into the ancestral realm.

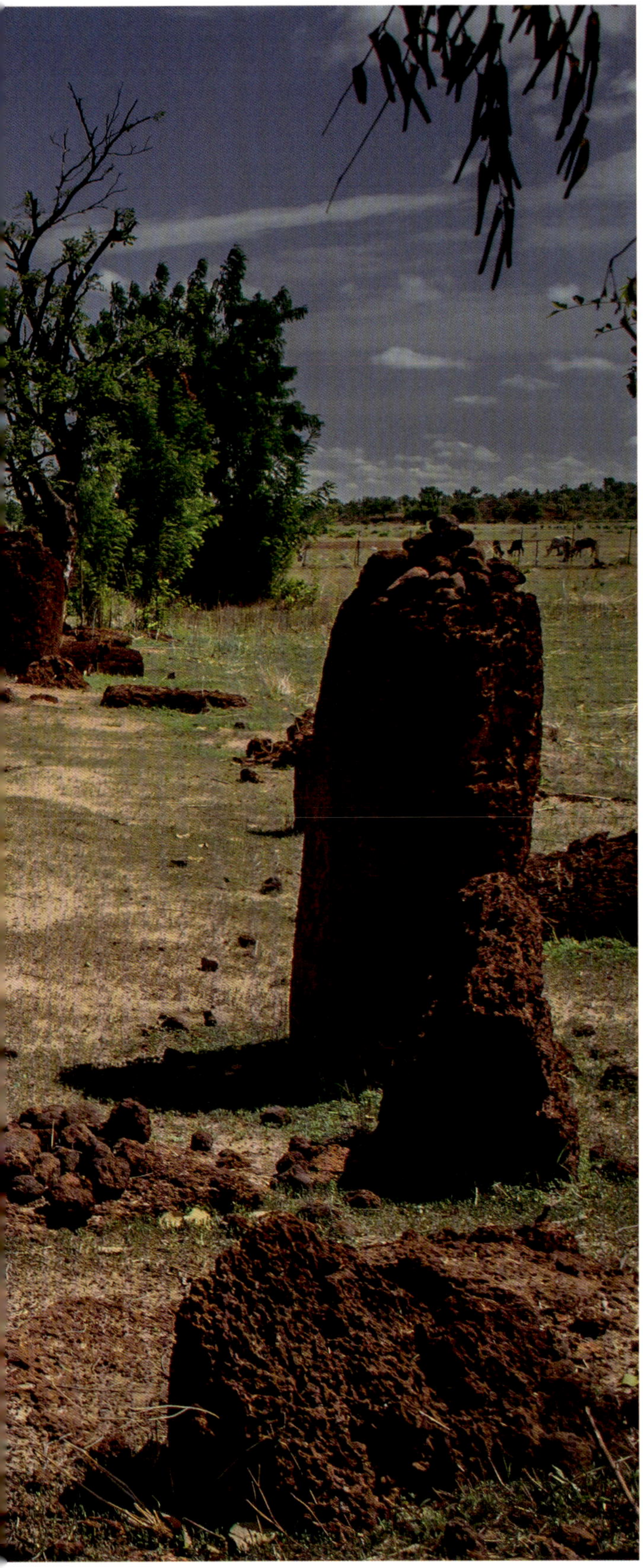

To step into the enigmatic stone circles of Senegambia is to cross the threshold between the physical and spiritual worlds. Over 1,000 of these monuments are scattered across 93 sites in the expansive borderlands between present-day Senegal and Gambia in West Africa. Today, scholars agree that these circles served as ceremonial burial grounds—powerful symbols for the living that reveal an extraordinary reverence for the dead.

For centuries, the deceased were interred here in carefully prepared graves, often in excavated pits or stone chambers beneath the circles. Some graves contain evidence of double or even multiple burials, suggesting that these resting places might have served whole families and communities. Particularly striking is the practice of secondary burial, where remains were ceremonially reburied after a period—archaeological findings of scattered and subsequently reassembled skeletal remains support this interpretation. The graves themselves were often richly adorned. Pottery, sometimes delicately crafted, and jewelry made from iron, copper, or even rare or imported materials accompanied the deceased. These grave goods likely symbolized not only the social status of the departed but also equipped them with the items they might need on their journey, easing their transition to the afterlife.

Central to these burial traditions was the belief that death is not an abrupt end but a transition to a new state. The societies of this region viewed death as a multi-phase process through which the deceased gradually entered the ancestral world. This began with physical burial, typically soon after death, followed by grand funeral ceremonies that marked the final integration of the deceased into the community of ancestors. Between these stages, ritual acts often took place to honor the spirit of the departed, maintain the person's connection with the living world, and to protect the community. Ceremonial dances, animal sacrifices, and offerings of food and other gifts to the dead played a vital role in these traditions. These rituals not only preserved the memory of the departed but also strengthened the bond between the earthly and spiritual realms.

Thus, the stone circles of Senegambia bear witness to both an unseen ancestral world, and a worldview that regarded death as part of a much larger journey—a journey in which the living community played an indispensable role.

Osun-Osogbo Sacred Grove

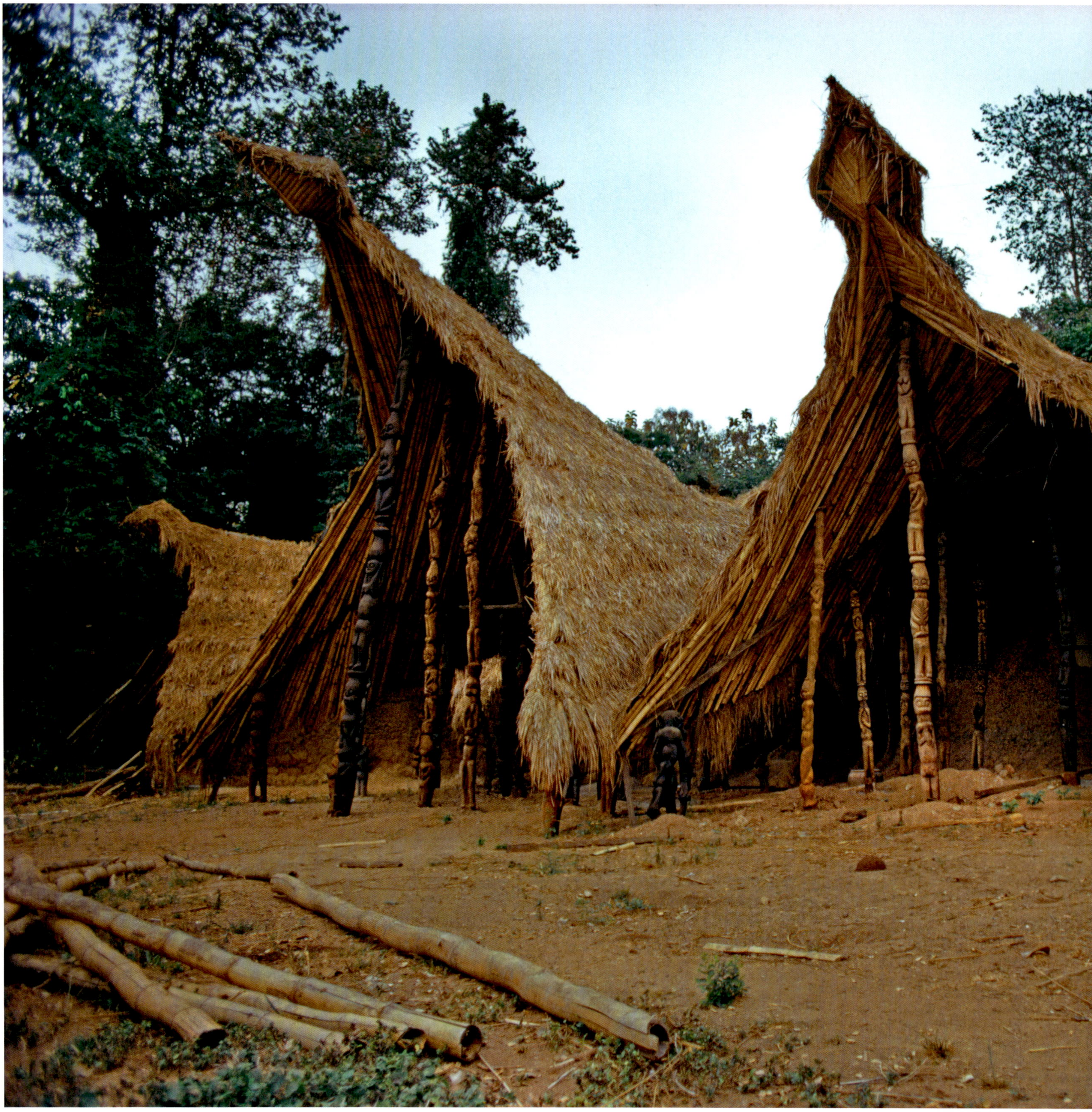

Founded: 17th century CE,
Osogbo, Nigeria

Gigantic sculptures protect this sacred place and fulfill a pact once made between a deity, a founding father, and an elephant hunter.

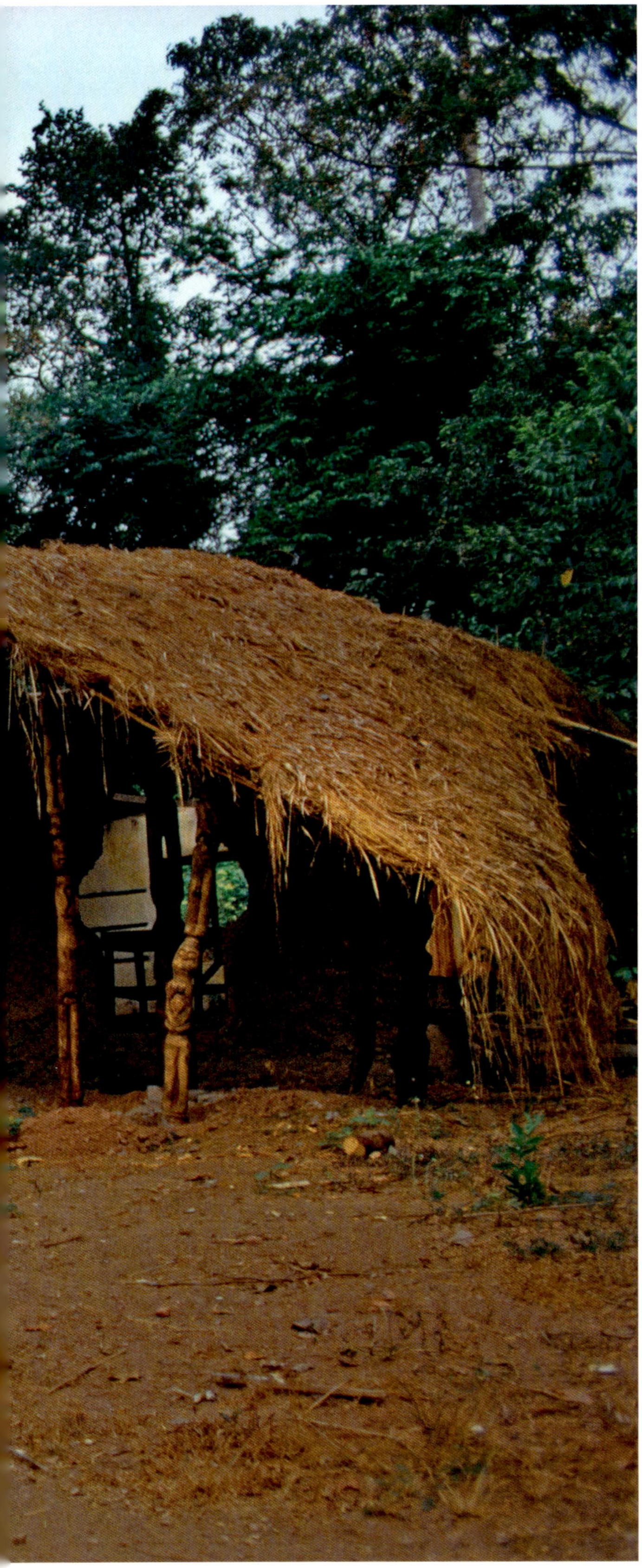

On the banks of the Osun River, hidden in one of West Africa's wild tropical forests, lies the Osun-Osogbo Sacred Grove. Its shrines and sculptures tell of the Yoruba people's belief in *orishas,* divine beings that reveal themselves to humans through rivers, trees, and forests. They are mediators between the faithful and the supreme creator god, Olodumare. Osun is one such *orisha:* as the goddess of water, fertility, and life, she is especially revered in this sacred grove.

The grove is a remnant of Yorubaland's once-widespread sacred groves, traditionally linked to the founding of towns. Regarding Osun-Osogbo, legend tells of a pact made 400 years ago between the goddess Osun, Osogbo's founder Larooye, and elephant hunter Olutimehin: if they protected the grove, she would safeguard their people. This agreement endures to this day. Home to over 40 shrines and sculptures, the grove hosts the annual Osun-Osogbo Festival. For 12 days, the Yoruba community honors its bond with the goddess Osun, starting with the Iwopopo, a symbolic city cleansing. After lighting the 16-armed candelabrum Ina Oloju Merindinlogun and the Iboriade, where rulers' crowns are consecrated, the festival culminates in a procession to the sacred grove, led by the Arugba, a young woman of royal descent who carries a ritual calabash filled with offerings for Osun. Once at the grove, the faithful lay flowers and fruits as offerings on the riverbank. Prayers are spoken to the gently rippling water, with the hope that their innermost wishes will be fulfilled. It is said that the water of the Osun River is capable of healing the sick, granting children to the childless, and offering protection to the weak.

When the grove faced the threat of deforestation in the mid-20th century, Austrian-Nigerian artist Susanne Wenger, also known as Adunni Olorisha, worked with local Nigerian artists and began restoring many of the shrines, as well as creating new sculptures dedicated to the Yoruba deities. The artists' commitment did not go unnoticed. In 2005, UNESCO added the Osun-Osogbo Sacred Grove to its World Heritage List, officially recognizing the forest and its shrines as a globally significant site. In this way, the pact to protect the grove was formally sealed, and the goddess Osun continues to reveal herself in its river, extending her protective hand over the Yoruba people.

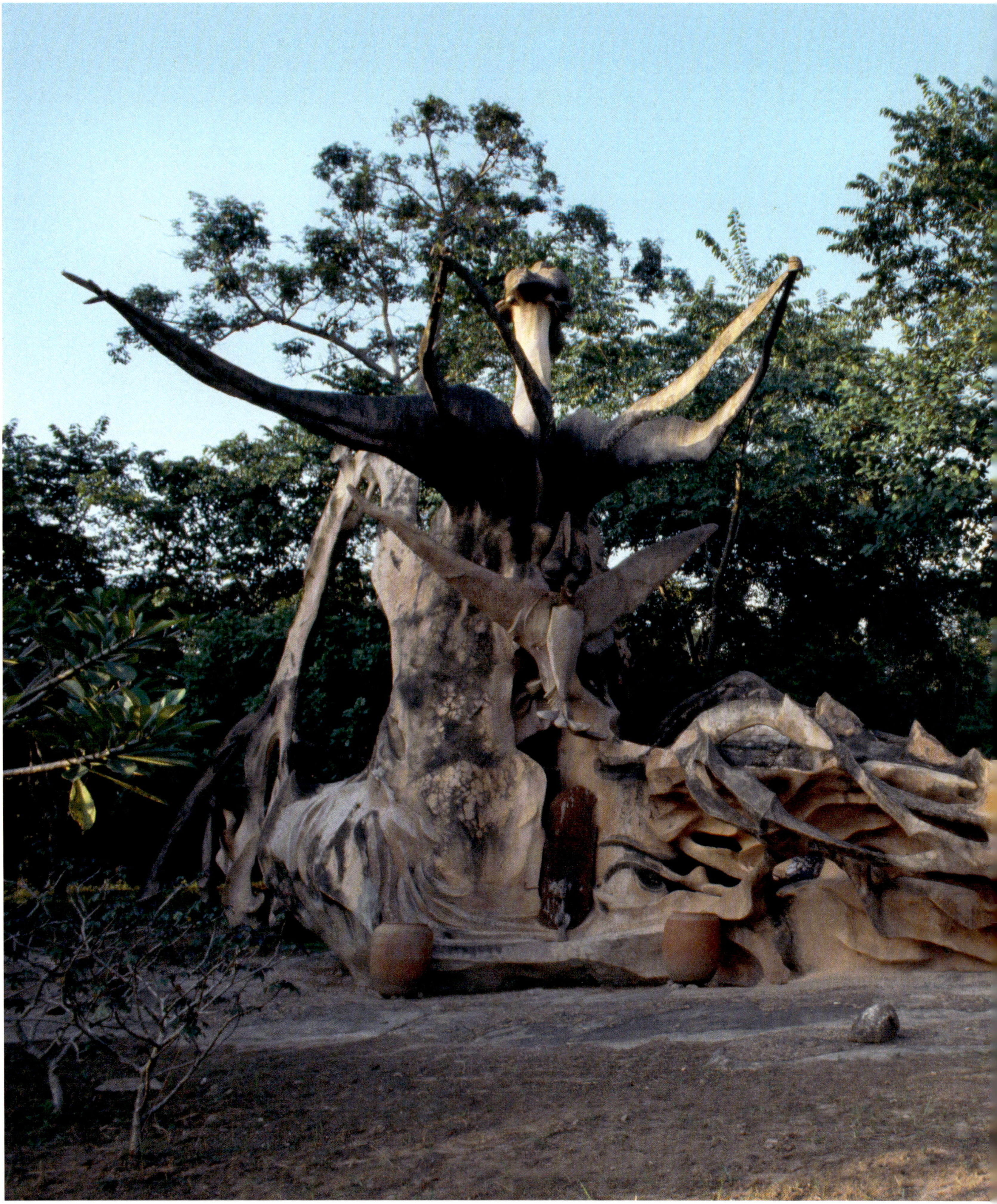

Above The impressive sculpture of the deity Iya Moopo, crafted by Adebisi Akanji and Susanne Wenger, offers divine protection over the Osun-Osogbo Sacred Grove.

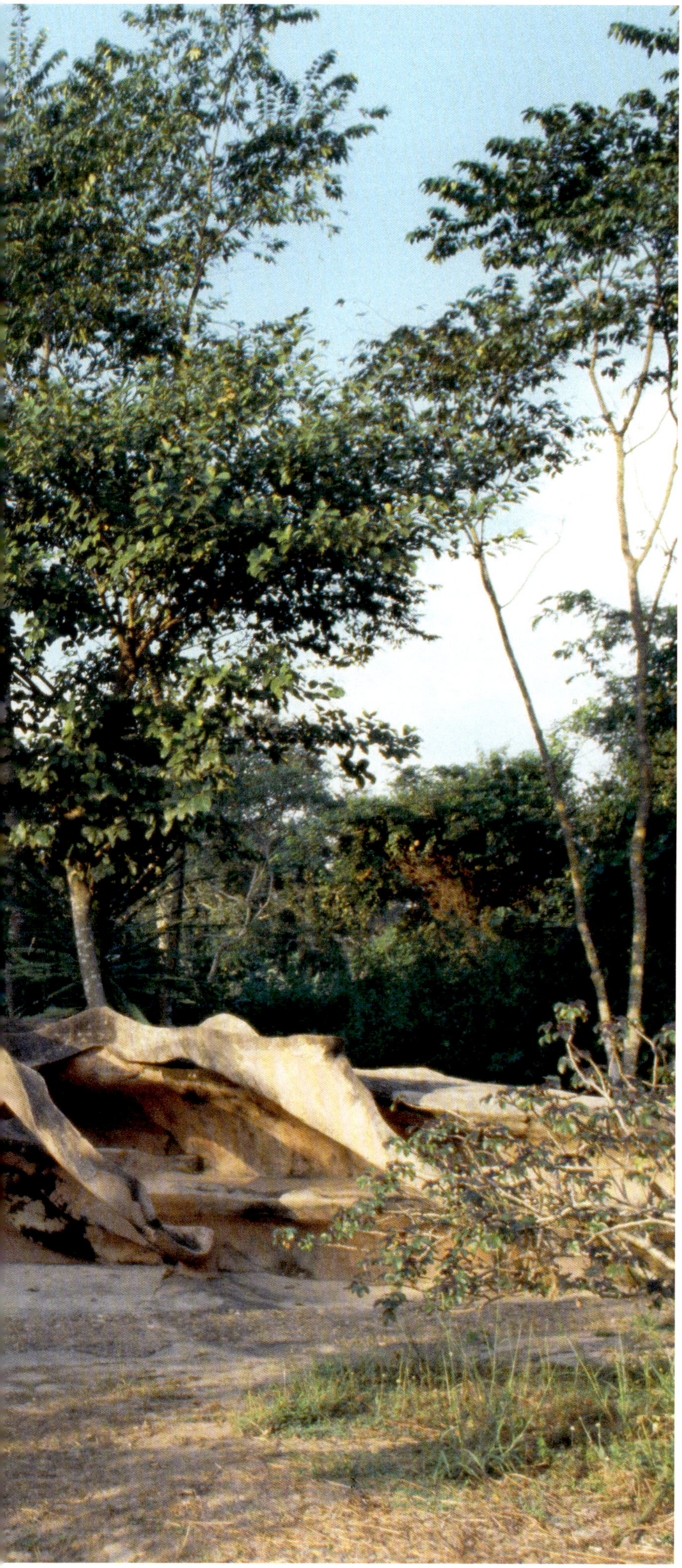

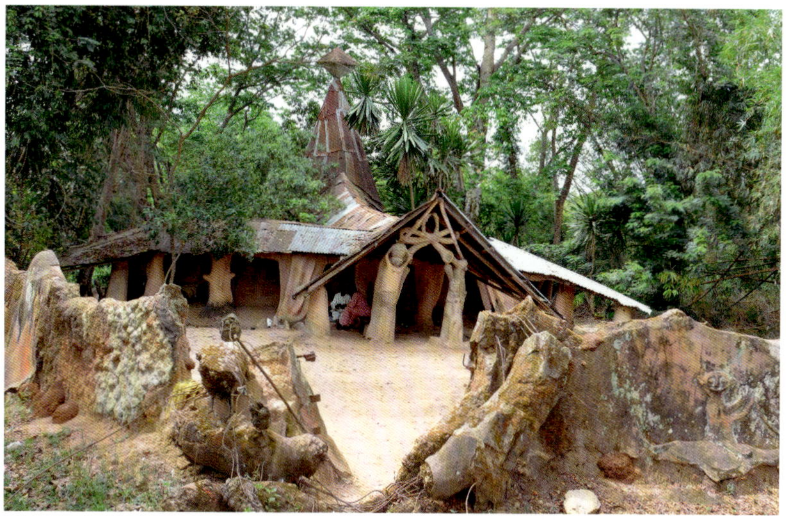

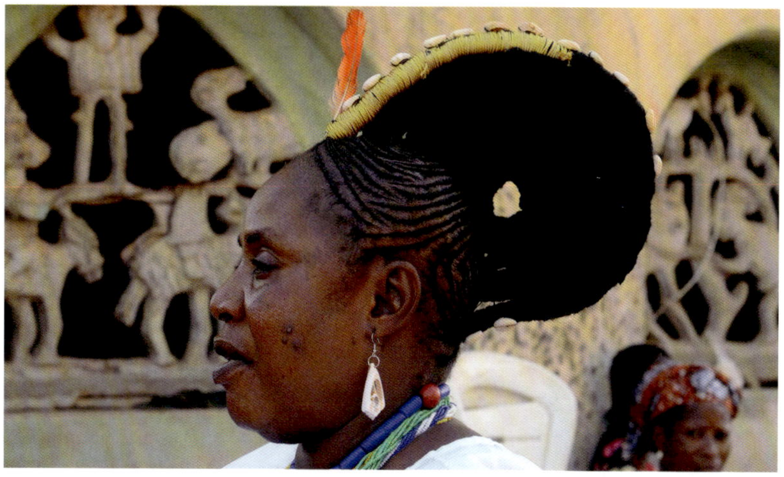

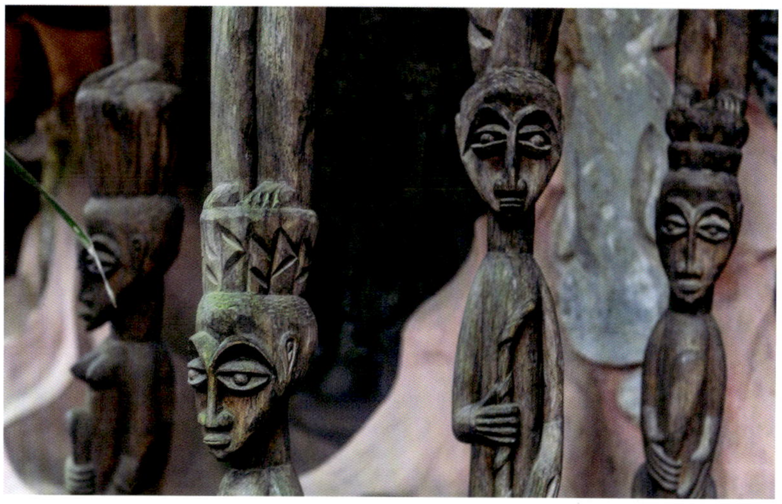

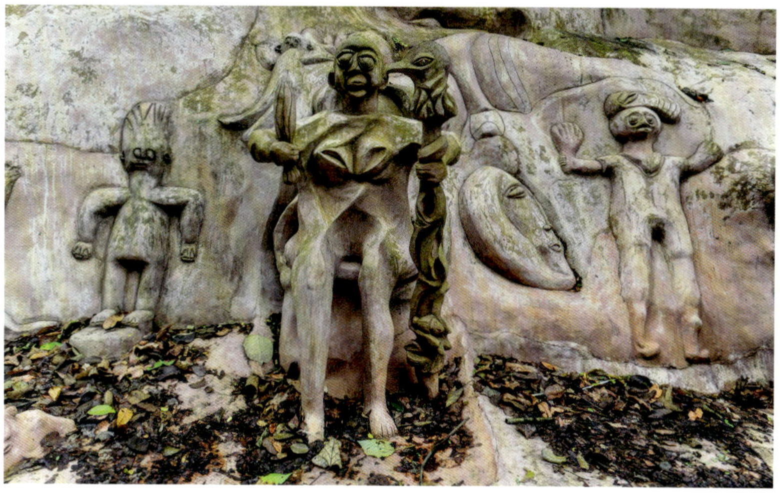

Top The goddess of water, fertility, and life resides in the grove.
Upper middle A worshipper dresses for the Osun-Osogbo Festival.
Lower middle The sculptures are dedicated to various deities.
Bottom The grove is a unique blend of sanctuary and art gallery.

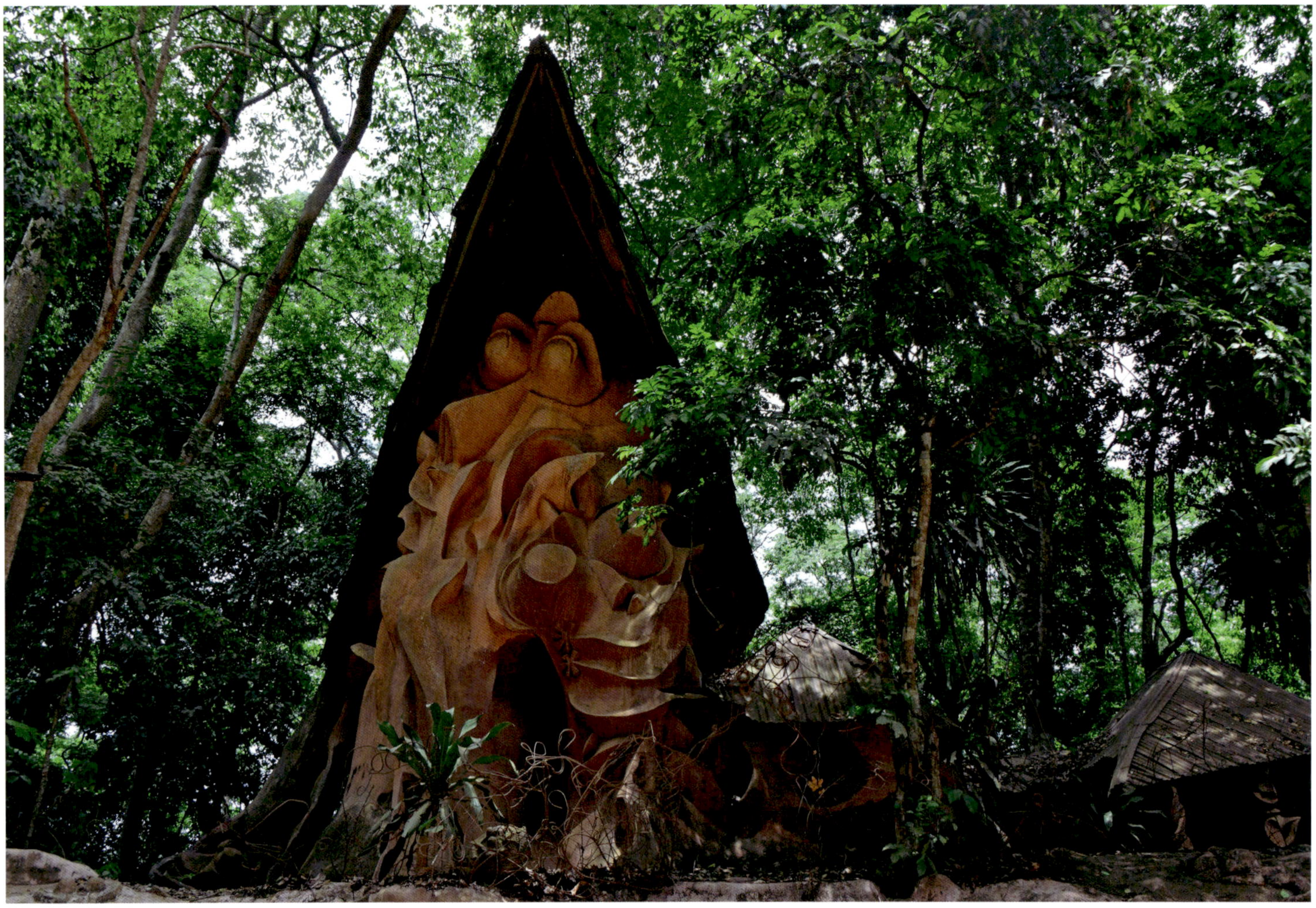

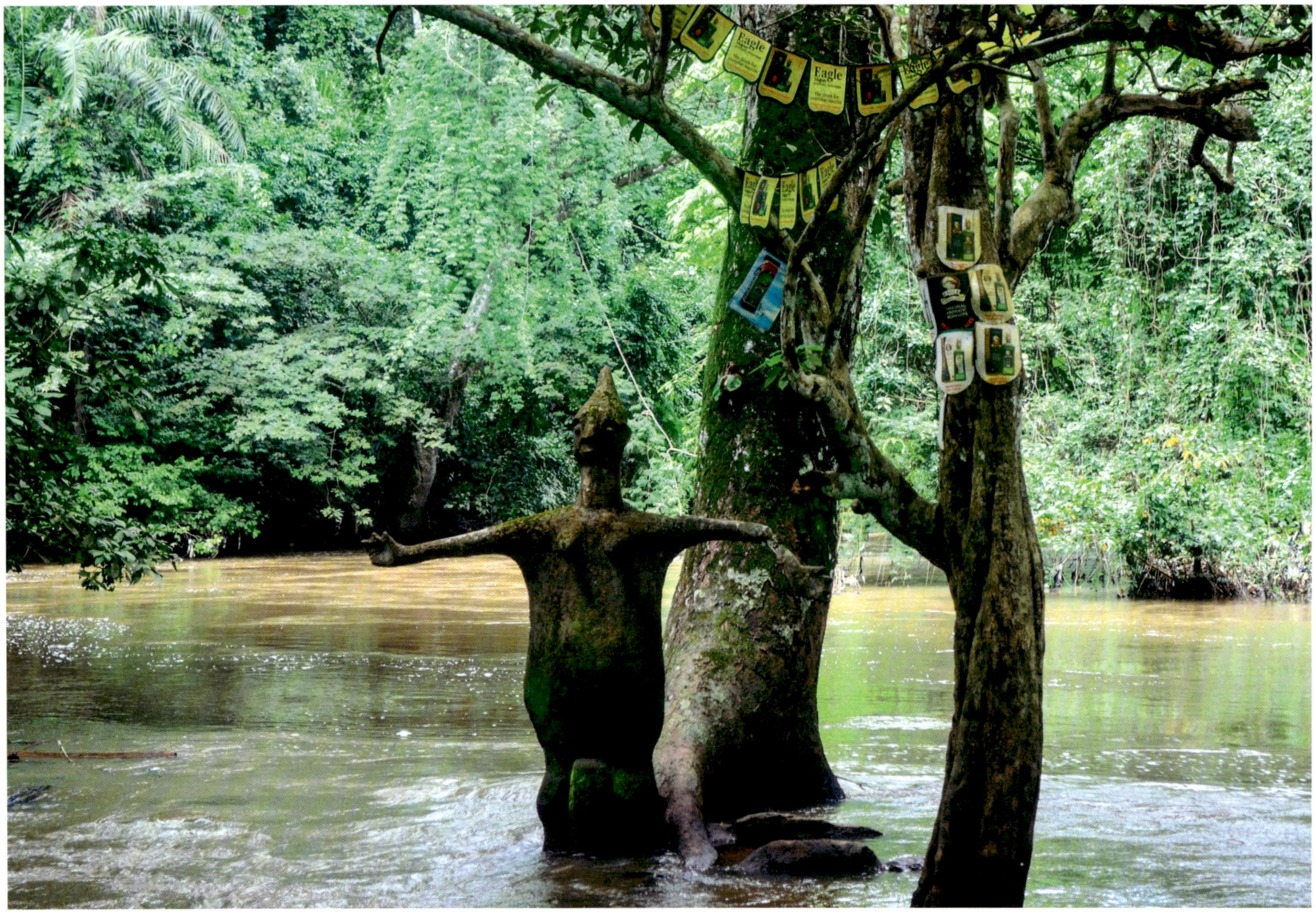

Top The massive sculptures protected the grove from deforestation by bringing it to UNESCO's attention. *Bottom* The water of the Osun River is considered healing and life-giving.

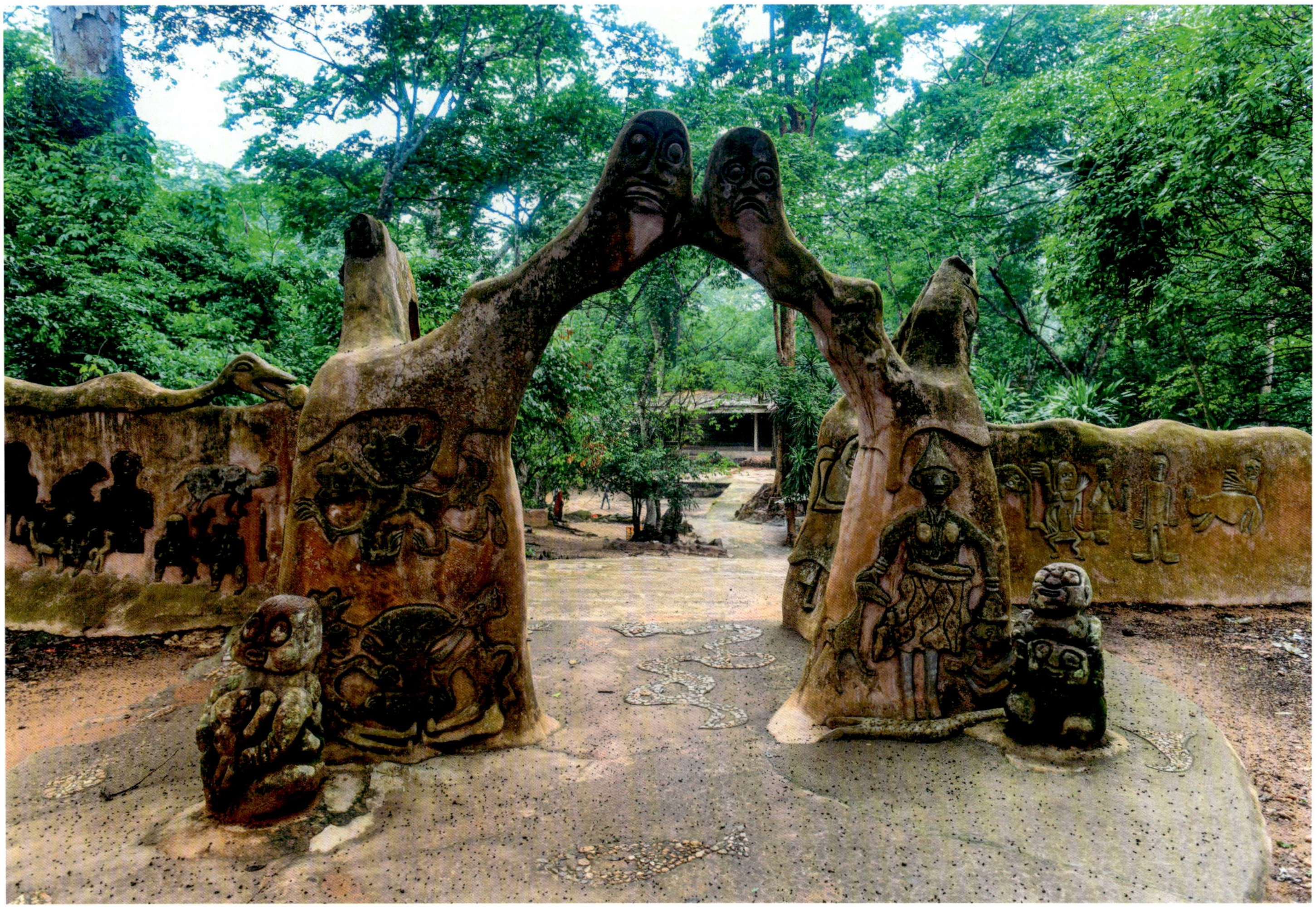

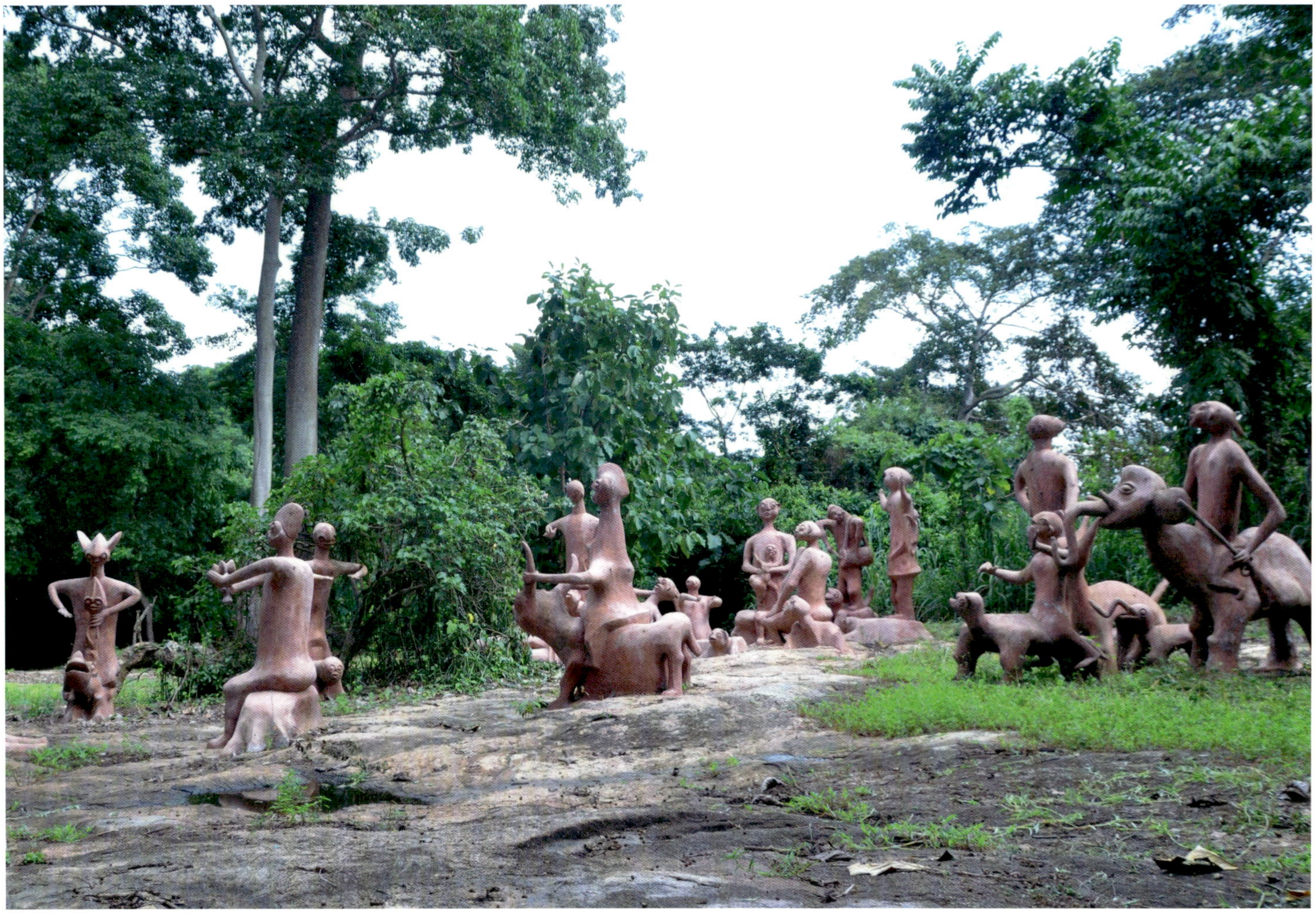

Top The Yoruba pantheon is as diverse as the grove's nature, a true refuge for various animal and plant species.
Bottom Only art-making is allowed—fishing and hunting are strictly forbidden within the grove.

Debre Birhan Selassie Church

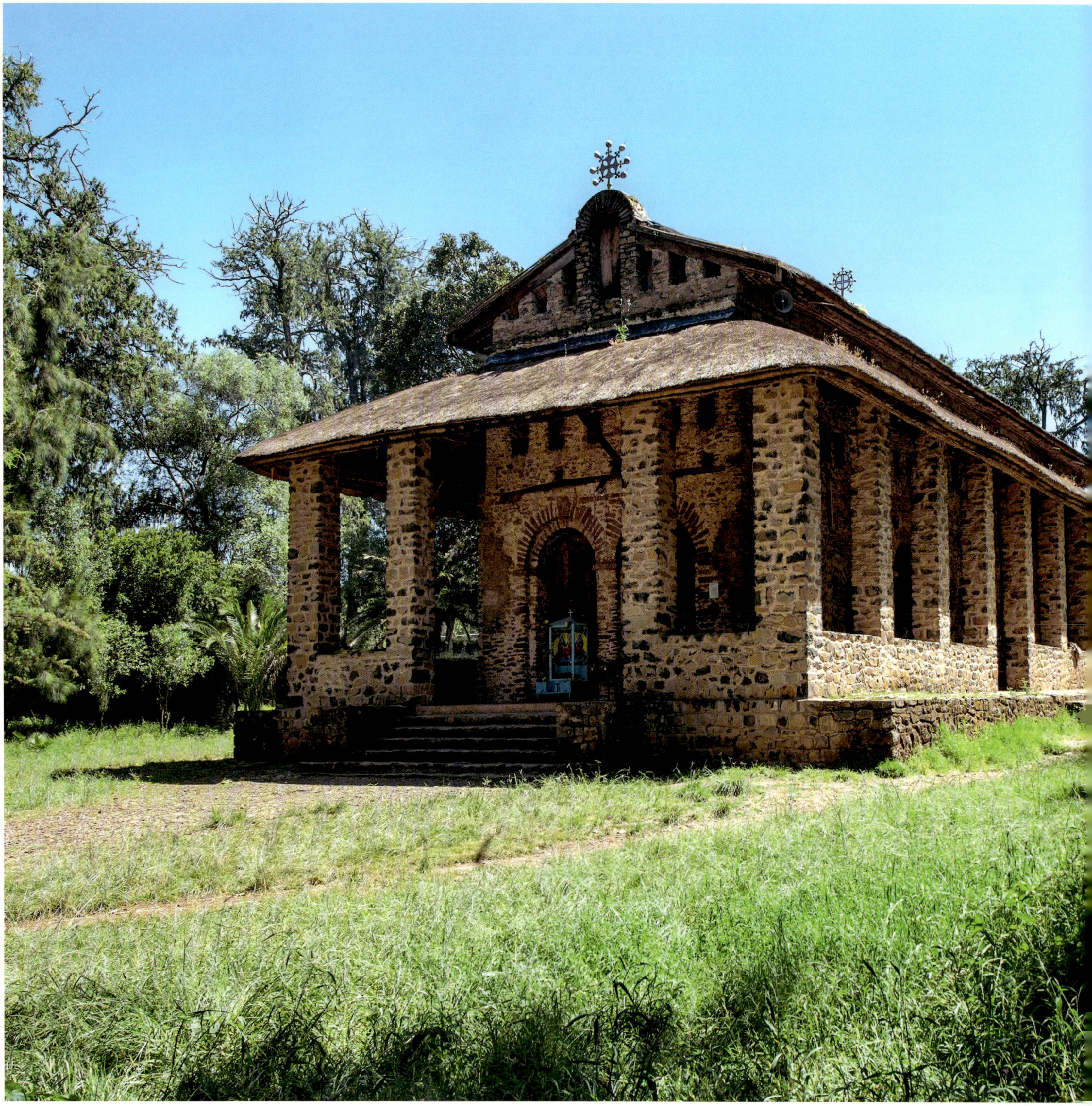

Built: 17th century CE, Gondar, Ethiopia

Beyond the entrance gate, which bears the symbol of the Lion of Judah, visitors embark on a journey into the profound depths of Ethiopian spirituality and artistry.

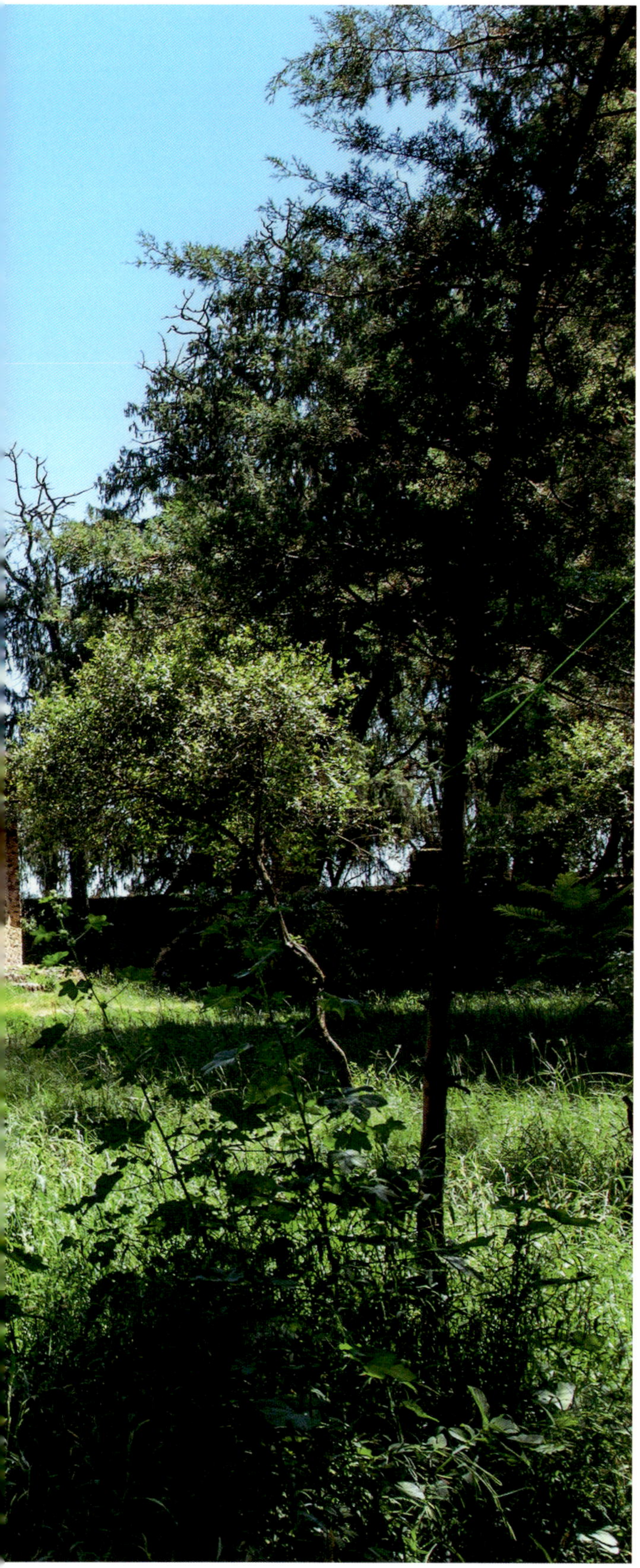

The story of Debre Birhan Selassie Church, which translates to "Mountain of the Light of the Trinity," is one of remarkable resilience. The original church was destroyed by lightning in the early 18th century, after which a sturdier and more elaborate construction was built on the same site. In the late 19th century, when the Dervishes, fighters of the Mahdist uprising from Sudan, invaded Ethiopia with the aim of establishing an Islamic state, they eventually reached Gondar. While attempting to desecrate Debre Birhan Selassie Church, legend holds that a swarm of enraged bees descended upon the attackers, driving them away. Thus, the church was spared, becoming the only one in Gondar to survive intact.

Among the treasures preserved are the church's stunning paintings, which are considered some of the most precious works of art in the Ethiopian Orthodox Church. From the wooden ceiling, the faces of 135 winged angels gaze down with their large, watchful eyes, creating a celestial canopy. The walls of the church are also richly adorned with frescoes, which leave no corner untouched. They depict key biblical narratives such as the Nativity, the Crucifixion, and the Resurrection of Christ. Viewers are also transported to the Garden of Eden, where Adam and Eve reside, and aboard Noah's Ark, surrounded by rescued animals. The Archangel Michael is portrayed wielding his sword in battle against evil, while Saint George is shown slaying the dragon with his spear. The vivid portrayal of hell is particularly striking: sinners, surrounded by blazing flames, endure torment at the hands of demonic creatures behind the tabernacle. This serves as a powerful reminder to stay on the righteous path. It is easy to imagine the profound effect these images had on the faithful—for centuries, these paintings did more than decorate the church; they brought scripture to life, transforming its walls into a visual gospel that guided, inspired, and warned generations of worshippers.

Surrounding the church is a protective stone wall with 12 round towers, symbolizing the apostles. The entrance gate forms a 13th tower, representing Jesus Christ, who is subtly depicted here as the Lion of Judah. In Revelation 5:5 it is written: "Behold, the Lion of the tribe of Judah, the Root of David, has triumphed." This sentiment seems to encapsulate the spirit of this remarkable church, which stands as a symbol of resilience, a visual Bible, and a fortress of faith in Gondar.

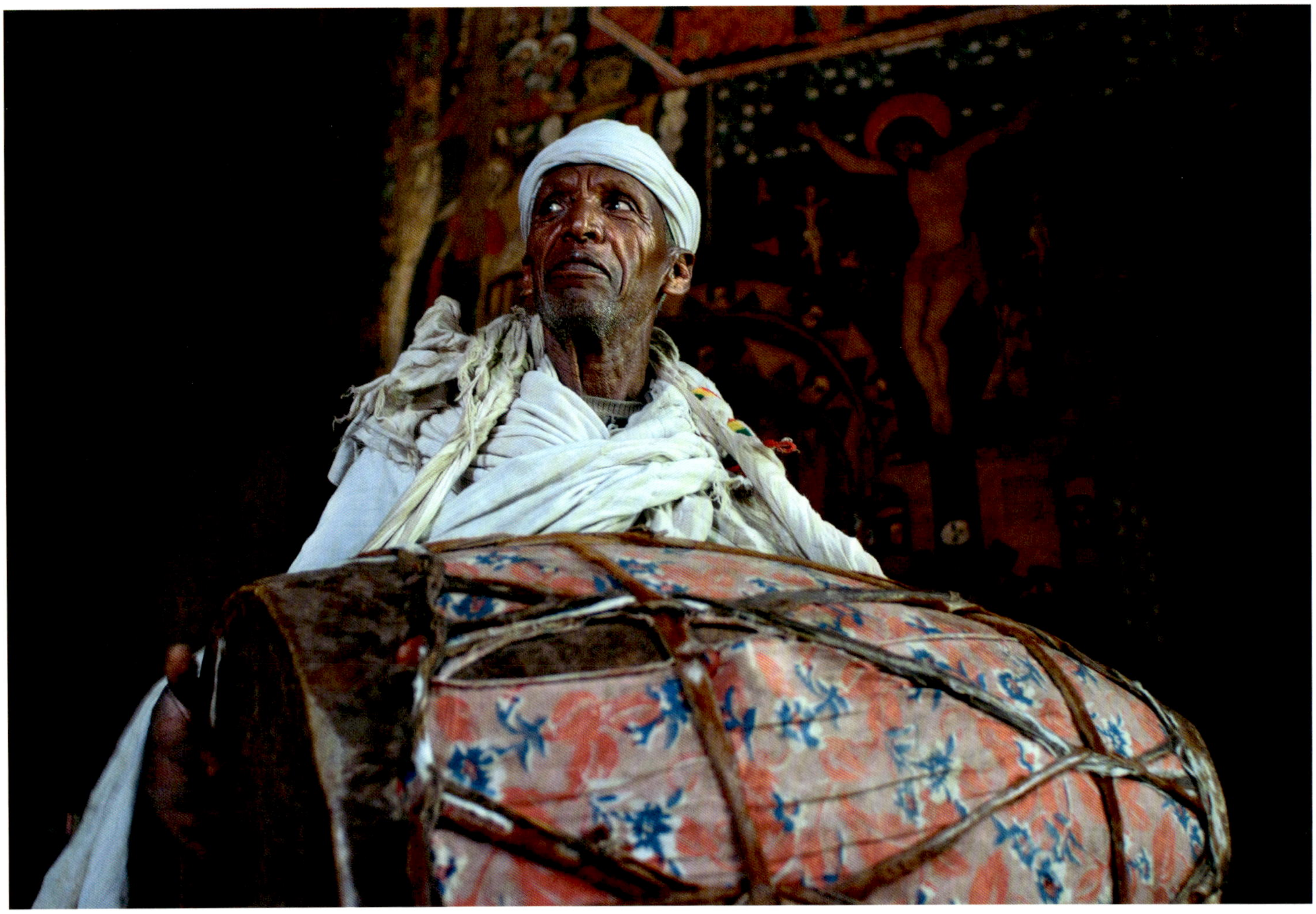

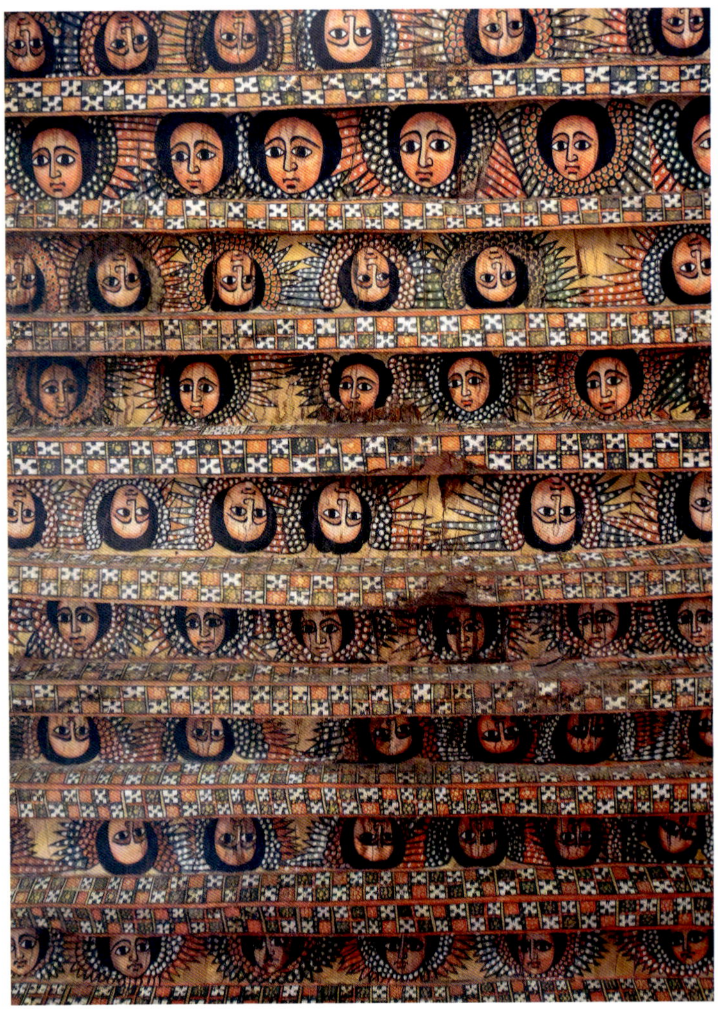

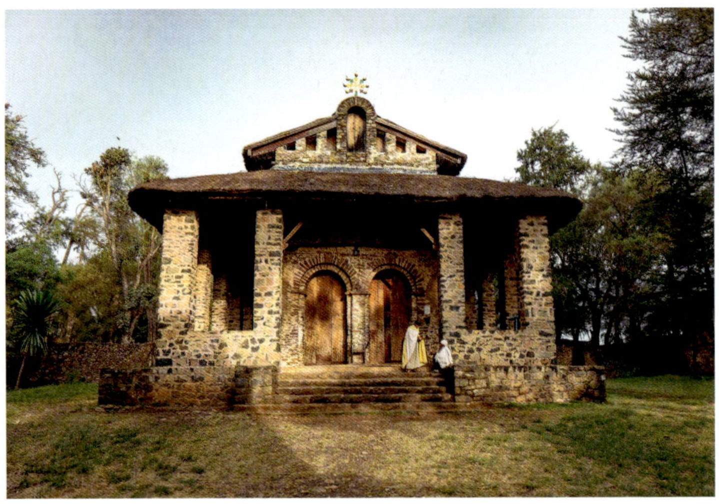

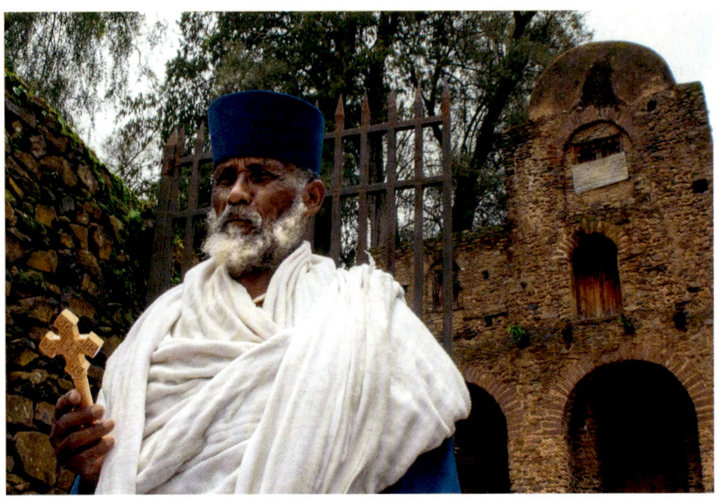

Gondar, Ethiopia

Top Debre Birhan Selassie Church remains an active house of worship.
Bottom images This church is one of Ethiopia's most important Christian legacies.
Opposite Cherubim, arranged in harmonious rows, completely cover the wooden ceiling.

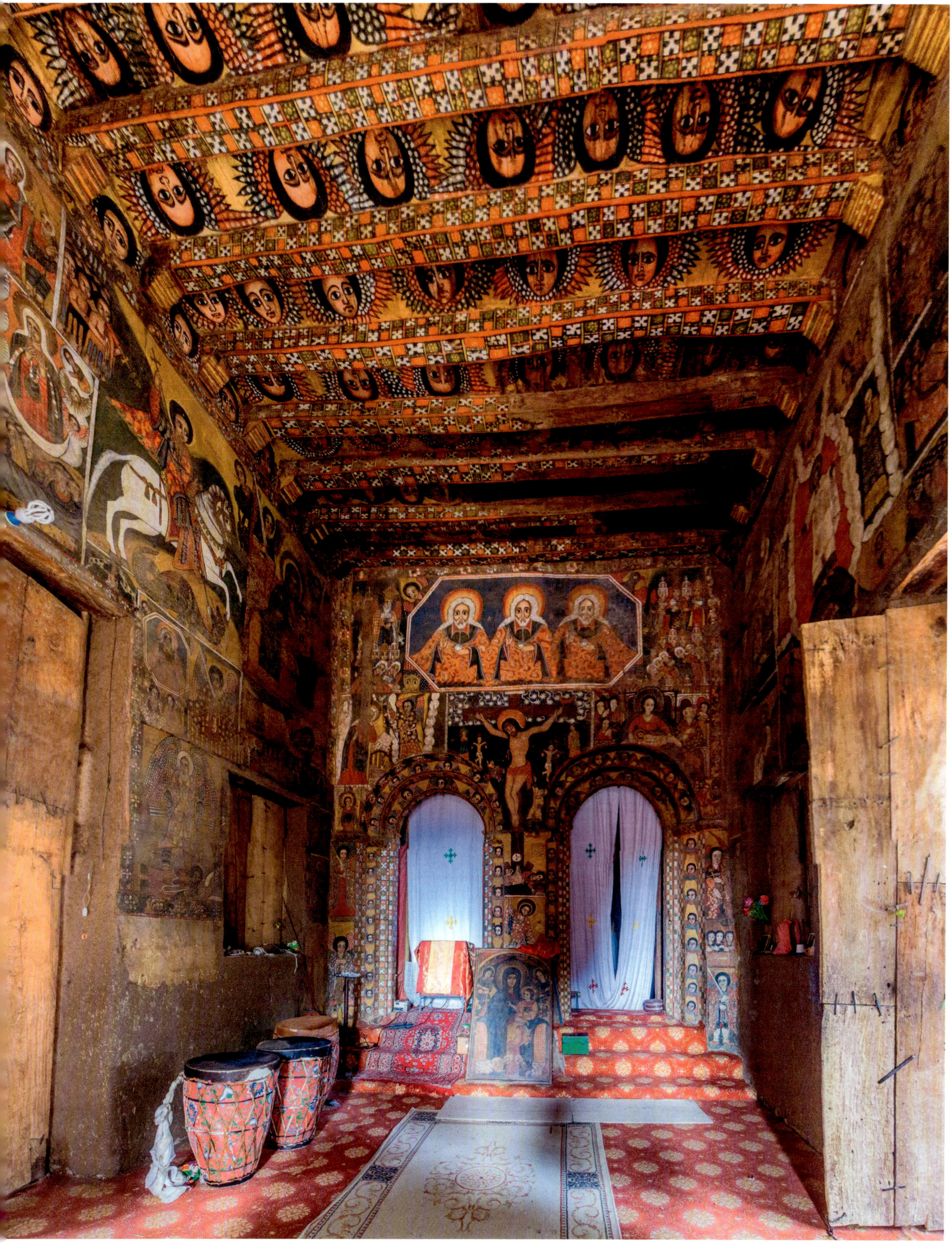

Rock-Hewn Churches of Lalibela

A New Jerusalem

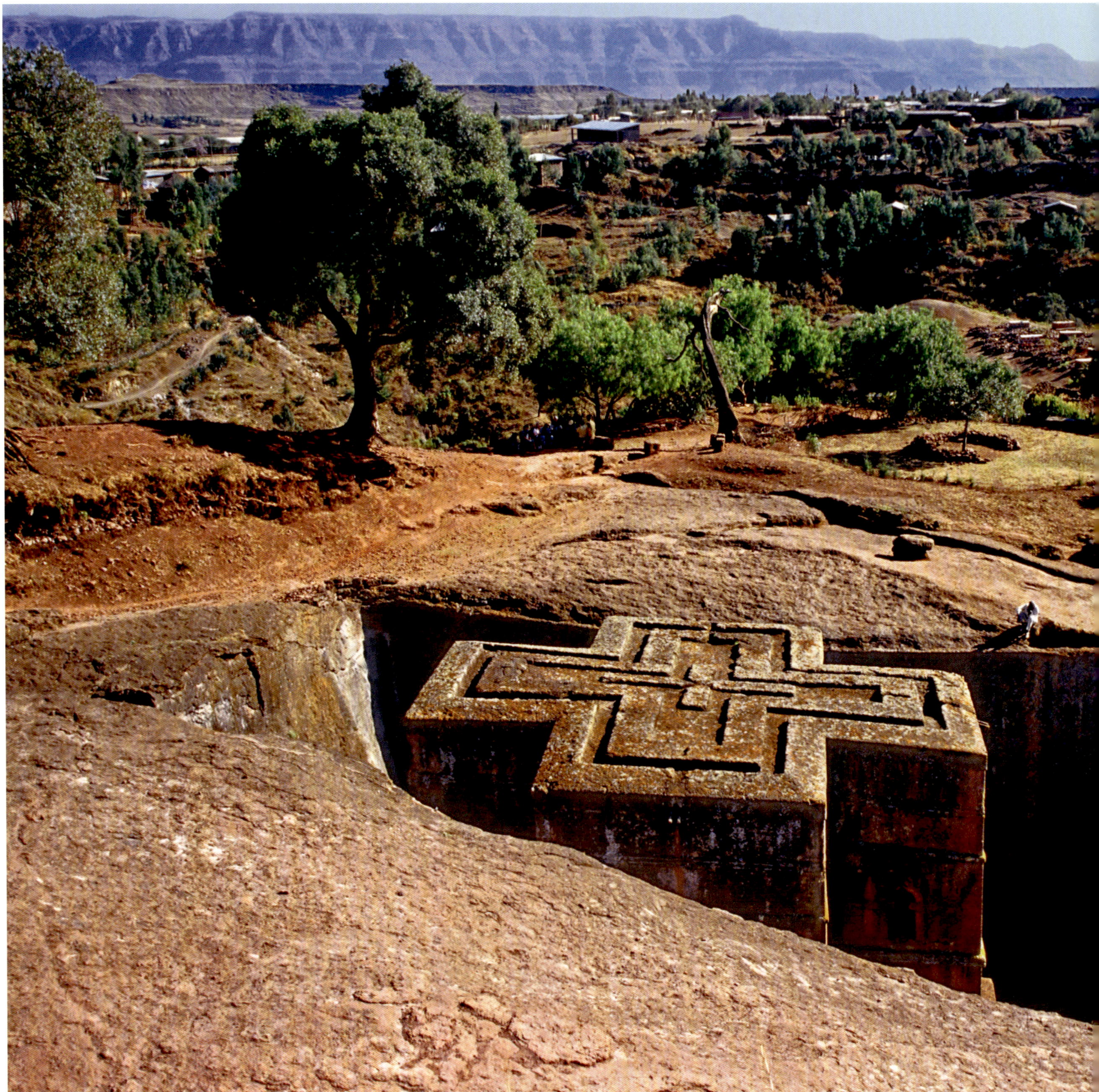

Built: 12th and 13th centuries CE, Lalibela, Ethiopia

These monolithic churches—11 in total—were each carved from solid volcanic rock.

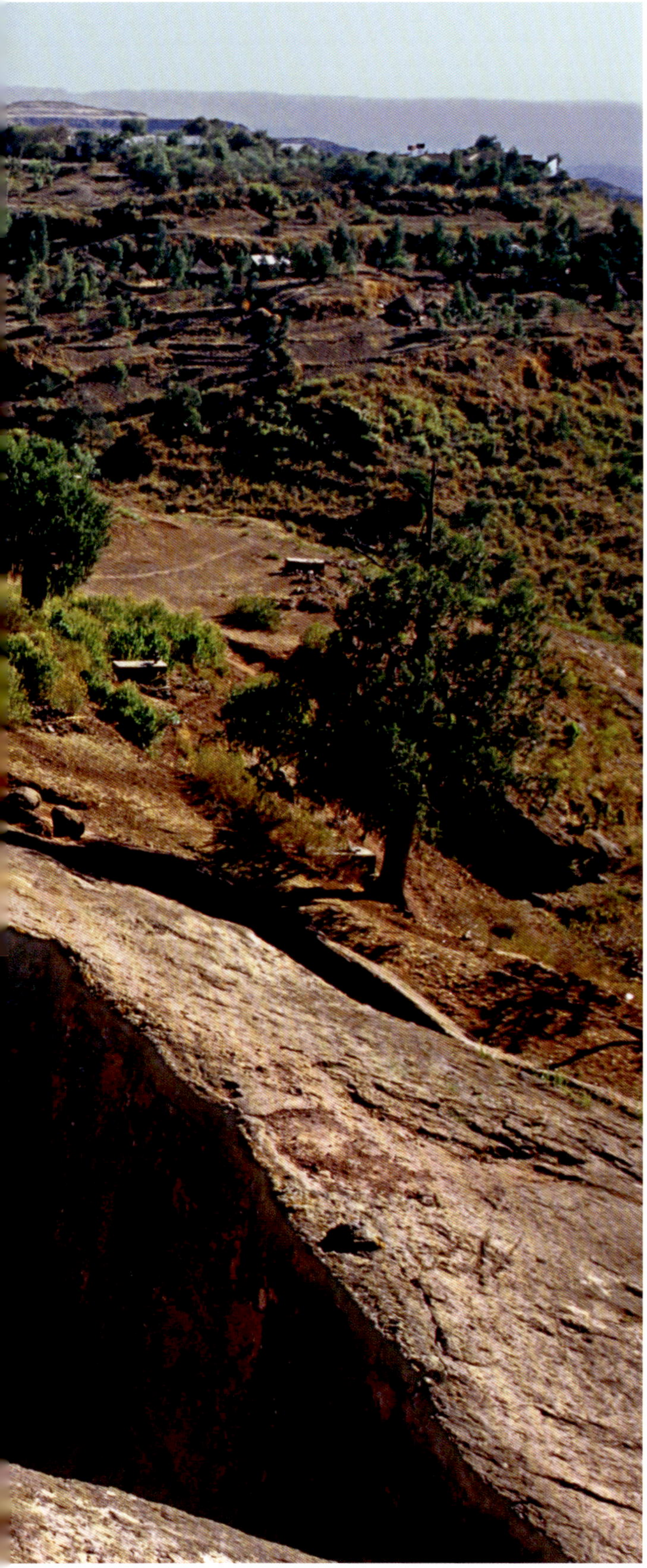

In the Book of Deuteronomy, we find the following proverb: "He is the Rock; His works are perfect, and all His ways are just." These words might well have provided inspiration for the 11 churches of Lalibela, which were constructed not stone by stone, but hewn from a single mass of rock. Their design follows strict geometric patterns; many, such as Bete Giyorgis, dedicated to Saint George, the patron saint of Ethiopia, are rectangular or cross-shaped. Entrance gates are found on three sides, a distinctive feature of Orthodox churches and symbolic of the Holy Trinity. Inside each church, one finds three sections. The first is reserved for priests, the second for mass, and the third, the holiest chamber, is where the Tabot—a replica of the Ark of the Covenant and the most sacred object in every Ethiopian Orthodox church—is kept. Pathways and tunnels connect the 11 churches, symbolizing the spiritual journey of every believer.

Thousands of pilgrims from across Ethiopia and the wider world travel to Lalibela each year, especially during major religious holidays like Timkat, which celebrates Jesus's baptism in the River Jordan. Central to this celebration is the solemn procession of the Tabot, which, on the eve of Timkat, is carried to a nearby body of water—in Lalibela, to a special baptismal pool created specifically for this feast—and guarded overnight. The following morning, priests bless the water, and the faithful sprinkle it over themselves to renew their spirits. The Tabot is then returned to the church, accompanied by hymnal singing, drumming, and dancing.

That Lalibela, said to have been built by King Lalibela as a second Jerusalem, is found in the remote area of northern Ethiopia is no coincidence. Although Christianity came to the Horn of Africa as early as the 4th century, by the 7th century much of North Africa had become Muslim, and pilgrimage routes to Jerusalem grew fewer. It was in Ethiopia's mountains, protected from conquest and persecution, that a distinct form of Orthodox Christianity evolved—with the rock-hewn churches of Lalibela at its heart. Today, these churches are a UNESCO World Heritage Site, and remain a vibrant center of living faith. Both in its physical form and spiritual significance, Lalibela comes remarkably close to embodying the kind of divine perfection spoken of in Deuteronomy.

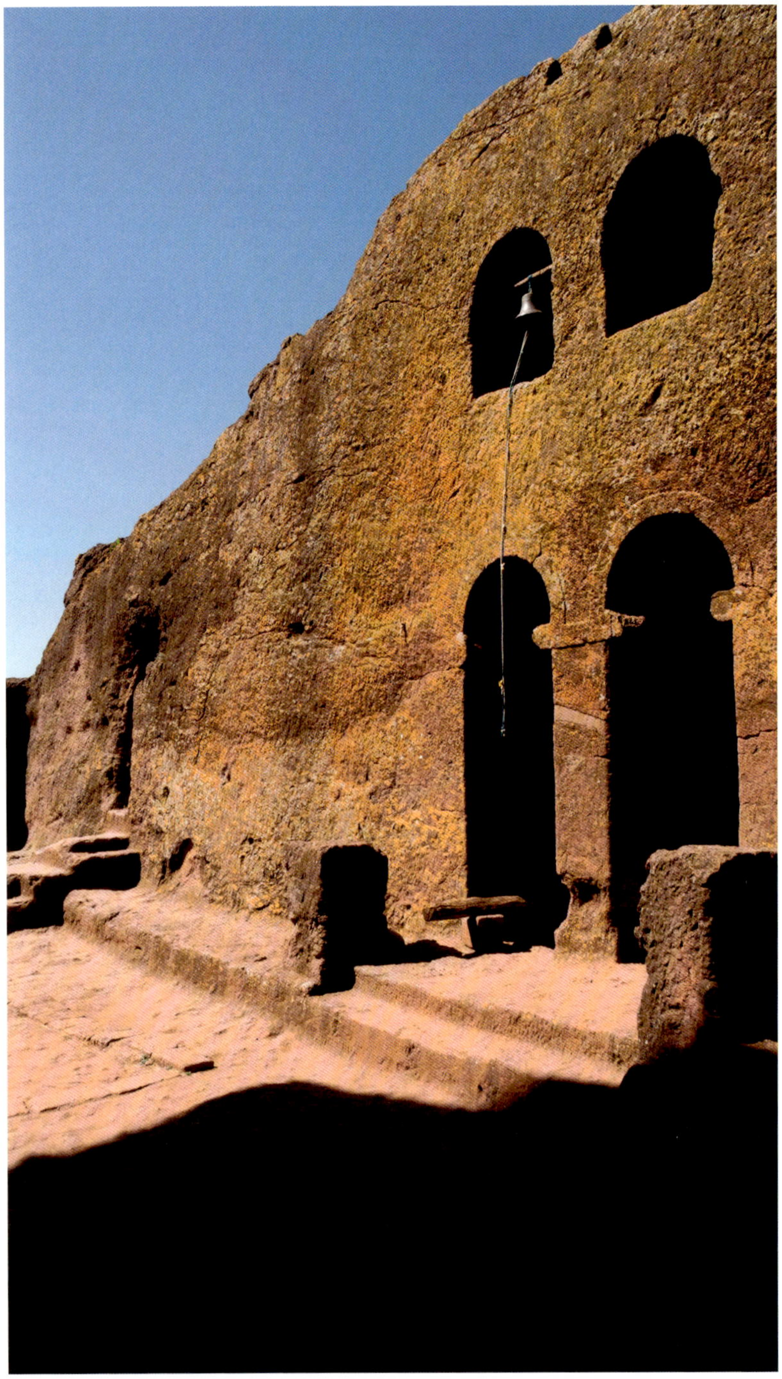

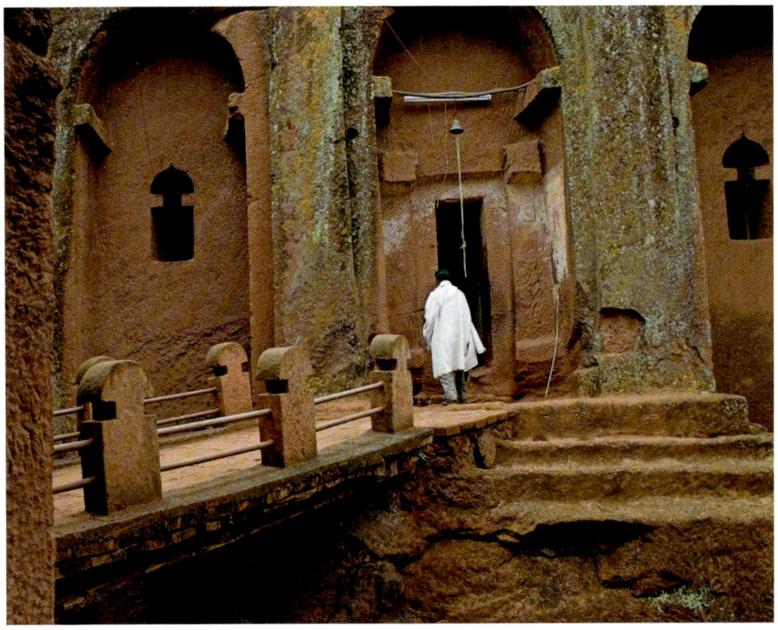

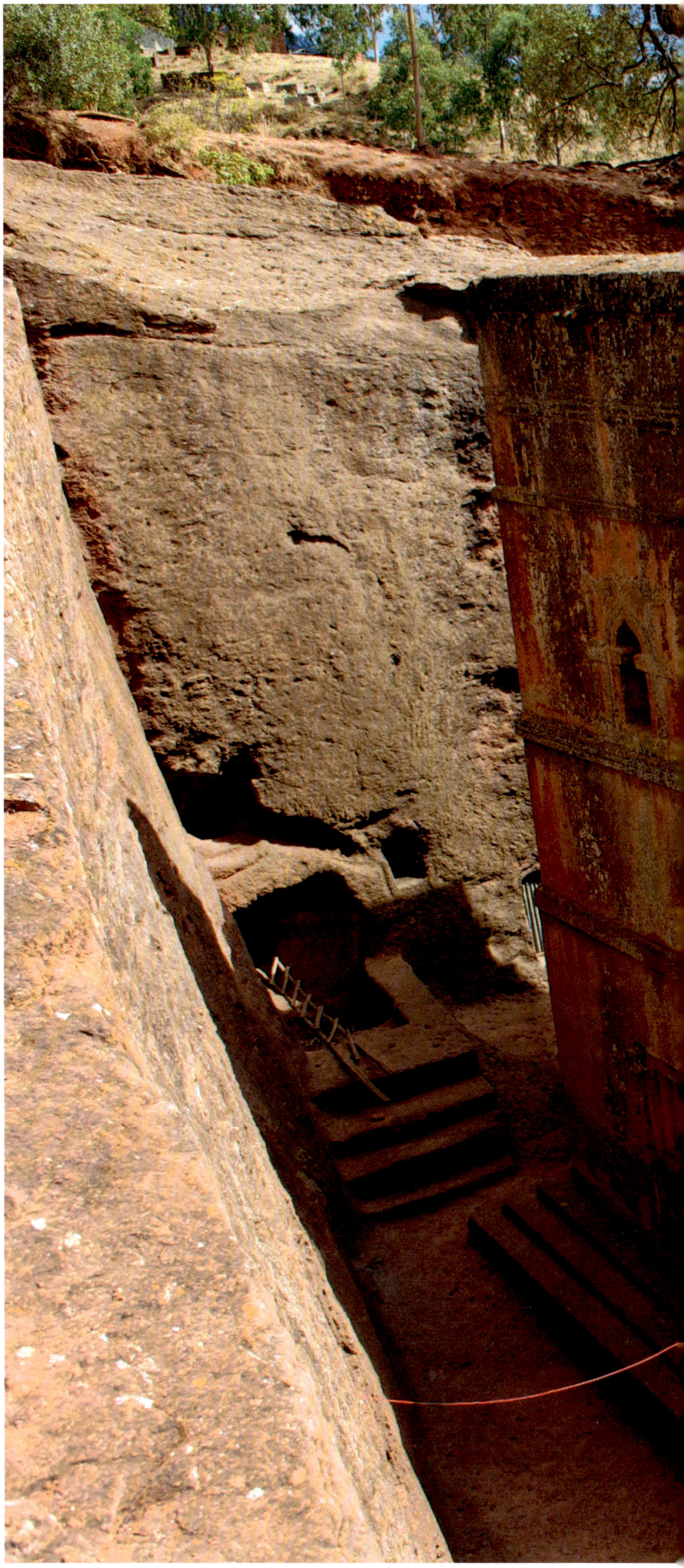

Top In the third chamber of each church lies the Tabot, a replica of the Ark of the Covenant.
Bottom Some of the Lalibela churches are surrounded by protective water trenches.

Lalibela, Ethiopia

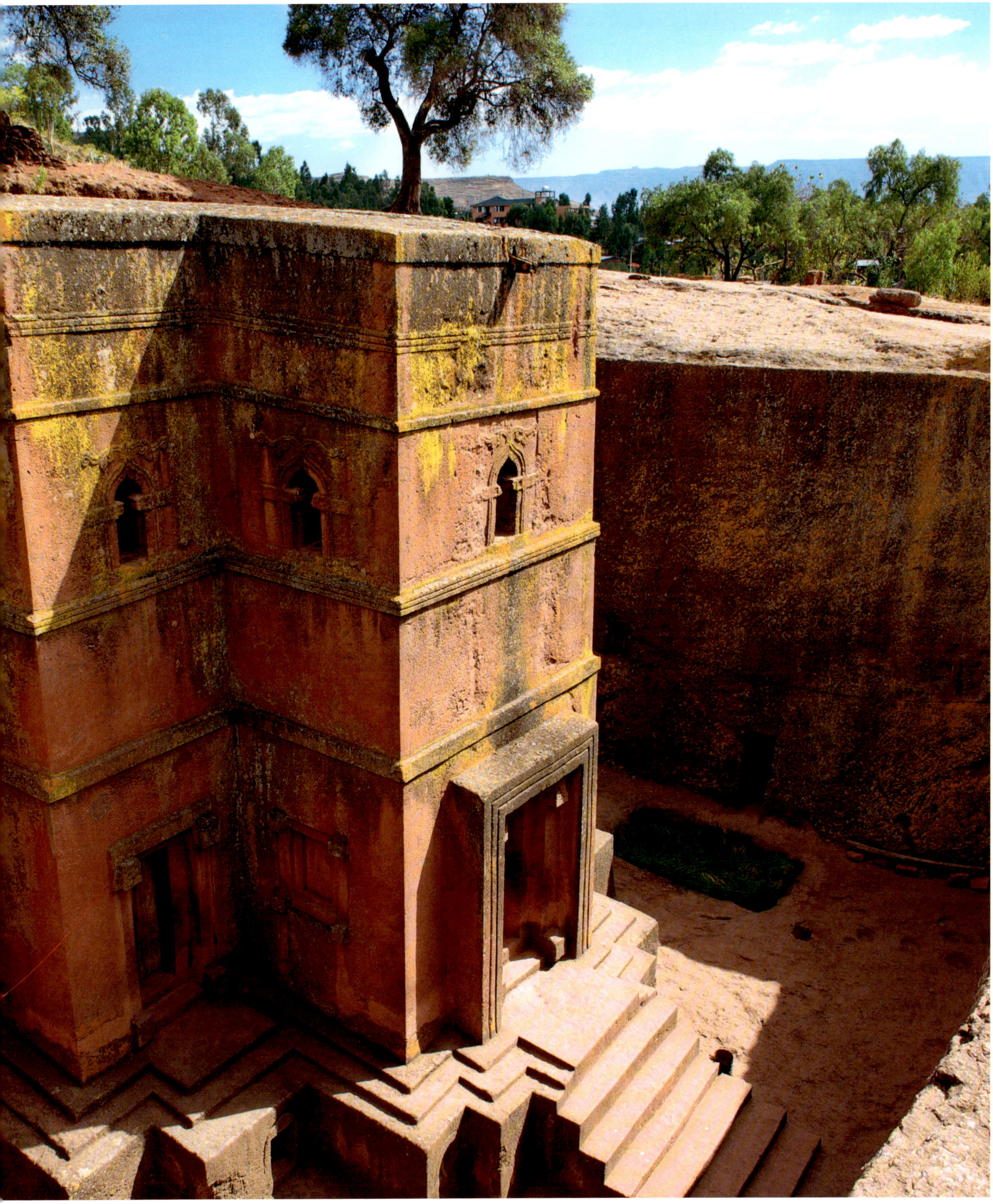

Above According to legend, angels helped King Lalibela and his workers complete the breathtaking rock-hewn churches with supernatural speed.

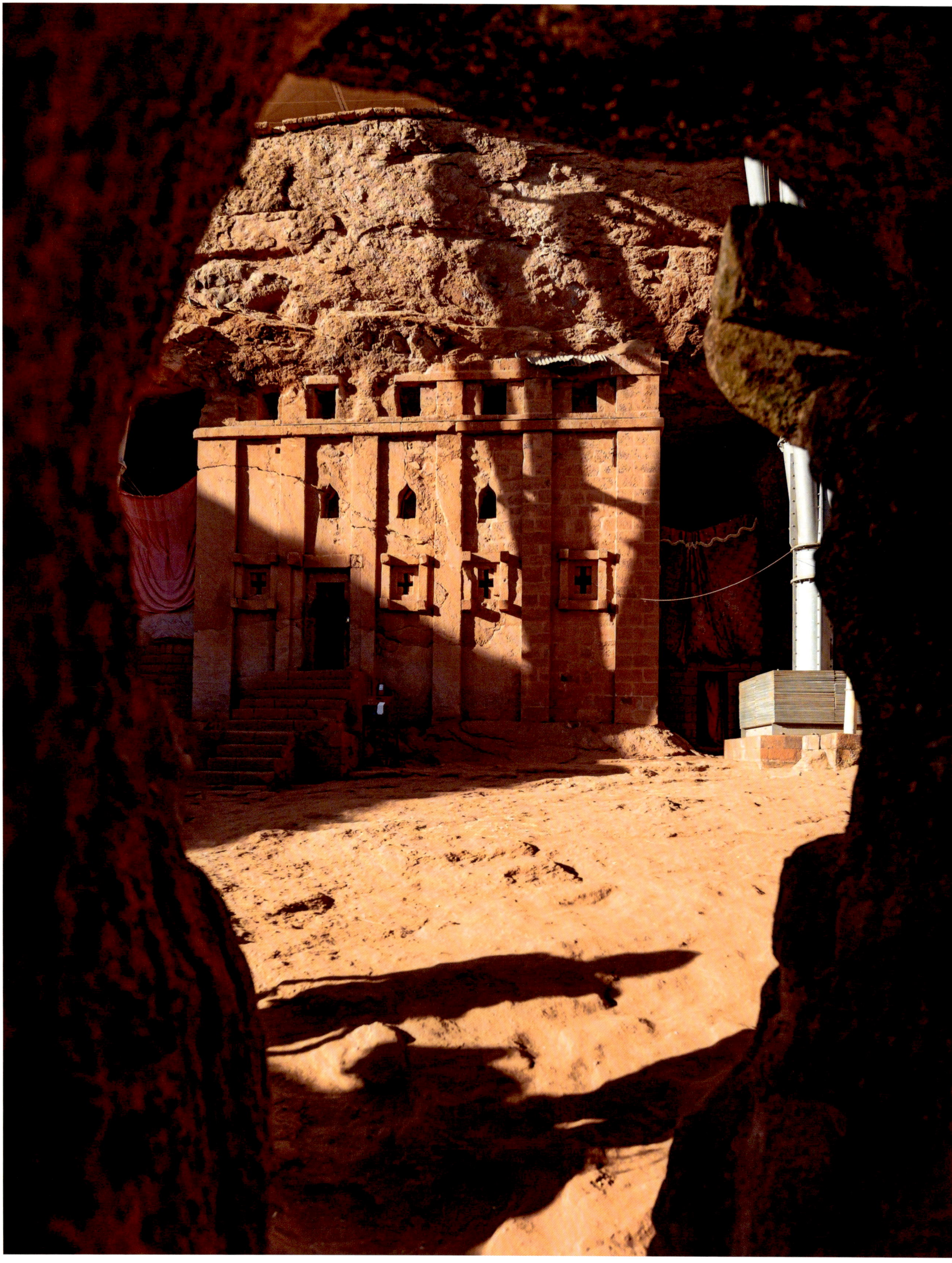

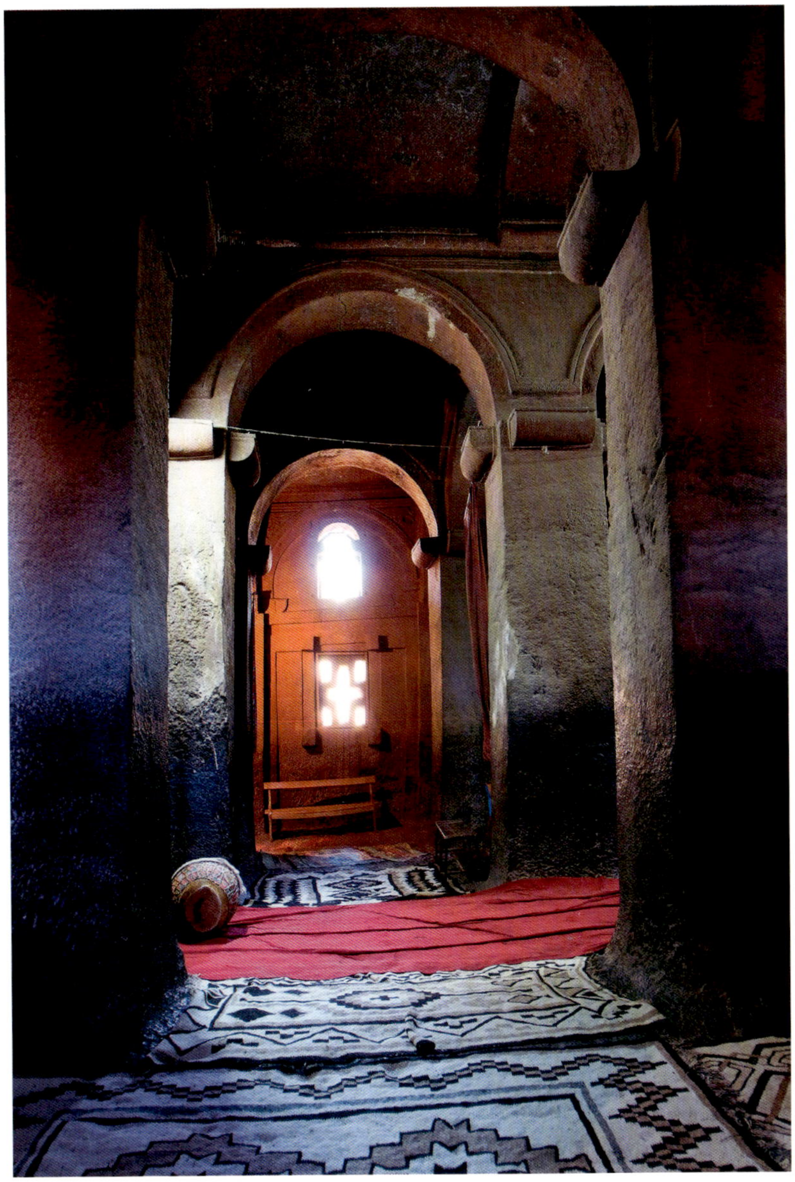

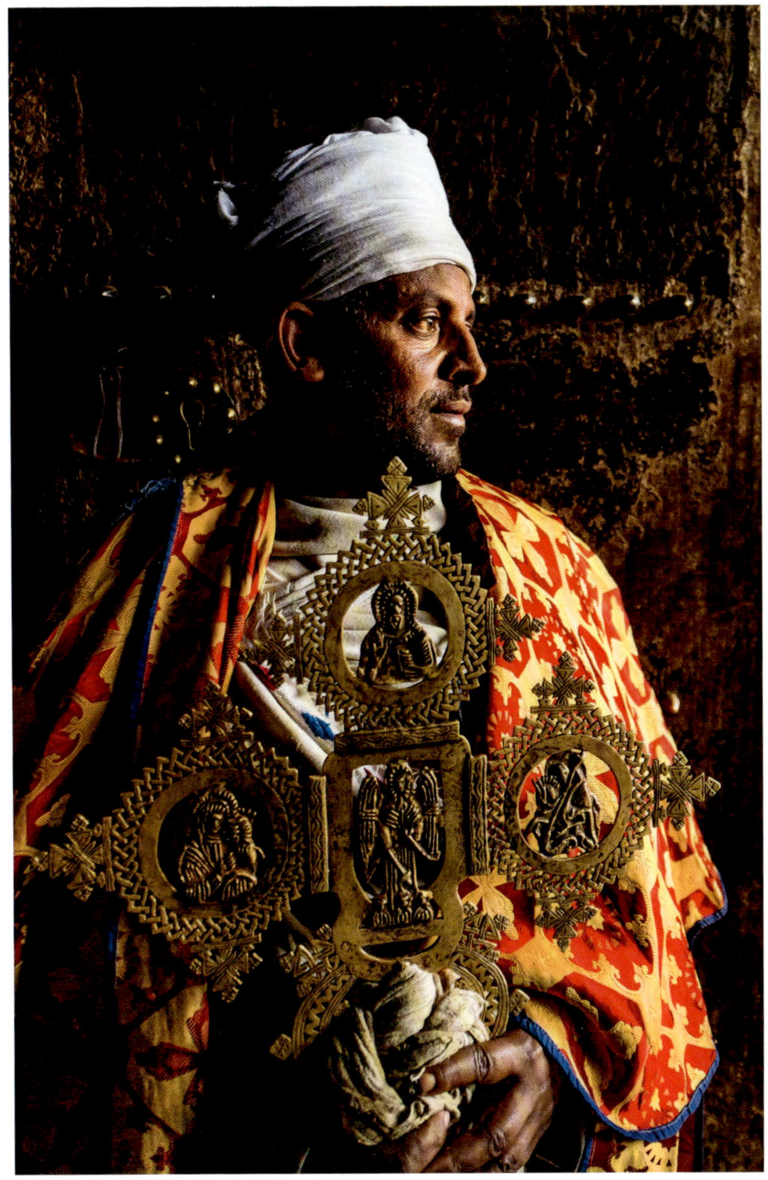

In the mountains, protected from persecution, a distinct form of Orthodox Christianity evolved—with the rock-hewn churches of Lalibela at its heart.

Opposite The churches were completely carved from the volcanic stone of Lalibela.
Above left The interiors of the rock-hewn churches are as artfully carved as the exteriors.
Above right The Lalibela Cross is an important part of the Tabot procession.

Abuna Yemata Guh

The Only Way is Up

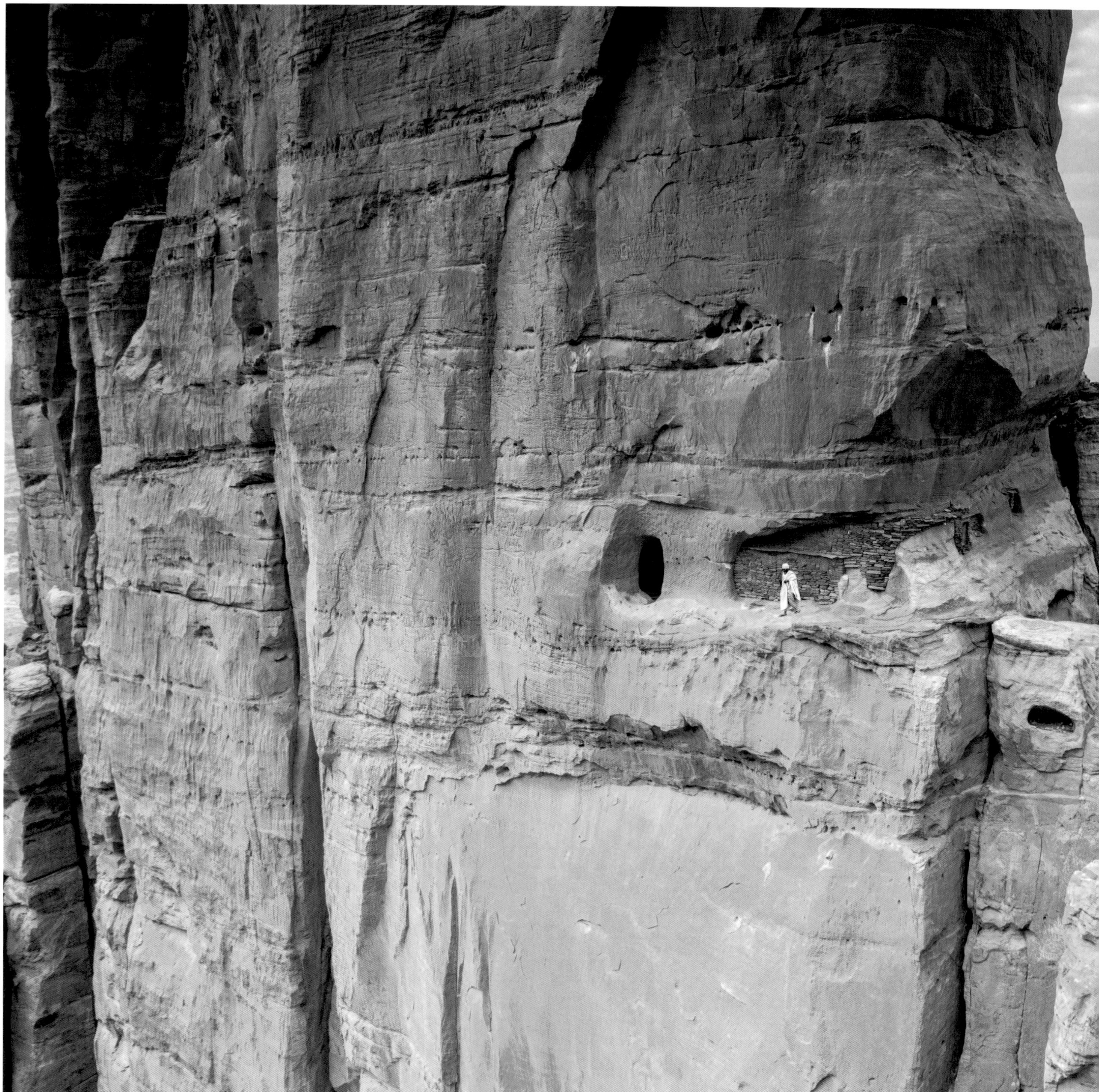

Tigray Region, Ethiopia

Built: 6th century CE,
Tigray Region, Ethiopia

Sheer cliffs, a wildly strenuous ascent, and breathtaking views accompany the route to the most elusive church in the world.

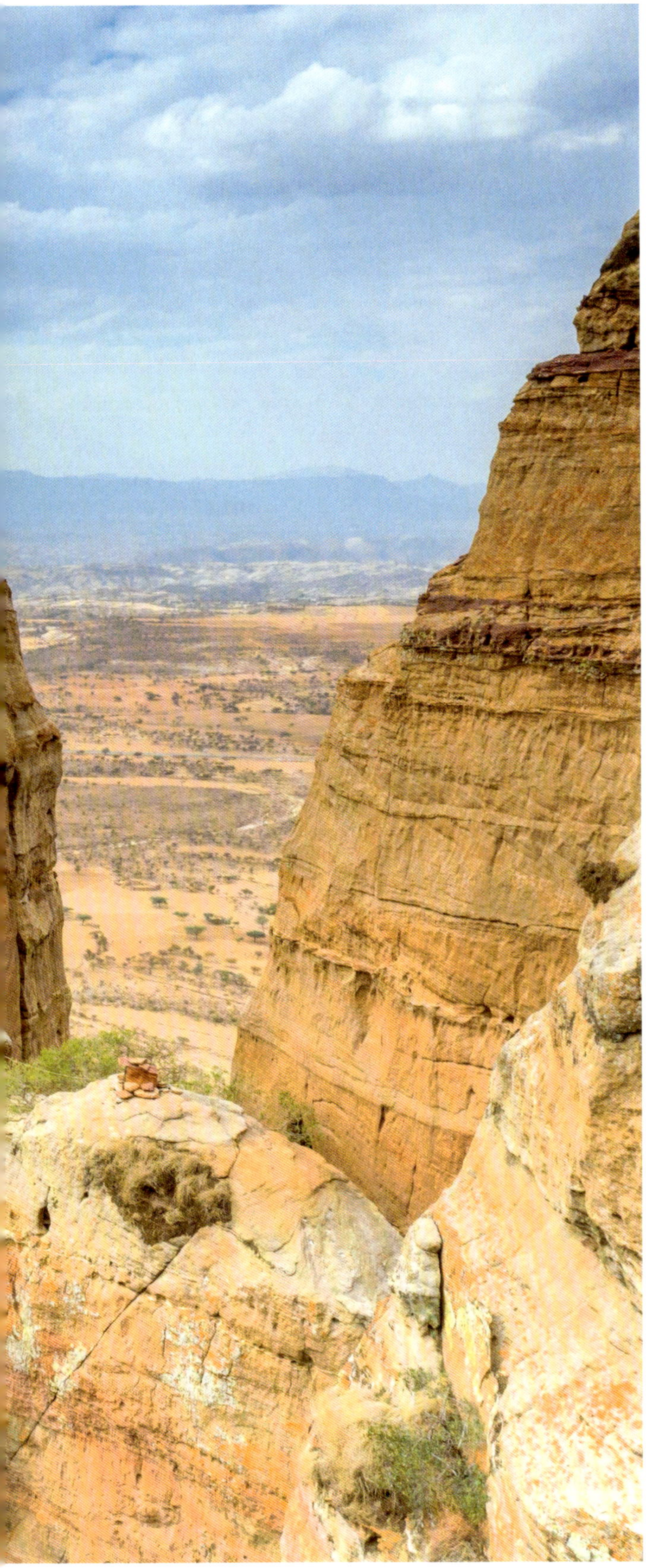

The climb to Abuna Yemata Guh is not for the faint of heart. True believers and curious visitors alike must traverse narrow paths along dizzying precipices, without ropes or safety gear, often relying on small handholds and footholds carved into the rock. There are no nets on this ascent, and whether one relies on faith or one's physical abilities—or some combination of both—the danger is great. But for those who undertake the risky pilgrimage, the reward is immense: stunning views of the vast plains of Tigray and spiritual replenishment inside the rock-hewn church.

The place is named for the 6th-century Saint Abuna Yemata, one of nine who traveled to Ethiopia from the Eastern Roman Empire to spread Christianity in the highlands. According to legend, Abuna Yemata withdrew to this mountainous solitude, spending his days in prayer and meditation—he is even believed to have carved the church out of the bare rock himself. Even today, centuries later, this cave church is regularly visited by believers who follow the saint's example, enduring the strenuous ascent for the privilege of praying here.

As unassuming as Abuna Yemata Guh might appear from the outside, its interior offers a vivid expression of faith. The walls and ceiling are covered with early Christian frescoes that depict angels, biblical heroes, and the Nine Saints, painted with vibrant colors. The dry climate and lack of exposure to sunlight have ensured that they have suffered little weathering over the centuries, and these bright paintings make the distant past feel present and alive.

From within, one can gaze through the entrance and contemplate the spectacular expanse and striking rock formations of the surrounding landscape. Priests are also present, with some making this dangerous yet rewarding journey on a daily basis for decades. They lead lives of devotion, protecting the church, conducting services, and safeguarding the church's precious treasure: irreplaceable manuscripts from centuries past, often written in Ge'ez, the ancient liturgical language of Ethiopia. These manuscripts contain ancient prayers, still used in services today.

On holy days like Fasika, the Ethiopian Easter, a particularly large number of believers make the ascent to Abuna Yemata Guh. As the priest offers his blessing to the gathered congregation, perhaps a prayer or two is sent heavenward for a safe descent. Indeed, plans are underway to make the route safer for visitors, but for now, the danger remains part of its spine-tingling draw. For where else but far above the earthly realm could one feel closer to the divine?

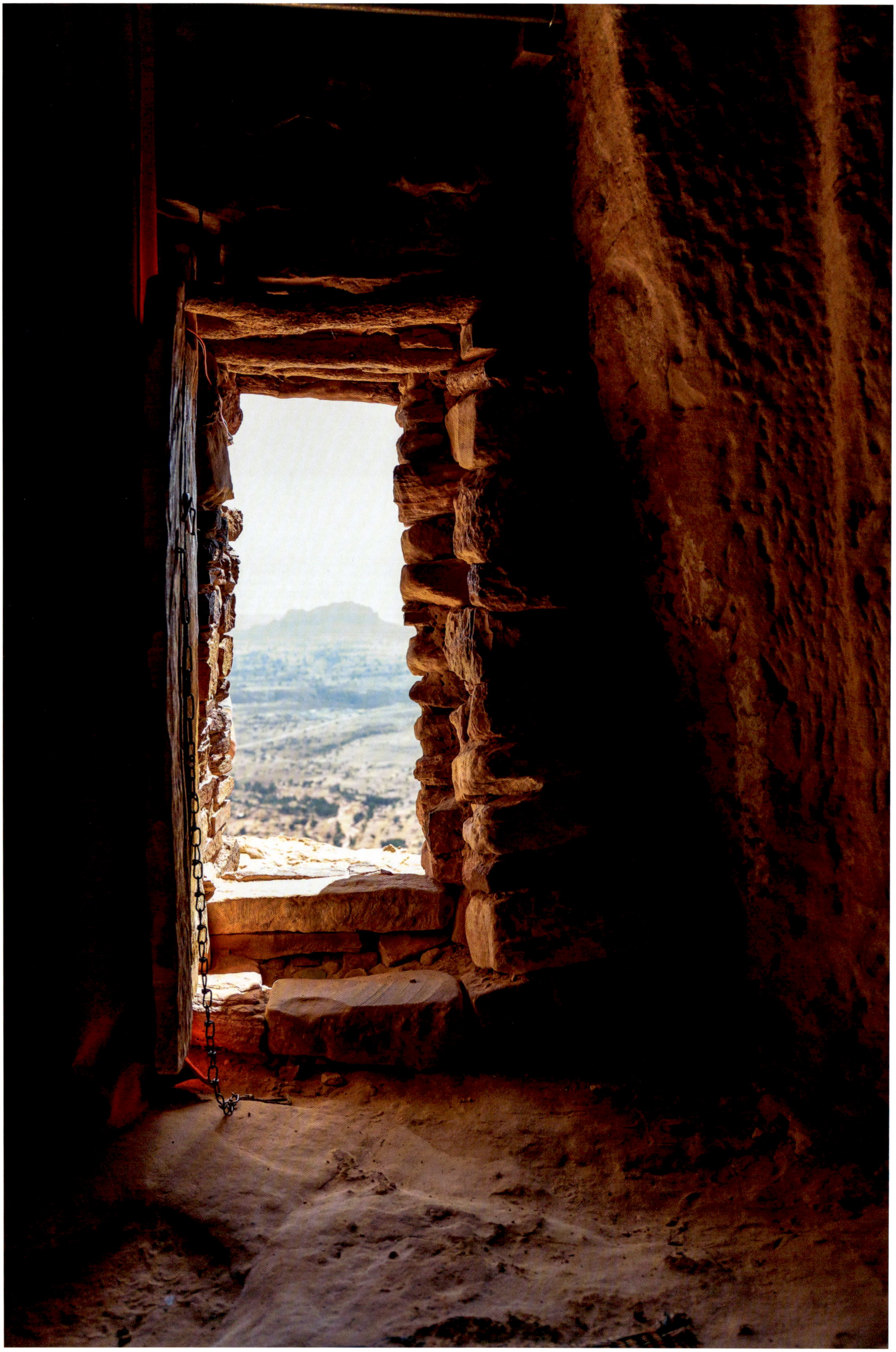

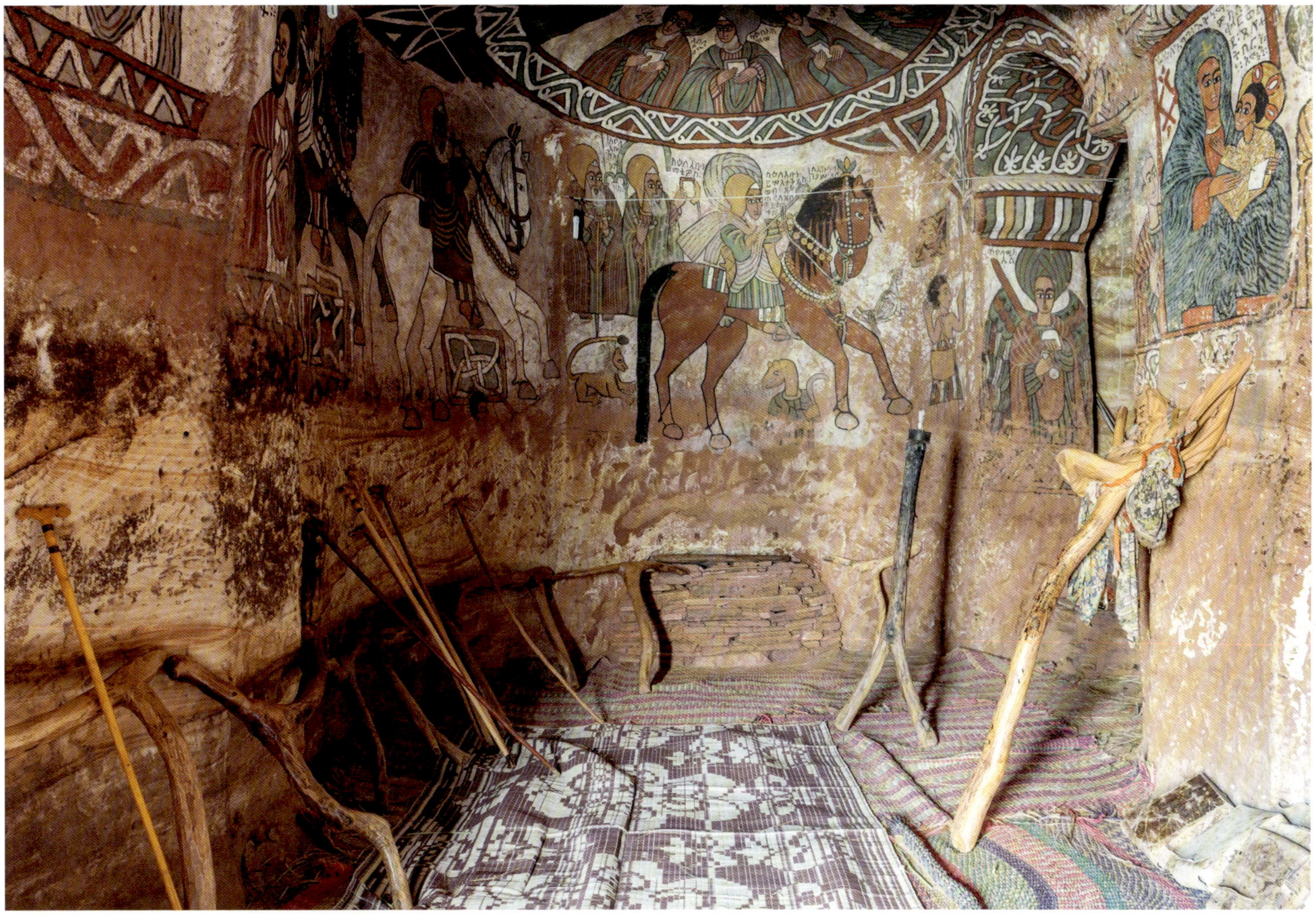

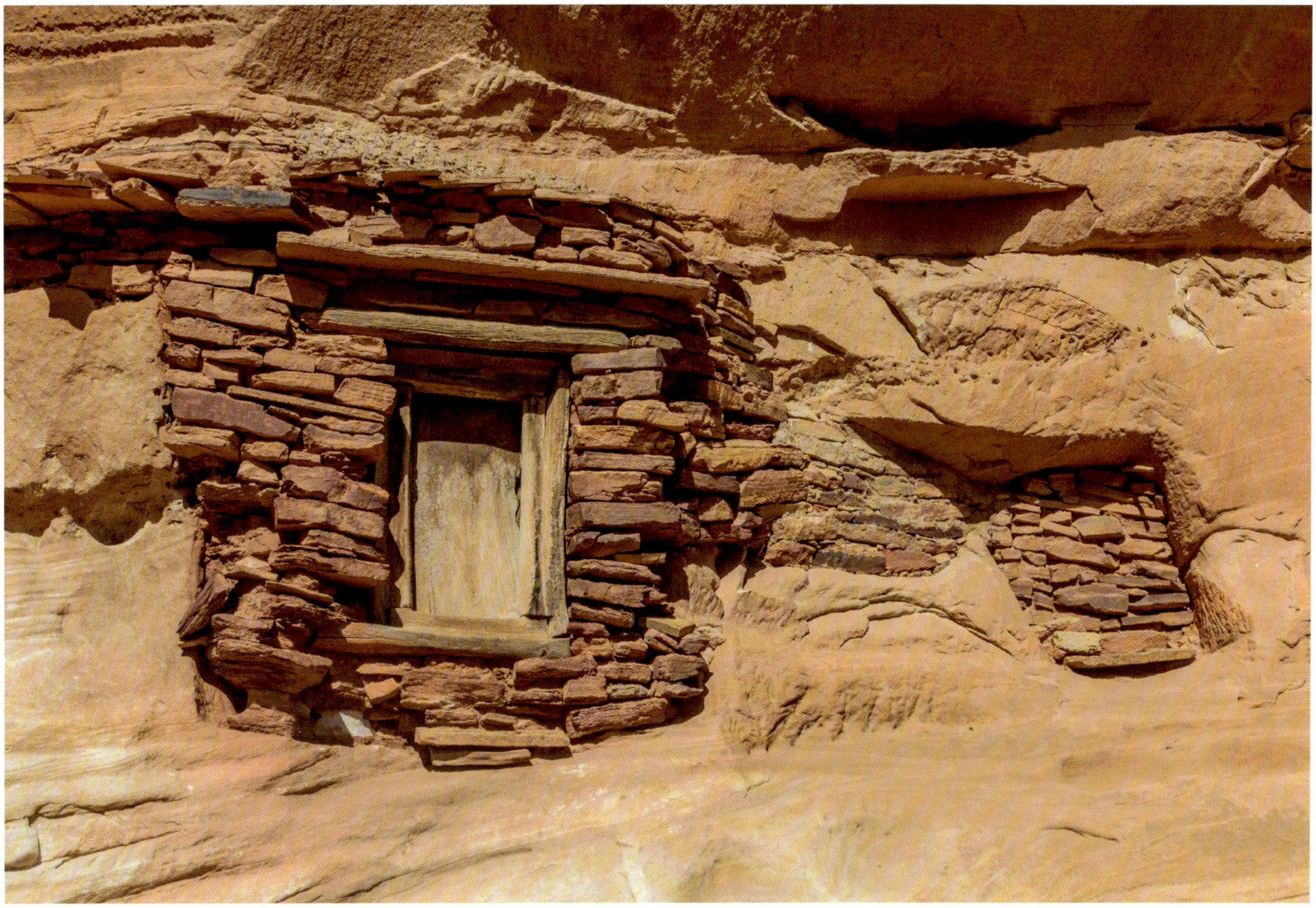

Opposite The lofty view from the high-built church lifts you into celestial realms.
Top The colorful frescoes are alive with symbols and biblical scenes.
Bottom It was in this remote mountain retreat that Saint Abuna Yemata sought refuge, dedicating his days to prayer and contemplation.

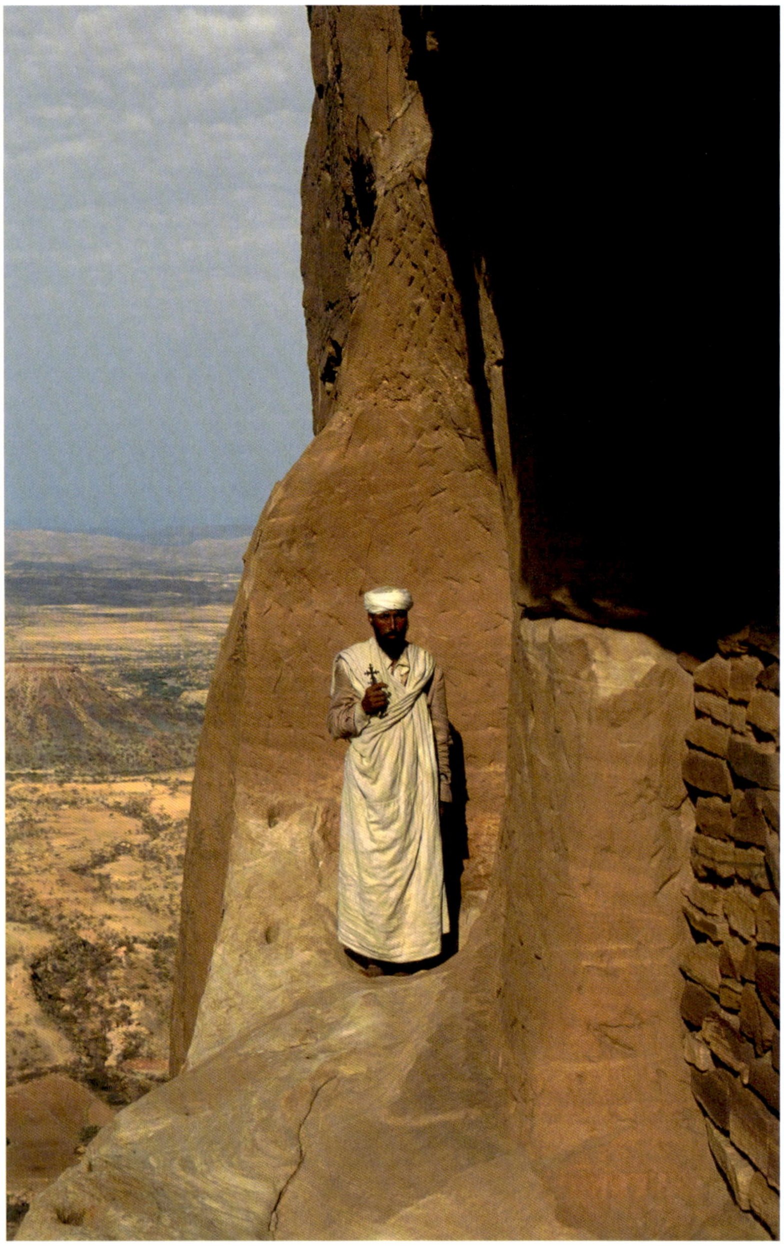

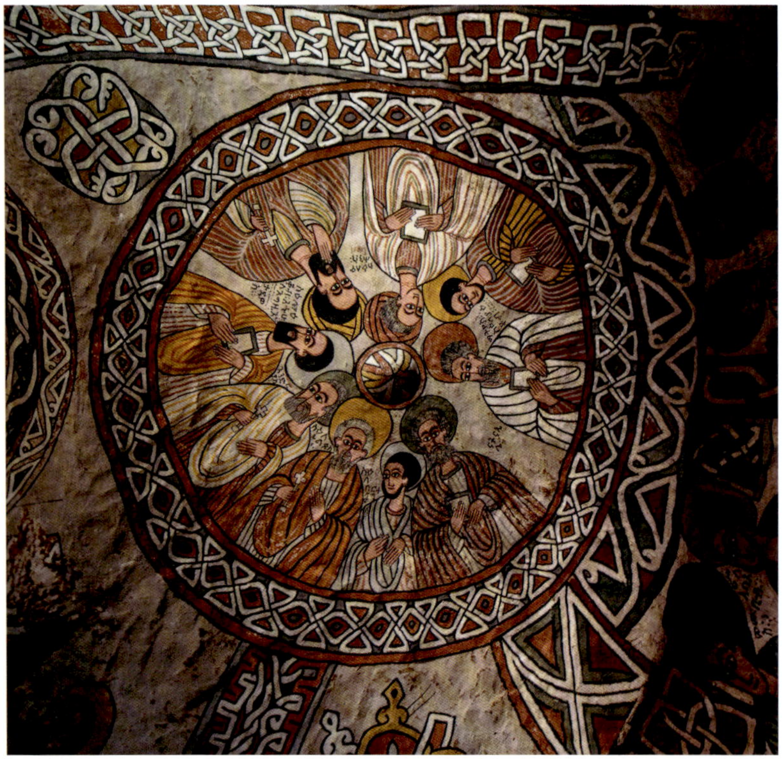

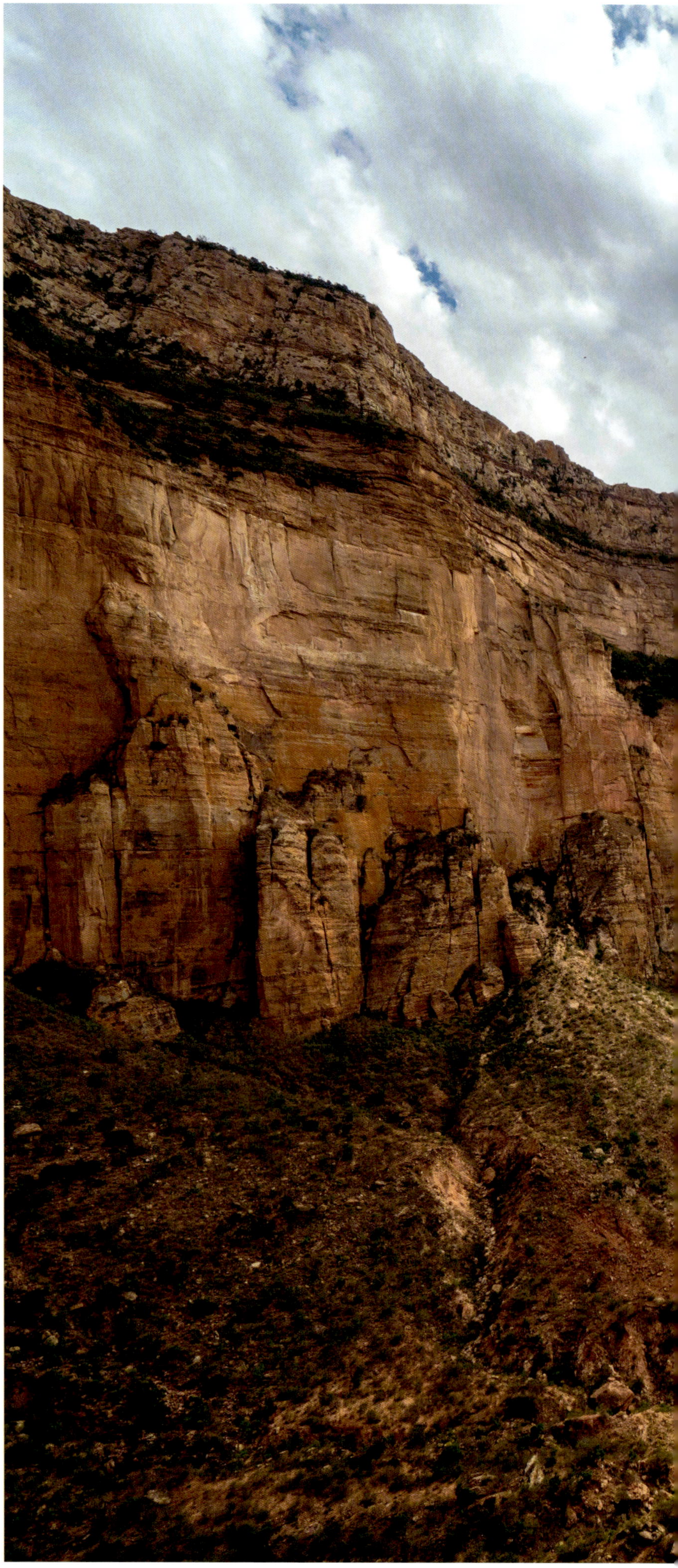

Top Far removed from the earthly realm, the priests offer blessings to anyone who dares the steep ascent. *Bottom* The Nine Saints, including Abuna Yemata, came to the region to spread Christianity.

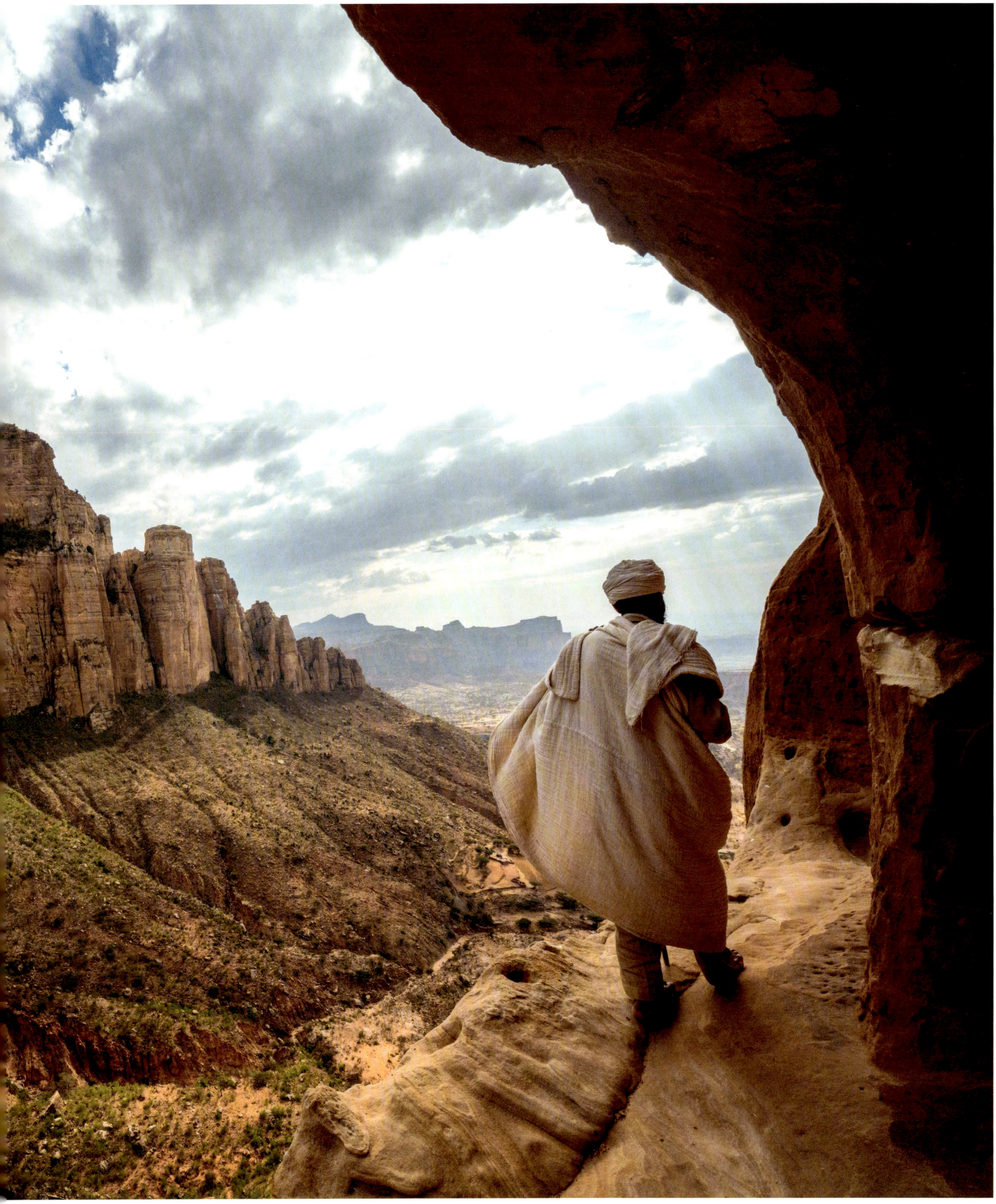

Above Given the view of the majestic Tigray Mountains surrounding this unique church, it's easy to lose oneself in meditation, spiritual gratitude, and admiration of all creation.

Al-Khazneh

A Treasury of History

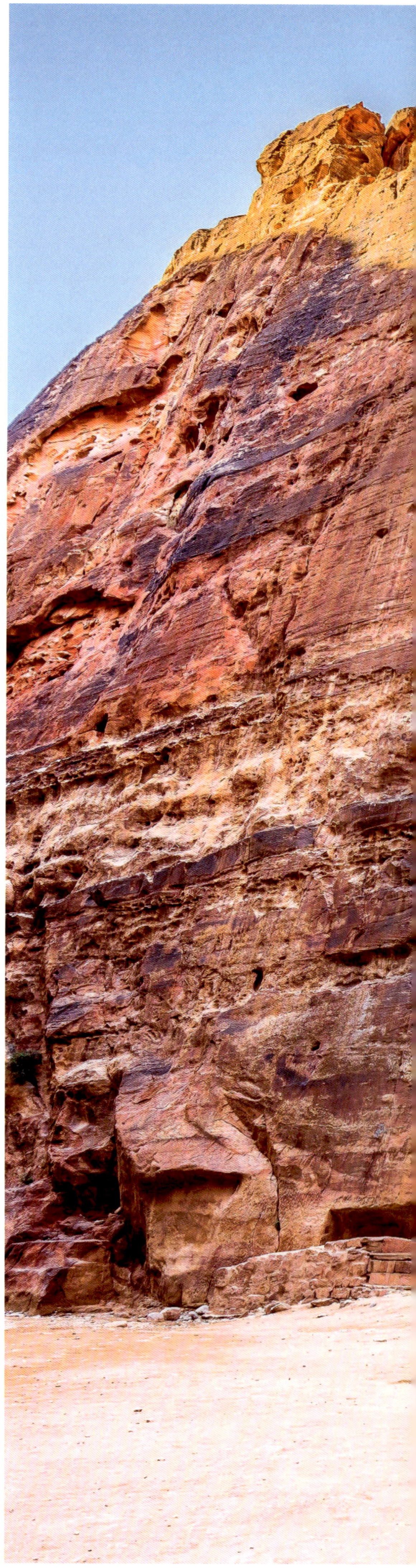

Built: 1st century BCE, Petra, Jordan

Recent discoveries by an international team of archaeologists are bringing to light, after 2,000 years, the secrets of the Nabataeans.

The Siq, a narrow sandstone gorge, stretches three-quarters of a mile (1.2 kilometers) and leads to the legendary Nabataean city of Petra. The millennia are clearly visible in the eroded layers of its rock. This natural corridor, a mere 6.6 feet (2 meters) wide at its narrowest point, offered access to and protection for a city that, 2,000 years ago, was a major trading center and a key stop for countless caravans. Traveling through the Siq today, one feels connected to these ancient travelers, can hear their voices and imagine the donkeys and camels laden with spices, incense, and silk. Then suddenly the rock road widens and the gorge opens up.

Al-Khazneh, or the Treasury, reveals itself in all its splendor, even larger and more impressive than imagined. A closer look reveals influences from many worlds—unsurprising, given the city's vibrant international connections. The Corinthian capitals on the columns, for example, show clear Greco-Roman inspiration. Mesopotamian, Egyptian, and Arabian influences can also be seen in the intricate reliefs, statues, and decorations throughout Petra. Ad Deir, or the Monastery, is arguably the most impressive Nabataean masterpiece after Al-Khazneh, and its facade also features a mix of stylistic elements. The Nabataeans skillfully adopted foreign ideas and fused them seamlessly with their own.

For a long time, it was merely suspected that Al-Khazneh was originally a royal tomb and later served as a temple. According to local legend, a treasure chamber (*al khazneh* in Arabic—a name given by the Bedouins) is hidden behind its exquisite facade—a myth fueled by the large stone urn at the top of the structure. In the hope that it was filled with gold and jewels, treasure hunters fired bullets at the urn to release the supposed treasure. Bullet holes, still visible today, bear witness to their efforts. Since 2024, there is more certainty as to Al-Khazneh's purpose. Using the latest technology, an international team of researchers discovered a hidden tomb behind the stone facade. Inside, they found the remains of 12 skeletons, likely buried in the 1st century CE. A particularly goosebump-inducing find was a ceramic vessel held in the hands of one of the skeletons, which strikingly resembles the kind of holy grail seen in *Indiana Jones and the Last Crusade*—a movie that was partially filmed in Petra.

Coincidence? Most certainly. But more importantly, these findings cast new light on the lives, beliefs, and burial practices of the Nabataeans, and hold the potential to greatly expand our understanding of their mysterious city and its beautifully preserved treasury of culture and history.

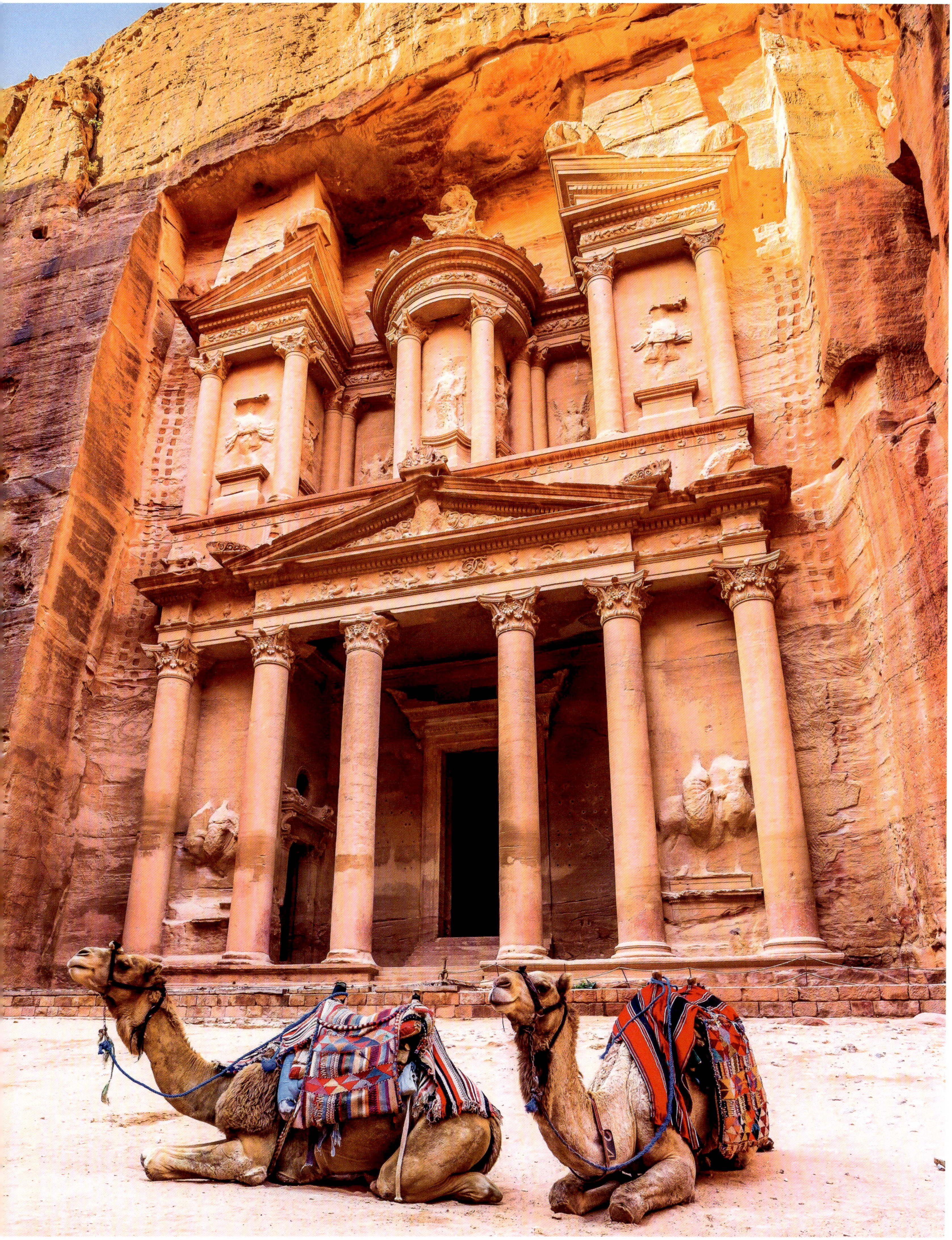

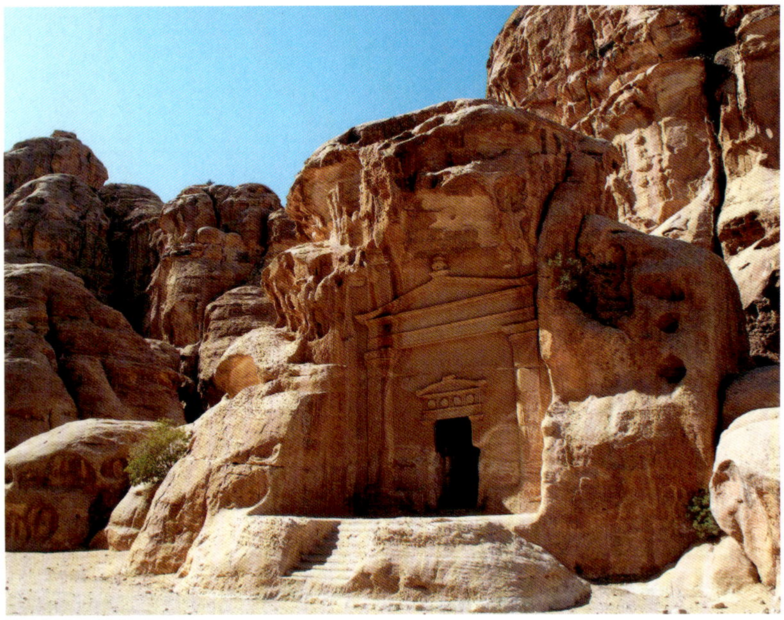

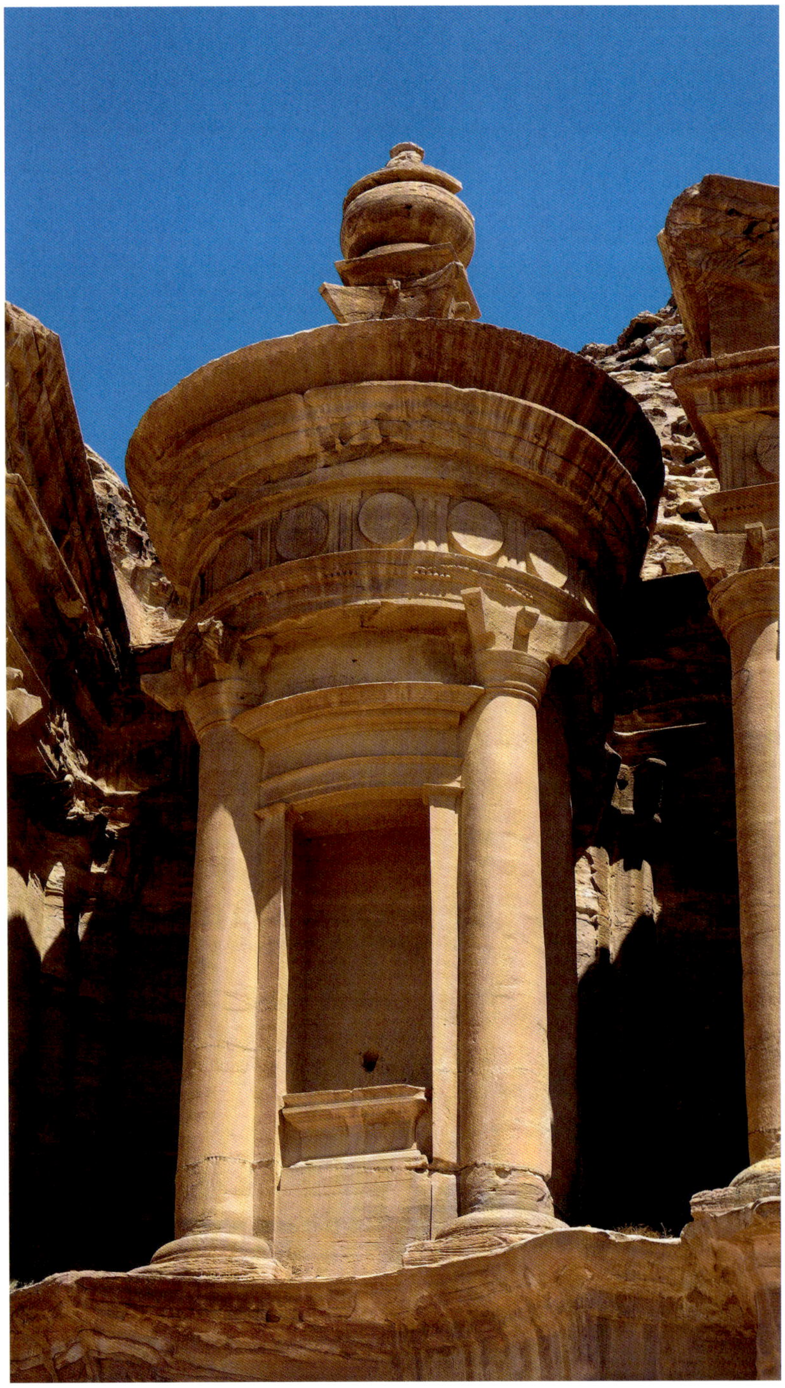

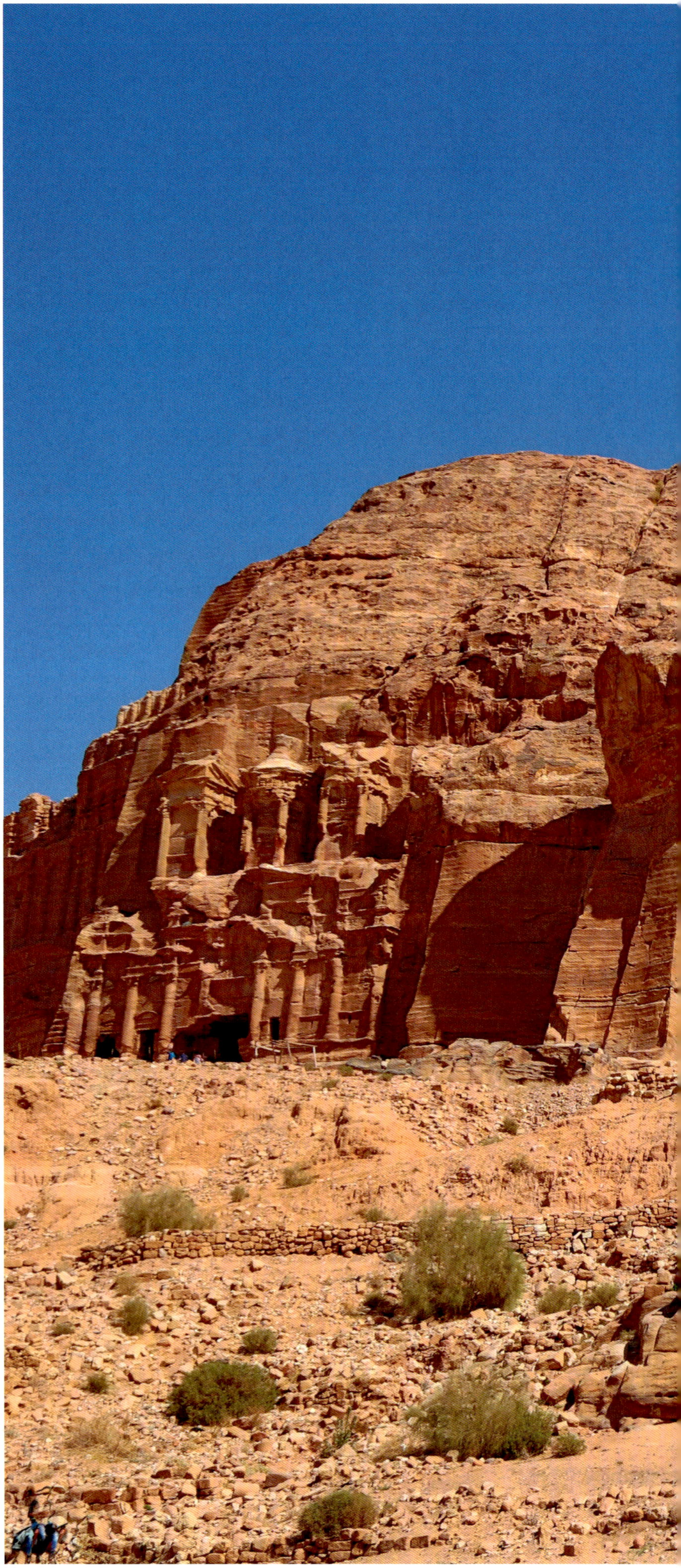

Top The city is often affectionately referred to as "the Rose-Red City" because of its colorful stone.
Bottom From the 4th century BCE to the 2nd century CE, Petra was a thriving trading hub, known for dealing in frankincense, myrrh, and many spices.

Petra, Jordan

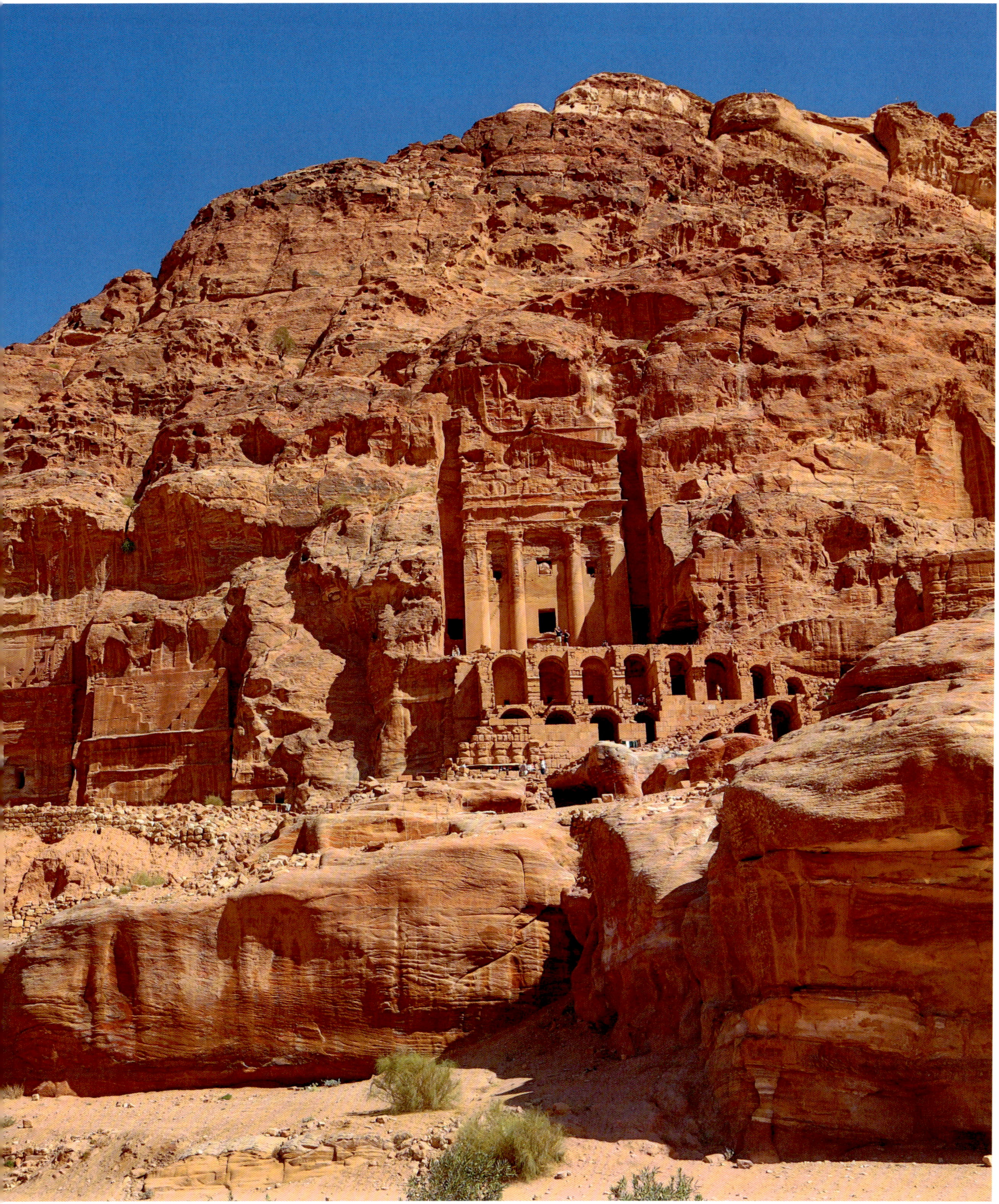

Above The architecture of the ancient rock-hewn city blends Nabataean, Greek, and Roman influences, serving as a testament to Petra's rich and diverse history.

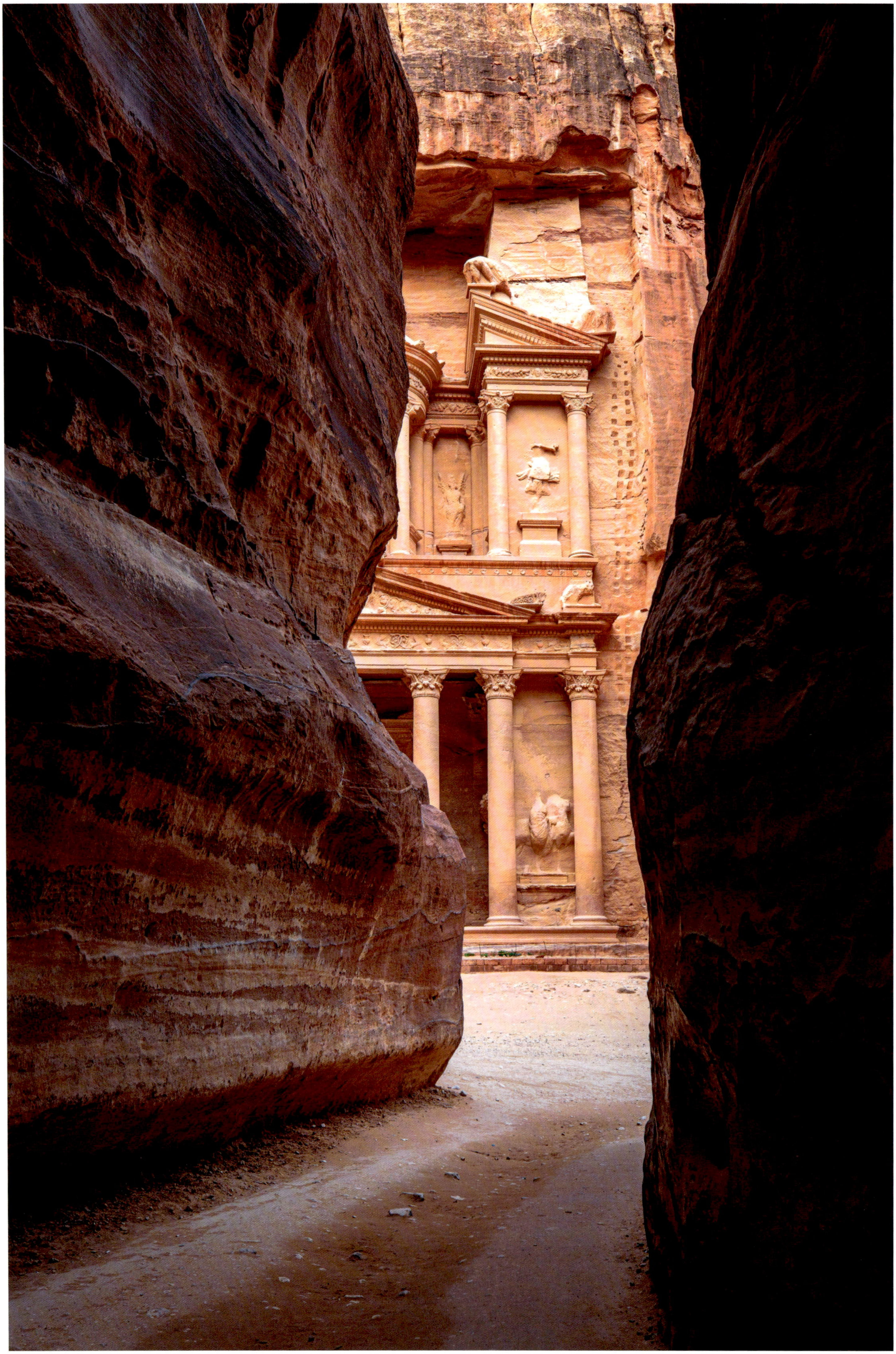

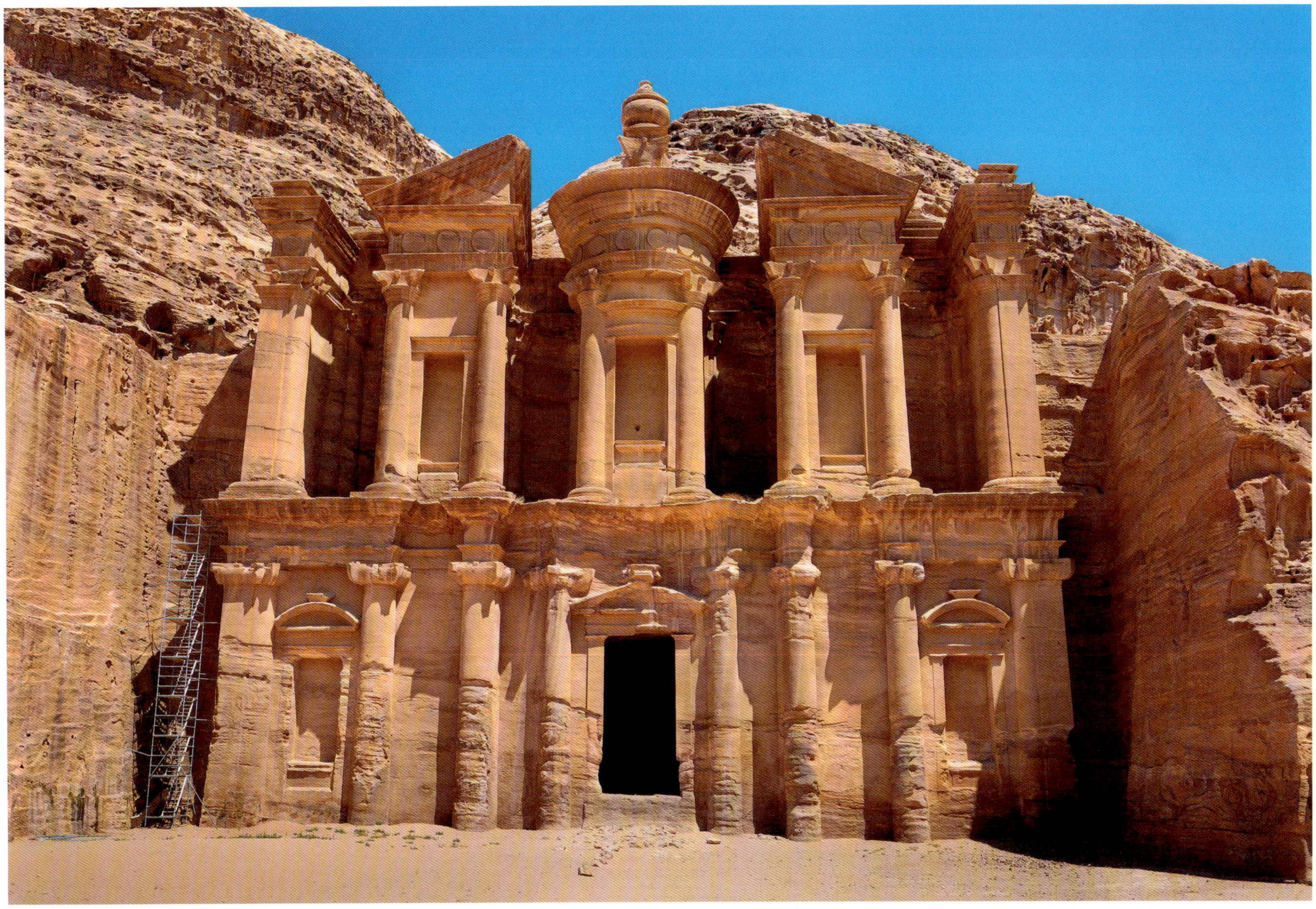

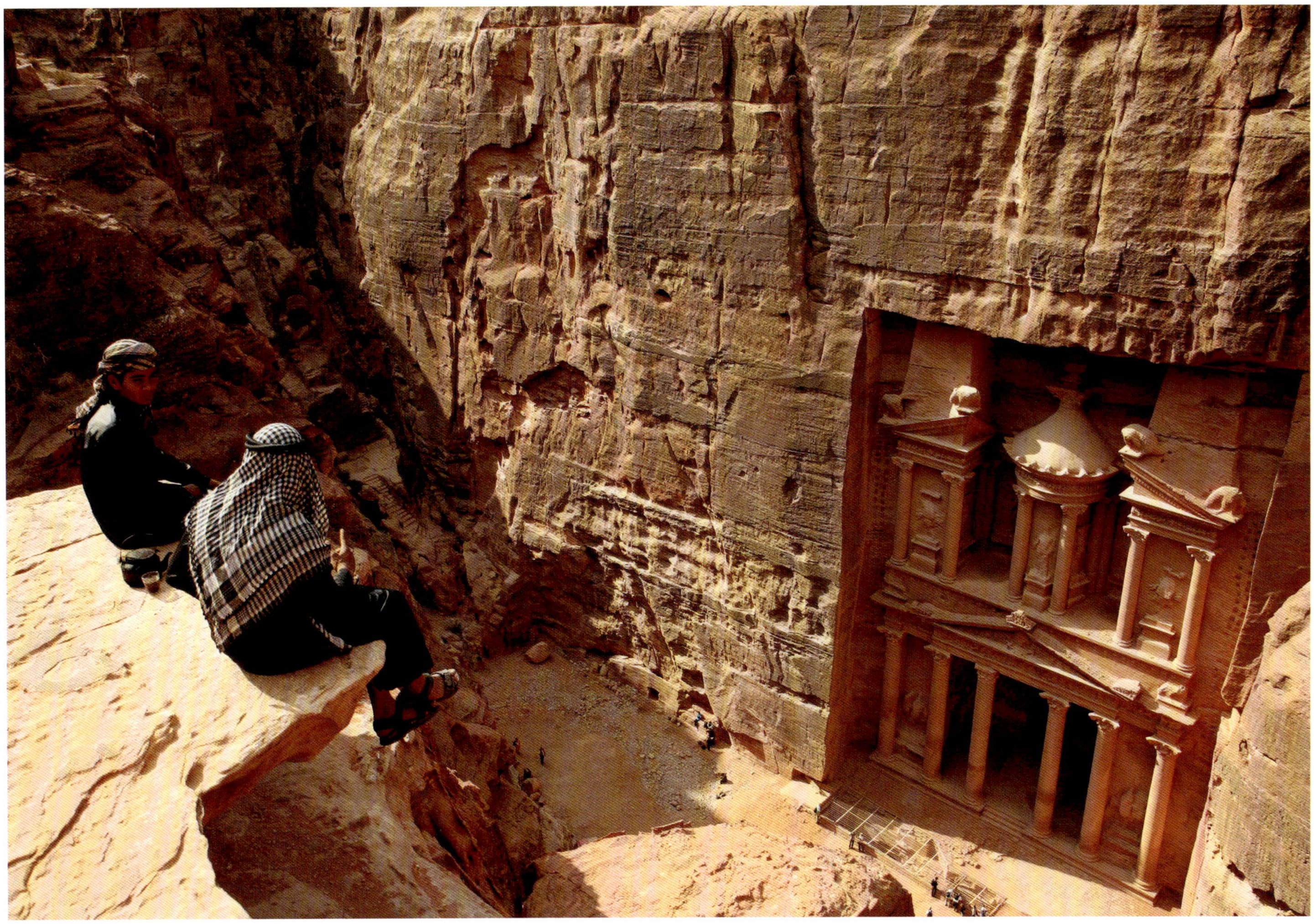

Opposite Those who emerge into the light after hiking through the narrow confines of the Siq are greeted by the spectacular sight of Al-Khazneh.
Top The monastery Ad Deir resembles Al Khazneh in its structure, style, and details.
Bottom The Treasury captivates with its grandeur, no matter the perspective.

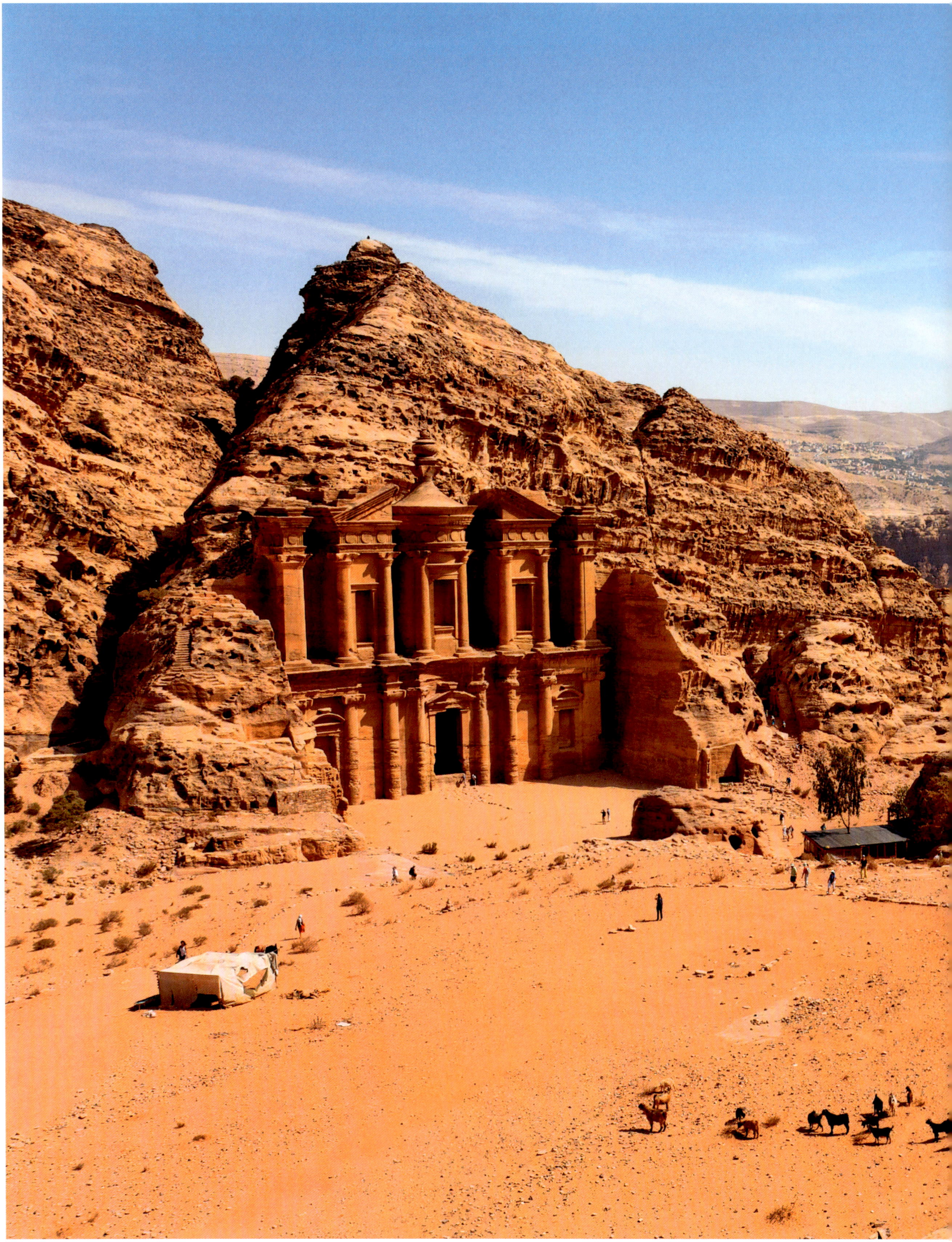

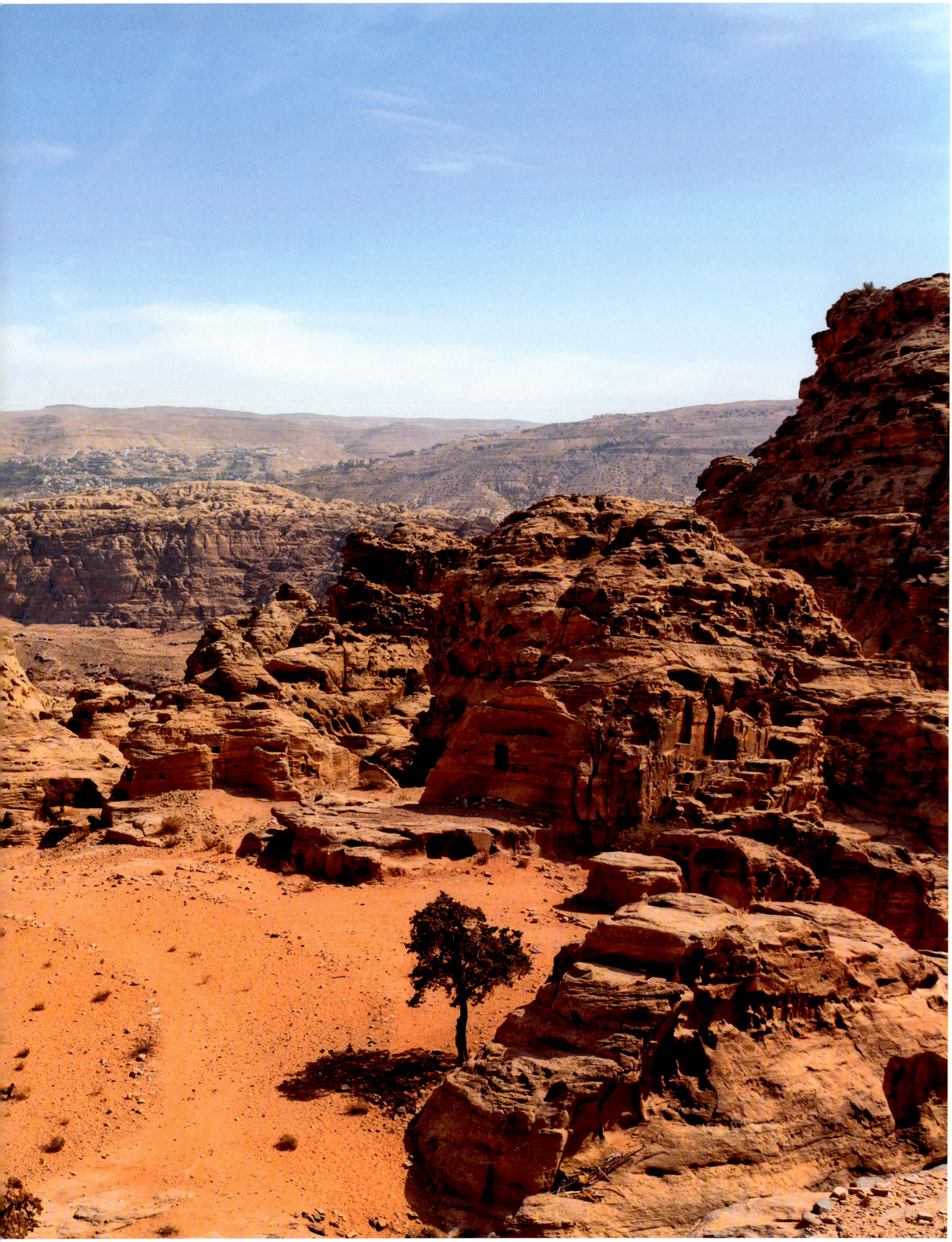

Western Wall

In the Eye of the Storm

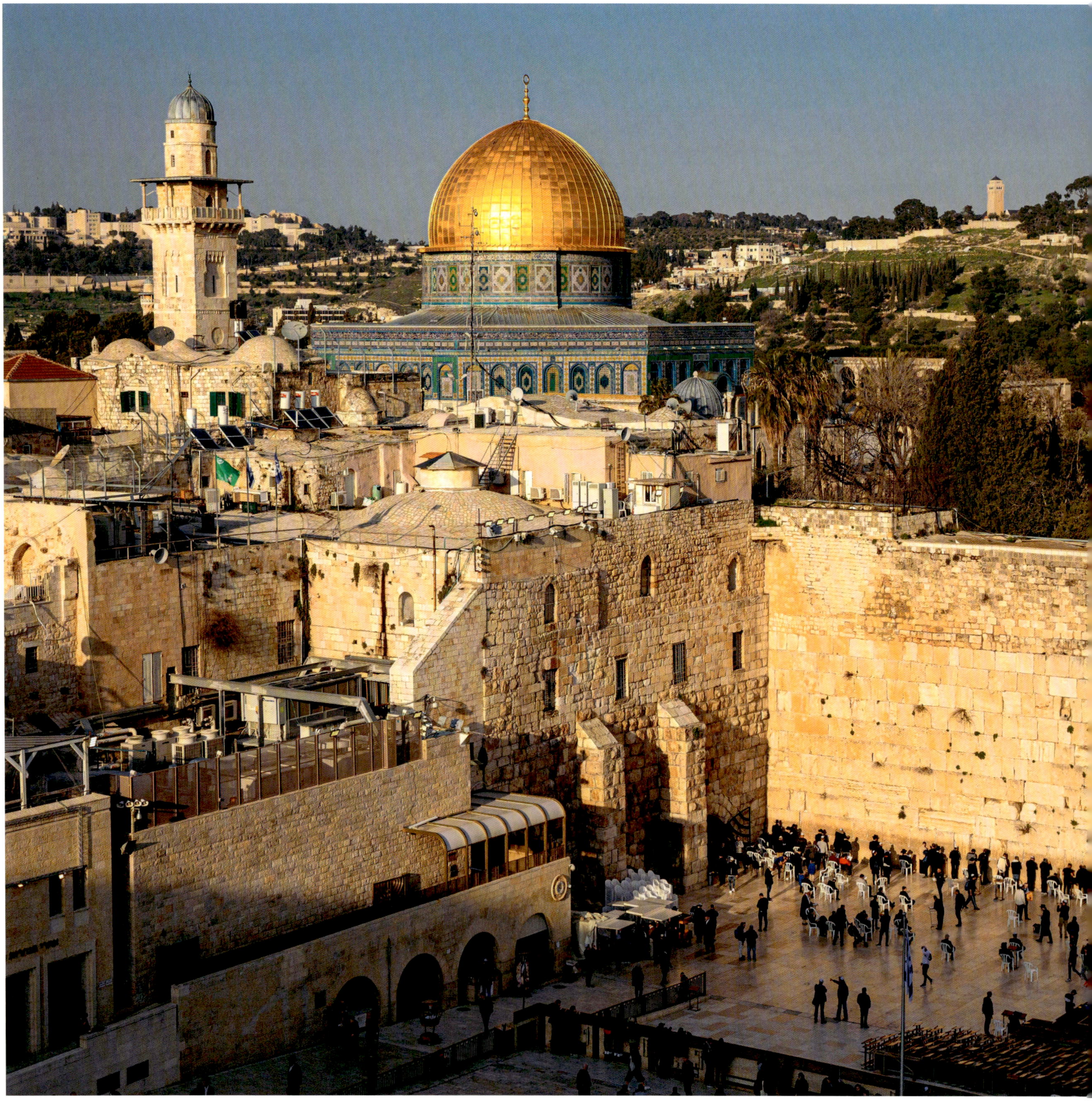

Jerusalem, Israel

Built: 1st century BCE,
Jerusalem, Israel

Where three world religions converge, these stones have stood sentinel for 2,000 years, bearing witness to sacred, profane, and hopeful days.

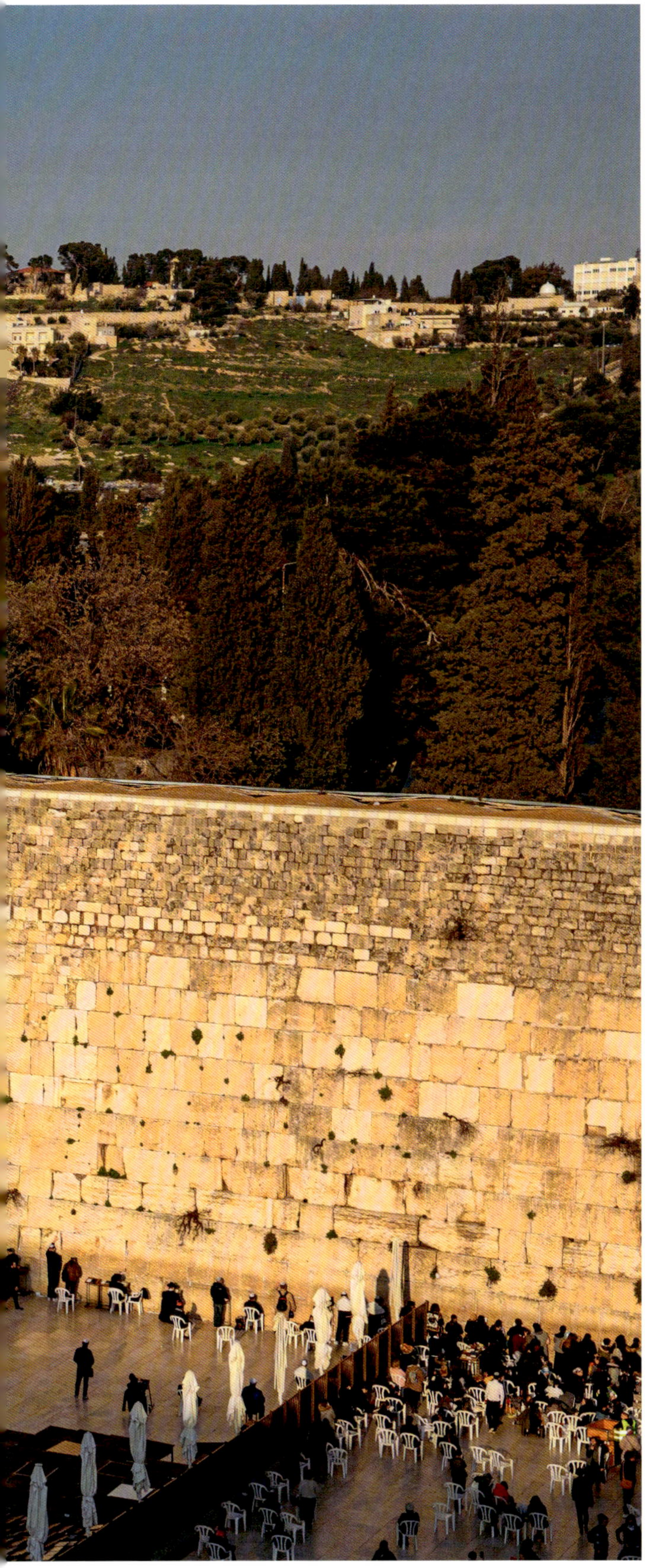

Small slips of paper, folded or rolled up and inscribed with prayers, petitions, and secrets, are tucked into the crevices of one of the most significant religious sites in human history. The Western Wall is the last remaining section of a retaining wall that supported the expanded platform of the Second Temple on the hill known to Jews as the Temple Mount and to Muslims as Haram al-Sharif. Its profound significance can only be fully appreciated within the broader historical context of Jerusalem.

Jerusalem is among the world's oldest cities, with traces of settlement dating back to 4000 BCE. In the 10th century BCE, King David conquered the city and established it as the capital of Israel. According to biblical tradition, his son Solomon built the First Temple to house the Ark of the Covenant. Following the division of Israel, Jerusalem became the capital of the Kingdom of Judah. Over the centuries, the city came under the rule of numerous empires. The Babylonians destroyed the First Temple in 586 BCE, and the Second Temple was destroyed by the Romans in 70 CE. In 1099 CE, the Crusaders captured Jerusalem—including the Church of the Holy Sepulchre, one of Christianity's holiest sites—and made the city the center of their Kingdom of Jerusalem. For Jews and Muslims, however, the Temple Mount holds immense spiritual significance. For Judaism, it is the sacred location of the First and Second Temples; for Islam, it is the site where the Prophet Muhammad ascended to heaven. This exact place where Muhammad departed is, in Jewish tradition, the place where Abraham was prepared to sacrifice his son Isaac. Around 700 CE, Muslims built the Dome of the Rock on this site and, shortly thereafter, the nearby Al-Aqsa Mosque, cementing Jerusalem as a key religious center for Islam.

For 2,000 years, the Western Wall has stood amidst this storm of history, through times of violence and uneasy peace. Although the section devoted to Jewish prayer is much smaller, the full surviving wall measures 1,601 feet (488 meters) and runs along the west side of the Temple Mount. Today, the Western Wall is open to all, regardless of their faith. Tourists mingle with Jewish worshippers, who traditionally gather here every Friday evening to celebrate the beginning of Shabbat, and Muslims visiting the place where Muhammad once tied the Buraq—the winged, horse-like creature that he rode during the Night of Ascension. The custom of placing small slips of paper between the cracks of the wall has become a cherished tradition, embraced by Jews and visitors of other faiths alike. Whichever God reads these messages could likely not tell which faith their authors belong to anyway—for in the end, humanity's hopes all circle back to love and peace.

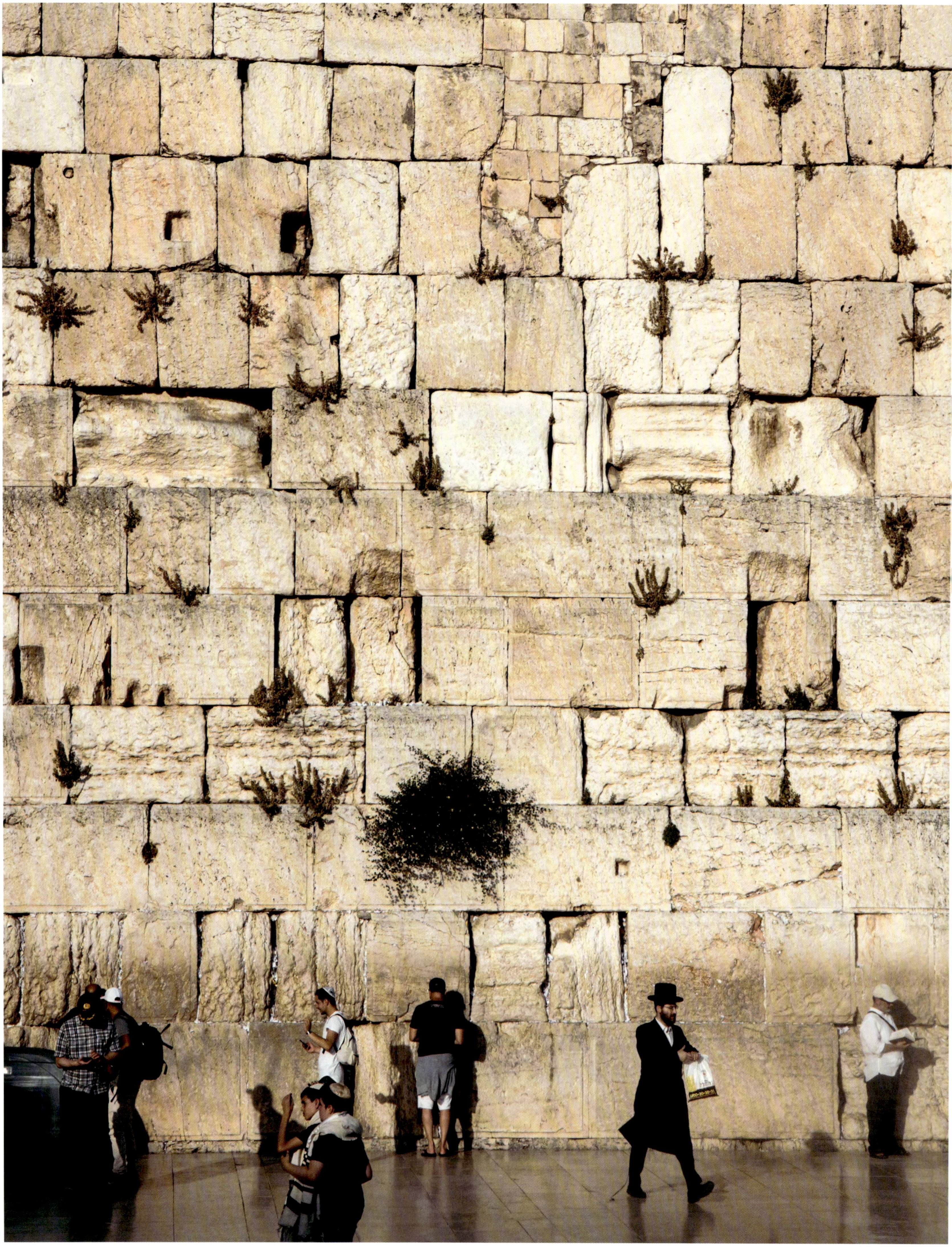

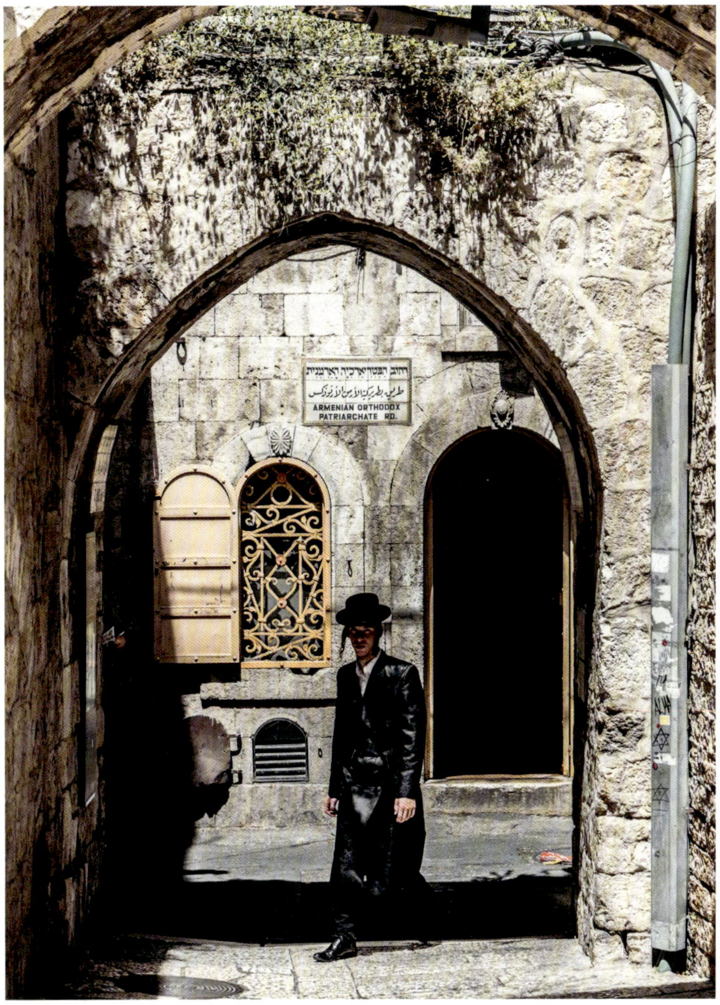

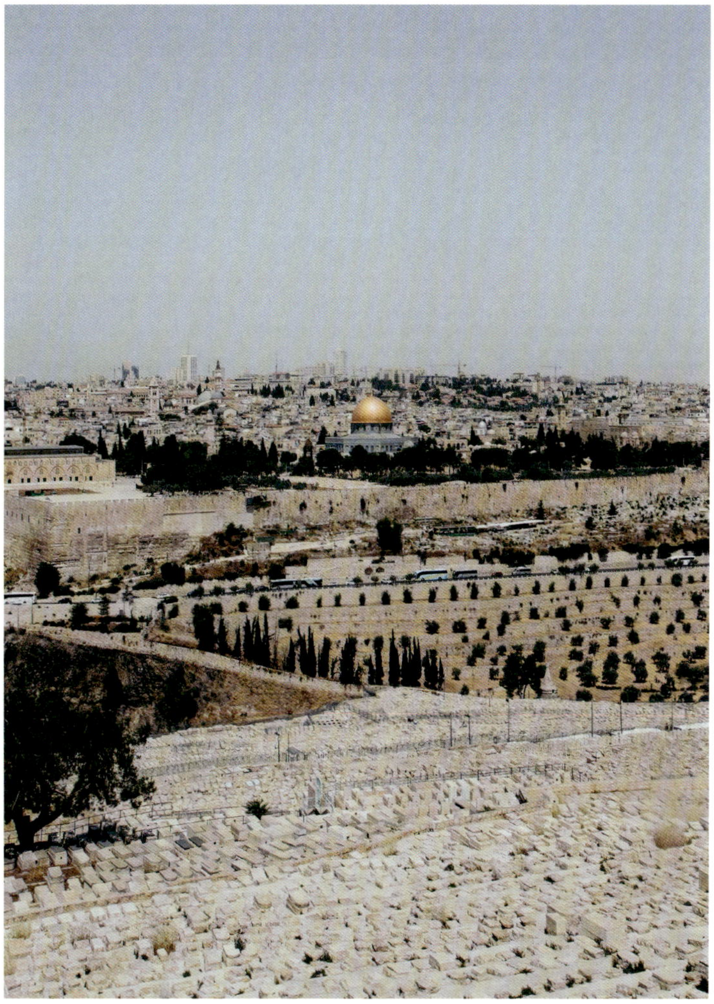
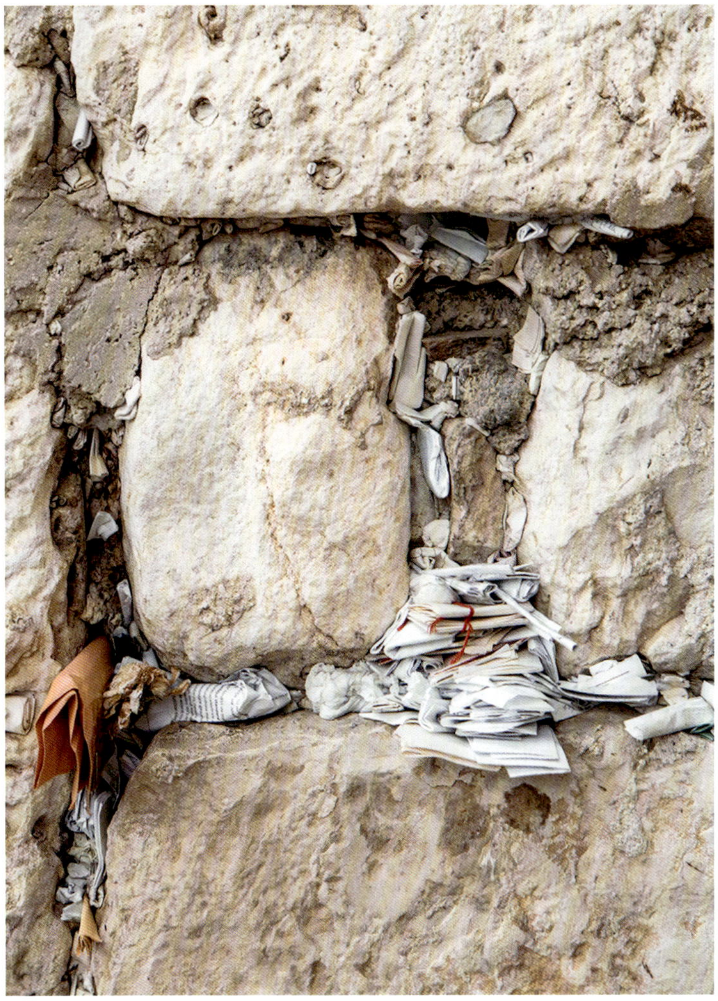
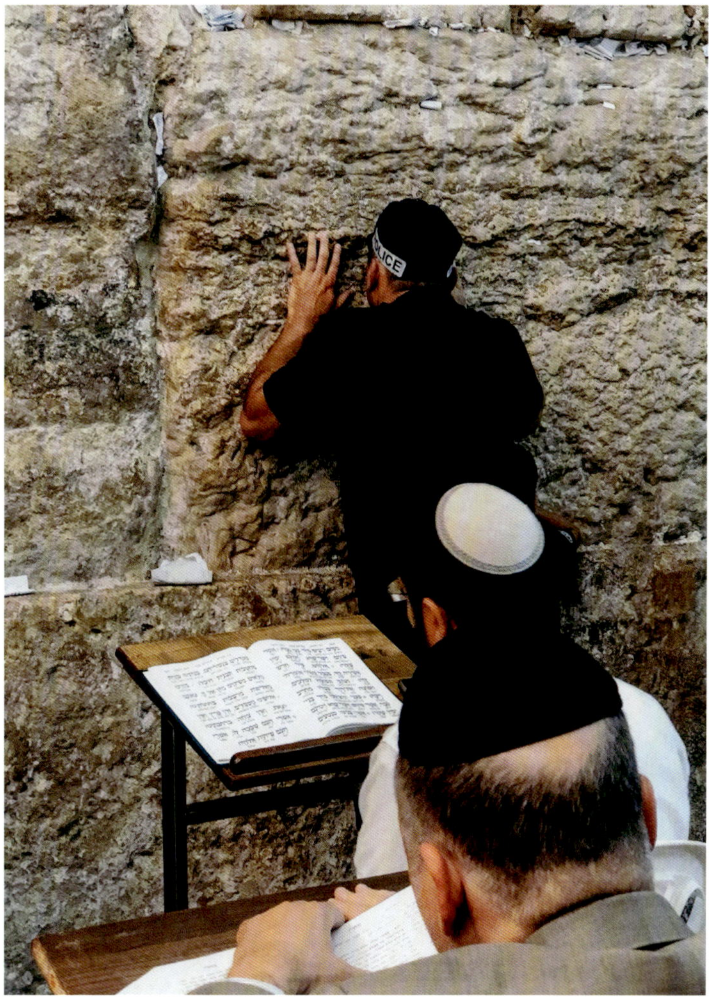

Opposite In these massive stone blocks live the memories of thousands of years.
Top left and right Jerusalem is considered the most important city in Judaism.
Bottom left Slips of paper are regularly buried on the Mount of Olives.
Bottom right Jews pray at the Western Wall, mourning the loss of the Second Temple.

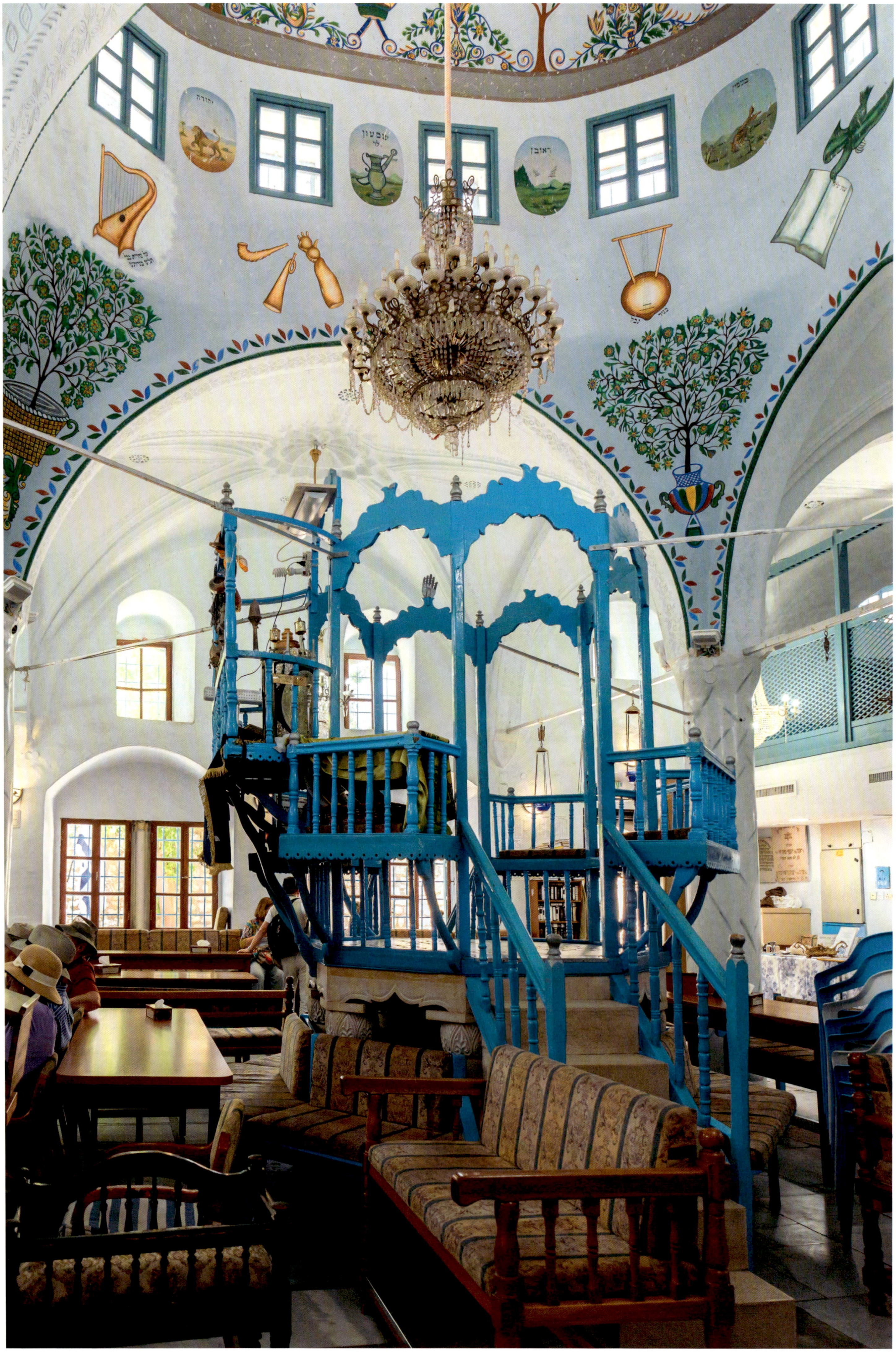

Abuhav Synagogue

Secrets of the Kabbalah

Built: 15th century CE, Safed, Israel

At the heart of Jewish mysticism, symbols narrate humanity's quest for the origins of creation.

Alongside Jerusalem, Tiberias, and Hebron, Safed ranks among the four holiest cities in Judaism. Nestled in the Galilee region of northern Israel, it is also a sacred center of Kabbalah, the Jewish mystical tradition. Among its most significant spiritual sites is the Abuhav Synagogue. Its entrance is tucked away in a labyrinth of ancient cobblestone alleys, their pale stones polished smooth by countless footsteps over the centuries.

Named for Rabbi Yitzhak Abuhav, a 14th-century Spanish Kabbalist, the synagogue's design adheres closely to Kabbalistic principles. As a mystical tradition, Kabbalah explores the mysteries of creation, the structure of the universe, and the relationship between humanity and the divine. The teachings of the Zohar, the central text of Kabbalah, have shaped religious practice in Safed and inspired the rich symbolism of the Abuhav Synagogue. Its arches and curves reflect the concept of cosmic balance. Within the sanctuary, four mighty pillars represent the letters of the divine Tetragrammaton YHWH, the sacred name of God. In Kabbalah, this name is considered the blueprint of creation and the key to divine revelation. Each of its four letters symbolizes an aspect of universal order: the concept of creation, its unfolding, the connection between the divine and material worlds, and the material world itself.

Every corner of the synagogue brims with symbolism, and the site reflects the Kabbalah's interest in numerology. Along the southern wall, three arks face toward Jerusalem. The central ark houses the synagogue's oldest and most revered Torah scroll, traditionally attributed to Rabbi Abuhav himself. This scroll is removed and read only three times a year—on Yom Kippur, Rosh Hashanah, and Shavuot. The synagogue's dome is adorned with four crowns: the crown of the Torah, the priesthood, kingship, and the crown of impending redemption—a reference to the Messianic expectation prevalent in 16th-century Safed—while the painted depictions of the 12 zodiac signs represent the 12 tribes of Israel. At the heart of the synagogue lies the blue *bima* (platform), featuring six steps representing the six weekdays and the spiritual preparation for the Sabbath. Its vibrant blue evokes the heavens, drawing the thoughts and prayers of worshippers toward God.

To this day, Safed remains an important destination for those seeking immersion in the mysteries of the Kabbalah. The doors of the Abuhav Synagogue stand open wide, offering a window into the enigma of creation and a place to ponder the questions in one's own heart.

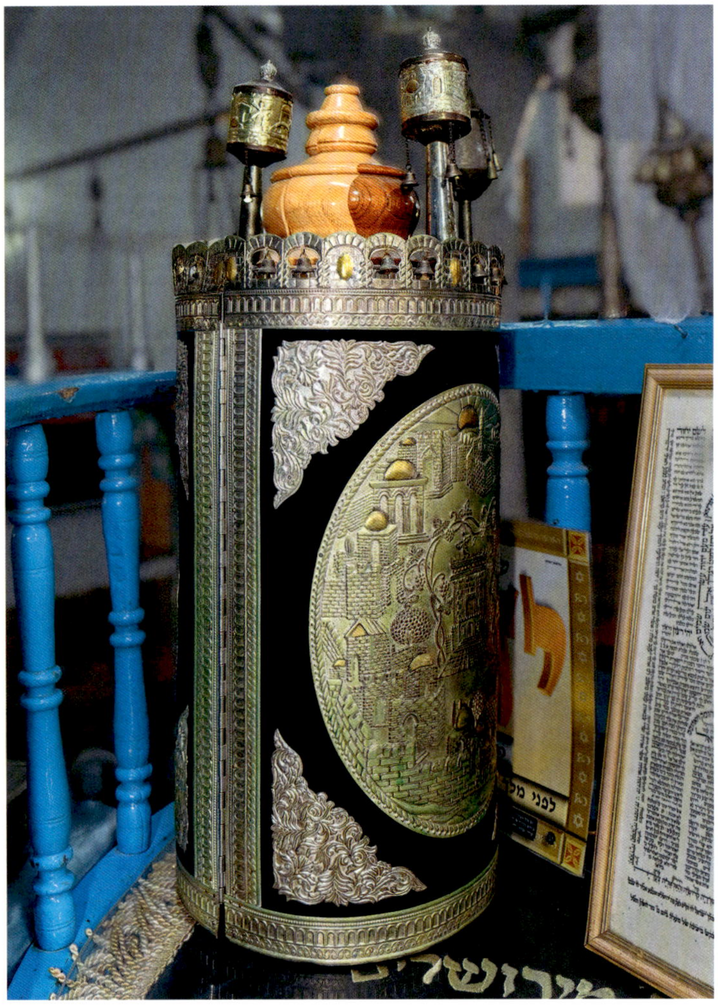

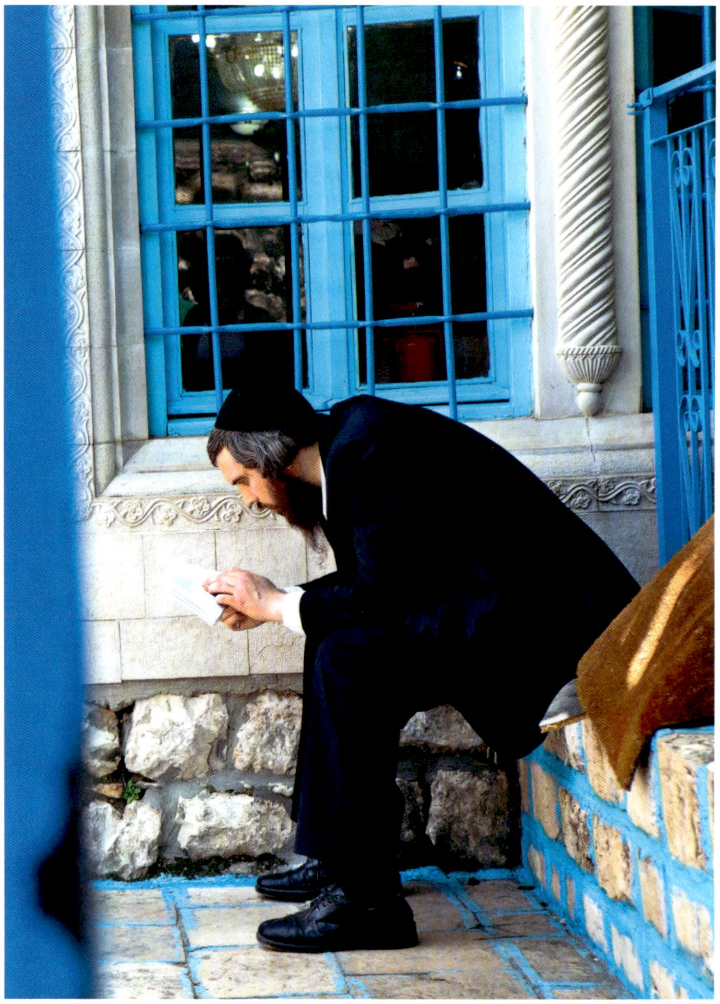

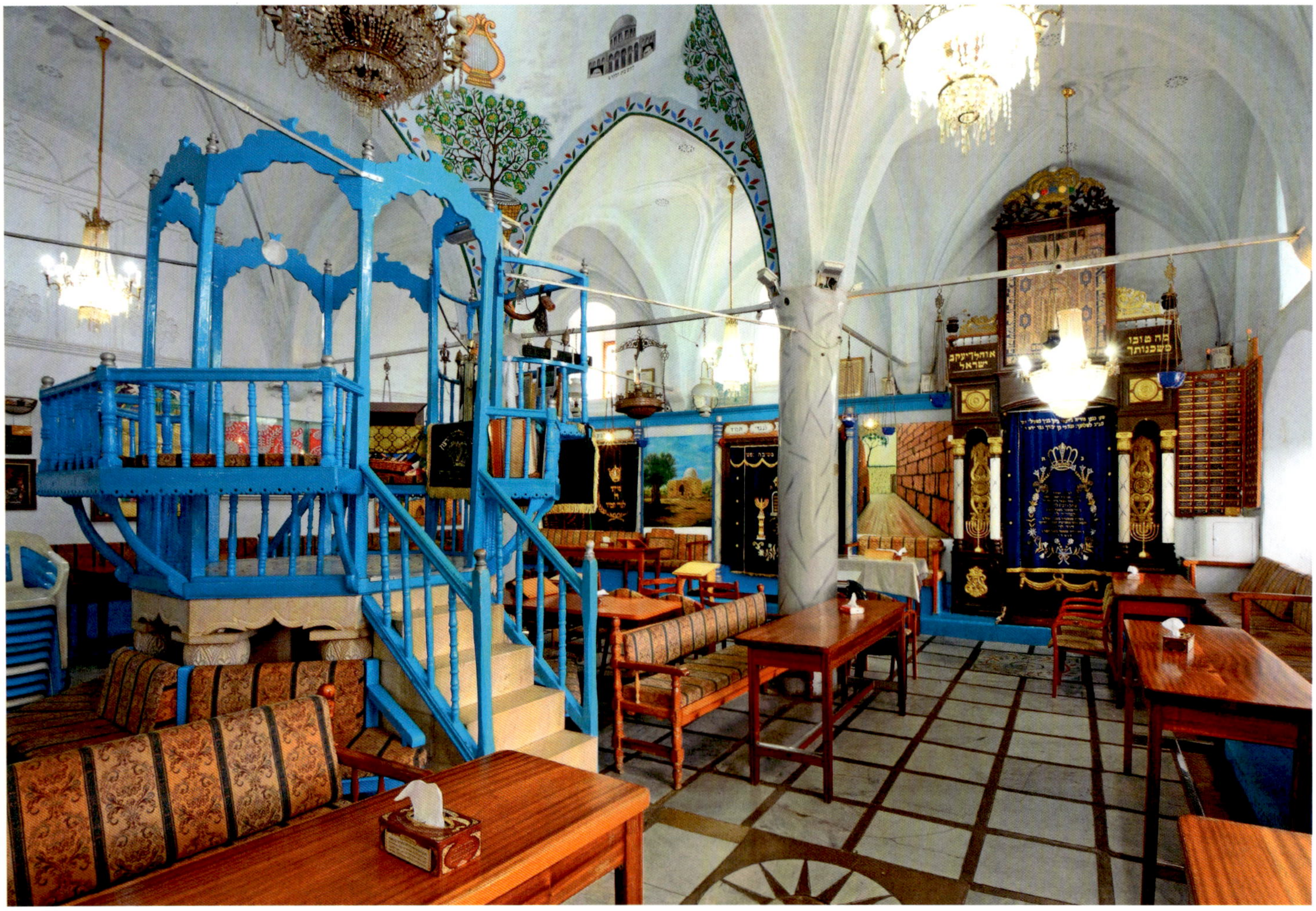

Top left The *aron ha-kodesh*, or Holy Ark, contains the Torah scrolls.
Top right The synagogue's characteristic blue extends into the outer area.
Bottom Kabbalistic symbolism infuses every corner of the Abuhav Synagogue.

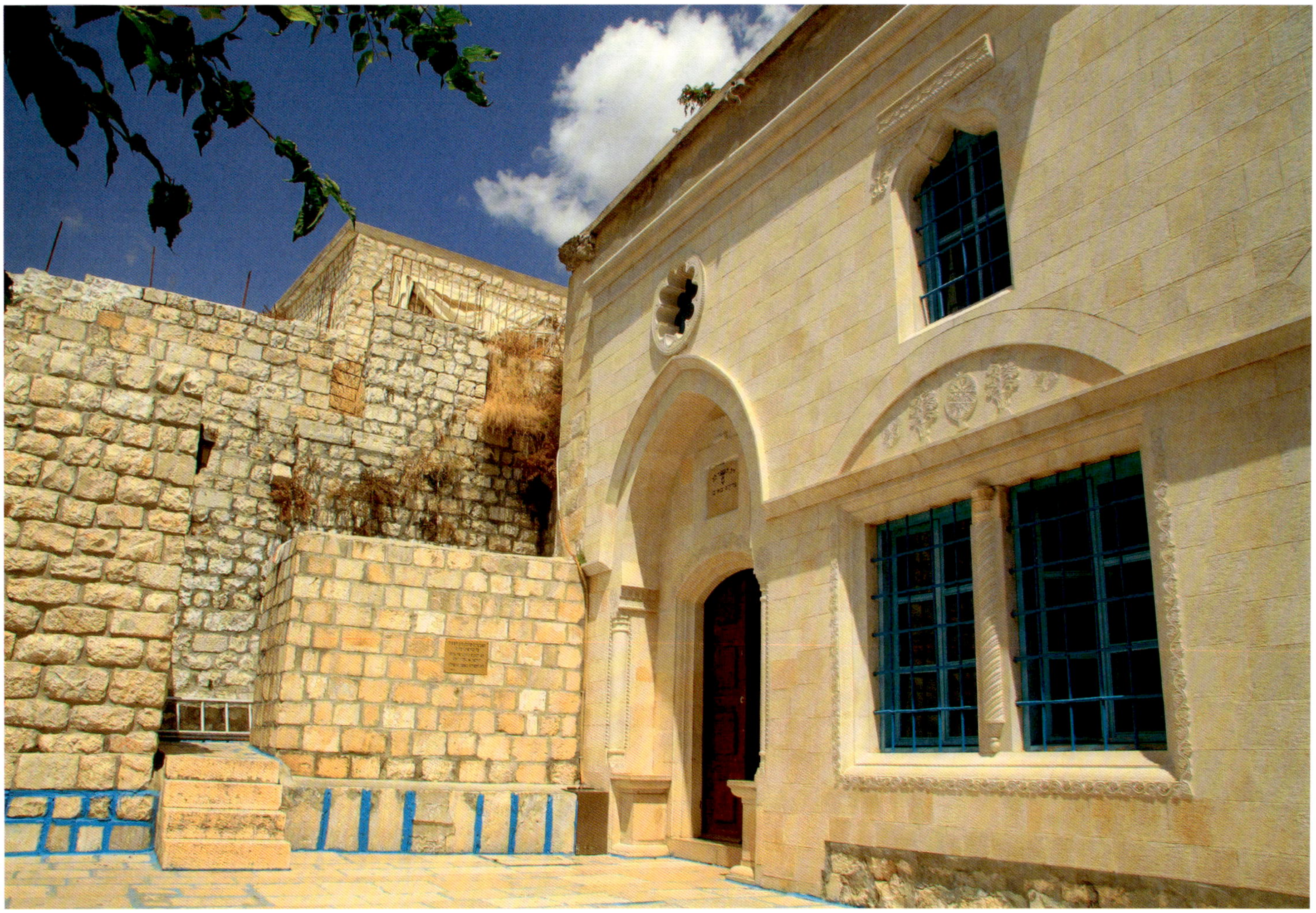

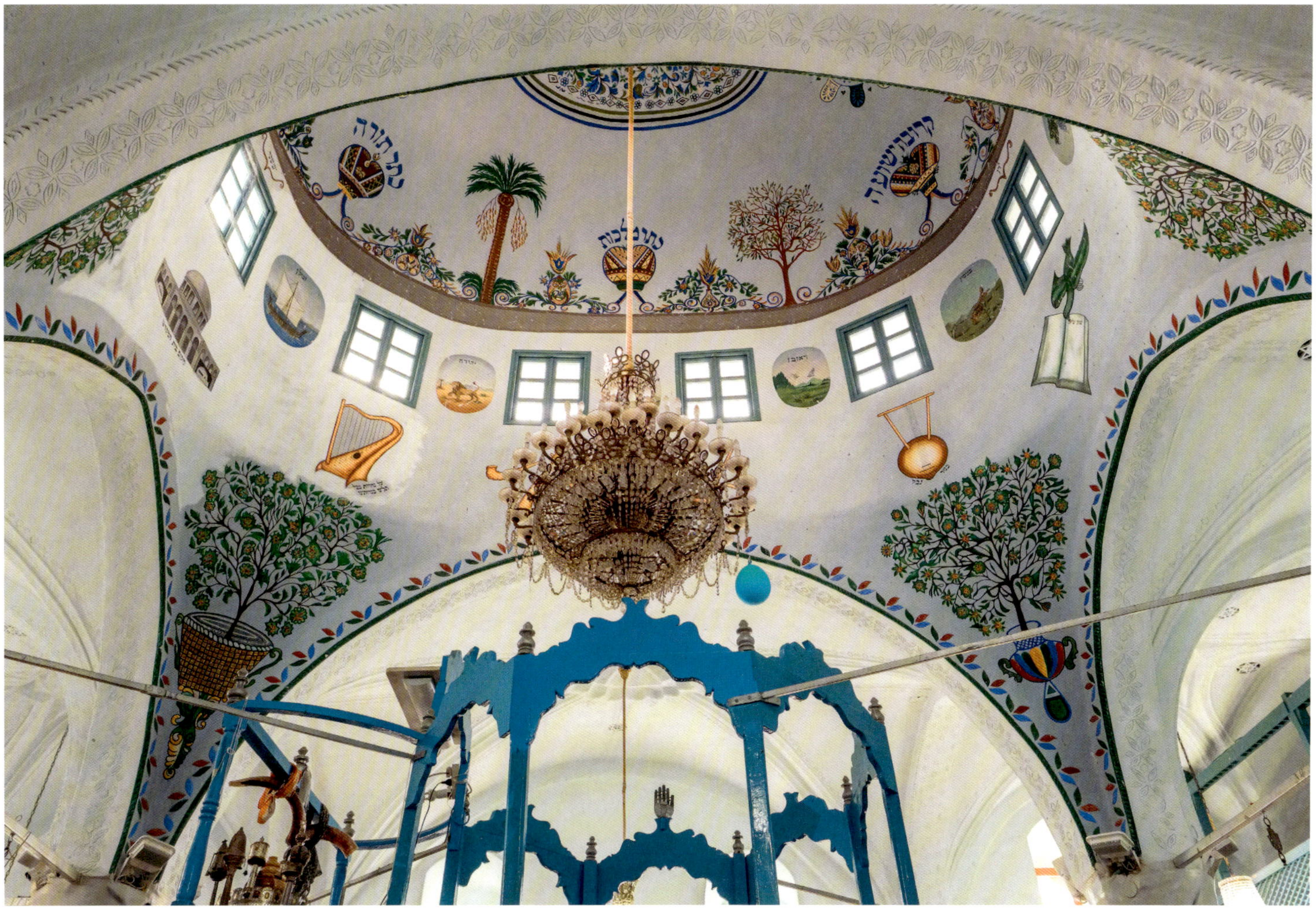

Top For followers of Kabbalah, Safed is one of the most spiritually significant places on earth.
Bottom The interior of the synagogue's dome is adorned with spiritual symbols.

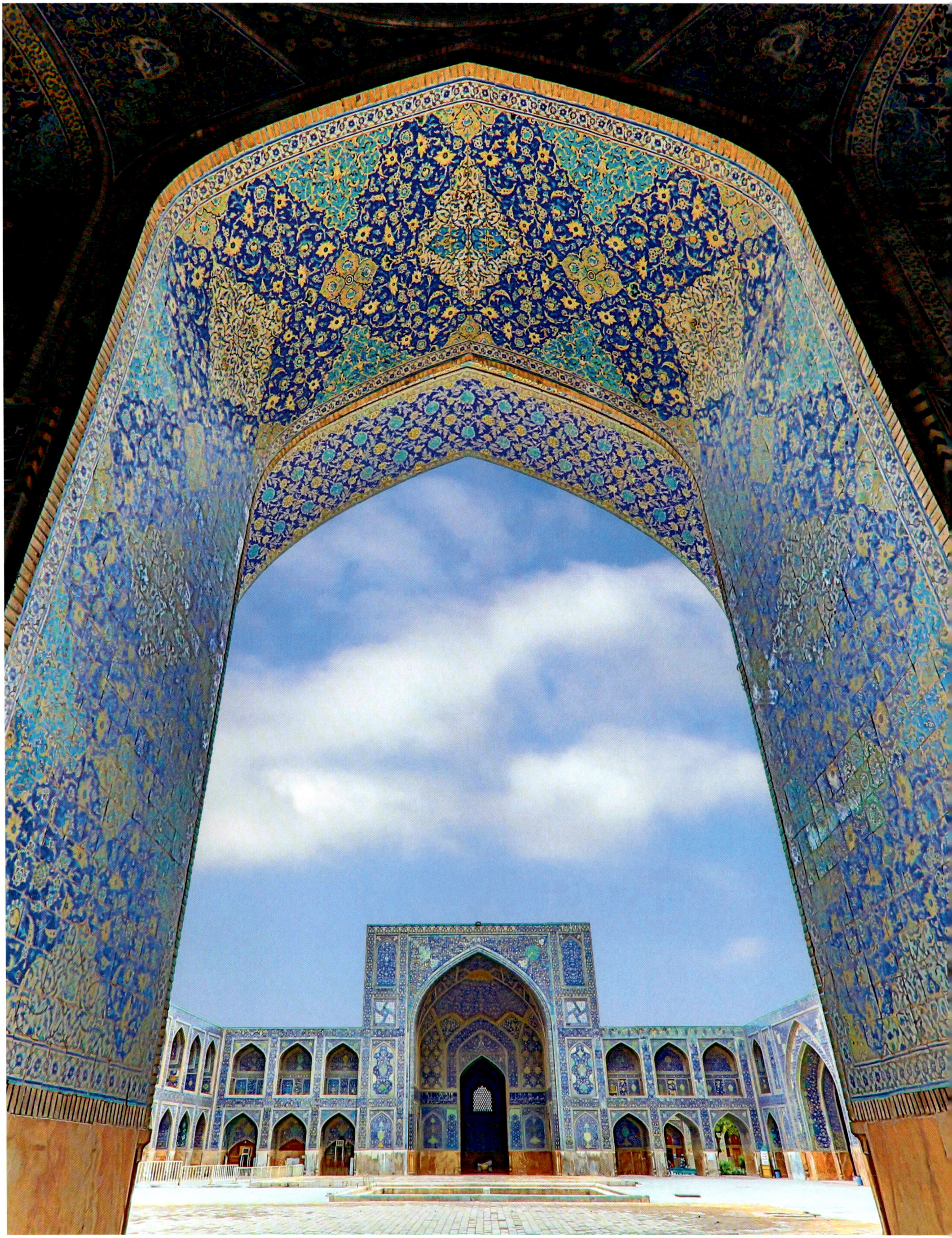

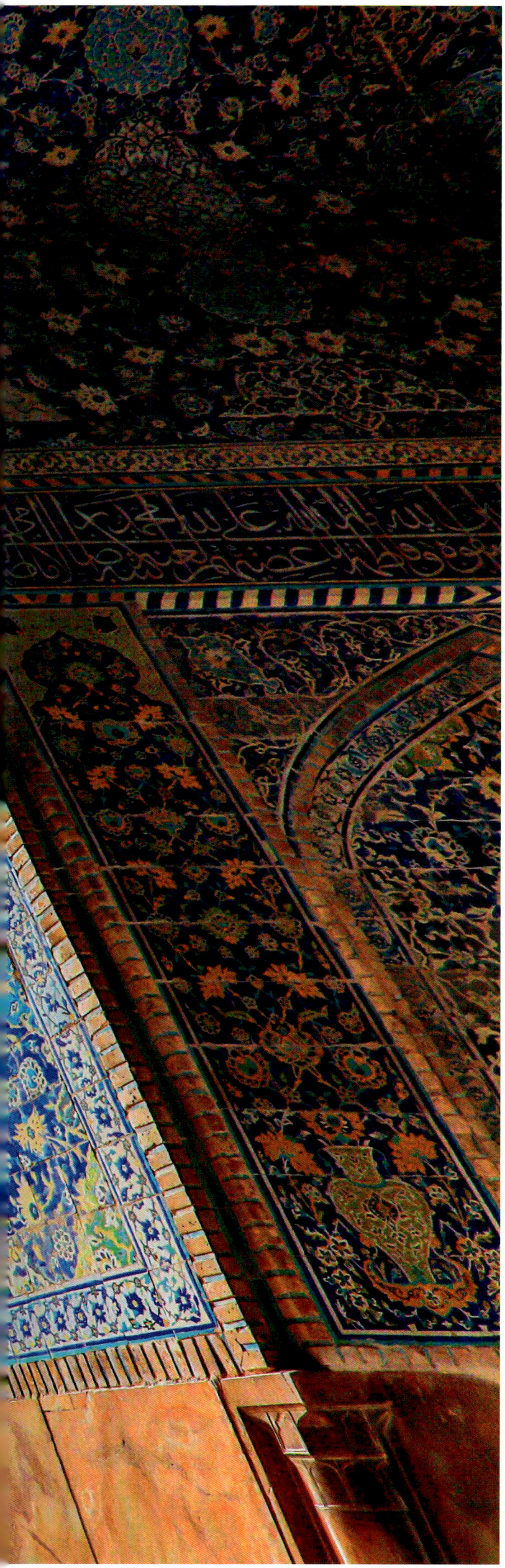

Shah Mosque

Turquoise for the Infinite Heavens

Built: 1611 – 1629 CE, Isfahan, Iran

The extraordinarily precise alignment of this mosque is a testament to the astronomical and mathematical expertise of its architects.

At the beginning of the 17th century, Safavid ruler Shah Abbas I was at the height of his power. His vision was to make his capital, Isfahan, spectacular and breathtaking, a city that would solidify Shia Islam—replacing the previously dominant Sunni Islam—as the religion of the people. To achieve this, he commissioned the construction of a magnificent mosque, designed to serve as the centerpiece of a new architectural ensemble at the heart of his royal city.

With the help of chief architect Shaykh Bahai, Abbas's vision was fulfilled. The Shah Mosque's 174-foot (53-meter) dome and its four triumphal minarets radiate in vibrant turquoise—a mystical color in Persian architecture, symbolic of a heavenly infinity. Inside, the mosque's vast and intricate tilework features geometric patterns, floral motifs, and calligraphic inscriptions that span its walls. Each tile was individually handcrafted, and it is said that the Safavids enlisted skilled artisans from across the Islamic world to create this masterpiece.

Visitors to the mosque are greeted by a monumental gateway, the *iwan*, flanked by two turquoise minarets. This grand portal, adorned with glazed tiles and gorgeous, maze-like calligraphy, leads to a vast courtyard. At its center lies a rectangular pool, reflecting the surrounding arcades and vibrant ornamentation. Here, worshippers pause for purification before prayer.

The path from Naqsh-e Jahan Square, which is oriented along a north-south axis, to the visually astounding main prayer hall, takes one through a gracefully curving corridor—an architectural marvel. To ensure that the mihrab, or prayer niche, and qibla (prayer wall) align with Mecca, the architects utilized their astronomical and mathematical expertise, building the majority of the prayer hall at a 45-degree angle. Seamlessly, the corridor guides visitors toward the correct orientation for prayer, harmonizing the geometry of the square with the mosque's spiritual axis.

Beyond its visual splendor, the Shah Mosque is renowned for its remarkable acoustics. The dome is a particularly resonant structure, allowing worshippers to hear the Imam's sermon (*khutbah*) without amplification. As holy verses from the Quran resonate within its walls, one might hear the recitation of Surah At-Tawba (9:18), which has inspired countless mosque builders and architects throughout Islamic history: "The mosques of Allah are only to be maintained by those who believe in Allah and the Last Day, establish prayer, give zakat, and fear none but Allah. It is they who are expected to be upon guidance."

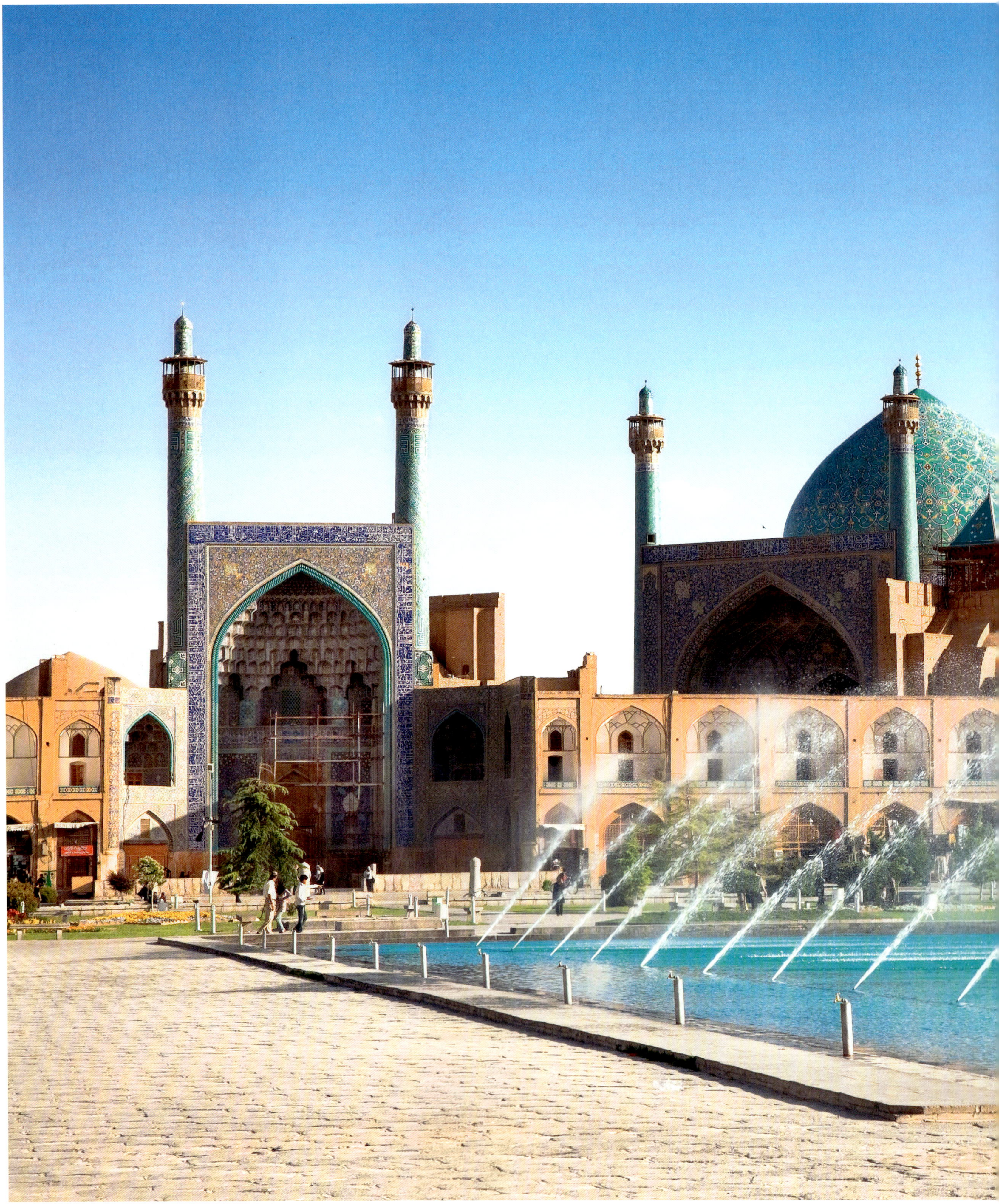

Above Is the water in the fountain turquoise because the mosque's dome is reflected in it? Regardless, in Islam, water is considered a precious gift from Allah.

Isfahan, Iran

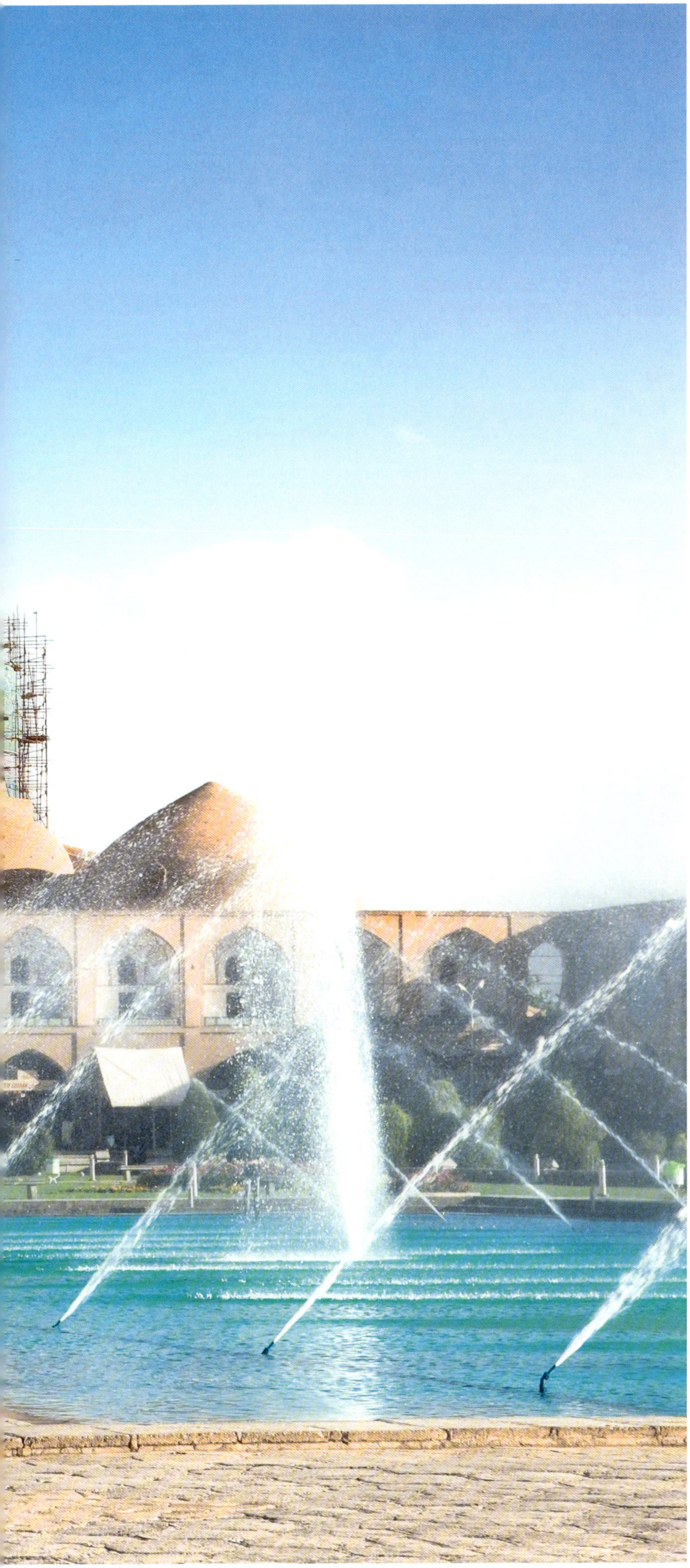

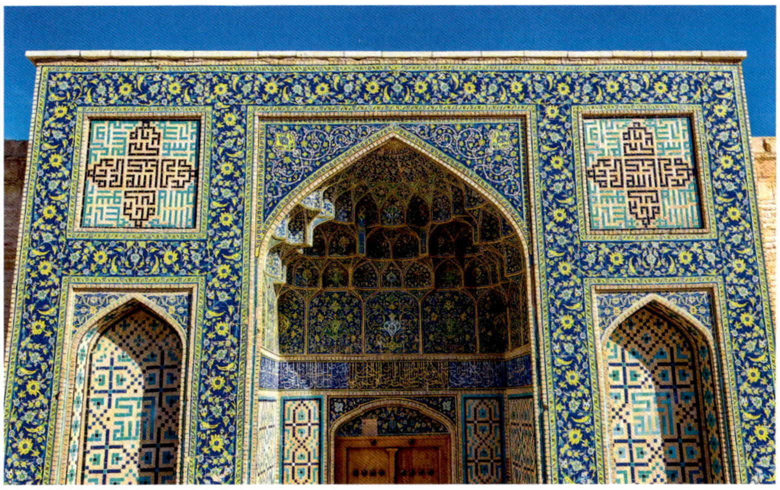

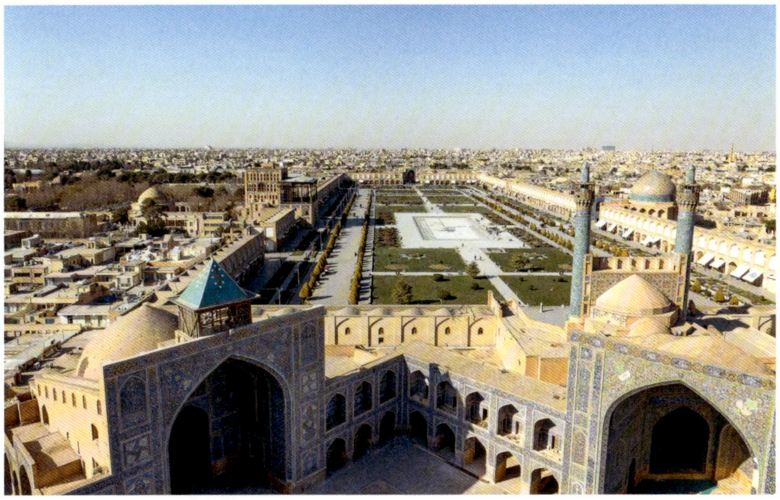

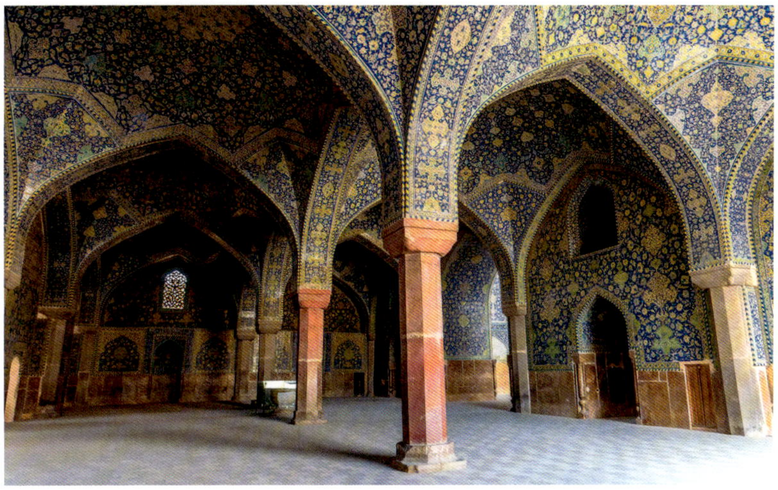

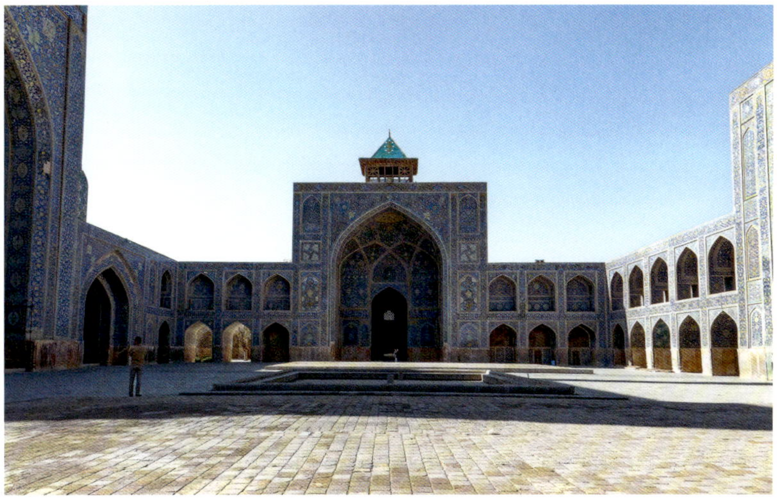

Top Intricate tile mosaics feature floral and geometric patterns.
Upper middle The mosque rises 170 feet (52 meters) above Naqsh-e Jahan Square.
Lower middle The full grandeur of the mosque unfolds inside.
Bottom Classical Islamic architecture defines the entire complex.

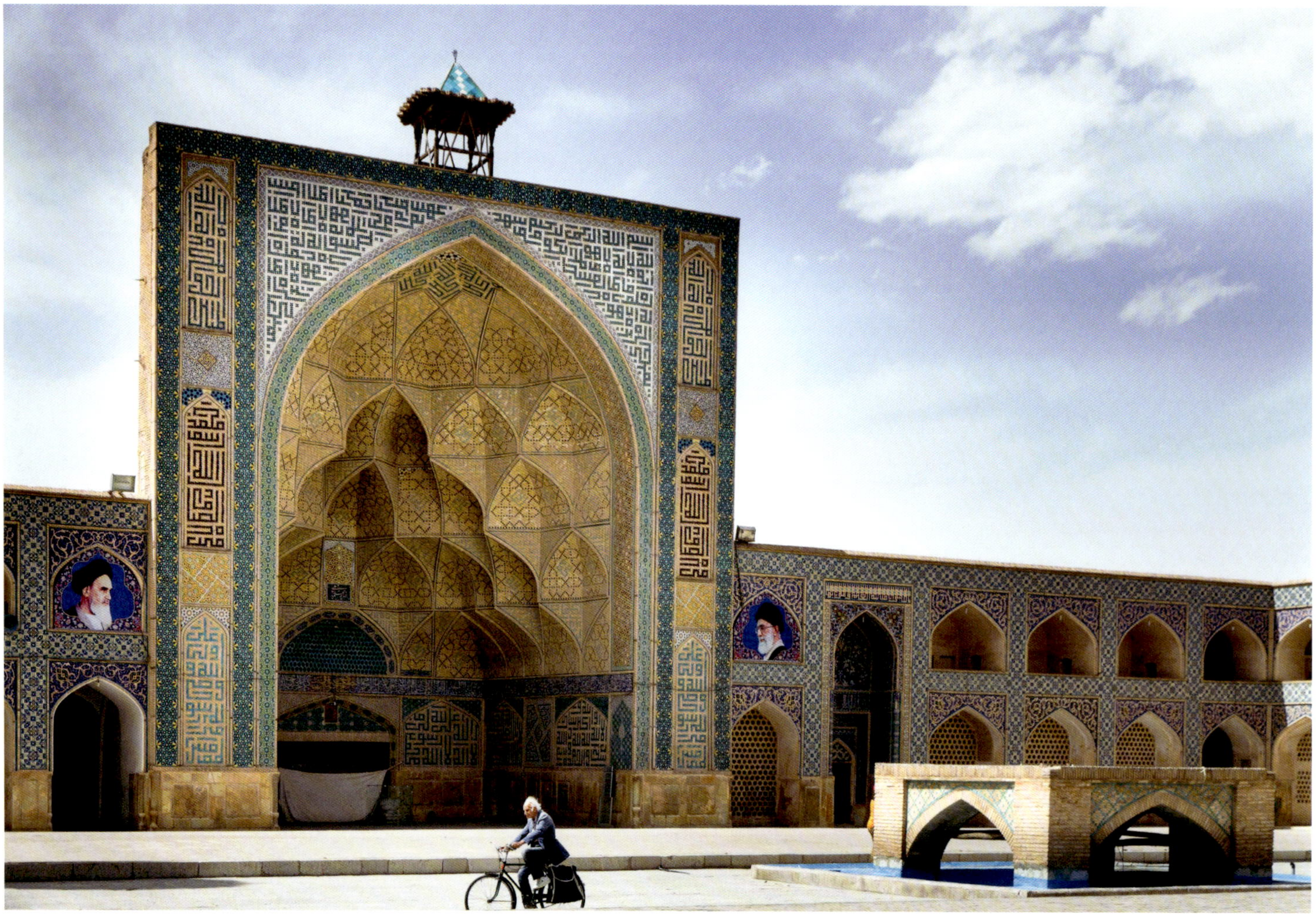

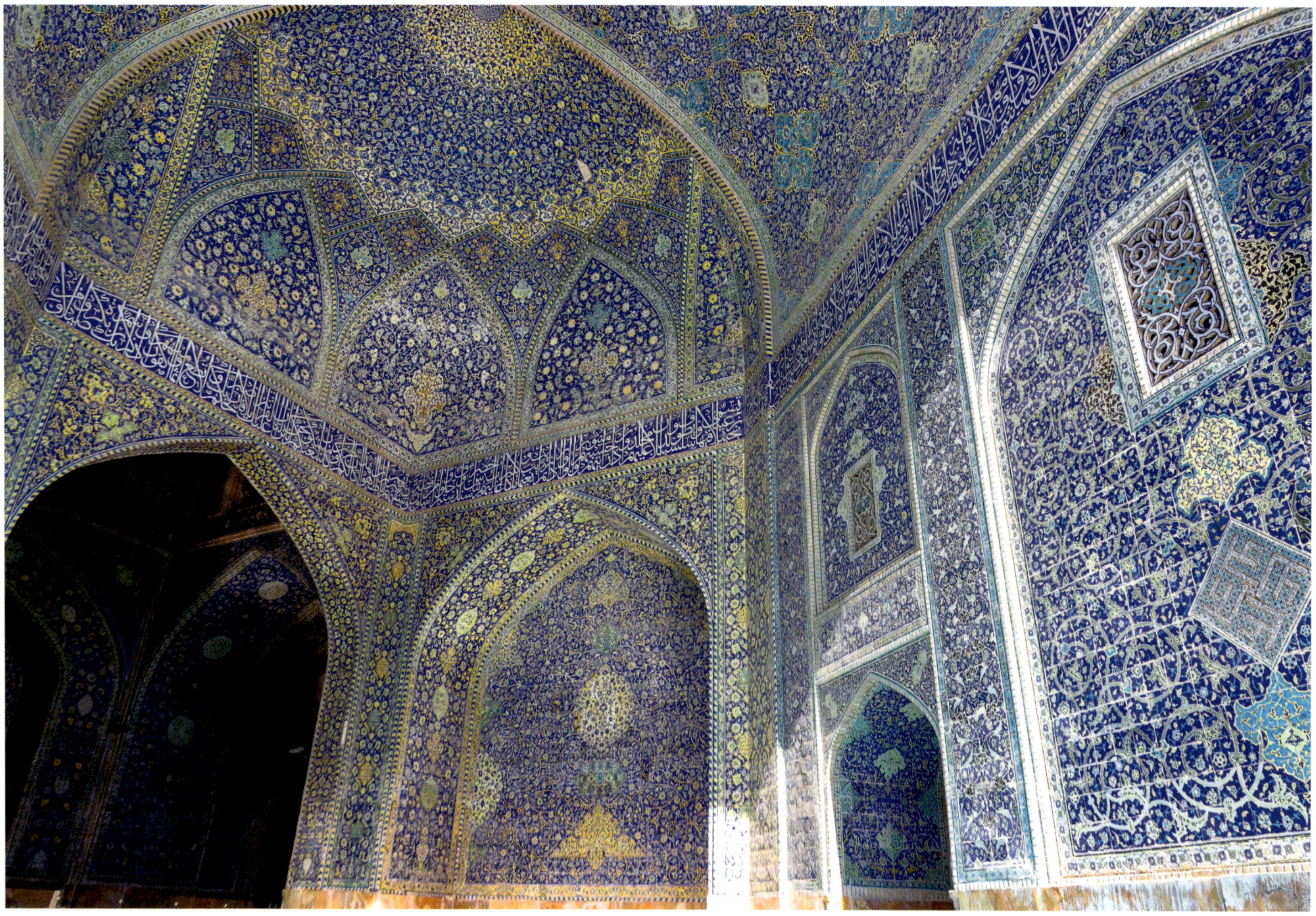

Top The *iwan* gateways outshine each other in their splendor.
Bottom Glazed tiles cover the mosque's surfaces.
Opposite Wondrous surprises are hidden in the courtyards, such as this golden tree.

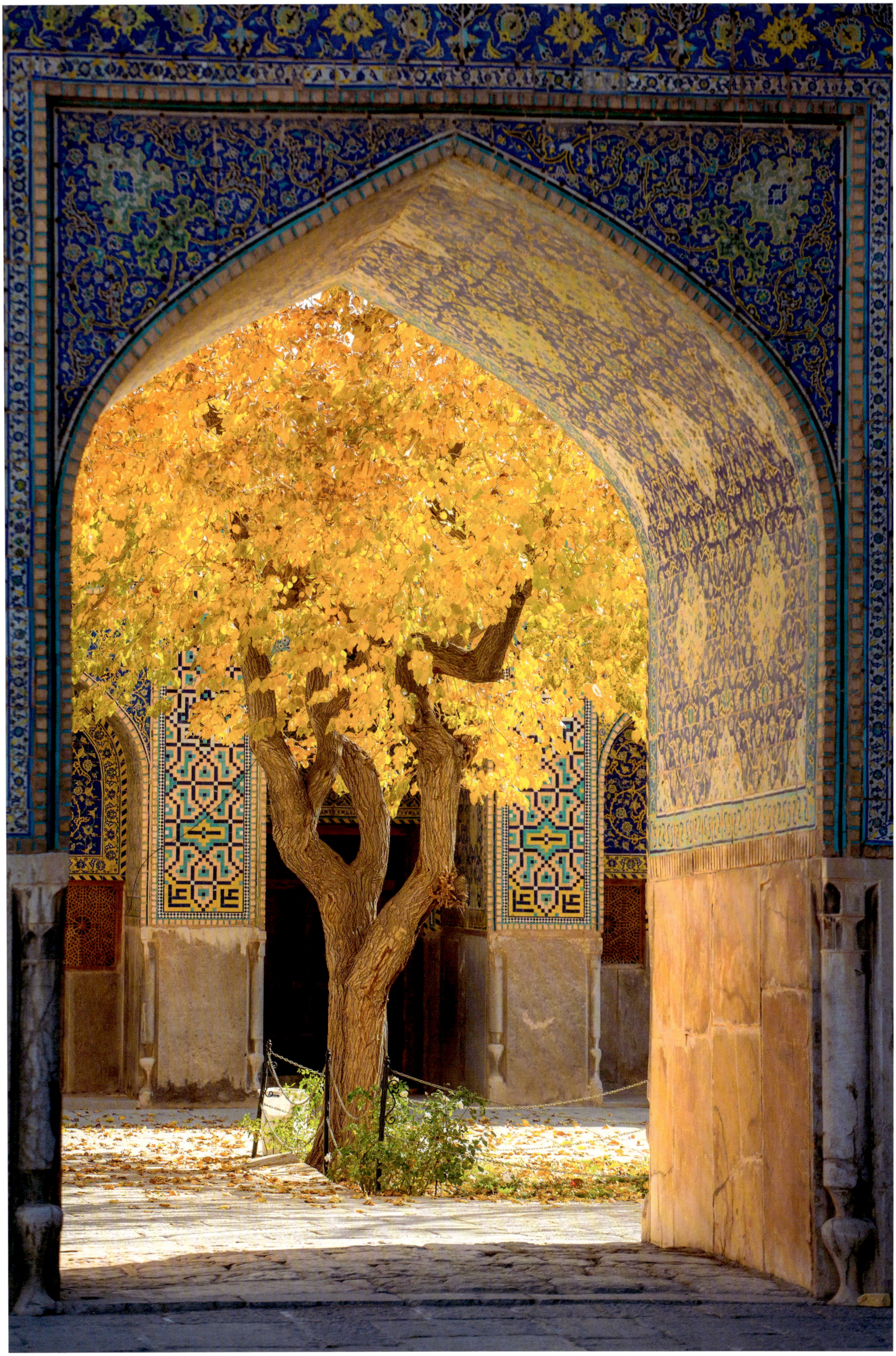

Rock Tombs of Naqsh-e Rostam

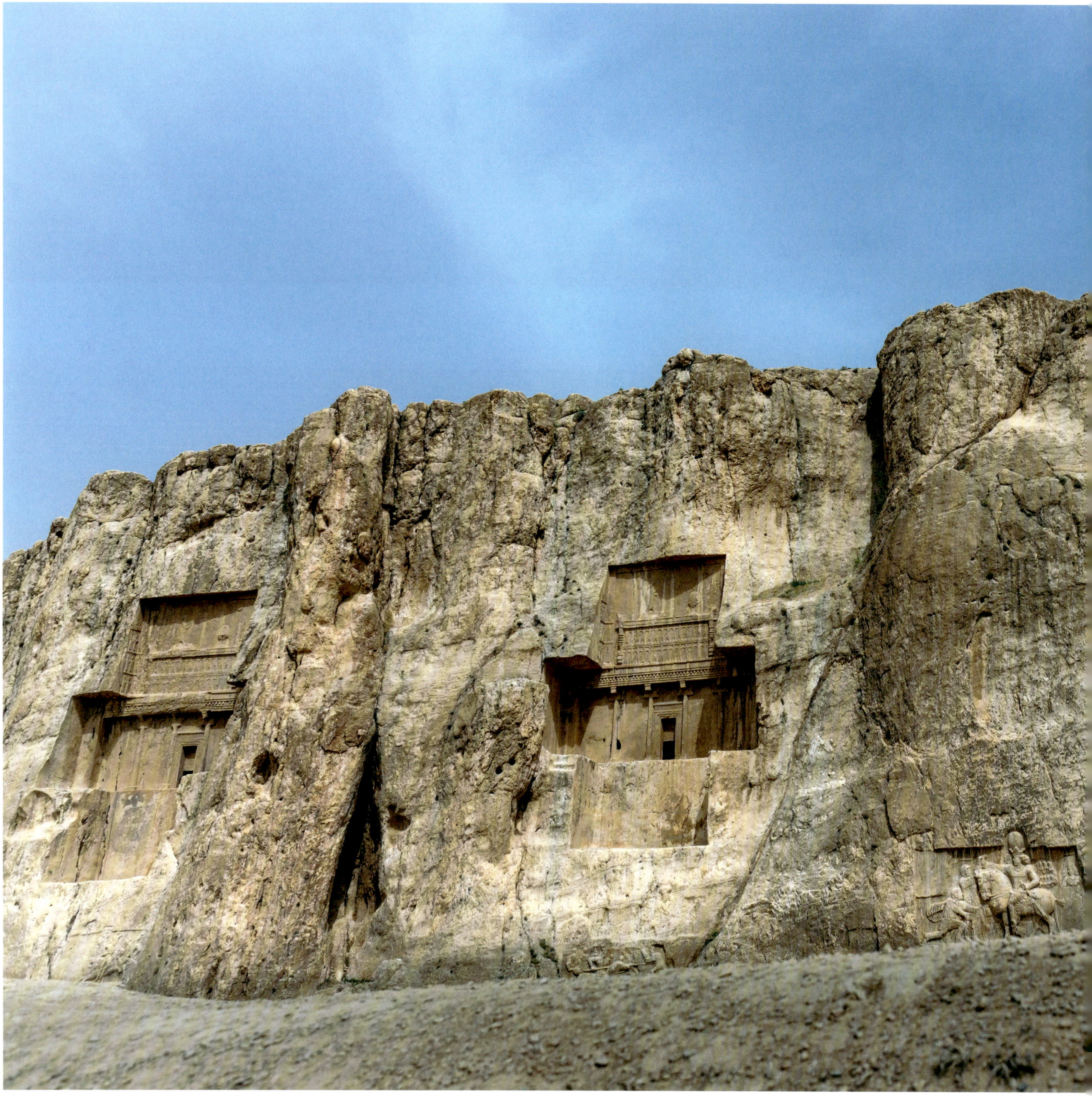

Built: ca. 490 – 404 BCE,
Marvdasht, Iran

The four kings buried here were revered as earthly representatives of Ahura Mazda, the Zoroastrian creator god.

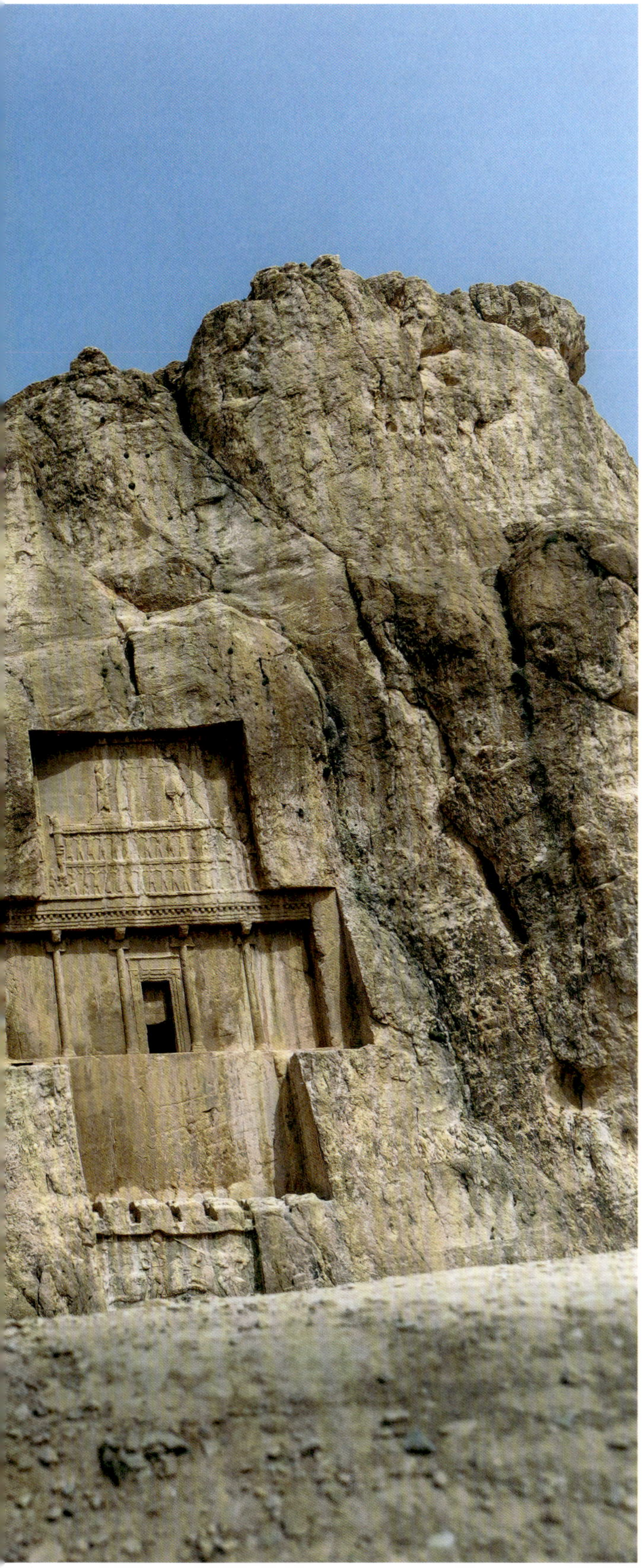

Four monumental rock tombs, carved cross-shaped into the sheer cliffs of the Kuh-e Rahmat ("Mountain of Mercy"), dominate the landscape of Naqsh-e Rostam. Here, surrounded by mountains and the deserts of southern Iran, lie the resting places of four of ancient Persia's most powerful rulers: Darius I, Xerxes I, Artaxerxes I, and Darius II. Exquisite reliefs above the entrances to the burial chambers depict these rulers, immortalized in stone alongside Ahura Mazda, the "Wise Lord" and chief deity of Zoroastrianism.

This religion, one of the world's oldest monotheistic faiths, is rooted in the teachings of the Persian philosopher Zarathustra, who is believed, depending on the source, to have lived sometime between 1500 and 500 BCE. In an age dominated by polytheistic traditions, Zarathustra proclaimed a revolutionary message: Ahura Mazda as the supreme god, the creator of the universe, the source of all that is good, and the embodiment of truth, wisdom, and light. Spenta Mainyu, the Good Spirit, and his adversary Angra Mainyu, the Evil Spirit, were locked in a cosmic struggle. At the center of this conflict stood humanity, endowed with free will and tasked with choosing good to uphold *asha*, the divine order. The tenets of Zoroastrianism are clearly outlined to guide the faithful: nurture good thoughts (*humata*), speak good words (*hukhta*), and perform good deeds (*huvarshta*).

Protecting *asha*—which also translates to "divine will"—was also the duty of the kings. This helped preserve the connection between the divine and mortal realms, much like the deeply revered element of fire. Every Zoroastrian fire temple contains an eternal flame, which must never be extinguished. The Ka'ba-ye Zartosht, a rectangular stone structure located below the tombs at Naqsh-e Rostam, may once have been such a fire temple. Its precise function, however, remains a subject of scholarly debate.

What is certain is that the majestic rock tombs of the Achaemenid kings at Naqsh-e Rostam were created during the first golden age of Zoroastrianism. The religion reached its zenith during the Sassanid era (224 – 651 CE), when it became a state religion. Islam began displacing it in the mid-7th century, yet Zoroastrianism did not vanish entirely. Today, Iran is home to approximately 30,000 practicing Zoroastrians. The world's largest Zoroastrian community now resides in India, descendants of those who fled persecution in Iran during the 8th and 9th centuries. Additionally, small diaspora communities exist in the United States, Canada, Australia, and Europe, continuing the long history of this faith based in good thoughts, good words, and good deeds.

Exquisite reliefs above the entrances to the tomb chambers depict these rulers, immortalized in stone alongside Ahura Mazda, the chief deity of Zoroastrianism.

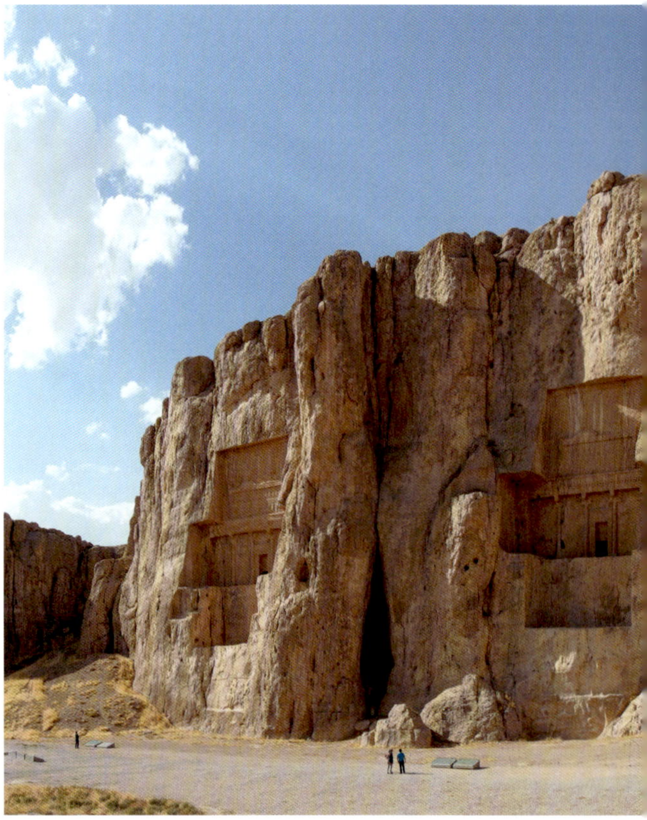

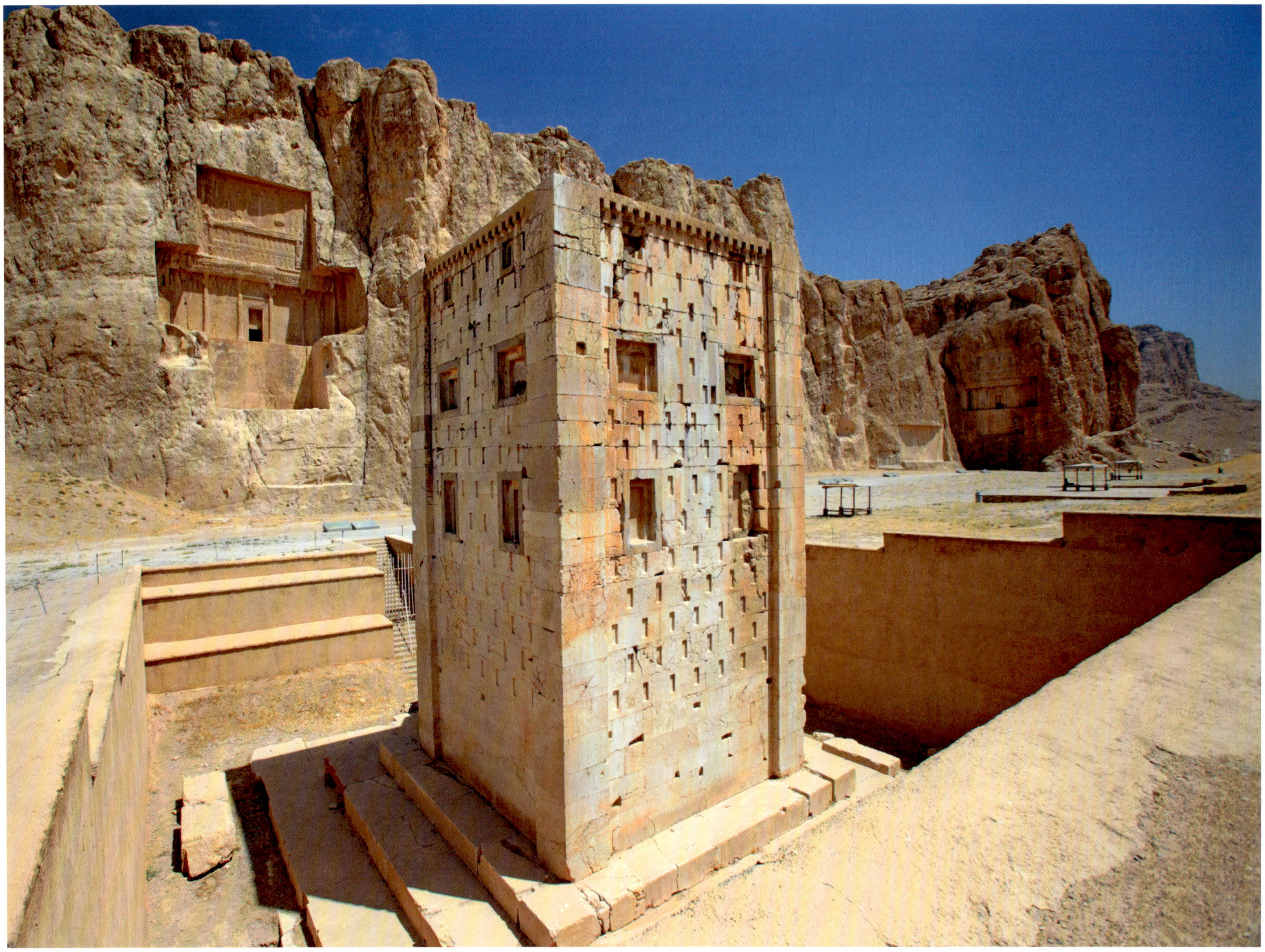

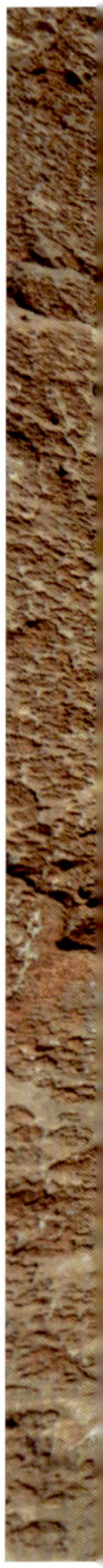

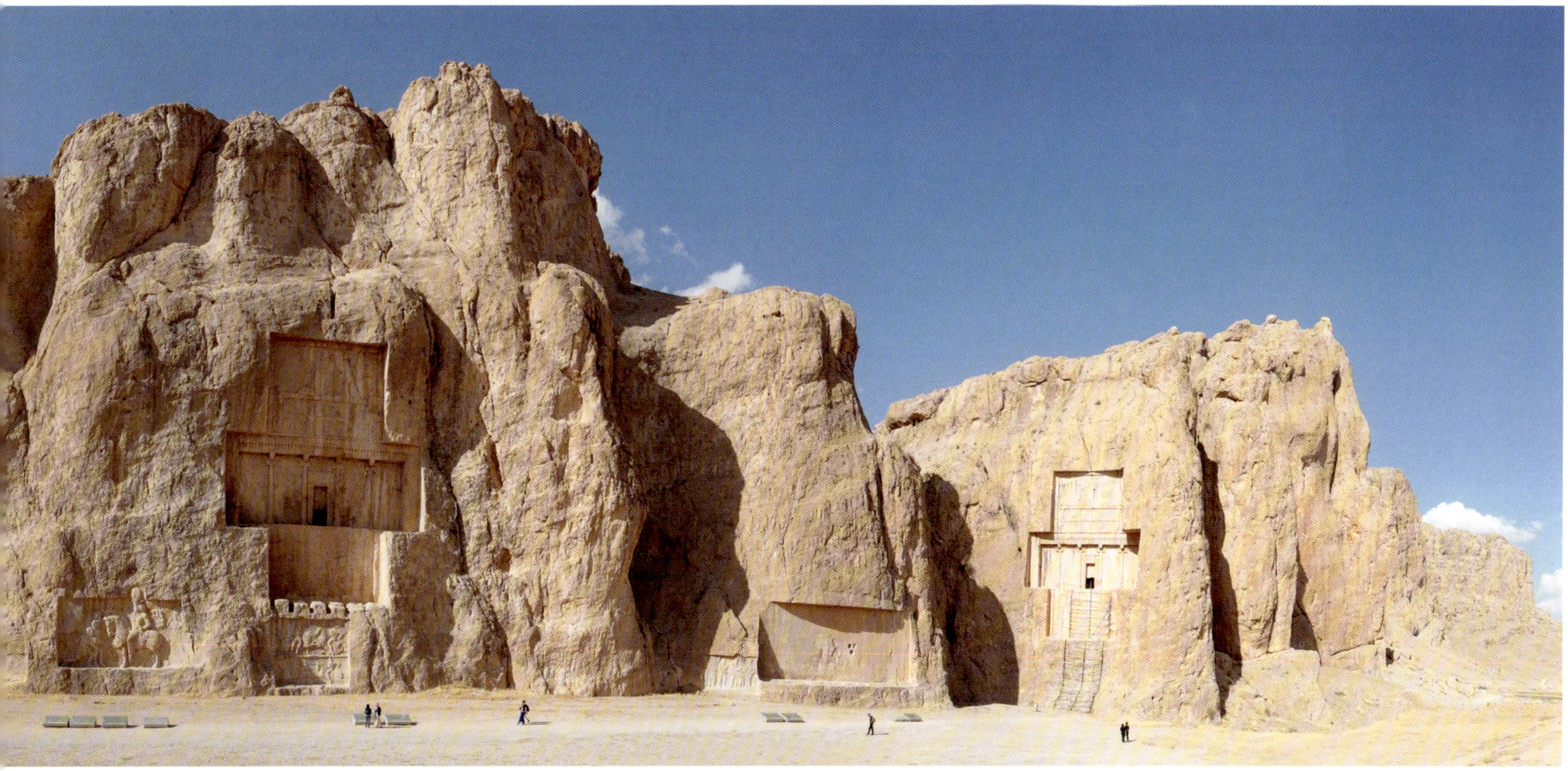

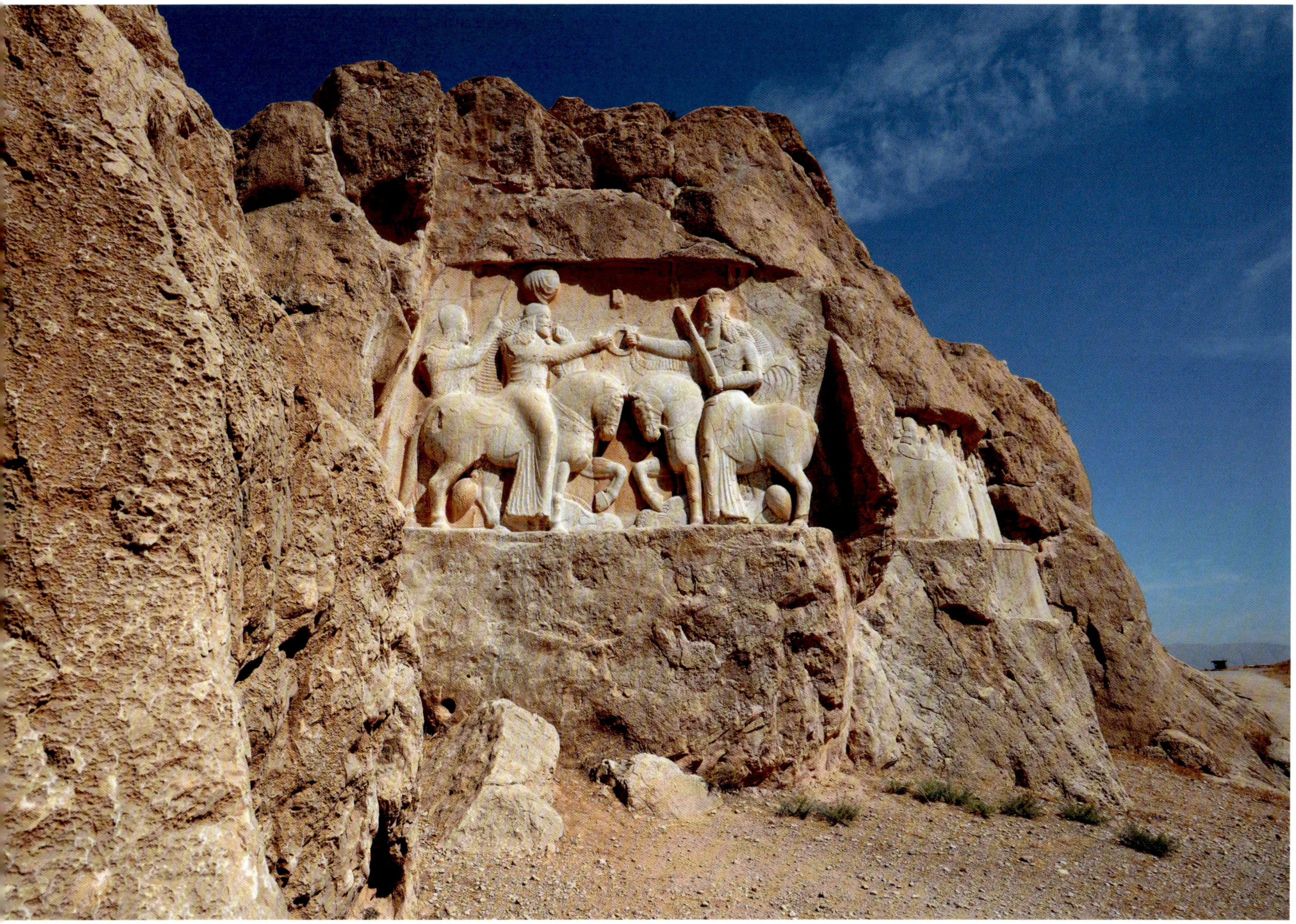

Top The kings buried here were tasked with guarding the divine order.
Left The Ka'ba-ye Zartosht is believed to have once acted as a sacred fire temple.
Right Majestic reliefs beautifully recount the grandeur of ancient Persia.

INDEX

ASIA
Imaginechina Limited / Alamy Stock Photo (p. 9)

Angkor Wat
imageBROKER.com GmbH & Co. KG / Alamy Stock Photo (p. 10), David Wall / Alamy Stock Photo (p. 12 top), hanohikirf / Alamy Stock Photo (p. 12 middle), Selena Daphne Taylor / selenadaphne.com (p. 12 bottom), LE PICTORIUM / Alamy Stock Photo (p. 13), mauritius images / ADS / Alamy Stock Photo (p. 14), mauritius images / Toby Adamson / Alamy Stock Photo (p. 15 top), Rob Arnold / Alamy Stock Photo (p. 15 middle), Jon Arnold Images Ltd / Alamy Stock Photo (p. 15 bottom)

Harmandir Sahib
Dan Glindemann / Getty Images (p. 16), Tuul & Bruno Morandi / Getty Images (p. 18), f9photos / Getty Images (p. 19)

Meenakshi Temple
mauritius images / Michele Falzone / Alamy Stock Photo (p. 20), IndiaPicture / Alamy Stock Photo (p. 21), Dmitry Rukhlenko – Photos of India / Alamy Stock Photo (p. 22 top), Prisma by Dukas Presseagentur GmbH / Alamy Stock Photo (p. 22 bottom), mauritius images / David South / Alamy Stock Photo (p. 23)

Fushimi Inari Shrine
Yanis Ourabah / Getty Images (p. 24), Kwanchai Khammuean / Kontributor / Getty Images (p. 26 top), Atlantide Phototravel / Getty Images (p. 26 middle), Simonlong / Getty Images (p. 26 bottom), Pavel Tochinsky / Getty Images (p. 27), mauritius images / Mirko Kuzmanovic / Alamy Stock Photo (pp. 28 – 29)

Seiganto-ji
David BERTHO / Alamy Stock Photo (p. 30), mauritius images / HSUEH-YI CHEN / Alamy Stock Photo (p. 32 top, lower middle), mauritius images / Mirko Kuzmanovic / Alamy Stock Photo (p. 32 upper middle), mauritius images / Little valleys / Alamy Stock Photo (p. 32 bottom), mauritius images / coward_lion / Alamy Stock Photo (pp. 33, 35 top), mauritius images / Pierrick Lemaret / Alamy Stock Photo (p. 34), mauritius images / Cristi Croitoru / Alamy Stock Photo (p. 35 bottom left), mauritius images / Zoonar GmbH / Alamy Stock Photo (p. 35 bottom right)

Kinkaku-ji
Planet One Images / Kontributor / Getty Images (p. 36), photography by Maico Presente / Getty Images (p. 38), Chiara Salvadori / Getty Images (p. 39 top), Wolfgang Kaehler / Kontributor / Getty Images (p. 39 bottom)

Hanging Temple of Hengshan
Imaginechina Limited / Alamy Stock Photo (p. 40), Andrew Marriott / Getty Images (p. 42), Tatiana Kashko / Getty Images (p. 43 top), Heckepics / Getty Images (pp. 43 bottom, 44 – 45)

Temple Complex on Mount Laojun
Imaginechina Limited / Alamy Stock Photo (pp. 46 – 49)

Red Clouds Golden Summit
Fabio Nodari / fabionodariphoto.com (pp. 51, 53), Ian.CuiYi / Getty Images (p. 52), Imaginechina Limited / Alamy Stock Photo (pp. 54 – 55)

Tiger's Nest
RooM the Agency / Alamy Stock Photo (p. 56), mauritius images / Christian Offenberg / Alamy Stock Photo (p. 57), mauritius images / Graham Prentice / Alamy Stock Photo (p. 58), mauritius images / Peter Adams Photography / Alamy Stock Photo (p. 59 top), Cindy Hopkins / Alamy Stock Photo (p. 59 bottom), mauritius images / Michael Rooney / Alamy Stock Photo (pp. 60 – 61)

Seokguram Grotto
mauritius images / Keitma / Alamy Stock Photo (p. 62), Klepo / Alamy Stock Photo (p. 64), Tuul and Bruno Morandi / Alamy Stock Photo (p. 65 top), Jon Arnold Images Ltd / Alamy Stock Photo (p. 65 upper middle), mauritius images / Natmac Stock / Alamy Stock Photo (p. 65 lower middle), mauritius images / Jasper van Zandbeek / Alamy Stock Photo (p. 65 bottom), mauritius images / Mei Choo Teo / Alamy Stock Photo (p. 66), Imaginechina Limited / Alamy Stock Photo (p. 67 top), mauritius images / Joshua Davenport / Alamy Stock Photo (p. 67 bottom)

Borobudur
mauritius images / robertharding / Alamy Stock Photo (p. 68), mauritius images / Ivan Vdovin / Alamy Stock Photo (pp. 70 top, 71), mauritius images / Tibor Bognar / Alamy Stock Photo (p. 70 upper middle), Jorge Fernandez / Alamy Stock Photo (p. 70 lower middle), mauritius images / Erik Seket / Alamy Stock Photo (p. 70 bottom), mauritius images / Pakorn Lopattanakij / Alamy Stock Photo (p. 72), mauritius images / Paul Kemp / Alamy Stock Photo (p. 73 top), mauritius images / Dima Fadeev / Alamy Stock Photo (p. 73 bottom)

Temples of Bagan
Lkunl / Getty Images (p. 74), mauritius images / Danita Delimont Creative / Alamy Stock Photo (p. 76),

mauritius images / M@rcel / Alamy Stock Photo (p. 77 top), Ian.CuiYi / Getty Images (p. 77 bottom), pavelp / Getty Images (p. 78 top), Snoofek / Getty Images (p. 78 bottom), Don Mammoser / Alamy Stock Photo (p. 79)

Shah-i-Zinda
mauritius images / travel4pictures / Alamy Stock Photo (pp. 81, 84, 85 bottom), mauritius images / Robert Preston Photography / Alamy Stock Photo (p. 82), Tuul and Bruno Morandi / Alamy Stock Photo (pp. 83 top, 85 top, 85 lower middle), mauritius images / antimo andriani / Alamy Stock Photo (p. 83 bottom), Richard Maschmeyer / Alamy Stock Photo (p. 85 upper middle)

THE AMERICAS
THP Creative / Getty Images (p. 87)

Temple of the Great Jaguar
Michel Gounot / GODONG / Getty Images (p. 88), ByronOrtizA / Getty Images (p. 90), diegograndi / Getty Images (p. 91 top), VW Pics / Kontributor / Getty Images (p. 91 bottom)

Temple of Kukulkán
Panther Media GmbH / Alamy Stock Photo (pp. 92, 94), mauritius images / Konstantin Kalishko / Alamy Stock Photo (p. 95 top), mauritius images / Stephen Crawford / Alamy Stock Photo (p. 95 bottom)

Metropolitan Cathedral of Brasília
Oscar Niemeyer @ VG Bild-Kunst, Bonn 2025: mauritius images / robertharding / Alamy Stock Photo (p. 96), Trajano Paiva / Alamy Stock Photo (p. 98 top), mauritius images / Nick Albi / Alamy Stock Photo (p. 98 middle), mauritius images / John Dambik / Alamy Stock Photo (p. 98 bottom), mauritius images / richard sowersby / Alamy Stock Photo (p. 99)

Sanctuary of Our Lady of the Rosary of Las Lajas
Rchphoto / Getty Images (p. 100), Panther Media GmbH / Alamy Stock Photo (p. 102), Diegograndi / Getty Images (p. 103 top), Mark A Paulda / Getty Images (p. 103 bottom)

St. Patrick's Cathedral
mauritius images / Patti McConville / Alamy Stock Photo (p. 104), mauritius images / Geza Kurka / Alamy Stock Photo (pp. 106, 107 bottom right), mauritius images / Egon Bömsch / imageBROKER (p. 107 top), mauritius images / Zoonar GmbH / Alamy Stock Photo (p. 107 bottom left)

Machu Picchu
Merrill Images / Getty Images (p. 108), photography by p. Lubas / Getty Images (p. 110 top), Bob Krist / Getty Images (p. 110 upper middle), Traveler1116 / Getty Images (p. 110 lower middle), Mindful Media / Getty Images (p. 110 bottom), Polhansen / Getty Images (p. 111), Jose Antonio Maciel / Getty Images (p. 112), Craig Hastings / Getty Images (p. 113 top), Henryk Sadura / Getty Images (p. 113 bottom)

Moai of Rapa Nui
Jenny Benoist / talesfromthelens.com (pp. 115 – 117)

EUROPE
mauritius images / Novarc Images / Dennis Schmelz (p. 119)

Monasteries of Meteora
mauritius images / funkyfood London – Paul Williams / Alamy Stock Photo (p. 120), Krle / Getty Images (p. 122), a_Taiga / Getty Images (p. 123 top), DEA / S. VANNINI / Kontributor / Getty Images (p. 123 bottom)

Monastery of Panagia Hozoviotissa
mauritius images / Constantinos Iliopoulos / Alamy Stock Photo (pp. 125, 126), mauritius images / Martin Molcan / Alamy Stock Photo (p. 127 top), Cavan Images / Alamy Stock Photo (p. 127 bottom), mauritius images / imagesandy / Alamy Stock Photo (p. 128), mauritius images / VASILIS VERVERIDIS / Alamy Stock Photo (p. 129 top), George Pavlopoulos / letterstobarbara.com (p. 129 bottom)

Hagia Sophia
mauritius images / Nattee Chalermtiragool / Alamy Stock Photo (p. 130), mauritius images / Antony McAulay / Alamy Stock Photo (p. 132), mauritius images / Stefano Politi Markovina / Alamy Stock Photo (p. 133 top), Gelia / Getty Images (p. 133 upper middle), Izzet Keribar / Getty Images (p. 133 lower middle), mauritius images / Gaetano Di Rosa / imageBROKER (p. 133 bottom), Panther Media GmbH / Alamy Stock Photo (pp. 134 – 135)

Sagrada Família
mauritius images / Witold Skrypczak / Alamy Stock Photo (p. 136), Panoramic Images / Alamy Stock Photo (p. 137), mauritius images / frantic / Alamy Stock Photo (p. 138), Bednorz-Images / achimbednorz.com (pp. 139 top, 140, 141 bottom), iWebbstock / Alamy Stock Photo (p. 139 bottom), mauritius images / Sattachit Phochanasrichai / Alamy Stock Photo (p. 141 top)

Milan Cathedral
Dovapi / Getty Images (p. 142), Bednorz-Images / achimbednorz.com (pp. 144 top, lower middle), Francesco Vaninetti Photo (p. 144 upper middle), Julian Elliott Photography (p. 144 bottom), Atlantide Phototravel / Getty Images (p. 145)

Chartres Cathedral
Julian Elliott Photography / Getty Images (p. 146), Bednorz-Images / achimbednorz.com (pp. 148, 149 top left, bottom), ValeryEgorov / Getty Images (p. 149 top right)

Mont-Saint-Michel Abbey
mauritius images / Earth Pixel LLC / Alamy Stock Photo (p. 150), MathieuRivrin / Getty Images (p. 152), mauritius images / Sen LI / Alamy Stock Photo (p. 153 top), Bednorz-Images / achimbednorz.com (p. 153 middle, 155 middle, bottom), Andia / Alamy Stock Photo (p. 153 bottom), Tuul and Bruno Morandi / Alamy Stock Photo (p. 154), mauritius images / goga18128 / Alamy Stock Photo (p. 155 top)

Hallgrímskirkja
mauritius images / Eric Nathan / Alamy Stock Photo (p. 156), mauritius images / Keren Su / China Span / Alamy Stock Photo (p. 157), mauritius images / Zeljka Burazin / Alamy Stock Photo (p. 158), imageBROKER.com GmbH & Co. KG / Alamy Stock Photo (pp. 159 top, bottom)

Cologne Cathedral
Westend61 / Getty Images (pp. 160, 163 top right), Bednorz-Images / achimbednorz.com (p. 162), Vladislav Zolotov / Getty Images (p. 163 top left), Hans-Peter Merten / Getty Images (p. 163 bottom)

St. Basil's Cathedral
Zoom-zoom / Getty Images (p. 164), Ayhan Altun / Getty Images (p. 166 top), mauritius images / Dimitar Chobanov / Alamy Stock Photo (p. 166 bottom), Vladislav Zolotov / Getty Images (p. 167 top), mauritius images / robertharding / Alamy Stock Photo (p. 167 bottom)

Borgund Stave Church
dave stamboulis / Alamy Stock Photo (p. 168), mauritius images / Kellee Kovalsky / Alamy Stock Photo (p. 171 top), Jan Wlodarczyk / Alamy Stock Photo (pp. 170, 171 bottom left), mauritius images / Guido Vermeulen-Perdaen / Alamy Stock Photo (p. 171 bottom right)

Blagaj Tekke
Mauka Travels / maukatravels.com (p. 172), mauritius images / RnDmS / Alamy Stock Photo (p. 174 top), mauritius images / Felix Lipov / Alamy Stock Photo (p. 174 upper middle, 177 bottom), mauritius images / Zoonar GmbH / Alamy Stock Photo (pp. 174 lower middle, 175), mauritius images / Bert de Ruiter / Alamy Stock Photo (p. 174 bottom), mauritius images / Ivan Batinic / Alamy Stock Photo (p. 176), mauritius images / Dario / Alamy Stock Photo (p. 177 top)

Sanctuary of Madonna della Corona
mauritius images / Simone Polattini / Alamy Stock Photo (p. 178), mauritius images / Novarc Images / Dennis Schmelz (p. 180 top), imageBROKER.com GmbH & Co. KG / Alamy Stock Photo (pp. 180 bottom, 181)

Pantheon
Image by Erik Pronske Photography / Getty Images (p. 182), PytyCzech / Getty Images (p. 183), Kathryn Donohew Photography / Getty Images (p. 184 top), ROMAOSLO / Getty Images (p. 184 middle), Image by Ramesh Thadani / Getty Images (p. 184 bottom), Francesco Riccardo Iacomino (p. 185)

St. Peter's Basilica
mauritius images / Aleksandr Ugorenkov / Alamy Stock Photo (p. 186), Wirestock, Inc. / Alamy Stock Photo (p. 188), Bednorz-Images / achimbednorz.com (pp. 189, 190, 191 top), mauritius images / Striking Images / Alamy Stock Photo (p. 191 bottom), mauritius images / robertharding / Alamy Stock Photo (pp. 192 – 193)

AFRICA AND THE MIDDLE EAST
tunart / Getty Images (p. 195)

Great Mosque of Touba
Friedrich Stark / Alamy Stock Photo (pp. 196, 200, 201 bottom right), MJ Photography / Alamy Stock Photo (pp. 198, 201 top), mauritius images / Zoonar GmbH / Alamy Stock Photo (p. 199 top), mauritius images / Luke Dray / Alamy Stock Photo (p. 199 bottom), Thierry GRUN / Alamy Stock Photo (p. 201 bottom left)

Great Mosque of Djenné
Donhype / Getty Images (p. 202), oversnap / Getty Images (p. 203), Olivier Martel Savoie / Getty Images (p. 204), bPoncho / Getty Images (p. 205)

Bou Inania Madrasa
mauritius images / travel4pictures / Alamy Stock Photo (p. 206), mauritius images / Marko Rupena / Alamy Stock Photo (p. 207), mauritius images / Andrey Khrobostov / Alamy Stock Photo (p. 208), mauritius images / Artur Szymczyk / Alamy Stock Photo (p. 209 top), mauritius images / Jens Benninghofen / Alamy Stock Photo (p. 209 middle), mauritius images / Nikreates / Alamy Stock Photo (p. 209 bottom), mauritius images / Ylan / Alamy Stock Photo (p. 210), mauritius images / Arterra Picture Library / Alamy Stock Photo (p. 211 top), mauritius images / Alessandro0770 / Alamy Stock Photo (p. 211 bottom left), imageBROKER.com GmbH & Co. KG / Alamy Stock Photo (p. 211 bottom right)

Temple of Philae
Panther Media GmbH / Alamy Stock Photo (p. 213), mauritius images / Jon Bower / Alamy Stock Photo (p. 214 bottom), mauritius images / Delphotos / Alamy Stock Photo (p. 215 top), eye35 stock / Alamy Stock Photo (p. 215 bottom), mauritius images / Ismael Khalifa / Alamy Stock Photo (p. 216 top), mauritius images / robertharding / Alamy Stock Photo (p. 216 upper middle), Janzig / Egypt / Alamy Stock Photo (p. 216 lower middle), mauritius images / Michael S. Nolan / Alamy Stock Photo (p. 216 bottom), mauritius images / John Dambik / Alamy Stock Photo (p. 217)

Stone Circles of Senegambia
Dan Grec / theroadchoseme.com (p. 218)

Osun-Osogbo Sacred Grove
mauritius images / Juliet Highet / Art Directors / Alamy Stock Photo (p. 220), mauritius images / Juliet Highet / ArkReligion.com / Alamy Stock Photo (p. 222), mauritius images / OMONIYI AYEDUN OLUBUNMI / Alamy Stock Photo (pp. 223 top, 225 bottom), NurPhoto / Kontributor / Getty Images (p. 223 upper middle), imageBROKER.com GmbH & Co. KG / Alamy Stock Photo (p. 223 lower middle), mauritius images / Michael Runkel / imageBROKER (p. 223 bottom), mtcurado / Getty Images (p. 224 top), mauritius images / Jbdodane / Alamy Stock Photo (p. 224 bottom), mauritius images / robertharding / Alamy Stock Photo (p. 225 top)

Debre Birhan Selassie Church
imageBROKER.com GmbH & Co. KG / Alamy Stock Photo (p. 226), mauritius images / Sergi Reboredo / Alamy Stock Photo (p. 228 top), Matthew B Holmes / travelationship.com (p. 228 bottom left, middle), mauritius images / Sergi Reboredo / Alamy / Alamy Stock Photos (p. 228 bottom right), mauritius images / Matyas Rehak / Alamy Stock Photo (p. 229)

Rock-Hewn Churches of Lalibela
Jarek Winniczek / Getty Images (p. 230), mauritius images / John Elk III / Alamy Stock Photo (p. 232 top), Lingbeek / Getty Images (p. 232 bottom), Dmitry_Chulov / Getty Images (p. 233), mauritius images / Christian Offenberg / Alamy Stock Photo (p. 234), mauritius images / Thomas Cockrem / Alamy Stock Photo (p. 235 left), mauritius images / Richard Dunwoody / Alamy Stock Photo (p. 235 right)

Abuna Yemata Guh
mauritius images / robertharding / Alamy Stock Photo (pp. 236, 241), mauritius images/Christian Offenberg/ Alamy Stock Photo (p. 238), Jorge Fernandez / Alamy Stock Photo (p. 239 top), mauritius images / Matyas Rehak / Alamy Stock Photo (p. 239 bottom), Ariadne Van Zandbergen / Alamy Stock Photo (p. 240 top), mauritius images / Novarc Images / Nicolas Marino (p. 240 bottom)

Al-Khazneh
mauritius images / Sorin Colac / Alamy Stock Photo (p. 243), mauritius images / Naeblys / Alamy Stock Photo (p. 244 top), mauritius images / Photiconix / Alamy Stock Photo (pp. 244 bottom, 247 top), mauritius images / Paul Brown / Alamy Stock Photo (p. 245), mauritius images / John Dambik / Alamy Stock Photo (p. 246), Yadid Levy / Alamy Stock Photo (p. 247 bottom), mauritius images / Robert Preston / Alamy Stock Photo (pp. 248–249)

Western Wall
mauritius images / John Dambik / Alamy Stock Photo (p. 250), Marlo Delforge / alongcameanelephant.com (pp. 252–253)

Abuhav Synagogue
mauritius images / Lev Tsimbler / Alamy Stock Photo (p. 254), mauritius images / Barbara Ash / Alamy Stock Photo (p. 256 top left), mauritius images / Evan Spiler / Alamy Stock Photo (p. 256 top right), mauritius images / Itsik Marom / Alamy Stock Photo (p. 256 bottom), mauritius images / Hanan Isachar / Alamy Stock Photo (p. 257 top), mauritius images / Aliaksandr Mazurkevich / Alamy Stock Photo (p. 257 bottom)

Shah Mosque
mauritius images / MehmetO / Alamy Stock Photo (p. 258), mauritius images / master2 / Alamy Stock Photo (p. 260), mauritius images / Leonid Andronov / Alamy Stock Photo (p. 261 top), Odette Haye (p. 261 upper middle, bottom, 262 bottom), mauritius images / Mr_Karesuando / Alamy Stock Photo (p. 261 lower middle), mauritius images / imageBROKER.com GmbH & Co. KG / Alamy Stock Photo (p. 262 top), mauritius images / Aliaksandr Mazurkevich / Alamy Stock Photo (p. 263)

Rock Tombs of Naqsh-e Rostam
Maximilian Haensel / @nanda_haensel (p. 264), mauritius images / EmmePi Travel / Alamy Stock Photo (p. 266), mauritius images / Alexander Ludwig / Alamy Stock Photo (p. 267 top), mauritius images / Leonid Serebrennikov / Alamy Stock Photo (p. 267 bottom)

This book was conceived, edited, and designed by gestalten.

Edited by Robert Klanten and François-Luc Giraldeau
Contributing editor: Marianne Julia Strauss

Text by Marianne Julia Strauss

Editorial Management by Anna Diekmann

Cover, design, and layout by Hy-Ran Kilian

Photo Editor: Madeline Dudley-Yates

Typeface: Cormorant Infant by Christian Thalmann

Cover image by Imaginechina Limited / Alamy Stock Photo
Back Cover image by Friedrich Stark / Alamy Stock Photo

Printed by aprinta druck GmbH, Wemding
Made in Germany

Published by gestalten, Berlin 2025
ISBN 978-3-96704-136-1

1st printing, 2025

For more information, and to order books, please visit www.gestalten.com

Die Gestalten Verlag GmbH & Co. KG
Mariannenstrasse 9 – 10
10999 Berlin, Germany
hello@gestalten.com

Bibliographic information published by the Deutsche Nationalbibliothek. The Deutsche Nationalbibliothek lists this publication in the Deutsche Nationalbibliografie; detailed bibliographic data is available online at www.dnb.de

This book was printed on paper certified according to the standards of the FSC®.

FSC www.fsc.org MIX Paper | Supporting responsible forestry FSC® C004592